PEOPLES OF AN ALMIGHTY GOD

THE ANCHOR BIBLE REFERENCE LIBRARY is designed to be a third major component of the Anchor Bible group, which includes the Anchor Bible commentaries on the books of the Old Testament, the New Testament, and the Apocrypha, and the Anchor Bible Dictionary. While the Anchor Bible commentaries and the Anchor Bible Dictionary are structurally defined by their subject matter, the Anchor Bible Reference Library will serve as a supplement on the cutting edge of the most recent scholarship. The series is open-ended; its scope and reach are nothing less than the biblical world in its totality, and its methods and techniques the most up-to-date available or devisable. Separate volumes will deal with one or more of the following topics relating to the Bible: anthropology, archaeology, ecology, economy, geography, history, languages and literatures, philosophy, religion(s), theology.

As with the Anchor Bible commentaries and the Anchor Bible Dictionary, the philosophy underlying the Anchor Bible Reference Library finds expression in the following: the approach is scholarly, the perspective is balanced and fair-minded, the methods are scientific, and the goal is to inform and enlighten. Contributors are chosen on the basis of their scholarly skills and achievements, and they come from a variety of religious backgrounds and communities. The books in the Anchor Bible Reference Library are intended for the broadest possible readership, ranging from world-class scholars, whose qualifications match those of the authors, to general readers, who may not have special training or skill in studying the Bible but are as enthusiastic as any dedicated professional in expanding their knowledge of the Bible and its world.

David Noel Freedman
GENERAL EDITOR

THE ANCHOR BIBLE REFERENCE LIBRARY

PEOPLES OF AN

ALMIGHTY GOD

Competing Religions in the Ancient World

JONATHAN GOLDSTEIN

ABRL

Doubleday

New York   London   Toronto   Sydney   Auckland

THE ANCHOR BIBLE REFERENCE LIBRARY

PUBLISHED BY DOUBLEDAY
a division of Random House, Inc.
1540 Broadway, New York, New York 10036

THE ANCHOR BIBLE REFERENCE LIBRARY, DOUBLEDAY,
and the portrayal of an anchor with the letters ABRL are trademarks of
Doubleday, a division of Random House, Inc.

Book design by Leslie Phillips

LIBRARY OF CONGRESS CATALOGING-IN-PUBLICATION DATA
Goldstein, Jonathan.
Peoples of an almighty god : competing religions in the ancient
world / Jonathan Goldstein.—1st ed.
p.   cm.—(The Anchor Bible reference library)
Includes bibliographical references and index.
1. Middle East—Religion.   2. God—Omnipotence—History of
doctrines.   I. Title.   II. Series.
BL1060 .G65   2001
291.1'72'093—dc21   00-065855

ISBN 0-385-42347-0

CONTENTS

PREFACE   *xi*
ABBREVIATIONS   *xiii*

1 *Peoples of an Almighty God* and the Israelite Example

1. Introduction   *3*
2. Authoritative Utterances on the Cosmic Might of the Deity   *6*
3. Stories of Divine Intervention in the Time of Adversity or of Other Challenge to the God's Power   *6*
4. Connected Histories   *7*
5. Prophetic Texts   *8*
6. Prayers Complaining of the Hostility or Inactivity of the God   *18*
7. Meditations on the Apparent Injustice of the Deity   *18*
8. Conclusion   *19*
   NOTES   *20*

2 The Babylonians as a *People of an Almighty God*

1. Introduction   *27*
2. Authoritative Utterances on the Cosmic Might of Marduk   *31*
3. Connected Histories   *31*
4. Stories of Divine Intervention in the Time of Adversity or of Other Challenge to the God's Power   *33*
5. Prophetic Texts   *37*
6. Prayers Beseeching the God to Be Appeased   *46*

7. Meditations on the Apparent Injustices of the Gods   *47*

8. Conclusion   *49*

   NOTES   *49*

3   *Peoples of a Nearly Almighty God:* The Egyptians and the Zoroastrian Iranians

1. Introduction   *62*

2. The Egyptians   *62*

3. The Zoroastrian Iranians   *67*

   NOTES   *70*

4   Jews and Babylonians, from the Reign of Ahaz to the Accession of Nabonidus (ca. 733–556 B.C.E.)

1. Introduction   *75*

2. From the Reign of Ahaz to the Fall of Zedekiah   *76*

3. The Metamorphosis of Isa 13:2–14:27   *83*

4. The Jews and the Babylonians, from the Fall of Jerusalem (586 B.C.E.) to the Accession of Nabonidus (556 B.C.E.)   *92*

   NOTES   *98*

5   The Reign of Nabonidus and the Fall of the Kingdom of Babylon (556–539 B.C.E.)

1. Introduction   *112*

2. Historical Sketch of Nabonidus's Reign   *113*

3. Religious Conflict with Nabonidus's Babylonian Subjects   *116*

4. Nabonidus Leaves Babylon   *129*

5. Nabonidus Returns to Babylon   *132*

6. Conclusion   *135*

   NOTES   *135*

6   Deutero-Isaiah's Reactions to the Career and Fall of Nabonidus and to the Policies of Cyrus   *154*

   NOTES   *162*

7   The Material History of the Babylonians and Jews from Cyrus to the Early Reign of Artaxerxes I (538–464 B.C.E.), except as Reflected by Daniel

1. Cambyses and the Babylonians   *167*

2. Cambyses's Reign, "Bardiya's" Usurpation, and the Wars of Darius to Suppress Rebellions   *168*
3. The Babylonians and Xerxes   *178*
   NOTES   *191*

8 Daniel 1–7 and Other Texts of the Babylonians and the Jews, 538–464 B.C.E.

1. Babylonian Responses to Deutero-Isaiah's Challenges   *203*
2. Strange Features of Daniel 1–7 as a Whole   *205*
3. Daniel 1   *210*
4. Daniel 2   *212*
5. Dan 3:1–30   *215*
6. Dan 3:31–4:34 (Dan 4:1–37 in Most English Bibles)   *215*
7. Dan 5:1–30   *217*
8. Daniel 6 (5:31–6:28 in Most English Bibles)   *222*
9. Daniel 7   *223*
10. Partial Solution of the Problem of Daniel 2: The Five-King Version   *224*
11. Solution of the Problems of Daniel 1 and of the Languages and Biblical Echoes in Daniel 2   *228*
12. Solution of the Problems of Dan 5:1–30   *229*
13. Solution of the Problems of Dan 3:1–30   *232*
14. Solution of the Problems of Dan 3:31–4:34 (4:1–37)   *233*
15. Solution of the Problems of Daniel 6 (5:31–6:28)   *235*
16. When Did Jews Come to Accept All the Stories of Daniel?   *237*
17. Partial Solution of the Problems of Daniel 7: The Three-Beast Version   *237*
    NOTES   *245*

9 The Jews and Babylonians from the Death of Xerxes I to the Eve of the Great Expedition of Alexander (465–334 B.C.E.)

1. Introduction   *264*
2. The Babylonians   *265*
3. The Jews   *267*
   NOTES   *278*

10 The Career of Alexander the Great

1. Introduction   *288*
2. Asia Minor, Syria, Palestine, and Egypt   *290*

3. Mesopotamia
4. Iran   *297*
5. Alexander's Last Years (327–323 B.C.E.)   *301*
   NOTES   *313*

11 How the Persians, Babylonians, and Jews Reacted
   to Alexander

1. The Religious Problems that Faced the Conquered Peoples   *324*
2. The Responses of the Persians   *325*
3. Sibylline Prophecy   *326*
4. Texts in Persian   *331*
5. Another Sibylline Prophecy   *341*
6. Later Persian Texts that Preserve Memories of Alexander   *345*
7. Summary: Reactions of the Persians, the Babylonians, and the Jews
   to Alexander   *347*
   NOTES   *348*

12 Babylonians, Jews, and Iranians under the
   Successor Dynasties

1. Introduction   *359*
2. The Babylonians and the Iranians to 301   *363*
3. The Jews and the Greeks to 301   *368*
4. The "Divided Empire" through the Aftermath of the Battle
   of Ipsos   *370*
5. The Four-Plus-Kingdom Version of Daniel 2   *371*
6. From the Aftermath of the Battle of Ipsos (301) to the Death of
   Antiochus I (261)   *378*
7. The Mixture Marriage (252), the War of Laodice (246–241), and the
   Mixture Version of Daniel 2   *383*
8. Events Affecting the Jews and the Babylonians, 238–223 B.C.E.   *392*
   NOTES   *393*

13 The Reigns of Antiochus III and Seleucis IV

1. Introduction   *405*
2. Antiochus III Consolidates His Rule   *405*
3. Antiochus III versus Ptolemy IV (the "Fourth" Syrian War)   *408*
4. Antiochus Crushes Achaios and Marches to Northwest India
   and Back   *410*

5. Antiochus III versus Ptolemy V (the "Fifth" Syrian War)   *411*
6. Events in Jerusalem, 201–198 B.C.E.   *412*
7. The Later Years of Antiochus III (198–187 B.C.E.)   *423*
8. The Four-Beast-Ten-Horn Version of Daniel 7 and the Reign of Seleucus IV (187–175 B.C.E.)   *427*
NOTES   *434*

14 The Reigns of Antiochus IV and V

1. The Civic Policy of Antiochus IV   *444*
2. Jason Usurps the High Priesthood   *445*
3. Menelaus Usurps the High Priesthood   *446*
4. Antiochus IV in Egypt   *447*
5. Jason's Coup at Jerusalem   *447*
6. Antiochus Sacks Jerusalem   *448*
7. Rome Forces Antiochus, Embittered, to Withdraw from Egypt   *449*
8. The Expedition of Apollonius the Mysarch   *450*
9. The Imposed Cult   *450*
10. The Four-Beast-Eleven-Horn Version of Daniel 7   *451*
11. The Forcible Implementation of the Decrees   *454*
12. The Testament of Moses   *455*
13. The Revolutionary Policies of Mattathias   *456*
14. Judas Maccabaeus's Career   *458*
15. The Supplementing of *1 Enoch* 90   *458*
16. How the Persecution Was Brought to an End   *460*
17. The Death of Antiochus IV   *461*
18. Embarrassing Factors   *461*
19. How the Festival of Ḥanukkah Came to Be   *461*
20. Daniel 8 and 9   *462*
21. The Akra Besieged   *465*
22. The Royal Government Reacts   *465*
23. Daniel 12:11–12   *466*
24. How the Siege of the Temple Mount Ended   *466*
25. Demetrius I Becomes King   *467*
NOTES   *467*

15 The Last Struggles of Judas Maccabaeus and Conclusion

1. Judas's Last Struggles   *474*
2. Conclusion   *476*
NOTES   *477*

APPENDIX: The Prophetic Zand   *479*
  NOTES   *482*

MAP 1: Palestine in the Hellenistic Period   *485*
MAP 2: Empire of Darius I   *486*
MAP 3: Alexander's Empire   *488*
MAP 4: Hellenistic States   *490*

BIBLIOGRAPHY   *493*

INDEX OF AUTHORS   *513*
INDEX OF SCRIPTURAL SOURCES   *519*
INDEX OF OTHER ANCIENT SOURCES   *538*
INDEX OF SUBJECTS   *552*

PREFACE

THE MOST IMPORTANT DISCOVERIES in this book are connected with a set of texts produced by Jews, Babylonians, and Persians in reaction to defeat and subjection to foreign rule. I begin to treat those texts and their historical background in chapter 4. To my mind, those discoveries are solidly based. In the course of my studies, I was so struck by the similarities between the Israelites (or Jews) and the Babylonians that I formulated the more speculative theories that fill chapters 1–3. Indeed, I have no claims to be an expert in Mesopotamian, Egyptian, or Iranian studies. Preliminary drafts of this book have received severe criticism from experts, and I have responded to it by modifying my treatment. I believe that my speculations are valuable enough to face criticism from yet more readers.

My errors are my own. I am deeply indebted to the following for generous help and criticism: A. Leo Oppenheim, William W. Hallo, John A. Brinkman, Janet Johnson, Matthew W. Stolper, Wilfred G. Lambert, Jan J. A. van Dijk, Michael Astour, Erle Leichty, A. Kirk Grayson, Tremper Longman III, Abraham Malamat, Hayim Tadmor, Erica Reiner, Robert Biggs, J. Renger, Paul-Alain Beaulieu, Nahum Sarna, and Irving Finkel. I must also acknowledge my debt to the pioneer in such studies, Samuel K. Eddy (*The King is Dead* [Lincoln: University of Nebraska Press, 1961]). The University of Iowa gave me excellent working facilities and frequent research leaves. This book has grown out of my course there, 16:108, National and Religious Resistance to Ancient Empires.

At first, I gave this book the title "Chosen Peoples," but specialists in Babylonian studies called my attention to the fact that Babylonians never claimed to have been chosen. However, both Israelites and Babylonians claimed their god was almighty.

Jonathan Goldstein
February, 2001

ABBREVIATIONS

ABC	*Assyrian and Babylonian Chronicles*
AJSL	*American Journal of Semitic Languages and Literature*
ANET	*Ancient Near Eastern Texts Relating to the Old Testament*
AS	*Assyriological Studies*
BHLT	*Babylonian Historical-Literary Texts*
CAD	*The Assyrian Dictionary of the Oriental Institute of the University of Chicago*
CAH	Cambridge Ancient History
CAH²	Cambridge Ancient History, 2nd edition
CAH³	Cambridge Ancient History, 3rd edition
CHI	*Cambridge History of Iran*
CHJ	*Cambridge History of Judaism*
CT	*Cuneiform Texts from Babylonian Tablets in the British Museum*
FGH	*Die Fragmente der griechischen Historiker*
HUCA	*Hebrew Union College Annual*
HZ	*Historische Zeitschrift*
IEJ	*Israel Exploration Journal*
JAOS	*Journal of the American Oriental Society*
JBL	Journal of Biblical Literature
JCS	*Journal of Cuneiform Studies*
JE	*The Jewish Encyclopedia*
JEA	*Journal of Egyptian Archeology*
JNES	*Journal of Near Eastern Studies*

JSOT	*Journal for the Study of the Old Testament*
JSOTSup	Journal for the Study of the Old Testament: Supplement Series
LÄ	*Lexikon der Ägyptologie*
MDOG	Mitteilungen der Deutschen Orient-Gesellschaft
MVAG	Mitteilungen der Vorderasiatisch-ägyptischen Gesellschaft
NABU	*Nouvelles assyriologiques brèves et utilitaires*
Oz	*"עז" for David,* Jerusalem, 1964
PAAJR	*Proceedings of the American Academy of Jewish Research*
PHPKB	*A Political History of Post-Kassite Babylonia*
RE	*Realencyklopädie für protestantische Theologie and Kirche*
RLA	*Reallexikon der Assyriologie*
SEHHW	*Social and Economic History of the Hellenistic World*
TAPS	Transactions of the American Philosophical Society
YOSR	Yale Oriental Series, Researches
VAT	Vorderasiatische Abteilung Tontafel, Vordersiatische Museum, Berlin
ZA	*Zeitschrift für Assyriologie und Vorderasiatische Archäologie*

PEOPLES OF AN ALMIGHTY GOD

My witnesses are you—declares the LORD—
My servant, whom I have chosen
To the end that you may take thought
and believe in Me
And understand that I am He:
Before Me no god was formed,
and after Me none shall exist—
None but Me, the LORD.
Beside Me, none can grant triumph.
I alone foretold the deliverance,
And I brought it to pass;
I announced it,
And no strange god was among you.
So you are My witnesses—declares the LORD—
And I am God.
Ever since day was, I am He;
None can deliver from my hand.
When I act, who can reverse it?
. . . I am your Holy One, the LORD
Your King, the Creator of Israel.

(Isa 43:10–15)[1]

—1—

Peoples of an Almighty God
and the Israelite Example

1. Introduction

T HE ANONYMOUS PROPHET whom we now call "Deutero-Isaiah" or
"the Second Isaiah" wrote the words on the facing page after Cyrus,
king of Persia, took Babylon in 539 B.C.E. Long before he wrote, the Israelites (or Jews) considered themselves to be the chosen people of almighty
God the creator. These words and others like them were to inspire the Jews for
centuries to preserve their own identity in the face of bitter adversity and defeat. In turn, the Jews preserved the religious literature that contained such
words, and they produced more.

In human history, not every people that was the victim of repeated adversity
preserved its identity and produced and preserved a religious literature. Most
ancient cultures and literatures have perished. Of those peoples in history who
survived and preserved a literature, many drew directly on the Bible of the
Jews.[2]

Historians naturally seek to explain this survival and this literary productivity of the Jews. There is a logical connection between the beliefs of the Israelites as a *people of an almighty god* and the peculiar phenomena of the
Jews' history and literature. Let us define a *people of an almighty god* as one
which believes that a god stronger than all other powers combined is ultimately committed to be their protector, though temporarily the people may
suffer adversity.

In the ancient world, all groups that we know of believed in gods. They

3

could see the uncontrollable forces of nature, capricious like human beings, now benevolent, now indifferent, now angry. They could see the capricious fortunes of their wars. They knew little of machines. For most human beings in the ancient world, the suggestion that nature and the fortunes of war reflected the operation of complex mechanisms working under immutable laws would have been ridiculous. For the ancients, gods with capricious or at least change-able minds—like human minds—had to be the powers that moved the phe-nomena of nature and history. And since the phenomena of nature and history so clearly exhibited contradictory clashing forces, for most ancient peoples the gods had to be many.

Peoples who lived under kings would believe in a king of the gods. But no power of nature prevails universally over all others: Waters erode mountains, mountains block winds, winds blow away the clouds, clouds obscure the face of the sun, the sun dries up the waters. Normally one or more of the gods would be the special protector or owner of the group who worshiped them. This was true of each of the city-states in the earliest known civilization in Mesopo-tamia, that of the Sumerians. Sumerian Ur belonged to Nanna, the moon-god;[3] similarly, in Greece, Athena was the protectress of the city-state of Athens. No people was always victorious in battle, however mighty the divine power pro-tecting it. Hence, just as no human king could be mightier than all other human forces combined, so for many ancient societies, including those of Sumer, Greece, and Rome, even the king of the gods could not have greater power than all other forces combined. If their special divine protector (like Nanna or Athena) was not the monarch ruling the gods, his or her power was still less.[4] All those societies were, by definition, not *peoples of an almighty god*. The Is-raelites were, at least those whose thought and experiences are reflected in the Hebrew Bible. As we shall see, there were other *peoples of an almighty god*. Such peoples did not have to have a monotheistic religion. If only that people's special divine protector was stronger than all other powers combined, they could believe in many gods. On the other hand, all *peoples of an almighty god* which we shall study were like the Jews in holding that their special divine pro-tector was the creator of the world.

The Jews shared with many if not all ancient peoples and sects the belief that God or the gods communicate their will for the present and the future to their worshipers, except during temporary episodes of wrath. Such communication can be through apparitions, dreams, omens, or prophetic revelations.[5] To my knowledge, the Epicureans are the only ancient sect who disbelieved in such communication between the gods and man.

The confidence imparted by the beliefs of a *people of an almighty god*, especially if that people is a small one, can fill their history with disastrous defeats. If that people is not conscious of any sin that might alienate their god, they may assume vast risks in war against stronger nations, in the belief that their god will not let them be defeated. Although we lack direct evidence to prove the point, it is probable that such beliefs led the people of the kingdom of Israel under their last kings to think that they were a match for the Assyrian Empire. If a king of Israel sought safety as a docile subject of Assyria, the members of his own people probably thought he was not worthy to be their king, and they would murder him and replace him with another. Finally, in 722 B.C.E. the Assyrians put an end to that kingdom.[6] A similar phenomenon probably accounts for the fall of the kingdom of Judah and for the disastrous defeats of the Jews in their multiple revolts against the Roman Empire. The stubborn rebelliousness of those two Israelite kingdoms and of the later Jews is enough to suggest strongly that a large majority of their populations throughout their history believed in an almighty God, even though there is abundant evidence in the Hebrew Bible that the religious views of Israelites were not monolithic and that some of them were polytheists.[7]

Indeed, in our world no human power has achieved world domination or even a century of uninterrupted victory. Defeat is not only a possibility but a recurrent reality. Yet the Jews and some other groups have believed themselves to be *peoples of an almighty god*. If such a people is to maintain its beliefs, it must solve two problems:

1. The supremacy of their god is not recognized by other peoples. It therefore must be revealed by some authoritative means.
2. Every *people of an almighty god* has suffered adversity, and other peoples have prospered. Some explanation must be provided for those facts. Especially difficult for such a people is a protracted period of adversity. How long could it take to expiate sin? Although the purposes of a god need not be fathomable by human beings, how long could a divine protector treat his people with inscrutable wrath?

Peoples who do not believe an almighty god protects them do not face these problems. There is no reason why the power of any of their gods should always be recognized by the rest of mankind. Adversity can come to such peoples through the other forces that are at least as strong as their divine protector.[8]

What intellectual structures did ancient *peoples of an almighty god* have to produce in order to solve those problems? Oral traditions from ancient times are scarce, tenuous, and probably contaminated by later accretions. For the most part we can examine the intellectual structures of ancient peoples only if they embodied them in writing that survives. So the question for us becomes, what kinds of literature did they have to create? Let us examine the literary products of *peoples of an almighty god*, taking our examples first from the Bible. We shall see later that the beliefs of such a people gave rise to much the same phenomena among the Babylonians. In this study I aim to present, not all aspects of the history and literature of the Jews and Babylonians and similar groups, but only those which arose from the fact that such nations were *peoples of an almighty god* according to my definition. Let us proceed to examine the types of literature that Jews produced because they were members of such a people.

2. Authoritative Utterances on the Cosmic Might of the Deity

A PEOPLE OF AN ALMIGHTY GOD WILL PRODUCE and preserve authoritative utterances to prove the cosmic might of their god as creator. Among the Jews, these utterances were usually the words of prophets speaking in the name of the deity.[9] However, human wisdom might be enough to confer authority upon a spokesman for the cosmic might of the creator.

3. Stories of Divine Intervention in Time of Adversity or of Other Challenge to the God's Power

THE TENDENCY TO TELL and preserve tales of the wondrous interventions of the gods is widespread among human cultures and may be even stronger in *peoples of an almighty god*. Even in times of prosperity, believers enjoy such tales. *Peoples of an almighty god* especially need them in times of adversity, to demonstrate how the deity acted (or still acts) in time of crisis. The mere memory of adversity can call into question the power of the god; present troubles can challenge the faith of believers even more, especially if an enemy displays his contempt for their almighty protector. If a story can show that even in time of adversity the god was (or still is) miraculously active, so much the better: While the Israelites were slaves in Egypt and Pharaoh showed his contempt for their God, the LORD inflicted plagues on the Egyptians and their king. When the kingdom of Israel was weak, God performed miracles through the prophet Elisha. When Israel was in exile, God performed miracles for Tobit and his family. Such tales can be embedded in continuous histories (as in Exodus and in 2 Kings) or can survive as separate compositions (as Tobit).

4. Connected Histories

OTHER PEOPLES EXIST and prevail in the course of human events. A *people of an almighty god* must produce explanations as to how their own god brought that about.[10] And if such a people were defeated or enslaved, their thinkers must explain how their god let them fall. In the narrative and prophetic books of the Bible, by far the most prevalent explanation is that sin within the LORD's people provoked his wrath so that he punished them. On the other hand, if they enjoyed a period of unequaled prosperity, as the Israelites did in the time of King David, their writers would try to explain why the god had been so pleased with them. Consequently, for such a people, the recording of events and of their interrelationships has one intensely practical purpose (though there may be many others): It is a means of learning how to gain prosperity and avoid adversity, by pleasing the god and avoiding sin.[11]

We call the recording of events and their interrelationships "history," and the recorder, we call a "historian." To record all events even in the life of one person is impossible. The historian has to make a selection. Often the interrelationships of events are not obvious; the historian must somehow infer them. Historians, consciously or unconsciously, have principles by which they select the facts worthy of being recorded and principles by which they infer the interconnections of events. We may call those principles of a historian his "philosophy of history." Human nature being what it is, anyone who writes the history of a people will find his own philosophy impelling him to select and record facts of their prosperity and of their adversity. But philosophies of history differ widely. Marxists have collected (or assumed) facts about who owns the means of production and have excluded theology from the inferences about the interconnection of events. The author of the books of Kings collected (or assumed) facts about what deity or deities the people worshiped and where and how they did so, and he used mainly theological explanations of the interconnections of events. In both cases, the writers collected and interpreted facts and deserve to be called "historians," though we can reject as inadequate or false the philosophy of history held by either. If a history records events throughout a protracted period (throughout a major war or a generation or centuries), we may call it a "connected history."

Peoples of an almighty god tend to write and preserve connected history, running through centuries. They may also desist from doing so, about periods when they believe their god has temporarily decided not to operate in human history. Thus, the Jews probably wrote no histories of the time between the events of the books of Ezra and Nehemiah and the events of First and Second Maccabees. Certainly they preserved no histories of that time.

The writing and the preservation of connected history are not traits shared by all peoples. Human beings universally enjoy stories, but connected history that narrates real events over long periods is a rarity in the early cultural productions of mankind. Although William W. Hallo has demonstrated that the Sumerians carefully recorded individual events, the judgment of Samuel N. Kramer still stands, that the Sumerians never produced any connected history.[12] Even the Greeks were slow to do so. Hecataeus of Miletus may have begun writing his histories at the end of the sixth century B.C.E.; Herodotus wrote in the mid-fifth, and only the last five books of his work can be called connected history.

The writers of the biblical histories believed they had the keys to the puzzles of history: They pinpointed the sins that provoked God's wrath and the merits that pleased Him, and for that reason they impress a modern reader with their lack of objectivity. We may call such historical works of a *people of an almighty god* "tendentious histories." A writer from such a people must believe that the facts of historical prosperity and adversity reflect the god's intentions, but he does not have to know what those intentions are. If that writer thinks he has not yet found the keys to the puzzling facts, those facts remain important for him and his people, and he may still collect them and set them down in a chronicle, leaving them for the present without theological interpretation. Such a chronicle, by default, will impress a modern reader with its objectivity. However, for historians of *peoples of an almighty god*, the main factors connecting events are theological (sin, merit, and the will of the deity), so that those objective chronicles will be defective as histories, inasmuch as they will record events but will mostly lack discussion of their interrelationships, as is the case with the series of Babylonian chronicles. Perhaps the Chronicles of the Kings of Israel and the Chronicles of the Kings of Judah, used as sources for the biblical books of Kings, were such "objective" chronicles.[13]

5. Prophetic Texts

A GOD'S PURPOSES in history are not always clear from the real or imagined course of events, even after a believer has written it up in a chronicle. Should one infer from the atrocities and the preaching recorded in Judges 9 that God does not wish the Israelites to be ruled by a king? Or should one infer from the atrocities and the preaching recorded in Judges 17–21 that God does wish them to be ruled by a king? Though *peoples of an almighty god* strive to learn the will of their deity through empirical observation of history, it is a risky procedure. The widespread belief shared by such peoples, that the god directly communicates his will, might seem to offer a safer course: The utterance of a true prophet or the diagnosis given by a veracious interpreter of dreams and omens should be able to reveal the god's will. The great Israelite prophets in times of adversity declared that God was angry because of two sets of sins, ritual and moral. Modern readers are especially impressed, and rightly so, by the preaching of Amos, Isaiah, and Micah against social injustice and against oppression of the poor.

Unfortunately, there could always be false prophets and mistaken or lying interpreters. Even a prophet who spoke to defend the oppressed was not necessarily a true prophet: The oppressed might be sinners who deserved their plight. There is one obvious way for human beings to test whether the utterances of a prophet or interpreter represent the will of the deity, although the amoral facts of history can create problems in applying the principle: If the prophet's or interpreter's predictions are flagrantly wrong, they certainly do not represent the will of the deity; if they are strikingly fulfilled, they probably do. The Israelite writers in the Bible certainly held that principle. We may assume that other *peoples of an almighty god* did so, too. Indeed, human beings urgently desire to know what the future will bring. Because the gods have power to determine the future, they can reveal it to their prophets and to omen interpreters. Although the revelation of a god's will did not in every case involve predictions of the future, prediction always was a prime function of prophets and omen interpreters,[14] so much so that in this book, as in common speech, we can use "prophecy" and "prediction" as synonyms.

Accordingly, one or more strikingly fulfilled predictions validate the authority of a prophet or interpreter. That is one reason why such peoples tend to record and preserve fulfilled predictions. If a prophet had even one strikingly fulfilled prediction,[15] the fact could be enough to induce his people to preserve all his utterances, in the belief that if many were still unfulfilled, ultimately the god would fulfill them. That is one reason why we have the prophetic books of the Bible.

Let us define a real prophecy or a real prediction as one made before the predicted event took place, as opposed to a pretended prophecy, one made after the fact, a *vaticinium ex eventu.* A real prophecy may be either true or false, in accordance with whether the event did or did not occur as predicted. Even a fulfilled real prophecy of disaster could satisfy the believer's craving to know the will of the god. Failure of the gods to communicate predictions of important events was disturbing for their worshipers. After the occurrence of an unpredicted important phenomenon in history, there was a strong incentive for prophets or interpreters or even ordinary believers to fabricate a *vaticinium ex eventu*, so as to show that their deity strikingly "predicted" it. The incentive existed also among peoples who did not have an almighty god.[16] The fabricators might pretend that the text had come down from the past but had been unnoticed or lost or hidden until the present.

A flagrant example of a report of a *vaticinium ex eventu* exists at 1 Kgs 13:2, 2 Kgs 23:15–18. These passages are embedded in Kings, a historical work which seeks to demonstrate that the temple of Jerusalem is the sole legitimate place at which to offer sacrifices to the LORD.[17] In that context, this fabricated report of a "prophecy" of the coming acts of King Josiah serves as a forceful demonstration of that point. The story of the prediction which now stands at 1 Kgs 13:2 probably arose in the time of Josiah, and the author of the book of Kings later took it and incorporated it into his own work.

Because the Israelite kingdoms both fell and their peoples went into exile, it is not surprising that the prophetic books that have been preserved teem with fulfilled real prophecies of destruction and exile. The prophets who wrote those books were themselves imbued with the belief that they belonged to a *people of an almighty god*. Hence, every one of them who predicted disaster also predicted that God would restore His people. That is another reason the Israelites so eagerly preserved their works. Of the prophets who wrote before Jeremiah and Ezekiel, not one predicted that the age of adversity would last long, even for the northern kingdom of Israel, which fell in 722 B.C.E. In the biblical traditions about earlier periods, God's wrath lasts 40 years or less. Jeremiah and Ezekiel were the first to predict a long period of punishment. Jeremiah took no note of the length of the period for the northern tribes; for Judah he predicted 70 years or three generations of rule by Babylonian kings. Ezekiel predicted for the northern tribes a period of 190 years or more; for Judah, he predicted the traditional 40 years.[18] For the postexilic prophets, the period of punishment is over or almost over. None predicts that it will last much longer. Nevertheless, even Jeremiah and Ezekiel underestimated the length of the age of punishment. It lasted for centuries. The glorious predicted restoration was supposed to come within at most 70 years after 586 B.C.E. Although in 538 Cyrus permitted the Jewish exiles in Babylonia to return to Judah and Jerusalem, the restoration fell far short of the prophets' predictions. Adversity continued, and the Jews went on paying tribute as subjects of their foreign rulers.

We should take note of the difficult position of the prophet or interpreter of omens from a *people of an almighty god* who announces the end of an age of adversity. He can only predict imminent glorious victories. For a small people like the Jews, glorious victories were improbable. At best, the audience would suffer only disappointment when the prophecies failed to be fulfilled, and the prophet would reply to the complaints of the disappointed with angry rebukes of them for their lack of faith and perhaps for their continued sins, on which he might blame the nonfulfillment. Indeed, one might think that postexilic Jewish prophets could hardly blame the delay in fulfillment on the present sins of the people, because repeated scriptural promises declared that after the end of the exile God himself would make it impossible for the people to commit the grievous sins that could incur such punishment.[19]

Even so, we find the prophet in Isaiah 56–66 angrily rebuking the people for lack of faith and for sin in a tone that contrasts with the lyric optimism of Isaiah 40–55. Perhaps he convinced himself that the fulfillment of the scriptural promises of inability to sin still lay in the future. The difference between Isaiah 40–55 and 56–66 has led scholars to hold that a single writer could not have produced both sections. If, however, Deutero-Isaiah lived on even a short time after uttering Isaiah 40–55, he would have had to face the challenges of the disappointed people and, unless he himself lost faith in his inspiration, would have had to respond with the changed tone of "Trito-Isaiah."[20]

There could, however, be worse results than mere disappointment. Early in the reign of the Persian King Darius I (522–486 B.C.E.), Haggai predicted (2:20–23) to the Jewish prince Zerubbabel that God was about to overthrow the power of all the Gentiles. If Jews as a nation had responded to Haggai by rising in revolt against the Persian Empire, they, too, would have been among the rebel nations crushed by Darius. Somehow, they refrained from revolt, perhaps leaving the matter to be accomplished by the "wind" or "spirit" of the LORD, as Zechariah (4:6) had urged to Zerubbabel. Even so, Zerubbabel thereafter disappears from history (liquidated by the Persians?), and both Haggai and Zechariah left their Jewish audiences disappointed, at least for the present.

Such failures of prophecy could only be a bitter challenge to a *people of an almighty god*. One might explain those failures by use of the belief that part of the punishment the god imposed in this age of wrath consisted in the absence of true prophecy.[21] But the god surely gave true revelations in an earlier period. Either he should communicate his will now, or he should have predicted the present long age of punishment in a revelation given during a time of favor. We can understand how strong an incentive that situation would provide for a member of such a people to fabricate a *vaticinium ex eventu* making that very prediction.

The *vaticinia ex eventu* in the Jewish Bible are peculiar. They are conspicuous by their rarity in the prophetic books. Though some of the references to exile in the preexilic prophets may be interpolated *vaticinia ex eventu*,[22] not one predicts a long exile and a long-delayed restoration. King Tiglath-pileser III (747–727 B.C.E.) of the Neo-Assyrian Empire took an old method, mass deportation of resistant peoples, and made it a systematic policy. From his reign on, exile was a real possibility for any population within reach of Assyria, and one did not require divine inspiration to predict it. Hence, most if not all the references to exile and restoration in the preexilic prophets may be authentic. The need to portray God as predicting a long period of punishment did not lead to the interpolation of *vaticinia ex eventu* into the texts of the preexilic prophets.

On the other hand, *vaticinia ex eventu* are conspicuously present in the Pentateuch, and the most important of them are direct results of the above-mentioned failure of prophecy: They predict a long period of punishment for the sins that were thought to have brought about the falls of the kingdoms of Israel and Judah, a period to be followed by acts of God's mercy and the eventual restoration of his people.

Deut 29:21–28 reflects knowledge of a protracted period of ruin and exile, and 30:1–10 contains a prediction of a glorious restoration and a reformation of the heart so that there never again should be a period of punishment. Deut 29:21–28 and 30:1–10 may be by different authors, because in 29:21–28 only a single land of exile is mentioned, whereas in 30:1 the exiled Israelites are said to be among plural nations. In any case, the editor of Deuteronomy has incorporated them together, and they serve to make up for the failure at least of the preexilic prophets to predict for the LORD's people a long period of punishment.

One should also take note of the strange context of Deut 29:21–30:10. Deut 29:21 follows awkwardly upon Deut 29:17–20, which speaks only of the destructive anger of the LORD against an idolatrous individual, clan, or tribe (expressed in the masculine singular), whereas Deut 29:21–30:10 speaks of the destruction and restoration of the entire nation (expressed in the masculine plural) and land (expressed in the feminine singular). On the other hand, Deut 29:21–27 has been shown to be a part of that same structure of curses in Assyrian treaties on which the author of the curses in Deut 28:15–68 drew, whereas Deut 30:1–10 is a mitigation of the curses, predicting repentance and restoration, and probably should not stand within the curses. Therefore, one might suggest that originally Deut 29:21–27 was intended to stand before 28:69 and was displaced, perhaps when the pieces of parchment making up a scroll were sewn together in the wrong order.[23] More likely, the displacement may have been deliberate: The writer of Deut 30:1–10 could have felt that 29:21–27 led up well to what he was writing. He may also have composed 29:28. Deut 28:69 would follow well upon 28:1–68, 29:21–27.[24]

Furthermore, Deut 30:1–10, with its message of future repentance, divine forgiveness, and restoration, would not follow well upon 29:19–20: in 29:19–20, the sinner is destroyed, and there is no room for forgiveness. It is in Deut 29:21–27 that sinners survive in exile. Deut 29:21–27 thus contradicts Deut 29:19–20. On the other hand, Deut 30:11 (addressed to the singular individual) would follow well on Deut 29:20. We may thus suggest the following as the original order of passages: Deut 28:15–68, 29:21–27, 28:69–29:20, 30:11. Thereafter, a writer moved Deut 29:21–27 to stand after 29:20 and wrote 30:1–10 and placed it just before 30:11 and perhaps added 29:28.[25] Deut 29:21 follows well upon 28:63–68, because "that land" in 29:21 is then the land mentioned in 28:63. As for the single land of exile mentioned in 29:27, it might be the Egypt of 28:68 or it might be a generic singular, meaning no more than "somewhere else."

If so, one might assign Deut 29:21–27 to the same stage of composition as Deut 28:15–68. At that stage, the writer knew of the devastation inflicted on the territory of the northern kingdom by the Assyrians, and of the exile of the northern tribes, and of idol worship by Israelites in exile. But he predicted a mass return to Egypt which never happened, though it may have been suggested by the events described in 2 Kgs 24:31–34. Therefore, the author of Deut 28:68 may well have written before the final fall of the kingdom of Judah in 586 B.C.E. and probably before the first deportation from Judah to Babylonia in 597, and Deut 29:21–27 would have been written at or before that time. The writer would then be a contemporary of Jeremiah and Ezekiel. Unlike Jeremiah and Ezekiel, he predicted a long punishment of unspecified duration. The writer of Deut 30:1–10, however, was as incautious as they: He gives no hint that the glorious restoration will be a gradual, long-drawn-out process.

The author of Leviticus 26 seems to have been more careful about predicting a rapidly moving glorious restoration. Was he cautious because of greater hindsight?[26] In Leviticus 26, repeatedly sevenfold punishment is threatened for violation of God's commandments (vv 18, 21, 24, 28). The land will be destroyed and the people scattered in exile (vv 32–33), perhaps for a time sevenfold that of the sin, and in any case for a long period of unspecified extent, in order to make restitution for failure to observe sabbatical years (vv 34–35, 43). Indeed, more than one generation will have to live and repent in exile (vv 39–40). The exiles, however, will benefit from God's covenant that made them his chosen people (vv 44–45), and eventually, after they have repented and atoned for their sin, God will remember his covenant with the ancestors and will remember the land (vv 41–42).

Especially in the context of Lev 26:3–13, an audience who knew the promises of the covenant and the predictions of the prophets needed no more hint of future glory than that promise that God would remember. Here again, the writer was cautious. He did not predict that God's remembrance would quickly bring the promised glory. The glory would come but might come slowly.[27]

If *b'ḥryt hymym* ("in the end of days") at Deut 4:30 means that the Israelites will perform full repentance only long after they have received punishment for their sin of idolatry,[28] then at Deut 4:25–31, too, there is a *vaticinium ex eventu* of a long period of punishment and of a restoration that might proceed slowly.

One who believes in the possibility of divinely inspired knowledge of the future can also hold that Moses, like Amos and the other prophets who wrote centuries after the revelations on Mount Sinai, could have predicted a period of punishment followed by glorious restoration. But can Moses have foreseen the long age of punishment that later prophets (who should have known of the revelations to Moses) failed to predict? Thus these passages of the Pentateuch must be *vaticinia ex eventu*.[29]

The purposes of an almighty god might on occasion be absolutely inscrutable to human beings. For example, he could allow his people to fall without their having sinned.[30] Psalm 44 reflects the agony of the LORD's people in such circumstances. Israelites would not have to suffer the full torment of Job if it could be shown that their god had predicted the disaster: It was part of his inscrutable plan, and it was temporary. Thus, ineradicably strong in Israelite tradition was the report that their ancestors had been enslaved in Egypt. The account in Genesis ascribes that slavery to no sin, not even to the sale of Joseph into slavery (Joseph's own descendants, too, were enslaved). But God is made to predict it and the subsequent liberation to Abraham (Gen 15:13–16).

Let us now focus our attention on a special type of composition containing one or more *vaticinia ex eventu,* which has been conspicuous in the history of *peoples of an almighty god,* although such compositions have been produced by other peoples as well. In these compositions, the real writer does not write in his own name or as a person of his own time. Rather, the real writer pretends that the author is a god who gave a revelation in the past or an ancient worthy who received revelations or omens in the past. Sometimes the composition really will be based on old material. Always, however, the writer will present his god or his ancient worthy as surveying the course of history through the relevant past down into the (often dreadful) present. To impress his audience with the prophetic power of the god or of the ancient worthy, the writer will give vivid details concerning the relevant past and the present. Then he goes on to predict a glorious future, which he is confident will come soon upon his real audience, though in some cases he will first predict a final peak of adversity to precede the glorious future.[31]

The real interest of the writer is in the present, which his pretended ancient worthy foresaw, and in the near future, which he himself believes he can foresee. Hence, I call these compositions "present-future prophecies," even though they frequently also involve the relevant past. The writer's details on the present are so vivid and his predictions of the future are so impossibly glorious that a modern trained historian has no trouble identifying the writer's own present, if only he has good enough sources on the writer's period. The following fictitious example will illustrate the nature of present-future prophecies and how a historian can analyze them.

Suppose an archaeologist in Israel should say he came upon a scroll in a cave by the Dead Sea. In the scroll were words ascribed to Moses, in which Moses predicted a time far off, when a tiny remnant of the Israelites will begin to return from exile to the Promised Land (i.e., the early Zionist immigration of the late nineteenth and early twentieth centuries). The sons of Japheth (i.e., Europeans) will begin to fly in the skies (the early airplanes) and kill one another wholesale by pouring down hot metal and noxious vapors (World War I), and the victorious family among the sons of Japheth will speak words of encouragement to the LORD's people (the Balfour Declaration of the British government, viewing with favor a national Jewish home in Palestine). The sons of Japheth will fight yet a more deadly war (World War II), and the most wicked of them (German Nazis) will slaughter the Jews. Yet the survivors in the Holy Land will set themselves free of foreign domination (the establishment of Israel in 1948). All nations will come to the mountain of the LORD and beat their swords into plowshares (the glorious future). Clearly the document would be a present-future prophecy, and the author could hardly have written much later than 1948.

I deliberately refrain from calling these compositions "apocalypses," although the term is widely used. The term and the still vaguer abstract noun "apocalyptic" are derived from the Greek title of the book of Revelation in the New Testament. The concepts arose from the efforts of scholars to understand that book, which indeed draws heavily upon the imagery and present-future prophecies in the book of Daniel. But Revelation itself is not a present-future prophecy. The author writes openly using what apparently is his own name, as a person of his own time. Many different streams in Jewish tradition converged to produce the book of Revelation. In origin those streams often were separate from one another. Tours or visions of the scenes of heaven could have a different origin from present-future prophecy. It is a mistake to label all the phenomena exhibited in Revelation (and others besides) as a single movement, "apocalyptic." Rather, it is better to banish the terms "apocalypse" and "apocalyptic." I shall do so.[32]

Unless somehow the deception inherent in writing a present-future prophecy comes to be suspected or exposed, such compositions can make an enormous impression upon their audiences, so accurate are the "predictions" of the pretended speaker. Believers therefore tend to preserve the text of present-future prophecies.[33] Present-future prophecies can be valuable historical sources, for sometimes they contain precise details of the writer's own past and present which have been preserved nowhere else.

In the prophetic books of the Bible as preserved by the Jews, there is not even one present-future prophecy, for the book of Daniel was preserved by them as part of the Writings (Hagiographa), not as part of the Prophets. Deuteronomy 28–30 and Leviticus 26, however, contain present-future prophecy. The disasters predicted there do have the function of deterring disobedience to the commandments, but the past and present defeats and humiliations of Israel are "predicted" in sufficient detail so as to inspire the real writer's contemporaries to have confidence in the predicted glorious restoration.

Even so, there is a significant difference between Deut 28–30, Deut 4:25–31, and Leviticus 26 on the one hand and, on the other, 1 Kgs 13:2, Daniel 2 and 7, and the Babylonian texts we shall examine later.[34] Like the major and minor prophets, the artistic authors of those Pentateuchal passages do not imply that the future was completely predestined. They do not give the names or the lengths of the reigns of the sinning or meritorious kings or describe the conquering enemies and the course of their campaigns in such detail as to make each "prediction" point uniquely to a period in the histories of Israel, Judah, Assyria, and Babylon. Where Daniel 2 and 7, as we shall see, "predict" that the god's people will be subjected to four empires in succession (Babylon, Media, Persia, and Alexander and his successors) and then will be liberated, the writers of the Pentateuch tell only of defeat, exile, and subsequent restoration. The differences between the Pentateuchal present-future prophecies and those others is one of degree, but it is real. Modern writers in speaking of "apocalyptic" do not include the present-future prophecies of the Pentateuch, but perhaps only because they lack the kind of fantastic symbolic imagery present in Daniel 2 and 7 and in Revelation.

Even the authors of the *vaticinia ex eventu* of Deuteronomy and Leviticus were not cautious enough to escape the theological problems of a *people of an almighty god*. Like Second Isaiah and Jeremiah and Ezekiel, they left no room for future disasters. They promised that God would never again inflict such punishment on his people. An aspiring postexilic prophet was in a difficult position: He could disappoint his audience by predicting imminent glory, or he could denounce his audience for the sins by which they were delaying that glory. Malachi (3:8–24) so singled out the sin of failing to pay the tithes and priestly dues and thus probably gave the impetus that ultimately produced the sect of the Pharisees, with their insistence on tithing. But payment of tithes in fact had no effect on the duration of droughts or of foreign domination. To denounce the Jews thus for their sins might also disappoint them; in addition, it could antagonize or bore them. Believers knew they were sinners: Why else were they suffering adversity? Prophets could tell them nothing that was new, indeed, nothing that seemed to be true. Is it any wonder that prophets became more and more rare (Zech 1:5), that the office of prophet fell into disrepute (Zech 13:2–6), and that new works of real prophecy ceased to be recorded and preserved? The long age of adversity probably also destroyed faith in the veracity of dream interpretation and in the Urim and Thummim; these, too, may have been used to predict, disappointingly, an imminent but unfulfilled glorious future.

Desperate indeed is the lot of a *people of an almighty god* who find that their deity is no longer communicating the truth to them.[35] How can they give a hearing to any contemporary prophet? There still were options open to a postexilic religious spokesman who believed he had a divinely inspired message. He could write a present-future prophecy, placed in the mouth of a worthy who lived when God was communicating. That spokesman might "predict" the long delay in restoration. He might explain why in the relevant past and in the present God did not seem to be acting in history. Thus, in *1 Enoch* 89:59–90:25 the sheep symbolizing the LORD's people, as part of their punishment for sin, are temporarily abandoned by God and turned over to seventy angelic shepherds who each in turn negligently tend the flock for a period. At the end of seventy periods (in the writer's own time, the 160s B.C.E.), the shepherds would be punished for their negligence and the LORD's people gloriously restored.[36]

There was another option for a postexilic spokesman. He could take what he believed to be his inspired vision of the future and give it the form of an interpretation of an earlier prophecy, delivered in the time when the god was communicating. These interpretations will take those earlier prophecies, which surely dealt with the present and future facing the earlier prophet, and will make them apply to the present and future facing the interpreter and his audience. Thus, in Daniel 9 Jeremiah's seventy years are reinterpreted as seventy weeks of years because the writer believes that his present is almost seventy weeks of years removed from Jeremiah's time and that the glorious future is imminent. Similar are the interpretive "commentaries" called *p^eshārīm* in the Dead Sea Scrolls from Qumran.

As far as I can tell, no ancient writer of a prophetic text from a *people of an almighty god* left room for multiple periods of future adversity. Such writers were intent on explaining how the deity could have allowed the troubles of the past and on predicting a glorious future. If more adversity should come, the text might be exposed as a false prophecy. Alternatively, the author (if still alive) or other believers might interpolate into his text new passages taking account of the unpredicted adversity so as to leave it possible that the predicted glories still lay in the future. I call this procedure the "supplementing" of a prophecy.[37] The procedure is necessarily deceptive. Even believers can be alienated if they find a trusted seer has tampered after the fact with the texts of prophecies. Therefore a supplementer must take care to make his additions and changes as inconspicuously as possible.

6. Prayers Complaining of the Hostility or Inactivity of the God

PEOPLES OF AN ALMIGHTY GOD often come to suffer the kind of adversity from which, according to their beliefs, their god should have protected them. Their predicament leads them to compose prayers of complaint, and a considerable number have been preserved. We have had occasion to mention Psalms 44 and 82.[38]

7. Meditations on the Apparent Injustice of the Deity

IN OUR DEFINITION of a *people of an almighty god* there was no requirement that the acts of their divine protector be ethically just. The god need only be powerful and ultimately committed to protect his people. Even Israelites and the pious King David could on occasion view God as powerful but unjust.[39] The biblical skeptic Qohelet (Ecclesiastes) questions the principle that God brings just retribution upon the righteous and the wicked of mankind, but he never questions God's power and never discusses His commitment to Israel. Nevertheless, the biblical prophecies and narratives overwhelmingly reflect the Israelite view that God is just. There were pagan *peoples of an almighty god* who believed that the god could be unjust. But even they tended to believe that their god should not only be ultimately committed to defend the nation, he should also protect its righteous individuals, just because he is so strong that no force can prevent him from doing so.

The problem of evil exists for any religion that teaches that some or all of the gods demand what is good, for if so, whence comes evil? Thus, meditations on the apparent injustice of the gods are not peculiar to *peoples of an almighty god*, but the problem of evil can be more acute for such a people and still more acute for a monotheistic one. *Peoples of an almighty god* have been conspicuous for producing such meditations. Most of the surviving examples treat the problem of the suffering individual rather than that of the suffering nation.[40] However, the prophet Habakkuk (1:1–2:17) asks God about Judah, the victim of outrages perpetrated by the wicked power of Babylon, and receives the answer that there will be a happy ending: retribution will eventually come. Tobit and Job and Wisdom 1–5 are similar. They pose the problem of the righteous individual sufferer and solve it by a happy ending. Alongside the happy ending, Job also has the message that God's purposes can be beyond human comprehension.

Like the present-future prophecies, the stories of Job and Tobit solve only the past problems of their heroes. They do not solve the problem of any adversity that will come in the future upon a righteous member of the *people of an almighty god*. Wisdom 1–5 does solve that problem, by placing ultimate reward and punishment after death.

8. Conclusion

WE HAVE NOW SHOWN how the character of the Hebrew Bible is a logical consequence of the impact of the course of events upon the minds of members of a vulnerable *people of an almighty god*.

Remarkable as is the continuously preserved literary legacy of the Bible, it confronts the historian with difficult problems. The Israelites wrote on perishable materials. We have no manuscripts from the time of Moses or David or even Amos. Books transmitted for centuries by being copied and recopied by scribes can have suffered interpolation and alteration. The book of Amos, ascribed to a prophet of the eighth century B.C.E., displays the characteristic beliefs of a member of a *people of an almighty god*, and I see no reason to dismiss the relevant passages as the work of later hands. When and how did the Israelites first become convinced they were such a people? Is the biblical account correct in tracing the belief to the time of Exodus and even back into the "patriarchal age"?

The beliefs of a *people of an almighty god* in their own cosmic importance are grandiose. Can the chief or theologian (Abraham) of a small clan have been the originator of those beliefs? Can a group of fugitive slaves from Egypt have been so impressed by their miraculous escape as to believe their god was almighty? Perhaps. One might, however, be tempted to guess that the grandiose beliefs came to the Israelites in a period of remarkable prosperity, such as the reign of David or Solomon. In any case, there is another ancient *people of an almighty god* for whom we have manuscripts going back to and before the time when they became such a people! Let us study the parallels and contrasts between those people and the Israelites.

NOTES

1 As translated in *The Prophets: Nevi'im* (Philadelphia: Jewish Publication Society of America, 1978), 451.

2 Certainly all Christian sects did. On modern religious developments among oppressed peoples, most of which drew on the Jewish Bible, see Vittorio Lanternari, *The Religions of the Oppressed: A Study of Modern Messianic Cults* (New York: Knopf, 1963).

3 See Samuel Noah Kramer, *The Sumerians* (Chicago and London: University of Chicago Press, 1963), 40–59, 83–84.

4 On Enlil, king of the gods of Sumer, see ibid., 119, 146–47; Thorkild Jacobsen, *The Treasures of Darkness: A History of Mesopotamian Religion* (New Haven and London: Yale University Press, 1976), 86, 117–18; and Wilfred G. Lambert, "The Reign of Nebuchadnezzar I: A Turning Point in the History of Ancient Mesopotamian Religion," in *The Seed of Wisdom: Essays in Honour of T. J. Meek* (ed. W. S. McCullough; Toronto: University of Toronto Press, 1964), 3–4. In the *Iliad,* Zeus, king of the Greek gods, is too strong for all the other gods (i.565–94); even so, he is not stronger than the combined power of fate and the rest of the gods (xvi.433–61; xxii.168–85, 208–13). Aeschylus's *Prometheus Bound* shows that classic Greeks of the fifth century B.C.E. still held that Zeus was not stronger than the combined power of fate and the rest of the gods. Neither Greek Zeus nor Roman Jupiter was the creator.

5 On the Greeks and Romans, see the old detailed work of Louis Bouché-Leclercq, *Histoire de la divination dans l' antiquité* (4 vols.; Paris: Leroux, 1879–82). On the peoples of Mesopotamia, see A. Leo Oppenheim, *Ancient Mesopotamia: Portrait of a Dead Civilization* (rev. ed.; Chicago and London: University of Chicago Press, 1977), 206–27. The phenomenon of prophecy is too widespread in the Bible to require references. The Israelites knew of other means of divine communication—dreams: Gen 15:12–16, 40:5–20, 41:1–6, Daniel 2; ephod, Urim and Thummim: Num 27:21, 1 Sam 14:3, 23:6, 9, 30:7, Greek 1 Kgdms 14:18, 41, and see Roland de Vaux, *Ancient Israel: Its Life and Institutions* (New York, Toronto, and London: McGraw-Hill, 1961), 352–53.

6 2 Kgs 15:17–17:6, Hos 7:3–7, 8:3–4, 10:3, 7; 13:10–11.

7   On the kingdom of Judah, see 2 Kgs 22:23–24, 23:29–25:26, Ezra 4:12, 15, 19. Jeremiah (7:1–15) had to argue against the belief in the invulnerability of Jerusalem, for which Isaiah was responsible (Isaiah 36–37). On the revolts against Rome, see Josephus, *War* vi.5.4.312–13, ii.16.4.390–94. The religious views of the ancient Israelites were not monolithic; see, e.g., Morton Smith, *Palestinian Parties and Politics that Shaped the Old Testament* (New York and London: Columbia University Press, 1971). Since we have seen that belief in an almighty god is compatible with polytheism, many even of those Israelites whom Smith calls "syncretistic" could have believed in an almighty god.

8   Thus a people that does not have an almighty god can easily explain adversity without assuming it has sinned. See the Sumerian lamentations in *ANET,* 455–63, 611–19. The Sumerian king list reported the defeat of each successive dynastic city-state without any hint that sin was the cause; see Thorkild Jacobsen, *The Sumerian King List* (AS, no. 11; Chicago: University of Chicago Press, 1939), and *ANET,* 265–66. The Athenians after their defeat by King Philip II of Macedonia in 338 B.C.E. believed that theirs had been the righteous cause and blamed Philip's victory on the capricious power of Tyche, the goddess of luck. To induce Tyche to side instead with them, they built her a temple and offered her sacrifices; see Jonathan A. Goldstein, *The Letters of Demosthenes* (New York and London: Columbia University Press, 1968), 248–49.

9   Amos 4:10, 5:8, 9:6, Gen 1:1–2:7, Isa 45:7, 11–12.

10   Amos 9:7, Isa 10:5–15, Jer 51:20–23, Gen 10:1–11:9, Deut 32:8, 1 Kgs 19:15–17, 2 Kgs 8:11–13.

11   Cf. E. A. Speiser, "Ancient Mesopotamia," in *The Idea of History in the Ancient Near East* (ed. Robert C. Dentan; New Haven and London: Yale University Press, 1955), 47–48.

The biblical books from Joshua through Kings do not merely narrate and explain the religious failure of the people and the collapse of the two kingdoms. In the favorable portrayals of Joshua and the Judges and of Kings David, Hezekiah, and Josiah, the books present examples for the future. The writer of 2 Kgs 25:27–30 takes pains to end his narrative with the glimmer of hope that came in his time: Babylonian King Awêl-Marduk's release of King Jehoiachin of Judah from prison. The writer believed that the history neither of the people nor of the dynasty of David was over. He could leave it to the texts of the prophets, of which he surely knew many, to predict full restoration; he was writing history, not prophecy. Here I disagree strongly with the views of Martin Noth in his *The Deuteronomic History* (JSOTSup 15; Sheffield: JSOT Press, 1981), 12, 97–98.

The reader can compare my definition of history in the next paragraph with that of Baruch Halpern in *The First Historians* (San Francisco: Harper and Row, 1988), 6–7. Also in the next paragraph I allude to how Marxists and biblical writers assume facts where evidence is lacking; cf. Halpern, *First Historians,* 128–30. Halpern's entire book is valuable.

12 Hallo, "Sumerian Historiography," in *History, Historiography, and Interpretation* (ed. H. Tadmor and M. Weinfeld, Jerusalem: Magnes Press, 1983), 9–20; Kramer, *Sumerians,* 34–39, and "Sumerian Historiography," *Israel Exploration Journal* 3 (1953), 217–18. The Sumerian King-List gives names of kings stretching over millennia but does not narrate events.

13 On the sources for the books of Kings, see Otto Eissfeldt, *The Old Testament: An Introduction* (New York and Evanston: Harper and Row, 1965), 285–86. On Babylonian "objective" chronicles, see chap 2, sec 3.

14 Fulfilled predictions were a criterion of a true prophet for the biblical writers: see, e.g., Deut 18:15–22, Gen 40:5–41:57, Jer 23:14–21; at Deut 13:2–4 there is an effort to take account of a problem in applying the principle.

Prediction was always a prime function of prophets: see, e.g., Yehezkel Kaufmann, *The Religion of Israel* (trans. and abridged Moshe Greenberg (Chicago: University of Chicago Press, 1960), 158, 353.

15 E.g., Amos predicted the earthquake (1:1, 8:8). Isaiah predicted that King Ahaz of Judah would not be overthrown (7:1–9) and that Sennacherib's army would not take Jerusalem (chaps 36–37).

16 On the probability that the famous fulfilled predictions of the Greek oracle of Delphi (reported by Herodotus and Diodorus) are *vaticinia ex eventu,* see Joseph Fontenrose, *The Delphic Oracle* (Berkeley, Los Angeles, and London: University of California Press, 1978), 111–14, 122–23, 124–28, 300, 302, 316–18, 348. A Greek example from the second century B.C.E.: Phlegon of Tralles, *FGH* 257, F 36, III. A Roman example from the Second Punic War: Livy xxv.12.

17 See Halpern, *First Historians,* 249–53; Eissfeldt, *The Old Testament,* 283–84.

18 Wrath for 40 years in earlier periods: Num 14:33–34, 32:13, Josh 5:6, Judg 13:1, and probably implied in 2 Kgs 1:31–37, 13:1–5; wrath for fewer years: Judg 3:8, 14, 4:3, 6:1, 10:8. Jeremiah: 25:11–12, 27:6–7, 29:10; with solemn emphasis he (29:28) announced to the exiles, "It [the exile] is long." Ezekiel: 4:4–6, 9. The Greek text of Ezekiel has 190 years; the Hebrew, 390. If Ezekiel's prophecy dates from 593 B.C.E. (the fifth year of the exile of Jehoiachin, as in Ezek 1:2) the 40 years would end in 553 (or in 557, measuring from 597) and if the 190 years ended at the same time, the 190 years would have begun in 743, ten years before the year of the war in which Tiglath-Pileser III carried off to Assyria the first exiles from the kingdom of Israel. The reading "390" of the Hebrew may be a later attempt to correct the text when it became obvious that the prophecy of 190 years had not been fulfilled. Since Cyrus allowed the exiles from Judah to return in 538, only some 48 years after the great defeat in 586, the 40 years for Judah could be allowed to stand, as an approximately correct round number.

19 Deut 30:1–8, Jer 31:31–40, 32:37–40; Ezek 11:17–20, 36:24–35. Cf. Isa 54:7–10, 60:1–22 (n.b. the hedging in 60:22, "in its time"), 61:8–9; Ezekiel 18, 33:10–20. See my article, "Even the Righteous Can Perish by His Faith," *Conservative Judaism,* vol. 41, no. 3 (spring, 1989), 62.

20 On Deutero-Isaiah, see chap 6. On the separation of Isaiah 40–66 from Isaiah 1–39 ("First Isaiah") and on the theories ascribing only Isaiah 40–55 to Deutero-Isaiah and assigning Isaiah 56–66 to "Trito-Isaiah," see, e.g., Eissfeldt, *The Old Testament,* 304, 332, 341–45; Claus Westermann, *Isaiah 40–66: A Commentary* (Philadelphia: Westminster Press, 1969), 8–9, 27–28, 295–308.

21 See Amos 8:11–12, Mic 3:6–7, Jer 23:35–38. The hunger for true prophecy is reflected in Joel 3:22.

22 The one flagrant example of an interpolation *ex eventu* is Mic 4:10. On Isaiah 13–14, see chap 4, sec 3. On Isaiah 40–66, see chap 6. On the Hebrew text of Ezek 4:4–6, 9, see n. 19. Isa 21:1–10 is an enigma. Even though it contains no mention of Assyria and seems to allude to Elam as an enemy rather than as an ally of Babylon, Isa 21:1–10 may be an utterance of the First Isaiah upon the fall of King Marduk-apla-iddina II (Merodach-Baladan) to Assyria in 703 or 700 B.C.E., or upon the disastrous fall of Babylon to Sennacherib in 689.

The mysterious *midbar yām* of Isa 21:1 may reflect the name of the "Sealand" district (*mât tamtim*), the home territory of Marduk-apla-iddina II. Cf. Raymond P. Dougherty, *The Sealand of Ancient Arabia* (YOSR Vol. XIX; New Haven: Yale University Press, 1932), 44–77, 169–70. Dougherty, however, accepts (169) the theory that Isa 21:1–10 refers to the fall of Babylon to Cyrus in 539 B.C.E. Why, however, should a Jewish author write of his anxieties as in Isa 21:3–6 if he is reporting the fall of Babylon to Cyrus? And why should he imply that the news has come from afar as in Isa 21:7? Those features fit well a fall of Babylon to Assyria in the time of the First Isaiah. Could the calls to Elam and Media in Isa 21:2 be calls of Babylon to unresponsive allies? The imperative addressed to Media (*ṣwry*) might mean "go to war" (from the root *ṣrr*), just as the imperative punningly addressed to Elam should mean "come to war." Babylon would then be summoning both Elam and Media against unnamed Assyria. Yehezkel Kaufmann came to many of these conclusions before me (*Toledot ha-emunah ha-yisre'elit,* Vol. III, Part 1 [Tel-Aviv: Bialik Foundation and Dvir, 1947], 181–82).

On the prediction at Isa 39:5–7 and the story in which it is embedded, see Bustenai

Oded, "The Babylonian Embassy Narrative (Isaiah 39 = 2 Kgs 20:12–18): Historical Event but Fictitious Prophecy?" *Shnaton* 9 (1985), 115–26 (in Hebrew with English summary, xiii). Oded shows that the story is probably true and that the prediction is probably by Isaiah or his followers, slightly modified by a reviser in the age of Judah's fall to Babylon. As Oded notes (125) a *vaticinium ex eventu* should be accurate, and the prediction in Isa 39:5–7 was inaccurate if one looked for its fulfillment after 597 or 586 B.C.E. To Oded's instances, one should add that Jehoiachin and his male descendants certainly were not castrated (1 Chr 3:17–20). Furthermore, if Isa 39:5–7 is a *vaticinium ex eventu,* it, with the rest of Isa 36:1–38:8, 38:21–39:8, was first embodied in the book of Kings and only later attached to Isaiah 1–35; see chap 4, n 8. One would infer that the prophecy, if fabricated, at first could not be directly introduced into the collection of works attributed to Isaiah; cf. Kaufmann, *Toledot,* vol. 3, part 1, 154–56.

Possible interpolated *vaticinia ex eventu* in the preexilic prophets: see Francis I. Andersen and David Noel Freedman, *Hosea* ("Anchor Bible," vol. 24; Garden City, N.Y.: Doubleday, 1980), 55–57.

23 Structure of curses: see Moshe Weinfeld, *Deuteronomy and the Deuteronomic School* (Oxford: Clarendon Press, 1972), 116–29; Deut 29:21–17 within that structure: ibid., 114–16; possibility of accidental displacement: cf. Jonathan A. Goldstein, *I Maccabees* ("Anchor Bible," vol. 41; Garden City, NY: Doubleday, 1976), 493.

24 The verses fit together well whether Deut 28:69 be taken as the conclusion of what would then precede it, or as the introduction to Deut 29:1–20.

25 The following should make the rearrangement of the text clearer:

The Existing Text of Deut 28:15–30:14

28:15–68 (addressed mostly to a singular "you"): If you disobey the commandments, you will suffer terrible punishments.

28:69–29:20 (addressed mostly to plural "you"): You have seen God's power and mighty deeds on your behalf. Therefore, you and your posterity should obey the terms of the covenant that He is about to make with you. The LORD will never forgive the Israelite idol-worshiper but will blot out his name from under heaven.

29:21–27 (addressed to plural "you"); Your descendants and future Gentiles will see that the sinful idolaters will survive in exile from their devastated land.

30:1–10 (addressed to a singular "you"): God will forgive and restore sinful Israel if it repents in exile.

30:11–14 (addressed to a singular "you"): Obedience to the covenant is not difficult; you know how to do it.

Suggested Rearrangement of Deut 28:15-30:14 to Recover the Original Text

28:15–68 (addressed mostly to a singular "you"): If you disobey the commandments, you will suffer terrible punishments.

29:21–27 (addressed to plural "you"): Your descendants and future Gentiles will see that the sinful idolaters will survive in exile from their devastated land.

28:69–29:20 (addressed to plural "you"): You have seen God's power and mighty deeds on your behalf. Therefore, you and your posterity should obey the terms of the covenant that He is about to make with you. The LORD will never forgive the Israelite idol-worshiper but will blot out his name from under heaven.

30:11–14 (addressed to a singular "you"): Obedience to the covenant is not difficult; you know how to do it.

A writer who found that Deut 29:20 left too little room for hope moved 29:21–27 to stand after 29:20, and the author of Deut 30:1–10 inserted his verses (addressed to a singular "you") just before 30:11: God will forgive and restore the sinner who repents in exile and obeys God's commandments.

26 I am still not convinced by the arguments for a late date for the Priestly Code. Nevertheless, if hindsight is the reason for the greater circumspection shown by the author of Leviticus 26, my observations here can be used to support the view that the Priestly Code, at least the portion containing Leviticus 26, is late.

27 The author of 2 Chr 36:21 did not feel the need for caution which seems to have shaped the predictions in Leviticus 26: He identified the period predicted in Leviticus 26 with Jeremiah's 70 years and (falsely) with the years that elapsed between the fall of Judah in 586 B.C.E. (on the date, see chap 4, n 44) and Cyrus' proclamation of 538.

28 The Masoretic accents at Deut 4:30 support that interpretation. Jeremiah's use of the phrase "at the end of days" shows that its meaning is relative to what the speaker had in mind: "at the end of the predicted course of events," which might be relatively brief (as at Jer 23:20) or long (as at Jer 30:25). Cf. E. Lipiński, *"B'hryt hymym* dans les textes préexiliques," *Vetus Testamentum* 20 (1970), 445.

29 Deut 32:1–43 is a special case. Placed as it is in the mouth of Moses, the poem looks like a *vaticinium ex eventu,* but the verses themselves make no claim that Moses is the speaker. Deut 32:12–15 presupposes that Israel is in the promised land. Rather, the poem may have been written as a meditation upon the fact of a glorious victory of Israel that followed upon a time of adversity (not on one described as long!). The verses know nothing of exile and may have been written in response to the Israelite victory mentioned at 2 Kgs 14:25–27 (an idiom in 2 Kgs 14:26 is the same as that in Deut 32:36), if not to a still earlier victory. For the editor of Deuteronomy, the poem was old and prophetic. Perhaps long before him it had been ascribed to Moses. The aforementioned failures of prophecy may therefore have had nothing to do with the inclusion of the poem in Deuteronomy.

30 See Isa 55:8, Hab 1:13–14, and cf. the book of Job.

31 There is a final peak at Dan 12:1. The writer of such a composition is interested in the present and is confident of the imminent glorious future. Therefore he cannot predict more than one additional period of adversity.

32 Cf. T. Francis Glasson, "What Is Apocalyptic?" *New Testament Studies* 27 (1980), 98–105; Robert L. Webb, " 'Apocalyptic': Observations on a Slippery Term," *JNES* 49 (1990), 115–26; P. R. Davies, "Qumran and Apocalyptic or Obscurum per Obscurius," ibid., 127–34.

33 On the supplementing of present-future prophecies, see the last paragraph of this section.

34 The Greek example preserved by Phlegon (*FGH* 257, F 36, III) belongs to the second category.

35 See n 20.

36 On the passage and when it was written, see chap 13, sec 6, pp. 416–23. Psalm 82 reflects the same view: The present evil state of the world is due to the negligence of God's culpable superhuman subordinates (*ēl, ĕlōhīm*), whom He will punish.

37 For examples of supplementing, see chaps 8, 12, 13, and 14, sec 10.

38 See p. 14 and n 36.

39 See 2 Sam 6:6–8.

40 It is possible that the author of Job intended the person of Job to be a symbol for the LORD's people. One might assume that to the author's mind the disastrous defeats of the Jews were out of proportion with whatever sins had been committed, that they went beyond the double dose mentioned at Isa 40:1 and even beyond the sevenfold dose mentioned in Leviticus 26. But the author of Job never hints that Job is a symbol for the nation. The book is better taken at face value, as a meditation on the problem of evil as it affects the individual rather than the nation.

On the other hand, the author of Tobit shows so much interest (3:3–5, 13:2–18, 14:4–7) in Israel's suffering and coming vindication as to suggest that his real concern is the problem of the suffering nation; see George W. E. Nickelsburg, *Jewish Literature between the Bible and the Mishnah* (Philadelphia: Fortress Press, 1981), 33.

2

The Babylonians as a
People of an Almighty God

1. Introduction

THE BABYLONIANS AT FIRST were not a *people of an almighty god,* and
their deity, Marduk, was not the supreme power in the universe,
stronger than any other combination of forces. Indeed, until Marduk
became supreme, no god in Mesopotamia held that position, and there was no
people of an almighty god there, as the documents of the times demonstrate.
Babylon and Marduk were both obscure before the unexpected rise to imperial
power of King Ḫammurapi (reigned ca. 1792–1750) of the First Dynasty of
Babylon. Even then, as Babylonians saw it, Marduk and his city had received,
by decree of the other gods, only supremacy on earth over all the peoples.
"This was a limited promotion by superiors, not a take-over. . . . Marduk was
made great 'among,' . . . not 'over' . . . the . . . gods."[1]

Though Ḫammurapi's empire had fallen completely with the defeat of his
fifth successor Samsu-ditana (ca. 1595 B.C.E.), politically Babylon remained
the chief city of southern Mesopotamia, the region that was then called
"Akkad" or "Sumer and Akkad." We shall follow modern usage and shall call
that region "Babylonia," and thus (unlike the ancients) shall use "Babylonian"
to mean both "of Babylon" and "of Babylonia." For our study, the usage is appropriate, because Sumer and Akkad were to take on a common identity, by
which most of the inhabitants took for granted that the King of Babylon was
the king of Akkad (or of Karduniash, the Kassite name for the territory) and
that Marduk was the supreme deity. For over four centuries (ca. 1595–1155),

the kings of the foreign Kassite Dynasty kept the city as one of their capitals. They respected the gods of Mesopotamia (including Marduk), but at least one member of the line, Kurigalzu (1332–1308), in a text, insisted on the supremacy of his own Kassite gods.[2]

In no document of a Kassite king is Marduk treated as supreme even among the gods of Mesopotamia. Under the Kassite dynasty, however, some Babylonian worshipers of Marduk seem to have felt that their own Marduk was indeed almighty among the gods. Such beliefs are attested by some texts of late Kassite times[3] and by the appearance in documents of those times of the personal name "Marduk-shar-ilâni," which means "Marduk is king of the gods." Nothing tells us how such beliefs began to grow among Babylonians under the rule of a foreign dynasty.[4] The fall of the last Kassite king to Kutur-nakhkhunte, king of Elam, in 1155 at first was a disaster for Marduk, too: His statue was carried off to Elam by the victors.

But there arose in Babylon a new line of kings, native to Mesopotamia, called the "Second Dynasty of Isin." The fourth king of this dynasty was Nebuchadnezzar I (1125–1104). Under him Babylon enjoyed a remarkable though brief episode of prosperity. Nebuchadnezzar I campaigned successfully in Elam and returned with the precious statue of Marduk. At least, so say documents surviving from the time and literary texts that became "classics" in Mesopotamia.[5] Let us define that term. A piece of literature is a classic if a considerable number of literate persons value it and make efforts to keep it in existence over the generations. Before the invention of printing, that meant that a classic was a work that was copied by scribes and that could be found in collections of books or tablets. Some classics were appreciated only by small sectarian circles. Others were treasured by kings or by chief priests and by their scribes. If copies of a work were written generations after it was composed and were found at more than one site (as is the case with the *Gilgamesh Epic,* the *Iliad,* and the book of Deuteronomy), that work is a classic.

From the reign of Nebuchadnezzar I on, Mesopotamian texts proclaim Marduk to be "king of the gods" and "lord of lords." The position of the Babylonians as a *people of an almighty god* and the creed, that Marduk was the supreme deity, marked a sweeping change in Mesopotamian religious beliefs and could not fail to meet opposition, especially during the first generations. The victories of Nebuchadnezzar I and his recovery of Marduk's statue provide a plausible political background for the rise of Marduk to be the almighty head of the Mesopotamian pantheon, though one is surprised at the permanence of that belief after the adversity suffered by Nebuchadnezzar's successors.[6] Texts survive which oppose the *supremacy* of Marduk and Babylon. They assert rather the older beliefs in the *importance* of the god Enlil (with or without the assembly of the other gods) and of Enlil's holy city of Nippur. Nippur was never important politically, and one could assert its religious, but not its political supremacy. And, by the older beliefs, even Enlil did not have the status of an almighty god.

Thus, a document from the reign of Nebuchadnezzar I seems to show prompt resentment over the new doctrines. It is a boundary stone from the vicinity of Nippur, and it begins with praise to Enlil. No other boundary stone begins with praise of any god. At the very beginning, Enlil's supremacy over the other gods is asserted in terms perhaps stronger than in any other text: "Enlil, the lofty lord, the aristocrat of heaven and underworld, the noble, the lord of all, king of the great gods, who has no god who can rival him in heaven or underworld, at the giving of whose command the Igigi [deities of Mesopotamia] show submission and reverently heed. . . . "[7] From the early career of the Babylonians as a *people of an almighty god* we shall find other instances wherein a text asserting the supremacy of almighty Marduk has a counterpart asserting the importance of Enlil.

The problems facing a *people of an almighty god* declared themselves immediately: The believer had to explain how Marduk's cosmic power, hitherto widely unrecognized, really had been supreme, and how Marduk and Babylon had hitherto so often appeared to have been humiliated in the course of events. Indeed, not just once but three times between the glorious reigns of Ḥammurapi and Nebuchadnezzar I, Marduk seemed to have been humiliated along with his city as foreign powers sacked Babylon and carried off his statue. King Murshilish I of the Hittites did so in ca. 1595 B.C.E.; King Tukulti-Ninurta I of Assyria, in ca. 1225; and King Kutur-nakhkhunte of Elam, in ca. 1160. All three instances were remembered, though with the lapse of time some inaccuracies could creep into the traditions.

I believe that Babylonian writers promptly responded to the challenge of these problems and produced literature in the typical forms of a *people of an almighty god*. In the reign of Nebuchadnezzar I, a Babylonian composed a present-future prophecy, the "Speech of Marduk," in which Marduk himself is the speaker: Marduk explains the great previous humiliations of his city, saying that he had chosen in each case to go abroad to reside with the enemy, but in the reign of Nebuchadnezzar I he will return forever.[8] Babylonian literary texts are often difficult to date, and I, an outsider to cuneiform studies, shall be presumptuous enough in the rest of this chapter to argue that important Babylonian texts in the forms of a *people of an almighty god* were composed during or soon after the rise of Marduk to supremacy, and very likely that means during or soon after the reign of Nebuchadnezzar I. However, my main thesis is only that the beliefs of a *people of an almighty god* lead eventually to peculiar courses of history and to the production of peculiar forms of literature. For that thesis, it is desirable but not necessary that Babylonians *promptly* produced those literary forms. Thus, even if my datings should be refuted, my main point can still stand.

Before we proceed to examine in detail the literary creations of Marduk's people, let us keep our discussion of the Babylonians parallel to our discussion of the Israelites, and let us note that the confidence imparted by the belief they were the *people of an almighty god* probably helped bring upon the Babylonians (just as upon the Israelites) a series of disastrous defeats in war. Neither the Israelites nor the Babylonians always acted on the belief that each was the *people of an almighty god*. A good many of the kings and commoners of both peoples could be men of little faith, perhaps taught by harsh experience. But other kings and commoners could follow their faith to disaster.

After the reign of Nebuchadnezzar I, Assyria (until her final weakening in the years 625–612) was the dangerous neighbor of Babylon. The Synchronistic History is an Assyrian document that narrates Assyrian conflicts with Babylonia, omitting all Assyrian defeats but telling of many instances in which Assyria defeated and humiliated Babylon. In two instances it probably tells outright lies. Nevertheless, it displays how its Assyrian author was impressed with the Babylonian tendency to "crime" (i.e., assertiveness and aggression against Assyria), and it is largely correct in telling of Babylonian defeats in battle. The Synchronistic History used as sources the inscriptions of the Assyrian kings, which present the same picture of the Babylonians as incorrigible rebels and perfidious enemies of Assyria.[9]

After the reign of Nebuchadnezzar I, there was to be much fighting between Elam and the Assyrian empire, but Babylonia (except when subject to an Assyrian king) seldom came into conflict then with her other powerful neighbor, Elam, though the history of enmity was remembered and the natural hostility of neighbors still existed. The Speech of Marduk predicted, falsely, that Nebuchadnezzar I would destroy Elam. Nevertheless, the Babylonians preserved that prophecy; it told them that almighty Marduk would be with them forever[10] (that promise, too, proved to be false in 689 B.C.E., when King Sennacherib destroyed Babylon and carried Marduk's statue off to Assyria). Thus, Babylonians could be led by their faith to believe they could defeat their most powerful neighbors. Often, instead, they suffered terrible defeats.

Let us turn now to the literature that the Babylonians produced as a consequence of their belief that they were the people of almighty Marduk.

2. Authoritative Utterances on the Cosmic Might of Marduk

PROBABLY THE MOST IMPRESSIVE of the literary compositions, in the eyes both of the ancient Mesopotamians and of modern readers, is *Enûma elish,* the Babylonian Creation Epic, which certainly reflects Marduk's supremacy in the pantheon and may well be a product of the reign of Nebuchadnezzar I. The epic proclaims Marduk to be the supreme power, greater than any other, creator of heaven and earth, king of the gods. It also proclaims Marduk's city, Babylon, to be the primeval city, home of all the gods. Enlil's name appears only in contexts expressing Marduk's power or Enlil's subordination, and Enlil's city, Nippur, is not mentioned at all. The text became a classic and was incorporated into religious ritual. Despite the political weakness of Babylon during the centuries after the reign of Nebuchadnezzar I, the theology of the Creation Epic became almost completely dominant in Mesopotamia, to the extent that of all the peoples there, to my knowledge only the Babylonians consistently exhibit the historical, theological, and literary patterns of a *people of an almighty god.* The Assyrians in the reign of Sennacherib, from 689 on to 681, did assume the beliefs of a *people of an almighty god* and modified Babylonian texts to reflect that status, but the phenomenon died with Sennacherib.[11]

3. Connected Histories

THE MESSAGE OF THE Creation Epic not only contradicted a religious heritage that was many centuries old. It also contradicted memories of the recent and remote past, preserved in earlier documents, stories, and poems. Other peoples than Marduk's Babylonians had ruled. Before Hammurapi's reign, Babylon had been insignificant, and in the middle centuries of the second millennium B.C.E. Marduk's city had suffered adversity.

Babylonian writers dealt with those problems using the patterns of a *people of an almighty god*, but in ways somewhat different from the Jews'. In the biblical histories only hints are given as to how and why God gave power to the great states of the remote and even the recent past. There is no good evidence that Babylonians wrote connected history before the rise of Marduk to supremacy.[12] One can argue that during or soon after the god's rise to be almighty a Babylonian historian produced the Weidner Chronicle, to demonstrate that the great Mesopotamian kings of the remote past enjoyed prosperity because of their pious devotion to Marduk and suffered adversity when they slighted him.[13]

The Weidner Chronicle takes for granted the absolute supremacy of Marduk; therefore, it cannot be earlier than the god's rise to be almighty.[14] On the other hand, it is preserved on a tablet from Ashur as well as in two fragmentary Neo-Babylonian copies. Thus, the text must antedate the fall of Ashur in 614. The copies of multiple origin prove that the chronicle became a classic text in Mesopotamia. Indeed, in order to have been accepted by the Assyrians of Ashur, it must already have been a classic for Babylonians.

It is unlikely that Marduk's theologians waited centuries to write a work like the Weidner Chronicle. As soon as they asserted that Marduk was supreme, they faced the necessity of explaining previous history to fit this doctrine. On the other hand, they could no more erase previous historical evidence than the author of 1 and 2 Chronicles could eradicate the historical books of the Bible extending from Joshua through 2 Kings. Nor did the theologians of Marduk in the reign of Nebuchadnezzar I and thereafter have to cover all of remembered history in their explanatory works. They had only to establish the principle of the primacy of almighty Marduk from early dynastic times, and believers could apply that principle for themselves. If the Weidner Chronicle is not itself the early work that Marduk's theologians could hardly avoid producing, the fact remains that no trace remains of such an earlier work, and no clue has been found within the Weidner Chronicle regarding its existence (as one could find clues to the existence of 1 and 2 Kings within 1 and 2 Chronicles). There is thus some reason to date the writing of the Weidner Chronicle in or soon after the reign of Nebuchadnezzar I, though one must be cautious when imputing consistency to Babylonian theologians.

Babylonian historians may have gone on to treat later periods in the same tendentious manner displayed in the Weidner Chronicle and in the biblical books of Kings, but if so, their works have not been found. What has been found demonstrates that there were Babylonian chroniclers who were not as sure of Marduk's purposes as the biblical historians were of the LORD's. Chronicle P is fragmentary; it covers from the mid-fourteenth century down to ca. 1220 B.C.E.[15] When complete, it may have included the reign of Nebuchadnezzar I. To judge by the surviving fragments, Chronicle P takes for granted the supremacy of Marduk but otherwise objectively narrates the humiliations suffered by the god and his city. A preserved passage tells how Tukulti-Ninurta I of Assyria despoiled Babylon and carried off the statue of Marduk and how under "Tukulti-Ashur" of Assyria Bêl (= Marduk) returned to Babylon.[16] Also preserved are passages telling how Elamites devastated Nippur and Akkad (Babylonia).

There survives a long set of "objective" Babylonian chronicles covering the reigns of the Babylonian kings from 747 to 539, with fragments of more such works extending down into the third century B.C.E. or even later, the period when Babylonia was under the rule of the Macedonian Seleucid Dynasty. As histories they are indeed deficient because they do nothing to explain the interconnections of events, as if the writers were not yet sure of this aspect of their philosophy of history. I believe that one reason why these chronicles were written is that the historians of the Babylonian *people of an almighty god* hoped that eventually the information in them would provide the key for understanding Marduk's purposes (perhaps even under Nebuchadnezzar I and certainly thereafter, Babylon suffered vicissitudes that did not lend themselves to easy theological explanation). There is in fact good reason to suppose that these chronicles were constructed by using information collected for the religious purpose of serving as a database for compiling a new astrological omen corpus.[17]

The so-called Dynastic Chronicle is not a connected history but is rather a king-list. It narrates no human events but only how the gods lowered kingship from heaven before the flood, how the flood occurred, and how the gods again lowered kingship from heaven after the flood. The badly preserved fragments treat reigns down into the eighth century B.C.E. or later; they say nothing of Marduk and mention Anu, Enlil, and Ea as establishers of kingship and presumably as creators.[18] The Dynastic Chronicle may thus be a relatively late example of a text written by one who did not accept Marduk's supremacy.

4. Stories of Divine Intervention in Time of Adversity or of Other Challenge to the God's Power

TO COPE WITH THE PROBLEMS raised by the course of history, Marduk's faithful also composed and preserved tales of how their god wondrously intervened to help them in times of adversity and punished mortals who slighted him. Such tales were written as separate from any work of connected history. There was a long literary tradition, going back to Sumerian times, for putting such tales in verse (whereas the Babylonian chronicles are all in prose). Scholars have come to call the tales in verse about historical figures "historical epics." The Bible, in contrast, contains no tales in verse of divine intervention. Mesopotamian writers also produced prose tales of divine intervention in which a king narrated his experiences; we shall call such stories "moralizing narratives in the first person."[19]

4a. HISTORICAL EPICS

Babylonian historical epics are poetic narratives written in the third person, each concerned with the activities of a king. With one exception, the surviving examples have as their main theme the supreme power of Marduk. It is he who grants prosperity to good kings and punishes those who slight him. We may expect that the writing of such texts began in the reign of Nebuchadnezzar I, and early examples should deal with him and his near predecessors. In fact, the earliest kings to be treated in the surviving fragments of Babylonian historical epics are the Kassite kings, Kurigalzu II (1345–1324) and Adad-shuma-uṣur (1218–1189), and enough survives of the texts to suggest that they were focused on Marduk. The opening lines of an epic on Nebuchadnezzar I himself are preserved, telling how the king lamented the absence of Marduk from Babylon. The poem must have gone on to describe Nebuchadnezzar's heroic campaign against Elam and his victorious return to Babylon with Marduk's statue. If so, that epic presented the king as successful and righteous. Most of the surviving passages of Babylonian historical epics tell how Marduk punished a sinful king.[20]

As we have seen, there remained partisans of the old religious order who did not welcome the idea of Marduk's supremacy. Some fragments survive which may be from an early Babylonian historical epic; if so, that epic, as an exception to the rule, has as one of its purposes the assertion of the power of Enlil and the other gods as at least equal to Marduk's, so as to deny Marduk's absolute supremacy.

The narrative is preserved on the obverse side of a late Babylonian clay tablet,[21] but we shall find reason to date the original composition of the text in the age of Nebuchadnezzar I. Despite the bad condition of the tablet, the general outline is clear. An Elamite king, whose name is not preserved on the obverse, comes to Enlil's holy city of Nippur and to Enlil's temple, the Ekur, and apparently (the passage is mutilated) succeeds in looting it. Thereupon, the king marches upon another temple, the Eadgege, intending to plunder it, too. But the *shêdu* (guardian angel or demon) of Esharra, the heavenly abode of the gods, descends to oppose him. When the king advances upon the statue of Ennundagalla, a subordinate god of Nippur,[22] the statue flashes like lightning and quakes, so that the king, intimidated, shrinks back. Nevertheless, the king orders his *nisakku* (high official)[23] to seize Ennundagalla's diadem. The *nisakku* fearlessly tries to obey and suffers miraculous disablement.

The Elamite king who was famous for humiliating Babylonia was Kutur-nakhkhunte. One might therefore guess that he is the king in the story, which then would demonstrate in typical fashion how Babylonian gods were active in a time of adversity. In fact, the identification is more than a guess.

On the reverse side of the same tablet is preserved a group of poetic religious "pronouncements." The first of them is mutilated, but enough survives to let us guess that the failure of a governor in Babylonia to perform some duty will cause the avenging *shêdu* to descend from above, and on earth the Elamite enemy will work evil, and the lordly god (Bêl; here, too, surely another name for Marduk) in wrath will allow evil to be plotted against Babylon. According to the second pronouncement, the failure of a governor to pronounce just decisions will cause the avenging *shêdu* to descend, the Elamite enemy will seize property, and Enlil will blaze with anger. According to the third, sins of certain functionaries will provoke all the gods to descend in a storm, and the heaven-god Anu, called here "creator" (*pâtiq-*), will bring destruction upon important temples of Babylonia.[24] The mutilated fourth pronouncement speaks of destruction and wrath and of the land of Enlil, and Kutur-nakhkhunte is mentioned in a rhetorical question, "Who is Kutur-nakhkhunte who did evil?" The mutilated fifth pronouncement speaks of conditions that brought trouble upon the Ezida, the temple of Nabû at Borsippa, and calls Nabû "protector of all" (*pâqid kishshat*). The last readable section on the reverse (lines 30–38) seems to be poetic narrative describing an Elamite invasion. Borsippa is mentioned as a target, and temples are reported to have been looted.

There is good reason to think that the material on the reverse of the tablet has a connection with the material on the obverse: Both are concerned with an Elamite king who invades and plunders Babylonia and with the avenging *shêdu* of Esharra. One is surely correct in using the mention of Kutur-nakhkhunte on the reverse to identify the king whose name does not survive on the obverse. Although it is conceivable that Kutur-nakhkhunte's acts became proverbial and could have been treated in a text composed much later,[25] the rhetorical question, "Who is Kutur-nakhkhunte?" is hardly the way one would write about a personality of the distant past. Later disasters to Babylonia could make the faithful lose interest in the atrocities of Kutur-nakhkhunte. After the Assyrian king Tiglath-pileser I (reigned 1115–1077) hit Babylonia hard,[26] Babylonian believers would have been concerned rather to explain that later disaster. In the pronouncements on the reverse of the tablet, we find an insistence on explaining the disasters by sin, typical of *peoples of an almighty god*, though not restricted to them. The most likely time for Babylonians to write an epic on evil Kutur-nakhkhunte was between the victory of Nebuchadnezzar I and the campaign of Tiglath-pileser I.

Other peculiarities of the tablet suggest an early date for the text. Though Marduk is prominent already under his alternative name, Bêl, he has no role in the narrative on the obverse and, in the pronouncements on the reverse, has to share the stage with Enlil, Anu, and Nabû. Anu and Enlil were the two leading deities of the Mesopotamian pantheon before Marduk became the almighty king of the gods. Also present as a moving force in history is the collectivity of the other gods in Esharra, again just as before the Babylonians became a *people of an almighty god*. The events on the obverse occur in Enlil's holy city of Nippur and at his temple, the Ekur. On the other hand, Nabû appears on the reverse, as god of Borsippa; his prominence in Borsippa begins in the age of Nebuchadnezzar I.[27] It would thus seem that on this tablet is another text opposing the idea of the supremacy of Marduk by insisting on the importance of Enlil and Nippur, a text that was written in the age of Nebuchadnezzar I and perhaps during his reign.

4b. Moralizing Narratives in the First Person

These are prose narratives in the first person in which kings tell of their experiences. The phenomena described are historical, legendary, and occasionally supernatural. The central theme of the best preserved example, the Cuthaean Legend of Narâm-Sin, is that a king must heed the diviners and abstain from aggressive imperialism or suffer dire consequences (Marduk is not mentioned in that text). The other representatives of the genre probably also taught religious lessons.[28]

Most of the surviving examples deal with kings who for Babylonian writers lay in the remote past, Sargon of Agade (ca. 2334–2279) and his grandson, Narâm-Sin (ca. 2254–2218). For those examples at least, Grayson's designation of the genre as *"pseudo-*autobiography" and Longman's of it as "fictional"[29] are justified. However, I do not see any way of excluding the possibility that a king could write such a composition about himself, so I prefer to use the term "moralizing narratives in the first person." For this genre, too, the age of Nebuchadnezzar I may have been a turning point. One of the surviving fragments treats a king of the Kassite period.[30] Another probably treats Nebuchadnezzar I himself.[31]

The preserved lines of the latter text begin by speaking of how Elamite kings crushed the last members of the Kassite Dynasty and how Kutur-nakhkhunte destroyed the cult-centers of Babylonia and carried off the statue of the great lord, Marduk. After a lacuna, the Babylonian king tells how he and his army were troubled (by defeat?): "They [the army?] saw, they searched the decision of Marduk." The king tells how he nevertheless resolved to go into battle against the Elamites, but "Irra, the strong god," smote his warriors with disease, so that the disconsolate king feared death and withdrew before the Elamite onslaught. In the last preserved lines the king is praying that "the heart of Enlil will be appeased . . . his anger mitigated."[32]

This text pays respect to Marduk but also tells how Irra the "strong god" smote the warriors of Babylon and presents the king who is probably Nebuchadnezzar I as praying for the favor of Enlil. It, too, would seem to spring from the movement that in the age of Nebuchadnezzar I and his early successors tried to resist the idea of the absolute supremacy of Marduk. If so, one may guess that the text ended by telling how Nebuchadnezzar I with the aid of Enlil and perhaps of Irra finally defeated the Elamites and recovered the statue of Marduk. If Nebuchadnezzar I wholeheartedly believed in Marduk's supremacy, this text is certainly pseudo-autobiography, composed during the reigns of the early successors of Nebuchadnezzar I, before the belief in Marduk's supremacy became fully dominant in Mesopotamia.

5. Prophetic Texts

MARDUK'S THEOLOGIANS SOLVED the problems of the repeated apparent humiliations of Marduk and Babylon also by fabricating a present-future prophecy, the Speech of Marduk, in which Marduk himself utters predictions on the eve of the glorious career of Nebuchadnezzar I.[33] Marduk tells how the three great humiliations occurred as a result of his own decrees: He himself, by his own decision, took up residence abroad, in the land of the Hittites,[34] at Ashur (the capital of Assyria), and in Elam, bringing prosperity to the land of the foreign enemy and adversity to Babylonia.

Significantly, Marduk says nothing of any cause that impelled him to make those fateful decisions, they were acts of his own free inscrutable will. Though Israelites might on occasion demand that God's decision be justifiable in human terms, the Mesopotamian peoples knew that the gods were too powerful for human beings and were free to make their own decisions, regardless of human ethical preconceptions.[35] Thus, we should not assume that the writer believed his audience would infer that Marduk made his fateful decisions in response to sin in Babylonia. Indeed, perhaps the writer from his knowledge of the periods could find no sin in them heinous enough to justify Marduk's desertion of his city.

After telling of his sojourns in foreign lands down to the eve of the career of Nebuchadnezzar I, Marduk turns to predict unambiguously the glorious reign of that king, though without naming him. "A king of Babylon shall arise," who will bring Marduk back forever to his city Babylon and to his temple Ekursagila and will be a great benefactor of other cities and temples in Babylonia. The writer's intentions are transparent in this text: Nebuchadnezzar I has not yet conferred those benefactions and the fabricator wishes him to fulfill "Marduk's predictions" by giving those grants to the cities and temples. Although the benefactions were indeed conferrable (and we may assume that Nebuchadnezzar I fulfilled the writer's hopes), writers of present-future prophecy typically predict an impossibly glorious future, and this instance is no exception. The return of Marduk and the other restorations are to be "forever." The reign of Nebuchadnezzar I is to be a golden age of abundance, prosperity, and glory. In fact, it fell far short of fulfilling that prediction.[36]

The Speech of Marduk was incorporated into a series of "classical tablets," and copies of this Babylonian document were found at the two Assyrian capitals of Ashur and Nineveh.[37] The Speech of Marduk does not indicate how the author wished the audience to think that it was communicated to human beings. There is ample evidence that the Mesopotamian peoples believed that Marduk could write on clay tablets,[38] and perhaps the original propagandists needed to do no more than to circulate a clay tablet of the speech, claiming that it had mysteriously appeared in Marduk's temple.

Another present-future prophecy survives, the Speech of Shulgi, which may well have been composed in the same period as the Speech of Marduk and in direct opposition to it. It, too, was preserved as a classic. It appears as the immediately following member in the series of clay tablets that contains the Speech of Marduk. Unfortunately, the text is badly mutilated, especially at its end, but enough survives to be interesting.

The speaker identifies himself as the "god Shulgi," favorite of the god Enlil and of Enlil's wife, the goddess Ninlil. The historical Shulgi reigned successfully ca. 2094–2047 over a large empire in Mesopotamia and Elam, as the second king of the Third Dynasty of Ur. Whereas Nebuchadnezzar I conducted only a successful campaign against Elam, recovering Marduk's statue, Shulgi completely subdued that country, and the Speech probably contains an allusion to that fact.[39] In his later inscriptions, Shulgi's name regularly appears with the determinative label "god," implying that he himself claimed divine status. Sumerian documents, centuries older than the Speech, prove him to have been a benefactor of Enlil's holy city of Nippur and of its shrines.[40] On the other hand, the Babylonian tradition of the Weidner Chronicle condemned him, surely anachronistically, for sacrilege to Marduk and for looting Babylon and Marduk's temple Esagila.[41]

The Speech of Marduk throughout stresses the importance of Marduk and Babylon, although it gives incidental mention to Enlil[42] and to Nippur.[43] In Babylonian, the Sumerian word *ekur* ("mountain house") is frequently used as a common noun, even though it is also the name of Enlil's temple at Nippur. But the speech of Marduk is peculiar in using *ekur* as an element in the names of temples of other gods than Enlil, for example in calling Marduk's temple "Ekursagila" instead of "Esagila."[44]

In contrast, so far as we can tell, the Speech of Shulgi does not mention Marduk at all and gives Enlil's city Nippur equal importance with Babylon. In the mutilated beginning lines, Shulgi claims to have received direct revelations from the sun god Shamash and from the great goddess Ishtar. Farther on, he speaks of the great extent of his empire and makes the false claim to have founded Nippur (unless the words mean that he strengthened the foundations of the city, that he rebuilt it). Repeatedly, he says, he carried out commands of Enlil and Ninlil to build and to go to war. These topics are expressed in the preterite (past) tense in the first two columns of the text.

Shulgi's surviving utterances in the remaining columns are all in the future tense, as predictions. For the real author, however, at least some were *vaticinia ex eventu*. A mutilated context refers to the Hittites and probably alluded to their sack of Babylon ca. 1595 B.C.E. A well-preserved context refers to the sack of Babylon in which spoils were carried off to Assyria, identifiable as the one perpetrated by Tukulti-Ninurta I. A third passage refers to a destruction of Nippur and a violent end to the reign of a king of Babylon; the events are identifiable: King Kidin-Hutrutash of Elam destroyed Nippur and in the same campaign put an end to the reign of King Enlil-nâdin-shumi of Babylon (ca. 1224 B.C.E.), the twenty-ninth of the thirty-six Kassite kings.[45] Clearly, by this point in the Speech, the writer has reached the reigns of the later Kassite kings of Babylon, a period on which our information is scarce.[46]

Unlike the Speech of Marduk, the Speech of Shulgi, to judge by its preserved portions, regards adversity as punishment for the sins of Babylonian kings and/or commoners. The last readable remnants of the Speech of Shulgi (column V, lines 16–30) deal with the prosperous reign of a king who rebuilt cities and shrines of lower Mesopotamia, including the shrines of Nippur. Thereafter, some thirty lines of text are missing. At what point did the writer of this present-future prophecy cease to write *vaticinia ex eventu* and begin to write predictions of a glorious future? The last preserved lines might refer to the reign of the king who would accomplish those future glories. If so, the Speech of Shulgi promised glory for one of the later Kassite kings, perhaps Enlil-nâdin-shumi's second successor, *Adad-shuma-uṣur,* who reigned for thirty years (1216–1187) and is known to have built at Nippur.[47] In that case, the Speech of Shulgi would have been written several decades before the Speech of Marduk.[48]

One should, however, note how the Speech of Shulgi overtops and differs from the Speech of Marduk. The great god Marduk openly treats events down to the reign of Nebuchadnezzar I as past; his predictions extend only into a brief period of the present and the future. Enlil's writer refuses to demean the great god Enlil by having him be the spokesman. Rather, he uses the deified mortal, Shulgi, as the speaker to glorify Enlil. Shulgi, going far beyond Marduk, foresees with accuracy what will happen over a period of many centuries. Enlil's writer puts no strain on the beliefs of his audience: No one has to assume that a tablet mysteriously appeared. Rather, a passage of the Speech of Shulgi (column II, lines 7'–9') implies that Shulgi had the text inscribed upon a wall in Nippur, where later it could be "discovered."[49]

Can Marduk's writer have allowed his great god to be overtopped by Shulgi? If the Speech of Shulgi had been written before the Speech of Marduk, one may be sure that Marduk's writer would have known of it, because such texts are not written to be kept private but to be published. One may also be sure that Marduk's partisan writer would have outdone Enlil's. Furthermore, why would one write such propaganda for Enlil and Nippur as the Speech of Shulgi under the Kassite Dynasty? The Kassite kings honored Enlil and Nippur as well as Marduk and Babylon. The question of the primacy of Marduk and Babylon over Enlil and Nippur arose in the reign of Nebuchadnezzar I.[50] We may infer, then, that the Speech of Shulgi was written at the earliest in the reign of Nebuchadnezzar I and that the last preserved reign in the Speech is not the one of the glorious future. It rather reflects the real past of the writer: One of the later Kassite kings, probably *Adad-shuma-uṣur,* rebuilt Nippur after the destruction of ca. 1224.[51] Enlil's spokesman would have to mention the fact. In the end of column V and in column VI, in lines now lost, the writer treated the disastrous fall of the Kassite dynasty and Babylon to Kutur-nakhkhunte of Elam and went on to the momentous reign of Nebuchadnezzar I, predicting for him the characteristic glorious future.

The Speech of Marduk and the Speech of Shulgi thus reflect the view of opposed "sects" in Mesopotamian religion. Nevertheless, both "prophecies" were so strikingly accurate that they impressed Nebuchadnezzar I and his contemporaries as well as posterity and were preserved as classic texts. We shall not be surprised to find that Jews and Christians could also preserve, side by side, present-future prophecies that were created by opposed sects within their religious heritages.

There are other fragmentary texts of Babylonian present-future prophecies. All of them are so mutilated that one cannot tell whom the writer designated as the speaker. To judge by the Speeches of Marduk and Shulgi, the speaker was always a god or an inspired or deified human being. It is worth noting that one of those mutilated texts, Text A,[52] has been conjectured to be a present-future prophecy that included (though with one scribal error) the reigns of the last Kassite kings of Babylon. One might then guess that with one other scribal error it went on to "predict" the reigns of the dynasty of Nebuchadnezzar I, down at least as far as the end in 1082 of the "bad" reign of his second successor, Marduk-nâdin-akhkhê.[53] Text A was found at Ashur and must have been written before the fall of that city in 614 B.C.E.

For two centuries after 1082 B.C.E., Babylon was in a dark age. No king of Babylon enjoyed a glorious reign, though a spokesman for the gods could venture to predict an end to adversity. Unless more of Text A should be discovered, we cannot tell how much further the author went in writing his present-future prophecy. Enough survives of another example, the mutilated "Uruk Prophecy," to suggest that it was written between 721 and 710 B.C.E., in the time of King Marduk-apla-iddina II. We shall consider farther on in our study present-future prophecies surviving from later periods of Babylonian history.[54]

The fragmentary nature of the evidence makes further inferences hazardous. Nevertheless, we have reason to believe that the existence of the Speech of Marduk provoked the writing of the Speech of Shulgi. We have no evidence of any Babylonian present-future prophecy earlier than the Speech of Marduk. Let us then cautiously suggest that Babylonians began to produce present-future prophecy because they had become a *people of an almighty god*.[55]

There is no sign that the Babylonians produced a literature of real prophecies on a scale like that of the Jews. Nevertheless, they knew of real prophets and of prophetic revelations, and some are preserved on clay tablets.[56] The Babylonian texts called "oracles" are messages from a god which a human intermediary, whom we can call a "prophet," addresses to a named individual, normally a king, in relation to a specific time and set of circumstances. Among these oracles are Babylonian analogues of the prophecies of Haggai, Zechariah, and the Second Isaiah, announcing the end of an age of adversity. Thus, an Old Babylonian oracle from Uruk survives, written ca. 1850 B.C.E., long before the Babylonians became a *people of an almighty god*. In it, a prophet announces to the king of Uruk (no name is preserved) that he has received a revelation from the goddess Nanaya proving that the age of adversity for Uruk is over; the prophet exhorts the king to hearken to the goddess.[57]

Two mutilated tablets in the British museum (Spartoli II, 987 and Spartoli III, 2) may preserve oracles from around the time of Nebuchadnezzar I or echoes of them. The texts are written in cryptic orthography, with allusive epithets that are hard to interpret. The style of writing is very late Babylonian.[58] We shall see, however, that the content shows that the texts were composed much earlier. Although both tablets are unique, it is clear that literate persons valued and preserved the texts over many generations, so that we may call them Babylonian classics.

Spartoli II, 987 is the written reply of Babylonians to a letter of Kutur-nakhkhunte.[59] The Babylonians reject the claims of the Elamite ruler to be their rightful king: No Elamite can reign over Babylon. Writing over three decades before the reign of Nebuchadnezzar I, the Babylonian author already takes for granted the supremacy of Marduk and calls him "king of the gods" (line 9); he implies (line 15) that any king of Babylon must endow Esagil (= Esagila). In lines 6–9, the writer reports that the gods have decreed that, instead of Kutur-nakhkhunte, one pleasing to them should rule. The basis for this assertion may well have been a prophetic revelation, whether to the writer or to someone else.

The Babylonians' brusque rejection of Kutur-nakhkhunte's claims proved to be disastrous for them. The Elamite king destroyed the city and carried off Marduk's statue.[60] However, his triumph was short-lived. His own son killed him, and the Babylonians recovered their independence. The Babylonians inferred that the revelation echoed in Spartoli II, 987 was true and that Kutur-nakhkhunte's temporary victory was an aberration of history (perhaps they viewed it as a temporary episode of Marduk's wrath against his own city). Thus, we can understand how the Babylonians came to preserve a piece of diplomatic correspondence which had had disastrous results.

Unless Jeremias's reading of Spartoli III, 2 is wildly wrong, that other mutilated tablet in the British Museum displays how believers in almighty Marduk in the age of Nebuchadnezzar I viewed the three great humiliations of Babylon. According to Benno Landsberger and Jan van Dijk, it too is a letter, despite its high-flown literary style, which resembles that of Spartoli II, 987.[61]

In the last fully intelligible passage of Spartoli III, 2, as rendered by Jeremias, the writer prays that merciful Marduk will restore Babylon and Esagil and addresses an exhortation to a king (again no name is preserved).[62] Before reaching this point, the writer has presented an elaborate exposition in which he relates, first, how Marduk, "lord of lords," struck down with his weapon a king of Babylon who "did not provide for . . ." (the direct object is lost; was it Esagila?).[63] Then he describes how three foreign kings plundered Babylon and "led water over Babylon and Esagil," destroying them, and how in each case Marduk brought it about that the foreign king's own son murdered him. One of the kings is an Elamite, cryptically named KU.KU.KU.MAL. We may guess, with Jeremias, that the author meant Kutur-nakhkhunte. Cryptic orthography and epithets make it still more difficult to identify the other two, but they may well be Tukulti-Ninurta I and Murshilish I. The figure of destruction by water could have been borrowed from the Babylonian Deluge myth and need not be taken literally.[64] If so, the text has the same three destroyers as the Speech of Marduk and belongs to the age of Nebuchadnezzar I and should not be dated later than the reign of Tiglath-pileser I (1115–1077). It has been suggested that the second of the cryptically named kings is Sennacherib of Assyria (704–681),[65] who literally destroyed Babylon by making water flood over it (in imitation of the Deluge story?) and later was murdered by his son.[66] But that identification is unlikely because it leaves unmentioned the first great humiliater of Babylon, the Hittite king.

In any case, the text asserts the supremacy of Marduk, "lord of lords"; the prayer to Marduk and the exhortation to the king suggest that the age of adversity is about to end. The writer cannot deny the humiliations suffered by Babylon, but in the typical manner of *peoples of an almighty god*, he calls to mind how Marduk was active even in those times of adversity, bringing doom upon the enemy kings, just as the God of Israel brought plagues upon the Egyptians while the Israelites were still slaves. A prophetic revelation to the writer or to someone else may well have given rise to his confident belief that the enemy kings fell through the action of Marduk. However, we cannot be sure of that, because the writer could have inferred his belief from the course of events. Babylonians welcomed the belief, whether derived from prophetic revelation or by inference, that almighty Marduk always punished grievously the perpetrators of atrocities against his city, and they preserved the text for centuries.

Particularly impressive as a text of a *people of an almighty god* and thus far unique in preserved Babylonian literature is the Erra Epic (also spelled "Irra" and "Era").[67] The names of the authors of most Babylonian literary pieces, including epics, are unknown. The Erra Epic presents itself as the word-for-word record of the revelation which Kabti-ilî-Marduk received in a dream,[68] with the approval of the god Erra. The author not only gives his own name and claims to present a divine revelation. He reflects the circumstances of his own time and makes a real prediction of the future, one which soon proved to be false. Therefore, the Erra Epic deserves to be classified as a real prophecy. It resembles many messages of the Israelite prophets in that it is not limited to prediction and in that so much of it serves to explain why the *people of an almighty god* suffered a time of troubles.

The poet in his time faced the problems that so often beset *peoples of an almighty god*. Although Marduk was stronger than any other combination of forces, Babylonia after the reign of Nebuchadnezzar I entered a dark age of adversity, characterized by internal strife, defeats in war, and attacks by predatory barbarians. Sins might have provoked Marduk to allow all that to come upon his chosen city, and Kabti-ilî-Marduk knew of sin in Babylonia. Evidently, however, he could see no way in which the sin could have been bad enough so to provoke merciful Marduk.[69] Rather, such disasters could have occurred only if somehow Marduk's attention had been diverted.[70]

The poet perhaps begins the Erra Epic with praise to Marduk. If so, his procedure would befit a member of a *people of an almighty god.*[71] He then goes on to explain how Erra, the cruel god of "scorched earth, raids, and riots,"[72] induced Marduk to go away to have his crown jewels cleaned, leaving Erra in charge (Tablet I). Erra then brought upon Babylonia the dark age of adversity, taking advantage of Marduk's absence (Tablet II and the beginning of Tablet III).

One might have expected the epic to end with Marduk's returning and putting an end to Erra's mischief. Kabti-ilî-Marduk's revelation told a different story. The poet may have reasoned that if Marduk could be distracted once for the Deluge and a second time for Erra's mischief, he might be distracted yet again. Perhaps the poet was strongly devoted to the worship of Erra. For whatever reason, the mischief ends thanks rather to Ishum, the god of fire, who was the vizier and constant companion of Erra. Ishum pleads with Erra to desist from destroying the righteous of mankind along with the wicked (end of Tablet III and Tablet IV). In Tablet V, we learn that Erra consented: Strife might continue among non-Babylonian peoples, but lasting internal peace and prosperity and victory with spoils and tribute would come to Akkad, "and unto distant days Babylon will rule the cities all." Erra thus promised in effect never again to bring such disasters upon Babylonia. The epic is revealed to Kabti-ilî-Marduk, and Erra promises that any house containing a tablet on which it has been engraved will be protected from evil even if Erra should be irate.[73] The message is clear: Though Marduk may be distractible, Erra never again will perpetrate such deeds on Babylonia.

Prominent among the disasters for Babylonia mentioned in the Erra Epic are the depredations of the semi-nomads called "Sutû" (Tablet IV, lines 54, 69, 133). At Tablet V, line 27, the poet speaks of the victory of crippled Akkad over the "mighty Sutû." He must have regarded them as important. The Sutû began to hit Babylonia hard in the reign of Adad-apla-iddina (1068–1047), the fourth successor of Nebuchadnezzar I. The unsettled conditions in the countryside prevented the observance of the New Year's rituals (Akîtu) of Marduk himself and of his son Nabû, for those rituals required the free movement of the statues of the gods to and from Babylon. King Nabû-apla-iddina of Babylon (ca. 885–852) claimed to have taken vengeance upon the Sutû and to have restored Akkad. That king had an active interest in literature, and perhaps the Erra Epic was written under him.[74] On the other hand, W. von Soden has sought to identify the strife in Uruk mentioned in Tablet IV, lines 52–62, with events known to have occurred in the reign of King Erîba-Marduk of Babylon (ca. 770–760), and other considerations lead von Soden to set the date of the writing of the epic between 765 and 763.[75]

Whenever it was written, the Erra Epic is a text of a *people of an almighty god* explaining how that deity, despite his power, allowed adversity to come upon his people. The idea of the distractibility of a god is a common phenomenon in polytheistic religions.[76] The distractibility of Marduk would not necessarily impair for the believer the principle that the god's power exceeded that of any other combination of forces (indeed, not all Babylonians may have agreed with the poet that Erra had distracted Marduk). Even Israelites could complain (metaphorically?) that their God was asleep.[77] Still, there is more logical rigor in the view that the power of a supreme deity should include indistractibility. The Jewish parallel to the Erra Epic at *1 Enoch* 89:59–90:25 does not have God being distracted; God deliberately turns wayward Israel over, as punishment, to seventy remiss angelic shepherds.

As usual with the texts of ancient *peoples of an almighty god*, the Erra Epic solved only the problem of past adversity and left nothing to explain the coming of evil times in the future. Whether the epic was written in the middle of the ninth or in the middle of the eighth century, the onrush of Assyrian power soon afterward brought disasters upon Marduk and his city.

The Babylonians were remarkable for their practice of and trust in divination through the interpretation of omens. It may therefore seem strange that we know of few Babylonian collections of fulfilled omen-predictions from the time of Nebuchadnezzar I on. Most of the texts that report historical omens treat events of the third millennium B.C.E.[78] Three factors may have operated. One was psychological: The Mesopotamian peoples never questioned the validity of omen-interpretation. They therefore saw nothing remarkable when an interpretation was fulfilled. Another factor was reality: We know that Mesopotamian divination was mere superstition and that any fulfilled omens came about by coincidence, surely rare.

Most important may have been a third factor. Modern scholars have given the name "astronomical diaries" to the genre of Babylonian texts, each of which contains a summary of the astronomical observations for a period of half-a-year and associates them with observations on meteorological phenomena, the height of the Euphrates at Babylon, commodity prices, and notable events in political, military, or cultic history as far as they affected Babylon. William W. Hallo believes that the diaries represent a deliberate effort to assemble a "database" on which to build a new astrological omen corpus, with astronomical or meteorological phenomena in the "protasis" column as the predictors and terrestrial events in the "apodosis" column as the predicted. Hallo also believes that the compilation of the diaries began in the reign of King Nabû-nâsir (= Nabonassar; 747–734) of Babylon. "As it happened, the new omen series was never written—perhaps because the scribes were never satisfied that they had collected sufficient data. Indeed, diaries continued to be written till about 50 B.C.E. . . . "[79] Hallo himself admits that the earliest known diary is of 652 B.C.E., well after the reign of Nabû-nâsir. On the other hand, we would not be surprised if members of the Babylonian *people of an almighty god,* who also put such faith in omens, began compiling diaries in or shortly after the age of Nebuchadnezzar I.

6. Prayers Beseeching the God to Be Appeased

MARDUK, STRONG AS HE WAS, failed to protect his people. On one occasion, Kabti-ilî-Marduk in his Erra Epic revealed that the cause had been Erra's distraction of Marduk. But even if all Babylonians accepted that explanation, Erra had promised never again to do so. On suffering more adversity, Babylonians had to conclude Marduk was angry. We may assume that they could not find in their past conduct any sin great enough to have caused such anger. Their sole recourse was to pray that the god be appeased. One such prayer[80] became an annual ritual at the end of the Akîtu, the long New Year's ceremony. Its words invoked the principal temples where Marduk was worshiped as well as all the main gods: Temples and gods are asked to say to Marduk (clearly, as the supreme deity), "Be appeased." We can read the pathetic plight of the Babylonian *people of an almighty god* from the words of the prayer, "Do not neglect Babylon. . . . The bolt of Babylon, the lock of Esagila, the bricks of Ezida restore thou to their places": Babylon has been neglected, and Esagila and Ezida have been violated. The prayer is a text of a *people of an almighty god*: Marduk is supreme; Enlil is his subordinate; Marduk even dwells in the Ekur, and Nippur as well as Babylon is his city.

The extant copies of the prayer are in the Emesal dialect of Sumerian with interlinear translation in Akkadian. Copies of the text were found at Assyrian Nineveh, dating from the reign of Ashurbanipal (668–627). Another copy was found at Babylon. Thus, the text became a classic of Mesopotamian religion by the seventh century B.C.E. With its classic status, its assumption of Marduk's supremacy, its invocations of so many deities of Mesopotamia as subordinate to him, and its interest in shrines of Mesopotamia beyond those of Babylon, one can say that the Babylonian Psalm to Marduk is a good polytheistic counterpart for the Israelites' Psalms complaining of their almighty God's hostility or inactivity. We cannot, however, assert that Babylonians began to compose such prayers only after they became a *people of an almighty god*. The origins of the genre can be traced back to the times of Hammurapi's dynasty. There are abundant examples of similar Babylonian psalms to other deities who never became almighty. Noteworthy are the psalms to Enlil, in which the other gods, including Marduk, are asked to pray to him.[81]

7. Meditations on the Apparent Injustice of the Gods

IN BABYLONIAN BELIEF, Marduk's acts did not have to be ethically justifiable to human beings. Nevertheless, as we have seen, there is a strong tendency in *peoples of an almighty god* to produce meditations upon what appears to be the injustice of the deity to the suffering righteous individual. Such texts usually present a righteous sufferer and follow his experiences and utterances through to a happy ending. Two such Babylonian literary works are interesting for our study.[82]

7a. LUDLUL BÊL NÊMEQI

Ludlul bêl nêmeqi ("I will praise the lord of wisdom")[83] is a meditation that takes for granted the supremacy of Marduk, beginning with praise to him. It is a long monologue, in which the noble Shubshi-meshrê-Shakkan, an upright person who had held wealth and high position, tells how he was forsaken by the gods, lost his position, and was beset by terrible misfortunes as he suffered from the hostility of human beings and from diseases against which prayer and exorcism proved to be of no avail, despite the righteousness of the sufferer and his devotion to the rites of the gods. Accordingly, he protests.

We can see here the problem of a suffering righteous member of a *people of an almighty god*: If Marduk is so strong, who but Marduk could be responsible for his troubles? In the poem, the victim does not directly say that Marduk caused his difficulties; he cautiously hints at the point, using pronouns and leaving their antecedent obscure: *"His* hand was heavy upon me." Next he tells of three dreams. Most of the content of the first is lost. In the second, a young priest, sent by Laluralimma of Nippur, purifies Shubshi-meshrê-Shakkan. In the third, a divine-looking young woman gives him a message of consolation, and the young exorcist Urnindinlugga the Babylonian (?—the word is mutilated), sent by Marduk comes to treat the sufferer.

At this point, his troubles abate, and he recognizes (Tablet III, lines 50–51) that ". . . The mind of my lord had quietened, and the heart of merciful Marduk was appeased." The poem goes on to present a detailed description of the sufferer's release from disease and gives Marduk credit for it. In Tablet IV the speaker elaborates on the importance of Marduk and of Marduk's wife Sarpânîtum in his cure: "Who but Marduk could have restored the dying to life? Apart from Sarpânîtum, which goddess could have granted life? Marduk can even restore life to someone already in the grave." Creatures everywhere, he says, give praise to Marduk. The preserved parts of the poem end with a joyful account of the speaker's restoration and of his offerings of thanksgiving in Esagil.

The names of Shubshi-meshrê-Shakkan and his benefactors Laluralimma and Urnindinlugga are characteristic of the period of the Kassite Dynasty. According to W. G. Lambert, the names "do not permit an earlier date, and stylistic considerations are opposed to one later."[84] Lambert, however, presents no stylistic consideration that would exclude the possibility that *Ludlul bêl nêmeqi* was written in the age of Nebuchadnezzar I, whose dynasty was the successor to the Kassites. A writer of moralistic fiction in the age of Nebuchadnezzar I could easily have chosen to give his characters names that had been common in the preceding century, the more so if he wished to imply that his hero had been a man who recognized Marduk's greatness before all Mesopotamia turned to do so. On the other hand, there is no difficulty for our theory on how the position of a *people of an almighty god* leads to the composition of these types of literature, because there is some attestation even from the Kassite period for the idea of Marduk's supremacy.

7b. THE BABYLONIAN THEODICY

The other Babylonian meditation on the apparent injustice of the gods is an "Enlil-text," one which does not mention Marduk and does not accept the idea of his supremacy. It is a dialogue between a sufferer, who exposes the evils of life and of current social injustice, and a friend, who tries to reconcile these facts with the established views on the justice of the divine ordering of the universe.[85] The speakers come to agree on a principle that would be uncomfortable for many members of a *people of an almighty god:* There is injustice among men because the gods created them that way. The creator gods are named. Marduk is not mentioned but rather the three who were the creator gods of Mesopotamia before Marduk was recognized as supreme: "Narru [= Enlil], king of the gods, who created mankind, and majestic Zulummar [= Ea], who dug out their clay, and mistress Mami [= Ninhursaga], the queen who fashioned them."[86]

The poem is an acrostic, giving the name of the poet, Saggil-kînam-ubbib. Since "Saggil" is another form of "Esaggil" or "Esagila," the name of Marduk's temple at Babylon, clearly the poet knew of great Marduk but chose to write of other gods. The composition of the Babylonian Theodicy is datable in a period when one can expect that Marduk's supremacy was still a matter of controversy, in the reign of a later member of the dynasty of Nebuchadnezzar I, Adad-apla-iddina (1068–1047).[87]

8. Conclusion

I HAVE STRIVEN TO SHOW how the position of the Israelites and the Babylonians as *peoples of an almighty god* gave rise to peculiarities in their historical experiences and in their literatures. I am the first to admit that many uncertainties are involved. I cannot read cuneiform and must rely on the translations of others. Not everyone will agree with my interpretations even of biblical passages. What I have called "Enlil-texts" long continued to be composed and treated as classics in Babylonia, whereas in the Bible no texts survive celebrating the importance of rivals to the God of Israel. Therefore, even if we cannot provide an answer, we must ask the question: How prevalent in Babylonia was the belief in Marduk's supremacy, even after the reign of Nebuchadnezzar I? In any case, it is clear that the overwhelming majority of Babylonians believed in Marduk's supremacy by the time of Nebuchadnezzar II (604–562 B.C.E.),[88] and that fact is fortunate, because especially interesting for our study are the histories and literary products of the Jews and the Babylonians from the sixth through the second centuries B.C.E., and we shall examine them later.

NOTES

1. Throughout the first five paragraphs of this chapter, I draw on Wilfred G. Lambert, "The Reign of Nebuchadnezzar I: A Turning Point in the History of Ancient Mesopotamian Religion," in *Seed,* 3–13, and Walter Sommerfeld, *Der Aufstieg Marduks* ("Alter Orient und Altes Testament," Band 213; Neukirchen-Vluyn: Verlag Butzon und Bercker Kevalaer, 1982). Lambert and Sommerfeld agree that Marduk is not known to have been treated in official royal inscriptions as the head of the pantheon until the reign of Nebuchadnezzar I (1125–1104 B.C.E.). Sommerfeld, however, maintained that nonroyal Babylonian texts so portrayed Marduk earlier, under the Kassite kings. The matter depends on the dating of the texts. Lambert presented argument to refute Sommerfeld's datings in his review article on *Der Aufstieg Marduks* ("Studies in Marduk," *Bulletin of the School of Oriental and African Studies* 47 [1984], 1–9). We shall find reason to believe that people of Babylon viewed Marduk as almighty already in the late Kassite period. For our purposes, the difference between Lambert's and Sommerfeld's positions is of little importance. The quotation at the end of the first paragraph of this chapter is from Lambert in *Seed,* 6. The quotation remained true for centuries after the fall of Hammurapi's dynasty, throughout the reigns of the Kassite kings; see John A. Brinkman, *Materials,* 252.

In early Mesopotamia, no city god was strong enough to give permanent protection to his city. The Sumerian king list reports the transfer of rule from city to city, without giving any reason: "X was smitten by weapons; its kingship was removed to Y" (*ANET,* 266). The Sumerian lamentations over fallen cities state explicitly that the fallen city was righteous and that no city can hold the favor of the gods permanently (*ANET,* 455–63, 611–19). On the god Enlil, see chap 1, n 4.

2   Most of the inhabitants took for granted that the king of Babylon was the king of (Sumer and) Akkad: See, e.g., Brinkman, PHPKB, 207 (cf. 189). See also the Synchronistic History and the Babylonian Chronicles, in Grayson, *ABC.* One must be cautious about asserting that there was near-universal belief in Marduk's supremacy before the Neo-Babylonian kings of the late seventh and the sixth centuries B.C.E., as Lambert warned me in a letter of August 7, 1990, calling attention to hostility to Marduk in, for example, Uruk. Indeed, in this chapter I myself call attention repeatedly to instances of opposition to the idea of Marduk's supremacy (pp. 46–47; 55; 56–62; 63–67, 82). But the opposition seems to have been attacking the dominant view. See my remarks in n 6 in reply to van Dijk's letter. Text of Kurigalzu: See Lambert in *Seed,* 8.

3   No document of a Kassite king: See Sommerfeld, *Aufstieg,* 160–74, and Lambert in *Seed,* 8. Some documents of late Kassite times: See sec 5 on Spartoli II, 987 and Spartoli III, 2. The Babylonian Creation Epic, too, may have been written under the later Kassite kings.

4   On the inscription of Agum II Kakrime, see n 6.

5   Besides the texts cited by Lambert in *Seed,* see A. R. George, Review of *Literarische Texte aus Babylon,* by Jan van Dijk, *Bibliotheca Orientalis* 46 (1989), 382–84, and Tremper Longman III, *Fictional Akkadian Autobiography: A Generic and Comparative Study* (Winona Lake, IN: Eisenbrauns, 1991), 139–41. Where I use the terms "classical" and "classic," William W. Hallo would prefer "canonical" and "canonical text."

6   Sweeping change: Lambert in *Seed,* 3–5; Sommerfeld, *Aufstieg,* 182–92. Cf. W. W. Hallo and J. J. A. van Dijk, *The Exaltation of Inanna* ("Yale Near Eastern Researches," 3; New Haven and London: 1968), 66–67. Against van Dijk's argument placing the change in the reign of Abi-eshukh (ca. 1711–1684), see Sommerfeld, *Aufstieg,* 108–9. In a letter to me of August 12, 1990, van Dijk wrote that it seems to him that Marduk never supplanted Enlil (= Bēl) in the pantheon, that perhaps Marduk did become "enlil" of the city of Babylon and of its realm, and, in that sense, "enlil" has a different meaning from "Enlil" of the pantheon. But if van Dijk's view were right, there would have been no need for the polemic texts in defense of the majesty of Enlil and the polemic assertions of the supremacy of Marduk (see nn 7 and 11 and secs 1 [pars. 5–6], 3 [last paragraph], 4a–4b, 5 [on the Speech of Shulgi], and 7b). A cuneiform text says that the Kassite king, Agum II Kakrime (ca. 1602–1585), recovered the statue of Marduk which had been carried off by the Hittites, a feat parallel to that of Nebuchadnezzar I. However, Benno Landsberger viewed the document as both apocryphal and corrupt (see Rykle Borger, *Handbuch der Keilschrift literatur* [Berlin: Walter de Gruyter, 1967], I, 406 [t33]; Landsberger, "Assyrische Königsliste und 'Dunkles Zeitalter,' " *JCS* 8 [1954], 65, n 160; and Longman, *Fictional*, 83–87, 221–24). Even if the report is true, the recovery of Marduk's statue by a king of a foreign dynasty ruling Babylon is not a plausible political background for the rise of Marduk to supremacy, especially inasmuch as no known document of a Kassite king asserts that supremacy.

7   Lambert in *Seed*, 10–11. Later texts supporting the supremacy of Marduk tell how Enlil's eye was plucked out or even how Enlil was ritually killed. See Thorkild Jacobsen, *The Treasures of Darkness: A History of Mesopotamian Religion* (New Haven and London: Yale University Press, 1976), 231; Alasdair Livingstone, *Mystical and Mythological Explanatory Works of Assyrian and Babylonian Scholars* (Oxford: Clarendon Press, 1986), 126–27, 149–50, 152–54.

8   See sec 5 (on the Speech of Marduk).

9   For a description of the Synchronistic History (= Chronicle 21), see Grayson, *ABC*, 51–56 (its outright lies: 52); its text: ibid., 155–70; its connection with the inscriptions of the Assyrian kings: ibid., 54, and Oppenheim, *Ancient Mesopotamia*, 161.

10   Babylonian conflict with Elam: At Babylonian Chronicle 1, col. IB, line 9 (*ABC*, 83), the king of Elam enters Sippar and perpetrates a massacre, but Sippar and the rest of Babylonia were then subject to Assyrian King Esarhaddon. Besides the Speech of Marduk, two other texts that gave the Babylonians confidence against Elam may have been based on prophetic revelations; see sec 5, on Spartoli II, 987 and Spartoli III, 2.

11   See Lambert in *Seed*, 3–11; Jacob J. Finkelstein, "Early Mesopotamia, 2500–1000 B.C.," in *Propaganda and Communication in World History,* ed. Harold D. Lasswell, Daniel Lerner, and Hans Speier (Honolulu: University Press of Hawaii, 1979–), I, 91–96; Jacobsen, *Treasures*, 169–70. Lambert (*Bulletin of the School of Oriental and African Studies* 47 [1984], 3–6) argues against Sommerfeld and W. von Soden, who hold that the Creation Epic arose under the Kassite kings. Ritual recitation of *Enûma elish* on the New Year's festival *(Akîtu):* see *ANET*, 332. During the ritual recitation, the statues of Anu and Enlil were covered up (Jacobsen, *Treasures*, 231). For the most part, even the writers of the mighty Neo-Assyrian empire recognized Marduk as the supreme creator; see Jacobsen, *Treasures*, 232–34, and below, p. 79. On Nabonidus and the people of almighty Sîn, see chap 5. English translation of the Creation Epic: *ANET*, 60–72, 501–3; see also F. N. H. Al-Rawi and A. R. George, "Tablets from the Sippar Library: II. Tablet II of the Babylonian Creation Epic," *Iraq* 52 (1990), 149–57.

12   Only hints are given in the biblical histories: See chap 1, n 10. No good evidence: See John Van Seters, *In Search of History* (New Haven and London: Yale University Press, 1953), 82–83, 90–91.

13   Weidner Chronicle: F. N. H. Al-Rawi, "Tablets from the Sippar Library: I. The 'Weidner Chronicle': a Supposititious Royal Letter Concerning a Vision," *Iraq* 52 (1990), 1–10 (newly discovered nearly complete text); Grayson, *ABC,* 145–51 (text and commentary), 43–45 (introduction), and Irving L. Finkel, "Bilingual Chronicle Fragments," *JCS* 32 (1980), 72–74.

14   Absolute supremacy: This seems to be the meaning of the fragmentary lines 19–27, 29, and is implied throughout by the fact that Marduk, not Enlil and the assembly of the gods, gives sovereignty to kings. Strangely, Lambert himself (in *Seed,* 7) does not draw the inference to put the Weidner Chronicle at his date for the rise of Marduk to supremacy, the reign of Nebuchadnezzar I. He asserts only that it is "certainly no earlier than the Cassite dynasty." Grayson, however, drew the inference ("Histories and Historians of the Ancient Near East: Assyria and Babylonia," *Orientalia,* N.S., 49 [1980], 180). Although Lambert (in *Seed,* 7) mentions the Weidner Chronicle to support his dating for the rise of Marduk to supremacy, it does not serve as a main basis for his arguments. Thus, it is not circular reasoning to infer the date of the Weidner Chronicle from that of the rise of Marduk to supremacy. The author of the Chronicle of the Early Kings must have agreed with the Weidner Chronicle, for he copied sections of it (Grayson, *ABC,* 47; Van Seters, *Search,* 84–85).

15   The Verse Chronicle of Nabonidus should not be classified with the chronicles but with the Babylonian historical epics; see Grayson, BHLT, 43. Chronicle P: See *ABC,* 50, 56–59 (introduction); 170–77 (text and commentary). Grayson classifies Chronicle P along with the Assyrian Synchronistic History as a "biased history," but he himself is the first to assert that it is hard to discover any bias in it (*ABC,* 50, 56–58). But see Van Seters, *Search,* 86–87.

16   The fragments of Chronicle P focus on Marduk and on no other god (col. III, line 8; col. IV, lines 5–6, 12; at col. IV, line 5, Marduk is *ᵈBêl rabû,* and at col. IV, line 12, he is *Bêl*). No King Tukulti-Ashur of Assyria is recorded anywhere else. Ninurta-tukulti-Ashur reigned in 1133, but if he returned a statue of Marduk to Babylon in 1133 (the one carried off by Tukulti-Ninurta I in ca. 1235), the statue carried off by Elamite King Kutur-nakhkhunte in ca. 1160 must have been a different one. We do not hear elsewhere of Babylonians having a statue of Marduk made to replace one carried off by an enemy.

17   On the objective chronicles, see A. K. Grayson, *Orientalia,* N.S., 49 (1980), 174–75, and *ABC,* 8–28. On their deficiency as histories, see p. 8, and cf. Joachim Krecher and Hans-Peter Müller, "Vergangenheitsinteresse in Mesopotamien und Israel," *Saeculum* 26 (1975), 28–29. W. W. Hallo holds that the objective chronicles are based upon the "astronomical diaries" and that the astronomical diaries had the religious function of serving as a database on which to build a new astrological omen corpus; see his articles, "The Nabonassar Era and other Epochs in Mesopotamian Chronology and Chronography," in *A Scientific Humanist: Studies in Memory of Abraham Sachs,* ed. Erle Leichty et al. ("Occasional Publications of the Samuel Noah Kramer Fund," 9; Philadelphia, 1988), 188–89, and "Compare and Contrast: The Contextual Approach to Biblical Literature," in *The Bible in the Light of Cuneiform Literature* ("Scripture in Context, III," ed. William W. Hallo, Bruce William Jones, and Gerald L. Mattingly (Lewiston/Queenston/Lampeter: Edwin Mellen Press, 1990), 13–14, as well as Van Seters, *Search,* 81–82. Though Grayson (*ABC,* 11) holds that the objective chronicles were written in response to an interest in the past for its own sake, I believe that their objectivity may be by default and that at least one purpose for writing them was religious; see p. 8. On the astronomical diaries, see also pp. 45–46. Babylonian writers of connected history may have had more than one reason for producing their works; cf. Hallo's discussion of the purposes for which the Mesopotamian kinglists were compiled, in *A Scientific Humanist,* 179–85.

18 On the Dynastic Chronicle, see *ABC,* 40–42 (introduction), 139–44 (transliteration, translation, and commentary); Finkel, *JCS* 32 (1980), 65–72 (containing the mention of Anu, Enlil, and Ea); and Hallo in *A Scientific Humanist,* 184–85.

19 Poetic sources seem to have been used in writing Chronicle P (see *ABC,* 57), but that fact does not impair the generalization that the poetic source was originally written as separate from any chronicle. See also n 15. I base the terminology and the descriptions partly on Grayson, BHLT, 7–8. However, Longman (*Fictional,* 45, 199, 203) has shown that the royal autobiographies are in prose, not in verse as Grayson supposed. For my disagreement with both Grayson and Longman, see p. 36.

20 See Grayson, BHLT, 42–45, 56–59, and *Orientalia,* N.S., 49 (1980), 186–87. According to Grayson, the main source for the Kurigalzu Epic is Chronicle P. Chronicle P, col. III, line 8, has "I *[made]* a canopy of pure gold for Marduk my lord." The Adad-shuma-uṣur Epic, col. I, line 10, has "Bêl, your help, who is like [you]?" Col. II, line 16, has "To Bêl, lord of [lords], let me pray that me alone he might not for[get]." See also col. II, lines 20–29, and col. III, lines 16–17. Mention is also made of Nabû (probably: col. III, lines 26–31), Nergal (lines 31–34) and Nusku (col. IV, line 6), but Marduk gets most attention. The mentions of Babylon and Esagil in col. II, lines 15, 19, 22, and 28, and of Marduk in line 29 render it certain that Bêl here is Marduk, not Enlil. Lambert (*Seed,* 9–10) describes another badly damaged narrative text with high-flown poetic imagery, telling of the aspirations of Nebuchadnezzar I and of Marduk's triumphant return from wicked Elam; the text dates from the Second Dynasty of Isin.

21 Spartoli 158 + Spartoli II, 962 in the British Museum, published in transliteration with translation and commentary by Alfred Jeremias, "Die sogenannten Kedorlaomer-Texte," MVAG 21 (1916), 85–93. Jeremias (ibid., 72, 76) calls the text "epic fragments," and Grayson (BHLT, 42, n 11, and *ABC,* 57) writes, "It is also possible that . . . Sp 158 + Sp II, 962 . . . are historical epic fragments." There is a later and somewhat better German translation, also with commentary, in Niels Stokholm, "Zur Überlieferung von Heliodor, Kuturnakhkhunte, und anderen missglückten Tempelräubern," *Studia Theologica* 22 (1968), 8–18. According to Jeremias (*Das Alte Testament im Licht des alten Orients* [3d ed.; Leipzig: Hinrichs, 1916], 280), the tablet is of Arsacid date (second century B.C.E. at the earliest). I owe this reference to Prof. Michael Astour. Most of the Babylonian historical epics are known from late copies. In those late periods, Babylonians, dominated by foreigners, treasured copies of the historical epics, probably in order to promote a sense of pride in themselves (Grayson, *Orientalia,* N.S., 49 [1980], 189, 192–93).

22 The late Babylonian series, AN = *(ilu) A-nu-um* (CT 24, Plate 28, line 64), identifies Ennundagalla as a servant of Marduk, but before the Babylonians became a *people of an almighty god* he may well have been a servant of Enlil of Nippur.

23 Stokholm, *Studia Theologica* 22 (1968), 10, n 41.

24 "Pronouncements" is my effort to render in English Jeremias's description of the sentences as "Sprüche." Jeremias identifies Bêl in Reverse, line 5, with Marduk. Stokholm (*Studia Theologica* 22 [1968], 10, n 48) states that "Bêl" was a name both of Marduk and of Enlil. Against his assertion, see "belu 1a.2," *CAD,* II (1965), 193b, and Sommerfeld, *Der Aufstieg Marduks,* 177, n 6 (extending onto 178). Jeremias read the title of the functionaries as *ša-bu-ru-ú,* but Wilfred G. Lambert in a letter of June 25, 1990, informed me that reading was wrong.

25 Cf. PHPKB, 90, n 476.

26 Roux, 279; PHPKB, 128–29.

27 Rykle Borger, "Gott Marduk und Gott-König Shulgi als Propheten: Zwei prophetische Texte," *Bibliotheca Orientalis* 28 (1971), 22.

28 See A. K. Grayson and W. G. Lambert, "Akkadian Prophecies," *JCS* 18 (1964), 8; BHLT, 7–8; *ABC,* 2–3; Erica Reiner in Wolfgang Röllig, *Altorientalische Literaturen (Neues Handbuch der Literaturwissenschaft,* ed. Klaus von See, Band I; Wiesbaden: Akademische Verlagsgesellschaft Athenaion, 1978), 176–80; Longman, *Fictional,* 116.

29 BHLT, 5, 8; see the title of Longman's work in n 5.

30 Published by W. G. Lambert as CT 46, nos. 49 and 50.

31 Published in Hayim Tadmor, "Historical Implications of the Correct Rendering of Akkadian *dâku," JNES* 17 (1958), 137–39. Tadmor did not identify the king who is the speaker, beyond asserting that he was one of the first four kings of the Second Dynasty of Isin (the dynasty of which Nebuchadnezzar I was the fourth king), and Grayson (BHLT, 8, n 11) leaves the same uncertainty. However, Brinkman (PHPKB, 106, esp. nn 571, 575) unhesitatingly identifies the speaker as Nebuchadnezzar I. See also Longman, *Fictional,* 194–95, 243 (English translation).

32 Instead of "decision of Marduk," Tadmor has "decision of the sun god," but his reading has been corrected by Brinkman, PHPKB, 106, n 575. Strangely, Tadmor's translation has "Nergal," where his transcription has "Irra." I retain the spelling "Irra" here because Tadmor used it, but see n. 67. As Brinkman informs me, *gashri,* translated by Tadmor as "strongest" should not be rendered by the superlative.

33 Edition with cuneiform text, transliteration, German translation, and commentary: Borger, *Bibliotheca Orientalis* 28 (1971), 3–13, 16–20, 21–22. See also Longman, *Fictional,* 132–42, 163–66, 233–35 (English translation).

34 Did Marduk, after being carried off by the Hittites, reside in their land? See Roux, 245–46; Benno Landsberger, "Assyrische Königsliste und 'Dunkles Zeitalter,' "*JCS* 8 (1954), 65, n 160; C. J. Gadd, "Hammurabi and the End of His Dynasty," chap v of CAH³, Vol. II, Part I (1973), 226.

35 See chap 1, pp. 18–19.

36 For the available facts on the reign of Nebuchadnezzar I, see PHPKB, 104–16.

37 Borger, *Bibliotheca Orientalis* 28 (1971), 3–4, 21.

38 See Daniel D. Luckenbill, *Ancient Records of Assyria and Babylon* (2 vols.; Chicago: University of Chicago Press, 1926–27), II, 243, and "The Black Stone of Esarhaddon," *American Journal of Semitic Languages and Literatures* 41 (1925), 165–67; see also my treatment of Daniel 5 below, chap 8.

39 Edition with transliteration, translation, and commentary: Borger, *Bibliotheca Orientalis* 28 (1971), 14–15, 20–21, 23–24. See also Longman, *Fictional,* 142–46, 163–66, 236–37 (English translation). Facts about the historical Shulgi: see Roux, 168–69; Kramer, *Sumerians,* 68–69; allusion: column II, line 20'.

40 Kramer, *Sumerians,* 47; cf. *ANET,* 584–86 (of Shulgi) and 583–84 (of Shulgi's father, Ur-Nammu). See William W. Hallo, *Early Mesopotamian Royal Titles* ("American Oriental Series," vol. 43; New Haven: American Oriental Society, 1957), 60–61.

41   See *ABC,* 48, 150, 154, and cf. the fragmentary chronicle from Uruk, Document 2 in Hermann Hunger, *Spätbabylonische Texte aus Uruk,* Teil I ("Ausgrabungen der Deutschen Forschungsgemeinschaft in Uruk-Warka," Band IX; Berlin: Gebr. Mann, 1976), 19–20.

42   Col. I, line 1.

43   Col. I, lines 2 and 9'.

44   See Borger, *Bibliotheca Orientalis* 28 (1971), 18, note on col. I, line 4'.

45   Borger, *Bibliotheca Orientalis* 28 (1971), 23.

46   Roux, 246–52, 263–65; the available information is collected in Brinkman, *Materials.*

47   No building texts are attested for the first two successors of Enlil-nâdin-shumi, but the next king, Adad-shuma-uṣur is known to have had work done on the Ekur; see Brinkman, *Materials,* 87–90, 146–52.

48   Cf. Borger, *Bibliotheca Orientalis* 28 (1971), 23.

49   Cf. Borger, *Bibliotheca Orientalis* 28 (1971), 22 (last paragraph).

50   Enlil and Marduk under the Kassites: Roux, 248, 249.

51   The destruction of ca. 1224: see n 45.

52   Grayson in BHLT calls the texts "Akkadian prophecies." Longman has presented detailed arguments to show how all known examples of Babylonian present-future prophecies are written as utterances of gods in the first person (*Fictional,* 131–32, 136–37, 143–44, 146–47, 150–52, 162–64).
    Text A has been published with introduction, transliteration, and translation in A. K. Grayson and W. G. Lambert, "Akkadian Prophecies," *JCS* 18 (1964), 7–16. See also Longman, *Fictional,* 152–66, 240–42.

53   Text A gives the number of regnal years but not the names of the kings who "are to" reign. For the hypothesis that the first preserved figures are those of the reigns of late kings of the Kassite Dynasty, first suggested by E. Weidner; see W. G. Lambert, *The Background of Jewish Apocalyptic* (London: Athlone Press, 1978), 10. If my guess is correct, the reigns and kings in the passages of Text A would be as follows: in First Side, col. II, lines 2–8, good reign of 18 years (scribal error for 15), Meli-Shipak (alternative reading of name: Melishikhu; 1186–1172); in col. II, lines 9–14, bad reign of 13 years, Marduk-apla-iddina I (1171–1159).

In col. II, lines 14–18, one ruler is treated, and another, in line 19. If the reigns predicted in Text A are to come close to fitting those known from the late kings of the Kassite dynasty, one of those two monarchs was not recognized in King List A. In fact, the bad king of lines 14–18 is described as a "nobody" and the length of his reign is unspecified. The king of line 19 is described as ephemeral, and the prediction is that "he will not be master of the land." One of those two rulers can be identified with Zababa-shuma-iddina (1158), and the other's name, absent from the king-list, is unknown to us.

The rest of the kings would be as follows: in col. II, lines 20–23, bad reign of three years, Enlil-nâdin-akhi (1157–1155); in col. III, lines 1–8, length of good reign not preserved, Marduk-kâbit-akhkhêshu (1157–1140); in col. III, lines 9–11, reign of 8 years (moral character not preserved), Itti-Marduk-balâṭu (1139–1132); in Second Side, col. I, length and character of two reigns not preserved, Ninurta-nâdin-shumi (1131–1126) and Nebuchadnezzar I (1125–1104); in col. II, lines 2–9, bad reign of three years, Enlil-nâdin-apli (1103–1100); in col. II, lines 10–20, bad reign of eight years (scribal error for 18), Marduk-nâdin-akhkhê (1099–1082). For the known facts on the late Kassite kings, see Brinkman, *Materials.* For those on the kings of the Second Dynasty of Isin, see Brinkman, PHPKB, 90–130. I have taken the dates from Oppenheim, *Ancient Mesopotamia,* 338.

Against Hallo's identification ("Akkadian Apocalypses," *Israel Exploration Journal* 16 [1966], 235–39) of the rulers in Text A with the kings of the Second Dynasty of Isin, from Marduk-nâdin-akhkhê (1099–1082) through Nabû-shumu-libur (1033–1026), see C. B. F. Walker, "A Chronicle of the Kassite and Isin II Dynasties," in *Zikir šumim: Assyriological Studies Presented to F. R. Kraus on the Occasion of His Seventieth Birthday* (Leiden: Brill, 1982), 417; Lambert, *Background,* 18, n 13; Brinkman, PHPKB, 129, n 762; Longman *Fictional,* 154; Longman, ibid., 155–62, argues in defense of Hallo's identification.

54 On the "Uruk Prophecy," see my article, "The Historical Setting of the Uruk Prophecy," *JNES* 47 (1988), 43–46, and cf. Paul-Alain Beaulieu, "The Historical Background of the Uruk Prophecy," in *The Tablet and the Scroll: Near Eastern Studies in Honor of William W. Hallo,* ed. by Mark E. Cohen, Daniel C. Snell, and David B. Weisberg (Bethesda, MD: CDL Press, 1993), 41–52. Beaulieu (45) admits my interpretation is possible but prefers his own, believing that it has the support of corroborative evidence. His interpretation, however, has grave weaknesses. We have no proof that in such prophecies the kings must have ruled consecutively, but that seems likely, especially in view of the texts that give the lengths of reigns. On Beaulieu's interpretation, between Erîba-Marduk and Nabopolassar the text would enumerate only six kings, though at least 21 ruled. Also, under his interpretation, the last king in the text must be Awêl-Marduk, son of Nebuchadnezzar II, who did not rule from Uruk and who was murdered after a very brief reign and was succeeded by Nabonidus, who was not a member of Nebuchadnezzar's dynasty. Thus, the prediction for the last king, "He will exercise . . . kingship in Uruk; his dynasty will endure forever," soon proved false. How could the text have been composed in the reign of Antiochus I (281–261 B.C.E.) as Beaulieu suggests?

55   The suggestion was made that *Textes cunéiformes du Louvre* 16:46 was a Sumerian present-future prophecy (W. W. Hallo, "Akkadian Apocalypses," *Israel Exploration Journal* 16 [1966], 242, n 79), but the text is now known to be part of the letter of Ninshatapada, daughter of King Sîn-kâshid of Uruk, to King Rim-Sîn of Larsa; see William W. Hallo, *Sumerian Historiography,* in *History, Historiography and Interpretation: Studies in Biblical and Cuneiform Literatures,* ed. H. Tadmor and M. Weinfeld (Jerusalem: Magnes Press, n.d.), 13–18.

Longman puts the present-future prophecies into the same classification as the moralizing narratives in the first person (see n 51) and holds that both are an organic growth from the nonfictional royal autobiographies such as we find in the inscriptions of the kings (*Fictional,* 199–200, 203, 210). But one should ask, what drove Babylonian authors to fabricate moralizing stories about kings long dead and to perpetrate the deceit of composing present-future prophecies? The predicaments that tend to beset *peoples of an almighty god* constitute a plausible answer. In any case, there is no necessary incompatibility between his view and ours.

56   On Akkadian real prophecies, which Grayson calls "Akkadian oracles" see BHLT, 13–14. On the prophecies from Mari and on Neo-Assyrian oracles, see Longman, *Fictional,* 179–82.

57   *ANET,* 604.

58   Both texts are published in transliteration and translation, with brief commentary, by Alfred Jeremias, "Die sogenannten Kedorlaomer-Texte," MVAG 21 (1916), 69–84, 92–97. On the style of writing, see Jeremias, ibid., 95, and above, n 21. In a letter of June 25, 1990, Wilfred G. Lambert concurs that the writing is late Babylonian, and warns me against trusting Jeremias's readings. In a letter of May 29, 1990, John A. Brinkman declares that the texts are "poorly understood."

59   See Jan van Dijk, "Die dynastischen Heiraten zwischen Kassiten und Elamern: eine verhängnisvolle Politik," *Orientalia,* N.S., 55 (1986), 159–70. Van Dijk's German translation (ibid., 166) of Spartoli II, 987, lines 7–18, renders obsolete Jeremias's translation of the same lines. So does Brinkman's English translation of lines 6–16 at PHPKB, 80–81.

60   Van Dijk, "Heiraten," *Orientalia,* N.S., 55 (1986), 169–70.

61   Ibid., 163 (n 10), 167, 169. Van Dijk, however (ibid., 169), groups Spartoli III, 2 with Spartoli II, 987 and with VAT 17020 as parts of a series of diplomatic exchanges dated before the fall of Babylon to Kutur-nakhkhunte. As read by Jeremias, Spartoli III, 2 speaks of the death of Kutur-nakhkhunte and therefore cannot be dated before the fall of Babylon to him. Erle Leichty kindly passed judgment for me on the style of the text.

62   Reverse, lines 9–10.

63   Obverse, lines 7–9.

64   On how the name Jeremias read as *Dûr-MAKH-ilâni* can be read as "Tukulti-Ninurta," see Michael C. Astour, "Symbolism in Genesis 14," in *Biblical Motifs,* ed. Alexander Altmann (Cambridge, Mass.: Harvard University Press, 1966), 82–83. In the text, Dûr-MAKH-ilâni is the son of *ᵐIR-ᵈÉ-a-ku,* which then would have somehow to be interpreted as an epithet for Shalmaneser I, father of Tukulti-Ninurta I. If the writer intended to allude to the Hittite sack of Babylon in ca. 1595, he did not know that the Hittite king at that time was Murshilish I. The name in Spartoli III, 2 is "Tudkhula," which would be only a slight distortion of the Hittite royal name Tudkhaliyash. Indeed, no Babylonian text records the name of the Hittite sacker of ca. 1595 (Roux, 245–46; Astour in *Biblical Motifs,* 89). There were four Hittite kings named "Tudkhaliyash," and the fourth of them may have been the last Hittite king to make an impression on the peoples of Mesopotamia; he was the contemporary and rival of Tukulti-Ninurta I (see A. Goetze in CAH³, Vol. II, part 2, 262, 290–94, but see also ibid., 265–66). Metaphorical use of the figure of the deluge: cf. Thorkild Jacobsen, "The Eridu Genesis," *JBL* 100 (1981), 526–27; William W. Hallo, "The Limits of Skepticism," *JAOS* 110 (1990), 194–97.

65   Hayim Tadmor ("Tid'al," *Entsiqlopediah miqra'it,* VIII [1982], 434–36) reads in Obverse, line 13, TU.UD.KHULA DUMU GAZ.ZA, "the offspring of evil, son of the killed one," who would be Sennacherib, son of Sargon II; Sargon II was killed in battle (Roux, 317).

66   Roux, 322–23; Simo Parpola, "The Murder of Sennacherib," in *Death in Mesopotamia,* ed. Bendt Alster (Papers read at the XXVIᵉ Rencontre assyriologique internationale = *Mesopotamia* 8; Copenhagen: Akademisk Forlag, 1980), 171–181; W. von Soden, *Nouvelles assyriologiques brèves et utilitaires* 1990 (No. 1; Mars), 16–17.

67   The best edition is that of Luigi Cagni, *L'Epopea di Erra* ("Studi semitici," 34; Roma: Istituto di studi del vicino oriente, 1969). For an English translation, see Cagni, *The Poem of Erra* ("Sources from the Ancient Near East," vol. 1, fasc. 3; Malibu: Undena, 1977). See also F. N. H. Al-Rawi and J. A. Black, "The Second Tablet of 'Ishum and Erra,' " *Iraq* 51 (1989), 111–22. According to Cagni, *Poem,* 14, there is no doubt that "Erra" is the correct reading of the name.

68   Tablet V, lines 42–44.

69   Sins in Babylonia: Tablet I, lines 120–23; Tablet V, line 6. On Tablet I, lines 131–40, Marduk expresses his concern for mankind and his regret that he allowed the deluge to occur!

70   Cf. Erica Reiner, "More Fragments of the Epic of Era: A Review Article," *JNES* 17 (1958), 45.

71   Ibid., 43–44; Cagni, *L'Epopea* 136. Cagni (*Poem*, 19–20, 27 [n 1]) argues strongly for taking Ishum, not Marduk, as the deity addressed at the beginning.

72   Jacobsen, *Treasures*, 227.

73   The text thereafter was inscribed on amulets; see Erica Reiner, "Plague Amulets and House Blessings," *JNES* 19 (1960), 148–55.

74   Roux, 298; Brinkman, PHPKB, 285–87; Cagni, 33–34, 37–45.

75   "Etemenanki vor Asarhaddon," *Ugarit-Forschungen* 3 (1971), 255–56, endorsed by Erica Reiner in Röllig, *Altorientalische Literaturen*, 208, n 23.

76   In the *Iliad*, Hera distracts Zeus from the Trojan War (xiv.157–xv.33); cf. also 1 Kgs 18:27.

77   Ps 44:24; contrast Ps 121:3–4. See Bernard Batto, "When God Sleeps," *Bible Review* 3–4 (1987), 16–23.

78   Oppenheim, *Ancient Mesopotamia*, 216–17. One of the Assyrian court astrologers of the early seventh century B.C.E., in dealing with celestial phenomena, refers to an omen series titled "How Nebuchadnezzar Shattered Elam" (Brinkman, PHPKB, 110 and n 599). As Lambert informed me in a letter, I. Starr published a text in *Archiv für Orientforschung* 32, 60 ff., which consists of omens including some about Ḫammurapi, Itti-Marduk-balâṭu (1139–1132), and Ashurbanipal (668–627).

79   Hallo, *Bulletin: The Society for Mesopotamian Studies* 6 (1983), 16, and in *A Scientific Humanist*, 188. The diaries have been collected, transliterated, and translated in Abraham J. Sachs, *Astronomical Diaries and Related Texts from Babylonia* (completed and edited by Hermann Hunger; 2 vols. and 2 vols. of plates; Wien: Verlag der Österreichischen Akademie der Wissenschaften, 1988–89).

80   The Psalm to Marduk (*ANET*, 389–90), and cf. Stephen Langdon, *Babylonian Liturgies* (Paris: Geuthner, 1913), 114–23.

81   Origins of the genre: See Stefan M. Maul, *Herzberuhigungsklagen: Die sumerisch-akkadischen Eršaḫunga-Gebete* (Wiesbaden: Harrassowitz, 1988), 4, 8–10. Psalms to Enlil in which the other gods, including Marduk, are asked to pray: ibid., 90–93, 112–16; see also the psalm to Adad, ibid., 148–54.

82   Strong tendency: See chap 1, pp. 18–19. On theodicy and its patterns in Mesopotamia, see Gerald L. Mattingly, "The Pious Sufferer: Mesopotamian Traditional Theodicy and Job's Counselors," in *The Bible in the Light of Cuneiform Literature* ("Scripture in Context III"; "Ancient Near Eastern Texts and Studies," vol. 8; Lewiston/Queenston/Lampeter: Edward Mellen, 1990), 305–336.

83   See the edition with introduction, translation, and commentary of Wilfred G. Lambert, *Babylonian Wisdom Literature* (Oxford: Clarendon Press, 1967), 21–62, 283–302; E. Leichty, "Two New Fragments of 'Ludlul Bēl Nēmeqi,' " *Orientalia,* N.S., 28 (1959), 361–63; and the revised translation by Robert D. Biggs, *ANET,* 596–601.

84   *Babylonian Wisdom Literature,* 20, 196–97; copies were found in the libraries of Ashurbanipal (ibid., 26).

85   Edition with introduction, translation, and commentary: ibid., 63–89, 302–10; revised translation by Biggs, *ANET,* 601–4.

86   Lines 276–78; on the identity of Narru and Zulummar, see *ANET,* 440, nn 3–4; on Mami, sister or spouse of Enlil, see Jacobsen, *Treasures,* 104–5.

87   See W. G. Lambert, "A Catalogue of Texts and Authors," *JCS* 16 (1962), 62, 67, 76.

88   Lambert in *Seed,* 3.

~ 3 ~

Peoples of a Nearly
Almighty God: The Egyptians
and the Zoroastrian Iranians

1. Introduction

I T WAS PRESUMPTUOUS for an author who is not an Assyriologist to write
the previous chapter. Still less am I competent in Egyptian and Iranian
studies. Nevertheless, if my study of *peoples of an almighty god* is to be
valid, I must discuss the Egyptians and the Iranians.

2. The Egyptians

IN SOME RESPECTS the Egyptians resemble the Babylonians and the Jews. In
others, they do not. Should we consider the Egyptians to be a *people of an
almighty god* under our definition? If we do, we shall have to account for the
striking differences. If we do not, we shall have to justify our exclusion of them
from the ranks of such peoples.

Let us consider first how the literary products of the Egyptians differed from
those of the Jews and Babylonians, bearing in mind how precarious is the survival of any Egyptian literature at all. The Egyptians wrote not on clay but on
perishable flimsy papyrus, and no continuous tradition of scribal copying preserved their writings beyond ancient times. One must be careful about general-
izing from what survives by chance.

2a. PRESENTATIONS OF THE COSMIC MIGHT OF THE DEITY

No single literary depiction of creation prevailed in Egypt to parallel Gen
1:1–2:3 or the Babylonian Creation Epic. The purpose of the Memphite Theol-

ogy of Creation[1] may have been to establish in the beliefs of all Egyptians these two points: that the god Ptah was the preeminent creator and that his city of Memphis was the earthly site of greatest cosmic importance. However, that purpose was not fulfilled. In Egypt several gods were credited with creating the world, not only Ptah, but also Thoth, Atum-Re', Amon-Re' and Khnum; and Khnum, Horus, Re', and Amon were credited with creating man.[2]

2b. Connected Histories and Stories of Divine Intervention

The most obvious difference between the intellectual productions of the Egyptians and those of the Jews and Babylonians is that the Egyptians produced no connected histories;[3] even stories of divine intervention are rare and mostly late.[4] There are no parallels to Babylonian historical epics and moralizing narratives in the first person. We demonstrated how *peoples of an almighty god* tend to write history in order to learn how to please the deity so as to prosper and to avoid adversity.[5] We also showed how stories of divine intervention were especially valuable in helping a *people of an almighty god* face adversity.[6] Before the time that Egyptologists call the "First Intermediate Period" (ca. 2181–2040), the geography of Egypt (desert, other difficult terrain, and sea) insulated her people from the kind of invasions to which the Israelites and the Babylonians were exposed, and the all but unchanging climate left the Egyptians largely free from natural disasters. The economic power of ancient Egypt long dwarfed the military resources of any invader.[7] These facts can account for the absence of connected histories and of stories of divine intervention from Egyptian literature: There were few if any ages of adversity to record or to face. Thus, we might have reason to consider the Egyptians to be a *people of an almighty god* despite their failure to produce these types of literature.

2c. Prayers Complaining of the Inaction
of the Great Gods of Egypt

Such prayers are conspicuous by their absence from the anthologies and the discussions of Egyptian religion. It would appear that none survive.[8] Can this, too, be an accident, due partly to the long periods without adversity and partly to the rarity of any texts surviving on papyrus?

2d. Meditations on the Apparent Injustice of the Deity

Such texts do not survive from ancient Egypt. Their absence may be due to the prevalence in Egypt of the belief in the judgment of the soul after death,[9] for that belief can solve the problem. Job and the righteous sufferers in the Babylonian literary pieces did not hold it, and even the author of the Jewish book of Wisdom had to argue against those who did not accept it.

Such are the differences between the Egyptians' literary products and those of the Babylonians and the Jews. But there are also parallels, notably in prophetic texts.

2e. PROPHETIC TEXTS

Texts beginning with Queen Hatshepsut (reigned ca. 1490–1469) of the Eighteenth Dynasty show the Egyptians believed that the gods communicated their will and also true predictions of the future through oracles and dreams. We are not told how the predictors in still earlier texts received their knowledge of the future; they, too, may have been thought to have learned the future through oracles or dreams.[10]

There are a few surviving reports of fulfilled real predictions, but by far the most interesting Egyptian texts for our study are the present-future prophecies. The earliest Egyptian present-future prophecy, the one ascribed to Neferti,[11] is in fact the earliest known representative of the type from any nation. Other Egyptian examples come from the much later periods when the inhabitants of the Nile valley suffered prolonged adversity.[12]

2f. CONCLUSION: THE EGYPTIANS WERE ONLY A PEOPLE OF A NEARLY ALMIGHTY GOD

Let us postpone our detailed examination of the Prophecy of Neferti and let us observe immediately that Egyptian literature differs sharply from the writings of the Jews and the Babylonians but has parallels to them in prophetic texts, especially in present-future prophecies. Greeks and Romans, too, produced present-future prophecies, and they certainly were not *peoples of an almighty god*.[13] One might be tempted to proceed to exclude the Egyptians from the ranks of such peoples, but our definition of the concept says nothing about the kinds of literature produced but depends on the religious beliefs of the peoples.

Let us consider the character of the gods worshiped by the Egyptians. Their theological concepts especially in the early periods before the rise of the Middle Kingdom (ca. 2040 B.C.E.) have what we might call a "lack of logical rigor": Contradictory views can be held side by side, even in a single text. Two deities can be said to be distinct persons, and yet they can be said to be identical.[14] Egyptians held that any of their deities could be killed.[15] Under such circumstances how can one assert with confidence that the Egyptians believed in a god stronger than all other forces combined? The conceptual imprecision also makes it difficult to deny that they believed in such a deity.

Throughout the history of ancient Egypt as an independent country, the king was held to be a god and, especially in the periods of the Early Dynasties (ca. 3100–2686) and the Old Kingdom (ca. 2686–2181), the king was presented in documents and on monuments as invincible.[16] Nevertheless, surely such kings were vulnerable enough so that most Egyptians did not really believe their king was stronger than all other powers combined.

Should we assert that the Egyptians held their entire pantheon was ultimately committed to protect them, and for that reason should we study the Egyptians along with the Jews and the Babylonians? The consensus of gods in a polytheistic pantheon was inherently unstable unless enforced by an almighty chief god. For example, though Zeus was king of the gods, he was not almighty, and the *Iliad* vividly displays how one group of Greek gods supported the Achaeans while the other group backed the Trojans.[17]

However, from the early reigns of the Twelfth Dynasty (ca. 1991–1895) and perhaps even from the late reigns of the Eleventh Dynasty (ca. 2040–1991), there is the rise of Amon, god of Thebes, to be identified with Re' as Amon-Re', supreme deity of Egypt, and Amon-Re' was viewed as the creator. If Egyptians held him to be stronger than all other powers combined, they would fit the definition of a *people of an almighty god*.[18] Again, however, we are faced by the lack of logical rigor in Egyptian texts and by the fact that the Egyptians believed that any and all members of the pantheon, including Amon-Re', could be killed.

Eventually, the Egyptians did come to suffer foreign domination, under the Hyksos kings (ca. 1674–1558). The Egyptians' religious explanation of this experience and of later such episodes can be used to exclude them from being considered a *people of an almighty god*. They blamed on the evil god Seth (later called "Typhon" in Greek) the fact of foreign domination, whether by Hyksos, Assyrians, Persians, or Macedonians and Greeks.[19] One must notice the contrast between the Egyptian texts and those of the Jews and Babylonians: The Hyksos and the other foreign conquerors were said to rule over Egypt with Seth and without Re';[20] Babylonians and Jews suffered because their great god sided with the enemy, whether on account of the sins of his people or through an act of the god's inscrutable will.

A people will not behave as a *people of an almighty god* as long as they have a dualistic religion, that is, as long as they believe that a second power is capable of withstanding the might of their greatest god (even if eventually that second power will fall), for they can and will blame adversity on the second power. Those medieval Christians and Jews who blamed adversity on Satan were not behaving as members of a *people of an almighty god*. Accordingly, we should view the ancient Egyptians in most periods as at most only a *people of a nearly almighty god.*

Even so, it is interesting that the Prophecy of Neferti, the very early Egyptian present-future prophecy, occupies a place in history rather like that of the Speech of Marduk. In the Prophecy, Neferti is made to predict to King Snefru of the Fourth Dynasty (reigned ca. 2613–2589) the rise and career of a king he names as Ameny (Amenemhet I, first king of the Twelfth Dynasty, who reigned ca. 1991–1962).

Snefru ruled at the very peak of the prosperous period known to Egyptologists as the Old Kingdom. Before the rise of Amenemhet I lay the long age of adversity Egyptologists call the "First Intermediate Period," from the Seventh Dynasty through the first kings of the Eleventh (ca. 2181–2040)[21] and the briefer span (ca. 1998–1991) which accompanied the fall of the Eleventh Dynasty and must in some way have lent itself to being portrayed in the Prophecy of Neferti as a time of disorder.[22]

Amenemhet I ruled during the very time of the rise of the god Amon to supremacy. The king's own name is a declaration of the fact, for it means "Amon is at the peak" or ". . . in front" or ". . . at the beginning."[23] Also significant is the king's Horus-name, *Whm-mswt,* "Repetition of Creation,"[24] reflecting at least his view of himself as founding a new dynasty. No text ascribes to Seth the evils of the First Intermediate Period or of the interval between the Eleventh and Twelfth Dynasties. Indeed, the Prophecy of Neferti itself contains an allusion to Seth in which he is not an enemy of Egypt.[25] The period was not one in which we have the right to call Egyptian beliefs "dualistic."

Neferti vividly describes to Snefru the coming age of adversity. He does not mention Amon by name but speaks of Re' as having hidden his face during the age of adversity and as being the one who is to act to "recreate" or "set in order" and thereby end the evil time. In this passage, the Egyptian root *(grg)* is not the same as the one for "creation" in the king's Horus-name *(Whm-mswt),* but it may be a synonym.[26] Neferti goes on to tell how King Ameny will arise and gloriously end the age of adversity.

In the Speech of Marduk, adversity for Babylon is a result of Marduk's withdrawal, and the speaker predicts Marduk's return and the glorious reign of Nebuchadnezzar I.[27] Similarly, Neferti says that adversity for Egypt involves the withdrawal of Re', and the restoration of her fortunes requires Re' to renew his creative action, and the prophet goes on to predict the glorious reign of Amenemhet I. The Prophecy of Neferti thus resembles a text of a *people of an almighty god:* The evil is not ascribed to other gods, but to the withdrawal of Re', who even before the rise of Amon to supremacy was the greatest of the

Egyptian gods, even if he was not stronger than all other powers combined. Did the writer of the Prophecy already identify Amon with Reʿ? Did he hold Reʿ to be stronger than all other forces combined? If he did, it is strange that he did not set forth explicitly doctrines that were new in Egyptian religion.

There are important differences between the Prophecy of Neferti and the Babylonian and Israelite texts. First, Neferti's ability to foresee the future is never connected in the text with either Amon or Reʿ. Second, though the text patently aims at justifying Amenemhet's position as king, there appears to be no effort to prove that despite Egypt's adversity Reʿ is still powerful. Reʿ's withdrawal, far from being presented as the cause, is presented only as one evil among many. In fact, as all Egyptians could see, the sun (Reʿ) went on shining during the time of troubles. His power was obvious. As Neferti said, if the troubles were to end, Reʿ must be the one to act.

Let us then grant that perhaps we should include the Egyptians of the period of Amenemhet I (the Middle Kingdom, especially the Twelfth Dynasty) among our *peoples of an almighty god*. With the fall of the Middle Kingdom, however, comes the tendency to ascribe adversity to Seth. From then on, it is certainly right to call the Egyptians only a *"people of a nearly almighty god."*

3. The Zoroastrian Iranians

BEFORE THE REIGN (from ca. 560 to 530 B.C.E.) of the famous Persian king, Cyrus, very little is known of the history of the Medes and the Persians, the two great Iranian peoples of antiquity, although the Medes joined the Babylonians in the final overthrow of the Assyrian Empire (614–609 B.C.E.).[28] The date of the great Iranian prophet Zarathushtra (called "Zoroaster" by the Greeks) is a matter of controversy, with some scholars accepting later Zoroastrian traditions placing his birth in the seventh or sixth century B.C.E.[29] and others, on the basis of the society reflected in his works, dismissing the later traditions as ill-founded and putting his life at some time during the Iranian bronze age (ca. 1700–1000).[30]

From the time of King Cyrus, however, the Iranians, especially the Persians, had profound impacts upon the Jews, the Babylonians, and the Egyptians. The teachings of Zarathushtra and of the persons who followed them left their marks on the literatures of those peoples, and the Zoroastrians in turn showed phenomena typical of such peoples and can be shown to have borrowed from the Babylonians.[31]

The decision to classify the Zoroastrians as a *people of a nearly almighty god* is straightforward. They have preserved a body of scripture called the

"Avesta," composed by or ascribed to Zarathushtra.[32] In the Avesta, their great god Ahuramazda is depicted as stronger than any other combination of powers; he is the creator of the world, of all beneficent forces, and of man.[33] At present, however, the world is in the age of "Mixture," when it contains both good and evil; at present, Ahuramazda has an evil twin rival, Angra Mainyu (later called "Ahriman" in the Pahlavi dialect of Iran). Ahriman can and does resist Ahuramazda, though eventually the age of "Separation" (of good from evil) will come, when Ahriman will be defeated and destroyed.[34] The dualistic teaching concerning the present age is sufficient reason to exclude the Zoroastrians from the class of *peoples of an almighty god:* For them all adversity can be said to have been caused by Ahriman.

But in other respects, the Zoroastrians came near being a *people of an almighty god.* The specialists called "magi" interpreted dreams and omens as messages from the gods and predictions of the future, a heritage that probably existed in the Iranian peoples long before the time of the prophet himself.[35] Zarathushtra uttered revelations (or is said to have done so) predicting events both of his own time and of later periods, and lost portions of the Avesta contained more such predictions.[36] We shall find later Zoroastrian seers composing present-future prophecies, some of which they ascribed to the prophet and another to a "sibyl" who lived in the remote past.[37] Zarathushtra preached a doctrine of dualism and also taught that human beings receive reward and punishment for their actions both immediately after death and at the resurrection which will come with Ahuramazda's final victory.[38] Therefore, the Zoroastrians could have existed as a *people of a nearly almighty god* without producing any prayers of complaint or meditations on the problem of evil,[39] and none survive from their hands.

Zoroastrian literature almost completely lacks historical texts, especially before the time of the later Sassanian kings (sixth and seventh centuries C.E.).[40] Cyrus had an inscription in Babylonian published, telling of his conquest of Babylon in 539 B.C.E., but it is in fact a text of the people of Marduk, for the priests of Marduk were glad to portray Cyrus as the agent of their god.[41]

The Persian king, Darius I (reigned 522–486 B.C.E.) came to the throne after violent struggles. First, there was the coup in which he and six other conspirators slew the person who had been reigning as king for six-and-one-half months, a man who claimed to be (and may have been) Bardiya, younger son of Cyrus and rightful occupant of the throne at the time he was murdered, because his older brother, King Cambyses, was then dead. Thereafter, there was the bitter series of wars, in which Darius crushed multiple revolts of the conquered peoples as well as a revolt of Persians who supported another pretender who claimed to be Bardiya.[42] If Darius was indeed a Zoroastrian,[43] very interesting for our study is the narrative of those struggles which he published in many languages, on perishable materials to be passed from hand to hand among his subjects, on imperishable stone to be read for ages by human beings, and on the inaccessible cliffside of Behistun to be read forever by the gods.[44] That narrative, whether truthful or mendacious, would constitute the great exception to the dearth of Zoroastrian historical texts.

We should at least suggest the possibility (even if we cannot prove it) that the Zoroastrians' dualistic beliefs constitute one reason why they, unlike the Babylonians and the Jews, lacked the incentive to write history. For them, adversity did not come from the the will of the creator but from the evil will of Ahriman. One did not have to study history to fathom the will of a deity whose ways were sometimes difficult for human beings to understand. Rather, Ahuramazda was known to be good, and Ahriman, to be evil.

Near Eastern rulers who were usurpers or whose title to the throne was dubious long before Darius had been publishing narrative justifications of their own royal legitimacy, and victorious Darius can be shown to have followed their patterns when he published his narrative.[45] But even when viewed in that perspective, his procedure had extraordinary aspects. His narrative was issued on papyrus in Aramaic and distributed to far corners of his empire. Aramaic was the official business language of the Persian Empire, but it was also widely understood among the subject peoples, both soldiers and civilians. Darius's Near Eastern predecessors did not, so far as we know, circulate narratives to be read by their far-flung subjects,[46] and none of his Persian successors produced a narrative like the inscription of Behistun, though more than one of them had to struggle to ascend the throne, and the last of them, Darius III (336–330), was only distantly related to the royal line. Can we account for these differences between Darius I and his predecessors and successors? Let us suggest a reason connected with our theories on *peoples of an almighty god,* even though we cannot prove that it brought about the differences.

According to Darius, his accession saw the greatest defeat of the forces of evil. Just when the forces of the "Lie" *(Drauga),* of Ahriman, seemed to be prevailing, they came closer than ever before to being completely routed by Ahuramazda and his supporters immortal and human.[47] Ahuramazda's final victory had not yet occurred, for the resurrection and the other events introducing the age of Separation had not yet come to pass. In his inscription, Darius himself expressed his expectation that the forces of the Lie would still be active in the future. Nevertheless, using our own terminology, we can say that Darius could have viewed himself as the ruler of a *people of an almighty god:* The events of his victories and subsequent reign for him exhibited the will of Ahuramazda, not that of Ahriman, and all peoples, Iranians and non-Iranians, should be told. He proceeded to tell them.

Darius's reign in fact marked the peak of Persian success. But his last years saw the defeat at Marathon of his expeditionary force, which sailed westward across the Aegean against Greece (491), and the rebellion of Egypt. His heir, Xerxes, was defeated in Greece and never came near duplicating his father's feat of rising from adversity to a spectacular height of prosperity. Still less successful were the subsequent Persian kings of the fifth and fourth centuries B.C.E. Ahriman seemed to be operating in the world, and history no longer could be taken as revealing the will of Ahuramazda. If the Persian kings were Zoroastrians, history for them no longer provided good material for sermons preached to an audience of their subjects and the gods.

NOTES

1   *ANET*, 4–6.

2   See Ludlow Bull, "Ancient Egypt," in *The Idea of History*, ed. Robert C. Dentan 22–25; Morenz, 51, 160–67, 183–85.

3   Connected histories in Egypt begin with Manetho (third century B.C.E.), who wrote in Greek and clearly borrowed his literary form from the Greeks. See Bull in *The Idea of History*, 20–21.

4   Stories of divine intervention: see John Wilson's translations and comments in *ANET*, 29–32. The text there on 29–31 was written when Egypt was under her last native kings and celebrates the power of the god Khonsu; the text there on 31–32 was written when Egypt was under the rule of the Macedonian Ptolemies and celebrates the power of the god Khnum. Papyrus Westcar when complete contained at least four wonder-tales. The first three told of the wondrous magical deeds of lector priests and did not connect the miracles with the gods, but the fourth tale involves Re' as well as Isis, Nephthys, Heket, Mesekhent, and Khnum and tells of a prediction to King Khufu of the Fourth Dynasty of the birth of members of the Fifth Dynasty, which would replace his. See Adolf Erman, *Die Märchen des Papyrus Westcar* (Berlin: W. Spemann, 1890) and *The Literature of the Ancient Egyptians* (reprinted; New York: Benjamin Blom, 1971), 36–47; William Kelly Simpson, "Pap. Westcar," *LÄ*, IV (1982), 744–46. The text survives in a unique manuscript written when Egypt was under the rule of a foreign dynasty, the Hyksos (ca. 1674–1558). Thus, all four wonder-tales of Papyrus Westcar may have served to help the Egyptians face adversity in a time when priestly magic was of no avail and the gods were not acting to set the country free.

5   See chap 1, pp. 7–8.

6   See chap 1, p. 6.

7   See Alan Gardiner, *Egypt of the Pharaohs* (Oxford: Clarendon Press, 1961), 33–44.

8   Cf. Morenz, 58–60.

9   See Morenz, 126–33.

10   See László Kákosy, "Orakel," *LÄ*, IV (1982), 600–6; A. Leo Oppenheim, *The Interpretation of Dreams in the Ancient Near East* ("Transactions of the American Philosophical Society," Vol. 46, Part 3; Philadelphia: American Philosophical Society, 1956), 187–89, 191–92, 194, 196, 200, 206–7, 209, 228, 242–45, 251–54; John A. Wilson, *The Culture of Ancient Egypt* (Chicago: University of Chicago Press, 1951), 169–70; Morenz, 68–69, 103–4, 124. There is a story of a god's revelation of his will through a dream to King Djoser of the Third Dynasty, but many scholars, including Oppenheim (*Dreams*, 189), regard it as a late forgery; others, however, think it may derive from an old written tradition (see Karola Zibelius, "Hungernotstele," *LÄ*, III [1980], 84).

11   Translated at *ANET*, 444–46; the table of contents of *ANET* as well as the translated text still give the inferior reading of the seer's name, as Nefer-rohu. Hans Goedicke attempted, without success, to deny that the work is a present-future prophecy *(The Protocol of Neferyt (The Prophecy of Neferti)* [Baltimore: Johns Hopkins University Press, 1977], esp. 1–14). An Egyptian text of ca. 1300 B.C.E. regards Neferti as a great predictor of future events (see *ANET*, 431–32). See also Donald B. Redford, Review of Goedicke, *JAOS* 100 (1980), 368–71, and Elke Blumenthal, "Neferti, Prophezeiung des," *LÄ*, IV (1982), 380–81.

12   For the texts and interpretations of them, see *Die sogenannte Demotische Chronik des P. 215 der Bibliothèque nationale zu Paris,* ed. Wilhelm Spiegelberg ("Demotische Studien," Heft 7; Leipzig: J. C. Hinrichs, 1914) and Peter Kaplony, "Demotische Chronik," *LÄ*, I (1975), 1056–1060 (includes discussion of other present-future prophecies); Karl-Theodor Zauzich, "Lamm des Bokchoris," *LÄ*, III (1980), 912–13; Ludwig Koenen, "Die Prophezeiungen des 'Töpfers,' " *Zeitschrift für Papyrologie und Epigraphik* 2 (1968), 178–209, "A Supplemental Note on the Date of the Oracle of the Potter," ibid., 54 (1984), 9–13, and "The Prophecies of a Potter; A Prophecy of World Renewal Becomes an Apocalypse," in *Proceedings of the Twelfth International Congress of Papyrology* ("American Studies in Papyrology," Vol. VII; Toronto: Hakkert, 1970), 249–54; see also Robert Schlichting, "Prophetie," *LÄ*, IV (1982), 1122–25.

13 See chap 1, pp. 3–6 and chap 1, n 16, where the last Greek example and the Roman example are both present-future prophecies.

14 See Henri Frankfort, *Ancient Egyptian Religion* (New York: Columbia University Press, 1948), 14–22; Morenz, 139–46.

15 See Morenz, 24–25.

16 See Wilson, *Culture,* 44–47, 72–73, 80, 83–85, 87–88.

17 On the Egyptian pantheon, see Morenz, 49–52, and the "Israel Stela," *ANET,* 377. Inherent instability: see chap 1, p. 4.

18 See Kurt Sethe, *Amun und die acht Urgötter von Hermopolis* ("Abhandlungen der Preussischen Akademie der Wissenschaften, Philosophisch-historische Klasse," 1929, Nr. 4; Berlin: Verlag der Akademie der Wissenschaften, 1929), esp. 11–12, 77–78, 111–12, 122–24; Eberhard Otto, "Amun," *LÄ,* I (1975), 243–45. The Hymn to Amon-Reʿ (*ANET,* 365–67) asserts his preeminence as creator of all, of man, the world, and the gods, but it also asserts (ibid., 365) that Ptah made Amon-Reʿ! One should note that Marduk, too, in the Babylonian Creation Epic was the son of Ea, but the Epic has all gods including Ea surrendering sovereignty to Marduk. There is no text proclaiming Ptah's surrender to Amon-Reʿ.

19 See Herman te Velde, *Seth, God of Confusion* ("Probleme der Ägyptologie," ed. Wolfgang Helck, Band VI; Leiden: Brill, 1967), 109–51; L. Koenen in *Proceedings of the Twelfth International Congress of Papyrology,* 250.

20 See *ANET,* 231.

21 Wilson, *Culture,* 104–24; CAH[3], Vol. I, Part 2, 189–201, 464–79.

22 Wilson, *Culture,* 130; CAH[3], Vol. I, Part 2, 492–95.

23 See Sethe, *Amun,* 11, 111; Eberhard Otto, "Amun," *LÄ,* I (1975), 237; Gardiner, *Egypt,* 126–27.

24 Jürgen von Beckerath, "Amenemhet I," *LÄ,* I (1975), 188.

25 See *ANET,* 446, n. 25; te Velde, *Seth,* 146.

26 *ANET,* 445; cf. Goedicke's discussion of readings and proposed translations of the passage (*Protocol of Neferyt,* 78). The difference between "create" and "set in order" does not matter for our study. The universe had not been destroyed during the age of adversity, so that the creative task in the new age was the restoration of order.

27   See chap 2, pp. 37–46.

28   See J. M. Cook, *The Persian Empire* (London, Melbourne, and Toronto: Dent, 1983), 1–10; Roux, 345–47.

29   Ilya Gershevitch, *Literatur,* 10–11 in *Handbuch der Orientalistik,* ed. B. Spuler, Erste Abteilung, Der nahe und mittlere Osten, Band IV: Iranistik, Abschnitt II, 2 Lieferung (Leiden/Köln: Brill, 1968–81), and M. A. Dandamaev, *Persien unter den ersten Achämeniden (6. Jahrhundert v. Chr.)* ("Beiträge zur Iranistik," ed. Georges Redard, Band VIII; Wiesbaden: Dr. Ludwig Reichert Verlag, 1976), 217.

30   Mary Boyce, HZ, I, 3, 189–91, and II, 1–3, 68–69.

31   See Morton Smith, "II Isaiah and the Persians," *JAOS* 83 (1963), 415–21, and below, chap 6 and chap 11, pp. 331–41.

32   On the *Avesta,* see Ilya Gershevitch, "Old Iranian Literature," in *Literatur,* I, 11–30.

33   See Boyce, HZ, I, 192–228.

34   In the Zoroastrian texts in the Pahlavi dialect, "Mixture" is *gumēzishn,* and "Separation" is *wizārishn;* see Boyce, HZ, I 229–46.

35   Herodotus i.107–8, 120; vii.19; Boyce, HZ, I, 11–12, 184, II, 67, 165, 213; on the magi, see E. J. Bickerman and H. Tadmor, "Darius I, Pseudo-Smerdis, and the Magi," *Athenaeum,* N.S., 56 (1978), 249–61.

36   Gershevitch in *Literatur,* I, 15–16; Boyce, HZ, I, 280–93, II, 254; cf. II, 183; Cook, *Persian Empire,* 156 and 254, n 32; lost portions of the *Avesta:* Boyce in *Literatur,* I, 49.

37   See Boyce, HZ, I, 287–89, 293, and below, chap 11, pp. 326–31 and 341–45.

38   See Boyce, HZ, II, 235–46.

39   Cf. ibid., 194–95.

40   See Gershevitch in *Literatur,* I, 25–26; Mary Boyce, "Middle Persian Literature," ibid., 57–60.

41   *ANET,* 315–16; similarly, in his Hebrew decree addressed to the people of the LORD God of Heaven (Ezra 1:2–4), Cyrus poses as the agent of the God of the Jews. On the Babylonian character of the "Cyrus Cylinder," see J. Harmatta, "The Literary Pat-

terns of the Babylonian Edict of Cyrus," *Acta Antiqua* 19 (1971), 217–31, and Hayim Tadmor in *Shilton paras,* 12–14.

42 Darius's rival the rightful heir: See Dandamaev, *Persien,* 108–232; Bickerman and Tadmor, *Athenaeum,* N.S., 56 (1978), 239–61. But the question still is not decided. See, e.g., Ilya Gershevitch, "The False Smerdis," *Acta Antiqua,* 27 (1979) 337–51; Cook in CHI, II, 215–17; Richard N. Frye, *The History of Ancient Iran* ("Handbuch der Alterumswissenschaft," Abteilung 3, Teil 7; München: Beck, 1984), 98–99. See also chap 7.

43 So argues Boyce (HZ, II, 78–131), but for the contrary view, see Dandamaev, *Persien,* 215–41, and cf. Cook, *Persian Empire,* 155–57.

44 Boyce, HZ, II, 78–80. Persian text and translation of the inscription at Behistun: Roland G. Kent, *Old Persian* ("American Oriental Series," Vol. 33; New Haven: American Oriental Society, 1950), 116–34. See also Elizabeth N. von Voigtlander, *The Bisitun Inscription of Darius the Great: Babylonian Version* ("Corpus Inscriptionum Iranicarum," Part I: Inscriptions of Ancient Iran, Vol. II: The Babylonian Versions of the Texts of the Achaemenian Inscriptions, Texts I; London: Lund Humphries, 1978); Jonas C. Greenfield and Bezalel Porten, *The Bisitun Inscriptions of Darius the Great: Aramaic Version* ("Corpus Inscriptionum Iranicarum," Part I: Inscriptions of Ancient Iran, Vol. V: The Aramaic Versions of the Achaemenian Inscriptions, etc., Texts I; London: Lund Humphries, 1982). Darius says he had copies of the text sent to all provinces (Behistun Inscription, Persian Version, col. IV, lines 88–92 [Kent, *Old Persian,* 130, 132]).

45 Bickerman and Tadmor, *Athenaeum,* N.S., 56 (1978), 241–43. On the narrative patterns of the commemorative inscriptions of the Assyrian kings, see A. K. Grayson, "Histories and Historians of the Ancient Near East: Assyria and Babylonia," *Orientalia* 49 (1980), 150–55).

46 On Cyrus, see the fourth paragraph above. He sent messages to subject peoples in their own languages, but addressed them in terms of their own religion and their own deities, whereas Iranian Ahuramazda is the sole god mentioned by Darius. There is no narrative in Cyrus's proclamation to the Jews, and even his inscription in Babylonian is poor in narrative content when compared with Darius's at Behistun.

47 Cf. Boyce, HZ, II, 90–97, 118–24. On the stratum from the reign of Darius in *Sibylline Oracles* iv, see chap 11, sec 5.

~4~

Jews and Babylonians, from the Reign of Ahaz to the Accession of Nabonidus (ca. 733–556 B.C.E.)

1. Introduction

MEDIEVAL JEWISH HISTORY and early modern Jewish history are fascinating because they present one *people of an almighty god* living in the same social system with another. In those periods, Jews existed as tolerated subject minorities in both Christian and Muslim states. Christians, too, existed as tolerated subjects in Muslim countries; Christian toleration of Muslim subjects was less common. The rival claims of *peoples of an almighty god* could not fail to lead to hostility and conflict. The minority people had to devise ways to survive. The rival claims also led to interesting examples of reciprocal influences and borrowings. The Jews as well as those Christians who lived in Muslim countries were instances of followers of "parent religions" dwelling as a minority among a majority who follow a "daughter religion" that acknowledges the legitimacy and former validity of the parent religion but claims to represent a superior later revelation.

In pre-Christian times, I know of no examples of a *people of an almighty god* living as a minority in the land of a daughter religion, but the Babylonian exile brought it about that the Jews came to live as a minority in the land of another such people, the Babylonians, and in this case, neither religion acknowledged the validity of the claims of the other: The followers of Marduk could not acknowledge the preeminent power of the God of Israel, and the Jews refused to grant even that Marduk was a god. There is, to my knowledge, no parallel for this equally interesting phenomenon in medieval and modern times. In much of the rest of this book we shall be studying the instances in which the Babylonians and the Jews affected one another and borrowed from one another.

2. From the Reign of Ahaz to the Fall of Zedekiah

WE MUST BEGIN at a surprisingly early point, because very important in the Jews' interactions with the Babylonians were the prophecies of the First Isaiah and the events that were seen as fulfilling them. In any case, the life and times of Isaiah were significant in the experience of the Jews as a *people of an almighty god*. The faith of Isaiah, a member of such a people, in his God never wavered; he was confident that the LORD would preserve at least a remnant of the people of Judah. However, the prophet himself gave his contemporaries ample reason not to share his confidence. From his own utterances they could infer that God was angry enough over their sins to allow them to fall to foreign enemies.[1]

From the known acts of King Ahaz of Judah (reigned ca. 743–727 B.C.E.) we can conclude that he lacked the faith of a convinced member of a *people of an almighty god*. His contemporary, the king of Israel, Pekah son of Remaliah, may have had that faith (as it proved, disastrously). The biblical narrative implies that Ahaz refused to join King Raṣyan ("Rezin," according to the traditional Hebrew vowels) of Aram and King Pekah in defying the might of King Tiglath-pileser III of Assyria. The armies of Raṣyan and Pekah invaded Judah in ca. 733 with the aim of replacing Ahaz with a king who would do their bidding. Isaiah predicted to Ahaz that the LORD would be with Judah: Ahaz would keep his throne, and within at most a few years both invading kingdoms would fall (7:14–16). Isaiah also strongly condemned the idea of seeking the aid of Assyria against Aram and Israel. Ahaz, however, showed his lack of faith. He sent a sumptuous bribe to Tiglath-pileser and declared himself the vassal of the Assyrian king, begging for his help.[2] Isaiah's predictions of the falls of Aram and Israel were promptly fulfilled, as Tiglath-pileser put an end to the kingdom of Aram in 732 and badly defeated Pekah, leaving him holding only the hill country of Ephraim.[3]

Pekah was soon murdered.[4] His successor was his slayer, Hoshea, but Hoshea himself rebelled against Assyria and fell into the hands of the Assyrian king, Shalmaneser V, and the last vestige of the northern kingdom of Israel had fallen to Assyria by 722 B.C.E.[5] Isaiah had predicted at the time of the same crisis in Ahaz's reign that Assyria would despoil Judah within at most a few years.[6] The predicted spoliation could be said to have come, but only much later, when Ahaz's successor, Hezekiah, rebelled against his Assyrian over-lord, Sennacherib, and Sennacherib punished the rebellion with a devastating invasion in 701.[7] Even with the delay in apparent fulfillment, the reign of Ahaz thus contained remarkably true predictions by the great prophet who held to the faith of a *people of an almighty god!*

However, it is worth noticing that (unlike Isaiah 6 and 8) Isaiah 7 is in the third person, as if Isaiah himself had not wished to tell of his somewhat inaccurate predictions. If so, unlike the prophet himself, his followers may have been so impressed by the ultimate partial fulfillment that they wrote up the narrative and incorporated it in the book of his prophecies.

Another prophecy of Isaiah was not preserved by the prophet's own circle but was strikingly enough fulfilled to be preserved in the book of Kings: the prediction in the time of Hezekiah (probably to be dated in 701 B.C.E.) that Sennacherib would go back to Assyria without taking Jerusalem. The author of Kings embedded the text of the prophecy in a narrative purporting to give the circumstances, and his composition was later also incorporated in the book of Isaiah.[8] The facts of Sennacherib's campaign and of the preservation of Jerusalem are matters of controversy, and some hold the whole story to be pious fiction, except for the report of Hezekiah's abject surrender in 2 Kgs 18:13–16.[9] I do not propose to solve the problems here, but I wish to point out features of the quoted prophecy which have received insufficient attention.

Though the quoted utterance predicts that the Assyrian king will not take Jerusalem, some of its content remained unfulfilled. The unfulfilled passages are very inconvenient for the point which the narrator wishes to make (that God defends the righteous remnant in Jerusalem). Contrary to the prophet's words in 2 Kgs 19:30–31 and Isa 37:31–32, the survivors of Jerusalem did not go out from the city walls to enjoy immediate prosperity. Rather, if, as some hold, the prophecy and its "fulfillment" came in 701 B.C.E., the survivors after Sennacherib's departure had to live in a devastated, depopulated, shrunken territory under Assyrian domination and after Hezekiah's death were ruled by his heir, Manasseh, whom Isaiah's circle and the author of the book of Kings could only view as wicked.[10] If, on the other hand, the prophecy and fulfilment came during a later expedition of Sennacherib (perhaps in 688/7), nearer the time of his own death in 681, it also occurred near the time of Hezekiah's death (687), so that the survivors would have been still worse off in their devastated country dominated by Assyria: They soon saw Hezekiah die, and they fell into the hands of Manasseh.[11] The author of Kings need not have known the true state of affairs in the aftermath of Sennacherib's departure; but though one might have expected him to write that the prophecy was fulfilled as Judah recovered and prospered during the fifteen more years he ascribes to Hezekiah's life-time,[12] he does not do so. And he eloquently describes Manasseh's wickedness.

The prophecy concludes with a "sign" for Hezekiah and his subjects: "This year you eat what grows of itself, and the next year what springs from that, and in the third year sow and reap and plant vineyards and eat their fruit" (2 Kgs 19:29, Isa 37:30). One would assume that a prophet offers a sign to let his audience know that divine power is operating to bring the prophecy to pass even before it is completely fulfilled by historical events.[13] No one has yet given a satisfactory interpretation of the sign, and I cannot give one myself.[14] Nevertheless, the words clearly predict that at least two years will lapse before deliverance is complete and are in character for Isaiah, who was equally cautious in his prediction to Ahaz: Deliverance would come, not immediately, but within about two years, implying that a king of Judah should patiently wait that long in near-impregnable Jerusalem for God to save him.[15] But the story of the repulse of Sennacherib as told by the author of the book of Kings has the deliverance of Jerusalem come immediately! However one interprets the biblical and Assyrian texts, Sennacherib and his army withdrew from Judah in much less than one year after Isaiah's prediction. How could the author of Kings have written a prophetic text which was so palpably false and inconvenient for his purposes?

Rather, we should infer that the narrator quoted a previously existing utterance of Isaiah, one that was too famous for him to alter; he himself did not fabricate the prophecy as an embellishment of his narrative. If, however, the prophecy was preserved and was famous, it must have been fulfilled in considerable measure: Sennacherib must have again menaced Jerusalem after first receiving rebellious Hezekiah's surrender of enormous reparations, and Jerusalem must have been surprisingly preserved in a manner which led people to believe that God brought to pass what Isaiah had predicted. Modern scholars have found it difficult to believe that Isaiah, after arraigning Jerusalem in chapter 1, would predict her deliverance, or that Hezekiah and his subjects, after being frightened into surrendering large sums in silver and gold and probably also large stores of arms, would then dare to face a siege. But there are parallels for Hezekiah's desperate resolution,[16] and the faith of a *people of an almighty god* has led to ventures still more rash. Isaiah, as prophet of such a people, could have seen in Hezekiah and at least some of his subjects in Jerusalem the mere remnant of the kingdom that God had pledged to preserve.

Thus, we may be sure that 2 Kgs 19:21–34 and Isa 37:22–35 are indeed by Isaiah. The prophet himself and his disciples may have excluded the utterance from their own collection of his works for whatever reason, perhaps because they considered it insufficiently fulfilled. Other circles, perhaps including the masses of Judah and some of the royal line, were fascinated by how far the utterance had been fulfilled and preserved it down to the time of the author of Kings.

Whatever deliverance had occurred in the reign of Hezekiah joined the thought patterns of the *people of an almighty god* and the fact that the immensely strong site of Jerusalem had indeed been surrendered before without a fight but had never fallen to siege from the time it became an Israelite stronghold. The result was the widely held belief that God would keep Jerusalem invulnerable.[17] Even the author of Kings, who wrote during the exile knowing that the belief had proved to be false in 586 B.C.E., included in his book 2 Kgs 19:34, and still later, the author of the book of Chronicles wrote 2 Chr 32:1–23!

The survival of Jerusalem was the more remarkable because Sennacherib in 689 took Babylon and razed it to the ground. For the moment, Sennacherib's Assyria usurped the Babylonians' status as a *people of an almighty god,* for Sennacherib transferred dust from ruined Babylon to the Akîtu temple of his city of Ashur. Assyrian hands revised the Creation Epic to have Anshar (identified with Ashur, god of Assyria) as the creator instead of Marduk. Sennacherib's son and successor, Esarhaddon, was quick to repent for his father's presumptuous treatment of Marduk and his city, with the result that we do not have to treat the Assyrians as a *people of an almighty god.* Indeed, their history and literature do not exhibit the patterns typical of one.[18]

We are poorly informed on the fifty-five year reign of Manasseh. He ruled longer than any other king of Judah or Israel and, in the judgment of the author of Kings, was also more wicked. The catalogue of Manasseh's sins (2 Kgs 21:2–17) guarantees that Isaiah's circle would have condemned him, too. The length of his reign was a troubling puzzle for pious observers and recorders of history. We are told that Manasseh worshiped Baal and Asherah and the Host of Heaven and that he shed much innocent blood.[19]

In Manasseh's time, the Assyrian Empire conquered Egypt (671–667), so that there was no power which could support weak Judah against the Assyrian colossus. Whatever deliverance had been granted Judah and Jerusalem when Hezekiah faced Sennacherib no longer was enough to impress Manasseh with the LORD's ability and willingness to defend his people. In a world of polytheistic peoples, Manasseh did what would be normal for most other heads of state: To protect his kingdom, he remained abjectly loyal to Assyria[20] and invoked more gods than before.[21]

Had Manasseh's idolatry included worship of Assyrian deities, one may be sure that the author of Kings or Zephaniah or Jeremiah or Ezekiel would have explicitly condemned him or his subjects for it. However, the chief deities of Assyria, Ashur and Ninlil and Ishtar, were thoroughly identified with Assyria, and no one could have besought them for protection in a time when Assyria was the menace. Nowhere do the biblical writers reprove the LORD's people for worshiping the gods of Assyria. Nowhere do they attack Assyrian gods, despite their readiness to denounce and ridicule the gods of the pagans.[22] Rather, Manasseh turned to gods long worshiped by the peoples of the immediate region, to gods long worshiped even by many in Israel and Judah.[23]

We are not surprised to find that Manasseh and some members of the LORD's people in a time of adversity could lose faith in the protective power of their great deity. Equally unsurprising is the fact that others could hold tenaciously to that faith and could angrily resist those who had lost it. It is likely that many of those "innocents" whose blood Manasseh shed were just such men of obstinate faith. One indeed wonders how Manasseh survived so long as king over a nation imbued with the beliefs of a *people of an almighty god.*

Manasseh's heir, Amon, who is said to have followed the same policies, had no such success. He was murdered after a very brief reign.[24] Any attempt to use our inadequate evidence to reconstruct the motives of the regicides can only be guesswork. The same is true of efforts to determine the motives of the powerful element in the population of Judah (called the "people of the land") which inflicted death upon the slayers of Amon and placed his 8-year-old son Josiah on the throne (640 B.C.E.).[25] How far did the psychology of a *people of an almighty god* affect the regicides or the "people of the land"?

Once Josiah reached maturity, his reign stood in vivid contrast to those of his two predecessors. The contrasts display the resurgent attitudes of a *people of an almighty god* led by a king and ministers acutely conscious that the subservient and polytheistic policies of Manasseh and Amon had roused the wrath of God. Josiah carried out a thoroughgoing monotheistic religious reform that enforced the teachings of Deuteronomy, a book steeped in the faith of a *people of an almighty god.* Josiah also pursued a strongly assertive foreign policy, as the Assyrian empire collapsed and fell between 614 and 609.[26]

The collapse of the superpower was sudden and must have been unexpected to most observers. Two new powers accomplished her overthrow: the Median kingdom of Cyaxares (reigned ca. 625–585) and the Neo-Babylonian kingdom of Nabopolassar (reigned 626–605). In an inscription, Nabopolassar himself says he was insignificant until Marduk made him king; clearly a revolution brought him to the throne of almighty Marduk's city. In the same inscription, he says that with the help of Marduk and Nabû he put an end to Assyrian cruelty and drove out the Assyrians and freed all Akkad.[27] Cyaxares's predecessor, whom Herodotus calls Phraortes, may already have attempted to capture Nineveh. Before that attempt, the Medes and the Babylonians had often tried to resist Assyrian domination but had never constituted a menace to Assyria herself.[28] Even so, Isaiah, who by 614–609 was long dead, had foretold the fall of Assyria (10:5–27). This great fulfillment of one of his prophecies joined the others to increase the awe with which the later generations in Judah must have viewed the power of the prophet's inspiration. According to Isaiah, Assyria had been God's punishing instrument but in her arrogance had gone beyond her mandate from God and perpetrated self-aggrandizing cruelty. Therefore she would fall, and the LORD's people would be freed from bondage to her. The prophecy, in 10:20, speaks of the present reliance on Assyria by the "remnant of Israel" (i.e., Judah) and therefore may have been composed during the reign of Ahaz. By 609, when the last hopes of Assyrian die-hards were crushed, the predicted destruction of Assyria was a fact.

Many in Judah rejoiced over her fall with the prophet Nahum and believed the LORD's proclamation through him (1:12–13) that all adversity was past. Others may already have wondered if God could ever forgive the sins of the reign of Manasseh. Some even of those, however, may have seen great hope in the successes of young Josiah and in his reform. All those bright hopes were dashed in Sivan (May or June), 609; Josiah fell in battle at Megiddo, fighting against an army led by King Neco II of Egypt, who was on his way to support Assyrian die-hards against the army of Nabopolassar, king of Babylon. Neco's efforts on behalf of the die-hards came to nothing, but Josiah was dead and his army, defeated.[29] Defenders of the dead king and his policies taught that even Josiah's righteousness was not enough to atone for the sins of Manasseh;[30] those not pleased by the reform would blame Josiah's death on the reform itself: his misguided zeal had angered the power (or powers) in heaven.[31]

Neco quickly deposed Jehoahaz, the immediate successor whom national organs of the Jews had set up as king of Judah, and put on the throne of Judah another son of Josiah, Eliakim, changing his name to Jehoiakim.[32] From 609 until 605 Judah was dominated by Egypt, but from 605 Jehoiakim and his subjects lay open to the might of Nabopolassar's Neo-Babylonian Empire, which had risen in the place of Assyria and had driven Egyptian power out of Asia; Jehoiakim's formal acceptance of the overlordship of the king of Babylon probably came in 603, during the second regnal year of Nebuchadnezzar II, who had been crown prince and military commander under Nabopolassar and had succeeded to the throne; the terms of submission involved the payment of tribute, but no Jews were exiled at this time.[33]

The turn of events was puzzling for the LORD's people. Already during 605,

Nebuchadnezzar's accession year, Jeremiah presented as the word of the LORD an assertion that the impending victory of the power from the north was the result of God's anger over sins of the people of Judah during 23 years, from the beginning of the prophet's career in the reign of Josiah down to the present. Judah, he went on to say, would be destroyed, and its people would be in servitude for 70 years.[34] But Jeremiah's must have been a lonely voice at the time. Few agreed with him about the sinfulness of the age or about the invincibility of Nebuchadnezzar as God's punishing instrument. The authority of great prophets seemed to oppose Jeremiah. For example, Isaiah had not predicted that another power would rise to take Assyria's place as the rod of the LORD's anger. He certainly had said nothing to suggest he foresaw Egypt's temporary mastery over Judah, and it is at least doubtful whether he had said anything to forecast Babylonian domination. Nahum, too, failed to foresee the rise of Egyptian and then of Babylonian power. Perhaps, then, both subjections of Judah were temporary episodes in God's plan. Many Jews surely held to the beliefs of a *people of an almighty god:* Even if Manasseh had sinned grievously, surely God should not long wreak his wrath on a later generation;[35] perhaps Josiah's defeat and death might be enough to atone. The belief in the impregnability to siege of Jerusalem was still widely held.

In December, 601, the Babylonian army attempted to invade Egypt. In a bloody battle, both sides suffered very heavy casualties. Nebuchadnezzar withdrew and spent the next year rebuilding his military forces. Jews could infer Nebuchadnezzar's empire was no permanent part of God's plan. Egypt was the earthly power that had put Jehoiakim on the throne and had some claim on his sympathies, but the beliefs of a *people of an almighty god* may well have been involved in the decisions of the king of Judah. Probably not faithlessness but faith in God impelled Jehoiakim to rebel against Nebuchadnezzar in ca. 600 and induced the prophets whom Jeremiah condemned as "false" to promise God's support against Babylon.[36]

Other concerns at first diverted Nebuchadnezzar from using his power to subdue rebellious Judah, but Jehoiakim lived to see his country begin to suffer, and only his death late in 598 saved him from the siege that the overwhelming Babylonian force placed around Jerusalem. His heir, Jehoiachin, after a reign of only three months showed his lack of faith in the doctrine of Jerusalem's impregnability and in the words of the false prophets. On 2 Adar (March 16), 597 B.C.E., he surrendered to Nebuchadnezzar. The victor took large spoils and deported Jehoiachin and many of the political, religious, and military elite to Babylonia. He appointed as king of Judah a son of Josiah, Mattaniah, renaming him Zedekiah and exacting from him an oath of allegiance.[37]

Zedekiah had to wonder what the LORD intended for him. Had the punishments inflicted on Josiah, Jehoahaz, Jehoiakim, and Jehoiachin been enough to expiate previous sin, so that God would now protect His people? The prophet Jeremiah himself may at first have given Zedekiah reason to think so.[38] Many of Zedekiah's subjects seem to have agreed.[39] But Jeremiah soon proclaimed, like Ezekiel, that Zedekiah's reign, too, belonged to an age of adversity. Jeremiah told the Jews exiled to Babylonia to resign themselves to long residence there, because the subjugation of the LORD's people to Babylon would endure for seventy years, for three generations of Babylonian kings.[40] But there were other prophets who could encourage the people of Judah and Jerusalem to believe there would soon be an end to adversity, though some seers looked not to King Zedekiah as ruler in the impending age of prosperity but to the exiled King Jehoiachin (= Jechoniah).[41]

How much did materialistic power politics and how much did religion move Zedekiah and his advisers? There is no reason to doubt Ezekiel's testimony that Zedekiah sought help from Egypt.[42] But Jeremiah, who unlike Ezekiel was in Jerusalem, does not inveigh against a pro-Egyptian party; his opponents are the "false" prophets and those who believed that God would not allow Jerusalem to fall.[43] Thus, it would seem that the advisers who pushed the weak Zedekiah to rebel did so from the religious faith of a *people of an almighty god*.

By 589, Zedekiah broke his oath of allegiance and took his kingdom into rebellion against Nebuchadnezzar. An Egyptian expedition gave only temporary relief to beleaguered Jerusalem. After a long siege, the city and Zedekiah fell to the Babylonians, probably in 586. A state that had rebelled more than once and a king who had violated his oath could expect no mercy. Jerusalem and the temple were destroyed, Zedekiah was cruelly punished, and thousands more Jews were deported to Babylonia.[44]

3. The Metamorphosis of Isa 13:2–14:27

THE GREAT ISAIAH had foreseen the fall of Assyria. Could he have failed to foresee the events of the late seventh and early sixth centuries? There is reason to think that admirers of Isaiah, including Jeremiah, came to believe that Isaiah had indeed predicted both the rise and the still-future fall of Babylon. Those admirers were able to prove their point, it seems to me, by taking an old manuscript of a real prophecy of Isaiah. They made only a few alterations at points where the manuscript may have been hard to read, to produce what we now have in Isa 13:2–14:27. Let me explain why I think so. The words ascribed to Isaiah in those chapters have many strange features.

The content of the passage is as follows. In 13:2–22 there is a description of the rising of merciless peoples from the distant mountains who will come upon "all the earth" on the "Day of the LORD" to punish the proud and the wicked in a catastrophic invasion, which will be accompanied by eclipses of the heavenly bodies and by earthquakes. In 13:17, at least some of the inexorable invaders are identified as the Medes. The invaders (and perhaps the earthquakes, too) will totally destroy Babylon (13:18–22). According to 14:1–2, the aftermath will see the restoration of Israel, as Gentiles bring the LORD's people back from exile; the Israelites will possess their former captors as slaves. In 14:3–21 there is a vigorous taunt song which the liberated Israelites are to recite concerning the slain king of Babylon, contrasting his former arrogance with his humiliation in death. In 14:22–23, God promises to destroy Babylon completely. Strangely, in 14:24–27 comes an abrupt oath of the LORD to "break Assyria [not Babylon!] in my land" and liberate his people.

The strange features of Isa 13:2–14:27 go far beyond the mention of Assyria in 14:24–27. First, the prophecy bears the title, "The 'Babylon' Pronouncement, a Prophecy of Isaiah Son of Amoz." Both halves of this title are odd. Isaiah's own words let us know that he prophesied in the reigns of Uzziah, Jotham, Ahaz, and Hezekiah, as does the editorial superscription to the book that bears his name. He certainly gave his predictions to Ahaz in ca. 733 B.C.E. Babylon in Isa 13:1–14:27 is portrayed as a cruel great power, but from Isaiah's birth to the rise of King Nabopolassar in 626 Babylon could with difficulty assert her independence and was more often the subject or victim of Assyria. Furthermore, in 13:19 Babylon is called "proud splendor of the Chaldaeans." It is at least doubtful that Isaiah could have used that expression of Babylon. In the eighth century Babylon had several kings of Chaldaean stock, including Marduk-apla-iddina II (Merodach-baladan), whose ambassadors came to Jerusalem in Isaiah's time. But during most of that century the Chaldaean tribes were enemies of the city of Babylon, and that hostility may have existed also in the opening years of the seventh century.[45] The Medes, too, are presented as a cruel great power in Isa 13:4–14, yet they were certainly no match for Assyria before the middle of the seventh century. Contrary to that passage, the Medes never overran the Near East, terrifying and slaughtering vast populations and destroying Babylon.

If Isaiah's prophetic vision really could penetrate the future, it should have been more accurate! And even if he did somehow predict the fall of a cruel Babylon to a cruel Media, what circle of Jews in the late eighth and early seventh centuries would have been interested enough to preserve a prediction that one distant power, then still small, would destroy another, also still small?

On the other hand, Jeremiah's generation bitterly resented the cruelty with which Nebuchadnezzar punished rebellious Judah, and they probably were impressed by his readiness to "kill his own people" (cf. Isa 14:20) by accepting heavy casualties in his battle of 601 against Egypt and in the siege of Jerusalem.[46] Had not Babylon, like Assyria, exceeded her mandate as God's punishing instrument? Such Jews believed that Babylon in turn should be punished, and they looked to the Medes, the only great power bordering on Babylonia, to be the agents of God's retribution.[47] How, then, can Isa 13:2–14:27 be the work of Isaiah? Rather, one would think, it must represent the ardent wishes of Jeremiah's generation, and somehow this later composition found its way into the collection of the works of Isaiah.

There is reason to think that the declaration of Isaiah's authorship in the second half of 13:1 (the verse that serves as the title of 13:2–14:27) reflects an editor's awareness of how incongruous the prophecy is as a work of Isaiah. The prophecies in the book of Isaiah can have circulated separately before they were brought together into a collection, and they could have received titles either while separate or when placed in the collection. Still, Isa 1:1 is a title for the whole book, "The Prophecies of Isaiah Son of Amoz. . . ." Even if that verse is the title of only chapter 1, would not one assume, in the absence of statements to the contrary, that all pieces which followed were also by Isaiah? Yet the editor found reason to attach (or leave in place) titles identifying Isaiah as the author not only of 13:2–14:27 but also of chapter 2.

One can guess why he did so. The glorious prophecy for Judah and Jerusalem in 2:1–5 follows somewhat incongruously on chapter 1, which is mostly an indictment of land and city, relieved somewhat by the promise that God will purge the dross and that the repentant will be redeemed. The title in 2:1 assures the reader that the author of 2:2–5 is indeed the same as the prophet of chapter 1. Similarly, the title of 13:2–14:27 may have been added or left in place because the editor wished to assure his reader that the same Isaiah who spoke to Ahaz also predicted the fall of Babylon, strange as it seems!

Even if we knew nothing of the history of the eighth and seventh centuries B.C.E., Isa 13:2–14:27 would still be strange as a prophecy primarily concerned with Babylon. Babylon is not mentioned in the passage until 13:19. At least one scholar has suggested that even in that verse *bbl* ("Babylon") may be an interpolation.[48]

Despite the incongruities of Isa 13:2–14:27, it is difficult simply to reject the information given in the title. The portrayal of the barbarians gathering to be the LORD's scourge on his Day is entirely in keeping with the teachings and diction of the prophecies that certainly belong to Isaiah. As in 13:5–18, the great prophet taught that God would purge the arrogant from the world and that his wrath would occasion great slaughter and destruction. As in 14:5–6, he also taught that the wicked empire of his day would be punished for wronging many nations, not just for injuring Israel.[49]

One might try to explain away the anachronisms: "Babylon" in Isa 13:2–14:27 might be a name for the Assyrian Empire (Assyrian kings on occasion called themselves "kings of Babylon," and elsewhere in the Bible a writer will use the name of one empire when he means another), and "Media" in our passage might be, not the name of an existing great power, but of a distant and barbaric people, and the mention of the Chaldaeans might be a later insertion.[50] Thus, Isaiah could have written most if not all of the passage.

Moreover, so effective is the taunt song in 14:3–21 that scholars have been reluctant to deny that Isaiah wrote it.[51] On the other hand, even defenders of 13:2–22 and 14:3–21 have held the Isaiah did not write 14:1–2, 22–23.[52]

The anachronisms, however, cannot so easily be explained away. Assyrian kings did on occasion take the title, "King of Babylon," but the title was used only in Babylon, not by non-Babylonian subjects of the empire. At 2 Kgs 15:19, "Pul," which may have been the Babylonian royal name of Tiglath-Pileser III, is used, but the writer still calls him "king of Assyria," not "king of Babylon." All biblical examples of anachronistic use of names for empires use the name of the earlier for the later, never the name of the later for the earlier.[53] Excellence of composition and agreement with the thought and diction of Isaiah in themselves do not guarantee that Isaiah was the author.[54]

The existing clues can be used to point to a better way to solve the problems of Isa 13:2–14:27, to show, first, that in most if not all of Isa 13:2–14:27 we have words of Isaiah himself, written not against Babylon and her king, but against Assyria and her king and against Nineveh, her capital; and to show, second, that Jews of the sixth century B.C.E. who admired Isaiah and longed for retribution upon Babylon found it possible to read the passage as referring to her.

The text itself makes Assyria the target of Isa 14:25. The mark of Assyria is on the rest of the verses, too. Although one passage in Jeremiah (50:31–32) denounces Babylon as the personification of "arrogance" *(zdwn),* the arrogance of the monarch in Isa 14:13 was hardly characteristic of the kings of Babylon, even of the spectacularly successful Nebuchadnezzar II. The books of Kings, Chronicles, and Ezekiel (who lived a quarter century in exile under Nebuchadnezzar) do not accuse Babylon or her king of arrogance. Even in Habakkuk and Jeremiah (outside 50:31–32) the charges are only of wrongdoing and cruelty. Assyria, not Babylon, is the arrogant power in the histories and prophecies covering the age of the first temple and the Babylonian exile.[55]

Evidence from Mesopotamia, including the inscriptions of the Assyrian and Babylonian kings, confirms the impression given by the Bible. The Assyrian kings boastfully report their great military conquests; the kings of Babylon tell of their constructive and peaceful accomplishments, especially of the building and repair of temples.[56]

Though there are protests in Habakkuk and Jeremiah against the cruelty of Babylon, that trait as reflected in Isa 14:3–6, 16–17 was characteristic rather of Assyria.[57] Nebuchadnezzar's father, Nabopolassar, in an inscription boasts of having put an end to Assyrian cruelty.[58] The books of Kings, Chronicles, and Ezekiel regard the Babylonian actions against Judah and her kings as just and make no accusations of cruelty. Even the book of Lamentations complains only of the cruelty of war and siege and does not accuse the Babylonians.

At Isa 14:8, the fallen tyrant is said to have done violence to the cedars of Lebanon. The Assyrian, Babylonian, and Persian kings all used those forests as a royal lumber reserve, so nothing can be concluded from this point.[59]

The Assyrian kings, not the kings of Babylon, conspicuously "murdered their own people" (Isa 14:20), grossly depleting the national manpower in war so that it is hard to find a trace of the Assyrians after the fall of their empire in 612.[60] By contrast, Babylonians survived for centuries as a subject nation after the fall of their kingdom in 539.[61]

The text of Isa 13:2–14:27 contains one more valuable set of clues indicating that the passage originally dealt with Assyria rather than Babylon. Apart from the title in 13:1, only 13:19 and 14:22 connect our passage with Babylon. What happens to 14:22 if we remove the word "Babylon" and insert references to Assyria and her capital, Nineveh? The verse comes to contain a stunning double pun: "I will wipe out from Assyria [*'aššūr*] name and remnant [*uš^e'ār*] and kith and [*nīn wa-*] kin from Nineveh [*ninua*]."[62] It is likely that the author at the end of 14:22 wrote, not "declares the LORD" *(n'm yhwh)* but "from Nineveh" *(mnynwh)*. The ease of the transition from one reading to the other is visible even in English transliteration. If a reader in the sixth century found "from Nineveh" inappropriate or somewhat illegible, he would immediately be led by the occurrences of "declares the LORD" in v 23 and in the first half of v 22 to read the same here at the end of v 22. Our context is the only one in Isa 1–39 in which multiple occurrences of *n'm yhwh* come so close together.[63]

If "Nineveh" originally appeared in 14:22, we may be sure that it also stood in 13:2, where the text now has *hr nšph* ("bare[?] hill"). *Nšph* ("bare"?) is a word of unknown meaning which occurs nowhere else in the Hebrew Bible. If the correct reading is "Nineveh," the prophecy no longer has an inappropriate beginning. Rather, as one would expect, it comes to the point immediately: A standard is to be raised on the hill of Nineveh, capital of Assyria, to make it the target of the gathering barbarian hordes.[64] Nineveh stood on two hills, now called "Kuyunjik" and "Nebi Yunus." What the two were called in antiquity is unknown,[65] but there is no evidence to show that one of them was not called the "hill of Nineveh." Indeed, Isaiah need not have known anything about the geographical nomenclature of Nineveh; it was common knowledge that standards used as signals to assemble were raised on hills.[66]

Moreover, the enigmatic end of Isa 13:2 can be used to confirm that the verse originally contained references to Assyria or her capital city. No one has yet produced a satisfactory interpretation of *pthy* (the construct state of *pthym*, perhaps "openings" or "gates") in the last clause of that verse, *wyb'w pthy ndybym* ("Let them enter the gates[?] of nobles[?]"). Whatever *pthym* are, Mic 5:5 contains good evidence that they are objects that Assyria was known to possess: *wr'w 't 'rṣ 'šwr bhrb w't 'rṣ nmrwd bpthyh*, "They shall waste the land of Assyria with the sword and the land of Nimrod in its *pthym.*"

As for Isa 13:19, "Babylon" there may be an interpolation by those later Jews who wanted to find a prophecy by Isaiah predicting the fall of that city; on metrical grounds alone one might suggest it is an interpolation.[67] And desires for retribution upon Babylon could have led such a Jew to misread (whether deliberately or unconsciously) "the pride of the arrogant" *(g'wn zdym)*[68] as "pride of the Chaldaeans" *(g'wn kṣdym).*

One can also easily explain the reference to the Medes in Isa 13:17. The same sort of eye that misread *nynwh* ("Nineveh") as *nšph* could have misread *gwy* ("nation") as *mdy* ("the Medes"), and he or a later hand could have added the particle *'t* which precedes the definite direct object.[69] The mention of an unnamed nation as God's punishing instrument is common.[70]

Sennacherib was the first king to make Nineveh the chief city of Assyria. Our reconstructed prophecy, too, treats Nineveh as the capital; therefore it cannot have been written before the reign of Sennacherib (704–681).[71]

This reconstructed original of Isa 13:2–14:27 is a cogent composition befitting Isaiah and his times and flows easily from clues in the extant text. There is more evidence in its favor: One later prophet can be shown to have read Isa 13:2–14:27 when it still was directed at Assyria, when it still said nothing of Babylon; and another later prophetic composition just as clearly drew on Isa 13:2–14:27 after it had been changed into a prophecy of the downfall of Babylon.

Zephaniah throughout his short book echoes the diction and ideas of Isaiah, and especially numerous are his borrowings from Isa 13:2–14:27.[72] Zeph 2:13–15 draws heavily upon that prophecy in the book of Isaiah. In Zeph 2:13, "He shall stretch his hand over the north and shall destroy Assyria and turn

Nineveh into desolation, arid as the desert," we have the same parallelism of Assyria and Nineveh as in our reconstruction of Isa 14:22, and the same arid devastation as in Isa 13:19–22. In both Zeph 2:14 and Isa 13:20 we have the mention of shepherds making their flocks lie down, though at Isa 13:20, in contrast to Zeph 3:14, the devastation is so great that the flocks will not lie down on the ruined site. According to both Zeph 2:14 and Isa 14:23, the *qpwd* ("bittern"?) will inhabit the ruins. In both Zeph 2:15 and Isa 13:21, wild beasts (or demons) will lie down on the site. If *qpwd* does indeed mean some kind of water bird, both at Zeph 2:12–13 and at Isa 13:19–22, 14:23, we have the incongruous prediction of both dry and watery devastation for the evil city. Where Isa 13:21–22 mentions ruined mansions, Zeph 2:14 mentions their windows, column-capitals, thresholds, and cedar-woodwork. Zeph 2:15 contrasts the previous prosperity of arrogant Nineveh with her impending humiliation and destruction; Isa 14:4–21 makes a similar contrast, about the king rather than about the city.

One must not be blind to the differences between Zeph 2:13–15 and the parallels in Isa 13:2–14:27. But so impressive is Zephaniah's debt throughout his book to that prophecy in the book of Isaiah, that he must have known the text. He may have had his own reasons for somewhat changing its predictions in his own 2:13–15, but perhaps the departures there from the prophecy in Isaiah are due to nothing more than Zephaniah's faulty memory of his source. In any case, Zephaniah attests that the version of Isa 13:2–14:27 which lay before him predicted the destruction of Assyria and Nineveh, not that of Babylon. Zephaniah also gives some attestation that in his time 14:1–2 stood in that prophecy, though perhaps not everyone will grant that the parallels between Zeph 3:9, 19–20 and Isa 14:1–2 are strong enough to justify that conclusion.[73]

Habakkuk prophesied at a time when Babylonian armies had begun to take spoils from Judah, at the earliest at a time well into the reign of Jehoiakim.[74] His words may reflect a text of Isa 13:2–14:27 wherein "Assyria" and "Nineveh" had been replaced by "Babylon." Just as Isa 14:3–20 predicts the humiliating downfall of the arrogant, cruel, and destructive power, so Hab 2:5–17 predicts the humiliating downfall of the greedy and destructive power. Both prophecies contain a taunt song *(mashal)* to be sung after the downfall of the tyrannical power (Hab 1:6–17, Isa 14:4–20). Both messages speak of the violence done to the Lebanon (Hab 2:16; Isa 14:8). Both complain of the tyrannical power's sins against plural nations, not just against the LORD's people (Hab 2:5, 8, 13; Isa 14:6, 16–17). In both, the tyrant is said to have sought to dwell on high (Hab 2:9; Isa 14:13). But even if Habakkuk read Isa 13:2–14:27, we cannot tell whether he read it as a prophecy against Assyria and used it as a model for his message against Babylon, or whether already in his time someone had changed the text to make Babylon the target.

The parallels to Isa 13:2–14:27 which run through Jer 50:1–51:58 demonstrate conclusively that the author or authors of the latter knew Isa 13:2–14:27.[75] He or they also knew Habakkuk 1–2.[76] Did the version which lay before the later writer or writers have Isaiah's original target, Assyria, or had it already been turned into a prophecy against Babylon? Close examination of Jer 50:1–51:58 gives an unequivocal answer.

Like Isa 13:1, Jer 50:1 both names the prophet who is supposed to be the author and gives Babylon as his target. However, Jer 50:2 does not have an equivalent for the "bare[?] mountain" *(hr nšph);* the writer fails to specify the place for raising the standard, unlike his or Jeremiah's practice elsewhere.[77] In other verses, the writer seems embarrassed with inability to read the word in Isa 13:2 designating the place for raising the standard. Though Nineveh stood on two hills, Babylon was flat. There was no reason to speak of the "hill of Babylon." A writer who had no model before him would have spoken rather of her tower, the famous ziggurat Etemenanki. Nevertheless, at Jer 51:25 Babylon is called the "mountain of the destroyer" *(hr hmšhyt)* and, for the future, a "mountain of burning" *(hr srph).* Nowhere else in Jeremiah is the image of a volcano used, and it does not seem appropriate in Jer 51:25. Let us rather note that *š* and *s* (written identically in ancient Hebrew) occur in *nšph, mšhyt,* and *srph,* and that *nšph* and *srph* both end in *ph.*

The conclusion seems inescapable: At some time before Jer 50:1–51:58 was written, a version of Isa 13:2–14:27 puzzled a reader. Either that reader was unable to read "Nineveh" in 13:2 (because the writing was blurred), or he was unwilling to do so. It is hard to believe that all the original references to Nineveh and Assyria in Isa 13:2 and 14:22 had become blurred. But believers in the great prophetic power of Isaiah could have had good reason to take advantage of any place in those verses which was hard to read or merely looked something like what they wanted to see. Either way they could (whether unconsciously or deliberately) alter the text without arousing too many suspicions among their contemporaries. Their beliefs could have driven them to remove legible or illegible references to Assyria and replace them by references to Babylon. Why? Because otherwise the great Isaiah's prophecy in 13:2–14:27 contained too many falsehoods.

True, Nineveh and Assyria were destroyed, and the king was killed, fulfilling the prophecy. But the civilized world had not suffered a cruel and devastating invasion by barbarians from the mountains to extirpate sinners (contrary to Isa 13:4–9). Contrary to Isa 13:9, there were no noteworthy eclipses (eclipses of the moon are common). There were no quakes in heaven or earth (contrary to Isa 13:13). Captive peoples did not return to their homelands, and certainly not the descendants of those deported from the northern kingdom of Israel, nor did the LORD's people possess their captors and oppressors as slaves (contrary to Isa 13:14, 14:1–2). The powers that conquered Assyria did not perpetrate merciless massacres of children (contrary to Isa 13:18). The final defeat of Assyria did not occur in the Holy Land (contrary to Isa 14:25).

There was a prophecy by Isaiah of the fall of Assyria (10:5–27) which had been completely fulfilled by 609 B.C.E.; it seemed even to predict Josiah's moment of prosperity (10:27) and Assyria's turning in her last struggles to rely on Egypt (10:26). If Isa 13:2–14:27 as a prophecy of her fall was not only superfluous but false, what could have been God's and Isaiah's purpose in revealing it? On the other hand, surely God and his great prophet should have given some forewarning and comfort to Israel concerning Babylon. Thus there were good reasons for the faithful to read Isa 13:2–14:27 as a prophecy against Babylon and even for them to alter the text deliberately. Whether innocently or deliberately, someone after the time of Zephaniah's prophecy did make that alteration. When?

Since 1878, most modern commentators have held that Jeremiah cannot have written 50:1–51:58,[78] on insufficient grounds, in my view.[79] Many scholars who deny that Jer 50:1–51:58 are by Jeremiah concede that the narrative at 51:59–64 transmits truly Jeremiah's deeds and words (except for implying that everything in 50:1–51:58 is his).[80] But Jer 51:62 resembles Isa 14:22–23 and 13:19–20 enough to justify the conclusion that Jeremiah himself drew on Isa 13:2–14:27.[81] And the deeds and words in that narrative are dated (51:59) in the fourth year of Zedekiah, ca. 593 B.C.E. Even if, as most modern commentators hold, members of the generation after Jeremiah wrote all of Jer 50:1–51:58 (and even Jer 51:59–64), they must have written before Cyrus of Persia conquered the Medes in 550, for otherwise the name of the Persians would have been prominent among those of the peoples in Jer 50:9, 51:11, 27–28.

Thus, at a time between Nebuchadnezzar's first harsh measures against the kingdom of rebellious Jehoiakim (ca. 599 B.C.E.) and 550 B.C.E., Isa 13:2–14:27 (which Zephaniah ca. 612 still knew as a prophecy of the fall of Assyria) was turned into a prophecy of the fall of Babylon to invaders, among whom were the Medes.[82] The prophecy brought some small comfort to the Jews who suffered the fall of the kingdom and the exile, and it was to have important effects in the future.

4. The Jews and the Babylonians,
from the Fall of Jerusalem (586 B.C.E.) to the
Accession of Nabonidus (556 B.C.E.)

THE LITERATURE THAT SURVIVES from the generation of Jews who saw and survived the disaster of 586 is typical of a *people of an almighty god*. All the authors take for granted that the LORD's wrath against Judah and Jerusalem brought about the catastrophe. A *people of an almighty god* could hardly have given any other explanation. The beliefs of their Babylonian captors could serve to reinforce this view: Babylonians knew that disaster could come upon Babylon only if Marduk was angry.

The chapters of the book of Lamentations were written in the immediate aftermath of the fall of Jerusalem, apparently to reflect the plight of the king (chapter 3), the nobles (chapter 4) and the general population of Judah and Jerusalem (chapters 1, and 5). The writer or writers took for granted that the LORD had inflicted punishment for the sins of an earlier generation (5:7), surely King Manasseh's. They also believed that present sins of the LORD's people must have contributed to produce divine wrath on such a scale, but they found it difficult to define what those sins could be (3:40). The present king, Zedekiah, was not to blame; he, too, had suffered punishment, largely for the sins of others (4:20 and chapter 3, especially 3:58). The writer knew of bloodshed caused by the sins of *prophets* and *priests* (4:13); we have no other information whatever on such incidents.

The prophets Jeremiah and Ezekiel were soon to loom large for having correctly predicted the catastrophe and for having denounced and defined sins of the present generation as the cause, but the chapters of Lamentations show no trace of the influence of either prophet. One would expect that an audience which had been led by Jeremiah or Ezekiel to repent would confess its sins of idolatry and immorality, but there is nothing of the kind in the book of Lamentations. In its chapters, prophets and their utterances are mentioned repeatedly (2:9, 14, 20, 4:13), yet in such a way as might lead one to believe that Jeremiah and Ezekiel never existed.

The state of mind that produced the book of Lamentations was uncertain what sins had enraged the LORD and was hardly conducive to the writing of tendentious history, but the writers of a *people of an almighty god* could not fail to feel the need to produce a narrative telling how the god's people roused his wrath. Only a quarter-century had elapsed when, in 561, in the reign of Nebuchadnezzar's son Awêl-Marduk (Evil-Merodach; 562–560), a Jewish writer produced the book of Kings,[83] a comprehensive effort to explain how the LORD in his wrath came to destroy both Israelite kingdoms for the failures of the peoples and especially of the kings to observe the commandments in Deuteronomy. Except for Hezekiah and Josiah, all kings in the narrative angered the LORD by tolerating the "high places," shrines for the offering of sacrifices other than the one chosen site, the temple of Jerusalem, in violation of Deut 12:1–14. But the decisive factors for the kingdom of Israel were the continual and rampant idolatry and pagan practices there, and the decisive factors for the kingdom of Judah were King Manasseh's idolatry and his other sins.[84] God himself caused Jehoiakim and Zedekiah to rebel against Babylonian rule, in order to bring about the destruction of their kingdom.[85] The author of the book of Kings, too, ignores Jeremiah and Ezekiel, although he told of many prophets and gave great prominence to Isaiah.

One might have thought the disasters of the years from 609 to 586 B.C.E. would have proved to the Jews that the power or powers in heaven were enraged at the reform which Josiah had carried out only a few years before, and that the book of Deuteronomy did not contain the word of God. Indeed, Jeremiah had to argue against Jews who so believed (chap 44).[86] At least two factors ensured that the impact of Josiah's reform and of the book of Deuteronomy would be lasting. First, whatever had been the content of its hortatory chapters when the book was brought before King Josiah,[87] they did predict the destruction and exile of a sinful Israelite kingdom. We have no way of pinpointing when the *vaticinia ex eventu* predicting a long exile[88] became part of the text of Deuteronomy; but, if they were not already in the text, there would be an ever stronger incentive for adding them as the years wore on after the first mass exile of Jews in 597. Thus, in the eyes of any Jew who believed that King Manasseh had committed unforgivable sins against the teachings of Deuteronomy, the book stood vindicated: Its threats had come true.

There was a second factor preserving belief in Deuteronomy. The course of events had strikingly vindicated the prophecies of Jeremiah and Ezekiel. According to their teachings, the reforms and even the death of Josiah had not appeased the wrath of the LORD over the sins of the past,[89] and sins in the present had enraged him still further. Judah and Jerusalem, said the two prophets, were doomed to fall, and fall they did. Some Jews still rejected the messages of Jeremiah and Ezekiel,[90] but those who kept the faith were greatly impressed with the words of the two vindicated prophets. Certainly the believing Jews of the generation of the exile preserved the prophecies of both. Jeremiah's diction and ideas contain numerous echoes of Deuteronomy, and Ezekiel's utterances reflect Deuteronomy and other priestly traditions he had studied.[91] Those who heard or read their prophecies could tell that the two inspired men who had predicted the fall endorsed the content of Deuteronomy. For that reason, too, believing Jews henceforth would regard the commandments in the book as the word of God and would dread the consequences of disobedience.

One other implication of the teachings of Jeremiah and Ezekiel had a lasting effect on the history and literature of the Jews, the belief that in this age of God's wrath, the LORD's people, punished by subjection to foreign masters, must not rebel against their foreign king. Unless and until God should signify that the full term of the sentence for sin had been served, the LORD himself would punish such rebellion as he punished Zedekiah and his kingdom. Subjection to Babylon is a milder alternative punishment for sin; if the LORD's people do not submit to it, they will incur instead as their sentence the dreadful content of Deut 28:15–68, 29:21–7.

This doctrine is not quite explicit in the books of Jeremiah and Ezekiel, but the ingredients that produced it are there. Jeremiah states that all peoples of the region, including the Jews, must submit to the rule of the king of Babylon for 70 years,[92] for three generations of kings,[93] and that for the Jews the compulsory submission is a punishment for their sins.[94] If a country refuses to serve the king of Babylon, the LORD will cause it to be destroyed.[95] If a nation submits to the yoke of Babylon, the LORD will let it survive on its own soil.[96] The final destruction of Jerusalem and the cruel punishment of Zedekiah occurred because Zedekiah during the siege did not surrender himself to the Babylonians.[97] Ezekiel denounced the Lord's people as a "rebellious house."[98] His message throughout chaps 2–24 and 33 was that sinful Jerusalem and Judah were doomed; King Zedekiah and his army would fall to the Babylonians because Zedekiah rebelled against Nebuchadnezzar, violating his oath and covenant of loyalty.[99] On the other hand, God would restore and liberate the exiles in Babylonia, even against their will.[100]

Two later Jewish writers drew these threads together. According to the author of the book of Kings, God makes Zedekiah rebel against Nebuchadnezzar, in order to bring destruction upon Judah, already doomed by sin. A later historian of the LORD's people, under the influence of Jeremiah and Ezekiel, has a different view. Of Zedekiah's sins, the Chronicler mentions first his failure to yield to Jeremiah's preaching. He then turns to ascribe the final destruction, first, to Zedekiah's own act of rebellion, in violation of his own oath and covenant, and, second, to the supposedly rampant paganism of the priests and people during Zedekiah's reign.[101] In so doing, the Chronicler echoes Ezekiel.

Under the rule of the Persian kings from 539 on, Jewish writers showed their belief that they were sentenced by their God to serve their Gentile overlord.[102] So dependably unrebellious were Jews as subjects of the Persian Empire and its successors, that they were valued as soldiers and stationed in rebellious areas.[103] No believing Jew wanted God to inflict upon his generation the punishment for rebellion against the foreign ruler which Zedekiah and his kingdom had suffered. One might use a modern metaphor: God had sentenced his wayward people to reform school or to a minimum security prison. The king of the pagan empire ruling the Jews was the warden. Rebellion against the warden would result in a sentence to the penitentiary or even to the death-house.

Under Babylonian rule, Jews were either exiles living in the heart of Babylonia or miserable poor farmers living in ruined Judah.[104] They were in no position to think of rebellion, so that we cannot tell whether they had already inferred from the teachings of Jeremiah and Ezekiel that the LORD would punish any rebellion against the pagan empire.

There is no direct evidence to tell us how the Jewish *people of an almighty god* in defeat reacted to the claims the victorious Babylonian *people of an almighty god*. Jeremiah's strange verse in Aramaic (10:11) may be a direct attack, in the Babylonian vernacular, on the claims of Marduk to be the creator. Biblical writers did not use against the deities of Assyria the sort of mocking hostility which we find in Jeremiah and Deutero-Isaiah against Babylonian Marduk *(Bêl)* and *Nabû*.[105] The nonviolent and nonmythical account of creation in Gen 1:1–2:3, ascribed by modern scholars to the Priestly Source (P), reads like a deliberate contradiction of the story of Marduk's violent creative victory in the Babylonian Creation Epic.[106] If P was indeed composed during or after the exile, its creation story would reflect the conflicting claims of the two *peoples of an almighty god*. The interest of the Second Isaiah in creation[107] has been traced with certainty to his reaction to Iranian influence,[108] but the competing claims of Marduk's people on behalf of their god may have contributed.

Deutero-Isaiah gloats over the prospect of the humiliation of Babylon (chapter 47) and quotes God as promising to restored Jerusalem and Judah glories that had been Babylon's, letting us see how the LORD's people had envied Marduk's Babylonians.[109]

After crushing rebellious Judah, Nebuchadnezzar saw no reason to be cruel to the Jewish exiles in Babylonia and the poor survivors in Judah. Jeremiah's generation bitterly resented the atrocities perpetrated by the Babylonians against Judah,[110] but nowhere do they complain of cruelty committed in the years after Judah had been defeated. Ezekiel prophesied in Babylonia down to 571 B.C.E. (the date given in 29:17) and wrote not a word against Nebuchadnezzar. Nebuchadnezzar's reign was mostly peaceful and remarkable for artistic achievements.[111] In an inscription, he boasts how he brought peace and prosperity to the mountains of Lebanon.[112] In Babylon he constructed the buildings, walls, and hanging gardens that made Babylon one of the wonders of the ancient world. He died in 562 after a long reign of 43 years.

The exiled Jews remembered all too clearly the dreadful manifestations of the LORD's wrath in the siege of Jerusalem and must have appreciated the contrast between those horrors and everyday life as subjects of Babylon. Many Jews probably shared in the prosperity of Nebuchadnezzar's long reign. They understood, however, that for a *people of an almighty god* subjection to a foreign king could only mean that their God was still punishing them.[113]

What did the exiled Jews experience in their worldly lives? What institutions did they set up to run their affairs? One would like to have such information to supplement the fairly abundant traces in literature of the intellectual structures they produced. There is no evidence, however, that any ancient Jew ever attempted to write the history of the exilic period. Historians of a *people of an almighty god* must explain disasters, but they do not have to give a detailed account of the age of lesser adversity that follows. The period of lesser punishment after the fall of Jerusalem was not worth recording until the first sign should appear of God's returning mercies.

The author of Kings wrote nothing of the exilic period in which he lived except to record at the very end of his book that first sign, how Awêl-Marduk released King Jehoiachin from prison and thereafter treated him with honor (2 Kgs 25:27–30). Jeremiah's preserved prophecies come to an end before Hophra (Apries), king of Egypt, was killed in 570;[114] indeed, they probably ceased soon after the fall of Jerusalem. They give us little information on the spiritually unproductive group of Jews who took refuge in Egypt and tell us nothing of the exiles in Babylonia after 586. Ezekiel, though he was active in Babylonia from 592 to 571, was totally uninterested in recording the experiences and thoughts of his audience. Little as we know of the experiences and institutions of the exiled Jews, we do know something of their thoughts, and those thoughts left their mark on the literature and the subsequent history of the LORD's people.

Let us turn to sketch what is known of the Babylonians as a *people of an almighty god* in the three decades that followed the destruction of Jerusalem. The reigns of Nabopolassar (626–605) and his son, Nebuchadnezzar II (605–562), were a last golden age for Babylon. Nabopolassar, a man with no previous dynastic connections, as king had liberated Babylonia from Assyria and had founded a new dynasty.[115] A historical epic celebrated his accession and his acts.[116] Chroniclers recorded the events of his reign and of his son's.[117] The circumstances of Nabopolassar's accession and the victorious character of both reigns would lead one to expect that Babylonians would follow their old patterns and compose present-future prophecies to prove the legitimacy of the new dynasty, to celebrate what it had already achieved, and to predict a glorious future for it.

The "Uruk Prophecy," a fragmentary present-future prophecy surviving on a damaged clay tablet from Uruk,[118] has been interpreted[119] as "predicting" the rise of Nabopolassar, the worldwide rule of Nebuchadnezzar, and the everlasting reign of the Neo-Babylonian dynasty. However, for the writer of the document, the present king and his future heirs probably were Marduk-apla-iddina II (Merodach-Baladan) and his descendants, and the text would then have arisen in the time between 721 and 700 B.C.E.[120] Other present-future prophecies, however, might have circulated to support the claims of the dynasty. Some Jews in exile, like the biblical Daniel and his friends, may have become literate in Babylonian. If so, they could have learned of the earlier present-future prophecies which had become classical literary texts.[121]

Jeremiah predicted 70 years and three generations of Babylonian imperial rule. Actually, it endured for a much shorter time. Nebuchadnezzar's grandson could hardly be said to have ruled. From the time of Jeremiah's prophecy, five kings reigned, though one might say that they belonged to only three generations. By 539 B.C.E., only 47 years after the fall of Jerusalem, the Babylonian Empire was dead.

Nebuchadnezzar's son, Awêl-Marduk (Evil-Merodach), succeeded him and reigned from 562 to 560. The Bible takes note of Awêl-Marduk for his kindness to exiled King Jehoiachin,[122] but the later Babylonian king, Nabonidus, and the historian Berossus wrote down their disapproval of him.[123] Awêl-Marduk did not prosper. After a reign of only two years he was murdered in a palace revolution led by his sister's husband, Nergal-shar-uṣur (called "Neriglissar" in Greek). Nergal-shar-uṣur became king. Nabonidus wrote approvingly of him. Nergal-shar-uṣur built temples and conducted a successful campaign into eastern Asia Minor (Cilicia) before dying in April 556.[124] His son, Labâshi-Marduk, a mere child, succeeded him. Nabonidus was to write that Labâshi-Marduk (his predecessor) was a minor who had not learned how to behave, one who sat down an the throne against the intentions of the gods; and Berossus calls the boy king "depraved" *(kakoêthês)*. Labâshi-Marduk reigned only during parts of the first two months of the Babylonian year 556/5 B.C.E. By May 25, 556, as a result of a plot of courtiers, he was beaten to death, and the conspirators made Nabonidus king.[125]

NOTES

1 Examples of Isaiah's confidence that God would preserve a remnant: 1:28, 2:1–5, 4:2–6, 9:1–6, etc.; examples of his declarations on the wrath of God: 1:20, 3:24; 5:5–7, 25–30, 6:9–13, etc.

2 2 Kgs 16:6–9, Isa 7–8; those chapters of Isaiah contain formidable difficulties, which I hope to treat elsewhere; for the present, see Herbert Donner's discussion of the sources and the events ("The Separate States of Israel and Judah," in Hayes-Miller, 422–32).

3 2 Kgs 16:9, 15:29.

4 2 Kgs 15:3.

5 2 Kgs 17:1–6; Donner in Hayes-Miller, 427, 432–34.

6 Isa 7:15–25.

7 2 Kgs 18:13–16; Bustenay Oded, "Judah and the Exile," in Hayes-Miller, 446–49.

8 Prophecy: 2 Kgs 19:21–34 = Isa 37:22–35; narrative: 2 Kgs 18:13–19:37, which, except for 18:14–16, is almost identical to Isa 36:1–37:38. On the account in Kings as the source of the version in Isaiah, see Otto Kaiser, "Die Verkündigung des Propheten Jesaja im Jahre 701," *Zeitschrift für die alttestamentliche Wissenschaft* 81 (1969), 305–15; John Gray, *I & II Kings: A Commentary* (2d ed.; London: SCM Press, 1970), 657–59; Otto Eissfeldt, *The Old Testament: An Introduction* (New York and Evanston: Harper and Row, 1965), 296, 328.

9 For extreme rejections of any historicity in the rest of that biblical narrative, see R. E. Clements, *Isaiah and the Deliverance of Jerusalem* (JSOTSup 13: Sheffield, England: JSOT Press, 1980), and the massive study of Francolino Gonçalves, *L'Expédition de Sennachérib en Palestine dans la littérature hébraïque* ("Publications de l'Institut orientaliste de Louvain," 34," "Études bibliques, nouvelle série," 7; Paris: Gabalda, 1986). For more balanced treatments, see Hayim Tadmor, "The Period of the First Temple, the Babylonian Exile, and the Restoration," in *A History of the Jewish People,* ed. H. H. Ben-Sasson (Cambridge: Harvard University Press, 1976), 142–46, and "Sennacherib's Campaign to Judah: Historical and Historiographical Considerations," *Zion* 50 (5745 = 1985), 65–80 (in Hebrew, with English summary); Oded in Hayes-Miller, 446–51; Gray, *I & II Kings,* 657–96; John Bright, *A History of Israel* (3d ed.; Philadelphia: Westminster Press, 1981), 284–88, 298–309; Brevard S. Childs, *Isaiah and the Assyrian Crisis* ("Studies in Biblical Theology," Second Series, 3; Naperville, Ill.: Allenson, 1967); Hayim Tawil, "The Historicity of 2 Kings 19:24 (=

Isaiah 37:25)," *JNES* 41 (1982), 195–206; Danna Nolan Fewell, "Sennacherib's Defeat: Words at War in 2 Kings 18.13–19.37," JSOT 34 (1986), 79–90; Mordechai Cogan and Hayim Tadmor, *II Kings* ("Anchor Bible," vol. 11; Garden City, N.Y.: Doubleday, 1988), 240–51; Halpern, *First Historians,* 209, 247; William H. Shea, "Rewriting Jerusalem History: Jerusalem Under Siege; Did Sennacherib Attack Twice?" *Biblical Archaeology Review* 25, 6 Nov.–Dec., 1999), 36–44, 64.

10   2 Kgs 21:1–18, 2 Chr 33:1–11; Tadmor in Ben-Sasson, 145.

11   William H. Shea, "Sennacherib's Second Palestinian Campaign," *JBL* 104 (1985), 401–18; Bright, *History,* 288, 310–13.

12   2 Kgs 18:2, 13; 20:1, 6.

13   Cf. 2 Kgs 20:8–11, Isa 38:22, 7–8.

14   If the sign refers to material reality, it was hardly remarkable that those shut up in Jerusalem would have to eat what grows of itself this year. Sennacherib's forces had been in Judah, capturing all the other fortified cities and surely disrupting agriculture, but had not yet put a tight siege around Jerusalem, so that foragers from Jerusalem could have gone out to gather that which grew of itself. But how could one confidently predict that in the next year besieged Jerusalemites would find some way to go out and forage? And how could that serve as a sign?

The word "that which grows of itself" or "aftergrowth" *(spyḥ)* is part of the vocabulary of the laws of the Sabbatical and Jubilee Years (Lev 25:5, 11). One therefore might infer that the sign was connected with those laws, though rabbinic tradition puts the events in the eleventh year of the Jubilee and in the fourth of the Sabbatical cycle, expressly excluding any involvement with the Sabbatical and Jubilee years *(Seder ʿolam rabbah* 23, 103–4 Ratner). We know that 164/3 B.C.E. was a Sabbatical Year; to judge by the evidence from the 160s B.C.E. and later, the nearest Sabbatical Years to 701 B.C.E. were 703/2 and 696/5; see Goldstein, *1 Maccabees,* 315–18. But the cycle of Sabbatical Years in the time of Hezekiah need not have been in step either with rabbinic chronology or with the cycle in the postexilic Jewish commonwealth.

I used to think that we have no other evidence whatever of the observance of the agricultural laws of the Sabbatical and Jubilee Years in the age of the kings of Israel and Judah. Now, however, Lisbeth S. Fried and David Noel Freedman have argued well *(apud* Jacob Milgrom, *Leviticus 17–27* [*Anchor Bible,* vol. 3A; New York, London, Toronto, Sydney, and Auckland: Random House, forthcoming], Comment F) to establish that the Sabbatical and Jubilee Years were observed in the age of the kings of Israel and Judah and thereafter; and that Sennacherib's siege of Jerusalem and Isaiah's strange prophecy occurred in 688; that 689/688 was a Sabbatical Year; and that 688/7 was a Jubilee Year. These dates do not fit the Sabbatical cycle that can be established from the data in 1 Maccabees and later sources, but we have already granted that the cycle of Sabbatical Years in the time of Hezekiah need not have been in step with the cycle in the postexilic Jewish commonwealth.

If the year of Sennacherib's campaign was indeed a Sabbatical Year and the year following was a Jubilee Year, and if the laws of Lev 25:1–12 were then so interpreted and were in force, the people in Jerusalem might indeed have eaten that which grew of itself in the first year and in the second, what sprang from that, the "second growth." And the prophet would be predicting almost immediate deliverance, as would befit the context: In the Sabbatical and Jubilee Years the people in Jerusalem would be free to forage, and in the third year they would be free to sow and reap. But the book of Kings elsewhere reflects knowledge of the laws of Deuteronomy, not of the laws of Leviticus. And the events predicted for the sign would be identical with the fulfillment; how, then, could they be a sign? If the year of Sennacherib's coming fell in a pre-Sabbatical Year and no Jubilee Year followed, the eating of the aftergrowth might be due to Sennacherib's campaigning, and the eating of the aftergrowth might be due to the Sabbatical Year. But again, how is that a sign, and how could the prophet be confident the besieged would be able to go out to forage? Any other position for the year of Sennacherib's campaign in the Sabbatical and Jubilee cycles lends itself still less to making the sign comprehensible. So, problems that I have not been able to solve remain, despite the good arguments of Fried and Freedman.

15 Isa 8:1–4; see n 2.

16 Cf. the desperate resolution of the Carthaginians after similarly surrendering their arms to Rome (Appian viii *[Lybikê]*.80–93.371–441).

17 Jer 7:4–8, Lam 4:12; cf. Joel 4:20–21 (postexilic).

18 Roux, 322–24; Jacobsen, *Treasures,* 167; B. Landsberger and J. V. Kinnier Wilson, "The Fifth Tablet of *Enuma Eliš,*" *JNES* 20(1961), 154–79; W. von Soden, "Gibt es ein Zeugnis dafür, dass die Babylonier an die Wiederauferstehung Marduks geglaubt haben?" *ZA* 51 (1955), 161–66. Even in a presumptuous text from the reign of Sennacherib, Ashur is not autocrat enough to judge Marduk: He puts Marduk on trial to be judged by other gods (von Soden, ibid., 161). On the *Akîtu* (New Year's festival), see chap 2, n 5. The Assyrianized version of the Creation Epic was composed in the reign of Sennacherib, the time that is so logical a setting for it. See Daniel D. Luckenbill, *The Annals of Sennacherib* ("The University of Chicago: Oriental Institute Publications," Vol. II; Chicago: University of Chicago Press, 1924), 140–142. Hayim Tadmor, "The Campaigns of Sargon II of Assur: A Chronological Study," *JCS* 12(1958), 82.

19 On the poor sources for Manasseh's reign, see the attempts to reconstruct the data by Bright, History, 310–13; Oded in Hayes-Miller, 452–56; and Tadmor in Ben-Sasson, 146–48. Manasseh's "atrocities": 2 Kgs 21:3, 5, 7, 16; cf. 23:12–13.

20   So the Assyrian sources imply, and even 2 Chr 33:11 does not say that Manasseh rebelled against Assyria; see Oded in Hayes-Miller, 454–56.

21   The Athenians and the Romans, despite their religious conservatism, proceeded in just this manner in times of crisis; see Martin P. Nilsson, *Geschichte der griechischen Religion,* I (3d ed.; München: Beck, 1967), 725–27; and Kurt Latte, *Römische Religionsgeschichte* (München: Beck, 1960), 258–62.

22   Attacks on Canaanite deities are too common to require examples. For attacks on the deities of neighboring peoples and Babylon, see Num 21:29, 1 Kgs 11:5, 7, Isa 21:9, 46:1, Jer 48:7, 13, 50:2, 51:44.

23   Cf. Morton (Mordechai) Cogan, *Imperialism and Religion: Assyria, Judah, and Israel in the Eighth and Seventh Centuries B.C.E.* ("Society of Biblical Literature Monograph Series," 19; Missoula, Mont.: Society of Biblical Literature and Scholars Press, 1974), 72–96; John W. McKay, *Religion in Judah Under the Assyrians 732–609 BC* ("Studies in Biblical Theology," Series II, 26; Naperville, Ill.: Allenson, 1973). Hermann Spieckermann published a massive effort to refute Cogan and McKay (*Juda unter Assur in der Sargonidenzeit* ["Forschungen zur Religion und Literatur des Alten und Neuen Testaments," 129; Göttingen: Vandenhoeck & Ruprecht, 1982]). Cogan, in turn, has refuted Spieckermann ("Judah under Assyrian Hegemony: A Reexamination of *Imperialism and Religion," JBL* 112 [1993], 403–14). Against Spieckermann, see also Francolino Gonçalves, *L'Expédition de Sennachérib,* 35–50, 73–101; and the reviews of Spieckermann's book by M. J. Mulder (*Bibliotheca Orientalis* 41 [1984], 173–77) and Stefan Timm (*Theologische Literaturzeitung* 110 [1985], 883).

24   2 Kgs 21:19–23.

25   2 Kgs 21:24; see, for instance, the guesses of Abraham Malamat ("The Historical Background of the Assassination of Amon King of Judah," *Israel Exploration Journal* 3 [1953], 26–29) and of William W. Hallo ("From Qarqar to Carchemish," *Biblical Archaeologist* 23 [1960], 60–61).

26   On Josiah's policies, see Oded in Hayes-Miller, 458–68; Tadmor in Ben-Sasson, 148–52; and Bright, *History,* 316–25. Except for 19:1, 20:1–4, 26:8–9, 15, 19, the passages of Deuteronomy reflecting the attitudes of a *people of an almighty god* are all in the hortatory passages at the beginning and end of the book (1:30–33, 2:4–39, 3:21–22, 24, 4:7, 19–20, 32–39, 6:18–19, 7:6–10, 18–22, 9:1–3, 10:14, 17, 11:2–7, 23–25, 27:9, 28:12–13, 15–69, 30:1–10, 31:6–8). Some such passages must have been in the book presented to Josiah, for he was so impressed by the threats and promises it contained that he was ready to kill to implement its provisions.

   On the fall of Assyria, see Roux, 372–77.

27 Farouk N. H. Al-Rawi, "Nabopolassar's Restoration Work on the Wall *Imgur-Enlil* at Babylon," Iraq 48 (1985), 3 (col. I), with translation, ibid., 5. "Shazu" in col. I, line 15, is a name for Marduk; see Creation Epic, Tablet VII, line 35.

28 Roux, 307–10, 311–12, 319–20, 321–23, 325–26.

29 2 Kgs 21:10–15, 22:1–23:30; Babylonian Chronicle 3, lines 66–69 (*ABC*, 96); Roux, 377; Abraham Malamat in *Age*, 205–6, and (for the date of Josiah's death) "The Last Kings of Judah and the Fall of Jerusalem," *IEJ* 18 (1968), 139, and "The Twilight of Judah: in the Egyptian-Babylonian Maelstrom," *Vetus Testamentum,* Suppl. 28 (1975), 125, n 5.

30 2 Kgs 21:10–15, 23:25–27, 24:3–4, Jer 15:4.

31 Jer 44:15–19; cf. the belief reflected at 2 Kgs 18:22 and Isa 36:7.

32 2 Kgs 23:30–35; Malamat in *Age,* 206–7. Malamat has revised his account of the events from the death of Josiah to the final fall of the kingdom of Judah, in his *Israel in Biblical Times: Historical Essays* (Jerusalem: Bialik Institute and Israel Exploration Society, 1983), 242–91 (in Hebrew).

33 Roux, 372–79; Malamat in *Age,* 207. The reports at 2 Chr 36:6–7 and Dan 1:1–4, that Jerusalem fell to a siege by Nebuchadnezzar in Jehoiakim's reign and that persons and temple vessels were then taken into exile, are false; see chap 8, pp. 210–12. On how the reports at Dan 1:1–4 and 2 Chr 36:6–7 came to be, see chap 8, sec. 11.

34 Hebrew and Greek Jer 25:1–11; see John Bright, *Jeremiah* ("Anchor Bible, Vol. 21; Garden City, N.Y.: Doubleday, 1965), 162–63. The Greek text is the more original. In it Jeremiah follows his early practice of not naming the menace from the north (as at 1:13–15, 4:6, 6:1, 22–26, 10:22), but in 605 no one in Judah could be ignorant of who ruled the great power from the north.

35 Isaiah on Babylonian domination: On Isa 39:6–7, see chap 1, n 21. The prevailing view among scholars is that Isa 13:1–14:27 as a prophecy against Babylon is not by Isaiah; see H. L. Ginsberg, "Isaiah: First Isaiah," *Encyclopaedia Judaica,* IX (1971), 55, and Otto Eissfeldt, *The Old Testament: An Introduction* (New York and Evanston): Harper and Row, 1965), 312. On the true origin of Isa 13:1–14:27, see pp. 83–91. Wrath wreaked on a later generation: Note the complaints later addressed to Jeremiah (31:28) and Ezekiel (18:2).

36 "False" prophets under Jehoiakim: Jer 26:7–16; Jehoiakim's defiance of Jeremiah (Jer 36:20–26) may well have stemmed from religious faith. Battle of December, 601: Babylonian Chronicle 5, Reverse, lines 6–7 (*ABC*, 101).

37 2 Kgs 24:1–17, Babylonian Chronicle 5, Reverse, lines 11–13 (*ABC,* 102).

38 23:3–8 where the name *yhwh ṣdqnw* ("the LORD is our righteousness") is equivalent to *ṣdqyhw* ("Zedekiah"). Much later Jeremiah seems to have tried, at 33:14–18, to correct this earlier mistake by giving the words another meaning.

39 Lam 4:20.

40 25:11–12, 27:6–7, 29:1–19, 28.

41 Jer 28:1–4.

42 Ezek 17:15 (cf. 29:6 and Jer 37:5, 7); see Malamat in *Age,* 215, 218–19.

43 Jer 28:1–17, 29:1–32; cf. Jer 7:4, 14:13, 26:1–24, Lam 2:14.

44 Zedekiah's reign and the fall of the kingdom of Judah: 2 Kgs 24:17–25:21, 2 Chr 36:10–20, Jer 39:1–11, 52:1–30; Malamat in *Age,* 211–21. Some date the fall and destruction of Jerusalem in 587; see Bright, *History,* 330, n 60. The matter depends on how the regnal years of the kings of Judah were reckoned by the biblical writers. Because our evidence is insufficient, there is no scholarly consensus on how to deal with the ambiguities and apparent inconsistencies. See Malamat, *IEJ* 18 (1968), 144–55, *Vetus Testamentum,* Suppl. 28 (1975), 132–42, and *Israel in Biblical Times,* 243–81 (in Hebrew); Tadmor, "Kronologiah," *Entsiqlopediah miqra'it,* IV (1962), 274–76, and "The Chronology of the First Temple Period," chap 3 of *Age,* 55–56; and the literature cited by Malamat and Tadmor.

45 See Brinkman, PHPKB, 262–64; Sidney Smith in CAH, ed. J. B. Bury, S. A. Cook, and F. E. Adcock, Vol. III (1st ed., reprinted with corrections; Cambridge: University Press, 1929), 47–50, 62–66.

46 Cruelty: Jer 50:17, 51:34, Lam 3:60–66. Casualties against Egypt: See p. 82.

47 Jer 51:11, 28. Cf. Roux, 351. Herodotus ascribes to a Babylonian Queen Nitokris a system of defense works aimed against the danger from Media (i.185). No such queen otherwise attested, but the defense-works were real. However, they may have been built in the reign of King Nabonidus as a defense against King Cyrus of Persia; cf. Raymond P. Dougherty, *Nabonidus and Belshazzar* ("Yale Oriental Series: Researches," Vol. 15; New Haven: Yale University Press, 1929), 38–62. Nabonidus reports how he feared the power of the Medes in the first year of his reign (556/5); see below, pp. 123–26.

48 Rudolf Kittel in his note ad loc. in *Biblia Hebraica,* ed. Rudolf Kittel (4th ed.; Stuttgart: Privilegierte Würtembergische Bibelanstalt, l949). There is no sign Kittel believed (with me) that Isa 13:2–14:27 was originally about Assyria, not Babylon. Did syntactical or metrical considerations lead him to his suggestion?

49 For parallels to Isa 13:5–18. see Isa 2:10–22 (though the prophet focuses on Judah, he means the entire human race; Bashan, the cedars of Lebanon, and the ships of Tarshish were all outside Judah), 6:11–13, 9:18–20, 10:22–23, 16:13, 17:1–6, 18:6, 19:2, 5–7, 23:11–12. For a parallel to Isa 14:5–6, see Isa 10:7.

50 Kaufmann, *Toledot,* Vol. III, Part 1, 175–81, and *The Religion of Israel from Its Beginnings to the Babylonian Exile,* translated and abridged by Moshe Greenberg (Chicago: University of Chicago Press, 1960), 382–83. My own position in many respects is close to Kaufmann's.

51 H. L. Ginsberg in *The Book of Isaiah: A New Translation* (Philadelphia: Jewish Publication Society, 1973), 14–15.

52 Ginsberg (ibid., 16–17) rejects 14:1–4a, 22–23; Kaufmann, only 14:1–2 (*Toledot,* Vol. III, Part 1, 178–81).

53 Ezra 6:22, Neh 13:6; Lam 5:6 is probably not an anachronism but an allusion to history (cf. Ezek 16:26–28, 23:3–12). Ezra 5:13 contains a correct designation of the date by Cyrus's Babylonian regnal year, in which he indeed bore the title "King of Babylon." Long before, he had ascended the throne of Persia. Babylonians, Egyptians, and Greeks spoke of the Persian Empire as "the Medes."

54 Thus, Ginsberg rejects 13:2–22 (in *Book of Isaiah,* 11–12), despite Kaufmann's list of its parallels to the authentic Isaiah (*Toledot,* Vol. III, Part 1, 179–80, n 28).

55 2 Kgs 18:19–35, 19:10–13, 21–24, Isa 10:7–16, 36:4–20, 37:10–13, 22–25, Zeph 2:15, 2 Chr 32:10–19.

56 Inscriptions: Speiser in *Idea of History,* 64–65; Grayson, *Orientalia,* N.S., 49(1980), 150–55, 160, 162–64, 170–71. Also noteworthy is the contrast between the position of the king of Assyria as high priest of the God Ashur and the humble position of the king of Babylon in religion and ritual; see Oppenheim, *Ancient Mesopotamia,* 99, and Roux, 367–68. Naturally, the kings of Assyria showed humility toward their own gods (Roux, 315; Julian Reade, "Ideology and Propaganda in Assyrian Art," in *Power and Propaganda,* ed. Mogens Trolle Larsen ["Mesopotamia: Copenhagen Studies in Assyriology," Vol. 7; Copenhagen: Akademisk Forlag, 1979], 340).

57 Nah 2:12–13, 3:1, 19.

58 Text: Stephen H. Langdon, *Die neubabylonischen Königsinschriften* (Leipzig: Hinrichs, 1912), 61; English translation at Roux, 347; see also the text cited in n 27.

59 2 Kgs 19:24, Isa 37:24, *ANET,* 282, 291, 307, Ezra 3:7.

60 Roux, 289–91, 293–98 (through the reign of Sennacherib; can Isaiah have observed any later reign?); still heavier casualties came later (Roux, 300–10).

61 Roux, 358, 374–90.

62 Bezalel Porten has called my attention to the fact that Isaiah elsewhere plays on the words *'ăšer, 'aššūr,* and the root *š°r* (11:11, 16). *Ninua,* the ancient pronunciation of "Nineveh" is abundantly attested in cuneiform documents.

63 But see Jer 3:12–14, 23:24, 28–29, 31:31–32, 36–37, 47:38–39, 51:24–25, Isa 52:5.

64 Cf. Isa 5:26–30, Jer 4:6, 51:12, 27. In the old Hebrew letters used in Isaiah's time, *nynwh,* "Nineveh," could look very much like *nšph.* See figure 1.

65 So I have been informed in a letter of March 14, 1984, from Prof. Erica Reiner, who consulted the staff of the *Chicago Assyrian Dictionary.*

66 Isa 30:17.

67 See above, p. 85, and n 48.

68 The phrase occurs a few lines earlier, in Isa 13:11.

69 In old Hebrew letters *gwy* and *mdy* are shown in figure 2. Consider the parallels in Jer 50–51 (see p. 90, and n 75 below). Jer 50:9 is derived from Isa 13:17, has the plural of *gwy,* and *'t* is absent, though one might expect it to be present. Jer 51:11 is also derived from Isa 13:17, has *mdy,* and *'t* is present. Jer 51:28 is also derived from Isa 13:17

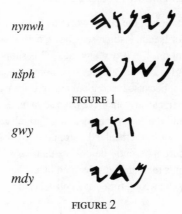

nynwh	ᗺᕽᎫᘔᎫ
nšph	ᗺᒍ᙭Ꭻ

FIGURE 1

gwy	Ꮇᕽᎍ
mdy	ᎷᐃᎫ

FIGURE 2

and has the plural of *gwy* without *'t* and has "the kings of *mdy*" with *'t*. Did the author of Jer 50:9 and 51:28 know a text of Isa 13:17 that did not have *'t?* Or do Jer 50:9 and 51:11, 28 merely show how easily a later hand could add or omit the particle? On the omission of it in biblical poetry see *Gesenius' Hebrew Grammar,* rev. E. Kautsch (2nd English ed., by A. E. Cowley; Oxford: Clarendon Press, 1949), 363, sec. 117b; Alfred M. Wilson, "The Particle *'et* in Hebrew," *Hebraica* 6 (1889–90), 140, 219. On the tendency of later scribes to add it, see Isa 14:4 with 1Q Isaᵃ 14:4, and E. Y. Kutscher, *The Language and Linguistic Background of the Isaiah Scroll (1Q Isaᵃ)* ("Studies of the Texts of the Desert of Judah," ed. J. van der Ploeg," Vol. VI; Leiden: Brill, 1974), 44.

70 Amos 6:14, Isa 13:4, Jer 5:15, 50:3, Deut 28:36, 49–50.

71 Sennacherib and Nineveh: Roux, 298. The ignominious details of the death of the tyrant in Isa 14:18–20 may reflect the death of Sennacherib's father and predecessor, Sargon; see Hayim Tadmor, "The 'Sin of Sargon,' " *Eretz-Israel* 5 (1958), 157–58 (in Hebrew), and H. L. Ginsberg, "Reflexes of Sargon in Isaiah after 715 B.C.E.," *Journal of the American Oriental Society* 88 (1968), 49–53.

The note in Isa 14:28 ("In the year that King Ahaz died came this oracle") might refer to 13:2–14:27 rather than to 14:29–32. It would then be yet another effort to set before the reader the remarkable character of 13:2–14:27. But, if so, the author of the note got his facts wrong; Ahaz died long before the reign of Sennacherib.

72 See H. L. Ginsberg, "Gleanings in First Isaiah," in *Mordecai M. Kaplan Jubilee Volume,* English Section (New York: Jewish Theological Seminary of America, 1953), 258–59. There Ginsberg correctly followed Kaufmann and regarded chap 13 as by Isaiah. Later (in *Book of Isaiah,* 11–12) he changed his mind and held that Isaiah could not have written it and that the author of that chapter borrowed from Zephaniah. Ginsberg's arguments can be refuted. With so great a number of borrowings in the book of Zephaniah from the book of Isaiah, one would be surprised to find any passages showing borrowings in the reverse direction. Our theory disposes of the anachronisms in Isa 13:2–14:27. Let us consider Ginsberg's other points.

1. The predicted devastation of the entire world by God's instrument is supposed to be out of character for Isaiah. Rather, see above, n 49.
2. "My proudly exultant ones" *('lyzy g'wty)* at 13:3 is supposed to be an inept borrowing from Zeph 3:11: Zephaniah uses the expression as a term of opprobrium (as Isaiah would have, because he condemned all pride); at Isa 13:3, the term is a compliment! However, can anyone have been so inept as to use a truly pejorative term as a compliment? Rather, words meaning "pride" and "glory" *(g'wh, g'wn)* and "exult" *('lz)* are not in themselves derogatory for Isaiah. At Isa 32:13 *'lyzh* ("mirthful") is no more inherently pejorative than *mśwś* ("delight") in the same verse. Isaiah condemns the attributes denoted by such words if they are found in the wrong persons at the wrong time. At Zeph 3:11, the proudly exultant ones are

Jerusalemites and are condemned. But *g'wn* is proper for God and he will confer it on his people (Isa 2:10, 19, 21, 4:2, 12:5; cf. Exod 15:7, Deut 33:26, Isa 60:15, Ps 47:5). In fact, Isa 13 displays Isaiah's own traits: *g'wh* is proper for God's punitive agents (v 13), but those agents will destroy the *g'wn* of arrogant tyrants (vv 11, 19).

3. Ginsberg holds that without Zeph 1:7 we should not know why the LORD's henchmen are called his "purified [guests]" *(mqdšy)* at Isa 13:3. But the metaphor at Zeph 1:7, though otherwise unknown to us, might have been familiar to the contemporaries of both Isaiah and Zephaniah. Furthermore, Zephaniah's metaphor treats the coming slaughter as "the LORD's sacrifice" *(zbḥ;* the Hebrew word means both "sacrifice" and "slaughter"). But the "purification" or "sanctification" in Isa 13:3 may have nothing to do with sacrifice; it may be a preparatory rite of war (cf. Jer 6:4, 22:7, 51:27–28; Mic 3:5, Joel 4:9, Josh 7:13).

4. Zephaniah speaks only of thick clouds (1:15); in Isa 13:10, 13, we read of heaven- and earth-quakes and eclipses. But even if Zephaniah's description of the Day of the LORD is milder (and briefer), how does that prove that Isaiah could not have written of eclipses and quakes? Isaiah certainly knew of eclipses and had lived through the earthquake in the reign of Uzziah (Zech 14:4, Amos 1:1, Isa 6:1).

We shall discuss immediately how Zeph 2:13–15 draws on Isa 13:2–14:27. The other passages in Zephaniah showing dependence on Isa 13:2–14:27 are 1:4 (on Isa 14:22), 1:7 (on Isa 13:3, 6), 1:11 *(hylylw;* on Isa 13:6), 1:15 (on Isa 13:9–10), 1:18 (on Isa 13:17–18), 2:2–3 (on Isa 13:9, 13), 3:8 (on Isa 13:4–5), 3:9 (on Isa 14:2, 3:19–20 (on Isa 14:1–2; but in Zephaniah, God, not the Gentiles, brings the captives back).

73   Ginsberg and Kaufmann might not accept our argument here (see n 52).

74   See Hab 1:6–10, 15–17; 2 Kgs 24:1–2.

75   I list here, first, the passage in Jer 50:1–51:58; second, the passage in Isa 13:1–14:27 on which it depends. I add any comments which I think necessary.

Jer 50:1; Isa 13:1, 19 ("Babylon" paralleled to "Chaldaeans"). Jer 50:2; Isa 13:2, 21:9; Jer 50:4–5; Isa 14:1–2 (though Jeremiah believed that the Gentiles would give up idolatry, he did not have Isaiah's enthusiasm for admitting them to the LORD's people). Jer 50:6–9; Isa 13:14, 14:2 (reference to the flock and to the captors of the LORD's people; Jeremiah hopes that the captors will be despoiled and annihilated [50:29, 35–37, 45], not that they will become slaves). Jer 50:9; Isa 13:4–5, 17.

Jer 50:10–13; Isa 13:19–20. Jer 50:14–16; Isa 13:15–18. Jer 50:16; Isa 14:22. Jer 50:16(end); Isa 13:14(end). Jer 50:17–18 does not draw directly on Isa 13:2–14:27, but Babylon there is paralleled to Assyria. Did the writer have some inkling that Isa 13:2–14:27 was originally about the fall of Assyria? Jer 50:19–20; Isa 14:1–3 (see on Jer 50:6–9). Jer 50:21, Isa 14:22 (the writer uses names from the Babylonian countryside, but the meaning of the passage is the same as that of Isa 14:22). Jer 50:22; Isa 13:4–5. Jer 50:23; Isa 14:4–6 (and 10:5). Jer 50:24; Isa 14:11–12. Jer 50:25–27 (Media not named!); Isa 13:17–19. Jer 50:26; Isa 14:22. Jer 50:28; Isa 13:14, 14:1–2. Jer 50:29–30; Isa 13:18. Jer 50:33–34; Isa 14:1–2 (however, for the writer in Jeremiah, only God himself, not the Gentiles, will release the captives; see on Jer 50:6–9).

Jer 50:35; Isa 13:19 (the target is identified as Babylon and the Chaldaeans). Jer 50:35–37; Isa 14:22 (the destruction of the enemy is essentially the same). Jer 50:38–40; Isa 13:19–22. Jer 50:41–42; Isa 13:4, 9, 17–18. Jer 50:44(end); Isa 14:27. Jer 50:44–45; Isa 14:24–25, 14:1–2 (the sheep of the LORD's flock will drag off their Babylonian captors as prey, and Babylon will be destroyed; see on Jer 50:6–9). Jer 50:46; Isa 13:13.

Jer 51:1; Isa 13:19. Jer 51:2–4; Isa 13:15–18. Jer 51:6; Isa 13:14. The metaphor of the cup of drunkenness in Jer 51:7 is Jeremiah's own (cf. 25:15–28), as is that of the balm in 51:8–9 (cf. 8:22, 46:11). Jer 51:8 ("howl" *[hylylw]*); Isa 13:6. Jer 51:9 ("abandon her"); Isa 13:14. Jer 51:10; Isa 14:1–2. Jer 51:11; Isa 13:17. Jer 51:12; Isa 13:2, 14:24 (and 21:8). Jer 51:17–19; Isa 21:9 (attack on idols). Jer 51:20–23; Isa 14:5–6 (and 10:5). Jer 51:24; Isa 14:24–26. Jer 51:25; Isa 13:2 (mention of a mountain). Jer 51:27–28; Isa 13:2–4 (raising a standard, nations, sanctification or purification [Hebrew root: *qdš*], making sounds). Jer 51:28; Isa 13:17 (Media). Jer 51:29; Isa 13:13 (earthquake) and 14:24–27 (God's plans). Jer 51:31; Isa 21:9. Jer 51:34–35; Isa 14:17 (and 10:7, 14). Jer 51:37; Isa 13:21. Jer 51:38–39; Nah 2:12–14.

Jer 51:39 again has the metaphor of drunkenness; see on 51:7. Jer 51:41; Isa 14:12. Jer 51:42; Isa 14:23. Jer 51:43; Isa 13:19–22. Jer 51:44; Isa 21:9 (fall of Babylon and her god[s]). The destroyer from the north in 51:48 is a motif of Jeremiah's own (1:14, 4:6, 6:1, etc.). Jer 51:49; Isa 13:14–15. Jer 51:50; Isa 13:14, 14:1. Jer 51:52; Isa 21:9. Jer 51:53; Isa 14:12–14. Jer 51:57 again has the metaphor of drunkenness (see on Jer 51:7).

Like Isa 13:19–23 alongside Isa 14:23 and like Zeph 2:13 alongside Zeph 2:14, the dry desolation of Jer 50:10–11, 38–40, 51:1, and 51:43 is incongruous alongside the flooding in Jer 51:42.

76 Jer 51:58 contains an unmistakable allusion to Hab 2:13.

77 Contrast Jer 4:6, 51:27; the location of the standard at Jer 4:21 is clear from the context.

78 Following K. Budde, "Über die Capitel l und li des Buches Jeremia," *Jahrbücher für deutsche Theologie* 23 (1878), 428–70; see Eissfeldt, *Old Testament,* 362.

79 See Kaufmann, *Toledot,* Vol. III, Part 2 (Tel-Aviv: Bialik Foundation and Dvir, 1948), 421–23, 467–69.

80 See John Bright, Jeremiah, 212, 259–60.

81   The verse from Jeremiah, like the passages in Isaiah, contains the verb *hkryt* ("wipe out," "cut off") and the removal of human and domestic animal inhabitants from the devastated site.

82   As a by-product of our research we can assert that Zephaniah and Jeremiah and Jews of the late seventh and early sixth centuries read Isa 14:1–2 and 22–27 as integral parts of Isa 13:2–14:27.

The repetitions and apparent disarray in Jer 50:1–51:58, far from being a sign of in-authenticity, not only are in character for Jeremiah (Kaufmann, *Religion of Israel,* 414–15). They also should reflect the difficulties of a prophet who believes in his own inspiration and in that of his predecessors but is not sure how to apply both in predict-ing the fall of Babylon. There is disarray and duplication in Isaiah, too. He produced both 10:5–27 and 13:2–14:27. In fact, it seems clear that 14:24–27 are out of place and belong after 10:27. After 10:27 the verses would supply the missing announcement of Assyria's destruction; in their present position after 13:2–14:23, the verses contradict the implication of 13:2–22, that barbarian invaders will destroy Assyria in her home territory. Isaiah himself was probably responsible for the disarray, out of inability to de-cide how the tyrannical kingdom would fall. His notebooks may have contained inter-mingled sketches of the various possibilities.

83   The date is given at 2 Kgs 25:27. Although our Bibles divide the book of Kings into First and Second, the work is a unit. Like Samuel and Chronicles, the book was di-vided when it was translated into Greek and its length became half again as long be-cause vowels, omitted in Hebrew, necessarily were included in Greek.

84   Israel: 2 Kgs 17:7–18; with 2 Kgs 17:16–17 compare Deut 4:15–19, 16:21, 18:9–14. Judah: 2 Kgs 21:2–16, 22:16–20, 23:26–27.

85   2 Kgs 24:1–4, 19–20.

86   Morton Smith ("The Veracity of Ezekiel, the Sins of Manasseh, and Jeremiah 44:18," *Zeitschrift für die alttestamentliche Wissenschaft* 87 [1975], 15–16) suggests that the cessation of the worship of the Queen of Heaven mentioned in Jer. 44:18 was an (unrecorded) "suspension of cults other than that of Yahweh, during the final siege of Jerusalem." Jeremiah on his side and his opponents on theirs were ardent upholders of a theology. Ardent theologians in debate can distort the proportions of time and events. If the cessation of the worship of the Queen of Heaven was brought about by Josiah's reform of 622, Jeremiah in Egypt after Jerusalem fell in 586 could accuse his opponents and their fathers and the kings (plural) of Judah of worshiping the Queen of Heaven (especially since *'ab* in Hebrew means both "father" and "ancestor"), and his opponents could say they had prospered until they had ceased to do so. But how could Jeremiah's opponents assert that their prosperity ended only when pressure of the final siege left so few animals and so little incense that sacrifices had to be reduced?

87   See n 26.

88   See chap 1, pp. 13–18.

89   Jer 15:4.

90   Jer 44.

91   See Kaufmann, *Religion,* 415–17, 432–35; *Toledot,* VII, 533–38, 562, 613–25.

92   Chaps 25 and 27, 29:10.

93   27:7.

94   25:8–9.

95   27:8.

96   27:11.

97   38:17–23; on these teachings of Jeremiah, cf. Kaufmann, *Religion, 422–24.*

98   2:5–8, 17:11, etc.

99   17:11–21.

100   20:32–44.

101   2 Chr 36:11–14.

102   Ezra 9:7–9, Neh 9:30–37.

103   See Jonathan A. Goldstein, *II Maccabees* ("Anchor Bible," Vol. 41A; Garden City, N.Y.: Doubleday, 1983), 144, 150–51.

104   Tadmor, "The Babylonian Exile and the Restoration," in Ben-Sasson, 160–64; Oded in Hayes-Miller, 476–86.

105   Isa 46:1–7, Jer 50:2, 51:44. Is Jer 51:42 a parody of the Creation Epic? Marduk's victory has been reversed, and the sea (Tiâmat) has covered Babylon!

106   See Ephraim A. Speiser, *Genesis* ("Anchor Bible," Vol. 1; Garden City, N.Y.: Doubleday, 1964), 8–11.

107   40:12, 21–22, 26, 28; 41:4, 42:5, 43:1, 7, 15; 44:2, 21, 24; 45:7–9, 12, 18; 48:12–13, 51:13.

108   Morton Smith, "II Isaiah and the Persians," *JAOS* 83 (1963), 415–21.

109   44:3, 45:3, 14, 48:22–23 (the Babylonian king Nabonidus in Deutero-Isaiah's own time set up inscriptions telling how his subjects kissed his feet; see *ANET,* 309), 54:3, 11–12, 60:5–17, 66:12. See also Tadmor in Ben-Sasson, 167.

110   Jer 51:34.

111   Roux, 350–51, 359–73.

112   *ANET,* 307.

113   See Zech 1:12, Ezra 9:7–9, 13; Neh 9:26–37, Dan 9:4–16.

114   See Jer 44:30.

115   Roux, 345–47.

116   Grayson, BHLT, 78–86.

117   Babylonian Chronicles 2–5 (*ABC,* 87–102).

118   Hermann Hunger and Stephen A. Kaufman, "A New Akkadian Prophecy Text," *JAOS* 95 (1975), 371–75; Hermann Hunger, *Spätbabylonische Texte aus Uruk, Teil I* (*"Ausgrabungen der Deutschen Forschungsgemeinschaft in Uruk-Warka,"* Band IX; Berlin: Gebr. Mann Verlag, 1976), 21–23.

119   By W. G. Lambert, *Background of Jewish Apocalyptic,* 10–11, 18–19.

120   See my article, "The Historical Setting of the Uruk Prophecy," *JNES* 47 (1988), 43–46, and on Beaulieu's counter-interpretation, see chap 2, n 54.

121   See chap 2, pp. 37–46.

122   2 Kgs 25:27–30, Jer 52:31–34.

123   *ANET,* 309; Berossus, *FGH* 680, F 9 (Josephus, *Against Apion* i.20.146–47).

124   *ANET,* 309; Babylonian Chronicle 6 (*ABC,* 103–4); Roux, p. 351.

125   Berossus, *FGH* 680, F 9 (Josephus *Against Apion* i.20.148–49); *ANET,* 309; Beaulieu, 139–42.

~5~

The Reign of Nabonidus
and the Fall of the Kingdom
of Babylon (556–539 B.C.E.)

1. Introduction

NABONIDUS'S NAME DOES NOT APPEAR in the Bible. Yet his reign was momentous for both *peoples of an almighty god*. Many Babylonian texts survive to tell us about the period. There are inscriptions by the king himself or set up in his name by his son as regent. Nabonidus's enemies, the priests and faithful of Marduk, were to turn against their own king and become loyal supporters of the foreigner, King Cyrus of Persia. They composed pieces of propaganda on Cyrus's behalf. One of these, the Verse Account, deserves to be called a historical epic, on Nabonidus and his sins. Another, the Cyrus Cylinder, narrates the sin and fall of Nabonidus and the accession of Cyrus after the manner of Assyrian and Babylonian royal inscriptions. Chronicle 7 was written to cover his reign and fall and the beginning of the reign of Cyrus (careful study of Babylonian chronicles has demonstrated their accuracy; unfortunately, only parts of Chronicle 7 survive). Of two fragmentary texts published by Wilfred Lambert, one (which we shall call "Lambert's Text") may be a chronicle on Nabonidus, and the other may be a historical epic on him. There is information on the king in a present-future prophecy (the Dynastic Prophecy) written in 331 before Alexander the Great won the battle of Gaugamela. Fragments on Nabonidus survive by the Babylonian historian Berossus, who wrote in Greek in the third century B.C.E. The Greeks Herodotus and Xenophon make brief but interesting allusions to the king. A fragment from Qumran, 4Q Prayer of Nabonidus (4QPrNab), purports to cover an episode in his life, and texts in Daniel 2–7 can be shown to reflect his reign. We shall not treat the Jewish texts in this chapter but shall turn to them later.[1]

Nabonidus's reign was fraught with controversy, and controversy has bedeviled modern efforts to reconstruct the course of events. Some of the difficulties may be due to modern inability or unwillingness to understand religious fanaticism. But much of the trouble stems from the tantalizing gaps, ambiguities, and outright contradictions in the surviving evidence. The dissertation of Paul-Alain Beaulieu[2] has made great contributions toward deriving from the difficult evidence the facts of the reign of Nabonidus and their chronology, as well as the truth concerning the king's character, policies, accomplishments, and failures. Beaulieu's work is fundamental, but he has committed errors. Therefore, we must study the sources ourselves to discover the facts on those aspects of Nabonidus's career that are important for our study of *peoples of an almighty god*. I shall first give a straightforward narrative of Nabonidus's reign, treating only the points where I am in agreement with Beaulieu. Then I shall give detailed discussions of the evidence on the points where I disagree with him, each headed by an italicized statement of my own view.

We shall have occasion repeatedly to allude to Babylonian chronological data, so we must pause here to explain the Babylonian system of reckoning. Babylonians gave the name "the beginning of the reign" to the period between the accession of a king and the next New Year's Day (1 Nisannu; in early spring). Modern writers now call that period "the accession year." The Babylonians numbered the next full calendar year as the first regnal year, so that all numbered regnal years began on 1 Nisannu and there was no overlapping among them.[3] Nabonidus's accession year began in May, 556; his first regnal year began on 1 Nisannu (March 31), 555.

2. Historical Sketch of Nabonidus's Reign

NABONIDUS WAS NOT of royal lineage but had enjoyed a distinguished career.[4] He was the only son of his parents,[5] and became king when he was at least well into his fifties.[6] So far as we know, even his enemies in their propaganda did not call him a foreigner. Only one surviving text can be read as denying that he was a Babylonian, and even it does not do so explicitly. Both Nabonidus and his father, Nabû-balâtsu-iqbi, bore pious Babylonian names. In his inscriptions, Nabonidus mentions his father as a man of distinction, too.[7] His mother, Adad-guppî, is quoted as claiming some credit for her son's career, as a result of which the great kings of the Neo-Babylonian dynasty had shown her honor.[8]

Nabonidus was involved in but did not instigate the conspiracy that brought about the death of Labâshi-Marduk; nevertheless, the conspirators (and very likely other persons of power in Babylonia) united to make Nabonidus king.[9] His previous distinction was probably the important factor responsible for his elevation to the throne. Despite the strange character of his reign, there is also evidence of his competence as king, in administrative documents and in his victorious military campaigns.[10]

Nabonidus and his mother were devoted worshipers of the moon-god, Sîn. Ekhulkhul, Sîn's great temple at Harran, had lain in ruins ever since it had been destroyed by the Medes in 610. From the moment of Nabonidus's accession, he and Adad-guppî believed he had the duty to rebuild Ekhulkhul speedily.[11] Nevertheless, the king found himself unable to do so, whether because of the opposition of his own subjects[12] or because the powerful Median army blocked the way to the ruined site.[13] Otherwise, down through his second regnal year Nabonidus, as a usurper, strove to demonstrate his legitimacy, displaying his military talent and especially his piety toward the gods of Babylonia.[14]

In the month Ayyaru of his third regnal year (May, 553), Nabonidus set out on a victorious campaign that took him through the mountains of Syria or Lebanon to Palestine or Transjordan, to Edom in southern Transjordan, and finally, by the first months of his fourth year, to a string of oases in northwestern Arabia, which he conquered.[15] Strangely, he made Têmâ, one of the oases, into his residence-city and stayed there. He was absent from his capital, Babylon, for ten years,[16] until 17 Tashrîtu of his thirteenth year (October, 543).[17] While Nabonidus was away, his only son, Bêl-shar-uṣur (Belshazzar), bearing the title *mâr sharri* ("son of the king"), presided over the government at Babylon and held command over the military forces in Babylonia.[18] The presence of the king was a prerequisite for the celebration of the rites of the Akîtu, the great Near Year's festival of Marduk, the creator.[19] Because Nabonidus was far away, the festival had to be omitted. Enemies of the king were indignant over these facts.[20]

In the royal inscriptions from the period of the king's long absence (Nab. 17, 3, 26, 19,[21] 12) Nabonidus speaks in the first person and honors Marduk in absolutely orthodox fashion. In Nab. 17, 3, and 19, he also tells of the actions he performed then in Babylonia, though he was away in Arabia (Nab. 12 is very short, and the relevant passage has been lost from the fragmentary Nab. 19). We are driven to the conclusion that the king performed those actions by proxy, through Bêl-shar-uṣur,[22] and there is strong reason to suppose that Bêl-shar-uṣur was the one who specified the content of those inscriptions, although they were drawn up in his father's name.[23] If so, we may conclude that except for the omission of the Akîtu, which only Nabonidus could rectify, Bêl-shar-uṣur scrupulously honored Marduk and refrained from offending the religious sensibilities of Babylonians.[24]

In the king's sixth year (550 B.C.E.), the Medes ceased to be a menace, as their king, Astyages, was overthrown by his rebellious vassal, King Cyrus of Persia. Though Cyrus would later defeat and depose Nabonidus, at first he seems to have been friendly to Babylonia and her king.[25] Nabonidus was still in Têmâ when his mother died, in his ninth year.[26]

In October of his thirteenth year (543), Nabonidus left Têmâ and returned to Babylon, confident in the might of Sîn, whom he thereafter proclaimed to be the greatest of the gods,[27] thereby slighting Marduk.[28] Bêl-shar-uṣur ceased to be in charge of the government at Babylon, though he still held important posts.[29] Documents show that Nabonidus deposed officials at Uruk who had served during Bêl-shar-uṣur's regency and that he appointed others in their place.[30] The king rebuilt Ekhulkhul and dedicated it with great pomp, probably in his fourteenth or fifteenth year.[31] He even declared Marduk's temple at Babylon, Esagila, to be a temple of Sîn.[32] His confidence in Sîn seems to have lasted into his sixteenth year. He assumed the grandiose title "King of the Universe" *(shar kishshati)* used before him by the kings of Assyria.[33]

Events late in his sixteenth year seem to have shattered his faith in Sîn. King Cyrus of Persia, now a superpower, began to menace Nabonidus and his kingdom. Marduk's faithful were bitterly hostile to their heretic king, and Marduk's priests under Nabonidus remembered how their predecessors with some success had invited foreigners (Assyrian Kings Shalmaneser III, Adad-nirâri III, and Tiglath Pileser III) to come to the rescue of Babylon and rule over her as kings.[34] The first indication of the king's misgivings is the recorded fact that Marduk's Akîtu was celebrated at the beginning of year 17.[35] Another sign that Nabonidus no longer had faith in Sîn was the king's removal of the images of many gods from shrines in outlying cities to Babylon, surely for fear they would fall into the hands of Cyrus and benefit him. Nabonidus's enemies could and did view the removal of the images as an insult to the deities.[36]

Nabonidus's repentant behavior toward Marduk was tardy and did not help him. The authors of the Verse Account and the Cyrus Cylinder, as far as we can tell, took no note of it. Although the Babylonian army battled Cyrus at Opis on the Tigris in Tashrîtu (early autumn, 539), Cyrus won. Sippar fell on the fourteenth, without a battle. Nabonidus fled. Cyrus's army entered Babylon on the sixteenth, again after so little resistance that both Chronicle 7 and the Cyrus Cylinder[37] can say there was none. From Jewish and Greek texts, one can infer that when Nabonidus marched out with the army to face Cyrus at Opis, he left Bêl-shar-uṣur in charge at Babylon, and that the crown prince was killed by the Persian army.[38] No known Babylonian source says so. Soon after the fall of Babylon, Nabonidus himself was captured there, and Cyrus began to reign over the city and land as king.[39]

For Marduk's faithful Babylonians, the conqueror acted as material and spiritual benefactor. He undid all of Nabonidus's objectionable innovations. He returned the images of the gods to their home shrines whence Nabonidus had taken them. There were other images of Mesopotamian gods who had, from times long before Nabonidus, been in exile from their home cities, together with the peoples who worshiped them. These images and peoples Cyrus restored to their homes, and he rebuilt their ruined temples.[40]

The period from the fall of Babylon in Tashrîtu, 539, to the Babylonian New Year in the spring of 538 was Cyrus's accession year, and thereafter began his first regnal year,[41] in the course of which he decreed that the LORD's temple, too, should be restored, at the king's expense, and that the LORD's people should return to Jerusalem.[42] Wherever possible, Cyrus posed as benefactor of the subject peoples, as restorer of an order which had been disturbed by the cruel course of history.[43]

3. Religious Conflict with Nabonidus's Babylonian Subjects

Nabonidus showed fanatical devotion to Sîn in his early reign and met bitter opposition from Babylonians. By the time he fell, both Nabonidus and his enemies agreed that the king's fanatical devotion to Sîn, god of the moon, and to Ekhulkhul, Sîn's temple at Harran, had provoked the most violent controversies.[44] Indeed, Nabonidus in the midst of almighty Marduk's people came to present himself as a member of almighty Sîn's people and attempted to impose his views upon his Babylonian subjects. Although Beaulieu acknowledges, as he must, that Nabonidus was devoted to Sîn already in his early reign, he believes that the king in that period muted his personal devotion in order to present himself as a legitimate and worthy king[45] of Babylon: "In the first part of his reign, nobody could charge Nabonidus with upsetting the cultural and religious foundations of Babylonia. . . . [46]

"There is evidence neither for a revolt among the clergy or the population nor for any early attempt to impose Sîn as supreme god."[47] Some of the evidence Beaulieu has acknowledged but underrated; some of it he has ignored.

Nabonidus could hardly have helped rousing controversy from his very accession, whatever his religious views. He came to power as a result of the murder of Labâshi-Marduk, grandson of the great Nebuchadnezzar. He soon faced opposition and wrote propaganda in reply (or had his scribes do so). Nab. 8, a stele set up at Babylon, is one such document. Beaulieu has dated it in Nabonidus's first regnal year, after the second Babylonian month, and therefore sometime between late spring, 555, and early spring, 554 B.C.E. It is the earliest of the king's datable inscriptions. As a stele, Nab. 8 was put up to be read by or to the public.⁴⁸ Though somewhat damaged, it is fundamental for understanding the subsequent events of the strange king's reign.

Nab. 8 begins with a sketch of history which conforms with the views of the Babylonian people, worshipers of almighty Marduk: Whenever ruin came upon either Babylon or her Assyrian enemies, it was because of the wrath of Marduk; Labâshi-Marduk perished and Nabonidus became king through the will of Marduk. Nabonidus did not choose at random the events illustrating this historical sermon.

For Babylonians, the worst enemy their city ever faced was the Assyrian king, Sennacherib, who captured it and razed it to the ground in 689 B.C.E.⁴⁹ Sennacherib was the son of King Sargon II. Like Nabonidus, Sargon and his descendants on the throne of Assyria displayed remarkable piety to Sîn and glorified Ekhulkhul.⁵⁰ Sennacherib's very name *(Sîn-akhkhê-erîba)* means "Sîn replaced [in me] the brothers [who died]." Nabonidus did not want his subjects to think he shared the sentiments of Sennacherib! Harran had been the last stronghold of the die-hards of Assyria. In the course of overthrowing Assyria and the dynasty of Sargon, the Medes also destroyed Harran and Ekhulkhul.⁵¹ Babylonians who hated Assyria may have welcomed that course of events.

In Nab. 8, the king first demonstrates his disapproval of Sennacherib and displays himself as sharing the beliefs of the Babylonian people of almighty Marduk; he presents Sennacherib as the instrument of the wrath of Marduk. Marduk brought about the destruction of his own temple Esagila and his own city Babylon, but he also avenged them (presumably because Sennacherib went beyond the mandate he had received from the god). Marduk saw to it that Sennacherib's own son murdered him.⁵² It was also Marduk who brought it about that the king of the Medes came to the aid of Nabopolassar, king of Babylon. The king of the Medes avenged Marduk's city by destroying Assyria as he swept through it (from 615 to 610 B.C.E.) "like a deluge" *(a-bu-ba-nish)*. Marduk's rage drove the Medes to destroy even the temples of Assyria, much to the horror of the pious Nabopolassar.⁵³ Among the ruined temples was Ekhulkhul, but Nabonidus preferred to mention that fact only later, after preparing the ground. Characteristically, Marduk's faithful did not have to approve of his rage; they only had to recognize it as irresistible. Here, at the end of column II, Nabonidus has associated himself with the great Nabopolassar in his respect for the supreme power of Marduk and in his dismay over the effects of that power on the temples of the gods in Assyrian territory.

Thereafter, he proceeds to tell with approval how a king of Babylon, with Marduk's permission, restored some of the ruined temples and also restored the proper image of Ishtar (Inanna) to Uruk. The king's name has been lost from the inscription, but he surely was Nebuchadnezzar.[54] The text is complete where Nabonidus tells of one last such act of piety by a predecessor, the restoration of the goddess Anunîtum to Sippar: Nergal-shar-uṣur accomplished it.[55]

Having given a selective summary of the pious acts of predecessors whom he respected and wished to present as models for his own conduct, Nabonidus goes on to report the death of Nergal-shar-uṣur and the succession "against the will of the gods" of that king's "unfit" and very young son, Labâshi-Marduk.[56] Three lines are missing which told of the murder of Labâshi-Marduk. Thereafter, Nabonidus reports how "all" then accepted him as king. He is king by the order of Marduk and is the real executor of the wills of Nebuchadnezzar and Nergal-shar-usur,[57] whereas Awêl-Marduk and Labâshi-Marduk were incompetent and unworthy to be their successors.[58]

The next passages reveal significant traits of Nabonidus's character. Babylonians were remarkable for their belief in the importance of astrological omens.[59] Nabonidus can serve as an extreme example of this fact. Early in his reign he was apprehensive over an astrological configuration involving the Great Star[60] and the moon (Sîn). In a dream, a man told him that the configuration boded nothing bad. In the same dream, King Nebuchadnezzar II himself appeared to Nabonidus and said to him, "Tell me what good signs you have seen." Nabonidus replied that he had seen in (another) dream(!)[61] the Great Star, the moon (Sîn), and Jupiter (Marduk) high in the sky, and the Great Star called him by name.[62]

Unfortunately, the lines that must have contained Nebuchadnezzar's reply interpreting the astrological dream are lost,[63] but the interpretation must have been favorable for Nabonidus. Remarkable here and elsewhere in Nabonidus's inscriptions is the king's reliance on his own resources, on his own observations, dreams, and interpretations. Unlike other Mesopotamian kings, he often omits any report that he consulted the numerous professional diviners and astrologers.[64] By narrating his dream, Nabonidus portrays Nebuchadnezzar himself, grandfather of the murdered Labâshi-Marduk, as endorsing the rule of the usurper who was implicated in the murder.

When the text resumes after the break, Nabonidus reports his elaborate procedures of prayer, while awake and in dreams, to several deities,[65] that he be granted a long life and a long reign. Especially he prayed that those gods secure for him the favor of Marduk. He saw the goddess Tashmêtum-Gula plead his case successfully before Marduk and says that thereupon "the wrath of Marduk, my lord, did calm down" *(i-nu-ukh lib ⁱˡᵘmarduk bêli-já).*[66] In so expressing himself, Nabonidus openly implies that he had reason to fear that Marduk was hostile to him. Babylonians would be unlikely to be loyal to a king to whom Marduk was hostile. If Nabonidus admits the possibility in his published propaganda, clearly he does so because it was too widely believed to be simply ignored or denied.

Next the king tells how, full of awe, he approached Marduk's own sanctuary and prayed, still with considerable diffidence, to Marduk himself for a long life and a long reign, promising in return to care lavishly for the shrines of the gods.[67] In columns VIII–IX, Nabonidus in the typical manner of a Babyonian king boasts of his generosity to the gods of Babylonia and to their temples, mentioning especially Marduk and Nabû and their temples, Esagila and Ezida.

By this point, Nabonidus has shown that the great Nebuchadnezzar approves of him. He has also displayed his reverence and loyalty to Marduk and Nabû and the other great deities of Babylonia. He can now return to the religious goal to which he was most passionately devoted, a matter to which he had cautiously alluded in column II: the restoration of Sîn's temple in Harran, Ekhulkhul. If it was meritorious for Babylonian Kings Nebuchadnezzar and Nergal-shar-uṣur to perform restorative acts for Ishtar at Uruk and for Anunîtum at Sippar, surely it should be meritorious for Babylonian King Nabonidus to restore Sîn's temple at Harran! Sound as the argument appears, careful reading of the text and attention to chronology reveal that Nabonidus was in an embarrassing predicament.

In columns I–IX Nabonidus seems to have narrated events in chronological order, reaching the New Year's festival of his first regnal year.[68] Thereafter, in column X, he tells of the command from Marduk, which he says came to him at or near the very beginning of his reign in 556 B.C.E., for he dates it 54 years after the destruction in 610 of Ekhulkhul. At that moment, says the king, Marduk entrusted to him the duty of restoring the destroyed or deserted temples of the angry gods. The predestined 54 years of Sîn's wrath are now over, and Marduk himself has ordered Nabonidus to restore to Ekhulkhul Sîn and the lesser deities associated with him (Ningal, Nusku, and Sadarnunna).[69]

How can this presentation of facts have been embarrassing for Nabonidus? To answer the question, let us first establish the chronology. Another document set up by authority of Nabonidus himself confirms the year-date for the destruction of Ekhulkhul,[70] as does Babylonian Chronicle 3. Chronicle 3 also gives Arakhshamnu (mid-autumn) as the month of the campaign of 610 B.C.E., which brought the fall of Harran.[71] One might think that Nabonidus measured the 54 years from the date in mid-autumn of the destruction to its anniversaries. Almost certainly, however, he counted the time by counting the numbered regnal years which had arrived since that date. This was the simplest way available to a Babylonian then. Nabonidus's own procedure is clear from an inscription set up by the authority of the king himself.[72] In that text, Nabonidus's mother, Adad-guppî, is made to count regnal years from the reign of Nabopolassar to the fourth year of Nergal-shar-uṣur, which was also the accession year of Nabonidus. As the sign that Sîn's period of wrath has ended, she gives her son's accession to the throne, which occurred by late May, 556.[73] Thus, the 54 years probably were counted down to Nabonidus's accession. They might even have been counted down to the beginning of that Babylonian calendar year, April 11, 556.[74] In either case, more than a year had elapsed by the time the king set up Nab. 8. Even if one reckons the 54 years down to the anniversary of the destruction in mid-autumn, over half a year had elapsed.

It was discreditable, indeed sinful, not to carry out the command of a god. Nabonidus could have said that the command had come to him shortly before he set up the stele, Nab. 8. Instead, he accepted the awkward position of admitting, without offering any excuse, that for more than a year he failed to carry out the god's order. Why? Only one answer suggests itself, that Nabonidus told his subjects earlier some other god than Marduk, probably Sîn, had commanded him to rebuild Ekhulkhul. If so, he could not erase his subjects' memory of what he had told them. Babylonian worshipers of Marduk might well oppose any pious acts to the deities of Harran, whom they could associate with the hated Assyrian Empire. Some Babylonians might well have been partisans of Labâshi-Marduk, too, in the belief that Marduk preferred him to Nabonidus. Later, in Nab. 25, column I, lines 10–22, Nabonidus was to record openly how his subjects' opposition blocked the rebuilding of Sîn's temple. In Nab. 8, early in his reign, the usurper king still had hopes of persuading the opposition: He claimed that Marduk himself endorsed Nabonidus and placed upon him the duty of restoring their temple to the deities of Harran. If such was the situation, it would have been extremely impolitic for Nabonidus to mention to his subjects that they themselves were his opponents. Hence, he presents no excuse for the delay. The king's protestations, however, are so earnest, they reveal to us that by the time he drew up Nab. 8, members of Marduk's people were strongly opposing their king's policies of honoring Sîn and his temple.

The immediate occasion for the setting up of Nab. 8 was probably the last act Nabonidus mentions: the depositing in Marduk's temple, Esagila, of an old cylinder seal bearing a eulogy of Sîn.[75] There was a temple of Sîn in Babylon. One would like to know whether taking an article sacred to Sîn and placing it in Esagila was to declare that Sîn was subordinate to Marduk. Or was it usurping Marduk's temple for the benefit of Sîn? When the stele was set up, a sheep was sacrificed and its liver examined for omens of the future. Characteristically, Nabonidus recorded in column XI the texts from Babylonian omen-literature that were relevant to the results obtained.[76]

From Nab. 8, we learn that Nabonidus exhibited the following important traits from early in his reign:

- From the very beginning of his reign, he was ardently interested in Sîn and in the deities who were Sîn's subordinates and also in Ekhulkhul.
- He believed in astrological and other omens.[77] He was ready to be his own interpreter of those omens.
- He undeniably evoked significant opposition among Babylonians.
- He already had reason to take precautions against widespread belief among his subjects that Marduk was hostile to him.
- He was willing, in a stele to be set up at Babylon, to give at least lip-service to Marduk's supremacy, but a careful reader of Nab. 8 can perceive that Nabonidus did so in order to serve the interests of Sîn.

The insecure king's reticence and fear of Marduk in Nab. 8 would lead us to expect he would be at least equally cautious in his other pronouncements down through his second regnal year (Nab. 2,[78] 7, 15, 18, 22). Indeed, he is careful to express piety to Marduk except in inscriptions solely concerned with the worship of Sîn at his holy city of Ur (Nab. 15, 18, 22); in those Marduk could well be left unmentioned. Nevertheless, Beaulieu finds remarkable restraint in the way Marduk is exalted in Nab. 2, 6, 7, and 8,[79] and he finds the glorification of Sîn in Nab. 18 beyond normal Babylonian practice.[80] One may infer that the king was giving lip-service to Marduk and passionate devotion to Sîn.

The worship of Sîn was certainly legitimate in Babylonia, especially at Ur, yet Nabonidus faced opposition even on a matter involving Sîn. Lambert's Text[81] expresses disapproval of how the king interpreted an astrological text in connection with the consecration of his daughter as Sîn's *entu*-priestess at Ur.

To confirm our inferences from the inscriptions of the early years and to learn more, we turn to Nab. 25, a document composed late in the reign of Nabonidus; Beaulieu dates it between the fourteenth and sixteenth regnal year.[82] It is a stele surviving in two copies, which the king set up by Ekhulkhul to be read by or to the public. He could hardly have written lies in Nab. 25 concerning well-known facts. Moreover, he would not have to conceal from the faithful worshipers of Sîn at Ekhulkhul the misguided opposition of mobs in Babylonia to his project of obeying a command of Sîn's to rebuild the temple at Harran. Those worshipers would regard his refusal to yield to such opposition as praiseworthy.

In Nab. 25 (unlike Nab. 8), Nabonidus directly contradicts the beliefs of the Babylonian people: Sîn is the greatest of the gods,[83] and Marduk is not mentioned. The king declares that the command in a dream to rebuild Ekhulkhul came just before he became king and from Sîn (not from Marduk), thus again allowing his audience immediately to perceive his potentially embarrassing delay in fulfilling the will of the gods. The king thereupon frankly admits that his subjects in Babylon, Borsippa, Nippur, Ur, and Larsa rioted against Sîn and brought upon themselves ruinous punishment, including civil strife, plague, and famine.[84] The context implies that Sîn was the power who inflicted punishment upon them, because Nab. 25 at its very beginning proclaims itself to be a narrative about "the operation of Sîn, greatest of the gods and goddesses." The punishment "decimated" the inhabitants of the country. Clearly there were many deaths, surely some inflicted by Nabonidus's government on behalf of Sîn. We can understand how Nabonidus was able to use his army against his own subjects. He had won victories in his early reign.[85] His victories must have enriched his army with plunder. Therefore, at first the army must have been strongly loyal to the king, willing to suppress opponents of his religious policies.

On the other hand, it is clear the usurper king had worked hard to impress his Babylonian subjects with his legitimacy. A report that they rebelled against him was inherently discreditable. He wished to inspire Marduk's people with reverence for Sîn. A demonstration that Sîn, though powerful, was hostile would be counterproductive. If only because they are potentially so embarrassing, the confessions of the king in Nab. 25 deserve belief.[86]

However, the king himself in a later document in which he surveys his reign seems to contradict some of the confessions he made in Nab. 25. Nab. 1 is preserved on cylinders from Sippar and Babylon. Beaulieu has dated it after Nab. 25, no earlier than year 14 and perhaps in year 16. In Nab. 1, as in Nab. 25, Sîn (not Marduk) is the supreme god whose wrath brought about the destruction of Harran and Ekhulkhul.[87] In Nab. 1 (like Nab. 8 and unlike Nab. 25) some special honor is paid to Marduk as a "great lord," and it is Marduk who in a dream gives the king the order to rebuild Ekhulkhul and bring the great lord Sîn to reside there.[88]

According to Nab. 1 (in agreement with Nab. 8), the dream came to the king "at the beginning of my reign" *(i-na ri-esh sharru-ú-ti-ja),* an expression that in a Babylonian royal inscription usually means "in my accession year."[89] Thereafter, Nabonidus reports that he replied to Marduk's command, objecting that the powerful Medes were surrounding Ekhulkhul. Marduk in turn countered with a prediction that the Median kingdom would cease to exist. "When the third year came to pass *[i-na shá-lu-ul-ti shatti ina ka-shâ-di],"* says Nabonidus, the gods (i.e., Marduk and Sîn) made Cyrus, the "young servant of the Median kingdom,"[90] rise in revolt. Does "when the third year came to pass" mean "at the beginning of my third regnal year"? Or is "the third year" a measure of how much time elapsed from the starting point? We shall find good reason to believe that the expression means "in my third regnal year."[91] But inasmuch as Nabonidus says that the starting point, his dream of Marduk and Sîn, came in his accession year, the third year after was in fact the third regnal year. Nabonidus goes on to relate that Cyrus overthrew Media and took her king, Astyages, prisoner, and thus the joint word of the divine great lord Marduk and of Sîn, luminary of heaven and earth, was fulfilled.[92] Thereupon, reports Nabonidus, without delay he assembled the resources of his kingdom and rebuilt Ekhulkhul and reinstalled there Sîn and the deities associated with him.[93]

Accordingly, in Nab. 1, the king presents a creditable excuse, the power of the Medes, for his delay down through year 2 to rebuild Ekhulkhul. He does not mention the rioting, the inherently discreditable excuse he had used in Nab. 25. He also fails to mention the strange facts that extended from year 3 into year 13, his absence from Babylon and his sojourn in Têmâ. Does he not thereby contradict his confessions in Nab. 25?

The account in Nab. 1, however, is itself full of chronological problems. In the first place, the third year after the accession year is the third regnal year, but the good witness of Chronicle 7 attests that Astyages fell to Cyrus in Nabonidus's sixth year.[94] This contradiction has troubled scholars.[95] Tadmor tried to demonstrate that *ina ri-esh sharru-ú-ti-ja* need not be a precise reference to the accession year, but rather is a vague expression, "in the early years of my reign."[96] But even if we supposed that the reported dream came two or three years before Nabonidus's sixth year, that is, in the third or fourth year, there would still be a contradiction between Nab. 1 and Nab. 8. Nab. 8 puts Marduk's command to rebuild Ekhulkhul in the king's accession year,[97] and Marduk's command in the dream reported in Nab. 1 can hardly be distinct from the former. Thus, it seems that the author of Nab. 1 intended *ina ri-esh sharru-ú-ti-ja* to be taken as "in my accession year," and the chronological difficulty mentioned at the beginning of this paragraph would remain unsolved.

Beaulieu[98] tries to remove the contradiction by suggesting that Cyrus's rebellion began in Nabonidus's third year but his victory came only with year 6. It is hard, however, to believe that the rebellion dragged on for more than two years without either succeeding or being suppressed. Herodotus's narrative[99] implies that Cyrus and the Persians quickly vanquished Astyages and the Medes.

Furthermore, by omitting the sojourn in Têmâ, Nab. 1 seems to imply that the king rebuilt Ekhulkhul immediately after the coming of year 3, or at least immediately after the fall of Media to Cyrus in year 6. Good evidence joins Nab. 25 in attesting that he could not have done so.[100]

These anomalies can be explained. Nab. 1 is not a stele that was set up for the public. It is a cylinder to be buried in a foundation deposit,[101] and its words are addressed to two sets of audiences: to the gods (Sîn,[102] Shamash,[103] and Ishtar-Anunîtum[104]) and to any later king who would come to rebuild their temples and would dig the cylinder up and read it.[105] Some of Nabonidus's contemporaries read copies, too.[106] At Babylon and Sippar, there was no point reminding either gods or men that Babylonians had impiously opposed Sîn. In Nab. 1, the king did not need to present an excuse for his failure to rebuild Ekhulkhul in years 3–13. We shall soon learn from Nab. 25 that he believed and proclaimed that he was away in Arabia in those years in obedience to Sîn's command. The gods did not need to be reminded of that fact, and Nabonidus could well have felt reluctant to mention his long absence in Têmâ to his contemporaries in Babylonia and to their posterity; his enemies had conjectured that the cause of it was madness or a loathsome disease.[107] In Nab. 1, however, if the king did not speak of the rioting of the Babylonians, he still needed to excuse his failure to rebuild down through year 2. Accordingly, he or his secretary thought up the excuse of Median power and contrived it to cover precisely those years.

Can that excuse have been the truth?[108] Had it been available at the time of Nab. 8, the king should have used it to avoid embarrassment. Perhaps the Medes surrounded the site of Ekhulkhul only after the time of Nab. 8. The pious king could hardly have presented in Nab. 1 a complete lie to Sîn and Marduk. Hence it is probably true that the powerful Medes had forces in the region of Harran during the early reign of Nabonidus, but that fact does not necessarily mean that they would have prevented Nabonidus from restoring Ekhulkhul. They might willingly have permitted him to do so, and the chief obstacle may have been the opposition of his subjects, as reported in Nab. 25. If the Medes had been recognized early as an impediment to the restoration, Nabonidus ought to have used the excuse of Median power in Nab. 25. The fall of the Medes is presented in Nab. 1 as a great illustration of the power of Sîn. The chief subject of Nab. 25 is the power of Sîn! Why, then, does the inscription say nothing of the fall of the Medes? There is a good indication that the excuse was not the truth but a tardy contrivance: the contradiction between Nab. 1, which puts the fall of the Medes in the king's third year, and Chronicle 7, which dates it in the sixth. It is best to assume that Nabonidus or his secretary muddled the chronology. The composer of Nab. 1 knew for what years the king needed an excuse but forgot or ignored the exact year of the Medes' fall. Therefore, the account in Nab. 1 provides no reason to doubt the confessions that the king made in Nab. 25.

One might suggest that a factor noticed by Tadmor produced the false chronology of Nab. 1. Mesopotamian kings in narrating great deeds tended to shrink the time over which they were accomplished, striving especially to pack them into the opening years and even months of their reigns.[109] But in Nab. 1 the events are not packed into the accession year and into year 1. The fall of the Medes comes at the beginning of year 3, and the rebuilding of Ekhulkhul still later.

Nabonidus's enemies, too, attest that in his early reign he enraged Marduk's people with his religious policies and, probably, also that he used violence against them. The Verse Account is easily datable, because it rejoices at its end that Cyrus is now king. Even in its fragmentary state, one can tell that it began with a list of the injustices, atrocities, and injuries which the king (Nabonidus) perpetrated upon his land and his subjects.[110] This list is probably a synopsis of the evils of Nabonidus throughout his reign, which serves as an introduction to the main narrative of the Verse Account, but the list surely would not omit misdeeds of his early years. In it appear the words, "The nobles he killed in war."[111] They are ambiguous. Did Nabonidus merely expose them to death in combat? Or did he wage war against his own noble subjects? Farther on in the list, there is a less ambiguous hint that executions were perpetrated by Nabonidus, in the fragmentary line, "their corpses on a dark/obscure place."[112] Other killings are recorded elsewhere in the text.[113] If some of the killings occurred in Nabonidus's early years, we have confirmation for our inference from Nab. 25, that the king used violence against his subjects then.

The main narrative of the Verse Account begins with line 17. The mere fact of his gaining power as king should have been proof that Nabonidus had the favor of the gods. Immediately in line 17, however, the Verse Account declares that Nabonidus's own protective deity *(shêdu)* became hostile to him. By the end of this paragraph, we shall see that the author is writing of events near the beginning of the king's accession year. Where Nab. 8 and Nab. 1 tell how Nabonidus was favored by revelations from Marduk and Sîn and how he formulated his policies in obedience to the gods' commands, the Verse Account says that his abominable religious innovations were on his own initiative.

Among the first of them was a hateful idol of Nanna (= Sîn).[114] Only after setting up the idol did Nabonidus announce his intention of rebuilding Ekhulkhul.[115] We have inferred from Nab. 8 that the king revealed that intention early in his accession year.[116] Therefore, Nabonidus must have set up the idol of Sîn still earlier in the accession year.[117]

We shall find other evidence that the idol roused resistance among Nabonidus's subjects.[118] Mass opposition to an idol in idolatrous Babylonia is conceivable; some idols were "improper."[119] One might, however, ask, If Nabonidus made a statue and called it Sîn of Harran, who in Babylon was competent to say it was an improper likeness? Perhaps the hatred was not merely against the statue, but against Sîn of Harran, a foreign deity with Assyrian associations. Indeed, the Verse Account implies that Nabonidus's deity was not Babylonian Sîn (= Nanna) but the foreign moon god Ilte'ri.[120]

Nab. 1 tells how the fall of the Medes, fulfilling the will of Sîn and Marduk, occurred "when the third year came to pass" *(ina shá-lu-ul-ti shatti ina ka-shâ-di)* and made it possible for the king to rebuild Ekhulkhul. In contrast, the Verse Account uses the expression *shalulti shatti ina kashâdi* to date Nabonidus's departure from Babylon for his long and disgraceful absence in Têmâ, while he left his son (Bêl-shar-uṣur) in charge. The departure seems to have been portrayed as the mad act[121] of a person damned by the gods. In fact, the departure occurred not long after the beginning of year 3.[122] Thus, the Verse Account has dated it correctly, and we infer that the author used *shalulti shatti ina kashâdi* to mean "at the beginning of the third regnal year." Therefore, in Nab. 1, too, the expression probably has that meaning. But the verse account also makes the departure follow close upon the completion of the rebuilding of Ekhulkhul, an event that occurred after year 13!

It is easy to understand how Nabonidus and the author of the Verse Account could each have put his own tendentious interpretation on the events of the king's reign. The problem is how to account for the one blatant error on a matter of fact, an error that might have discredited the Verse Account. The rebuilding and the procession from Babylon that brought the statues of the deities of Harran back to their temple were ostentatious public acts of Nabonidus's later reign. How could a Babylonian writer fail to know that they occurred after the king's return from Têmâ?

Two considerations go far toward solving this difficulty. Just as the writers of royal inscriptions tended to crowd the great deeds of the king into the opening years of his reign,[123] so the enemies of Nabonidus wished to show him as thoroughly wicked from the beginning, to demonstrate that he always favored Sîn and never revered Marduk. There was logic in the picture of Nabonidus that emerged: It was evil to favor Sîn over Marduk; retribution came upon the evil king in his mad project to desert Babylon for years and live in Têmâ. This portrait of Nabonidus, so advantageous for the propaganda of his enemies, could be drawn by the simple and convincing procedure of writing a parody of the king's own confessions. We should therefore not be surprised that the Verse Account is in considerable measure such a parody, especially of Nab. 1,[124] even when the writer could hardly have been ignorant that the chronology was false.[125]

The writer of the Cyrus Cylinder did not intend to supply a survey of Nabonidus's reign. He may have referred only to the outrageous acts perpetrated by the king from the time he returned from Têmâ. Nevertheless, the mutilated beginning of the Cylinder (lines 1–8) resembles the mutilated beginning of the Verse Account (col. I [line 1] through col. II [line 15]). Though nothing in the surviving portion of the Cylinder alludes to how Nabonidus had opponents killed, such killings may have been mentioned in the missing parts of the opening lines.

Chronicle 7 says nothing about such incidents. However, we may assume that the rioting was serious enough to dismay Nabonidus but was still not on the scale of the wars and rebellions recorded by Babylonian chroniclers.

Even Nab. 25 does not say that the issue over which the Babylonians rioted during the early reign of Nabonidus was the supremacy of Sîn over Marduk, though it may already have been. Was the issue only hatred for the idol or for the "foreign" deity and his temple at Harran and his Assyrian associations? For whatever reason, there was rioting against Sîn, and Nabonidus took vigorous action against his opponents and killed some of them.

Good evidence also attests that Nabonidus himself in year 2 was uncomfortable over the contradiction between his passionate belief in the supremacy of Sîn and his obligations as king of Babylon that required him to assert the supremacy of Marduk. Those obligations included his participation in the celebration of the *Akîtu*. Two inscriptions of year 2, Nab. 2 and Nab. 6, contain prayers unparalleled in any other pronouncement of a Babylonian king.[126] Nabonidus begs Shamash, the sun god, that his residence remain fixed in Babylon and that he find satisfaction in strolling through her streets,[127] that he spend much time in Marduk's Esagila and Nabû's Ezida,[128] and that he always participate in the New Year's ceremony of Marduk, the supreme god.[129] Should we infer instead that the prayers reflect anxiety felt by Nabonidus at Têmâ: his homesickness and guilt-feelings for omitting the *Akîtu*?

We should not. Nab. 2 and Nab. 6 both tell how Nabonidus in person saw to the rebuilding of Ebabbar, the temple of Shamash, the sun god, in Sippar. Lambert's Text dates that rebuilding in Nabonidus's second year (554–553), long before the departure to Têmâ.[130] Nab. 6 was composed *before* Shamash (i.e., his cult-statue) had taken up residence in the restored temple.[131] There is, indeed, another document, Nab. 3, in which Nabonidus makes a similar claim, that he in person saw to the rebuilding of Ebabbar, the temple of Shamash in *Larsa* in his tenth year, when he could only have supervised the operation by proxy, from Têmâ, through his son. But nothing indicates that Nab. 2 and Nab. 6 were composed after the king's departure for Têmâ. Had he felt homesick and guilty in Têmâ, he would have prayed to *return* to Babylon and to *resume* participation in the *Akîtu*.[132] His anxiety in Nab. 6 and Nab. 2 fits well with the anxiety of his early reign, which Nab. 8 attests.[133]

Against the evidence assembled here for the rioting and its suppression during the early regnal years and for Nabonidus's belief then in Sîn's supremacy, Beaulieu can set the following facts:

1. The early inscriptions pay some, though restrained, respect, to Marduk and say nothing of radical religious reforms.[134]
2. No known archival text from the early reign attests rioting or suppression.[135] Rather, archival texts show that Nabonidus himself established offerings at Sippar for the dwelling there of Marduk and his consort and reinstated at Uruk offerings for Marduk's temple.[136]
3. Even the very late Nab. 1[137] in surveying the reign says nothing about Babylonian resistance. Instead, as his excuse in Nab. 1 for delaying to rebuild Ekhulkhul in his early reign, the king pleads that the powerful Medes were blocking his way to the site of the ruined temple.[138]

Accordingly, Beaulieu[139] discounts the evidence of Nab. 25 on the rioting, holding it to be merely Nabonidus's (invented?) excuse for his delay in rebuilding Ekhulkhul. Not one of these points is cogent. In reply, we can urge the following points:

1. Nabonidus never denied that Marduk was a god. Even in year 15, after his return from Têmâ, he provided for offerings at Sippar to Marduk and his consort.[140] The bone of contention was whether Sîn was inferior to Marduk or was his equal or even his superior.
2. The available archival texts come mostly from Uruk and Sippar.[141] If Nabonidus's religious innovations involved only Sîn's prestige relative to Marduk's, they could well have had no effect on the cults of those two cities.[142]
3. All the significant early inscriptions were written to be displayed in Babylonia, at Babylon (Nab. 8), Ur (Nab. 18), and Sippar (Nab. 2, 6, 7).

Babylon and Ur are singled out as centers of rioting in Nab. 25, and even Sippar may be included among the unnamed cities alluded to there.[143] We are not surprised that the frank admissions on the stele at friendly Harran (Nab. 25) do not appear even in Nab. 1, late as it is; the text was inscribed on cylinders deposited at hostile Babylon and Sippar, and we have explained the allusion to the power of the Medes as a late contrivance.

We conclude that Nabonidus indeed showed fanatical devotion to Sîn in his early reign and forcefully suppressed bitter opposition.

4. Nabonidus Leaves Babylon

Nabonidus's fanatical devotion to Sîn was the cause that drove him to leave Babylon in his third regnal year and to spend ten years in Arabia. Beaulieu[144] admits that religious reasons account for the king's long stay in Têmâ, but he holds that the expedition which began in year 3 and ended in Arabia was undertaken for imperialistic purposes. Beaulieu has not properly understood the king's own statements bearing on the topic, and he has not paid careful attention to the dates of the texts in which Nabonidus displays "imperialistic" designs.

Let us examine the sources.

The most important text bearing on the king's purpose in leaving Babylon and going to Arabia is Nab. 25. In that inscription, immediately after telling of the rioting Babylonians and their fate, the king relates how he himself left Babylon for Arabia and the oases of Têmâ, Dadanu, Padakku, Khibrâ, Yadikhu, and Yatribu and how he spent ten years "moving about" in that area.[145] Other texts show that during the ten years Têmâ served as his residence-city.[146] The king marks the transition from the rioters to himself only by the conjunction *u* ("and," "but"). He has told, only shortly before, of Sîn's command to rebuild Ekhulkhul. Now he speaks of his own stay in Arabia, which delayed his fulfillment of that command by at least ten years. Surely Nabonidus did not wish the reader to ascribe that potentially discreditable delay to the king's own caprice or to his having been intimidated by the rioters. Rather, he intended the reader to construe the cause of the departure to Arabia in the same manner as the punishment of the rioters: Both were results of Sîn's will.[147]

Nabonidus in this passage does not say how Sîn communicated his wishes. Babylonians learned the will of the gods through dreams and omens. Farther on in Nab. 25, the king may imply that he received Sîn's orders in a dream.[148]

Whether he received them by dream or omen, this fanatic would zealously comply. Nabonidus succeeded in taking Têmâ and the other oases. If he had some material goal there, as modern writers have guessed, would he not have expressed his gratitude to Sîn and the other gods for having granted it to him? Why should we not take the king mostly at his word as to the reason why he went to Têmâ?[149] The only obstacle is the (misguided) unwillingness of modern readers to accept a fanatic's statement on what his faith has made him do. The audience of Nab. 25, consisting of the worshipers of Sîn at Ekhulkhul, could only praise the king for obeying Sîn's command, even if his obedience delayed the rebuilding of the temple. Later we shall inquire whether the king had a reason to seek the divine message which sent him to Arabia.

In Nab. 25, the king goes on to report that despite his absence in Têmâ, he remained secure and his kingdom remained stable and prosperous because Sîn ordered the other deities to see to it.[150] Then, says Nabonidus, after ten years he received on the seventeenth day of the month Tashrîtu the dream or omen allowing him to return to Babylon.[151] If Nabonidus's return to Babylon occurred because of a dream or omen,[152] the fact confirms our inference that his departure from the capital, too, occurred because of a dream or omen.

Again Nabonidus in Nab. 25 makes a confession that is potentially discreditable and therefore deserves belief. Indeed, one would assume that kings who are loved by the gods do not receive messages from them to abandon the capital city. The Verse Account dwells upon this very point to discredit the king. Its author surely included the departure for Têmâ among the facts which substantiated his charge at the very beginning of the main narrative,[153] that the gods were hostile to Nabonidus. The Verse Account says nothing of religious motives for the king's departure, implying that the cause was Nabonidus's own perverse inclinations, just as with his idol of Sîn and with his intention to rebuild Ekhulkhul.[154] We have now treated the only sources that bear directly upon Nabonidus's reasons for going to Têmâ.

Although Nab. 25 lets us infer that the king went off to Têmâ in obedience to a dream or omen, the inscription provides no answers to two important questions. Babylonians usually received omens after seeking them. They also deliberately sought to have dreams bringing messages from the gods. Why should Nabonidus have asked Sîn whether he should leave Babylon? Why should the king have so phrased his question, that the answer by dream or omen directed him to distant Têmâ? Têmâ probably was a place sacred to Sîn, but so was Ur, and so, especially, was Harran. We can find clues to the answers in what we have already learned from the king's own inscriptions.

We have evidence enough to justify the conclusion that this member of almighty Sîn's people was in an untenable position at Babylon, where, as king, he had the duty of participating in the *Akîtu* of almighty Marduk's people.[155] Beyond that strain on his religious conscience, he had had to face the rioting of his subjects at Babylon and even in Sîn's city of Ur.[156] If residence at Babylon and even at Ur was intolerable, Harran was no better an option for Nabonidus. Although the powerful Medes might have given him permission to rebuild Ekhulkhul, how could a king of Babylon permanently reside at a place surrounded by a Median army?[157] Nabonidus' faith in Sîn was to increase greatly. After returning to Babylon from Têmâ, he told (in Nab. 1) how Marduk and Sîn had used Cyrus to destroy the power of the Medes. From then through year 16, Nabonidus so trusted in the power of Sîn that he might even have defied Cyrus who by then was far stronger than the Medes had been.[158] But even then, in drawing up Nab. 1, he knew that early in his reign he and his subjects did not dare to provoke the powerful neighbor to the north.

If he moved to a distant region in obedience to a message from Sîn, the king would no longer have to prove false to his principles by participating in the rite celebrating Marduk's supremacy; he would no longer be in a region experiencing the wrath of Sîn; he would even have an excuse for not attempting the hazardous task of using an army recruited from people under Sîn's wrath to drive the powerful Medes away from Harran. The distant place to which the king would move should be pleasing to Sîn. The territories to the east and north of Nabonidus's kingdom were controlled by the formidable Medes and by their Persian vassals. To the south there was only the Arabian desert. Far to the west, under no great power and accessible to the Babylonian army, lay northwestern Arabia, an area known for moon worship, within which lay Têmâ. Têmâ itself may have been an important center of the moon-cult, though the fact is still unproved.[159] Is it any wonder that Nabonidus sought a divine message directing him, first, to make conquests in northwestern Arabia and, then, to reside there? While he lived at Têmâ, Nabonidus still wished to enjoy the prerogatives of a Babylonian king and used his resources in treasure and forced labor to embellish the site, as the Verse Account complains.

In the king's sixth year, Cyrus of Persia put an end to the Median Empire and apparently had no objection to letting Harran go to the Babylonians. But Nabonidus remained bound to his residence in Têmâ. He was a slave to dreams and omens, and perhaps we should believe his claim[160] that the divine message to return to Babylon came only after ten years. Nabonidus may still have been reluctant to face the dilemma at Babylon which the *Akîtu* posed for him. In his ninth year, his mother died, and his son conducted the funeral rites.[161] Throughout the king's absence, Bêl-shar-uṣur succeeded in maintaining order, especially by scrupulous respect to Marduk and abstention from honoring Sîn beyond ordinary Babylonian practice.[162]

We have thus accounted for Nabonidus's long absence from Babylon, and we have confirmed that long before his thirteenth regnal year he was fanatically devoted to Sîn's supremacy among the gods, a fact that could have been no secret to his subjects. Beaulieu, like many moderns, underestimates the power of religious fanaticism. Rather, he holds that the king's motive must have been to add a wealthy region to his empire. Beaulieu's argument takes note of the ancient texts that testify to the wealth of Têmâ and other western Arabian oases.[163] He also cites the utterances of Nabonidus which reveal the king's military interests and his efforts to connect himself with the Assyrian tradition of empire-building.[164]

Nabonidus certainly showed military interests from the beginning of his reign and had to use his military ability when he conquered Têmâ. But otherwise the evidence assembled by Beaulieu does not prove his point, and other evidence refutes it. In Nab. 25 the king dwells upon the wealth that Sîn and the other gods provided his kingdom during his stay in Têmâ. Yet he says nothing about wealth from Arabia. Instead he mentions that region and its people only to say that the god Nergal in those years brought defeat upon the Arabs and put an end to their predatory raids.[165] The silence on the wealth of Arabia is eloquent![166] Furthermore, both utterances of Nabonidus which connect him with the Assyrian tradition of empire building (Nab. 1 and Nab. 14) date from the period of the king's maximum confidence in the power of Sîn, in years 13 to 16, which followed the return from Têmâ. They cannot be used as clues to his opinions during the period in which he indeed passionately believed in Sîn's supremacy but had not the faith that the moon god would enable him to prevail over his own subjects and over the Medes.

5. Nabonidus Returns to Babylon

In year 13 (543/2), Nabonidus returned to Babylon because he believed Sîn had authorized him to do so. From the time of his return until his repentance (probably late in year 16), Nabonidus was confident that Sîn's might would make him invincible. He tried to compel his subjects to recognize Sîn as the supreme god. Beaulieu has ignored the king's own statements[167] on why he returned and has also failed to make some points that are important for our study.

Those statements of the king imply that he eagerly sought the divine message that released him from Têmâ, but also that he did not fabricate it—he honestly waited for it. It is easy to find reasons for his eagerness. He was already quite old, and his heir, Bêl-shar-uṣur, was clearly no zealot for Sîn. If Nabonidus was to act for the greater glory of the moon god, time was pressing.[168]

On the other hand, we can be sure that no menace from Cyrus and the Persians drove the king to return to Babylon from Têmâ. Trustworthy evidence indicates that Cyrus first moved against Babylonia in Nabonidus's seventeenth regnal year, not in his thirteenth. Most important, from the eve of his return far into year 16, the king had full confidence in the power of Sîn to protect Babylonia.[169] Defense of the realm could well have been left to Bêl-shar-uṣur. Furthermore, a famine can hardly have been a reason driving Nabonidus to return. The king's late inscriptions boast, on the contrary, of abundance,[170] and again, the king's son could well have coped with a famine.[171] The theme of the might and supremacy of Sîn runs through all of Nab. 25. Clearly, the king there seeks to indoctrinate his subjects with his own belief. There could hardly be a more forceful statement of Sîn's supreme power in heaven and on earth than Nab. 25, col. II, lines 14–42. Until he repented and turned to Marduk and the other gods of Babylonia, Nabonidus seems to have remained true to that statement.

The most extreme manifestations of his faith probably had to wait until he fulfilled Sîn's command to rebuild Ekhulkhul. Immediately upon his return to Babylon, he took the reins of power from Bêl-shar-uṣur and deposed and replaced officials.[172] He overrode any opposition to the rebuilding of Ekhulkhul and accomplished the deed. Nabonidus's assumption of the title of the Assyrian kings, "King of the Universe," indicates he believed that with Sîn's help he might equal their conquests. Even the king's enemies noted how he now showed no fear of Cyrus and Persia. They accused him of falsely boasting of conquests in Cyrus's territories.[173] Earlier in his reign, when he had prayed for aid in his wars, he had turned to Shamash[174] and probably to Marduk.[175] Now for aid in war he prayed only to Sîn.[176]

We have no evidence whatever that Nabonidus made real conquests in his last years. But he certainly proclaimed in Babylonia that Sîn was supreme among the gods.[177] If his somewhat diffident policies down through year 2 led to his execution of "Mardukist martyrs," all the more should his policies after the return from Têmâ. The king gives us no evidence of such executions. As long as he was confident in Sîn, he had no reason to record Babylonian opposition. After his repentance, he probably did his utmost to have his subjects forget the fact that he had persecuted Marduk's faithful. The surviving portions of the Cyrus Cylinder are ambiguous. They attest that Nabonidus in his late reign oppressed Marduk's faithful[178] and perhaps slew some: The inhabitants of Babylonia were "like corpses."[179] Unfortunately, the portions of the Verse Account and Chronicle 7 that probably told of such atrocities are lost. We shall find more evidence of them elsewhere.[180]

When we come to use the Jewish texts reflecting the reign of Nabonidus, we shall want to know what happened to Bêl-shar-uṣur in the last years of the reign. It is clear that the king's son had done nothing zealous for Sîn during Nabonidus's absence. If Bêl-shar-uṣur now no longer was de facto chief executive, and if some officials who had served under him were replaced, was all that simply a matter of the king's return? Or did the king formally demote his son and show him his displeasure?[181]

There is very little evidence to answer these questions. Archival texts from Sippar, from years 14 and 15, show that Bêl-shar-uṣur still was receiving there prerogatives of a coregent.[182] Let us see what can be learned from the king's latest preserved utterances. Three important inscriptions are later than the rebuilding of Ekhulkhul, Nab. 1, Nab. 4*, and Nab. 5. Nab. 5 commemorates the king's restoration of the ziggurat of the Egishnugal temple complex in Ur. Nab. 1 and Nab. 4* each narrate several building operations, but the last in each is the restoration of Eulmash, the temple of the goddess Anunîtum in Sippar-Anunîtum. Many copies of Nab. 1 were found at Sippar, and copies of Nab. 4*, which says nothing about the ziggurat of Ur, were found in the ruins of that tower. Beaulieu infers[183] that Nab. 4* and the building operations it commemorates must therefore be earlier than the completion of the restoration of the ziggurat. Archival texts show there were important royal building activities in Sippar in year 16, and Beaulieu suggests that the restoration of Eulmash was among them.[184] If so, Nab. 1 and Nab. 4* are of year 16 or later, and Nab. 5 is later than Nab. 4*.

These texts can cast light on Bêl-shar-uṣur because at the end of Nab. 5 and at the end of each narrative in Nab. 4* the king prays that his son have a long life and have no sin. The text of Nab. 1 is complete and contains no such prayer. Nab. 4* and Nab. 5 thus attest that Bêl-shar-uṣur was alive and that the aging king was still favorably enough disposed toward him to view him as his heir. If Nab. 1 is later than Nab. 4* and Nab. 5, one might infer that by the time Nab. 1 was composed Bêl-shar-uṣur was either dead or out of favor.

Nab. 1 and Nab. 4* both contain versions of how the king restored the temple Ebabbar of Sippar, and the version of Nab. 4* is the more elaborate. A foundation inscription for a restored building of Nabonidus would contain an elaborate text describing how the king restored it, for example Nab. 6, on Ebabbar of Sippar. If the king wished to parade his other building operations in the foundation text of a structure, he would present briefer "recapitulatory reports."[185] The narratives on that temple in Nab. 1 and Nab. 4* are thus both briefer recapitulations of Nab. 6.[186] The fact that Nab. 4* is the more elaborate says nothing about priority.

There is good evidence that Nab. 4* is later than Nab. 1. Nab. 4* itself, at the ends of each of its sections, describes its contents as copies taken from other inscriptions. It was not composed as a foundation text to be placed in newly restored Eulmash, but rather as a propagandistic presentation of the deeds of Sîn.[187] The closing formula of Nab. 1, on the other hand, addressed to any future king who would restore the building and would dig down to discover the inscription, reveals that it was composed as the text to be placed in the foundations of Eulmash.[188]

So far as we can tell from his inscriptions, then, Nabonidus throughout his reign viewed Bêl-shar-uṣur with favor, as his heir. If he was concerned that his son might sin,[189] He showed the very same concern about himself and his subjects.[190]

6. Conclusion

AMPLE EVIDENCE THUS SHOWS that religious motives were responsible for Nabonidus's strange behavior and that the king tried to force Marduk's people to change their religion. By the beginning of his seventeenth regnal year, he had repented, but too late. The hostility of the Babylonians to their king caused the easy fall of his kingdom to Cyrus. The supremacy of Marduk or Sîn among the Assyro-Babylonian gods was a matter of concern only for those who worshiped that pantheon. Nabonidus in his reforms for the glory of Sîn did not touch the Jews or the other conquered peoples. Nevertheless, Jews observed the strange events, and their reactions to what they saw and heard had profound and lasting effects.

NOTES

1 To designate the inscriptions of Nabonidus, I adopt here the system used by Hayim Tadmor ("The Inscriptions of Nabunaid: Historical Arrangement," AS 16, 351, n 2):

Nab. 1–15   Stephen H. Langdon, *Die neubabylonischen Königsinschriften* ("Vorderasiatische Bibliothek," Vol. IV; Leipzig: J. C. Hinrichs, 1912), nos. 1–15, 218–97). There is an English translation by A. Leo Oppenheim of Nab. 8 at *ANET,* 309–11.

Nab. 3*   A. Schott in Julius Jordan, *Erster vorläufiger Bericht über die von der Notgemeinschaft der deutschen Wissenschaft in Uruk-Warka unternommenen Ausgrabungen* ("Abhandlungen der Preussischen Akademie der Wissenschaften, philosophisch-historische Klasse," 1929, Nr. 7; Berlin: Verlag der Akademie der Wissenschaften, 1930), no. 30 (62–63)

Nab. 4*   S. Langdon, "New Inscriptions of Nabuna'id," *American Journal of Semitic Languages and Literature* 32 (1915–16), 102–17

Nab. 16   L. W. King, *Babylonian Boundary Stones and Memorial Tablets in the British Museum* (London: British Museum, 1912), no. 37 (128–29)

Nab. 17   P. Dhorme, "La Fille de Nabonide," *Revue d'assyriologie et d'archéologie orientale* 11 (1914), 105–17

Nab. 18   Albert T. Clay, *Miscellaneous Inscriptions in the Yale Babylonian Collection* ("Yale Oriental Series. Babylonian Texts," Vol. I: New Haven: Yale University Press, 1915), no. 45 (66–75)

Nab. 19   *Oxford Editions of Cuneiform Inscriptions,* ed. S. Langdon, Vol. I: *The H. Weld-Blundell Collection in the Ashmolean Museum,* Vol. I: *Sumerian and Semitic Religious and Historical Texts,* 32–37

Nab. 20   Sidney Smith, "Miscellanea," *Revue d'assyriologie et d'archéologie orientale* 22 (1925), 57–66

Nab. 21   Leon Legrain, *Royal Inscriptions and Fragments from Nippur and Babylon* ("The Museum of the University of Pennsylvania: Publications of the Babylonian Section," Vol. XV; Philadelphia: Museum of the University of Pennsylvania, 1926), no. 80 (46–47)

Nab. 22   C. J. Gadd and L. Legrain, *Ur Excavations: Texts, I: Royal Inscriptions* ("Publications of the Joint Expedition of the British Museum and of the University of Pennsylvania to Mesopotamia"; London: Harrison and Sons, 1928), no. 187

Nab. 23   A. Leo Oppenheim, "The Interpretation of Dreams in the Ancient Near East," *Transactions of the American Philosophical Society,* N.S., 46 (1956), 192

Nab. 24   C. J. Gadd, "The Harran Inscriptions of Nabonidus," *Anatolian Studies,* 8 (1958), 46–56. There is an English translation by A. Leo Oppenheim at *ANET,* 560–62.

Nab. 25   Gadd, *Anatolian Studies* 8 (1958), 56–69. There is an English translation by A. Leo Oppenheim at *ANET,* 562–63.

Nab. 26   Henry W. F. Saggs, "A Cylinder from Tell al Lahm," *Sumer* 13 (1957), 190–95

In addition, I designate the documents written by Nabonidus's enemies as follows.

Verse Account: For the transliterated text, see Sidney Smith, *Babylonian Historical Texts Relating to the Capture and Downfall of Babylon* (Hildesheim and New York: Georg Olms, 1975; reprint of edition of 1924), 83–87, with translation, 87–91. Better translations are given by Benno Landsberger, "Zu neuveröffentlichten Geschichtsquellen der Zeit von Asarhaddon bis Nabonid," *ZA* 37 (1926–27), 88–94, and by Oppenheim in *ANET,* 312–15.

Cyrus Cylinder: For the text, see P. R. Berger, "Der Kyros-Zylinder mit dem Zusatzfragment BIN II Nr. 32 . . . ," *ZA* 64 (1975), 192–234; there is an English translation by Oppenheim in *ANET,* 315–16.

CONVERSION TABLE

Tadmor	Beaulieu	Tadmor	Beaulieu
Nab. 1	Inscription 15	Nab. 13	Inscription 18
2	8	14	19
3	9	15	4
4*	16	16	14
5	17	17	7
6	5	18	2
7	6	19	11
8	1	20	B
9	Fragmentary Version of	21	A
	Adad-guppî Inscription)	22	3
10	D	23	F
11	C	24	Adad-guppî Inscription
12	12	25	13
		26	10

The "Nabonidus Chronicle" is Babylonian Chronicle 7 in *ABC* (text, translation, and commentary at *ABC*, 104–11; introduction, ibid., 21–22. There is also a translation by A. Leo Oppenheim at *ANET*, 305–7. On the reliability of Chronicle 7, see Dougherty, *Nabonidus*, 111–27. On the reliability of Babylonian Chronicles in general, see Grayson, *Orientalia* 49 (1980), 173–75, and *ABC*, 10–14.

Lambert's Text: fragment that may be a chronicle: W. G. Lambert, "A New Source for the Reign of Nabonidus," *Archiv für Orientforschung* 22 (1968–69), 1–8. Fragment that may be a historical epic: idem, "Nebuchadnezzar, King of Justice," *Iraq* 27 (1965), 1–11; so suggests Tadmor, quoted by Jonas Greenfield in *Shilton paras*, 304, n 5.

The Dynastic Prophecy was published in BHLT, 31–37.

On the Qumran text and Daniel, see chap 8.

2 *The Reign of Nabonidus, King of Babylon 556–539 B.C.* ("Yale Near Eastern Researches," 10; New Haven and London: Yale University Press, 1989). Beaulieu has done well in establishing the chronology of Nabonidus's royal inscriptions and uses a new system to designate them, as far as possible numbering them in their chronological order, as Inscription 1, Inscription 2, etc. I, however, retain the system described in n 1 because it has been used by earlier scholars and because it keeps to the old numbering of Langdon, *Die neubabylonischen Königsinschriften*, where fifteen of the texts are published. See conversion table above.

3 Elias J. Bickerman, *Chronology of the Ancient World* (Ithaca, N.Y.: Cornell University Press, 1968 or 1980) 66.

4 Nabonidus's lineage: Nab. 25, col. I, lines 7–9; Megasthenes *apud* Abydenos, *FGH* 685, F 6.4 (Eusebius *Praeparatio evangelica* ix.41.4); cf. Beaulieu, 88–89. In view of that testimony, one should not take literally Nab. 1, col. II, line 7, where Nabonidus writes as if he were a descendant of rulers who preceded him (including the Assyrian kings Ashurbanipal and Shalmaneser III), calling them "my forefathers" *(ab-bi-e-a);* contrast Julius Lewy, "The Late Assyro-Babylonian Cult of the Moon and its Culmination at the Time of Nabonidus," *HUCA* 19 (1945–46), 418, n 74.

Nabonidus's earlier career: Raymond Philip Dougherty, *Nabonidus and Belshazzar* ("Yale Oriental Series: Researches," Vol. XV; New Haven: Yale University Press, 1929), 29–42, and especially Beaulieu, 78–86.

5 Nab. 25, col. I, line 7; Nab. 24, col. I, line 40, and col. II, line 13; Beaulieu, 67–68.

6 Beaulieu, 76–78.

7 Surviving text: the Dynastic Prophecy, col. II, line 12 (Grayson, BHLT, 32–33), calls his reign *palê Ḥarran,* "the dynasty of Harran." Nabonidus's father: Dougherty, 16–18, 27; however, outside Nabonidus's inscriptions, no confirmation has been found for his assertions about his father's distinction (Beaulieu, 68).

8 Nab. 24, col. II, lines 45–50 *(ANET,* 561); see W. Röllig, "Erwägungen zu neuen Stelen König Nabonids," *ZA* 56 (1964), 236–37. Scholars have held that Adad-guppî had been priestess or even high priestess of the god Sîn at Harran (Édouard Dhorme, Review of *Inscriptions,* by H. Pognon, *Revue biblique* 5 [1908], 130–35, and "La mère de Nabonide," *Revue d'Assyrologie et d'archéologie orientale* 41 [1947], 1–21; Dougherty, 20–28). The evidence does not suffice for making that assertion. Against Dhorme and Dougherty, see Röllig, *ZA* 56 (1964), 236–37; Tadmor, "The Historical Background to Cyrus's Proclamation," in *Oz,* 453; Julius Lewy, "The Late Assyro-Babylonian Cult of the Moon and its Culmination at the Time of Nabonidus," *HUCA* 19 (1945–46), 407, and especially Beaulieu, 70–75; Beaulieu's further inferences concerning Adad-guppî: 75–79.

9 Nab. 8, col. IV, line 37 through col. V, line 13 *(ANET,* 309); Berossus, *FGH* 680, F 9a (Josephus, *Against Apion* i.20.148–49); Megasthenes *apud* Abydenos, *FGH* 685, F 6b (Eusebius *Praeparatio evangelica* ix.41.4): τὸν δ κηδεστὴς ἀποκτείνας Νιγλισάρης λείπει παῖδα Λαβασσοάρασκον. τούτου δ'ἀποθανόντος βιαίωι Μόρωι, Ναβαννήδοχον ἀποδεικνῦσι βασιχέα, προσήκοντά οἱ οὐδέν. ("Nergal-shar-uṣur, his brother-in-law, slew him [Awêl-Marduk]. [On dying,] he [Nergal-shar-uṣur] left a child heir, Labâshi-Marduk. After the latter was killed through violent means, they designated Nabonidus king, though he [Nabonidus] was unrelated to him"). Such is the correct reading and translation of the passage. The text may still be somewhat defective because it leaves the fact of Nergal-shar-uṣur's death to be inferred (where I have inserted it in brackets).

The relevant passage from the Armenian version of Eusebius *Chronika* (Karst's German translation is at *FGH* 685, F 6a.13) clearly was based on a text identical to that in *Praeparatio evangelica* and contains a series of errors. For λείπει παῖδα Λαβασσοάρασκον it has "He had one surviving son," as if the Greek had [τούτῳ] λείπεται παῖς. The Armenian translator probably also took Labâshi-Marduk to be the son of Awêl-Marduk, although in the Greek only Nergal-shar-uṣur can be the subject of λείπει, and the child (παῖδα) must be his. The historical present λείπει must mean "[on dying,] he left." Since that sentence in effect reports Nergal-shar-uṣur's death, he cannot be the subject of the next finite verb, ἀποδείκνυσι or ἀποδεικνῦσι. In view of Nab. 8, col. V, lines 1–7, a large mass of people made Nabonidus king, so that finite verb must be third person plural, and its subject must be the implied perpetrators of violence who slew Labâshi-Marduk. Finally, the Armenian translator misrendered προσήκοντά οἱ οὐδέν as "although it [the kingdom] did not belong to him." Dougherty, too (*Nabonidus,* 77) misconstrued the passage. In fact, in Abydenos's Ionian Greek, the enclitic third person dative pronoun οἱ need not be reflexive (see Raphael Kühner and Bernhard Gerth, *Ausführliche Grammatik der griechischen Sprache: Satzlehre* [2 vols.; 3d ed.; Hannover and Leipzig: Hahn, 1898–1900], I, 565–66). We thus eliminate any testimony by a historian that Nergal-shar-uṣur while alive designated Nabonidus to be king. If Nergal-shar-uṣur had done so, Nabonidus himself would have made the claim, loudly, in Nab. 8 and elsewhere.

Nabonidus himself says (Nab. 25, col. I, lines 7–9), according to Beaulieu's translation (67), "I am Nabonidus, . . . who has nobody. In my mind there was no thought of kingship." Beaulieu notes (ibid.) that this means Nabonidus could claim the support of no one and had not coveted the kingship before the coup which destroyed Labâshi-Marduk. For a detailed discussion of Nabonidus's accession, see Beaulieu, 86–90. Beaulieu (90–104) also assembles evidence to argue that Nabonidus's son, Bêl-shar-uṣur (Belshazzar) was ringleader in the conspiracy and that Nabonidus was selected to be king because he was still vigorous and his accession would secure the succession for Bêl-shar-uṣur. If that were so, would Nabonidus have said, "I am Nabonidus . . . who has nobody"?

10   Beaulieu's book contains the fullest available study of the administrative documents of Nabonidus's reign. On the prosperity of business during his reign, see Hildegard Lewy, "The Babylonian Background of the Kay Kâûs Legend," *Archiv Orientální* 17, Part 2 (1949), 58, n 133. Clearly he was victorious in at least two campaigns. On his campaign or campaigns in Cilicia (*Khume,* southeastern Asia Minor) see Babylonian Chronicle 7, col. I, line 7 (*ABC,* 105); Nab. 8, col. IX, lines 31–37 (*ANET,* 311); and Beaulieu, 22, 116–17. On his campaign in Arabia, see Verse Account, col. II, lines 22–26 (*ANET,* 313) and Nab. 25, col. I, line 45 through col. II, line 2 (*ANET,* 562).

11   Nab. 25, col. I, lines 12–14 (*ANET,* 562); Nab. 24, col. I (line 39) through col. II (line 21) (*ANET,* 561); Beaulieu, 46–50, 64–65, 113, 137.

12   Nab. 25, col. I, lines 14–20.

13   Nab. 1, col. I, lines 24–25.

14   Beaulieu, 110–37.

15 Beaulieu, 165–69; on Nabonidus's campaign in Edom, see pp. 155–56, and John R. Bartlett, *Edom and the Edomites* ("Journal for the Study of the Old Testament: Supplement Series," 77; Sheffield, England: JSOT Press, 1989), 157–61.

16 Beaulieu, 169–74. The ten years were counted from Nabonidus's departure from Babylon (see n 74). Têmâ can be found in northwest Arabia on Map 2.

17 Beaulieu, 163–65.

18 Beaulieu, 186–97. On the name "Belshazzar," see chap 8, n 21.

19 Above, chap 2, p. 3; *ANET,* 331–34; Beaulieu, 186–87.

20 Verse Account, col. II, lines 10–11 (*ANET,* 313); Chronicle 7, years 7, 9, 10, 11.

21 For the date of Nab. 19, see Beaulieu, 30–31.

22 Beaulieu, 187. Cf. n 26.

23 Beaulieu, 50–54, 62–65.

24 Cf. Beaulieu, *The Reign of Nabonidus, King of Babylon (556–539 B.C.)* (Diss. Yale, 1985; Ann Arbor: University Microfilms, Order No. DA8612940; copyright, 1986), 316.

25 Chronicle 7, col. II, lines 1–4; Nab. 25, col. I, lines 38–45, esp. line 42; Cyrus was king of the Medes during most of Nabonidus's years in Têmâ (see Gadd, *Anatolian Studies* 8 [1958], 76–77; W. Röllig, *ZA* 56 [1964], 228–29). Langdon, Oppenheim (*TAPS,* N.S., 46 [1956], 250), and Beaulieu (108) read Nab. 1, col. I, lines 28–30, as calling Cyrus Marduk's servant, but see n 90.

26 Chronicle 7, col. II, lines 13–15; Nab. 24, col. III, lines 5–7. Nab. 24 reports that the king participated in his mother's funeral. He can have done so only by proxy, through Bêl-shar-uṣur. We have just seen in Nab. 17, 3, and 19 the same kind of report of royal actions performed by proxy.

27 Nab. 25, col. II (line 13) through col. III (line 6). Beaulieu, 58–62.

28 Beaulieu, 54–63, 212–13, 214–19.

29 Beaulieu, 159–60. A. C. V. M. Bongenaar has published evidence showing that Bêl-shar-uṣur was still receiving royal prerogatives from Sippar in the summer of Nabonidus's fifteenth year ("The regency of Belsazzar," *Nouvelles assyriologiques* *brèves et utilitaires,* June, 1993, Item No. 41). In a letter to me of September 27, 1994, Beaulieu accepts Bongenaar's evidence and says that Bêl-shar-uṣur may have continued to be coregent with his father into year 15 and perhaps his power then was restricted to Sippar, since the evidence of the continued coregency comes solely from Sippar. Beaulieu's speculation, that two archival texts hint that Bêl-shar-uṣur was far from Sippar and even outside Babylonia (204–5), is unfounded (Bongenaar, *NABU,* June 1993, Item No. 41). On Bêl-shar-uṣur's possible role in the final struggle against Cyrus, see p. 116.

30 Beaulieu, 160–62.

31 Nab. 25, col. III, lines 21–31; Nab. 1, col. I (line 50) through col. II (line 25); Beaulieu, 205–9. On the discrepant chronology in Nab. 1, see pp. 122–25. On the possible contradiction at Nab. 8, col. X, lines 12–24, see n 69. On the one in the Verse Account, see pp. 126–27. Nab. 24 must have been addressed to a knowing audience, because it was set up at Ekhulkhul when that temple was dedicated. The inscription contains what purports to be an autobiography of the king's mother, Adad-guppî. Nab. 24 itself agrees with the report in Chronicle 7 (see n 26), that she died in year 9. Yet she is made to say in Nab. 24, col. II, lines 11–12, *a-mat (d.)XXX shàr ilani(MESH) iq-ba-a at-ta-'a-id-ma a-mur a-na-ku,* which Oppenheim (*ANET,* 562) and others have rendered, "I heeded the words which Sin, the king of all the gods, had spoken to me, and I saw (them come true)," where the words in parentheses have been added by the translator in the belief they are implied. The passage would imply, falsely, that Ekhulkhul had been restored by year 9. Beaulieu (208–9) is content to say that Nab. 24 belongs to the genre of pseudo-autobiography and that the passage is fiction. But to present such a fiction to the knowing audience at Ekhulkhul would have been absurd.

In fact, *CAD,* I, Part II (1968), 5–27 (s.v. *amâru*) lists no instance where the verb "see" is used elliptically to mean "see fulfilled." One might cite as a parallel 2 Kgs 7:2, 19, but even there, not the bare verb "see" occurs, but "see with your eyes." The passage rather is to be translated, "The word of Sîn, king of the gods, which he spoke, I heedfully received." See *CAD,* XI, Part I (1980), 4b–5a (s.v. *na'âdu,* 4); for the adverbial translation, "heedfully," cf. the use of the Grundstamm of *na'âdu* in hendiadys (ibid., 1b-2b). For *a-mur* as "I received" see *CAD,* I, Part II, 6b. One might object that the examples cited there are of written messages, so that the verb "see" was appropriate, whereas here Sîn is said to have spoken. But Adad-guppî says (Nab. 24, col. II, line 5) Sîn spoke to her in a *dream,* so that here, too, the verb is appropriate. See also the examples of *amâru* used of ominous phenomena, *CAD,* I, Part II, 14.

32 Nab. 4*, col. II, lines 16–21, etc.; Nab. 5, col. II, lines 9–11; Beaulieu, 61, 219.

33 Nab. 1, col. I, line 2; Nab. 14, line 1, as read at Beaulieu, 214 (cf. Verse Account, col. V, lines 4–7); Beaulieu, 141, 217.

34   Cyrus a menace: Cyrus Cylinder, lines 12–14; Chronicle 7, col. III, lines 1–4, as read at Grayson, *ABC,* 282; Beaulieu, 219–20.

Hostility to Nabonidus: Cyrus Cylinder, lines 1–11, 19; the Verse Account is not explicit on the point, but its whole tendency implies such bitterness. On indications that Marduk's faithful colluded with Cyrus to bring about the fall of Nabonidus, see Harmatta, *Acta Antiqua* 19 (1971), 226–27, 230, and Tadmor in *Shilton paras,* 10–12. Assyrian kings: Tadmor, ibid., 11 and 254, n 49.

35   Chronicle 7, col. III, lines 5–8. Nothing tells us directly whether the *Akîtu* had or had not been celebrated in years 14–16. Verse Account, col. II, lines 10–11, might mean that the *Akîtu* had been celebrated in year 15 or 16, after the rebuilding of Ekhulkhul, but it may only refer to the celebration in year 17. At Verse Account, col. II, lines 10–11, Nabonidus is quoted as having said, "Till I have achieved this [the building of Ekhulkhul], . . . I shall omit (all) festivals, I shall order (even) the *Akîtu* to cease." Illogically, Beaulieu (208) took this to mean that the resumption of the *Akîtu* would *precede* the building of Ekhulkhul.

36   Removal: Chronicle 7, col. III, lines 9–12; Beaulieu, 220–24, and "An Episode in the Fall of Babylon to the Persians," *JNES* 52 (1993), 241–61. Strangely, Beaulieu takes no note of how the events in year 17 imply that Nabonidus had lost faith in Sîn and had repented and had turned to Marduk and the other deities of Babylonia.

Enemies' view: Chronicle 7, col. III, lines 9–12, when contrasted with lines 21–22; cf. Verse Account, col. VI, lines 12–15, and Cyrus Cylinder, lines 9, 30–32.

37   The king's flight: Chronicle 7, col. III, lines 12–15. No resistance: Cyrus Cylinder, col. III, lines 15–16 (*ANET,* 306), Verse Account, Line 17 (*ANET,* 315).

38   See chap 8, pp. 220–21.

39   Chronicle 7, col. III, lines 16–28; Cyrus Cylinder, lines 17–end. On the events of the last regnal years and the accession of Cyrus as king of Babylon, see Tadmor in *Shilton paras,* 8–13.

40   Cyrus Cylinder, lines 17–end; Verse Account, col. vi.

41   See chap 5, p. 113.

42   Ezra 1:1–4, 6:2–5; Elias Bickerman, *Studies in Jewish and Christian History,* Part One (Leiden: Brill, 1976), 72–108.

43   See Tadmor in *Shilton paras,* 12–15; A. Leo Oppenheim in *The Cambridge History of Iran,* Vol. II, ed. Ilya Gershevitch (Cambridge: Cambridge University Press, 1985), 542–54.

44   Nab. 25, col. I, lines 1–22 (*ANET,* 562); Verse Account, col. I, line 17 through col. II, line 17, and col. V, lines 16–22 (*ANET,* 313, 314); Cyrus Cylinder, *ANET,* 315.

45   137–38.

46   138; see also Beaulieu, 49–50.

47   Beaulieu's dissertation, 105.

48   Date of Nab. 8: Beaulieu, 21–22. Beaulieu's dating rests on the secure basis of evidence from archival texts and must prevail over the efforts of Hildegard Lewy (*Archiv Orientální* 17, Part 2 [1949], 51–53) and Tadmor (*AS* 16, 355, n 25) to derive a later date from the combination of astronomical phenomena mentioned at Nab. 8, col. VI (line 31) through col. VII (line 4). The king himself there says he saw the phenomena in a dream, so that there is no good reason to take the description as reflecting a real configuration in the sky.

On the content and purpose of Nab. 8, see A. Leo Oppenheim, TAPS 46 (1956), 203–5; Beaulieu, 20–22, 89–90, 104–7, 110–15.

49   Roux, 322–23.

50   See J. Lewy, *HUCA* 19 (1945–46), 453–61.

51   Roux, 376, 382.

52   Nab. 8, col. I (*ANET,* 309); cf. chap 2, pp. 45–46.

53   Nab. 8, col. II (*ANET,* 309); on the deluge figure, cf. chap 2, pp. 42–43.

54   Nab. 8, col. III (*ANET,* 309); Nebuchadnezzar: See Beaulieu, 21, but note that the Uruk Prophecy can no longer be used as evidence that Nebuchadnezzar restored the proper image of Ishtar to Uruk (see my article, "The Historical Setting of the Uruk Prophecy," *JNES* 47 [1988], 43–46).

55   Nab. 8, col. IV, lines 14–33 (*ANET,* 309).

56   Nab. 8, col. IV, lines 34–41 (*ANET,* 309).

57   Nab. 8, col. V, lines 1–24 (*ANET,* 309).

58   Ibid., lines 25–34 (badly mutilated). Beaulieu (104, 110–11, 112, 114–15) read col. V, lines 1–34, and other passages as showing that Nabonidus viewed himself as competent *militarily* in contrast to his two incompetent predecessors.

59   Isa 47:13–14; Oppenheim, *Ancient Mesopotamia,* 224–25.

60   A bright star; Oppenheim (*ANET,* 309–10) did not determine its identity.

61   See Oppenheim, TAPS, N.S., 46 (1956), 205.

62   Nab. 8, col. VI.

63   Ibid., lost beginning of col. VII.

64   H. Lewy, *Archiv Orientální* 17, Part 2 (1949), 56. See, e.g., Nab. 1, col. I, lines 50–52, and col. II, lines 60–61; Nab. 7, col. II, lines 2–32; Nab. 18, col. I, lines 1–21; Nab. 25, col. I, lines 11–14 (*ANET,* 562). Nabonidus's enemies, too, recognized the fact (Verse Account, col. V, lines 9–14 [*ANET,* 314]; cf. W. G. Lambert, "A New Source for the Reign of Nabonidus," *Archiv für Orientforschung* 22 [1968–69], 3–4).

65   See Oppenheim, TAPS, N.S., 46 (1956), 205; Erica Reiner, "Fortune-Telling in Mesopotamia," *JNES* 19 (1960), 24, n 2.

66   Nab. 8, col. VII, lines 1–38 (*ANET,* 310).

67   Nab. 8, col. VII, line 39 through col. VIII, line 1 (*ANET,* 310). The passage is difficult and has troubled translators. See Oppenheim in *ANET,* 310, n 11, and cf. Langdon, Nab. 8, 281, H. Lewy, *Archiv Orientální* 17, Part 2 (1949), 70. In Nabonidus's quotation of his own prayer to Marduk at Nab. 8, col. VII, line 49, the king describes himself as *la mu-da-a-ka.* H. Lewy (*Archiv Orientální* 17, Part 2 [1949], 70) rendered the phrase as "the one who did not know thee," so as to have the king confess that hitherto he had not known or worshiped Marduk (cf. Beaulieu, 89, 137). Nabonidus had been a courtier (Nab. 24, col. II, lines 45–48; Beaulieu, 78–79) and could hardly have avoided knowing or worshiping the great god of Babylon. In a letter of August 5, 1987, Erica Reiner assures me that H. Lewy's translation would require some such form as *la mūdûka,* and that Oppenheim, Langdon, and Beaulieu (89, n 18) were right to take *mu-da-a-ka* as first person singular stative and to render the phrase as "me, the ignorant"; see *CAD,* X, Part II (1977), 166b, 168a.

68   See Beaulieu, 22.

69   Nab. 8, col. X, lines 1–31 (*ANET,* 311). Nab. 8, col. X, lines 12–24, might seem to contradict Beaulieu's well-established dating for the rebuilding of Ekhulkhul as no earlier than year 14. Oppenheim translated the passage (*ANET,* 311), "As to the temple Ekhulkhul in Harran which was in ruins for 54 years—through a devastation by the Manda-hordes the(se) sanctuaries were laid waste—the time (predestined) by the god, the moment for the appeasement (to wit) 54 years, had come near, when Sîn should have returned to his place. Now, Sîn, the crown-bearer, did return to his place and remembered his lofty seat. . . ." Does the report that "Sîn did return to his place" mean that Ekhulkhul had been rebuilt by the time the king drew up Nab. 8? Not necessarily. Langdon (indefensibly) interpreted the passage to mean "Sîn *wished* to return to his place" (*Königsinschriften,* 285). Tadmor (*AS* 16, 355–56) interpreted Oppenheim's rendering to mean that the moon (Sîn) in its eighteen-year cycle (54 = 3 × 18) had returned to the position in the sky which it had occupied in the year of the destruction. It could also mean that the invisible presence of Sîn, which had left earth for heaven at the time of his wrath (Nab. 24, col. I, lines 7–8), had now returned to earth and to ruined Harran.

70 Nab. 24, col. I, lines 6–9 (*ANET,* 560).

71 Lines 59–64 (*ABC,* 95; *ANET,* 305).

72 Nab. 24.

73 Col. I, lines 29–44.

74 Nabonidus appears to have counted the ten years of Nab. 25, col. I, line 26, in the same manner. In truth, by the time Nabonidus received the omen releasing him from Têmâ in Tashrîtu of year 13, ten regnal years had arrived since the beginning of his campaign and his departure from Babylon in year 3. For the method of counting probably used by Nabonidus, see p. 113. Beaulieu (152–53) disagrees, holding that the ten years were counted by reference to a calendar year that began with Sîn's *Akîtu* festival. According to him, that festival fell on 17 Tashrîtu, and the ten years were the ten complete years from that date in year 3 to that date in year 13. There is, however, no evidence that Nabonidus counted time in that manner. Let us suppose that in Nab. 25 the king employed the calendar year that began on 17 Tashrîtu. A count by the method which he is known probably to have used would have numbered eleven years: 17 Tashrîtu came eleven times between Nabonidus's departure, early in year 3 (spring) and his return, after 17 Tashrîtu of year 13. Beaulieu has also misread the interval, as beginning with the campaign in Arabia (the misreading involved him in difficulty on 169). Rather, the interval began with the departure from Babylon, *on the road to* the Arabian oases.

75 Nab. 8, col. X, lines 32–47.

76 See Oppenheim's parenthetic note at the end of his translation of Nab. 8 (*ANET,* 311). Beaulieu (114) believes that the omen texts at the end of Nab. 8 reflect the military interests of the king.

77 Cf. Nab. 7, col. I, line 11.

78 Beaulieu was wrong to date Nab. 2 during Nabonidus's sojourn in Têmâ. See below, n 132.

79 Beaulieu, 46–50, 53, 137.

80 Beaulieu, 48–49, 137.

81 Obverse, col. III, lines 2–9; Beaulieu, 129–31.

82 32.

83 Col. I, lines 1–6, 27–30.

84 Col. I, lines 10–22.

85 See n 10.

86 To get around difficulties incurred by his own hypotheses, Lambert ("Nabonidus in Arabia," *Proceedings of the Fifth Seminar for Arabian Studies,* 58–62) suggests that Sîn's priests at Harran were infuriated when Nabonidus in his late reign sought reconciliation with Marduk; they put on the stele "a full statement of Nabonidus's most extreme, but by then abandoned, doctrine of Sîn as king of the gods." The suggestion is improbable, because the stele also glorifies Nabonidus as no disaffected clergy would.

87 Col. I, lines 8–13, and col. II, lines 26–27, 33, 41.

88 Col. I, lines 18–22.

89 Cf. Tadmor, *AS* 16, 352.

90 The antecedent of the suffixed possessive pronoun in col. I, line 29, can be only the Median king. See M.-J. Seux, "Cyrus serviteur de Marduk?" *Revue biblique* 76 (1969), 228–29.

91 See p. 126.

92 Col. I, lines 23–35.

93 Col. I, line 38 through col. II, line 25.

94 Col. II, lines 1–4.

95 See Tadmor, *AS* 16, 351–54.

96   Ibid., 352–53.

97   See nn 5–6.

98   109.

99   i.126–28.

100   The rebuilding of Ekhulkhul must have been mentioned in Chronicle 7. Even in its broken state, Chronicle 7 excludes the possibility that Ekhulkhul was rebuilt before year 11. Abundant evidence attests the king's absence from both Babylon and Harran from year 3 into year 13 (see Beaulieu, 149–203).

101   See Nab. 1, col. II, lines 43–46; col. III, lines 8–10, 43–45. On the various purposes of cylinders see Paul-Richard Berger, *Die neubabylonischen Königsinschriften,* ("Alter Orient und Altes Testament," Band 4/1; Kevalaer: Butzon & Bercker; Neukirchen-Vluyn: Neukirchener Verlag, 1973), 99–101, and Richard S. Ellis, *Foundation Deposits in Ancient Mesopotamia* ("Yale Near Eastern Researches," 2; New Haven and London: Yale University Press, 1968), 110; Beaulieu, 18–19.

102   Col. I, line 26.

103   Col. III, line 11.

104   Ibid., line 38.

105   Ibid., lines 43–45.

106   The author of the Verse Account had read Nab. 1 (see p. 127). The cylinder from Babylon bearing Nab. 1 was not buried in a foundation deposit but was found in the "Museum" of the royal palace (Beaulieu, 18–19, 34).

107   See Verse Account, col. IV (*ANET,* 314), and Dan 4 and 4Q Prayer of Nabonidus, treated at chap 8, pp. 205–10 and 215–17.

108   Beaulieu (109) takes the power of the Medes to be the true reason for Nabonidus's delay in building Ekhulkhul.

109   "History and Ideology in the Assyrian Royal Inscriptions," in *Assyrian Royal Inscriptions: New Horizons in Literary, Ideological, and Historical Analysis,* ed. Frederick Mario Fales ("Orientis antiqui collectio," XVII: Rome: Istituto per l'Oriente, centro per le antichità e la storia dell'arte del Vicino Oriente, 1981), 14–25, esp. 22–24.

110 Col. 1, lines 1–16.

111 Col. I, line 2.

112 Col. 1, line 11.

113 Col. III, lines 3–4.

114 Col. I, lines 17–29.

115 Col. I, line 19 through col. II, line 16.

116 See 204–5; cf. Nab. 1, col. I, lines 18–27.

117 Beaulieu treats the idol only at 218, in his discussion of Nabonidus's policy in his last years, without saying anything about its date in the early reign.

118 See 346.

119 See, e.g., Nab. 8, col. III, lines 27–36.

120 Col. I, line 23; col. V, line 11; J. Lewy, *HUCA* 19 (1945–46), 425–33.

121 The fragments of col. IV show the king was regarded as mad.

122 Lambert's Text, col. IV, lines 57–61.

123 See n 109.

124 We have considered three paragraphs above some of the parallels and contrasts which show that the Verse Account contains parody of Nab. 1. One should also note the following. According to Beaulieu (207) the expression *shalulti shatti ina kashâdi* is found in Babylonian texts only in Nab. 1 and the Verse Account. Whereas in Nab. 1 respect is shown to Marduk in that the command to rebuild Ekhulkhul comes from him, the polemicist in the Verse Account takes advantage of the religious result of Nabonidus's absence in Têmâ and writes that the king resolved to omit all festivals, even the *Akîtu,* until Ekhulkhul was rebuilt (col. II, lines 10–11). Nabonidus's deity who granted him revelations was not even Babylonian Sîn but a god unheard of before named Ilte'ri (col. I, line 21; col. II, lines 2–3; col. V, line 11). In Nab. 1, Marduk himself used "Ekhulkhul" as the name of Sîn's temple. The author of the Verse Account writes as if Nabonidus assigned the name to the shrine (col. II, line 7). Both in Nab. 1 and in the Verse Account, the text dwells on how the king built Ekhulkhul from its foundations to its peak or roof-parapet and set a statue of a wild bull in or in front of the structure (Nab. 1, col. II, lines 8–9, 14–15; Verse Account, col. II, lines 13–15). Compare also Verse Account, col. II, lines 4–7, with Nab. 1, col. I, lines 21–22.

125 Beaulieu (207-8) agrees that the Verse Account contains parody of Nab. 1. Tadmor recognized long ago (in *Oz*, 459, n 22) how the Verse Account is a parody of Nabonidus's confessions but failed to use the fact to solve the chronological difficulty. For Tadmor in *AS* 16, 354–55, *shalulti shatti ina kashâdi* is an idiom, a vague expression, "when the time came," "when the cycle was completed," and the order of the Verse Account is topical rather than chronological. Scholars have pointed out the improbability of his theory that it is an idiom and have noted the clear indication of lapse of time in col. II, lines 16–17 (Lambert, "Nabonidus in Arabia," 59). One could add the fact that the Verse Account ends chronologically, with Cyrus's victory and its consequences.

126 See Tadmor, *AS* 16, 359, n 42. Beaulieu takes no note whatever of these prayers and misdates Nab. 2. See below, n 132.

127 Nab. 6, col. II, line 47.

128 Ibid., line 48.

129 Ibid., lines 49–52; Nab. 2, col. II, lines 27–34.

130 Lambert, *Archiv für Orientforschung* 22 (1968–69), 1; cf. Berger, *Königsinschriften,* 111.

131 Nab. 6, col. II, lines 14–17.

132 Consequently, Nabonidus's prayers concerning the *Akîtu* are no reason to date Nab. 2 and Nab. 6 after the departure for Têmâ; contrast Berger, *Königsinschriften,* 112. Beaulieu (11–12, 14, 27, 42) dates Nab. 2 during the period of the king's sojourn in Têmâ, perhaps in year 6. His argument, however, is very weak. First (11–12) he reads Nab. 2 with CT 22:68. In Nab. 2, the king says he purified *(te-bi-ib-ti-shu)* the temple of Bunene in Sippar. The letter CT 22:68 is undated, but Bêl-shar-uṣur is the sender, acting in place of the king; therefore it belongs to the period of Nabonidus's sojourn in Têmâ. The letter deals with the temple rituals of Bunene and mentions doorposts *(sippu)* and perhaps requires that they be purified *(lu [eb-bu])*. Beaulieu then says that the text called "Rituals of the *Kalû*" speaks of rituals performed upon the doorposts of a temple undergoing restoration. Thereupon, he argues that Nab. 2 is "the only inscription of Nabonidus which specifies that rituals of purification were required as part of the restoration of a sacred building, and letter CT 22:68 is to our knowledge the only archival text from Sippar which makes a direct allusion to such rituals." He draws the conclusion that the act of purification in the letter is the same as the one mentioned in Nab. 2. But his evidence is exceedingly flimsy: The verb "purify" does not survive in CT 22:68 (it has been restored by the editor); doorposts and rituals were mentioned in the "Rituals of the *Kalû*," but there is no proof purification was; and Nab. 2 says nothing of doorposts. Finally, Beaulieu (14) notes that the archival text CT 55:329 records that bricks were delivered in the Ebabbar of Shamash at Sippar in the sixth year of Nabonidus. If they were delivered in the Ebabbar, how can Beaulieu suggest as he does that the bricks were for the restoration of the Ekurra of Bunene?

133 See 202–5.

134 Beaulieu, 46–50.

135 Beaulieu, 63, 184.

136 Beaulieu, 121, 135–36, 137–38.

137 Beaulieu, 34, 211–12, dates it no earlier than year 14 and perhaps in year 16.

138 Col. I, line 24.

139 62–63, 184.

140 Beaulieu, 135–36.

141 Beaulieu, 6.

142 Cf. Beaulieu, 219 (on the last years of the reign).

143 Col. 1, lines 14–21.

144 174–85.

145 Col. I, lines 22–27.

146 Nab. 25, col. II, line 5 (*ANET,* 563); Chronicle 7, Col. II, lines 5, 10, 19, 23 (*ANET,* 306); Verse Account, Col. II, Lines 22–29 (*ANET,* 313).

147 Oppenheim correctly translated *u-she-ri-qa-an-ni-ma* at Nab. 25, col. I, line 23, by "made me leave," but Gadd's rendering, "I hied myself," can be defended.

148 Col. II, line 12 (see especially Oppenheim's translation, *ANET,* 563a); col. III, lines 1–3).

149 Note, however, the skepticism of Beaulieu, 183–84. Beaulieu there dismisses as a principal motive for the conquest of northern Arabia Nabonidus's possible interest in Arabian moon-cults, and he refuses to take seriously the king's confessions in Nab. 25. On his theory, that the motive was imperialistic, see pp. 225–27. Against the hypotheses of Dougherty (*Nabonidus,* 138–60) and others, that Nabonidus had materialistic purposes in going to Arabia, see also Lambert, "Nabonidus in Arabia," 60–64. Lambert himself (60–62) supposes, on the basis of Nab. 25, col. I, lines 14–25, and Verse Account, col. II, lines 10–11, that Nabonidus was dismayed at his subjects's contempt for Sîn and its consequences and therefore chose to separate himself from them; he also deliberately disrupted Marduk's New Year's festival by his absence. But Lambert can suggest as the reason why the king went to Têmâ, not to Harran, only the consideration that Ekhulkhul was in ruins. Nabonidus, however, early in his reign (in Nab. 8) publicly acknowledged his duty to rebuild Ekhulkhul. To fail to do so by voluntarily choosing to live at Têmâ would have been discreditable. Part of Lambert's hypothesis is tenable. See below, on the anxieties that drove Nabonidus to seek a message from Sîn.

150 Col. I (line 27) through col. II (line 10).

151 Col. II (line 11) through col. III (line 10).

152 Beaulieu (203) even ignores the reason that the king himself gives for his return!

153 Verse Account, col. I, lines 17–18.

154 This consideration disposes of the argument of Beaulieu, 184, par. 1.

155 See n 19.

156 Nab. 25, col. I, lines 14–22.

157 See pp. 122–25.

158 See pp. 115–16 and 133.

159 See Julius Lewy, *HUCA* 19 (1945–46), 425–449, with Beaulieu, 175–78.

160 Nab. 25, col. II (line 11) through col. III (line 10).

161 See n 26.

162 See pp. 114–15.

163 181–83.

164 110–15, 143–47; connecting self with the Assyrian tradition: 137–43 (citing Nab. 1, 8, 14, 24, and the Cyrus Cylinder), 178–81. In Nab. 8, however, the king does nothing to associate himself with the Assyrian kings; he alludes to Sennacherib (col. I, lines 35–41) by way of condemnation.

165 Col. I (line 43) through col. II (line 2) (*ANET,* 562b).

166 Yet Beaulieu remarks (183) that Nab. 25 "propagandizes the economic advantages wrought by the conquest of northern Arabia." He cites (183) Röllig's remarks on the passage of Nab. 25 ("Erwägungen zu neuen Stelen König Nabonids," *ZA* 56 [1964], 246–52); they, too, say nothing about wealth or economic advantages.

167 Nab. 25, col. II (line 11) through col. III (line 6).

168 Cf. Beaulieu, 203.

169 See the next two paragraphs. Contrast Beaulieu, 201. His evidence for the existence of a Persian threat to Babylonia by year 13, from the mutilated passage on year 10 at Chronicle 7, col. II, lines 21–22, is extremely weak. Chronicle 7, col. III, lines 5–16, attests how Cyrus's army invaded Babylonia and took the capital in year 17 (autumn, 539). Unfortunately, years 13–15 are missing from Chronicle 7, and only a few words are legible from year 16, and even they are weak evidence for a Persian threat, though Beaulieu (219–20) so uses them. Berossus is explicit: Cyrus moved against Nabonidus in the Babylonian king's seventeenth year after having conquered "all the rest of Asia" (Josephus, Against Apion i.20.150 = *FGH* 680, F9a).

The accounts of Herodotus and Xenophon might seem to place the beginning of Cyrus's campaign against Babylon soon after his conquest of western Asia Minor in 546. Both accounts, however, are chronologically vague, and Herodotus (i.177–78.1) in fact agrees with Berossus: Cyrus made war on the "Assyrians" of Babylon only after conquering all the rest of Asia. Even Xenophon has time elapse between the Persian conquest of western Asia and the invasion of Babylonia, though one would not guess from his narrative (*Cyropaedia* vii.4.16) that the interval was measured in years: Cyrus after conquering western Asia Minor "proceeded on the road toward Babylon" and conquered Greater Phrygia and the Cappadocians (central and eastern Asia Minor) and the Arabians and finally came with his huge force against Babylon. Xenophon's late, vague, and partly fictitious account has no weight against the other evidence. Cf. Roux, 386–87; Tadmor in *Oz,* 464–66, and in *Shilton paras,* 8–9.

170 Nab. 16 and 25.

171 Contrast Beaulieu, 203.

172 See above, nn 29, 30.

173   Verse Account, col. V, lines 4–7.

174   Nab. 6, col. II, lines 32–46 (cf. Nab. 2, col. II, line 27); Nab. 7, col. II, lines 46–49.

175   Nab. 21, col. II, lines 17–19; Beaulieu (38–39) was unable to date Nab. 21. But it gives highest honor to Marduk and next honors Sîn, in a manner that must be earlier than the king's return from Têmâ.

176   Nab. 1, col. II, line 37, but cf. col. III, line 50 (not for aid for himself!). In praying for himself in Nab. 1 to Shamash and Anunîtum, the king does not ask for aid in war (col. II, lines 11–21, 39–42).

177   Nabonidus's exaltation of Sîn in this period: See Beaulieu, 54–63, 212–19.

178   Lines 1–11.

179   Oppenheim was wrong at line 11 to insert in parentheses the word "living" to produce his translation, "like (living) dead."

180   See chap. 6, p. 180, and chap. 8, pp. 206–7.

181   Cf. Beaulieu, 63–64.

182   See n 29.

183   209–10.

184   9–11, 211–12.

185   Cf. Beaulieu, 210–11.

186   Cf. Beaulieu, 55.

187   Nab. 4*, col. III, line 79; Beaulieu, 17–18, 55–58.

188   Beaulieu, 210.

189   Cf. Beaulieu, 213–14.

190   Nab. 5, col. II, lines 13–30.

~6~

Deutero-Isaiah's Reactions
to the Career and Fall of Nabonidus
and to the Policies of Cyrus

THE REIGN AND FALL OF NABONIDUS, the benevolent policies of
Cyrus,[1] and the events of the 75 years that followed are reflected in the
first seven chapters of the book of Daniel, texts that have perplexed believers and scholars. We shall devote a later chapter to the problems of that part
of Daniel. For the present, we shall study events and utterances of the years
from 553 to 465 B.C.E. without using or treating the evidence in the book of
Daniel.

We have examined in considerable detail the propaganda that Marduk's
faithful wrote after Cyrus's victory.[2] They rejoiced over Nabonidus's fall and
viewed Cyrus as Marduk's chosen vindicator. In Isaiah 40–66,[3] we have the
words of a Jew who wrote at the time of Cyrus's victory and its aftermath,
viewing the events as the LORD's liberation and vindication of Israel. The
author's name is not preserved. We call him Deutero-Isaiah.

It is likely that Deutero-Isaiah, who never names Nabonidus, was writing already in that Babylonian king's third regnal year (553 B.C.E.). This probability
can be inferred from the puzzling chapters, Isaiah 34 and 35. Scholars have
recognized that stylistically and thematically they belong with Isaiah 40–66.[4]
Why, then, do they stand in Isaiah 1–39, with the words and deeds of First
Isaiah?

There are other riddles in these two chapters. Isaiah 34 begins as if it were
directed against all Gentile nations and contains so many echoes of Isa
13:2–14:27 and Jer 50–51[5] that one would think it was directed especially

against a great power that had wronged the LORD's people, such as Assyria or Babylon. Yet in vv 5–6 it presents the vast wrath of God as being poured upon puny Edom. One might hesitate over whether Jeremiah borrowed from Isaiah 34 or the author of Isaiah 34 borrowed from Jeremiah, except for the fact that Isaiah 34 presents itself as the announcement of the fulfillment of an earlier written prophecy, for "the scroll of the LORD" in v 16 surely is a copy of the scroll mentioned in Jer 51:59–63. The expectation that the prophecy should focus on Babylon or Assyria is heightened by what follows in Isaiah 35: a prediction of the return of the exiles through a miraculous second exodus in which the desert flows with streams and blooms. This chapter, too, teems with borrowings from the first Isaiah and from Jeremiah.[6]

Though the evidence is fragmentary and does not suffice for proof, it leads to an attractive hypothesis that can explain all the strange features of Isaiah 34–35. In the book of First Isaiah, in the prophecy against Babylon, Deutero-Isaiah could read God's promise that Babylon would fall in the reign of a king who ruined his own land and slaughtered his own people (14:20). Nabonidus by the time of his third regnal year had perpetrated ruin and slaughter upon Babylonians faithful to the supremacy of Marduk! In the same prophecy, Deutero-Isaiah could read the promise (14:25) that God in his own land and on his own mountains would smash the tyrannical power.[7]

As far as we know, after the last exilings of people from conquered Judah,[8] Babylonian kings and their armies long stayed away from the Holy Land. But Nabonidus in May of his *third* regnal year mustered his army and marched westward. After campaigning in the mountains of Syria or Lebanon, he and his army did something in "Amurru," in areas that had been *territory of Israel and Judah,* though we cannot tell whether they were east or west of the Jordan. Thereafter, the Babylonian forces moved on to attack the land of *Edom.*[9] At last a Babylonian army, led by a king who had slaughtered Babylonians, had entered the territory in which the LORD had promised to smash the tyrannical power! By campaigning in that region, Nabonidus was leaving his rear vulnerable to the Medes. Nabonidus and his predecessors on the throne had feared those dangerous neighbors.[10]

Jews, including Deutero-Isaiah, could well have had great expectations, because First Isaiah and Jeremiah, in the same contexts and in others,[11] predicted a glorious return from the exile to follow the fall of the enemy. One might think that the early reign of Nabonidus and even the year of Cyrus's victory over him were too early for a Jew to look for the fall of Babylon and the return to Zion. Had not Jeremiah predicted a seventy-year period of servitude to the king of Babylon (25:11–12, 29:10)? But Deutero-Isaiah, if not other Jews, viewed seventy as a round number, not to be taken literally. Jeremiah had also told the LORD's people that they would have to serve Nebuchadnezzar, his son, and his grandson "until the time of his own land shall come" (27:6–7). The reigns of Nebuchadnezzar's son (Awêl-Marduk) and grandson (Labâshi-Marduk) were past when Nabonidus became king! Accordingly, we can guess with considerable probability that Deutero-Isaiah originally wrote Isaiah 34–35 to predict a fall in the Holy Land of Nabonidus and Babylon, to be followed by an exodus of Jews from Babylon through a watered desert, in fulfillment of the words of Isaiah and Jeremiah. Those hopes failed to be realized. The Medes did not take advantage of their opportunity to attack the Babylonian Empire, and Nabonidus won victories in Edom and Arabia.

The prophet, however, seems to have found it possible to cover up his error. Edom, now hated by the Jews for its actions during and after the fall of Judah,[12] had been devastated by Nabonidus. We can guess that Deutero-Isaiah added references to Bozrah and Edom in Isa 34:5–6, so that what had been an oracle on the fulfillment of the prediction (in Isa 13:19 and Jer 50:40) of the destruction of Babylon became an oracle on the fulfillment of the prediction (in Jer 49:17–18) of the destruction of Edom.

If our guesses are correct, Deutero-Isaiah composed his original version of Isaiah 34–35 to a large extent because he thought he was observing the ongoing fulfillment of Isa 13:2–14:27. Again, we can guess that Deutero-Isaiah possessed a scroll of the works of First Isaiah, to which Isaiah 36–39 had not yet been added from the book of Kings.[13] For convenience in presenting his own discovery, that again the words of the great prophet of the eighth century were being fulfilled, Deutero-Isaiah could have written the original version of his own utterances at the end of that scroll and then modified that version to refer to Edom.

If so, the failure of his expectations must have been disappointing and embarrassing for Deutero-Isaiah. For some years, as far as we can see, he refrained from publishing further statements on impending fulfillments of the prophecies of Isaiah and Jeremiah. During those years, he may have studied them all the more and may have sought to collect more texts ascribed to First Isaiah. In particular he may have copied into his scroll 2 Kgs 18:13–20:19, so that it now stands at Isaiah 36–39. If so, our hypotheses have explained why Isaiah 34 and 35 stand where they do.

The march of events eventually led Deutero-Isaiah to produce the great poetry of Isaiah 40–48 as loud assertions that the great predictions were being fulfilled, of the LORD's victory over Babylon and of his vindication of Israel. Talented as he was, the poet nevertheless made great use of borrowed rhetoric!

His reactions to Cyrus's victory strikingly echo the Babylonian propaganda for the Persian king and also Zoroastrian texts. Just as strikingly, they again copy the words of great prophets of Judah.

Morton Smith has exhibited in detail the strong parallels between Isaiah 40–48 on the one hand and the Cyrus Cylinder and Zarathushtra's *Yasna* 44 on the other.[14] Where Babylonians claimed that Marduk chose Cyrus as his liberating agent for Babylon, Deutero-Isaiah borrowed many of their turns of phrase to assert, rather, that the LORD chose Cyrus as his agent to liberate his people from Babylon. Where Zoroastrians claimed that Ahuramazda was the creator and Cyrus was his agent,[15] Deutero-Isaiah used many of their turns of phrase to assert the same of the LORD. Many descriptions of Ahuramazda by Zoroastrians resembled descriptions of the LORD by Jews, but Deutero-Isaiah was sure the two deities were not identical.[16] He appears to have been confident that Cyrus would come to believe in the God of Israel.[17]

Cyrus's victory and the course of events and the pronouncements of Babylonians and Persians by themselves could never have roused the prophet to produce Isaiah 40–48. Jews could easily regard the fall of Nabonidus as an accident of history rather than as a liberating act of their God. Jeremiah had predicted seventy years of servitude to Nebuchadnezzar and his heirs.[18] Should not the number be taken literally? Since the fall of Jerusalem in 586 only forty-seven years had elapsed, and even from the city's fall in 597 only fifty-eight years had passed, and from Jeremiah's first utterance concerning the seventy years in 605, only sixty-six years. Only what he saw as the fulfillment of great prophecies gave Deutero-Isaiah the confidence to adopt Babylonian propaganda and Zoroastrian doctrine to preach that his own God had roused Cyrus to act. Indeed, he himself loudly and repeatedly boasted that Cyrus's victory over Babylon had been predicted far in advance by the LORD (surely through his own prophets)—and by no one else.[19]

Babylon's fortifications were famous. Nabonidus had enjoyed good relations with Cyrus.[20] If the fall even of Jerusalem to siege was unexpected,[21] how much more was Cyrus's capture of Babylon with so little fighting that Marduk's propagandists could claim there had been none! Though Babylonians were proud of the ability of their omen-interpreters and prognosticators to predict the future,[22] no pagan had published a prediction of the event, not even the clergy of Marduk who had colluded with Cyrus to bring about his practically unopposed entry into Babylon.[23] Otherwise, Deutero-Isaiah would never have been able to make his loud, repeated boasts.[24]

So important does the prophet regard the LORD's prediction of Cyrus's victory, that he gives it a special name; he calls it "the First Things" *(Ri'shonot)*.[25]

Where and when did Deutero-Isaiah think the LORD had made the prediction? Nowhere does the prophet claim that his own mouth uttered it. Indeed, he says it was made long before his own time.[26]

Our studies have shown us where Jews could go to claim that the God of Israel long before 539 B.C.E. predicted the fall of Babylon. The LORD had done so already in the eighth century B.C.E., through his great prophet Isaiah (13:2–14:27, 21:1–10).[27] He had done so in the seventh century, through his prophet Habakkuk,[28] and early in the sixth century, through his prophet Jeremiah.[29] Deutero-Isaiah must have found most remarkable the earliest of these utterances, the one through First Isaiah. Well he might. We have seen[30] how in fact that prophet was the source for Habakkuk, Zephaniah, and Jeremiah. Now Deutero-Isaiah could read the words of them all, and he must have found most striking the accuracy of the words of First Isaiah.[31]

Though Cyrus was a Persian, his kingdom was still called the Kingdom of the Medes, and the subjects of the Persians were to call them the "Medes" for centuries thereafter.[32] In Isa 13:17–19 stood a prediction that Babylon would fall to the "Medes." It did, indeed! In Isa 14:13–14 the prophet had said of the tyrant king that he had aspired to ascend to heaven and to vie with God. It took only a little imagination to apply that description to Nabonidus's theological arrogance in his religious reforms. In Isa 14:20 the prophet had said of the vanquished king of Babylon that he had slaughtered his own people.

Nabonidus indeed had massacred devoted worshipers of Marduk. In Isa 14:21 the prophet had called for the slaughter of the sons of the tyrant king, in punishment for the sins of their ancestors. Bêl-shar-uṣur had indeed been slain by the enemy as Babylon fell.[33] More obscure were the words of Isa 21:1–10, but they still mentioned Media and Elam and predicted the doom of Babylon and her idols. Cyrus's own kingdom, before his great conquests, was situated in territory that had belonged to Elam, and Elamite was destined to be an official language of the Persian Empire.[34]

The dazzling fulfillments in 539 B.C.E. were of Isa 13:2–14:7, of which Jeremiah 50–51 were in any case imperfect echoes.[35] Cyrus's own early policy and the promise at Isa 14:1–2, of the restoration from exile of the LORD's people, gave Deutero-Isaiah reason to hope, from the moment of Cyrus's victory, that the Persian king would fulfill that promise, and only several months had elapsed when Cyrus in 538 issued his proclamation calling for the rebuilding, at the king's expense, of the LORD's temple in Jerusalem by his people, restored from exile. Is it any wonder that Deutero-Isaiah boasted loudly of the predictive power of his God and was able to pass over in silence the aspects of Isaiah's prophecies that failed to be fulfilled?[36] If our guesses about Isaiah

34–35 are correct, this was the second time he accepted the risk of announcing that Isa 13:2–14:7 were in the process of being fulfilled.

Can we be sure that Deutero-Isaiah had mostly Isa 13:2–14:27 and 21:1–10 in mind when he challenged the pagans to show their gods to be equal in predictive power? Would one not then expect to find Isaiah 40–66 and especially Isaiah 40–48 full of quotations of the earlier prophecies and of allusions to the king who had slaughtered his own people? There are no allusions to that king, and at first sight the possible quotations may seem unimpressive. But Deutero-Isaiah would not have to repeat the First Things in his own prophecies if, as we have supposed, he carried around with him a scroll of the prophecies of First Isaiah and if he deliberately published his own prophecies as an appendix to such a scroll—just as we find them today. Our hypotheses thus have given an explanation for the puzzling composition of the book of Isaiah, consisting as it does of the prophecies ascribed to First Isaiah (1–33), the two early prophecies of Deutero-Isaiah (34–35), the traditions on First Isaiah from 2 Kings (36–39), and the rest of the prophecies of Deutero-Isaiah. Furthermore, on careful examination, the array of possible echoes from Isa 13:2–14:27 and 21:1–10 in Isaiah 40–66 proves to be suggestive enough.[37]

Though Hebrew tenses, especially in prophetic poetry, are ambiguous, there is good reason to hold that all of Deutero-Isaiah's prophecies in chaps 40–66 were composed and uttered *after* the fall of Babylon to Cyrus. This dating is certainly true of the passages in which he boasts that only his God predicted Cyrus's victory over Babylon.[38] Few would dare to utter such speeches while Nabonidus still reigned; any Jew or Babylonian who publicly predicted Nabonidus's fall then faced capital punishment for treason. Marduk's faithful in their propaganda for Cyrus tell how the gods deserted Nabonidus's kingdom, but they say nothing of acts against him by his subjects.

Scholars have made much of the fact that Deutero-Isaiah predicts, falsely, that Babylon will be destroyed, her people exiled, and Marduk and Nabû humiliated (46:1–2, 47:1–15); does that not prove that the prophet delivered at least those passages before Babylon fell to Cyrus and received kind treatment from him?[39] It does not. In the case of Marduk and Nabû, Deutero-Isaiah may have been following his convictions and expecting the humiliation of the idols predicted in Isa 21:9(end), now that the city had fallen in fulfillment of the rest of the verse.[40] Despite Cyrus's kind treatment of the city of Babylon, the prophet could still have been awaiting the destructions predicted by the earlier prophets.

Furthermore, there are other ways of understanding Isa 46:1–2 and 47:1–15 than as unfulfilled predictions. Isa 46:1–2 may mean only that Babylon has fallen and that the images of Bêl and Nabû have been paraded through the streets of the city in honor of victorious Cyrus. The heavy images have wearied the beasts of burden carrying them, but the two deities have done nothing to save even their own images from such humiliation, in contrast to the LORD God of Israel (vv 3–5), who has always carried his people and now has rescued them. The "captivity" of v 2 may mean no more than such a parade, or it may refer to the notorious past instances in which victors carried off the images of the gods of Babylon.[41]

Similarly, though the prophet in Isaiah 47 may look to the still unfulfilled promises of the enslavement of Babylon at Isa 14:2, the chapter need only reflect the subjection of Babylon to Cyrus. However kindly Cyrus treated Babylon, the city was his "slave," and he had the right to treat her as such.

In fact, Cyrus liberated neither the Babylonians nor the Jews. Rather, he brought them both under his own rule, beginning what scholars now call "the Persian period" of the histories of the two *peoples of an almighty god.*[42] For the Jews it extended from 539 to 333 B.C.E.; for the Babylonians, from 539 to 331.

Deutero-Isaiah soon suffered embarrassment because of the extremely incomplete fulfillment of his own predictions and those of the earlier prophets. Skeptics must also have been quick to point out to him that Jeremiah's seventy years had not yet elapsed. Isa 45:9–13 and 50:2 may be aimed at such persons. The failure of Deutero-Isaiah's glorious pronouncements to materialize naturally enraged his disappointed audience, who vented their frustration upon him (50:6–11).

Let us turn to the chapters which many scholars ascribe unnecessarily to "Trito-Isaiah." In fact, they are easily ascribable to the same prophet as Isaiah 40–55. The delay in complete fulfillment may have evoked the hint at Isa 56:1–2, that present sin was the impediment. It may also have evoked the attack on bad leaders at Isa 56:9–12 and the bitter and probably exaggerated denunciations of what seem to be described as present sins in 57:1–59:15. There is a clear response to the delay in Isaiah 62, and in 63:11–64:12, the prophet himself takes the part of the disappointed people; nevertheless, in chapter 65 he presents a reply from God that blames the sinners of the present, but again there is a promise of miraculous glories for the righteous members of the LORD's people.

Contrary to Deutero-Isaiah's predictions,[43] neither Cyrus, nor, at first, God and those who returned from the exile rebuilt the temple. Let us examine the evidence on this strange phenomenon and do so in the light of a significant historical parallel. The gods, said Nabonidus, had ordered him to rebuild the temple of Sîn, yet for years he left the task undone. Then, after he had carried out the rebuilding, he invented an excuse blaming the delay on outsiders, upon the powerful Medes who had been surrounding the site.[44] Just so, Cyrus told the Jews to rebuild the LORD's temple in Jerusalem, but the task was long left undone,[45] and long after it had been accomplished the author of Ezra 4 blamed the delay on outsiders, on the "enemies of Judah and Benjamin." He presented documentary evidence to support the accusation. But his reasoning is bad. The documents he quotes in 4:7–22 have nothing to do with the temple.[46]

Firsthand evidence, in the prophecies of Haggai and Zechariah, much earlier than the clumsy inferences of the author of Ezra 4, suggests a different reason for the delay. In the "second year of King Darius" (521 B.C.E.)[47] Haggai quoted (1:2) God himself as recognizing that "This people has said, 'The time has not come—the time for the House of the LORD to be built,' " and in the same year, some five months later, Zechariah quoted (1:12) the Angel of the LORD as speaking of seventy years of his wrath against Jerusalem and Judah. We have called attention to the uncertainty over the point from which Jeremiah's seventy years should be measured. It is hard to see how the "enemies of Judah and Benjamin" could succeed in blocking the rebuilding of a temple which Cyrus himself had decreed, but it is easy to see how the anxieties of pious Jews could delay fulfillment of that project. Many could have believed that it was not safe to complete the rebuilding of the temple until the seventy years predicted by Jeremiah should have elapsed from the time of its destruction.[48]

By the time Isaiah 66 was being written, Deutero-Isaiah probably was dismayed by the exceedingly incomplete fulfillment of his predictions and was unwilling to use invective against pious Jews who were afraid to complete the rebuilding of the temple. In that chapter he responded to the situation by declaring that a rebuilt temple was unnecessary and by again attacking the impious and predicting their doom and the future glory of Jerusalem and of the righteous Jews.

Thus, Deutero-Isaiah had to issue statements to cope with the failure of his predictions. But there is no trace in Isaiah 40–66 that he ever had to retract or alter his challenging boast, that only the God of Israel had predicted the victory of Cyrus. Deutero-Isaiah was a highly public preacher. Could Babylonians turn a deaf ear to his challenges? Even if they did, their own belief that the gods reveal the future through omens and dreams must have driven them to try to show that great Marduk had predicted Cyrus's triumph. We shall see later that they indeed attempted to do so.[49]

The prophet of Isaiah 40–66 published the chapters as we have them, as an appendix to Isaiah 1–39. We cannot tell whether he wanted any of his own words to be taken as those of First Isaiah or whether he made no secret of the fact that he himself was writing as a contemporary of Cyrus. In the early second century B.C.E. Jesus ben Sira wrote words clearly reflecting his belief that the author of Isaiah 40–66 was identical with the Isaiah who preached in the eighth century B.C.E.[50] Pious Jews reading the book of Isaiah had probably arrived at the same belief only a few generations after Deutero-Isaiah's death!

NOTES

1 On Nabonidus and Cyrus see chap 5, pp. 114–16.

2 The Verse Account and the Cyrus Cylinder; see chap. 5, pp. 125–26, and chap. 6, pp. 133–34.

3 So I believe, though many scholars assign Isaiah 56–66 to another author, "Trito-Isaiah." See chap 6, 160–61. Farther on in this chapter I shall present more argument for my position.

4 E.g., John L. McKenzie, *Second Isaiah* ("Anchor Bible," Vol. 20; Garden City, N.Y.: Doubleday, 1968), 6, 11–12; Eissfeldt, *The Old Testament,* 327–28.

5 The parallels are as follows. To 34:1–2, 13:2–5, Jer 50:2a. To 34:3, 13:9, 11–12, 15–16, Jer 51:4. To 34:4, 13:13. To 34:5, Jer 50:25, 35–37. To 34:6–7, Jer 50:27, 51:40. To 34:7, Jer 50:11. To 34:8, Jer 50:15, 28, 51:6, 35. To 34:9–10, 13:19–20, Jer 50:12–13, 40, 51:36, 43. To 34:11–14, 13:21–22, Jer 50:39, 51:36. To 34:15, 14:23. To 34:16, Jer 51:59–63. To 34:17, 14:23.

6 To 35:1, 12:3. To 35:2, 29:17, 33:9, Jer 50:19. To 35:4, 34:8, Jer 50:15, 28, 51:6, 35. To 35:5–6, 29:18, Jer 31:7. To 35:6b, 11:15, 12:3, Jer 31:7–8. To 35:8, 11:16, Jer 31:8, 50:5. To 35:10, Jer 31:10–12.

7 Slaughter: see chap 5, pp. 116–29. On Isa 13:2–14:27, see chap 4, pp. 83–91.

8 2 Kgs 25:8–21, Jer 52:12–30.

9 See chap 5, pp. 113–16; Beaulieu, 166–69, treats the fragmentary sources (Chronicle 7 and Lambert's Text). See also Bartlett's account, cited above, chap 5, n 15.

10 See chap 5, pp. 113–29. Nebuchadnezzar and his successors put up elaborate fortifications to defend against the Medes. See lines 68–69 of Nebuchadnezzar's inscription, Langdon, *Die neubabylonischen Königsinschriften,* 166; Herodotus i. 185, Xenophon *Anabasis* i.7.15, ii.4.12; Harmatta, *Acta Antiqua* 19 (1971), 223, 227–28; Tadmor in *Shilton paras,* 8–9.

11 Especially in Isa 11:11–12, 14:1–2; Jer 31:7–14, 50:4–5, 19, 51:5–6, 10.

12 Ps 137:7, Lam 4:21, Obadiah, Jer 49:7–22, Ezek 25:12–14, 35:1–15, 36:5.

13 The book of the First Isaiah originally ended with chap 33; see Eissfeldt, *The Old Testament,* 296, 304, 328.

14 "II Isaiah and the Persians," *JAOS* 83 (1963), 415–421. On 416a, Smith errs in making Isa 45:14 (wrongly cited as 15:14) a parallel to Cyrus Cylinder 13 and 18. The parallels in Isaiah 40–48 to those passages are 41:2, 25. Isa 45:14 is rather a promise that Judah and Jerusalem are to get the sort of wealth that used to flow to the Mesopotamian capitals and used to be the subject of the boasts of Mesopotamian kings.

15 We may assume that Persian Zoroastrians made this claim for Cyrus, though no surviving text says so. On what is known of Cyrus's position in Zoroastrianism, see Boyce, *HZ,* II, 49–69.

16 See Isa 45:7 (Ahuramazda was not the creator of evil) and 45:4 (Cyrus did not know the LORD).

17 45:3–7, 42:1–8 (cf. Smith, *JAOS* 83 [1963], 416, n 6).

18 See pp. 82–83.

19 Isa 41:1–4, 21–29, 44:6–8, 24–28, 45:20–21, 46:8–11, 48:3–15.

20 See chap 5, n 25.

21 See chap 4, n 17.

22 Cf. Isa 47:12–13.

23 See Tadmor in *Shilton paras,* 10–12, and in *Oz,* 466–67; Harmatta, *Acta Antiqua* 19 (1971), 226–27, 230.

24 For the same reason, Deutero-Isaiah cannot have known of a Persian prophecy promising Babylon to Cyrus in the name of Ahuramazda, though the possibility has been suggested by Elias Bickerman and Morton Smith (*JAOS* 83 [1963], 420; cf. Boyce, *Zoroastrianism,* II, 43–47).

25 M. Haran, *Congress Volume = Vetus Testamentum,* Suppl. 9 (1963), 137–40.

26 41:26, 44:7–8, 45:21, 46:10, 48:39.

27 See chap 1, n 22, and chap 4, pp. 83–91.

28 See pp. 89–90.

29 See pp. 89–91.

30 Chap 4, pp. 83–91.

31 Cf. Haran, *Vetus Testamentum,* suppl. IX (1963), 137–40; Ginsberg, *Book of Isaiah,* 11–12, 18.

32 See M. A. Dandamaev, *Persien,* 94–95. Nabonidus himself called Cyrus "King of the city of the Medes"; see Nab. 25, col. I, line 42, and chap 5, n 25.

33 See pp. 220–22.

34 Tadmor in *Shilton paras,* 5, 12–13; J. Hansman in *Cambridge History of Iran,* II, 25–34; J. M. Cook, ibid., 230.

35 In Jeremiah 50–51, Habakkuk, and Zephaniah, there is nothing that can be interpreted as a reference to Nabonidus or Bêl-shar-uṣur.

36 Cyrus's proclamation to the Jews: Ezra 1:2–4, 6:2–5. It probably came shortly after the beginning of his first regnal year, in spring, 538 B.C.E.; see Tadmor in *Oz,* 471–2, n 67.

   Unfulfilled aspects of Isaiah 13–14: worldwide disasters (13:5–17); Median cruelty (13:17–18); Babylon destroyed like Sodom (13:19–22); the Gentiles bring back all the exiles of the LORD's people to their homeland (14:1–2); Babylonians become slaves of Israelites (14:2); defeat of the Mesopotamian great power in the Holy Land (14:24–25). The humiliation of Babylon's idols, predicted at Isa 21:9, also had not occurred, though Deutero-Isaiah may have been able to interpret events so as to assert fulfillment of that prophecy, as we show farther on in this chapter. Cyrus, the large Jewish population in Babylon, and Deutero-Isaiah himself would have suffered and perhaps perished had Babylon been destroyed like Sodom!

37 I list here first, before a double slash, the source passages; then, after the double slash, the echoes in Isaiah 40–66. In addition to Isa 13:2–14:27 and 21:10, I place among the sources echoed some other passages from the First Isaiah and from Zephaniah and Jeremiah, the imitators of Isa 13:2–14:27.

   Isa 11:6, 9 // 65:25. Isa 11:12, *qbṣ* ("assemble [the dispersed]") // 43:5. Isa 11:15–16, Jer 50:5 (the road for the exiles' return) // Isa 40:3–4, 42:16, 43:19–20, 49:11, 57:14, 62:10 (cf. 35:8). Isa 11:12, 13:2 (raising a standard to assemble the nations to do God's work) // 62:10. Isa 13:4 ("Hark, the uproar") // 66:6. Isa 13:5 ("from a far country") //

46:11. Isa 13:5 ("weapon[s] . . . to destroy") // 54:16. Isa 13:6 ("Wail ye") // 65:14. Isa 13:11 ("tyrants") // 49:25. Isa 13:17 ("I will stir up the Medes"), Jer 50:9, 51:1, 11 // Isa 41:2, 25, 45:13. Isa 13:19 ("Babylon . . . the beauty of the Chaldaeans' pride") // 62:3 ("[Jerusalem] shall be a crown of beauty in the hands of the LORD"). Isa 14:1 ("The LORD will have compassion") // 49:10, 13, 54:8, 10, 60:10. Isa 14:1 ("[The LORD] will yet choose Israel") // 41:8–9, 44:1–2, 48:10. Isa 14:1 (aliens shall be added to the house of Jacob) // 56:3, 6–8. Isa 14:2 (Gentiles will bring Israelites back to their homeland) // 49:22, 60:3–4, 9, 66:20. Isa 14:2 (the Israelites' captors will become their slaves) // 49:22–23, 60:10, 12, 14, 16, 61:5, and cf. 45:14. Isa 14:24 (the LORD's counsel to humiliate Mesopotamian power shall come to pass) // 46:10.

Isa 21:2(end) // 51:11 (cf. 35:10). Isa 21:6, 8 ("watchman," "watchtower") // 52:8. Isa 21:9 // 46:1–2, 47:1–15, and the other passages ridiculing Babylonian idols (40:19–20, 42:17, 44:9–20, 45:20). Zeph 2:15 ("I am and there is none else beside me") // Isa 47:8, 10.

38 See p. 157.

39 See, e.g., M. Smith, *JAOS* 83 (1963), 417; Westermann, *Isaiah* 40–66, 180, 189.

40 Such humiliation was also predicted at Jer 50:2, 51:44.

41 See chap 2, p. 30.

42 As usual, in chaps 6–9 I shall present only those aspects of the histories and literatures of the Jews and the Babylonians which resulted from the fact that they were *peoples of an almighty god*. Others have treated the period in some detail. For the Jews, see, e.g., *The Cambridge History of Judaism,* ed. W. D. Davies and Louis Finkelstein, Vol. I (Cambridge: Cambridge University Press, 1984); *Shilton paras;* Tadmor in Ben-Sasson, 168–81, and in *Historiah shel Eretz Yisrael,* ed. Yisra'el Eph'al, (Jerusalem: Keter and Yad Yitzkhak ben Tzvi, 1982–), Vol. II (1984), 251–327; Geo Widengren in Hayes-Miller, 489–538; Bright, History, 360–411; Kaufmann, *Toledot,* 51–546. For the Babylonians, see, e.g., CHI, II (1985), 529–87; CAH², IV (1988), 53–63, 73–75, 112–38; Roux, 405–12.

43 44:28, 60:13, 61:4.

44 See the discussion of Nab. 8, Nab. 25, and Nab. 1 in chap 5, pp. 117–25.

45 Cyrus's command: Ezra 1:2–4, 5:13–15; cf. 6:2–5. Left undone: Ezra 5:16.

46 See my *II Maccabees* ("Anchor Bible," vol. 41A; Garden City, N.Y.: Doubleday, 1983), 174–75.

47 On the chronology, see chap 7.

48 On Jeremiah's seventy years, cf. Tadmor in *Historiah shel Eretz Yisrael,* II, 261–63. His entire treatment of the return is good (ibid., 251–64). In fact, the rebuilt temple was probably dedicated a safe seventy years after its destruction; see chap 7, p. 176.

49 See chap 8, secs 1, 4, and 10.

50 See Sir 48:22–25. With Sir 48:24, cf. Isa 40:1–2, 57:18, 61:2–3, 66:10; with Sir 48:24, cf. Isa 40:1–2, 57:18, 61:2–3, 66:10.

~7~

The Material History of the Babylonians
and Jews from Cyrus to the Early Reign
of Artaxerxes I (538–464 B.C.E.),
except as Reflected in Daniel

1. Cambyses and the Babylonians

W HATEVER DEUTERO-ISAIAH MEANT in gloating over the humiliation of Marduk and Babylon in Isa 46:1–2, 47:1–15, as far as we know, Cyrus and his heir, Cambyses, treated the god and his city with respect and kindness. There is only one possible exception. Let us examine the evidence on it.

Babylonian documents were dated by the year of the reigning king. The dates of documents show that Cyrus made Cambyses coregent king of Babylon while he himself in the documents bore the title "King of the Lands" *(shar mâtâti)*. The texts displaying this situation extend from the beginning of Cyrus's first regnal year (spring, 538 B.C.E.) well into the month of Tebetu (to January, 537). After that period, Babylonian documents under Cyrus are dated by the regnal years of "Cyrus, king of Babylon and king of the lands."[1] Why did Cambyses's coregency come to an end? The only evidence is a mutilated section of Babylonian Chronicle 7.[2]

The passage suggests that "Cambyses, the son of Cyrus" came to his installation as king of Babylon (under Cyrus) armed and in Elamite dress, contrary to Babylonian ritual, with embarrassing consequences that required compromises on the part of Cambyses and perhaps on the part of the Babylonian priests. Those consequences could have contributed to Cambyses's loss of his position as coregent.[3] Whatever the truth may be, nothing else indicates that

Marduk's worshipers were disappointed in or disaffected from Cyrus and Cambyses. The author of Chronicle 7 himself clearly favored the pious Cyrus.

Contrary to Deutero-Isaiah's expectations in Isaiah 47, Cyrus and Cambyses treated Babylon as a privileged community and certainly not as a slave.[4] The date formulas of the documents from Babylonia show that there the Persian conqueror and his heir bore titles presenting them as legitimate indigenous rulers, not as foreign conquerors, and presenting Babylon as the king's own territory, not as a conquered land. If Cambyses indeed committed a faux pas in 538, it hardly disturbed this friendly relationship between Babylon and her Persian rulers.[5]

2. Cambyses's Reign, "Bardiya's" Usurpation, and the Wars of Darius to Suppress Rebellions

CYRUS WAS KILLED while on campaign in 530 B.C.E., and Cambyses became king. In his own reign (530–522), he undertook expensive wars, conquering Egypt in 525 and failing in 524 to subdue "Ethiopia" (the modern Sudan) and the Oasis of Ammon.[6] Herodotus reports[7] that the Persians themselves were to remember Cambyses as a "master" or "tyrant" *(despotês)* who was "harsh" in contrast to the "fatherly" Cyrus. If Cambyses was harsh to the highly privileged Persians, he must have been harsh also to the less privileged Babylonians and other conquered peoples, who surely were taxed to pay for his wars. The later king, Darius I (reigned 522–486), was to write an account of the events through which he became king and consolidated his rule. In that account, Darius implies that Persians, Medes, and some if not all of the conquered peoples were discontented with Cambyses.[8]

In 522 Cambyses began to return from conquered Egypt to his capitals. He had been away too long. Besides Cambyses, Cyrus had a younger son, Bardiya, called "Smerdis" by Herodotus. According to Darius I and the Persian informants of the Greek writers Herodotus (mid-fifth century B.C.E.) and Ktesias (late fifth to early fourth century), Cambyses had had his brother killed some years before 522, but the fact that he was dead had been concealed, and in 522 an imposter pretended to be Bardiya. Darius says that the pretender was really a Magus, Gaumata. Modern scholars have cast grave doubts on the possibility of such concealment and imposture.[9] In any case, a Bardiya, whether the real one or an imposter, rose in revolt in the heart of Persia against Cambyses on March 11, 522, and was proclaimed king on July 1; documents from Babylon show that he was recognized as king there by May if not earlier.[10]

At the outset of his reign and perhaps at the outset of his revolt, this Bardiya proclaimed that all nations under his rule would be free for 3 years from military conscription and from taxes.[11] Such a policy quickly won this Bardiya the loyalty of the vast majority of the subjects of the empire, both among the Persians and among the conquered peoples. The swing of loyalty to this Bardiya became all the stronger with the sudden death of Cambyses (was it suicide?), leaving Bardiya, if really alive, as the rightful heir.[12] Babylonians unhesitatingly dated their documents by the years of Bardiya, and they may have viewed him as favorably as they had viewed Cyrus.

However, this Bardiya reigned only until Sept. 29, 522. On that day, seven noble Persian conspirators succeeded in murdering him. The seven came to an agreement as a result of which one of their number, Darius, became king,[13] and the others were to hold high rank in the realm. Thereafter, Darius had to put down numerous revolts. Not only many of the conquered peoples rose against him, but also many of the Persians.[14]

Cyrus had only two sons. The death of Cambyses and the murder of this Bardiya brought a sure end to the male line of Cyrus. In general, the fall of an imperial dynasty leaves the way open for reassertions of the national independence of subject peoples, for revolutions by submerged classes, and for the ambitions of would-be new rulers of the empire.[15] Even righteous foreign rule is still foreign and provokes some ethnic resentment. However, beyond these general truths, the beliefs and previous experiences of the Babylonian and Jewish *peoples of an almighty god* probably contributed to how they reacted to the extinction of Cyrus's line. Why should Marduk and the LORD let Babylon and the Jews be ruled forever by foreigners?

Babylonians at the time of the murder of Bardiya could have reviewed the record of the foreign dynasties who had ruled over Babylon and had done so sometimes at the invitation of Marduk's priests. Much earlier, three enemy kings had carried off Marduk's statue and destroyed Babylon and then had been murdered by their own sons, and Marduk had returned to a restored, independent Babylon.[16] Closer parallels, involving Assyrian kings, were available. Shalmaneser III in 851 and Adad-nirâri III (reigned 810–783) were invited to become kings of Babylon, but did not take the office.[17]

Tiglath-Pileser III became king of Babylon by invitation in 728, but died the following year; his son, Shalmaneser V (726–722), inherited the Babylonian title. But the next king of Assyria was Sargon II (721–705), and the propagandistic character of his name (*sharru-kîn,* "the king is legitimate") suggests that he was a usurper.[18] In his reign, some Babylonians welcomed the "Babylonian independence movement" led by the Chaldaean, Marduk-apla-iddina II,[19] though others regarded the Chaldaean as a foreigner and an enemy; Marduk-apla-iddina reigned over Babylon for eleven years (721–710).[20] When he was driven out, King Sargon II of Assyria became king of Babylon (710–705), but he was killed in battle, and his heir was Sennacherib, the great enemy of Babylon, who destroyed her in 689.[21] Babylon was not to have a dynasty of her own again until the decline of Assyria and the rise of the Chaldaean dynasty of Nabopolassar in 626, which was soon followed by the extinction of the Assyrian dynasty.

The lesson of such history could well be that Marduk may use briefly a benevolent or punitive foreign agent of his will but not for long, and the descendants of such agents could be grievous sinners against the god and his city. If almighty Marduk acted to wipe out a sinful foreign dynasty, it might be safe for his people to assert their freedom. As soon as the news of Bardiya's death reached Babylon,[22] Nidintu-Bêl led the Babylonians in revolt against the Persian Empire. The rebel king claimed he was Nebuchadnezzar, son of Nabonidus,[23] names connecting him with independent Babylon's most glorious ruler and with her last monarch, a sinner indeed, but one who had repented.

Babylonians rallied behind this pretender, Nebuchadnezzar III. They began to date their documents to his accession year, not to the accession year of Darius (documents had to be dated by the years of the reigning king). Darius did not entrust to a subordinate the suppression of the dangerous revolt of these privileged subjects. In person he led his army against them, managed to cross the flooding Tigris, and won a crushing victory on Dec. 13, 522, but Nebuchadnezzar III and his people went on resisting. On Dec. 18, Darius again won overwhelmingly at Zazannu on the Euphrates. The pretender fled to Babylon, but Darius took the city, captured him, and slew him and forty-eight Babylonian nobles.[24]

While Darius was at Babylon, according to his own account, Persis, Elam, Media, Assyria, Egypt, Parthia, Margiana, Sattagydia, and Scythia rose in revolt.[25] Thus, even after their own defeat, Babylonians could see civil war among the dominant Persians and their Median partners as well as ethnic revolts among the conquered peoples tearing the empire apart. Surely Marduk was driving the Persians mad and freeing his people!

Such reasoning led Babylonians to retain their hopes even after the fall of Nebuchadnezzar III. Darius in his account goes on to tell us that while he was in Persis and Media suppressing the revolts there, the Babylonians became rebellious for the second time, again under a pretender, who again claimed to be Nebuchadnezzar, son of Nabonidus. According to Darius, he really was an Armenian, Arakha, son of Haldita. Documents from Babylonia show Nebuchadnezzar IV reigning there in August,[26] but Darius sent an army under Intaphernes which crushed the revolt by Nov. 27, 521. Darius had the pretender and his nobles executed, and the outer wall of Babylon may have been demolished.[27]

Herodotus reports,[28] early in the reign of Darius, a Babylonian rebellion and a siege of the city which lasted some [21] months and ended only when the Persian officer Zopyros cut off his own nose and ears and thereby claimed to be deserting from the Persian king who had "mutilated" him; after Zopyrus won the trust of the Babylonians, says Herodotus, he opened the gates of the city to Darius' army. There is no way to fit Herodotus's account into the detailed chronology Darius himself gives at Behistun of his early reign, and there is no room in the dates of Babylonian documents from later in his reign for a Babylonian pretender.[29] Herodotus (or his informant) must have been mistaken, perhaps by confusing Darius's generation with Xerxes's.[30]

Within a year from "Bardiya's" usurpation, Darius had silenced all rebellion within the realm. In the strongly organized empire that Darius set up, Babylon was tightly controlled and heavily taxed and remained quiet throughout the rest of his long reign, which lasted until 486.[31]

If Babylonians could infer that Marduk was driving the Persians mad and freeing his people, could not Jews draw the corresponding inference about the LORD? If they had rebelled, they in their weakness would have suffered the cruel fate of the much stronger victims of victorious Darius. As a *people of an almighty god* they might have braved impossible odds, especially if they read Isa 50:2 and 63:3–4 as rebukes for leaving to God the struggle for their liberation.

The belief derived from Jeremiah and Ezekiel, that for the present Jews must obey the foreign ruler God had placed over them,[32] was no longer a sure deterrent to suicidal revolt, for God's sentence of Israel to servitude was not permanent. By the time "Bardiya" seized power in 522, over seventy years had passed from the time of Jeremiah's two pronouncements (25:11–12, 29:10) on the term of punishment as well as from the time of the exiling of King Jehoiachin. Surely there existed cautious Jews who believed that the seventy years were measured from the destruction and exile of 586. Such cautious Jews probably also noted that the incomplete fulfillment of the predictions of the true prophets was proof that they were still living in an age of God's wrath, when God would punish them severely for not obeying their foreign ruler. Cautious Jews could draw the same inference from the prevailing poverty and recurrent crop failures (Haggai 1:6, 9–11; Zech 8:10). But there was no assurance that the views of cautious Jews would prevail.

In the books of Haggai and Zechariah we have utterances delivered during those very times, and in the book of Ezra we have a later narrative reporting some of the events. To use that valuable information, one must have a proper understanding of the widely misunderstood chronological data contained in the books. Beginning with the reign of Cyrus, the Persian administrative bureaus adopted the calendric practices of the Babylonians.[33] Darius became king after "Gaumata" was slain on Sept. 29, 522. Accordingly, by the Babylonian reckoning, the time from then through the last day of Addaru, 521 (April 13), was Darius's accession year; his first regnal year began on April 14, 521, and his second, on April 3, 520. The earliest of the prophecies of Haggai and Zechariah is dated in the second year of Darius on the first day of the sixth month (Hag 1:1). As we shall see, those prophecies presuppose a background of continuing or recent widespread rebellions in the Persian Empire. Darius crushed the rebellions by Nov. 27, 521. How then, could Haggai and Zechariah speak as they did if their prophecies are all dated after Sept. 7, 520?

Elias Bickerman[34] perceived the truth: that Darius and his Jewish subjects did not follow the Babylonian practice but dated his accession from the moment "Gaumata" began to usurp the throne (a usurper is illegitimate and can have no accession and no regnal years), so that Darius's second regnal year began on April 14, 521. Indeed, Darius himself says so in his inscription at Behistun, even though one might wonder at his display of an apparent contradiction: He says that *after* he himself became king,[35] "Gaumata" usurped Cambyses's throne,[36] and then Darius goes on to say that he himself became king *after* the slaying of the usurper![37] What Darius meant was no absurdity; rather, by his own reckoning, his own accession year and first regnal year contained the period during which the usurper occupied the throne. Babylonians, on the other hand, did not at first recognize Darius as king after the murder of "Gaumata." Rather, they followed their own Nebuchadnezzar IV until Darius crushed their revolt in December. If only for this reason, they reckoned 522/1 as the accession year of Darius, and the Persian bureaus, as usual, followed the Babylonian practice as soon as Babylon was reconquered.

Bickerman's argument for his interpretation of the chronology is based upon the content of the prophecies of Haggai and Zechariah, not upon Darius's own statement, and contains a flaw.[38] Nevertheless, it is possible to construct a valid argument for Bickerman's interpretation on the basis of the words of the two prophets. To do so, one must take note of the problems a Jewish prophet had to face early in the reign of Darius.

Any Jew who claimed then to be a prophet had to deal somehow with the glaringly incomplete fulfillments of the words of earlier prophets whom most if not all Jews recognized as true spokesmen for the LORD. We have seen[39] how

Deutero-Isaiah was troubled by the failure of many of his own prophecies (based upon Isa 13:2–14:27 and 21:1–9 and their echoes in Jeremiah 50–51) to be fulfilled. Darius's victories made it look as if those prophecies were at last beginning to come true.

Cyrus had posed as liberator of conquered Babylon, had shown respect to her gods, had conferred privileges upon the city, and even had spared the life of Nabonidus. He had permitted and encouraged a return of Jews from the exile to rebuild the LORD's temple, but neither he nor Cambyses had seen to the completion of either the return or the rebuilding (unlike pious Jews, the Persian kings had no reason to fear acting before the passing of Jeremiah's seventy years). In December 522, however, Darius took rebellious Babylon, slew her king, and treated her with the sort of cruelty that could be viewed as a real beginning of the fulfillment of Isa 13:2–14:27, 21:1–9, and Jeremiah 50–51. Less than a year later, rebellious Babylon fell again, another of her kings was slain, the outer wall of the city may have been destroyed (in fulfillment of Jer 50:15, 51:30, 44, 58), and the city was condemned to servitude (in fulfillment of Isa 47:1–15).

Nothing tells us how Darius treated the gods of defeated Babylon, but he probably did nothing to show them respect in 522 and 521. The mere defeat of the rebel city was humiliation enough for her tutelary deities. At least to that extent, Isa 21:9, Jer 50:2, 51:44, 47, 52, and Isa 46:1–2 had been fulfilled. Civil wars were going on as predicted at Jer 51:46. In Isa 13:2–14:27, Jeremiah 50–51, and Isaiah 40–66, the prophets predicted that other wonders would accompany the fall of Babylon. The partial fulfillment of their prophecies gave Jews reason to expect that the other wonders would soon come to pass,[40] and, with them, the things promised in Jeremiah 31 and 33, for, if those promises were to reach fulfillment before the passing of seventy years after the destruction of 586, what better time could there be for it than the aftermath of the complete fall of Babylon?

Accordingly, in 522–521 believing Jews expected that heaven and earth would quake (Isa 13:13, Jer 50:46, 51:29); Babylon would be destroyed (Isa 13:19–22, 14:22–23, Jeremiah 50–51 passim); there would be a complete return of the exiles to their land (Isa 14:1–2, Jer 33:7, 50:28, 33–34, 51:10, 50); there would be peace and quiet throughout the earth (Isa 14:7, Jer 50:34; cf. 30:10, 33:9, 46:27), as the LORD's people, their sins forgiven (Isa 14:1, Jer 50:20 [cf. 33:8], Isa 40:2), would come to rule over their oppressors, who would become their slaves (Isa 14:2; cf. Jer 50:45); Gentiles would become converts on a large scale (Isa 14:1, 56:6–8); the LORD's people would sing and rejoice, and there would be bucolic and agricultural prosperity, and there would be multitudes of people and domestic animals in Jerusalem and the cities and villages of Judah (Jer 31:12–13, 23, 27, 33:13); the wealth of nations would flow to Jerusalem (Isa 60:5–12, 61:6; cf. Jer 33:9). There would be a new temple (Jer 33:11, Isa 56:7 and 60:7,[41] Ezek 40:5–43:11), which God himself would glorify (Isa 60:13), and there would be an everlasting kingship for the dynasty of David beginning with a person called a "Shoot of Righteousness" as well as an everlasting priesthood for the Levitical priests (Jer 33:14–25).

Logic has driven us to conclude that in 522–521 believing Jews would look forward to the imminent fulfillment of these prophecies. The prophecies of Haggai and the prophecies of Zechariah dated in the second year of Darius conspicuously look forward to the fulfillment of the same prophecies, often echoing their language, as we shall see. By September 520, however, though Babylon had fallen, she had not been subjected to the LORD's people. It was clear that Babylon was not going to be destroyed; that neither heaven nor earth had quaked; that not all the LORD's people had returned from exile; that Darius had silenced the major rebellions so that there was no longer hope for the collapse of his empire, but there was not peace throughout the earth;[42] that Israel and Judah were not dominating their oppressors; that multitudes of Gentiles were not becoming converts; that Jerusalem was not overflowing with people, cattle, and prosperity;[43] that the wealth of nations was flowing to Darius, not to Jerusalem.

The incomplete fulfillment of the comforting words of true prophets as usual served as proof that Israel's and Judah's sins still were not forgiven. Even the new temple was not yet finished, and the representative of the dynasty of David, Zerubbabel, had been governor, but not king. How could Haggai and Zechariah predict imminent fulfillment of the unfulfilled in 520/19? Thus, the second year of Darius, in which they uttered their optimistic prophecies, must be 521/0.

Let us now see how Haggai and Zechariah look forward to fulfillment of the earlier prophecies and echo their language. We shall follow the same order of topics as in the paragraph above where we listed the expectations of believing Jews in 522–521.

According to Hag 2:6–7, heaven- and earth-quakes are imminent, and God will destroy "the strength of the Gentile kingdoms." The prophet twice uses the Hebrew root *hpk*, regularly employed in mentions of the destruction of Sodom, the root Isaiah used at 13:19 in comparing the destruction of Babylon to that of Sodom. Zechariah calls (1:10–11) for a return of the exiles in language echoing Jer 50:4–5, 8, 28, 51:6, 51:45, 50, and Isa 48:20. Zechariah hears (1:11) supernatural informants report that the earth is "quiet," using the same verb Isaiah used at 14:7 to describe the aftermath of the fall of Babylon's king. Zechariah predicts (13:9) that God will quickly forgive the "sin of that land," the land of Judah. Haggai predicts that God will bring about the collapse of pagan king-doms and hints at imperial power for the Jewish prince Zerubbabel (2:22–23), and Zechariah says (2:12–13) that God will see to it that the Jews, formerly en-slaved, will despoil their spoilers. He also predicts that Gentiles will become converts (2:15), the LORD's people will sing and rejoice (2:14), and Jerusalem and Judah will overflow with prosperity and multitudes of people and cattle (2:8). According to Haggai (2:7), the wealth of nations will flow to Jerusalem.

Both prophets believe in and encourage the speedy completion of the new temple. Haggai (2:9) has God promising that the glory of the second temple will be greater than that of the first. Haggai, enthusiastically (2:21–23),[44] and Zechariah, somewhat guardedly (3:8, 4:6–10a, 12–14, 6:9–13), speak to or of Zerubbabel as the next link in the dynasty of David, and Zechariah gives reve-lations (3:1–10, 4:1–3, 11–14, 6:9–13) confirming the legitimacy of the power of the high priest. Zechariah's ambiguous epithet for alluding to Zerubbabel or to anyone else who proves to be the next link in the dynasty is the word "Shoot" from Jer 33:15.

In Isa 13:2–14:27, Jer 50–51, and Isaiah 40–66, all these consummations, to which the Jews looked forward in the second year of Darius, were presented as accompaniments of the fall of Babylon. Thus, even though Haggai and Zechariah never mention Babylon, they are reacting to her fall.[45] If the fall of Babylon had not been in the immediate background, they, too, might not have dared to insist on the rebuilding of the temple before it was clear that Jere-miah's seventy years had passed. If they had not pressed the matter in 521, in the disappointing background of the year 520 they might not have called for the rebuilding. We can thus be confident that "the second year of King Darius" in their date formulas is 521/0, not 520/19.

Unlike the Babylonians, the Jews did not rise in revolt against Darius. We have observed factors that could have driven them to disastrous rebellion. Probably most dangerous of all were Haggai's promises to Zerubbabel (2:21–22), of royal Davidic glory for him and of an imminent end of Gentile empires. Not long afterward, Zerubbabel disappears from our historical sources. Some scholars have taken this evidence as proving that Jews did re-volt and that the Persians at least eliminated Zerubbabel.[46] It is inherently un-likely, however, that our Jewish sources would have concealed an unsuccessful Jewish rebellion. Rather, the tendency would have been to publicize the fact and to ascribe it to some sin of the ringleaders; if no other sin could be found, the defeat could still be blamed upon Jews' rising in revolt before the end of Jeremiah's seventy years. Furthermore, Darius thereafter treated the Jews kindly, as if they were thoroughly loyal subjects. There is therefore no reason to believe that there was a Jewish rebellion in the early reign of Darius.[47]

What prevented the Jews from sharing the fate of the Babylonians? Probably several factors combined to save the Jews.

1. During the tumult of the early reign of Darius, Jeremiah's seventy years, if measured from the destruction of 586, were still far from over.
2. Haggai himself, despite knowing prophetic passages like Isa 50:2 and 63:3–4, did not tell Jews to aid the LORD in his work by rebelling; rather, he implied (2:6–7, 21–23) that all would be accomplished by God.
3. Zechariah delivered a message of the LORD (4:6b–10a) forcefully forbidding Zerubbabel to engage in armed revolt and promising that God's "spirit" or rather, his Wind would bring to that prince (and to the Jews) the promised fulfillments.[48]
4. As the year went by, the events of 521/0 made it increasingly clear that God was not fulfilling the glorious prophecies of the true prophets, so that, as we have noted, by 520/19, Jews no longer had dangerous tendencies to go into revolt.

By the time Jeremiah's seventy years were clearly over, by the fifth month of 516/5 (assuming, as we have, that the destruction of Jerusalem was in August 586/5), there was no indication whatever that the Persian Empire would collapse. Our assumed date in 586 B.C.E. for the destruction involves us in a chronological problem. According to Ezra 6:18, the second temple was finished on 3 Adar of Darius's sixth regnal year. If this means the sixth year by the reckoning in Darius's inscription at Behistun and in Haggai and Zechariah, the date is Feb. 21 or March 22, 516 (the year was intercalary and had two Adars). That date would be before the seventieth anniversary of a destruction in 586, and that fact would argue for dating the destruction in 587. However, the date at Ezra 6:15 could come from records kept by Jews at Babylon, who dated according to Babylonian practice (the passage is in Babylonian Aramaic). If so, the date of the completion of the second temple would be March 12, 515, a safe seventy years and almost seven months after the destruction.

Even the passing of Jeremiah's seventy years and the completion of the temple brought no indication that God was fulfilling the glorious predictions of the true prophets. Most believing Jews were driven to an important inference: Because of their sins, despite Jeremiah's promises of a definite limit of seventy years to their punishment, they were still living in an age of God's wrath, in which he would punish them severely for rebellion against the foreign rulers he had placed over them. Jews continued to believe they were the *people of an almighty god,* but their important inference long preserved them from incurring punishment for rebellion.[49]

"Ahasuerus" in the book of Esther is certainly the Hebrew equivalent of the name the Greeks rendered as "Xerxes," and the author certainly meant the king by that name to be Xerxes I (486–465), the heir of Darius I.[50] There is a strong case for saying Esther is fiction.[51] If, however, there is any truth in the book, it serves as one more proof that Jews in this period would not rebel: Though threatened, by royal decree, with massacre and looting (3:13), the Jews do nothing to defend themselves until the king decrees that they may do so (8:3–13). Whatever the reason for Mordecai's refusal to obey the king's command to bow down to Haman (3:2–5),[52] he clearly had no intention to rebel and on one occasion had saved the king's life (2:21–23).

At Ezra 4:6, we read that at the beginning of the reign of Xerxes, the "people of the land" (i.e., the Samaritans; see 4:2, 4, 10) wrote an accusation against the inhabitants of Judah and Jerusalem. Ezra 4:1–24 consists of sententious propaganda, an effort to prove that throughout the reigns of the Persian kings from Cyrus through Artaxerxes I the "people of the land," the "enemies of Judah and Benjamin," acted against the interests of the returned exiles in Judah and Jerusalem and were responsible for the long delay in the rebuilding of the temple.[53] For his assertion, the writer can quote only one piece of documentary evidence, a letter from authorities at Samaria to Artaxerxes I, a message which argues that Jerusalem should not be refortified and says nothing about the temple.

The writer of Ezra 4:1–24 may have heard a true report of a letter of accusation sent to Xerxes, but he does not quote it. We can suspect, even if we cannot prove, that he invented the written accusation sent to Xerxes, in order to bridge the embarrassing gap between his evidence from the reign of Artaxerxes I and the alleged events under the reigns from Cyrus to Darius. Even if Xerxes received a letter accusing the Jews, it is most unlikely that it spoke of present unrest. Otherwise, the persons who wrote to Artaxerxes I in opposition to the fortification of Jerusalem would have cited that recent instance. Instead, they mention the rebelliousness of Jerusalem in "ancient" times, before the destruction of Jerusalem in 586 B.C.E. (4:15, cf. 4:19).

Apart from the book of Esther and Ezra 4:6, nothing tells us of the history of the Jews in the reign of Xerxes. Can the silences on that reign (and on the reigns of the Persian kings after Artaxerxes I) cover up unsuccessful Jewish rebellions? That would be contrary to the whole tendency of biblical Jewish historiography: It does not hide defeats but presents them vividly and searches diligently for the sin that provoked God into letting his people fall. Jews wrote history of the reign of Xerxes's heir, Artaxerxes I (465–424), in the books of Ezra and Nehemiah. If they did not write and preserve an account of the reign of Xerxes, his times were neither so catastrophic nor so prosperous for the Jews as to serve as exemplifications of the intervention of God.

Thus, the Jews' inference, that God himself demanded that they serve loyally the pagan ruler he had placed over them, long protected them from suffering the fate of rebels against the Persian kings. No such inference protected the Babylonians. Let us turn to study their further misadventures.

3. The Babylonians and Xerxes

QUIET UNDER DARIUS from the end of 521 until his death in 486,[54] the people of Babylonia at first patiently bore the yoke of his son and heir, Xerxes, who reigned from 486 to 465. However, they soon went into revolt, though the evidence is tantalizingly scarce. Three Babylonian documents are dated in the summer from 15 Abu into Ululu of the accession year of King Bêl-shimânni; two of the texts are from Borsippa and one from Dilbat. Another ten are dated in the summer and early autumn between 4 Abu and a time shortly after 29 Tashritu of the accession year of King Shamash-erîba. Two of those are from Babylon and seven from Borsippa; another does not say where it was drawn up, but surely, not far from Babylon.[55] Mention of an accession year in the date of a Babylonian document means that a new king has taken the throne, and thus either that the previous king has died or abdicated and his heir has inherited the throne, or that there has been a revolution.

Persons mentioned in those documents are known to have lived late in the reign of Darius and early in the reign of Xerxes.[56] No heirs of either Persian king could have borne the Babylonian names "Bêl-shimânni" or "Shamash-erîba." Clearly Bêl-shimânni and Shamash-erîba were pretenders who rebelled late in the reign of Darius or early in the reign of Xerxes.

The pretenders would have been presumptuous enough if they each had claimed only to be king of Babylon, a city of Xerxes's realm. The great Babylonian kings had been content to be called no more than that. Each pretender bears that relatively modest title in the date of at least one document.[57] But in the dates of most of the surviving texts the two rebels bear the grandiose imperial titles, "King of Babylon and the Lands" or "King of Babylon, King of the Lands," hitherto borne by the kings of the Persian Empire; "King of the Lands" has imperial Assyrian antecedents.[58] Did the pretenders' aspirations go beyond independence to imperial glory? In the vast and powerful Persian Empire, aspirations of a Babylonian pretender to independence would be presumptuous enough, and any aspirations of his to imperial rule, all the more so. Such presumption in Babylon, so often conquered, should be ascribed to the faith of a *people of an almighty god.*

Can we pinpoint the dates of the presumptuous pretenders? An uninterrupted series of date-formulas in documents from Babylonia shows that there can have been no rebellion there late in the reign of Darius (who died in November 486) or in Xerxes's accession year (486/5) or first regnal year (485/4).[59] One of the three documents dated by Bêl-shimânni speaks of a period of time extending from the month Addaru (February-March) of the "first year" (surely meaning the first year of the previous reign) until the end of Abu (July-August). Addaru was the last month of the Babylonian year. Accordingly, the accession of Bêl-shimânni must have occurred in Xerxes's second regnal year, and the equivalents for the two readable dates, 15 Abu and 1 Ululu, in that year are Aug. 6 and Aug. 21, 484. The day and month are broken off from the date of the third tablet of Bêl-shimânni, but its content shows it to be of Abu or early Ululu (midsummer).[60] Bêl-shimânni's reign must have been very short, because Babylonian documents were dated by the second year of Xerxes as late as 6 Duzu (June 28) and resume being dated by Xerxes no later than 25 Second Ululu (Oct. 14).[61]

It is harder to ascertain the year of Shamash-erîba's accesssion. Several approaches have proved to be wrong. Mariano San Nicolò suggested that Shamash-erîba reigned just after Bêl-shimânni, but evidence of which he was ignorant refutes him. If we look only at the day-numerals and month-names now known to us, the days and months of Bêl-shimânni's reign fall within those of Shamash-erîba's. Two pretenders cannot have reigned simultaneously over Babylon and Borsippa, so the two must have reigned in separate years.[62]

Another delusory approach was based on incomplete evidence on the changes in the titles borne by Xerxes in the dates of Babylonian documents. In dating their documents by the regnal years of Cyrus, Babylonians had referred to him by the titles "King of Babylon, King of the Lands." The title "King of the Lands" was not new; it had been used by loyal Babylonian subjects addressing letters to their foreign but to them legitimate king, Assyrian Ashurbanipal.[63] The combination, "King of Babylon, King of the Lands," thus presented Cyrus as Babylonia's own king. It also displayed the privileged status of Babylon, as if she were not a conquered territory. The combination continued to be used under Cyrus's successors down into the early reign of Xerxes.[64]

Between the third month (June-July) and the fifth (August) of Xerxes's first regnal year, Babylonian scribes began to give Xerxes in the date-formula only the title "King of Persia and Media," thus apparently displaying Babylon's status as a conquered territory. Nothing tells us whose decision produced the change; we may guess that it was by royal order. Shortly thereafter, perhaps in response to protests, the formula was changed to give Xerxes the titles "King of Persia and Media, King of Babylon, King of the Lands," thus perhaps recognizing Babylon's privileged position, while still displaying her subordinate status.[65]

Until recently, it seemed that after Xerxes's fourth year (482/1), "King of Babylon" ceased to appear in the Babylonian date-formula, and that his title became solely "King of the Lands." Scholars yielded to the temptation to view the omission of "King of Babylon" as punishment for Babylonian rebellion and put Shamash-erîba's accession in Xerxes's fourth year.[66] Newly published documents and new collations of others previously known now reveal that the titulary of Xerxes in the date-formulas used by Babylonian scribes can reflect no consistent policy whatever. Although most dates after year 4 give Xerxes only the title "King of the Lands," tablets from that period attest also "King of Babylon, King of the Lands,"[67] as well as "King of Persia" alone,[68] "King of Persia, Media, and the Lands,"[69] and "King of Persia, Media, King of Babylon and the Lands."[70] Hence, we no longer can use the changes in Xerxes's titulary to put Shamash-erîba's rebellion in Xerxes's fourth year.[71]

One piece of evidence can exclude that rebellion from Xerxes's fourth year. A tablet in the British Museum, written at Babylon, bears the date 15 Ululu. The year numeral is messy but is probably 4. If Xerxes was recognized as king in Babylon in Ululu of his fourth regnal year, Shamash-erîba cannot have reigned then.[72] Can we put the rebellion in a later year? We cannot exclude that possibility by what we know of the persons mentioned in the documents dated in the reign of Shamash-erîba. Those persons could have lived on from Xerxes's early reign through all of his twenty-one regnal years. However, there are published tablets that are dated between 4 Abu and early Arakhshamnu (the days and months attested for Shamash-erîba) in Xerxes's twelfth,[73] sixteenth,[74] seventeenth,[75] and nineteenth[76] years. Among the unpublished tablets there should be some to exclude still other years of Xerxes from being the year of Shamash-erîba.

On the other hand, a few Babylonian documents are known from Xerxes's third regnal year (483/2 B.C.E.). Not one of them is dated between 4 Abu and early Arakhshamnu.[77] That year could have been the one of Shamash-erîba's rebellion.

The date formulas of Babylonian documents thus let us know that rebellions occurred and failed, but they leave some uncertainty about the year of Shamash-erîba's reign, and we would like to know more about the motives of the rebels and about the course of events. Greek writers do not mention the names of Bêl-shimânni and Shamash-erîba, but they confirm that the Babylonians rebelled in Xerxes's reign and that Xerxes subdued and punished them. Greek writers also hint at facts that could have driven Marduk's people to revolt.

Ktesias of Knidos, of the late fifth and early fourth century B.C.E., is generally regarded as unreliable,[78] but he served as physician to the Persian King Artaxerxes II (reigned 404–359) and had ample opportunity to learn the stories told by the royal family and upper-class Persians. Many if not all distortions in his accounts of Xerxes and later kings can be ascribed to his informants or to his own lapses of memory rather than to any mendacity of his.[79] His works have perished, but their content survives through excerpts made by other writers, especially by Photius, the Greek scholar of the ninth century C.E. Some of the errors in those excerpts are the result of Photius's carelessness or misunderstanding of the text.

Let us examine what Photius's summary of Ktesias has to say about a Babylonian revolt in Xerxes's early reign. After telling of the death of Darius I and Xerxes's accession, of the grandees under him, and of Xerxes's wife and children,[80] Photius's summary says, "Xerxes marched against the Greeks," and gives reasons why. The account[81] continues as follows:

> Before marching,[82] he went to Babylon and felt an eager desire to tour[83] the tomb of Belitanas. Mardonius [Xerxes's able and powerful brother-in-law] made it possible for him to do so. Xerxes was unable to fill the sarcophagus with oil as prescribed by the inscription.[84] He departed and rode to Ekbatana. There news reached him that the Babylonians had rebelled and had killed Zopyros, their governor. Such is Ktesias' account of the events, unlike that of Herodotus. What Herodotus tells[85] concerning Zopyros (except that his mule gave birth), Ktesias says Megabyzos accomplished. This Megabyzos was Xerxes's son-in-law, husband of his daughter Amytis. In this manner Megabyzos took Babylon. Xerxes granted him many rewards, including a golden millstone weighing 6 talents, the most valuable royal gift in Persian history. Xerxes, after mustering a Persian army of 800,000 (not counting the chariotry) and 1,000 triremes, set out against Greece.

Clearly, Ktesias reported a Babylonian rebellion early in Xerxes's reign, when he was in Ekbatana, shortly before his march on Greece. Xerxes probably departed against Greece from his capitals in Iran in April 481 B.C.E., at the beginning of his fifth regnal year.[86] Only in the aftermath of the Persian defeat in the battle of Mykale (August 479), in his seventh year, did he return from the West.[87] Ktesias reports only one rebellion. The revolt of Bêl-shimânni could not be said to have occurred shortly before the march on Greece, and it was very brief, so that Ktesias might never have heard of it and could have passed over it in silence. We infer that the rebellion reported by Ktesias is that of Shamash-erîba. If the report is correct and if Xerxes was away in the west from year 5 to August of year 7, those years did not contain the reign of Shamash-erîba.

Photius's summary asserts that Herodotus mistakenly took events of Xerxes's reign in which Megabyzos (= Megabyxos) was prominent and moved them into Darius's reign and ascribed the prominent role to Zopyros. Whether that judgment was explicitly voiced by Ktesias or is Photius's inference, it may well be correct,[88] but it gives only a partial explanation for Herodotus's story. Shamash-erîba's reign is attested only within 4 months, nowhere near the supposed 21 months of the siege. If Herodotus's tale originated from Shamash-erîba's rebellion, nothing tells us how the story of a 21-month siege grew up. The later the rebellion occurred, the closer it would be to the time Herodotus carried on his research, and the less likely he would be to make such errors.

Besides Ktesias, only Plutarch among Greek writers directly attests a Babylonian revolt under Xerxes. However, Arrian (ca. 95–175 C.E.), in his history of the conquests of Alexander the Great says that Xerxes destroyed the temple of Bêl and other Babylonian shrines "when he returned home from Greece."[89] Such sacrilegious multiple destructions, if they occurred, were surely punitive. If Arrian is right and if the destructions were a consequence of Shamash-erîba's relatively brief rebellion, it must have occurred in Xerxes's seventh or eighth year. On the whole, it seems more likely that Arrian and any sources of his from the 330s B.C.E., the time of Alexander, were mistaken,[90] than that Ktesias and his informants in the 390s were wrong about the order of the events.

We have now established that two Babylonian pretenders rebelled in the reign of Xerxes, Bêl-shimânni certainly in year 2, Shamash-erîba possibly in year 3, and both made the presumptuous claim to rule the whole empire. Xerxes in those years was preparing a vast campaign against Greece.[91] He had a huge army. By January 484, still in his first regnal year, he had suppressed a rebellion in Egypt.[92] The Babylonians had suffered grievously from the rebellions of the two pretenders at the beginning of Darius's reign. What drove them to try twice more? Even if the rebels were a *people of an almighty god,* we ought to ask that question. Let us examine first the Babylonian evidence, then the Persian, and then that provided by Greek writers.

From the Babylonians we have only the date-formulas of the documents. We now know that the Persians could tolerate some departures from uniformity in those formulas. Again nothing tells us what determined those formulas; we may guess they resulted from royal decisions. Even so, the percentage of literate Babylonians was small. The scribes and the few readers of the documents may well have been indifferent to the content of the dating formula, a perfunctory form. But however small the significance of the formula in itself, it may well have reflected Persian policies that enraged the people of almighty Marduk. A Persian king who took as his title, "King of Babylon, King of the Lands," may have had a general policy of giving the impression that he honored Babylon and that he ruled by the grace of Marduk. If he chose to be called only "King of Persia and Media," perhaps he had a general policy of slighting Babylon and her god. Even if his title was "King of Persia, Media, King of Babylon and the Lands," it could reflect a general policy of asserting the subordination of Marduk and his city. On the other hand, the title most attested in the dating-formulas of the later reign of Xerxes, "King of the Lands," is a title of Babylonian origin,[93] which could be viewed as asserting merely the fact of imperial rule without declaring the subordination of the god or his city, and we might then have an explanation for Babylonian rebellions in the early years of Xerxes and for Babylonian acquiescence later.

From the Persians we have a document, the interpretation of which has provoked vigorous controversy, Xerxes's "Daiva Inscription" from Persepolis, referred to by specialists as "XPh." Carved on stone tablets, it is trilingual, in Old Persian, Elamite, and Babylonian.[94]

In the inscription Xerxes begins with praise of Ahuramazda, the creator (lines 1–6) and goes on to identify himself and his ancestors (lines 6–13). In lines 13–28 he lists the many countries over which he is king. Included among them are Babylonia, Egypt, and the "Ionians [= Greeks] who dwell by the sea and those who dwell across the sea." Lines 28–41 are the part that may cast light on the Babylonian rebellions. Here is a translation[95] of them:

> Thus speaks King Xerxes: When I became king, there is among these countries listed above one which was in revolt. Afterwards, Ahuramazda bore me aid; by the favor of Ahuramazda I smote that country and put it down in its place.
>
> And among these countries there was [a place] where previously *daivas* were worshiped. Afterwards, by the favor of Ahuramazda, I destroyed that sanctuary of the *daivas,* and I made proclamation, 'The *daivas* shall not be worshiped!' Where previously *daivas* were worshiped, there I worshiped Ahuramazda in accordance with ritual law.[96]

In lines 41–46, Xerxes claims that by the favor of Ahuramazda he righted wrongs. In lines 46–56 he preaches to posterity that respect for Ahuramazda's law and worship of him in accordance with ritual law will confer blessedness. In lines 51–55 he prays that Ahuramazda will protect him, his dynasty, and his land.

The Babylonian version diverges significantly from the Persian and the Elamite in the paragraphs we have translated. Where the Persian has "one which was in revolt," "that country," and "it," the Babylonian has the plural. We should seek a reason why.[97]

In Zoroastrian texts the word *daiva* refers to an evil deity who must not be worshiped.[98] The Babylonian version renders the Persian plural word by *lemnû* ("evil ones"). Xerxes does not name the rebellious country or countries, nor does he say where the *daivas* were worshiped. Some scholars have asserted that the *daivas* are Marduk and other gods of Babylon.[99] Others have denied the possibility and have held that Xerxes was purging heterodox Iranian worship.[100]

Although the evidence does not suffice for certainty, I would like to propose my own hypotheses. Xerxes, using the Persian historical present tense, says that the unnamed country was in revolt at the time of his accession. Of only one country which had been subject to the Persians do we know that it was in revolt then. Herodotus reports[101] that Egypt rebelled in the fourth year (487/6 B.C.E.) after the Battle of Marathon. With a vagueness resembling that of Xerxes, Herodotus writes,[102] "After Xerxes was persuaded to march on Greece, he first, in the second year [485 B.C.E.][103] after the death of Darius, marched against those who were in rebellion and defeated them," but then the Greek historian's account becomes specific, "putting Egypt under more severe subjection than in the reign of Darius." Accordingly, the country in revolt should be Egypt. An inscription in Egypt shows that Xerxes had subdued the country by January 484.[104]

Xerxes's list of lands ruled by him gives clues to the date of the *Daiva* Inscription. He claims control of Egypt; therefore, the country is no longer in revolt, and the year is 485 or later. On the other hand, he says he rules the Greeks of Asia and the islands, a claim he could no longer make after the Battle of Mykale in August 479. He is unlikely to have had the inscription drawn up in his absence, after he marched out of Iran on his campaign against the European Greeks in April 481.

Can the *daivas* be gods of Babylonia? Can this inscription of between 485 and 481 be connected with the revolt of Shamash-erîba? An attack by Xerxes on the gods of Babylon could either have provoked a Babylonian revolt or have been punishment for one. If the attack on the Babylonian gods was the provocation and not a response to rebellion, we have to ask why Xerxes would single out Babylonian gods for persecution. None of his non-Iranian subject peoples worshiped Ahuramazda! Furthermore, the Persian kings otherwise tolerated the religions of the subject peoples, a fact which might indicate that the *daiva* worshipers must have been Iranians.

If, however, the attack on Babylonian worship was punishment for a religiously motivated Babylonian revolt, we can understand how Xerxes might ban worship of Marduk and destroy a Babylonian shrine.[105] Babylonians repeatedly exhibited the characteristic rebelliousness of a *people of an almighty god*. We know that they rebelled twice during Xerxes's reign. But the *Daiva* Inscription itself might seem to exclude the possibility that Xerxes's attack on *daiva*-worship was a response to Babylonian rebellion. He claims that in his early reign Ahuramazda aided him in two great acts: the reconquest of a rebellious land and the suppression of *daiva*-worship. We have argued that the rebellious land was Egypt. But if the suppression of *daiva*-worship was punishment for a Babylonian revolt, there were two rebellious lands! Surely Xerxes should have expressed himself differently. He should have been explicit about the second rebellion, the one of the *daiva* worshipers![106]

We can, however, imagine how events in Babylon could have resulted in what Xerxes says. The insults to Marduk implied or reflected in the documentary date-formulas could have been enough to provoke the revolt led by Bêl-shimânni. When we look at the information preserved by Greek writers, we shall find other possible insults that Marduk's faithful could have resented. The two readable dates of Bêl-shimânni's reign fall within a mere 16 days; the broken tablet might extend the reign to 26 days.[107] Babylon probably still had her famous fortifications.[108] If the pretender fell so quickly, chances are he put up no effective resistance. Intimidated, he may have surrendered, or other Babylonians may have opened the gates to Xerxes.[109] If Bêl-shimânni's movement collapsed very quickly, costing the Persians little or nothing, it might not deserve the name "rebellion." Then neither Xerxes nor Ktesias need have mentioned it. But the pretender and his supporters may have proclaimed it to be a holy enterprise in the name of Marduk. Then Xerxes would have reason to suppress the cult of "Evil Gods" even while mentioning no Babylonian revolt.

Persian multilingual royal inscriptions could be exposed on cliffs or buried in the earth to be read by gods or by remote posterity. They could also be circulated on perishable writing materials to be read immediately by the king's subjects. Darius, too, after suppressing revolts preached the supremacy of

Ahuramazda in many languages to the non-Iranians ruled by him.[110] For Babylonians, if not for others, Bêl-shimânni's revolt, however brief, could have been a noteworthy event. It may be for that reason we find that Xerxes or his propagandist in the Babylonian version of XPh told the Babylonians and their gods that plural countries (i.e., Egypt and Babylonia) rebelled.

On the other hand, there was only one region which Xerxes, even in the Babylonian version, accuses of being a seat of *daiva*-worship, and he claims to have destroyed only one sanctuary of *daiva*s.[111] If that shrine was in Babylon, Xerxes did not regard Egyptian deities as *daiva*s, perhaps because Egyptian priests were somehow able to dissociate their cults from the rebellion, whereas in Babylon deities may have been inextricably involved with Bêl-shimânni. We shall soon consider the evidence on which Babylonian shrine was destroyed.[112]

If Xerxes, in the aftermath of Bêl-shimânni's fall, banned Babylonian worship and destroyed a Babylonian shrine, his action could have provoked the longer rebellion, the one under Shamash-erîba, and we would have more reason to date that revolt in Xerxes's third regnal year (483/2 B.C.E.), before he left Iran to march on Greece, just as Ktesias says.[113] We could also explain the subsequent course of events. Xerxes wanted to conquer the Greeks. He did not wish to be tied down by protracted fanatical Babylonian resistance. Once Shamash-erîba was put down, the Persian king no longer insisted on suppressing Babylonian worship or on provocative date-formulas. The *Daiva* Inscription had been buried in foundations. What it says of Xerxes's deeds was, indeed, still true and could remain unaltered, even if Babylonians rebuilt the destroyed shrine.

Scholars have argued that Xerxes in writing of *daiva*s cannot have meant Babylonian gods. Our hypotheses remove most of their objections. Let us consider the arguments of theirs which still remain.

1. *Daiva* originally meant "deity"; as a pejorative term it is Zoroastrian and refers to Iranian deities whose worship was condemned by Zarathushtra. Xerxes throughout seems to be referring, not to foreign, but to domestic Iranian cults: After eradicating *daiva*-worship from its seat, in that same place he worships Ahuramazda according to ritual law![114]

   This argument of Ugo Bianchi's is not cogent. It begs the question. Henrik Nyberg and Geo Widengren have rightly written[115] that non-Iranian gods could hardly be called *ahura* or *baga* (the normal terms used for deity by the Persian kings and by Zoroastrians). Xerxes could use for them only the word *daiva*. Bianchi cites Widengren's and

Nyberg's point but says it is inconclusive. All he brings against it, however, is a statement which does nothing to refute it: "In many cultures one can speak of attacking foreign deities without having a special term for 'god whose worship is banned.' "[116]

2. Cyrus boasted he had the aid of Babylonian Marduk. One can even argue that Persians identified Marduk with Ahuramazda. How, then, could Xerxes regard Babylonian deities as *daiva*s?[117] This point is even less cogent. As long as Babylonian deities aided the ruling Persian dynasty, the kings could gratefully respect them and perhaps identify Marduk with Ahuramazda. If, however, the gods of Babylon became the focus around which their worshipers organized a rebellion, they joined the forces of the "Lie," the forces of evil, and became *daiva*s.

3. Xerxes says, "where previously *daiva*s were worshiped, there I worshiped Ahuramazda." Mary Boyce[118] sees not the smallest likelihood that Xerxes could have worshiped Ahuramazda in Esagila. We shall soon, however, find evidence that the destroyed shrine was, not Esagila, but the one atop the ziggurat (staged tower) of Babylon.[119] A ziggurat served as an artificial mountain in the level flood plain of Babylonia. Persians were known to conduct their worship of Ahuramazda on the peaks of mountains.[120]

Let us turn now to examine the evidence Greek writers provide on what could have provoked Babylonians to rebel in the reign of Xerxes and what were the consequences of the unsuccessful revolts. Long before Xerxes decreed a change in the documentary date-formulas, Babylonians could have felt that the Persian kings were insulting Marduk and them. Persians developed a "philosophy of history" that was unflattering to Marduk and to Babylon. As their royal inscriptions show, they held that imperial power was a divine gift. Their spokesmen said that the first great empire had been that of the Assyrians; the second was that of the Medes; and the third, which presumably would last forever, was that of the Persians. Persian literature does not survive to tell us this, but Greek tourists were hearing it from their Persian guides in the mid-fifth century B.C.E.

Herodotus was one such tourist. Persians may have laid claim to world empire. If so, as a proud Greek, Herodotus refused to grant that the Persians ruled the world, but he was willing to transmit their claim that first the Assyrians held the empire of Asia for 520 years, then the Medes for 128, and finally the Persians with no limit specified. Ktesias agrees, though his figures are different: Assyrians, over 1,300 years, Medes, over 282.[121]

Hence, by the time Herodotus pursued his research, in the reign of Artaxerxes I (465/4–425), Persians held that the empire of Asia, perhaps of the world, had belonged first to Assyria, then to Media, now to Persia, and never to Babylon. (Even Nebuchadnezzar II, the greatest of the Babylonian kings, had feared the Median Empire.)[122] There is no reason to think that this Persian philosophy of history arose during the reign of Artaxerxes I, after the Greeks had driven the Persians out of Europe and much of western Asia. The focus on Assyria and Media, indeed, suggests that the idea had its origin among the Median conquerors of Assyria and was further developed when Cyrus the Persian conquered the Medes in 550 B.C.E., eleven years before he conquered Babylon in 539. That background, rather than any intent to insult Marduk and his city, would explain why Babylon was unmentioned. But the Persian boast that ignored Babylon was very hard for proud worshipers of Marduk to bear. Hence, for the Babylonians, the Persian dynasty could not and did not remain Marduk's favorites. Already in 522 Babylonians had welcomed the would-be kings who each pretended to be Nebuchadnezzar, son of the repentant Nabonidus.

By the 480s, more than documentary date-formulas and the Persian philosophy of history may have been taken as insults to Marduk. We left unexplained part of Ktesias's account of a Babylonian revolt.[123] What were the "tomb of Belitanas," the "sarcophagus," and the "inscription"? "Belitanas" may well be the Greek transcription of "Bêl-ittanu," a common Babylonian personal name ("Bêl gave [him to his parents]"),[124] but we hear nothing elsewhere of a tomb of a human Bêl-ittanu at Babylon. The details, and perhaps a better text, can be found at Aelianus *Varia historia* xiii.3.

Aelianus reports that Xerxes "dug his way" *(diaskapsas)* into the "tomb of ancient Bêl" *(tou Bêlou tou archaiou . . . to mnêma)* and found a glass sarcophagus containing a corpse lying in olive oil. The level of the oil was some three inches short of reaching the top. On a stele alongside was inscribed, "He who opens the tomb and does not fill the sarcophagus will suffer ill fortune." Xerxes had oil poured in, but no matter how much oil was added, the level in the sarcophagus failed to rise, and the king thereafter suffered ill fortune.

The story is bizarre. Here, instead of the tomb of Belitanas, the tomb is of ancient Bêl, who can only be Marduk himself. "Belitanas" in the version of Ktesias preserved by Photius may be "Bêl" followed by the Babylonian epithet heard by Ktesias and translated in Aelianus's version as "ancient," but if so, I have not been able to find what that epithet could have been. In any case, Babylonians did not think that Bêl was dead, and they built him no tomb. We know nothing of the use of olive oil in embalming in the ancient world, either among

Babylonians or elsewhere.[125] And the unchanging oil-level passes belief. To my knowledge, there is no way to explain how the story arose, whether among Greeks, Persians, or Babylonians. On the other hand, there may be confirmation for some aspects of the tale. When Xerxes reports "I destroyed [*viyakanam*] that sanctuary of the *daiva*s," his verb literally means "I *dug* apart." [126] It may not be coincidence that Aelianus reports that Xerxes *"dug* his way into" the tomb. Xerxes's damage to a Babylonian holy place would then be attested both by Xerxes himself and by Aelianus's version of Ktesias's account.

There are other possible clues in Strabo, who drew directly or indirectly on the same passage of the unabridged Ktesias when he wrote,[127] "There [in Babylon] also stands the tomb of Bêl *[ho tou Bêlou taphos]*, now demolished (Xerxes had it torn down, as it is said). It was a square pyramid of fired brick, one stadium high and one stadium in length and breadth."

The huge pyramid described by Strabo, drawing on the unabridged Ktesias, can be only the great ziggurat of Babylon, Etemenanki.[128] Its pyramidal shape must have led Greek tourists to think that it, like Egyptian pyramids, was a tomb. Greeks knew how tomb-robbers in Egypt "dug their way" into pyramids. But there was no need to dig one's way into the shrine atop a ziggurat, and Babylonians did not use them as tombs.

If Greeks drawing false analogies to Egyptian pyramids nevertheless somehow created the legend preserved by Ktesias and Aelianus, did a kernel of fact serve as its origin? There is a plausible way to combine the clues in our possession. Perhaps Etemenanki, with the shrine at its top, was a rallying-place for Bêl-shîmannî and his followers. If so, Xerxes may already have viewed the shrine as a center of *daiva*-worship and may have destroyed it, as he says in his inscription. Alternatively, he may have toured the conquered tower and dug into it or otherwise impaired its structure. Either way, he could have outraged Babylonians and provoked the revolt of Shamash-erîba. On suppressing that, Xerxes may have destroyed the shrine atop Etemenanki, if he had not done so already.

Did Xerxes do more damage to holy places in punishing Babylonian rebellion? Herodotus reports on Babylon one generation after Shamash-erîba's revolt. Modern scholars have misread Herodotus and asserted that Xerxes carried off the great statue of Marduk,[129] and they even went beyond all evidence to say that he had it melted down or destroyed.[130] Careful reading of Herodotus proves that Xerxes left the statue of Marduk in place and carried off some other one.[131] Herodotus gives no indication that either Marduk's temple Esagila or the ziggurat was damaged, and that fact fits well with our surmise, that once the revolt of Shamash-erîba was put down, Xerxes stopped persecuting Babylonian religion and allowed the destroyed shrine to be rebuilt.

Strabo, however, in the passage we have reproduced, quotes a report that Xerxes had the tower torn down, and Arrian, too, says that Xerxes destroyed shrines in Babylon which were still ruined when Alexander the Great captured the city.[132] Ktesias, however, around the beginning of the fourth century B.C.E., joins Herodotus in saying nothing whatever about shrines destroyed by Xerxes at Babylon. On the contrary, though he states that Etemenanki and other temples were in ruins, he attributes the fact to the ravages of time. It is easy to explain how the authorities of Arrian and Strabo, writers of the time of Alexander, could have transmitted erroneous information. If Etemenanki and other holy places were in ruins through neglect, the fact was discreditable to Babylonians. Knowing that Xerxes in fact had perpetrated a destruction at Babylon, Marduk's faithful would prefer to blame all that devastation on him, the more so as the avowed aim of Alexander's expedition against the Persian Empire was revenge for the sacrileges perpetrated by Xerxes in Greece.[133]

Plutarch alone preserves a curious tradition: "[Xerxes,] furious over a Babylonian revolt, defeated them and then decreed that they were not to bear arms but should play the lyre and the flute, maintain brothels, engage in retail trade, and wear long flowing tunics."[134] The story seeks to explain "unmanly" Babylonian practices that need have had no connection with punitive acts of Xerxes, but it may also contain a memory of humiliating decrees imposed upon Marduk's people after the defeat of Shamash-erîba.

We thus can be sure that Babylonians rebelled twice under Xerxes and were punished. We have reason to believe that Xerxes destroyed the shrine atop Etemenanki, though he later allowed it to be rebuilt. He also made off with a colossal golden statue from Esagila and killed the priest who tried to prevent him.[135] Whether Xerxes did further damage to Babylon and degraded the status of Babylonia within the empire is uncertain.[136] But whatever the truth may be, Xerxes's deeds were enough to provoke great resentment among Marduk's faithful. They surely were delighted when he suffered ignominious defeats at the hand of the Greeks in 480 and 479 B.C.E., and still more when he was murdered in 465. After some struggles, Artaxerxes I managed to become king (465/4–425).[137]

We would like to know the reactions of Babylonians to their misadventures under Darius and Xerxes. How did they maintain their faith in Marduk? Some of their thinking survives in a surprising place, the biblical book of Daniel. We turn now to study evidence there.

NOTES

1 A. Leo Oppenheim in CHI, II, 545, 549, 558 (an oath formula confirms the evidence of the dates); Dandamaev, *Persien,* 101–2; Tadmor in *Oz,* 469, n 62, and 471–72, n 67; Jerome Peat, "Cyrus 'King of Lands,' Cambyses 'King of Babylon': the Disputed Co-regency," *JCS* 41 (1989), 199–216.

2 Col. III, lines 23–28.

3 Oppenheim in CHI, II, 554–59, took the incident to be part of the celebration of the *Akîtu* of 538 B.C.E. Against Oppenheim, see Amélie Kuhrt and Susan M. Sherwin-White, "Xerxes's Destruction of Babylonian Temples," in *Achaemenid History II: the Greek Sources,* ed. Heleen Sancisi-Weerdenburg and Amélie Kuhrt (Leiden: Nederlands Instituut voor het Nabije Oosten, 1987), 75.

4 See Cyrus Cylinder, lines 20, 22–30, 38–43.

5 For a general treatment of the Babylonian evidence, see Oppenheim, CHI, II, 529–559. On the date-formulas, see Tadmor in *Shilton paras,* 11.

6 Herodotus iii.1–26; Cook, *Persian Empire,* 46–49.

7 iii.89.3.

8 Inscription at Behistun, Persian, par. 10 (col. I, lines 33–35); Dandamaev, *Persien,* 125–26, 144–47. On the inscription, see pp. 68–70.

9 See chap 3, n 42.

10 Darius at Behistun, Persian, par. 11 (col. I, lines 35–43); Herodotus iii.61–62; Cook, *Persian Empire,* 50 and 237, n 14.

11 Herodotus iii.68; Dandamaev, *Persien,* 134–35.

12 Herodotus iii.64–66; Darius at Behistun, Persian, par. 11 (col. I, line 43; see Dandamaev, *Persien,* 146–51); Cook, *Persian Empire,* 49–55.

13 Darius at Behistun, Persian, par. 13 (col. I, lines 55–61), and par. 68 (col. IV, lines 80–86); Herodotus iii. 68–88; Cook, *Persian Empire,* 54–55.

14 Darius at Behistun, Persian, pars. 16–54 (col. I, line 72 through col. IV, line 36); Herodotus iii.150–60; Cook, *Persian Empire,* 55–57; Dandamaev, *Persien,* 128–32.

15   Cf. Elias Bickerman, Review of *Persien,* by Dandamaev, *Athenaeum* 56 (1978), 415.

16   See pp. 42–43.

17   Tadmor in *Shilton paras,* 11 and 254, n 49.

18   Roux, 310.

19   The Merodach-baladan of 2 Kings 20:12–19, Isa 39:1–8.

20   Roux, 311–12; John A. Brinkman, "Merodach-Baladan II," in *Studies Presented to A. Leo Oppenheim* (Chicago: Oriental Institute of the University of Chicago, 1964), 6–40; my article, "The Historical Setting of the Uruk Prophecy," *JNES* 47 (1988), 43–46.

21   Roux, 314–18, 322–23.

22   By Oct. 3 (Parker-Dubberstein, 15).

23   Darius at Behistun, Persian, par. 16 (col. I, lines 77–81).

24   Darius at Behistun, Persian, pars. 19–20 (col. I, line 83 through col. II, line 5); ibid., Babylonian, secs. 18–19 (lines 36–40); dating by accession year of Nebuchadnezzar III: Parker-Dubberstein, 15. See now Muhammad Dandamayev, "The latest evidence for Nebuchadnezzar III's reign," *N.A.B.U.* 7 (1993), 8–9 (Item No. 11), for a document written at Borsippa, in which Nebuchadnezzar III was still recognized as king on Feb. 1, 521 B.C.E.

25   Ibid., Persian, par. 21 (col. II, lines 5–8); see Map 2; Persis is the nuclear territory of the Persians, the province of Fars in the southwest of modern Iran.

26   Parker-Dubberstein, 16; Dandamaev, *Persien,* 130.

27   Darius at Behistun, Persian, pars. 49–50 (col. III, lines 76–92); Herodotus iii.159; Dandamaev, *Persien,* 130; wall: Herodotus iii.159, but see n 108.

28   iii.150–60.

29   Muhammad A. Dandamaev, *Slavery in Babylonia from Nabopolassar to Alexander the Great* (DeKalb, IL: Northern Illinois University Press, 1984), 15–16, lists 1,501 published documents dated in the reign of Darius I, though he does not quote the individual dates. See also George G. Cameron, "Darius and Xerxes in Babylonia," *AJSL* 58 (1941), 319.

30   See below, on the revolt of Shamash-erîba as possibly reflected in Herodotus's account.

31   Herodotus iii.92; Cook, *Persian Empire,* 66–90; Roux, 407–8; Cameron, *AJSL* 58 (1941), 319.

32   See pp. 94–95.

33   See chap 5, p. 113; Bickerman, *Chronology,* 24, and *Studies in Jewish and Christian History,* Part III (Leiden: Brill, 1986), 327–28.

34   Ibid., 331–36. Unfortunately, Eric and Carol Meyers (*Haggai, Zechariah 1–8* ["Anchor Bible," vol. 25B; Garden City, N.Y.: Doubleday, 1987]) ignore Bickerman's study, but see H. Tadmor in *Historiah shel Eretz-Yisrael,* II, 260–61. Earlier scholars, too, recognized that the background presupposed by the utterances of Haggai and Zechariah requires that the "second year of Darius" mentioned there be the year of the revolts narrated by Darius at Behistun. See, e.g., Albert Ten Eyck Olmstead, *History of Syria and Palestine to the Macedonian Conquest* (New York and London: Charles Scribner's Sons, 1931), 560–67, 572–74, and "Darius and His Behistun Inscription," *American Journal of Semitic Languages and Literatures* 55 (1938), 400–403, 409–12; Leroy Waterman, "The Camouflaged Purge of Three Messianic Conspirators," *JNES* 13 (1954), 73–78; Bright, *History,* 369, n 66 and 370, n 67.

35   At Behistun, par. 10 (col. I, lines 27–28).

36   Ibid., par. 11 (col. I, lines 35–42).

37   Ibid., par. 13 (col. I, lines 55–61).

38   Bickerman (*Studies,* III, 332) finds Zech 1:7–11 absurd if uttered on 24 Shebaṭ in the second year of Darius (Feb. 15, 520), over two months after the second fall of Babylon. In that passage, supernatural observers report that the earth is quiet. What Jerusalemite at that date needed a supernatural informant for the fact? But Bickerman has missed the prophet's point. The supernatural observers report to God and his angel, not to human beings, and the report is not what is important, but the protest it provokes from the angel, against the continuing desolation of Jerusalem and Judah after seventy years, at a time when the rest of the earth is at peace.

39   In the last ten paragraphs of chap 6 and the fourth paragraph of this chapter.

40   In the next notes and parentheses, I omit most references to the passages in Isaiah 40–66. Those passages correspond to passages from Isaiah 13–14 and 21 and can be found with the help of chap 6, n 37.

41 By 522, Cyrus was long dead, so that Deutero-Isaiah's predictions of a temple built by him could no longer be fulfilled.

42 Darius at Behistun, Persian, pars. 71–75 (col. V, lines 1–33).

43 Hag 1:9–11, 2:15–17, Zech 8:10.

44 In 2:23, Haggai undoes for Zerubbabel and his dynasty the doom pronounced upon his ancestor Coniah (= Jehoiachin) at Jer 22:24.

45 Another clue to this fact are the echoes of Isa 35:3–4 at Hag 2:4–5 and Zech 8:9, 13. Isaiah 35 is intended as the aftermath of the fall of the hated power (originally Babylon) in Isaiah 34. See chap 6, pp. 154–56.

46 See Albert Ten Eyck Olmstead, *History of the Persian Empire* (Chicago: University of Chicago Press, 1948), 136–42; E. and C. Meyers, *Haggai and Zechariah,* 352–53.

47 Kind treatment by Darius: Ezra 5–6. See also E. and C. Meyers, *Haggai and Zechariah,* 12–13, 370.

48 Zech 4:6b-10a intrudes between the prophet's confession, in v 5, of his ignorance of the meaning of the seven lights of the candelabrum and the angel's explanation of it in v 10b. See, e.g., David C. Peterson, *Haggai and Zechariah 1–8: A Commentary* (Philadelpnia: Westminster, 1984), 237–39. E. and C. Meyers (*Haggai and Zechariah,* 241–43, 265–73) have not succeeded in explaining away the incongruities.

If the passage is out of place, can we find an original context for it and explain why it stands where it does? There is a probable original setting. In 6:1–8, Zechariah sees four chariots, each drawn by a set of horses of different coloration, and is told that they are the four winds of heaven which go out after presenting themselves before the LORD. Thereupon, three wind-chariots go out to their normal stations, to the north, the west (read in 6:6 *'l 'hry hym* or *'l 'hwr* for *'l 'hryhm;* cf. E. and C. Meyers, *Haggai and Zechariah,* 325–26), and the south. By elimination, we may infer that the remaining wind-chariot is that of the east wind, *Qādīm,* the "Wind of the LORD" (see especially Isa 27:8b, Hos 13:15, and also Exod 10:13, 14:21, Isa 40:7, 59:19, Ezek 17:10, 19:12, Jonah 4:8, Ps 48:8), which helped destroy the Egyptians at the Red Sea (Exod 14:21). At first the horses of that chariot get permission from God to wander through the earth, but then God or the angel calls upon the prophet to notice that those horses have gone to the northland and have "deposited [or "stationed"] My Wind *(hēnīhū et rūhī)* in the northland."

Ancient versions and most modern translations take *hēnīhū et rūhī* as something like "they have appeased [or "satisfied"] my spirit" (cf. Ezek 5:13, 24:13). However, we have here a context dealing with winds, and the word in Hebrew for "spirit" is also the word for "wind," and the verb *hēnīḥū* can easily mean "set down," "deposit," or "station." At 2 Chr 1:14, 9:25, it is used of the stationing of military resources; see also Lev 16:23, Num 17:19, 19:9, Deut 26:4, 10, 1 Kgs 8:9, Ezek 37:1, 40:2, 44:19. E. and C. Meyers (*Haggai and Zechariah,* 316) do render *hēnīḥū* as "they have placed"!

In the text as we have it, Zechariah's vision of the four chariots ends with 6:8, and it is hard to see what the point of the vision could be (see E. and C. Meyers, *Haggai and Zechariah,* 330–31, 334–35). But perhaps originally there was more in the text. From the time of Jeremiah, believing Jews viewed the northland as the seat of Gentile imperial power, because the roads to Babylonia from Judah ran northward. From this prophetic perspective, Babylon and Persia, too, were in the northland. If God's destructive weapon, the east wind, now resided in the northland, and if Zechariah's message to Zerubbabel was "Do not use human force; God's Wind is in the process of destroying Gentile empires," how better could he express it than by saying, "Not by military might *(ḥyl)* nor by power, but by My Wind, says the LORD of Hosts" (Zech 4:6)? Zech 4:6–10a follows beautifully after 6:8. Furthermore, if the verse that originally followed 6:8 began with the same words as 4:6a, "He answered [or "spoke up"] and said to me as follows" *(wyʿn wyʾmr ʾly lʾmr),* one can easily understand how the eye of an ancient scribe in one of the commonest scribal errors leapt from 4:6 to the passage after 6:8 and mistakenly copied it after 4:5. We can also imagine that he perceived his error after reaching 4:10a and copied the passage he should have written after 4:5, but on reaching 6:8 he remembered he had already copied out what we now have in 4:6b–10a and skipped over the passage.

49 See pp. 94–95. The inference is reflected in Ezra 9, Neh 9:6–37, and Dan 9:2–20, especially in the sense of sin that pervades those passages. Cf. Frye, *History,* 114.

50 See Carey A. Moore, *Esther* ("Anchor Bible, vol. 7B; Garden City, NY: Doubleday, 1971), 3–4.

51 See Moore, *Esther,* xlv–xlvi; cf. Elias Bickerman, *Four Strange Books of the Bible* (New York: Schocken, 1967), 171–210.

52 See ibid., 178–80.

53 See my *II Maccabees,* 174–75. Against the view that Ezra 4:6 is evidence of a major catastrophe that befell the Jews, see also Widengren in Hayes-Miller, 525–26.

54 See n 31.

55 F. M. Th. de Liagre Böhl, "Die babylonischen Prätendenten zur Zeit des Xerxes," *Bibliotheca Orientalis* 19 (1962), 110a, 111b–113a. Böhl's article contains unfortunate slips and misprints. There is an urgent need for a fresh treatment of the two Babylonian rebel kings. One tablet dated under Shamash-erîba is an administrative text with no mention of where it was written (Mariano San Nicolò and Arthur Ungnad, *Neubaby-lonische Rechts- und Verwaltungsurkunden,* Vol. I [Leipzig: Hinrichs, 1935], no. 786). In a communication of April 30, 1990, Matthew Stolper wrote me, "The place might be deduced from the prosopography. One line refers to an item in Babylon; another has a personal name that might be from Dilbat. To all appearances, [the tablet was drawn up] somewhere in the north, but at which site is not certain from the contents." The latest published date of a document under Shamash-erîba is 29 Tashrîtu (Böhl, ibid., 113a; Arthur Ungnad, "Neubabylonische Privaturkunden aus der Sammlung Amherst," *Archiv für Orientforschung* 19 [1959–60], 76). I have heard that a slightly later date under Shamash-erîba was read on a tablet from Borsippa once owned by Lord Amherst of Hackney. The tablet has been sold, and its present location is unknown. The precise date upon it is for its present owner to publish.

56 Persons on documents dated by Bêl-shîmannî: A. Ungnad, "Bêl-sîmanni, Ein neuer König Babylons und der Länder," *Orientalistische Litteratur-Zeitung* [sic] 10 (1907), 466; on documents dated by Shamash-erîba: Ungnad, *Archiv für Orient-forschung* 19 (1959–60), 74–76.

57 George G. Cameron, "Darius and Xerxes," *AJSL* 58 (1941), 325.

58 On the imperial titles and the Assyrian antecedents, see the third paragraph below and n 63.

59 Cameron, *AJSL* 58 (1941), 319–23(line 1); Ungnad, *Archiv für Orientforschung* 19 (1959–60), 76.

60 Böhl, *Bibliotheca Orientalis* 19 (1962), 112.

61 M. San Nicolò, "Parerga Babylonica XIII-XIV," *Archiv Orientální* 6 (1933), 336; Böhl, *Bibliotheca Orientalis* 19 (1962), 111b–12a, but Böhl's dates must be corrected as above.

62 Böhl, *Bibliotheca Orientalis* 19 (1962), 110, refuting San Nicolò, "Parerga Bab-ylonica XIII–XIV," *Archiv Orientální* 6 (1933), 335–37.

63 For a time during 539 and 538, Cyrus bore only the title "King of the Lands"; see the second paragraph of this chapter. Earlier use of the title "King of the Lands": Tad-mor in *Shilton paras,* 11. His references, ibid., 254, n 53, contain errors. The examples are Letters 259–60, 274, 894, and 920 in Leroy Waterman, *Royal Correspondence of the Assyrian Empire,* Parts I-II (Ann Arbor: University of Michigan Press, 1930).

64 Cameron, "Darius and Xerxes," *AJSL* 58 (1941), 319–24; Böhl, *Bibliotheca Ori-entalis* 19 (1962), 110–11.

65   Oppenheim in CHI, II, 566.

66   Böhl, *Bibliotheca Orientalis* 19(1962), 111; Cameron, *AJSL* 58 (1941), 323–24.

67   Simonetta Graziani, *I Testi mesopotamici datati al regno di Serse (485–465 a. C.)* ("Istituto universitaria orientale—Napoli," supplemento n. 47 agli *Annali*—vol. 46 [1986], fasc. 2; Roma: Herder, 1986), nos. 71 (year 12) and 75 (year 14).

68   Graziani, no. 40 (year 5).

69   Graziani, no. 41 (year 5).

70   Graziani, nos. 67 (year 5), 69 (year 10), 72 (year 12).

71   Cf. Kuhrt and Sherwin-White in *Achaemenid History II, 72*–73; Matthew W. Stolper, *Entrepreneurs and Empire* (Leiden: Nederlands historisch-archaeologisch Instituut te Istanbul, 1985), 9, n 25. Böhl (*Bibliotheca Orientalis* 19 [1962], 113) used another argument to place Shamash-erîba's accession in Xerxes's fourth year. In the tablet he calls "Berlin Nr. 615" (i.e., Mariano San Nicolò and Arthur Ungnad, *Neubabylonische Rechts- und Verwaltungsurkunden,* Vol. I [Leipzig: Hinrichs, 1935], no. 615), a period of six months is defined as the time from Arakhshamnu, the eighth Babylonian month, of Shamash-erîba's accession year *adi ṣîtishu,* "until his outmarch." (If the reading just cited is correct, there might be a parallel text in Albert T. Clay, *Business Documents of Murashû Sons of Nippur Dated in the Reign of Darius II (424–404 B.C.)* ["The Babylonian Expedition of the University of Pennsylvania, Series A: Cuneiform Texts," Vol X; Philadelphia: Department of Archaeology and Palaeontology of the University of Pennsylvania, 1904], no. 1, lines 6–7, *sha a-di mukh-khi a-ṣi-e sharri.*) According to Böhl, "until his outmarch" must mean the king's trip to Borsippa during the *Akîtu,* which fell at the beginning of the month of Nisannu, the first of the Babylonian year. Only in an intercalary year with a second Addaru could six months elapse between Arakhshamnu and Nisannu, and the only such year in Xerxes's early reign was year 4. However, Böhl simply accepted San Nicolò's and Ungnad's reading of *adi ṣîtishu.* In a communication of April 23, 1990, Matthew Stolper informed me that the sign which Böhl read as *ṣi* looks more like *tup* in the autographed copy of the tablet (*Vorderasiatische Schriftendenkmäler der Königlichen Museen zu Berlin,* Vol. VI, ed. Arthur Ungnad [Leipzig: Hinrichs, 1908], no. 173). Furthermore, my search of the articles *aṣu* and *ṣîtu* in *CAD* reveals no support for Böhl's interpretation of *ṣîtishu.* Perhaps the king's march out to war is what is meant. That may usually have occurred in Ayyaru, the second month (see Babylonian Chronicles 3, lines 1, 16, 31, 58 [*ABC,* 91–95], and 5, obverse, line 21 [*ABC,* 100]; cf. 2 Sam 11:1 and 1 Chr 20:1, where the Hebrew cognate of *ṣîtu* occurs). The time from Arakhshamnu to Ayyaru is six months in non-intercalary years.

72   Tablet BM 35526, collated for me by Irving Finkel of the British Museum.

73   Graziani, nos. 71–73.

74   Graziani, nos. 47–56.

75   Graziani, nos. 61, 76–77.

76   Graziani, no. 79.

77   Graziani, nos. 28–30. In a letter of Feb. 8, 1990, Matthew Stolper writes that he knows of no documents of Xerxes's third year dated within the months and days attested for Shamash-erîba.

78   See J.M. Cook in CHI, II, 205–6, and *Persian Empire,* 21–22.

79   Cf. Ilya Gershevitch, "False Smerdis," *Acta Antiqua* 17 (1979), 345–46; Frye, *History,* 84; Olmstead, *Persian Empire,* 380; George G. Cameron, "The Persian Satrapies and Related Matters," *JNES* 32 (1973), 55–56.

80   FGH 688, F 13.25

81   Ibid.

82   Greek: *proteron.*

83   Greek: *idein.*

84   Below I shall treat the cryptic references to Belitanas and to the inscription.

85   Herodotus iii.150–160; see p. 171.

86   W. W. How and J. Wells, *A Commentary on Herodotus* (2 vols.; Oxford: Clarendon Press, 1912), II, 144–45; Andrew Robert Burn, *Persia and the Greeks* (2d ed.; London: Duckworth, 1984), 317.

87   Herodotus ix.101–8.

88   Cf. Walter Baumgartner, "Herodots babylonische und assyrische Nachrichten," *Archiv Orientální* 18 (1950), 100.

89   Plutarch: see n 134; Arrian Anabasis vii.17.1–2.

90   See below, pp. 187–90.

91   Herodotus vii.20.

92   Herodotus vii.7; T. Cuyler Young, Jr., "The Consolidation of the Empire and Its Limits of Growth under Darius and Xerxes," chap 2 of CAH², IV: *Persia, Greece and the Western Mediterranean, c. 525 to 479 B.C.* (1988), 73.

93   See n 63.

94   See Kent, *Old Persian,* 112. Kent's Old Persian text and English translation are there on 150–52. For the texts in all three languages and a German translation, see Ernst Herzfeld, *Altpersische Inschriften* (Berlin: Reimer, 1938), no. 14, 17–35. Oppenheim's English translation of the Babylonian text is at *ANET,* 316–17.

95   Based on Kent's translation of the Old Persian.

96   In the final prepositional phrase I follow Martin Schwartz, "The Religion of Achaemenian Iran," chap 14 of CHI, II, 689.

97   However, in the next translated paragraph, corresponding to "[a place]" and "that sanctuary," the Babylonian, too, has the singular, contrary to the assertion of Hans Hartmann, "Zur neuen Inschrift des Xerxes von Persepolis," *Orientalistische Literaturzeitung* 40 (1937), 159, and to the translations of both Herzfeld (34) and Oppenheim (*ANET,* 317).

98   Schwartz, CHI, II, 689.

99   E.g., Hartmann, *Orientalistische Literaturzeitung* 40 (1937), 158–59; Henrik S. Nyberg, *Die Religionen des alten Iran* (Leipzig: Hinrichs, 1938), 364–66; Geo Widengren, *Die Religionen Irans* (Stuttgart: Kohlhammer, 1965), 138; É. Duchesne-Guillemin, "Die Religion der Achämeniden," *Acta Antiqua* 19 (1971), 27.

100   E.g., Ugo Bianchi, "L'Inscription 'des daivas' et le Zoroastrisme des Achéménides," *Revue de l'histoire des religions* 192 (1977), 12–16; Boyce, HZ, II, 174–75; Schwartz, CHI, II, 690–91, states both views without taking sides.

101   vii.1.3.

102   vii.7.

103   Herodotus's informant probably reckoned Xerxes's accession year as the first year, and his first regnal year as the second.

104 Olmstead, *Persian Empire,* 215.

105 Cf. the treatment of the Jews and Jerusalem by Antiochus IV as analyzed in my *I Maccabees,* 122–59, and my *II Maccabees,* 89–112. One could also cite the parallels of the destructions of the temples of Jerusalem by Nebuchadnezzar and Vespasian.

106 Cf. Schwartz, CHI, II, 690, last paragraph.

107 Böhl, *Bibliotheca Orientalis* 19 (1962), 112.

108 The destruction of the walls of Babylon in the reign of Darius reported at Herodotus iii.159 probably belongs to the reign of Xerxes. See n 88. Even later, Herodotus, writing in the reign of Artaxerxes I (465/4–425), reports the existence of Babylon's double circuit of walls (i. 181.1).

109 Cf. the behavior of the Jews of Jerusalem described in my *I Maccabees,* 122, 208.

110 See pp. 69–70.

111 See n 97.

112 Below, pp. 187–90.

113 Cf. the procedure of Antiochus IV against the Jews when he believed that their religion had driven them to be rebels, as analyzed in my *I Maccabees,* 122–25 and my *II Maccabees,* 89–112. Antiochus's persecution of the Jews then provoked a Jewish revolt.

114 Bianchi, *Revue de l' histoire des religions* 192 (1977), 12–14; cf. Boyce, HZ, II, 175.

115 Nyberg, *Religionen,* 366; Widengren, *Religionen,* 138.

116 *Revue de l' histoire des religions* 192 (1977), 12.

117 Ibid., 14–15.

118 HZ, II, 174–75.

119 See n 132 and Herodotus i.181.3–5; Friedrich Wetzel and F. H. Weissbach, *Das Hauptheiligtum des Marduk in Babylon, Esagila und Etemenanki* (Leipzig: Hinrichs, 1938), 81–82.

120   Herodotus i.131.2, where Persian "Zeus" is Ahuramazda; Boyce, HZ, II, 179–80, esp. n 10.

121   Herodotus i.4.3–4, 95, 130; Ktesias, FGH 688, F 1.2, F 5–7 (= Diodorus ii.2, 32.5–34.6).

122   See chap 6, n 10. Heleen Sancisi-Weerdenburg ("Was There Ever a Median Empire?" in *Achaemenid History III: Method and Theory,* ed. Amélie Kuhrt and Heleen Sancisi-Weerdenburg [Leiden: Nederlands Instituut voor het Nabije Oosten, 1988], 197–212) has cast grave doubts on the institutional solidity of the Median Empire and on the accuracy of Herodotus's account of it. In fact, there are practically no sources on the presence or absence of institutional solidity in the Median Empire. Sancisi-Weerdenburg might, however, have taken note of Jer 51:28 (cf. Jer 25:25 and 51:11), which bears witness that Media was a "kingdom of kings" with a structure of subordinate officials. Whatever its structure, Media was powerful, as is attested not only by Nebuchadnezzar's apprehensions and by Herodotus but also by a variety of Greek and non-Greek witnesses. There is the Greek expression "Medize" for siding with the great power to the east. There are the expectations of Jeremiah and the reviser (see chap 4, p. 84) of Isa 13:17, that Babylon would fall to the Medes. On Nabonidus's fear of the Medes, see pp. 122–23. The Three-Beast Version of Daniel 7 is a Babylonian witness that in the fifth century B.C.E. Babylonians remembered a great Median Empire, contemporary with the Neo-Babylonian; see chap 8, pp. 237–44. See also M. A. Dandamayev, Review of *Achaemenid History,* Vols. I-III, in *Bibliotheca Orientalis* 46 (1989), 678.

123   Pp. 181–82.

124   See Johann Jakob Stamm, *Die akkadische Namengebung* (Leipzig, 1939; reprinted, Darmstadt: Wissenschaftliche Buchgesellschaft, 1968), 138.

125   See Mau, "Einbalsamierung," *RE,* V (1905), 2113–14. Persians are known to have embedded corpses in wax (Herodotus i.140) and Babylonians to have buried them in honey (ibid., chap 198). Olive oil is not mentioned at Homer Odyssey xxiv.71–73 or at Herodotus ii.87, and in neither text is the oil *(aleiphar)* used as an embalming fluid in which the unburnt corpse is immersed.

126   Kent, *Old Persian,* 178, 208.

127   xvi.1.5(738); cf. Diodorus xvii.112.3.

128   See Wetzel and Weissbach, *Hauptheiligtum,* 14–56, 79–85, and Henri Frankfort, *Kingship and the Gods* (Chicago: University of Chicago Press, 1948), 322–23.

129   E.g., M. A. Dandamayev, "Babylonia I. History of Babylonia in the Median and Achaemenid Periods," *Encyclopaedia Iranica,* III (1989), 329b.

130 E.g., Boyce, HZ, II, 164; Olmstead, *Persian Empire,* 237; Schwartz, CHI, II, 690; Oppenheim, ibid., 566, n 1, accepts the faulty interpretation, though he holds the report to be false.

131 See Sherwin-White in *Achaemenid History* II, 71–72.

132 Arrian iii.16.4, vii.17.2. In Babylonian documents nothing suggests that Xerxes damaged Esagila in any way. Babylonian evidence does show that Esagila was in disrepair in the times of Alexander and his successors (Babylonian Chronicle 10, Obverse, line 6, and Reverse, lines 13, 33 [*ABC,* 116–18; see also Grayson's commentary there]), but also that Marduk's priests were able to function in the temple. See Matthew W. Stolper, "The Governor of Babylon and Across-the-River in 486 B.C.," *JNES* 48 [1989], 294–96; *Entrepreneurs and Empire,* 9, n 24. Amélie Kuhrt (CAH2, IV, 133) is wrong in saying that the references in classical authors to Xerxes's destructive acts in Babylon are all due to misunderstanding the report at Herodotus i.183.3 of his removal of a colossal statue. Modern authors were guilty of such misunderstanding, but nothing shows that the ancient writers misconstrued mere removal of a statue as a destruction of temples. Under our interpretations, Xerxes himself and Aelianus's version of Ktesias testify to a destructive act of Xerxes. Such a punishment for religiously inspired rebellion is just what one would expect in an ancient empire.

133 Ktesias: FGH 688 F 1.9.4–9 (= Diodorus ii.9.4–9). How writers of the time of Alexander could have transmitted erroneous information: cf. A. B. Bosworth, *A Historical Commentary on Arrian's History of Alexander* (Oxford: Clarendon Press, 1980–), I, 314). Beyond the effects of mere neglect, the ziggurat may have suffered when irreverent Babylonians quarried its bricks. Cf. Wetzel and Weissbach, *Hauptheiligtum,* 79–80.

134 Plutarch, *Regum et imperatorum apophthegmata (= Sayings of Kings and Commanders)* 173c.

135 Herodotus i.183.2–3.

136 Evidence and argument for: Herodotus iii.159 (if the events belong, not to the reign of Darius, but to that of Xerxes); Olmstead, *Persian Empire,* 237, 293; Oppenheim in CHI, II, 565–67. Argument against: Kuhrt in CAH², IV, 135–38.

137 Ktesias, FGH 688, F 13.33–14.35; Olmstead, *Persian Empire,* 289; Cook, *Persian Empire,* 127.

~8~

Daniel 1–7 and Other Texts
of the Babylonians and the
Jews, 538–464 B.C.E.

1. Babylonian Responses to Deutero-Isaiah's Challenges

D EUTERO-ISAIAH LETS US KNOW that at first his challenges to the pagans went unanswered.[1] No pagan people, including the Babylonians, could show that its deity and its prognosticators had predicted the fall of Babylon to Cyrus. But Babylonians eventually made that very claim for Nebuchadnezzar II, possessed by some god of the city. The Greek writer Abydenos, surely drawing on the Babylonian historian Berossus, preserves[2] the following story:

> Thereafter,[3] it is said by the Chaldaeans, as Nebuchadnezzar went up to the palace, he was possessed by some god and spoke loudly the following words, "I, Nebuchadnezzar, predict to you, O Babylonians, that a disaster is coming which neither my ancestor Bêl nor his queen Bêltis can persuade the fates to avert. A Persian mule shall come, using as allies your own deities. He shall bring on slavery. To blame for that might be[4] a *Mêdês,*[5] the Assyrian boast. Would that before he . . . my countrymen, a whirlpool or a sea took him and utterly destroyed him, or would that he turned to other roads and was borne along through the desert, where there are no towns and no paths trodden by men but beasts have their habitation and birds rove, and would that he wandered banished and alone among crags and torrents; would that before these thoughts came into my mind, I had met with a better end." Upon uttering this prophecy, Nebuchadnezzar immediately vanished, and his son, Awêl-Marduk, became king.

In Greek, as in biblical Aramaic, "Chaldaean" means "Babylonian astrologer."[6] Here we may assume that the astrologers were priests of Marduk. I have put ellipsis dots at the point where the text is corrupt. It has, inappropriately, the commonplace verb *dounai,* which here would be translated "gave." The context would require something like *doulôsai* ("enslaved"), or, taking "my countrymen" as subject of a passive verb rather than as object of an active one, something like *doulôthênai* ("were enslaved") or *damênai* ("were subdued"). The "Persian mule" is a clear allusion to Cyrus, who conquered Babylon and reportedly had a Persian father and a Median mother.[7]

But who is the *Mêdês* who might be to blame? Is he a Mede? One could suggest that Astyages, the last Median king and reputedly the grandfather of Cyrus, was to blame for failing to suppress the young Persian king, his own vassal. From Babylonian Chronicle 7, we learn that Ugbaru, the governor of Gutium, was at the head of Cyrus's army that captured Babylon. "Gutium" in Babylonian texts of the first millennium B.C.E. is a vague geographical and directional term, usually referring to the east, but sometimes to the north.[8] Both Media and Assyria are north of Babylon, and scholars have identified "Gutium" in Chronicle 7 with one or the other.[9]

"Ugbaru" has been taken as equivalent to "Gubaru," and "Gubaru" in Greek transcription is "Gobryas." "Gobryas" is a Persian, not a Median name.[10] Even though the subjects of the Persians frequently called them "Medes," in this context the mule is Persian, and, if the one to blame was Persian, he, too, should receive that ethnic designation. But even if "Mede" is the correct reading and refers to Astyages or Gobryas, and even if Gobryas's "Gutium" was Assyria, we still have no explanation for "the Assyrian boast." We may be sure that Greek readers of Herodotus and Ktesias knew no more explanation than we—an indication that the story is authentically Babylonian, not an invention of Greeks.

Indeed, we can be confident that Babylonians fabricated the tale long after Deutero-Isaiah spoke and that during Cyrus's reign no Babylonian knew of Nebuchadnezzar's "prophecy." The pronouncement is vehemently anti-Persian, speaking of Cyrus's reign as a disaster that imposed slavery on Babylonia. Marduk's priests gladly collaborated with Cyrus and wrote propaganda speaking of him as savior of Babylonia. Nothing indicates that Babylonians were disaffected in the early reign of Cambyses. The story cannot have arisen before 525 and the discontent provoked by Cambyses's expensive warfare, and perhaps not until the strife that followed Cambyses's death in 522. The tale also exhibits a striking loss of faith in Marduk's omnipotence: The "fates" can act against his will, and he cannot persuade them to avert the evil coming upon

Babylon. But Marduk's faithful faced Deutero-Isaiah's challenges already in 539. They can hardly have waited until 525 to present a reply in an effort to maintain their faith unimpaired. Surprisingly, in the biblical book of Daniel there is strong evidence showing that Marduk's priests long before 525 came up with a record of a spectacular "prophecy," by a Babylonian, of the fall of Nabonidus.

2. Strange Features of Daniel 1–7 as a Whole

THE WRITERS OF THE FINAL VERSION of the book of Daniel were all pious Jews, strongly convinced of the righteousness of what they were doing. That fact does not prove that they were infallible or inspired. There are many strange aspects to what they preserved and presented in Daniel. We shall find those aspects converging to show that Daniel 2–7 is based upon Babylonian originals with surprisingly few alterations, whereas chap 1 is later than chaps 2–6 and was created by Jews. Let us examine the oddities of chaps 1–7 of Daniel.

Ethnically, Nabopolassar and his dynasty were Chaldaeans. At Dan 2:4, it is taken for granted that Chaldaeans speak Aramaic. By the time of Nebuchadnezzar, Aramaic-speakers were a large part of the population of Babylon. Probably Aramaic was already the chief vernacular of the city.[11] If Jews were the original writers of Daniel 2–7 and wrote for Jews, why are those chapters in Babylonian Aramaic,[12] not in Hebrew? The fact is all the stranger since Daniel 1, 8–12 are in Hebrew.[13]

Daniel 2–7 strongly resembles recognized Babylonian literary genres. Chapters 2 and 7 contain present-future prophecy, a type also attested for Jews, but we have seen[14] that the Jewish examples that have any claim to be preexilic or exilic differ significantly, in their relative lack of specificity, from Daniel 2 and 7 and from the Babylonian specimens. The narratives of Daniel 3–6 are heavily poetic in flavor,[15] even if, as we have them, they can be viewed as prose. Dan 3:1–30, 5, and 6 report, in the third person, how kings came to regret insults to a god and attempts to injure his worshipers. Dan 3:31–4:34 is a narrative in the first person on how the Exalted God taught Nebuchadnezzar to humble himself. We should recognize immediately the traits of Babylonian historical epics in Dan 3:1–30, 5, and 6 and those of a Babylonian moralizing narrative in the first person in 3:31–4:34.

Some badly mutilated fragments of a scroll found at Qumran preserve what was originally another piece of an analogue of Babylonian moralizing narratives in the first person. The piece is in Aramaic and is now called "4Q Prayer of Nabonidus."[16] One can restore some of what is missing on the basis of context and of the characteristic repetitiousness of biblical Hebrew and Aramaic narratives. To go beyond that is hazardous. Here is a translation of what is readable, with the probable restorations in brackets:

1. The words of the prayer which Nabonidus, king[. . .]
2. with grievous leprosy by the decree of God in Teman[. . .]
3. was stricken for seven years, and from the time that I was like[. . .]
4. And, as for my sin, he forgave it. A diviner, who was a Jew from[. . .]
5. "Compose a narrative and write in order to confer honor and greatness on the name of G[od . . ."]
6. I was stricken with grievous leprosy in Teman [by the decree of God . . .]
7. for seven years I was praying to gods of silver and gold, [bronze, iron,]
8. wood, stone, clay, because I [thought] that [they were] gods.[. . .]

The king's name appears in shortened form, as *nbny* ("Nabunay"). In Aramaic, names are frequently shortened in this manner so as to leave a mere fragment of a root before the "hypocoristic" ending *ay*.[17] But in Babylonian shortened names ("hypocoristics"), elements that are entire words are omitted, and never does a mere fragment of a root precede the hypocoristic ending, *-â* or *-ia*. Tēmān in the Hebrew Bible is a descendant of Esau or a region of Edom, and is distinct from Tēmā, a descendant of Ishmael and a region of Arabia, but Tēmān is mentioned fifteen times and Tēmā only five, so it is not surprising if a Jewish author or scribe substituted the former for the latter. The name of the Jewish diviner does not survive. It may or may not have been Daniel or Belteshazzar. In line 5 we must have the words of the Jewish diviner. In lines 6–8 the king again speaks. The stress, that the king's gods consist of inert raw materials, is typically Jewish.[18]

The following three sentences are true of Nabonidus. (1) He was a fanatic who set up an image of his god despite opposition and imposed his religious views upon his subjects on pain of death.[19] (2) He abandoned his capital city for so long a period that hostile subjects circulated reports that he was mad or diseased.[20] (3) His son was Belshazzar (= Bêl-shar-uṣur).[21] Babylonian records render it absolutely impossible that the same three sentences fit Nebuchadnezzar II. Even some Jews knew that the "diseased" king who abandoned his capital for years was Nabonidus.[22] Yet Dan 3:1–30 presents Nebuchadnezzar II as a fanatic who set up a great image in Babylonia and demanded of his subjects, on pain of death, that they worship it. Daniel 4 presents him as a king who became a demented animal and abandoned his capital for seven years; Daniel 5 presents Belshazzar as the son of Nebuchadnezzar. Surely somehow in Daniel 3–5 traits of Nabonidus have been transferred to Nebuchadnezzar!

Dan 1:7 tells the reader that "Belteshazzar," "Shadrach," "Meshach," and "Abednego" were names that Ashpenaz, Nebuchadnezzar's chief eunuch, gave to the Israelite boys, Daniel, Hananiah, Mishael, and Azariah. Surely, then, the names are Babylonian. Indeed, in the stories of the book, Babylonians use those names to speak of Daniel and his friends and to address them (Dan 3:12–14, 20, 26a, 28, 29; 4:5–6, 16[19], 5:12). Here there are two anomalies:

1. After Pharaoh gave Joseph an Egyptian name (Gen 41:45), the narrative of Genesis, written by and for Israelites, goes on using the name "Joseph," never again employing the Egyptian name. But the narrative of Daniel thereafter usually calls Daniel's three friends by their "Babylonian" names, even when a Babylonian is not the speaker (2:29, 3:16, 19, 22, 23, 26b, 30; exceptions: 1:19, 2:17), and frequently employs even Daniel's "foreign" name.

2. Thousands of Babylonian clay tablets have been found containing names of persons, but not one mentions a Shadrach, Meshach, Abednego, or Belteshazzar. No satisfactory etymology has as yet been suggested for "Shadrach" and "Meshach."[23] Some commentators have suggested, rightly, that the Jewish writers of our text of Daniel have deliberately deformed Babylonian names.[24] The fact is quite transparent in the case of "Abednego," a deformation of *'Abed-Nabû* ("slave of Nabû").[25] Jews tended to deform personal names if they contained the names of "idols." They did so in obedience to Exod 23:13, "You shall not mention the names of other gods; it shall not be heard from your mouth." The writer of 1–2 Samuel so deformed Israelite names containing the divine name *Ba'al,* substituting for it *bōshet* ("shame"), because (like Hosea in 2:18) he took the word to be the name of a pagan deity.[26] The Tosefta attests later Jewish deformations of idolatrous placenames.[27]

The fact of this Jewish tendency and the characteristics of the Aramaic alphabet lead to easy explanations of the Babylonian names of Daniel and his friends, explanations partially confirmed by their alleged Hebrew equivalents. "Shadrach" and "Meshach" in Aramaic both end in *k*. The conspicuous divine name that ends in *k* is "Marduk." "Shadrach" contains the two letters *d* and *r,* which in the Aramaic script of the times were identical or almost so. Surely the original order of the letters in the name was *rd* as in "Marduk." The *m* of "Marduk" has been omitted, probably as a deliberate mutilation of the pagan divine name.

The Babylonian syllable *sha* means "of" or "the one of" or "the one who." Several classes of Babylonian names begin with *sha-* followed by the name of a deity.[28] According to the book of Daniel, the Hebrew equivalent was "Hananiah" ("The LORD graciously gave [him to his parents]"). The alleged equivalent suggests that the unmutilated Babylonian name was Sha-Marduk ("Marduk's [boy]" or "Marduk's [man]") or Sha-Marduk-shu ("He is Marduk's). "Sha-Marduk" is closest to "Shadrach," but the systematic studies of Babylonian names[29] do not mention as a Babylonian name type *"sha* followed by the bare name of a god." Perhaps they overlooked it because, to my knowledge, only one example has been found, but for our purposes, one example is enough, especially since it is precisely the name "Sha-Marduk."[30] The alternative, "Sha-Marduk-shu," is of a type well attested in the sixth and fifth centuries B.C.E., but, to my knowledge, no example has been found of such a name with Marduk as the deity.[31] In Daniel, the final pronoun, shu, is missing from the name, but we could guess that Jews omitted the pronoun to avoid uttering a sentence that said the name-bearer belonged to a false god, even one whose name was mutilated.

This solution for "Shadrach" points the way toward solving the puzzle of "Meshach." That name, too, ends in *k,* and we are entitled to assume that all three of the first letters of Marduk's name have here been deliberately omitted.[32] The alleged Hebrew equivalent, Mishael, probably is a phonetic variant of *Misha' 'el* ("God is Salvation").[33] This fact, along with the *m* and the *sh* at the head of the name, leads us quickly to the very common Babylonian name, Mushêzib-Marduk ("Marduk is Savior").[34] The epithet *mushêzib* could hardly have been unfamiliar to readers of the Aramaic of Daniel, because the word came into Aramaic and occurs at Dan 6:28. *Mushêzib* was probably mutilated deliberately to *Mish-* in order to avoid letting the name say that a being (even one whose name was mutilated) was savior, other than the LORD.[35]

Daniel's name, Belteshazzar, is much less puzzling. Its consonants are readable as *blts'sr, balâṭsu-uṣur* ("preserve his life!"). Here mutilation has removed the divine name that stood at the beginning, surely *Bêl* ("lord"), the epithet of Marduk, so that the name originally meant "Bêl, preserve his life!"[36]

Having solved the puzzle of the names, we are left with a strange fact: The Babylonian names of the pious Israelites, Daniel and his friends, express piety to Marduk and Nabû, the supreme deities of Babylon!

Also odd is the way the text of Daniel 1–5 insists repetitiously that Belteshazzar is Daniel (1:7, 2:26, 4:5[8], 16[19], 5:12). One would have thought that the introductory notice at 1:7 was sufficient. In a similarly repetitious manner, the text of Daniel 7 insists that the author is Daniel (7:1, 2, 15, 25). Who needed so many reminders? Should we not assume that the characters in the chapters originally bore only the Babylonian names?

A King Darius the Mede in chap 6 could be expected to use Iranian vocabulary. But the tales in Daniel 1–5 and the vision in Daniel 7 purport to be set in the Babylon of Nebuchadnezzar and Belshazzar, and the account in 3:31–4:34 poses as a work of Nebuchadnezzar himself. Those chapters contain so many Persian words as to arouse suspicion. Officials bear Persian titles! [37] Even in the last months of the reign of Nabonidus so much Persian influence on Babylonia would have been surprising.

Jews, in adopting Babylonian stories as their own, could have added some Jewish flavor to the wording. In fact, however, there is surprisingly little that is unambiguously Jewish. One could expect Jews to use their own characteristic ways of referring to their God, even when quoting pagan characters. Striking in Daniel 2–7 is the complete absence both of *YHWH* ("Lord"), the proper name of the God of Israel, and of its substitute, *'ădōnāy* ("Lord"). Elsewhere in the biblical narratives, except in Esther,[38] both Israelites and pagans freely use the proper name.[39] The absence of the other most usual appellation for the God of Israel, *'Ělohim* ("God") might be ascribed to its being an idiomatic Hebrew common noun, a plural of majesty, whereas chaps 2–7 are in Aramaic, where plurals of majesty were less common. The word for "god" in these chapters is *'ĕlāh,* the singular of the Aramaic cognate, here used without any accompanying divine name. The Hebrew singular *'ĕlōāh* similarly occurs without a divine name in the Bible,[40] but *ilu* ("god"), too, occurs in Babylonian texts referring to a specific but not named deity.[41]

Epithets that Jews used of their God, Babylonians employed of Marduk and Sîn. "The god of the gods"[42] is an expression that befits polytheists and in Daniel comes appropriately from the mouth of a pagan king, though Moses uses it in Deuteronomy. Likewise attested both in the Bible and in Babylonian texts are expressions like "the god of my fathers,"[43] "the god of Daniel [or of some other named person or persons],"[44] "god" with a possessive adjective,[45] "the god of heaven,"[46] and "a god in heaven."[47] The same is true of "exalted god" or "most high god"; even if translators are correct in rendering Hebrew and Aramaic *'elyōn* and Aramaic *'ilāyā* and *'ilā'āh,* used as nouns, as "the supreme one" or "the most high" rather than "the exalted one" or "the lofty one," the expression befits polytheists at least as well as monotheistic Jews, and good evidence shows that Jews adopted those epithets from pagans.[48] One should not be surprised to find Daniel speaking of *"a* great God"; the expression is indeed used in the Hebrew Bible for the God of the Jews.[49] "King of Heaven" (Dan 4:34) is found nowhere else in the Hebrew Bible[50] but is attested in Babylonian.[51] "Lord of Heaven" (Dan 5:23), too, does not occur elsewhere in biblical Hebrew or Aramaic but is attested in Babylonian.[52] The epithet "Lord of Kingdoms" (or "Lord of Kings") is found in the Hebrew Bible only at Dan 2:47; it is attested in Phoenician, Aramaic, and in Ptolemaic and Seleucid texts.[53]

"He who lives forever" (Dan 4:31) may be a Jewish epithet,[54] but Babylonians, too, viewed immortality as an attribute of deity.[55] As Jews took oaths saying "As the LORD lives," so Babylonians swore "By the life of Nabû."[56] Marduk was the lord of life.[57] "Heaven" at Dan 4:23 may be the earliest occurrence of the use of that word as a substitute for "God," so common in I Maccabees, the New Testament, and rabbinic literature. Nevertheless, Babylonians knew of the power of Anu, god of the sky, and believed it had been vested in Marduk;[58] if Marduk ruled, Heaven ruled. Clearly the divine names and epithets contain few if any Jewish touches. Other examples of possible Jewish flavoring are better considered when we examine the chapters one by one. Let us proceed to do so, in two stages. First, we shall present the anomalous features of each chapter. Later, we shall construct hypotheses that turn the supposed anomalies into rational procedures of propagandists.

3. Daniel 1

THE VERY BEGINNING of the book clashes with known facts. It asserts (1:1–4) that Nebuchadnezzar, *king* of Babylon, besieged and took Jerusalem in the *third* year of King Jehoiakim of Judah and carried off to Babylonia ("the land of Shinar") some of the *temple vessels*[59] and noble Israelite *children*. The editor of Jer 25:1 equates the accession year or perhaps the first year of Nebuchadnezzar[60] with the *fourth* year of Jehoiakim. There is a problem in giving absolute dates for events under the last three kings of Judah: The sources do not give us enough evidence to decide conclusively how the regnal years of those kings were reckoned by the biblical writers.[61] But no matter how the years were reckoned, one can show that there is no room in history for what is reported at Dan 1:1–2.

The last kings of Judah in designating their years used an "accession-year" system, similar to that employed in Babylon.[62] It is still uncertain whether those kings of Judah counted their regnal years from the beginning of the month of the vernal equinox (called "Nisan" by Jews who adopted the Babylonian month-names) or from the beginning of the month of the autumnal equinox (called "Tishri" by those Jews).[63] Jehoiakim became king some three months after the death of his father, Josiah,[64] and Josiah was killed in the month of Sivan (May-June) 609 B.C.E.[65] If the kings counted from Nisan, Jehoiakim's accession year ran from late summer or early autumn 609, to Nisan 608, and his third year was 606/5. If they counted from Tishri, and if Jehoiakim became king before 1 Tishri, his accession year ran for a few days in late summer 609, and his third year was 607/6; if they counted from Tishri and if he became king after 1 Tishri, his accession year ran from Tishri 609, and ended with the coming of the next Tishri, and his third year was 606/5.

Babylonian records show that Nebuchadnezzar did not become king until 1 Ululu (Sept. 7) 605, though he was active beforehand as crown prince *(mâr sharri)*. The detailed Babylonian Chronicle renders it impossible that he could have besieged and taken Jerusalem in 607 or 606.[66] The Babylonian chronicler does report[67] that Nebuchadnezzar in his accession year (1 Ululu 605 to end Addaru 604) marched about victoriously[68] (or unopposed[69]) in Khattu (i.e., in the area of Syria and Palestine). Apart from the extreme unlikelihood that Nebuchadnezzar could have reached Jerusalem, besieged it, and taken it in the days between his assumption of the kingship on 1 Ululu and 1 Tishri, that report, too, excludes a victorious siege of Jerusalem and conspicuous plundering in Jehoiakim's third year, because the Babylonian chroniclers carefully told of sieges and important acts of looting.

Furthermore, the author of the book of Kings took care to note every instance wherein Israelites or temple vessels were carried off into exile. For him they were proof that the LORD was furious with His people. The author certainly regarded Jehoiakim as a provoker of divine wrath (2 Kgs 23:37)! There was another incentive for the author of Kings to record the carrying off of property and noble children from Judah, if that had occurred in the reign of Jehoiakim: It would have been a partial fulfillment of the prophecy of Isaiah which had been carefully recorded at 2 Kgs 20:16–18. Yet, despite those incentives, the narrative of 2 Kgs 23:34–24:6 contains no report of such events in the reign of Jehoiakim (2 Kgs 23:34–24:6). Jeremiah was in Jerusalem at the time, yet he says nothing of Jerusalem falling to siege in the king's third year. But if that event truly occurred, surely people of Judah would have asked Jeremiah why the LORD was so angry, and the "facts" of Dan 1:1–4 would have been reflected in the prophet's book.

Worse, there is a contradiction within the narrative itself of Daniel 1–2! Daniel, Hananiah, Mishael, and Azariah are said to have been carried off from Jerusalem by King Nebuchadnezzar in the third year of Jehoiakim (1:1–4, 6). Thereupon the king has them go through a three-year course of study, and they are said to have completed it (1:5, 18). The story implies that only thereafter, in Nebuchadnezzar's *second* year, did Nebuchadnezzar have the dream which Daniel was to interpret (2:1). Even if Nebuchadnezzar captured Jerusalem early in his accession year, which began in September, a completed course of three years would put any later events not in the king's second year but in his third at the earliest! Jews in antiquity were aware of the biblical inconsistencies and tried to solve them by giving special meanings to the chronological data of Dan 1:1 and 2:1,[70] a procedure justifiable only for those to whom it is axiomatic that the narrative is true.

4. Daniel 2

THE STORY OF NEBUCHADNEZZAR'S DREAM fits the historical Nebuchadnezzar. The writer has not given him the traits of Nabonidus, who so often dared to be his own omen- and dream-interpreter instead of turning to experts.[71] Nebuchadnezzar here is portrayed as pious, if a bit cruel and extreme in his demands on prognosticators. The plot and wording seem to echo Gen 41:1–44.[72] Even the worship[73] Nebuchadnezzar accords Daniel points to a Jewish writer, who in 2:46–47 was reporting fulfillment of Isa 45:14. But nowhere in the Hebrew Bible is there a parallel feat of mindreading, nor even a parallel revelation of a hidden fact to a seer who prayed for that.[74] Such prayers and revelations are characteristic of Babylonia and especially of Nabonidus.[75]

Daniel's prayer of thanksgiving for divine enlightenment (2:20–23) might seem to follow Jewish patterns, but Babylonian parallels are abundant.[76]

An idol-worshiping Babylonian king could well dream of a colossal statue, but would the image-hating God of the Jews send a dream in the shape of an idol, even one destined to be smashed by the stone? Furthermore, the imagery of the dream is inappropriate for "Daniel's" interpretation of it. The successive kingdoms are supposed to destroy and replace their predecessors. How then can they be represented by the levels of a single statue? One might have expected, rather, a row of statues each of which toppled its predecessor like a row of dominoes.

The interpretation of a symbolic vision should explain all features of it and only those features. When we compare the details of Daniel's interpretation of the dream in vv 37–45 with the supposedly accurate description of it in vv 31–35, we find strange discrepancies. Daniel's interpretation introduces matter that was not symbolized in the description and matter that was not in the description at all.

In the dream, the statue has five levels: (1) head of gold, (2) breast and arms of silver, (3) belly and hips of bronze, (4) thighs of iron, and (5) [lower] legs partly of iron, partly of "clay." In fact, the Aramaic word *(ḥsp)* properly means "earthenware," "baked clay," not "moist, moldable clay."[77] The feet of the statue, if made even partly of moldable clay, might well have collapsed under the weight of the heavier upper levels, made of metal. If the stone *pulverized* the statue (v 35), surely no part of the image consisted of plastic clay! We shall find that even a later supplementer of the prophecy in Daniel 2 intended to speak of earthenware, but the text as we have it in vv 41 and 43 (products of the latest supplementer) clearly speaks of moist clay. "Clay" is said to be brittle in v 42 but is called miry in vv 41 and 43. In such a situation, it is best to translate *ḥsp* by the ambiguous word, "clay."

In his interpretation (vv 37–40) Daniel assigns ordinal numerals only to the first four levels. In v 41, he assigns no numeral to the partly iron, partly clay legs and goes on in vv 41–42 to divide that level into legs and toes, though toes were not mentioned in his description of the dream. Though in the interpretation the third kingdom is to "rule the whole world," nothing in the vision symbolizes the fact. Rather, that kingdom is represented by the base metal, bronze, and by the inglorious belly and hips. Iron can symbolize the strength of the fourth kingdom, but even Daniel does not say the king saw the thighs of the statue smash its upper levels! Some ancient metal statues are known to have had earthenware cores in their legs,[78] and their legs thus were indeed partly metal, partly clay, but the text itself admits that iron never *mixes* with clay. The description of the statue contains no mention of such unnatural mixture, yet it receives prominent mention in vv 41 and 43!

Furthermore, Daniel's interpretation in vv 37–38 has the golden head symbolize Nebuchadnezzar alone, a king *(mlk),* and contains nothing to reflect his four Babylonian successors. Though the other levels of the statue are said to represent kingdoms, nothing is done to have the head reflect a kingdom or dynasty *(mlkw)*. Even Jews later knew at least of Nebuchadnezzar's first successor, Awêl-Marduk (2 Kgs 25:27)!

We shall see that the kingdom symbolized by the breast and arms of silver is certainly the Median Empire. That empire was larger than the Babylonian, was feared by the Babylonians, and never injured the Jews.[79] If a Jew is speaking, why does he describe the Median Empire as inferior to Nebuchadnezzar's?

Although in vv 39–43 the levels below the head of the statue are all interpreted as *kingdoms,* v 44 begins, "In the days of those *kings [malkhayyā]."* The consonants of the word for "kings" *(mlky')* can also be read as "kingdoms" *(molkhayyā),* the plural of *molk-,* a word now well attested in Daniel,[80] but the writer is unlikely to have used it here. In v 44 when he wishes to say "kingdom," he repeatedly uses instead the word *malkhū*. Indeed, if the writer meant "kingdom" here, he expressed himself illogically. We shall see[81] that the four kingdoms that are said here to be destined to hold power after the fall of Babylon are the empires of the Medes, the Persians, Alexander the Great, and his successors. Babylon fell to Cyrus in 539 B.C.E. Alexander's successors began to hold power in 323. According to the writer, the Persians *ended* the sway of the Medes (by ruling the whole earth, v 39), and Alexander ended the Persian Empire (v 40). Before the successors could rule, Alexander had to be dead. The great fifth kingdom is to come into existence with the fall of those successors. What sense, then, does it make to date the rise of that kingdom "in the days of those [plural!] kingdoms," a period over two centuries long?

The sequence of gold, silver, bronze, and iron deserves comment. That sequence of four metals, in that order, is a permanent fact of chemistry and (since the beginning of the iron age) of economics. Each metal is chemically nobler, less corrodable, and more valuable than those that follow it, and all four are tougher and more valuable than the earthenware and clay that follow them in Nebuchadnezzar's dream. Strange as it seems, despite the facts of chemistry and economics, the full ordered sequence has not been found in any cuneiform text. The earliest approximately datable occurrence of that ordered sequence is in *Works and Days* 109–201 by the Greek poet Hesiod, who wrote at some time between 725 and 650 B.C.E. In Hesiod the metals characterize successive races of human beings. The Greek poet clearly was not the first to use the sequence; in his poem he has interrupted it after the bronze race by inserting a race of heroes (vv 156–73) corresponding to no metal whatever. Hesiod is known to have drawn on Near Eastern traditions and may well have done so in this case.[82]

Important parallels for the sequence of metals exist in the Hebrew Bible. One is an utterance of Deutero-Isaiah, "For bronze I will bring gold, and for iron I will bring silver; and for wood, bronze, and for stones, iron" (Isa 60:17). Deutero-Isaiah wrote in Babylon only some seventy years after the purported time of Daniel 2. We shall see that Deutero-Isaiah wrote within a still smaller margin before the date at which the original of Daniel 2 was written. The other parallel in the Hebrew Bible for the sequence of metals is at 1 Chr 29:2. In both places, not clay but wood and stone appear as materials inferior to the four metals.

Nebuchadnezzar's confession of admiration for the power of "your God" (2:47) has parallels both in the Hebrew Bible and in Babylonian texts. Daniel is made "chief prefect over all the wise men of Babylon" (2:48), a function in which he would have had to participate in pagan practices.[83]

Daniel's friends, Hananiah, Mishael, and Azariah, play no active role in Daniel 2, though they are mentioned at 2:13, 17–18, 49. Otherwise, the narrative is terse and concentrated upon the main characters. Dan 3:1–30 is similarly concentrated upon the king and upon Shadrach, Meshach, and Abednego, and Daniel is absent. Can the stories in Daniel 2 and Dan 3:1–30 have had separate origins? Can a later editor have brought the dream-interpreter's friends into Daniel 2 so as to tie together narratives that were originally separate?

5. Dan 3:1–30

THE STORY OF THE THREE MEN in the fiery furnace, if it is about Jews in Babylon, is strange, too, and not only because of the confusion of Nebuchadnezzar with Nabonidus.[84] In the book of Daniel as we have it, the events of chap 3 follow those of chap 2. After the miraculous events of chap 2, Nebuchadnezzar should have known better than to challenge the God of the Jews and his worshipers! Daniel in chap 2 was closely associated with his three friends, and the narrative there leaves him "at the king's gate." Why, then, was he not involved in the events of chap 3?

One can suggest that the Greek names of several of the musical instruments[85] merely reflect the fact that Babylonians imported or copied Greek instruments, but the phenomenon is strange enough to arouse suspicion.[86]

Bar-ʾĕlāhīn ("angel," literally, "son of gods") in v 25 can be a Jewish expression,[87] but it is also the equivalent of Babylonian *mâr-ili* ("superhuman being," "demon").[88] In reading of the protective angel in 3:28, we should recall the *shêdu* who protected the Mesopotamian temple at Nippur.[89] Nebuchadnezzar's praise of the god of Shadrach, Meshach, and Abednego (3:28) for sending his angel to save them can be compared with Nabonidus's praise of Sîn for coming down from heaven on his behalf.[90] For the trust that the three Jews placed in their god (3:28), one can cite the parallel of Adad-guppî's trust in Sîn.[91] Nebuchadnezzar's assertion, "No other god can perform such a rescue" (3:29) has a parallel in Nabonidus's statement of the uniqueness of the miracle of Sîn.[92] On the other hand, the repeated stress that the image was of gold (3:1, 5, 7, 10, 12, 14, 18) may well be a touch added by Jews.[93]

6. Dan 3:31–4:34 (Dan 4:1–37 in Most English Bibles)

THE STORY HERE of Nebuchadnezzar's madness and absence from humankind cannot be true. There is no room for it in the Babylonian Chronicles and in the abundant other records from Babylon. From the time Nebuchadnezzar became king in 605 B.C.E. no Jew could ignore his existence and the state of his health, yet neither Jeremiah nor Ezekiel refers to the king's madness, nor is it reflected in 2 Kings or in 2 Chronicles.

However, the story here has parallels in Nabonidus's absence in Têmâ as reported in Nab. 25 and in Nabonidus's leprosy in Teman as told in 4Q Prayer of Nabonidus. The parallels are too vivid to be coincidental. Nevertheless, there is a discrepancy between the king's own account in Nab. 25 and the two legends transmitted by Jews. Nabonidus himself says he spent ten years in Têmâ. According to Dan 4:13(16), 20(23), 22(25), and 29(32), the period of Nebuchadnezzar's insanity was seven years. According to 4QPrNab, lines 2–3, Nabonidus in Teman suffered grievous leprosy for seven years. The discrepancy could easily have arisen from Babylonian public opinion. Nabonidus's absence from Babylon began with a military campaign.[94] A warlike king could stay for a long period away from his capital, but after Nabonidus had stayed three years in Têmâ without fighting any war, his puzzled subjects could easily come to speculate that he was insane or suffering from a loathsome disease. The king's report of ten years would then reflect the time that elapsed between his departure from Babylon and his return, and the seven years of Dan 4 and 4Q Prayer of Nabonidus would be the result of the rumors that began to circulate after 3 years of royal absence. If so, we have more reason to regard Dan 3:31–4:34 (4:1–37) as a Jewish adaptation of Babylonian material.

It is possible that the king's words at 4:5(8), that Daniel's "name is Belteshazzar like the name of my god," are an innocently ignorant Jewish attempt to provide authentic pagan color. Inasmuch as the name as it stands ("Preserve his life!") contains no name of a god, the remark is a blunder. But its presence might reflect a stage in which the name with its Babylonian divine element still stood unmutilated, as "Bêl-balâtsu-usur," and, if so, in the original we would have Nabonidus acknowledging Bêl (Marduk) as his god.

If Nebuchadnezzar had experienced the events of chaps 2 and 3, he should have known that Jewish wonder-workers operated through the power of but one god. Yet the king twice says (4:5[8]–6[9]) that Daniel "has within him the spirit of holy *gods*" (plural! the Aramaic is *'ĕlāhīn qaddīshīn)*. Even if Jews wrote the story we have here with no knowledge of chaps 2 and 3, one would think they would have put the singular into the king's mouth. One can, however, argue that in Aramaic the plural *'ĕlāhīn* ("gods") is a plural of majesty, like the Hebrew cognate *'ĕlōhīm,* to be treated as a singular,[95] so that this point is inconclusive.

The tree-symbolism of the king's dream is found both elsewhere in the Bible[96] and in the pagan ancient Near East, including Mesopotamia.[97] In the king's boast (4:27) there are echoes of Babylonian royal inscriptions.[98]

There is nothing peculiarly Jewish about Nebuchadnezzar's prayer of thanksgiving to the Exalted One (4:31–32[34–35]) and words of praise to the King of Heaven (4:34[37]).[99]

7. Dan 5:1–30

THE CHAPTER OPENS with a falsehood, in calling Belshazzar "king." Ample Babylonian records show that he bore only the title "son of the king," though he presided at Babylon over the government during his father Nabonidus's long absence.[100] From that falsehood the text passes in 5:2 to perhaps another, speaking of Nebuchadnezzar, not Nabonidus, as the father of Belshazzar. There is a chance that the passage is not in error, because Semitic 'b ("father") can also mean "ancestor" or even "unrelated remote royal predecessor."[101] Although we have noted the falsity of the report in chap 1, that Nebuchadnezzar took temple vessels from Jerusalem in the reign of Jehoiakim, one might plead that the vessels mentioned in 5:2–3 were taken in 597 or 586.[102]

Belshazzar is said to have had the insolence to use those vessels to serve the participants in a licentious and idolatrous banquet (5:2–4), until he was terrified by the sight of a hand writing a mysterious inscription on the wall (5–7). Greater was his dismay when none of his pagan experts could read it (8–9). The queen (i.e., probably the queen-mother) suggested that Daniel-Belteshazzar be summoned (5:10–12), and he was indeed successful (13–29) in reading and explaining the inscription as a divine rebuke of Belshazzar and a prediction of doom for him and his empire.

Again in 5:4 and 23 we have the Jewish touch, of stressing that the gods of the pagans consist of inert raw materials. In 5:7, 16, and 29, however, we probably have a survival of authentic Babylonian information. He who read and interpreted the handwriting on the wall was to be promoted to be *third* in the kingdom. When Joseph and Mordecai won the favor of their sovereigns, they became *second* in the kingdom.[103] Bêl-shar-uṣur was second in the kingdom while he presided for the absent Nabonidus, so that anyone whom Bêl-shar-uṣur (= Belshazzar) rewarded could be only third.[104]

In 5:11 again we have a pagan declaring that Daniel "has within him the spirit of holy *gods* [plural!]."[105] In the same verse there is altogether too much protest that Nebuchadnezzar was Belshazzar's father. Literally, the end of the verse says, "In the days of your father, enlightenment and intelligence and wisdom like the wisdom of gods was found in him, and King Nebuchadnezzar, your father, appointed him chief of the magicians, enchanters, astrologers, and diviners, your father, the king." Did the writer have to overcome doubts in his audience or doubts of his own?

In 5:18–22 we have repeated allusions to a king who can be only Nabonidus though he is called Nebuchadnezzar in 5:18. Nebuchadnezzar did not receive the kingship by an act of a god but rather by inheritance from his father. It was Nabonidus who could and did claim that Marduk and Sîn had conferred the royal office upon him.[106] Not Nebuchadnezzar but Nabonidus was famous for the sort of arbitrary behavior mentioned in 5:19. Not Nebuchadnezzar but Nabonidus was absent from his capital for so long that his subjects circulated rumors that he was an insane beast, as described in 5:20–21.[107] Not Nebuchadnezzar but Nabonidus was the father of Bêl-shar-uṣur.[108] Daniel and his friends always speak courteously to a king, addressing him by his title,[109] but at 5:22 Daniel addresses the supposed king only as "you, his son, Belshazzar." Do we have here a survival from an earlier stage of the narrative, wherein the author knew Belshazzar's true status?

The account of the handwriting on the wall puzzled readers already in ancient times. Daniel reads the inscription as consisting of four words. The consonantal text has *mn' mn' tql wprsyn* (5:25; Aramaic, like Hebrew, could be written without vowels; the medieval Masoretes supplied vowels as follows: *"mᵉnē mᵉnē tᵉqēl ūpharsīn"*). When, however, Daniel proceeds to interpret the inscription (5:26–28), where one would think the diviner is quoting each word individually and explaining it, Daniel does nothing to reflect the repetition of *mn'*. He explains *mn'* by an active verb, *mᵉnāh* ("has numbered"), derived from the same root, and his full interpretation is "God has numbered the days of your reign and brought it to an end." The seer explains *tql* by a passive verb, *tᵉqīltā* ("you have been weighed), derived from the same root, and his full interpretation is "You have been weighed on the scales and have been found wanting." Instead of *wprsyn* (a word with a plural noun-suffix) Daniel quotes a word without suffix, *pᵉrēs,* and explains it first by a passive verb, *pᵉrīsat* ("has been broken") and then by singular nouns, *māday uphārās* ("Media and Persia") and his full interpretation is "Your kingdom has been broken and given to Media and Persia."

The vagaries of oracular punning and of insertion of vowels by the ancient witnesses and by the Masoretes[110] might account for some of the grammatical inconsistencies, but the omitted repetition of *mᵉnē* and the omitted plural suffix were so serious that all ancient translations of 5:25 as well as the paraphrases by Josephus,[111] Jerome,[112] and a scribe of the old Greek version[113] quote only the three words *mn' tql prs* (providing them with vowels). Noteworthy is the fact that even Josephus translates all three words as singular nouns, "number," "weight," "thing broken off."[114]

Many modern scholars accept the reading of the ancient translations and paraphrases, but they have not given due weight to the difficulty of explaining how the Aramaic text could have arisen, with its embarrassing inconsistencies. Even if a stupid scribe somehow made such "errors," the next reader could have corrected them. The Aramaic text as we have it must have been firmly established, beyond "correctability." [115]

Charles Clermont-Ganneau [116] suggested paths to a good solution. He noticed that the words read out by Daniel in 5:25 can be taken as the names of weights or sums of money (money consisted of weighed pieces of metal). I would modify Clermont-Ganneau's scheme, as follows: *mn'* can be read as "mina" (50 or 60 shekels),[117] *tql* as the Aramaic word for "shekel," and *wprsyn* as Aramaic for "and halves [or "fractions"] of a shekel [rather than of a mina]." Inasmuch as in a list of weights one would expect to have them in ascending or descending order, Clermont-Ganneau himself was tempted to take *prs* as "half a shekel," but he was deterred by clear instances in Assyrian and Aramaic where it meant "half a mina" and by an ancient half-mina weight labeled *prs*.[118] Eissfeldt,[119] however, removed much of the reason for hesitating, by showing that *prs* ("half," "fraction") might take its meaning from its context. If the immediate context is "mina," *prs* means "half-mina"; if "shekel," the word could mean "half-shekel." A half-mina weight labeled *prs* could not be mistaken for a (much smaller) half-shekel weight. There may be cuneiform texts in which *persu* or *parsu* means "half-shekel."[120] However, though I made considerable efforts and had the help of a distinguished Assyriologist,[121] I was not able to find any such text. On the other hand, there is no doubt that *parsu* means "bit" or "fragment," and in an Old Assyrian text on weighing out tin, the word is used to express "in small bits."[122] Either way, the *prsyn* of the handwriting on the wall become pieces of little or no value.

Albrecht Alt [123] noticed that the practice of ancient accountants, to abbreviate the names of weights or sums of money, leaving only their first letter, would explain the inability of the pagan savants to decipher the writing, as well as the immediate acceptance won by Daniel's reading of it. The decipherment was the more difficult because the usual abbreviation for "shekel" was *š* rather than the Aramaic *t*.[124] When the pagans saw on a wall, not in a context of accounting, *mmšpp,* they could make nothing of it, but once Daniel read it out as a list of *mmšpp* or sums of money, all would recognize that he was right. The plural ending on *wprsyn* reflects the repeated *p,* and the *w* ("and") is usual in giving sums where a fractional unit follows a whole unit.[125]

The author might have intended the inscription to be a mere list of weights. But scholars have rightly looked for it to have been a widely known saying and to have contained symbolism.[126] Already Clermont-Ganneau [127] was aware of the expressions in the Babylonian Talmud,[128] "a mina, son of a *p^{e}rās*" for a distinguished son of an undistinguished father and "a mina, son of a mina," for a distinguished son of a distinguished father. Such an expression could have been current earlier in Babylonia, and, if so, it would be natural to take the weights as symbolizing kings of the Neo-Babylonian dynasty, and scholars have done so,[129] but have been hampered by regarding the *prsyn* as half-minas.

On recognizing them as half-shekels or still smaller bits, we get, in effect, "a mina, a mina, a shekel, and two[130] pieces of small change." One who has read Nab. 8 carefully will perceive immediately how that formula resembles Nabonidus's assessment of his Neo-Babylonian predecessors. Nabopolassar[131] and Nebuchadnezzar[132] were great; Nergal-shar-uṣur was respectable despite his relatively short reign of less than 4 years (August 560 to late April or early May 556);[133] and Awêl-Marduk and Labâshi-Marduk were ephemeral and contemptible.[134]

We have taken note of Nabonidus's need to legitimize the fact that he usurped the throne as a result of the murder of Nebuchadnezzar's grandson. Nabonidus could well have published a propaganda slogan: The now-extinct dynasty had consisted of "two minas, a shekel, and two worthless *p^{e}rāsīn*." The author of chapter 5 would then have shown sharp wit in turning Nabonidus's slogan into a prophecy of doom for Nabonidus's sole heir.

According to Dan 5:30, Belshazzar was killed on the very night of his feast. Babylonian Chronicle 7 says that Cyrus in the month Tashrîtu of Nabonidus's seventeenth year won a battle at Opis and thereafter there was no effective resistance, and on the sixteenth day of the month Babylon fell without a battle and Nabonidus himself returned to Babylon and was captured.[135] No Babylonian source in our possession tells us what happened to Bêl-shar-uṣur when Babylon fell to Cyrus. The Verse Account mentions Nabonidus's "eldest [son],"[136] so a report of the crown prince's death may have been lost through the mutilation of the Verse Account.

In Herodotus's narrative,[137] Cyrus likewise won a battle not far from Babylon, but the Babylonians in their heavily fortified and well-stocked city were ready to face a long siege. At first Cyrus was baffled, but then he diverted the water of the Euphrates, which flowed through the middle of Babylon, and his army penetrated the city through the now shallow streambed. The inhabitants, who were observing a festival, were taken by surprise, and the city fell.[138]

Xenophon in his *Cyropaedia* i.4.6–vii.5.34 tells a story of "Assyria" (i.e., Babylonia) in the reign of Cyrus which contains legend and fiction, but also some fact, where the fall of Babylon is concerned. Without naming names, he writes of a wholly fictitious good old king [139] of "Assyria" and of his evil young son and successor.[140] The young king won the enmity of the nobleman, Gobryas, and of the subject prince, Gadatas.[141] Gobryas and Gadatas went over to Cyrus.[142] The two were in Cyrus's army when he came down upon Babylon.[143] Noticing the strength of her fortifications, Cyrus promptly set about digging trenches to divert the flow of the river and completed the project. At the time of a Babylonian festival, during which all in the city were accustomed to drink and revel the night through, Cyrus, under cover of darkness, took a large force and opened the trenches to divert the river, which thus became fordable for his army. Gobryas and Gadatas led the way, fought their way into the palace, and slew the king. Cyrus took and disarmed the city.[144]

After the battle of Opis there was no way the people in Babylon could know what had happened to Nabonidus. If they should be convinced he was dead or a captive, his son could become king. No Babylonian evidence says that Bêl-shar-uṣur dared to take that step, and in all probability he did not. Nevertheless, he could have been in charge at the city as it prepared to face siege, and public opinion, in the absence of news of Nabonidus, could have regarded the prince as king when he was killed, as we find him both in Daniel and in Xenophon.[145] Belshazzar's feast could have been the festival mentioned by Herodotus and Xenophon. It is hard, however, to believe that within sixteen days Cyrus could have decided to divert the Euphrates and could have carried out the project, though perhaps it is not impossible. If the story of the diversion is true, one can easily imagine how it could have been omitted from Babylonian Chronicle 7, and if it is false, one can easily imagine how it could have grown up.

The Babylonian propagandists who worked for Cyrus wished to show that a miracle of Marduk brought about the fall of the city for her benefit; they did not wish Cyrus's conquest of Babylon to be viewed as the result of a royal stratagem that involved death and destruction for her inhabitants. On the other hand, by the time of Darius I, Persian rule was seen as no blessing. Marduk and his priests then would have needed to be cleared from complicity in Babylon's fall. Babylonians could have preferred to tell a story, whether true or false, that blamed the disaster on Cyrus's stratagem. Persians were unconcerned about Marduk's honor. They could welcome either a story about Marduk's complicity in their victory or one about Cyrus's resourcefulness.

Thus, Dan 5:1–30 was written against the background of the fall of Babylon to Cyrus and parades the sins of *Nabonidus's* heir Bêl-shar-uṣur. Bêl-balâtsu-uṣur's reading and interpretation of the handwriting on the wall probably present propaganda of Nabonidus and then parody it to predict the doom of his dynasty. The Jews welcomed the fall of Babylon but had no grievances against

Nabonidus, whose name was forgotten in the Bible, though it was known at Qumran. How, then, could a Jew have been the original author of the story?

8. Daniel 6 (5:31–6:28 in Most English Bibles)

THE GAP THAT SERVES as a paragraph division in the Aramaic text connects the notice in 6:1(5:31) of the accession of Darius the Mede as king of Babylon with the story of Daniel in the lions' den, not with the story of Belshazzar's feast. On the other hand, the text as we have it (like the text of 2:1, which is separated from Dan 1:21 by a gap in the script) begins with an *and,* which shows that pains have been taken to link the story here with the one in chap 5. Both the gap and the effort to bridge it suggest that the notice of Darius's accession was originally no part of the story of Belshazzar's feast.

Whatever the original context of Dan 6:1(5:31), the verse contains a puzzling falsehood. Before Babylon fell to Cyrus, her king was Nabonidus, not Belshazzar. If Belshazzar was killed when Babylon fell, the rightful king of the city was the conqueror, Cyrus the Persian, not a person called "Darius the Mede." Babylonian, Persian, and Greek records render it completely impossible that a King Darius the Mede ruled over Babylon during the reigns of Nabonidus, Cyrus, and Cambyses.[146] Though *Nabonidus* may have been 62 years old at the time of his accession over Babylon,[147] neither Cyrus nor Cambyses could have been.[148]

More puzzles come in 6:2–3(1–2), with the assertion that Darius set over his kingdom 120 satraps. The word *satrap* entered Babylonian,[149] Aramaic,[150] and Greek[151] as a loanword, with spellings reflecting its Median form, *xshathrapân.* The Old Persian form was *xshaçapâvan.*[152] However the Medes may have used the term, their empire is unlikely to have contained as many as 120 satrapies.[153] Cyrus is reported to have ruled through satraps,[154] but not until *Persian* Darius I do we hear of an elaborate system of satrapies, and he had not 120, but 20.[155] Throughout the chapter, the hero receives the name "Daniel," no longer the Babylonian name "Belteshazzar." The change might be appropriate, because the king is no longer a Babylonian but a Mede. But in 6:4(3), Daniel is called "this Daniel," as if he had been introduced for the first time in 6:3(2), a clear hint that Daniel 6 was originally separate from Daniel 1–5. The hero could originally have been a Babylonian holy man, not a Jew named Daniel.

Darius's ministers, jealous of brilliant Daniel for outshining them, seek to entrap him by concocting a proposal that the king for thirty days ban all prayer to any god or man except to the king himself, on pain of being cast into the lions' den, and the king accepts the proposal (6:3–10[2–9]). The conspirators know that Daniel will not cease from his habitual daily prayers to his God. The writer does nothing to induce the reader to believe that the ministers made such a proposal and that the king accepted it.[156] The proposed ban goes far beyond even the decrees that Antiochus IV imposed upon the Jews in 167 B.C.E.[157] The story must have arisen at a time when such arbitrary decrees on religion were thought possible. No other evidence supports the suggestion that under a Median king prayer was forbidden. Even under the Persian kings, the only possible parallel is Xerxes's prohibition of the worship of *daivas*.[158]

Daniel felt obliged to pray to his God three times a day (6:11[10]). Although Jews later copied Daniel's practice and regarded it as obligatory,[159] there is no other warrant for it in the Hebrew Bible.[160] However, a Babylonian text composed before the time of Nabonidus strongly recommends praying daily.[161]

There is nothing peculiarly Jewish about Darius's hope that Daniel's God will protect him (6:17[16]). The god who sent his angel to protect his worshiper (6:23) need not have been the god of the Jews.[162] However, the king's proclamation requiring his subjects to revere Daniel's powerful Deity (6:27–28[26–27]) may contain Jewish touches.[163]

9. Daniel 7

THE VISION OF THE four beasts terrified the seer (7:28), who bears the name Daniel throughout.[164] The text gives the vision a false date in the first year of *King* Belshazzar of Babylon. Belshazzar was never king.

Since the seer is a Jew presumably writing for Jewish posterity, we should expect his vision to contain Jewish touches. In fact, however, it is thoroughly pagan. The cosmic imagery is taken from the Babylonian Creation Epic, a source antithetical to Jewish Scripture. The Creation Epic tells a myth of a violent process of creation. Gen 1:1–2:3 tells how an omnipotent God without resistance created by his mere words. The parallels between Daniel 7 and the Creation Epic deserve to be stressed.[165]

The Creation Epic is an account of the wars of the younger gods against their progenitors, Apsu (the sweet waters) and Tiâmat (the sea),[166] who seek to destroy them as disturbers. The god Ea succeeds in killing Apsu, and Ea's son, Marduk, is born and grows to great majesty.[167] Thereupon, Anu, *god of heaven, creates the four winds which disturb Tiâmat.*[168] Daniel's vision begins with *the four winds of heaven stirring up the sea* (7:1). *Tiâmat* responds to the disturbance by *creating monsters* to fight against the gods.[169] In his vision, Daniel sees four *monstrous beasts emerge from the disturbed sea* (7:3). Marduk in his majesty has *fire blaze forth from his lips;*[170] he is *clothed with the rays of ten gods;*[171] on his way against Tiâmat, Marduk has *lightning go before him* and *fills his body with a blazing flame.*[172] The fifth tablet of the Epic is mutilated and may have lost a reference to *a court of the gods taking its seats* after Marduk's victory. Certainly, later in the Epic the gods set up a sanctuary at Babylon, *containing a throne, and they take their seats there, with Marduk as their chief.*[173] Daniel in his vision sees *thrones set up for a court and an Ancient One takes his seat as judge; his throne was fiery flames with wheels of blazing fire. A surging stream of fire flowed forth from where he sat.* Marduk *kills* Tiâmat and *tramples her monsters.*[174] Daniel in his vision sees *at least one of the monsters slain* (7:11).

There are serious discrepancies in chap 7 between the description of the vision on the one hand (7:2–14) and, on the other, Daniel's questions about it (7:16, 19–22) and the interpretations he receives (7:17–18, 23–26). They are just as strange as the discrepancies in chap 2. The examination of those discrepancies in chap 7 and of other strange aspects leads directly to hypotheses for solving the puzzles of the chapter, so let us postpone study of the discrepancies to the sections containing those solutions. Let us now turn to suggest how to solve the enigmas of chap 2.

10. Partial Solution of the Problems of Daniel 2: The Five-King Version

CHAPTER 2 WILL PROVE to contain a present-future prophecy that has twice been supplemented. We have set forth the principles for analyzing such compositions, and the reader will do well to review them.[175] We have noted how the image in the dream is an inappropriate symbol for representing successive empires.

It is easy, however, to suggest a configuration that the image in Daniel 2 could appropriately symbolize. A dynasty or an empire can be viewed as depending on its latest ruler for its survival. The Neo-Babylonian Empire did depend on Nabonidus; with his fall, it fell. Nabonidus was the fifth king of that empire in the series that began with Nebuchadnezzar, and to some extent he posed as an heir of Nebuchadnezzar's dynasty.[176] Hence, it would make sense to view the statue as representing the Neo-Babylonian Empire, and the five different levels of the statue seen by Nebuchadnezzar, as the five *kings* who ruled,[177] from his time on: Nebuchadnezzar, Awêl-Marduk, Nergal-shar-uṣur, Labâshi-Marduk, and Nabonidus. On that hypothesis, we shall find the symbolism of the dream entirely appropriate, and we shall discover that the *description* of the dream has not been changed at all. All supplements have been put into the *interpretation*.

Suppose great King Nebuchadnezzar in a Babylonian work has a dream predicting that he will have four indigenous successors, who will be, compared to him, degenerate; that the third king to succeed him will be base and depraved; that the fourth king after him will be a monstrously cruel weakling; and that after those four a superior ruler will come from outside and take over the empire. Progressive degeneracy can be symbolized by a succession of progressively baser raw materials; weakness, by brittle earthenware; cruelty, by iron. Babylonian observers did indeed regard Awêl-Marduk as inferior to Nebuchadnezzar; even moderately successful Nergal-shar-uṣur had so brief a reign as to be obviously inferior to his illustrious father-in-law. Labâshi-Marduk was condemned both by Nabonidus and by Berossus. One might object that the sequence of metals symbolizes Awêl-Marduk by silver, as if he were superior to Nergal-shar-uṣur, whereas Berossus and Nabonidus unequivocally regard Awêl-Marduk as bad. However, Babylonians could differ in evaluating Awêl-Marduk, just as they differed in evaluating Cyrus.[178] Cruelty and weakness certainly can characterize Nabonidus. Both the Cyrus Cylinder and the Verse Account display Nabonidus's cruelty; the Cyrus Cylinder at its beginning calls him a weakling; and Babylon's fall was a clear demonstration of Nabonidus's weakness. Both the Cyrus Cylinder and the Verse Account present Persian Cyrus as Marduk's agent for the salvation of Babylon and as Babylon's own king.

The symbolism of Daniel 2, construed in this manner, fits perfectly the sentiments of Marduk's worshipers at the time Babylon fell to Cyrus. There is more reason to believe that the dream described in 2:31–35 was originally part of a story of a prediction to Nebuchadnezzar of his four degenerate successors and of the victory of Cyrus. Marduk's worshipers had a strong incentive to produce such a story, in answer to the challenges of Deutero-Isaiah! World literature and human history contain many parallels for such a tale. God revealed to King Jehu of Israel that he would have four successors from his own family.[179] The Delphic Oracle revealed to King Gyges of Lydia that he would have five such successors; to King Arkesilas of Cyrene, that he would be a member of a line of eight monarchs; and to King Kypselos of Corinth, that he would have two such successors.[180] The fourth story in Egyptian Papyrus Westcar tells of a prediction to King Khufu that his son and his grandson would rule after him, but then rule would pass to another dynasty.[181] King Allah-ed-din Muḥammad of Persia (1199–1220) saw himself in a dream, having a head of gold, with other parts of his body being made of silver, bronze, lead and tin, to symbolize himself with four successors.[182]

We have seen that the symbolism of Daniel 2 is un-Jewish and, even as interpreted by "Daniel," unsuitable for Jewish purposes. Should we not adopt the hypothesis that Daniel 2 is based upon an original in which Babylonian Bêl-balâtsu-usur, not Jewish Daniel, interpreted Nebuchadnezzar's dream so as to predict to him that Babylon would fall to Cyrus in the reign of Nabonidus? The text of the description of the dream, on that hypothesis, still survives intact. On the basis of the strangenesses of the present text, on the basis of what we know of the history of the times, and on the basis of the numerous parallels in world literature, we can reconstruct the original Babylonian text of the interpretation of the dream, as well.

To remove all anomalies and get the original Babylonian text of the interpretation, we merely have to make the interpretation conform to the vision and perform a few other operations. First, we must translate the word for "kingdom" *(mlkw)* in 2:39–41 and in 2:44 as "reign," rather than "kingdom," or else remove its feminine suffix to leave masculine "king" *(mlk)* and change the feminine adjectives and verb-forms to masculines. Then, in 2:39 (first half) Bêl-balâtsu-usur predicts to the king that Awêl-Marduk will succeed him but will be inferior. The second half of 2:39, with its mention of a "kingdom which shall reign over all the earth," has been doctored by a later supplementer, as we shall show.[183] In its original form, 2:39(second half) merely predicted that Nergal-shar-usur would succeed Awêl-Marduk. We shall show how the same supplementer has altered 2:40. Labâshi-Marduk, a mere child, was depraved and base like corrodable iron, but he was not strong. He destroyed no other kingdom. The monstrously cruel weakling Nabonidus and his fate were the subject of 2:41, but in vv 41–43 we also have partly the work of the same supplementer and partly the work of another.[184] In the original, earthenware symbolized weakness and iron symbolized cruelty, rather than the "firmness" we now find in Dan 2:41.

Cyrus began to reign as king of the Persians in 559,[185] in the reign of Nergal-shar-usur, at a time when two more of Nebuchadnezzar's inferior successors were still to come to the throne. Thus, the statement in 2:44 is correct, that *"In the days of those kings* the God of Heaven will set up a reign [or "a king"] . . . that will put an end to all these reigns [or "kings"]. . . ."* The rest of 2:44 has suffered tampering to make it fit with a later supplement, which dealt with a succession of empires, each with a different ethnic base. We may be sure that to that supplement belong the words, "nor shall its sovereignty be left to another *people."* During the reigns of Cyrus and his son, Cambyses, the Babylonians regarded the Persian kings as men of their own and avoided mentioning the ethnic difference. Perhaps the Babylonian original had "The God of Heaven [i.e., Marduk] will set up a king, and his dynasty *[mlkwth]* shall never be destroyed. He shall bring these kings to an end, and his dynasty shall last forever."

Let us call this reconstruction of the Babylonian original of Daniel 2 the

"Five-King Version" of the chapter. It must have been circulated by the priests of Marduk some time after Deutero-Isaiah loudly proclaimed that only the God of the Jews had predicted the victory of Cyrus over Nabonidus. There may indeed have been a real prophecy to Nebuchadnezzar by a Babylonian seer named Bêl-balâṭsu-uṣur, predicting that Nebuchadnezzar would have four successors. Religious propagandists in a time when their deity seems not to be communicating have a strong tendency to make use of predictions revealed by the god when he still was communicating. If the priests of Marduk were already reading a story of how Bêl-balâṭsu-uṣur interpreted Nebuchadnezzar's dream, they had only to doctor it a little, by putting in the symbolism of the cruel weakling, so as to turn it into a story of how Marduk and his dream-interpreter, over sixty years before the event, had predicted the fall of Nabonidus. We, who do not believe in Marduk, may be sure, however, that no Babylonian seer really predicted to Nebuchadnezzar that there would be a cruel weakling followed by Cyrus. A Babylonian prophecy so accurate has to be a forged prophecy, produced after the fact by Marduk's faithful.

We can date the forgery within fairly narrow limits. It had to follow the loud boasts of Deutero-Isaiah and had to be written when Nabonidus was regarded as totally bad. By 522 B.C.E., a Babylonian pretender was posing as Nabonidus's son.[186] Thus, we must date the Five-King Version between 538 and 522, and probably closer to 538 because of the Babylonians' need to answer the taunts of Deutero-Isaiah. How would Jewish observers react to such propaganda circulated by Marduk's faithful only shortly after 538? Knowing how Deutero-Isaiah had challenged all other religions, they might regard it as a simple forgery, and probably some Jews did, at first. On the other hand, when the Five-King Version was published, between 538 and 522, Nebuchadnezzar had been dead for a quarter-century or more. A whole generation had passed. Jews were known to have been given government posts under the Neo-Babylonian kings. Jews could infer that if the story in Daniel 2 was true, the dream-interpreter must have been a Jew. A Jew named Daniel may well have served Nebuchadnezzar as one of his court magicians. Jews only had to say that Bêl-balâṭsu-uṣur was in reality the Jew, Daniel, and that Daniel's prediction was one more foundation for Deutero-Isaiah's boast, that only the God of the Jews had predicted Cyrus's victory.

The dream-interpreter's three friends are no essential part of the story of the miraculous dream-interpreter and probably were brought in by the editor who combined Daniel 2 with (originally separate) Daniel 3. If, however, the three were included in a Babylonian stage of the story, their names were not Hananiah, Mishael, and Azariah (as 2:17 has them), but Sha-Marduk, Mushêzib-Marduk, and 'Abed-Nabû.

11. Solution of the Problems of Daniel 1 and of the Languages and Biblical Echoes in Daniel 2

THERE WAS ONE DIFFICULTY to claiming that Bêl-balâṭsu-uṣur was the Jew, Daniel. The original Babylonian propaganda, the Five-King Version, dated the seer's interpretation of Nebuchadnezzar's dream in Nebuchadnezzar's second year, 604/3 (Dan 2:1). Babylonian magic and divination were complicated, partly secret techniques, ridiculed[187] by Jews and certainly not studied in the land of Judah. In Babylonia one had to have the king's permission to study the art. We do not know how long it took to train a Babylonian diviner. J. Renger wrote me,[188] "There is little evidence available. One unpublished text mentions eleven years as the time required for the education of a scribe. But for *bārû* and *mashmāshu* [diviners] we do not know of a specified time for their training. But my guess is, it was closer to the eleven years of the scribes than to the three mentioned in Daniel. Perhaps the three years there only refer to a particular phase of Daniel's and his friends' education. But you have to consider that a divination expert or magician in the first millennium B.C. was able to write and read, which certainly could not be achieved in three years—to judge from modern experience."

Thus, even as a prodigy Daniel would have had a hard time learning to be a Babylonian diviner in fewer than three years of study. Yet, according to the records, Jews had been exiled to Babylonia first in 597, after the last month of Nebuchadnezzar's *seventh* year, long after the king's dream.[189] Jews who believed that Bêl-balâṭsu-uṣur was a Jew produced a solution: There had been an earlier exile, one in the reign of Jehoiakim. We know that Jewish documents prove that to have been impossible, but our reasoning never occurred to the sort of Jew who innocently took the Babylonian propaganda as true but insisted the seer was an Israelite.[190]

The author of Daniel 1 was careful about one thing in giving his date for the supposed captivity in the reign of Jehoiakim. He knew that the course in Babylonian magic took a minimum of three years[191] and that Bêl-balâṭsu-uṣur interpreted Nebuchadnezzar's dream in the king's second year, which he appears to have regarded, correctly, as 603/2. A captivity taken in the third year of Jehoiakim, no matter how reckoned,[192] would allow the prodigy Daniel to complete the course by 603/2. If the author had such precise chronological knowledge and cared so much for accuracy, it is most unlikely that he made the error of saying that Nebuchadnezzar was king of Babylon in Jehoiakim's third year (it is improbable that by "king" he meant "future king"). Rather, he must have given Nebuchadnezzar his correct title at the time, "son of King Nabopolassar of Babylon."[193] We must attribute the error to later Jewish scribes, who had never heard of Nabopolassar (who is not mentioned in the Bible) and knew of Nebuchadnezzar only as king. Later Jewish scribes committed a similar error in chap 5.[194] It is possible that in the original of 1:3–18, "the son of the king" stood wherever we now have "king." By the time of 1:19, however, Nebuchadnezzar was king and is so called, and perhaps the author felt no need to mention the death of old Nabopolassar. Alternatively, the king mentioned in 1:3–18 is Nabopolassar, and a mention of his death has been lost from the text.

We have now solved the internal difficulty of Daniel 1–2, that after three years of study, Daniel interpreted the dream in the king's *second* year. It is easy to see how Jews, after reading Daniel 1, readily accepted Daniel 2 as part of their own sacred literature, even though Marduk's faithful had written it in Babylonian Aramaic (or translated it from Babylonian into Aramaic)! However, Daniel 1, as an introduction to sacred literature, had to be written in Hebrew. The Jewish adopters of Daniel 2 went on to turn Dan 2:1–3a into Hebrew, but they felt it excusable to leave the words of the Chaldaean prognosticators in Aramaic, and thereafter they spared themselves the labor of translating. Their procedure seems to have been similar to that of the Jewish compiler and writer of Ezra: He wrote in Hebrew but spared himself labor in 4:7–6:18 by quoting Aramaic documents and Aramaic narratives without translating them. The Jewish adopters added a few touches of their own, drawing on the language of Gen 41:8, 15 in Dan 2:1–3; and perhaps on Gen 41:16 in Dan 2:27–28 and on Gen 41:25, 28 in Dan 2:45(end).

When did few if any Jewish voices remain to say that the Five-King Version of Daniel 2 was a forgery? When did the overwhelming majority of Jews agree that Bêl-balâtsu-uṣur was the Jew Daniel? There are at least two clues in Daniel 1 itself. First, at Dan 1:21 the author takes the trouble to say that Daniel survived[195] down through the first year of King Cyrus. The author must have wanted to make room for stories about his hero which were supposed to have occurred almost as late as that. There are such stories, and we shall be able to discover the dates at which they were composed. A second clue in Daniel 1 is the fact that the author wished to demonstrate that Hananiah, Mishael, and Azariah were also brought to Babylon in the third year of Jehoiakim. We shall be able to date the composition of the story in Daniel 3 about them. Let us turn to solve the problems of Daniel 3–6.

12. Solution of the Problems of Dan 5:1–30

BABYLONIANS, NOT JEWS, had strong grievances against Nabonidus and could be expected to parody his propaganda and predict the doom of his dynasty. Most of the puzzling features of the story become completely understandable as soon as we assume that originally it was propaganda of Marduk's worshipers against Nabonidus and Bêl-shar-uṣur. Let us adopt that hypothesis and see how we can then resolve the difficulties of the chapter.

We have shown [196] that it is probable Jewish scribes mistakenly "corrected" a reference to Nebuchadnezzar son of King Nabopolassar of Babylon into one to King Nebuchadnezzar of Babylon. Similarly, here they could have turned the king's son Bêl-shar-uṣur into King Belshazzar.

No Babylonian propagandist could have written the reference to vessels taken from the temple of Jerusalem by Nebuchadnezzar, the king's father (Dan 5:2). It can be only a Jewish touch. But the whole story is built around Belshazzar's sacrilegious behavior toward sacred vessels. Something of the sort must have been present in the Babylonian original. Marduk's propagandists bitterly accused Nabonidus of asserting that Esagila, Marduk's own great temple, really belonged to Sîn! [197] We know that in the last weeks of his reign Nabonidus repented and showed honor to Marduk. [198] All other evidence in our hands shows that Bêl-shar-uṣur treated Marduk with reverence and tact. [199] Marduk's worshipers might well have wanted explanations why the king's repentance was not accepted, why Babylon fell, and why Bêl-shar-uṣur was slain. A fabricated story could answer all three questions, if it asserted that Nabonidus removed precious vessels from the temple of Marduk and if it then implied that the king never returned them to their rightful place and if it went on to assert that his heir used those vessels in a licentious feast. However scrupulous Bêl-shar-uṣur may have been in revering Marduk, Nabonidus's previous behavior and his heir's fate could have made the story credible. According to Xenophon, [200] the men who killed the "young king" (i.e., Bêl-shar-uṣur) also slaughtered those who were with him. Thus, there could have been no one left alive to contradict the story of Bêl-shar-uṣur's sacrilege.

There is good reason to think that the original story of Belshazzar's feast is intimately connected with the Five-King Version. By telling the tale, Marduk's worshipers could show how that version was fulfilled. After the battle of Opis, Bêl-shar-uṣur was acting sovereign at Babylon, and he was a potential sixth king in the series that began with Nebuchadnezzar. However, he provoked the wrath of Marduk. Marduk sent a miraculous hand that wrote upon the wall the slogan once used by Nabonidus to characterize the dynasty of his predecessors. The writing was in abbreviated form, and no one could read it until Marduk's holy man, Bêl-balâṭsu-uṣur read it out and interpreted it as a prediction of doom, and that very night, Bêl-shar-uṣur was slain, leaving the fifth king without an heir, and Babylon fell, so that Nabonidus was no longer a king.

I would reconstruct what stood in the original of Dan 5:2–4 as follows:

2 Under the influence of the wine, Bêl-shar-uṣur ordered the gold and silver vessels that his father had taken out of the sanctuary at Babylon [or "the sanctuary of Marduk"] to be brought, so that he and his nobles, his wives, and his concubines might drink from them. **3** The gold [and silver][201] vessels that his father had taken out of the sanctuary at Babylon [or "of Marduk"] were then brought and the king and his nobles, his wives, and his concubines drank from them. **4** As they drank, they praised Sîn, Ningal, Nusku, and Sadarnunna.

The last three names are those of the deities regularly associated with Sîn.[202] Babylonians were familiar with the history of Nabonidus and his son. They had no need to name Bêl-shar-uṣur's father as Nabonidus in 5:3. Jews, on the other hand, might feel a need to supply the father's name, and we shall see soon that they may have found a misleading clue to convince them that he was Nebuchadnezzar. As Jews viewed the matter, if a miraculous hand appeared and wrote a prophetic inscription on the wall, it could not have been on behalf of Marduk and his temple, but only on behalf of the LORD and His. Had not Deutero-Isaiah been able to boast that only his God had predicted the fall of Babylon? The names of the idols, Sîn, Ningal, Nusku, and Sadarnunna, meant nothing to Jews. Far better it was to substitute for those names the contemptuous Jewish formula, "gods of gold and silver, bronze, iron, wood, and stone." Similarly, "Sîn, Ningal, Nusku, and Sadarnunna" stood in the original of 5:23, where we now have "gods of silver and gold, bronze, iron, wood, and stone, who do not see, hear, or know anything." In 5:7, 16, and 29, we have exactly the right terminology: He who read and interpreted the handwriting on the wall for the *king's son* Bêl-shar-uṣur would be promoted to be *third* in the kingdom. In 5:11, the pagan queen properly says that Babylonian Bêl-balâṭsu-uṣur has within him the spirit of holy *gods*.

A strong clue to the truth of our hypothesis, that Dan 5:1–30 was originally Babylonian propaganda against Nabonidus and his son, may exist in the excessive references to Belshazzar's father (>b) in 5:11, "In the days of *your father* enlightenment and intelligence and wisdom like the wisdom of gods was found in him, and *King Nebuchadnezzar, your father,* appointed him chief of the magicians, . . . *your father, the king.*" The storyteller of Daniel 5 is an artist. It is unlikely an artist would perpetrate such a sentence.

Scribal errors can produce overloaded passages in handwritten texts. One common scribal error arises when a scribe mistakenly copies a gloss, a marginal explanatory note of a reader (or even of the original author), into the main body of the text. Marginal explanatory notes might be difficult or impossible to inscribe on clay tablets, but the Aramaic of the book of Daniel was written on the ancient equivalent of paper, where such notes are easy to insert. Though the third reference to Belshazzar's >b looks awkward in English, in Aramaic its position is normal for the subject of the verb "appointed." The first and third references cannot be glosses. They are unspecific mentions of "your father," a surprisingly ambiguous term when addressed in a Semitic language to a king or crown prince, because it can mean not only "father" and "ancestor" but also "royal predecessor." [203]

In fact, the author of Dan 5:11 knew of Bêl-balâṭsu-uṣur's feat and promotion to high office as told in Daniel 2, a story not of Nabonidus, the prince's father, but of Nebuchadnezzar, his more remote royal predecessor. The middle reference, naming Nebuchadnezzar, is likely to be a gloss by a knowing Babylonian. The text as originally written lacked that middle reference, though the gloss is a correct reflection of Daniel 2. However, once the 'b in 5:11 was identified with Nebuchadnezzar, a Jewish reader ignorant of Babylonian history would find nothing to prevent him from giving the same identification to the 'b in 5:2, 18–22, as we have it in the present text of Daniel.

In 5:22 Bêl-balâṭsu-uṣur observes complete decorum in addressing Bêl-shar-uṣur as the king's son and not as king.

So much for solving the difficulties of Dan 5:1–30. Can we date the writing of the original version of the tale? It shows knowledge of Daniel 2, and therefore can be no earlier than the time between 538 and 522 B.C.E. when that story was written. (We shall treat later [204] the seeming allusion in Dan 5:18–21 to Dan 3:31–4:34[4:1–37].) Dan 5:1–30 presents both Nabonidus and Bêl-shar-uṣur as unforgivable sinners: Nabonidus never restored the vessels to Marduk's temple; his son used them in a licentious feast. Therefore the story should be earlier than the revolt of in 522 of Nidintu-Bêl, who found it useful to pose as Nabonidus's son. [205]

13. Solution of the Problems of Dan 3:1–30

THE STORY OF Shadrach, Meshach, and Abednego in the fiery furnace is best understood as an Aramaic equivalent of a Babylonian historical epic. It tells of Marduk's miraculous triumph over the *temporarily* wicked king, *Nabonidus; Marduk's* angel protects Sha-Marduk, Mushêzib-Marduk, and Abed-Nabû from the flames. The names of the rescued men, the epithets of the god, and even his angel are all at least as appropriate to Marduk and his worshipers as they are to the LORD and his.

The original writer of Dan 3:1–30 may have known the story of the Five-King Version of Daniel 2, of how Bêl-balâṭsu-uṣur interpreted Nebuchadnezzar's dream in 604/3 B.C.E., but nothing prompted him to import a reference to the great dream-interpreter into a story from the reign of Nabonidus (556–539). Originally, the two tales were completely separate.

Unlike the writer of Dan 5:1–30, here the author takes pains to show how the king repented of his cruel treatment of Marduk's faithful worshipers and showed reverence to the deity (3:26–30). Between 538 and 522 B.C.E., Marduk's worshipers viewed Nabonidus and his son as wicked. Hence, we must date the Babylonian original version of Dan 3:1–30 in or after 522. The Babylonian pretenders who rebelled in the reign of Xerxes made no effort to pose as descendants of Nabonidus. Hence, we may infer that efforts to pose as the heir of the last independent king of Babylon and to mitigate his well-known sins by portraying him as repentant should be dated close to 522. By that time, Babylon had been under Persian rule for seventeen years; it is conceivable that the Babylonian rebel pretenders gave some of their subordinates Persian titles, and a Babylonian writer could make the slip of giving such titles to officials of Nabonidus.

We are now familiar with how Jews would approach such a miracle-tale: If the story were true, it could only be an act of the LORD on behalf of Jews. A version of Daniel 1 may already have been written in order to allow Jews to believe that the hero of Daniel 2 was none other than the Jew, Daniel. Jews could have imported into that version of Daniel 1 the references to Hananiah, Mishael, and Azariah, alias Shadrach, Meshach, and Abednego. Having accepted Daniel 2, the same sort of Jew could import into that chapter the references to Daniel's friends, so as to tie the miracle-tales together.

We have seen in the previous section how references to Nabonidus could have become references to Nebuchadnezzar in Dan 5:1–30, and perhaps ignorant Jews needed no more hint than that to change the king's name from the original "Nabonidus" in the story of the fiery furnace to the present "Nebuchadnezzar." With the lapse of time, Jews would forget Nabonidus. His name in Aramaic, like Nebuchadnezzar's, began with the letters *nbw*. On reading Nabonidus's name, a Jew would tend to see the name he expected, "Nebuchadnezzar." The process may have been encouraged by the use of shortened names in Aramaic. In 4Q Prayer of Nabonidus, the king bears the shortened name, *nbny*. According to the same procedure of shortening, "Nebuchadnezzar" would become *nbky*. In the Aramaic script of the time, *k* was easily confused with *n*.

14. Solution of the Problems of Dan 3:31–4:34 (4:1–37)

THE STORY OF THE king's madness is an Aramaic equivalent of a Babylonian moralizing narrative in the first person. It tells how *Marduk* humbled the pride of the *temporarily* wicked king, *Nabonidus,* who learned his lesson, so as to end the chapter with a declaration of faith in Marduk, king of heaven. The strange features we noticed in section 6 are just what one would expect in a Babylonian work. The dream of the tree (4:7–14) may have been patterned on the very omen that drove Nabonidus to leave Babylon for Têmâ (of which no description survives).

Like the Babylonian original of Dan 3:1–30, that of Dan 3:31–4:34(4:1–37) with its elaborate royal acknowledgment of the might of the supreme god was a painstaking demonstration that the once-wicked King Nabonidus repented. In contrast, the allusion at Dan 5:18–21, to how the proud king was punished by years of madness, contains no reflections of that royal acknowledgment; rather, our restored version of Dan 5:2–3 implies that even after recovering his sanity Nabonidus failed to restore to the temple of the supreme god the vessels he had taken from it.

Accordingly, Dan 5:18–21 would reflect, not the royal acknowledgment in Dan 3:31–4:34(4:1–37) but rather only the rumors that Nabonidus's long absence in Têmâ provoked (rumors which his return to Babylon did not extinguish, especially because his return at first was followed by the king's very worst "sins against Marduk"; only in the very last weeks of his reign, when threatened by the advance of Cyrus, did Nabonidus tardily repent and show full honor to Marduk). Thus, the story of the king's madness, based on rumors current in Babylon, was known to the author of the tale of Bel-shar-uṣur's feast when he wrote before the revolt of Nidintu-Bêl in 522, but that author did not know the version here in Dan 3:31–4:34(4:1–37). The considerations that enabled us to date the story of the fiery furnace in or not long after 538 B.C.E. serve to assign the version here of the story of the king's madness to the same period; the processes by which Jews adopted the story and changed Nabonidus into Nebuchadnezzar are the same for both tales.

We should try here also to ascertain the origin of 4Q Prayer of Nabonidus.[206] Like Dan 5:1–30, those scanty fragments contain a clearly Jewish touch in the reference to "gods of silver and gold, bronze, iron, wood, stone, clay." Like Dan 3:1–30 and Dan 3:31–4:34(4:1–37), 4Q Prayer of Nabonidus shows Nabonidus as repentant. Jews had no interest in clearing the reputation of Nabonidus. The simultaneous existence of Dan 3:31–4:34(4:1–37) and 4Q Prayer of Nabonidus would be enough to provoke skepticism: Could both stories be true? Perhaps both were fabrications! The 4Q Prayer of Nabonidus may have arisen in the following manner. Jews could have had more than one reaction to the publication of the Babylonian miracle tale of the king's madness. One sect of Jews could identify Bêl-balâṭsu-uṣur with the Jew Daniel and adopt the story as their own. Another group could regard the tale as false and could counter it with another, likewise based on Babylonian rumor, that the king, instead of being mad, had a loathsome disease and owed his recovery to religious prescriptions given him by a Jew, who, for all we know, may have been named neither Daniel nor Bêl-balâṭsu-uṣur. In the book of Daniel, Daniel is not said to have been a healer. Jews would not have composed a tale to compete with Daniel 4 before it existed. Therefore, 4Q Prayer of Nabonidus is of 522 B.C.E. at the earliest. Interest in Nabonidus can hardly have existed much later.

15. Solution of the Problems of Daniel 6 (5:31–6:28)

BY USING THE HYPOTHESIS that the stories were originally Babylonian, we have solved the problems of Daniel 2–5. The tale of Daniel in the lions' den contains nothing that a Jew could not have written. Nevertheless our hypothesis is useful for solving the problems of that story, too.

We have seen that no Median King Darius ever ruled over Babylon, that daily prayer, as in 6:11(10), 14(13), is a Babylonian trait; that an elaborate satrapy system such as is mentioned in 6:2–3(1–2) is not attested until the reign of Persian Darius I; that King Xerxes I of Persia is the only Iranian king in the period from the sixth through the fourth century B.C.E. who is known to have issued a decree forbidding worship; and that his decree may well have been aimed against the worship of Babylonian gods.

Let us add one more fact: For centuries after Cyrus the Persian conquered the Medes, his empire and that of his successors was called "the Empire of the Medes"; there are abundant instances of Greeks doing so, and, in their parlance, to support the Persian realm against the resistance of the Greeks was to "Medize."[207] Deutero-Isaiah took the mention of the Medes at Isa 13:17 to refer to Cyrus,[208] and Nabonidus called Cyrus's realm "the city of the Medes."[209] Egyptians, too, referred to Persian rule as the rule of the Medes.[210]

If there never was a truly Median King Darius who ruled over Babylon, and if the original author was well informed, in speaking of Darius the Mede he must have meant a Persian king. There were three Persian kings named Darius, but only of Darius I do we hear that he had any conflict with Babylonians. On the basis of the evidence that we have, it is legitimate to conclude that if a Babylonian author wrote of a Persian royal decree prohibiting prayer, he knew of Xerxes's decree against *daiva*-worship. Whoever the author was, he wrote at a time when Jews or Babylonians would welcome a report that an Iranian king had acknowledged the power of the LORD or of Marduk; consequently, he wrote while the Persian Empire still existed. By the time of the reign of Darius I (522–486 B.C.E.) a child prodigy who interpreted a dream in Nebuchadnezzar's second year (603/2) would have been at least an octogenarian. Nothing in the story indicates that the pious hero who braved the lions was extremely old.

We now have enough clues to reconstruct a background against which Daniel 6(5:31–6:28) may well have been written. Xerxes may well have forbidden Babylonian worship. He certainly put down the revolts of Bêl-shîmannî and Shamash-erîba. By then he could be viewed by Marduk's worshipers as the great enemy. From the outset of his reign, Xerxes was faced by the daunting prospect of living up to the colossal achievements of his father, Darius I, achievements that far outweighed some real defeats. Xerxes's inscriptions copy those of Darius and clearly show Xerxes's concern to be a fit son of his father. Xerxes's anxiety must have increased manyfold after his enormous disaster in Greece in 480–479 B.C.E. By then, he was the great failure among Persian kings, in contrast to his father, the greatest success.

As soon as Xerxes issued a decree forbidding Babylonian worship, there would be a good occasion for Babylonian propaganda showing that the great Darius, in contrast, never willingly attacked Babylonian worship. Rather, when Darius was tricked into doing so, he was sorry, and Marduk's angel protected the god's worshiper from the lions. That worshiper could well have borne the fitting name, "Bêl-balâtsu-uṣur" ("Bêl [= Marduk], preserve his life!"). It is unlikely, though possible, that the original author intended the hero to be none other than the now-elderly Bêl-balâtsu-uṣur who interpreted Nebuchadnezzar's dream. No one would need to write propaganda against the "great failure" after his ignominious death by assassination in 465 B.C.E. Thus, the original of Daniel 6(5:31–6:28) should be dated between the decree against *daiva*-worship early in Xerxes's reign and his death.

We can tell how Jews would react to the story: If the miracle happened, only the LORD could have wrought it, on behalf of a Jew, and this Bêl-balâtsu-uṣur must have been Daniel. By the time of Xerxes's death three-quarters of a century had elapsed since the fall of Babylon. If not already then, surely only a few decades later, Jews and even Babylonians could have jumped to the conclusions that the man who braved the lions was the seer who interpreted Nebuchadnezzar's dream and was not in advanced old age but rather served an ephemeral Darius the (ethnic) Mede to whom Babylon fell before passing under the rule of Cyrus. One could easily believe that the reign of an elderly Mede was brief, and thus we could explain how and why an editor within a few decades of Xerxes's death composed 6:1(5:31) to link the story of the man in the lions' den to the one about the handwriting on the wall. We shall find[211] that both Babylonians and Jews later came to believe that after the Babylonian Empire and before the Persian, a Median realm held sway.

The huge number, 120, of Persian satrapies in 6:2–3(1–2) probably reflects not the large-scale organization of the Persian Empire into satrapies, but the fact that chiefs of smaller regions were also called "satraps."[212] No one has found a source to confirm the three "presidents" in 6:3.

16. When Did Jews Come to Accept All the Stories of Daniel?

THE AUTHOR OF Daniel 1 took the trouble to say that Daniel survived down to the first year of King Cyrus. He probably did so to make room for the story of Daniel, Darius the Mede, and the lions' den.[213] The Jewish author of Daniel 1 and the Jewish editor of Daniel 6(5:31–6:28) worked when all the errors involved could have been made, surely at least some decades after the original Babylonian story of Bêl-balâṭsu-uṣur in the lions' den was written in the reign of Xerxes. Using evidence in the Bible, we can give a date for the latest time at which Daniel 1 could have been composed. Like Daniel 1 (and unlike Jeremiah, Ezekiel, and 2 Kings), 2 Chr 36:6–7 says that Nebuchadnezzar made war on Jehoiakim, arranged to exile at least one Jew, and carried off temple vessels, which he placed in his temple or palace at Babylon. Most scholars believe that Dan 1:1–2 depends on 2 Chr 36:6–7. But we have found good reason for the author of Daniel 1 to fabricate that account soon after the publication of the Five-King Version. I see no reason why the author of Chronicles, who probably wrote much later, would invent an account so incompatible with Jeremiah, Ezekiel, and 2 Kings. But if Dan 1:1–2 already existed and was widely accepted by Jews, the Chronicler would readily copy it and did so.

The author of Chronicles traces the priestly families and the dynasty of David down to some time between about 400 and the middle of the fourth century B.C.E. He shows no knowledge of the conquests of Alexander the Great, which began in 334. Thus, we may date the Chronicler between about 400 and 334.[214] Consequently by that date and perhaps considerably before it, Jews must have accepted Daniel 1 and with it all of Daniel 1–6, as stories of the miracles of the LORD, not of Marduk, on behalf of Jews, not Babylonians.

17. Partial Solution of the Problems of Daniel 7: The Three-Beast Version

BY THE TIME JEWS accepted all of Daniel 1–6, the Babylonians had produced another prophecy purporting to come from Bêl-balâṭsu-uṣur. The Babylonians had good reason to do so. The Five-King Version of Daniel 2 no longer gave any hope to Marduk's worshipers. Nabonidus had long been overthrown, yet Marduk's faithful were suffering under the harsh rule of Darius and Xerxes. Could great Bêl-balâtsu-uṣur have failed to foresee this time of troubles? Basing themselves in part on the sacred Creation Epic, believers in Marduk produced the comforting present-future prophecy that was the original version of Daniel 7. The strange features of that chapter give us the clues by which we can reconstruct the Babylonian original.

In Daniel 7, unlike Daniel 2, we have appropriate imagery for a vision on the succession of empires, a topic of great interest in the times of Daniel and Bêl-balâtsu-uṣur, when empires rose and fell, and the LORD's and Marduk's peoples came under subjection. The successive monsters of the vision symbolize empires, as is clear from the interpretation of the vision (7:17). What empires are meant has been a matter of controversy since ancient times. They are not named in Daniel 7.[215]

In interpreting a symbolic present-future prophecy, one should pay attention both to the pretended present and to the actual present faced by the writer. The pretended present is the regime of Belshazzar as acting king at Babylon, a period of a few days just before the fall of the city to King Cyrus of Persia. We have seen[216] how public opinion could have assumed that Nabonidus was dead or in captivity and could have viewed Bêl-shar-uṣur as king. Thus, even a Babylonian writing a present-future prophecy some decades later could have given a date-formula in which the crown prince bore the royal title. Nevertheless, we shall soon find that the original author knew that Nabonidus was the only king of his dynasty. The original date-formula must have been something like "in the days of Bêl-shar-uṣur, the son of the king," which a Jewish editor or scribe changed to "in the first year of King Belshazzar."[217] The actual present of the original version remains to be determined.

Let us examine the descriptions of the beasts, one by one.

> **4** The first was like a lion but had the wings of an eagle. As I looked on, its wings were plucked off, and it was raised from the ground and set on its feet like a man and given the mind of a man.

Daniel was a member of a people victimized by the Neo-Babylonian Empire. For a Jew in his time, the first monster empire ought to be Babylon's, yet the monster turns human and is raised up from the ground, heavenward! Neither in history nor in Jewish imagination was Babylon so rewarded. Babylon after Belshazzar's death went into irreversible decline, and in Jewish legend and in the New Testament book of Revelation, Babylon became the symbol of evil!

It is noteworthy that the first beast is a common stereotype of Babylonian art, the lion-griffin. Like all of the monsters, it is inhuman. In the vision, the griffin's inhumanity consists of its wings, its going on all fours, and its beastly mind. It becomes human by losing its wings, by standing erect on two feet, and by getting a human mind. The first beast has no specified number of body parts. The meaning of multiple body parts is revealed in 7:24: They signify multiple kings of a dynasty. In 7:4, a single beast, a dynasty of a single king, made humane, is contemplated. Nebuchadnezzar's dynasty might have been considered beastly by Jews, but it had five members, of whom one, Awêl-Marduk, was remembered for being kind to the captive Jewish king Jehoiachin. Only one dynasty had a single king who was regarded by his subjects as beastly but "turned human": Nabonidus persecuted the worshipers of Marduk but later repented.[218] Therefore, the first beast symbolizes only Nabonidus and his empire. Jews did not suffer at the hands of Nabonidus; again we find that the original author must have been a Babylonian.

> 5 And behold, another beast, a second one, which was like a bear and stood alongside;[219] it had three fangs[220] in its mouth among its teeth; it was told, "Arise, eat much meat!"

Though one would expect all the empires in Daniel 7 to be successive, in truth the first two are simultaneous. The fact does not depend upon my translation, "alongside," of the words *lištar had,* usually rendered "to one side" or "on one side." The formula "thereafter" *(bāʾtar dᵉnāh)* occurs in 7:6 between the description of the second beast and that of the third, and in 7:7 between the description of the third beast and that of the fourth, but not in 7:5 between the description of the first beast and that of the second. The author has shown that time elapsed between the sightings of the other beasts, but not between the sightings of the first and second. A further indication of the same fact is the presence of the formula "As I looked on, behold" *(hāzēh hăwēt waʾărū)* in 7:2, 6, 7, and 13, but not in 7:5; the seer did not have to wait or look in a different direction to catch sight of the second monster.

Although the word *tinyānāh* ("a second one") in 7:5 might imply that the bear came after the griffin, the word could have been added by a scribe who thought an ordinal number was missing, because one is present in v 4. In fact, an ordinal number is superfluous if *ʾŏḥŏrī* ("another") is present, as it is in v 6, where no ordinal number occurs. If a scribe added "a second one," he was probably Babylonian, because we shall discover[221] that later both Babylonians and Jews held the mistaken belief that after the Babylonian Empire and before the Persian, a Median realm held sway. Jews were more likely to take from Babylonians than vice versa.

Why does the second beast have three fangs in its mouth? From 7:24 we know the meaning of multiple body-parts: They signify the multiple kings of a dynasty. The empire that was simultaneous with the Neo-Babylonian Empire (including the first regnal years of Nabonidus) and had three kings (Cyaxares, Phraortes-Khshathrita, and Astyages) was that of the Medes.[222] The writer views the Medes as dangerously "voracious." Jews had no reason to complain of Median "voracity," but Babylonians built elaborate fortifications against a Median attack that never came, and Nabonidus spoke of his own fear of the Medes![223]

> 6 Thereafter, as I looked on in the night vision, behold, another one, like a leopard, and it had on its back four wings like those of a bird; the beast had four heads, and dominion was given to it.

If the first two beasts represent Nabonidus's Babylonia and Media and are succeeded by the third, the third must symbolize imperial Persia. That beast has four wings and four heads. What wings mean is clear from the first beast: Wings are an attribute of beastliness. The symbol of Nabonidus's beastly empire had only one pair of them. The symbol of the Persian Empire has two pairs because it was even more beastly: Nabonidus repented and showed honor to Marduk. Darius crushed the rebellions of "Nebuchadnezzar III" and "Nebuchadnezzar IV" and gave no privileges to Babylonia. Xerxes crushed the rebellions of Bêl-shimânni and Shamash-erîba. Though he apparently stopped enforcing his decree against *daiva*-worship, he showed no honor to Marduk. Babylonians, not Jews, had reason to consider the Persian Empire monstrous.

What multiple body-parts mean is clear from 7:24. The four heads must symbolize four kings. Darius's view prevailed, that the ephemeral Bardiya of 522 was an impostor. Hence, the Persian Empire ultimately had ten, eleven, or twelve kings (Xerxes II and Sekyndianos were each murdered after reigning only a few months in 424/3; neither was recognized as king in Babylonian documents). The fourth Persian king was Xerxes I! The author of Daniel 7 is well informed; he knows that Nabonidus's empire and the Median Empire were contemporary, and he knows that three kings ruled the Median Empire. He could leave the third beast with a mere four heads only if he wrote before a fifth Persian king was securely in power. The heir of Xerxes I, Artaxerxes I, was securely in power by summer, 464.[224]

The writer is explicit in 7:7: The fourth beast came *after* the third beast. There could be a fourth beast only after the Persian Empire fell, and by then there had been many more than four Persian kings. Immediately we recognize that everything about the fourth beast both in the description of the vision

(7:7–8) and in the interpretation (7:19–26) must be supplement, and later[225] we shall explain how and when the supplementing was done. Let us call the Babylonian original of Daniel 7 "the Three Beast Version." Can we reconstruct it on the basis of what is preserved? We can do so with considerable probability.

The writer of a present-future prophecy often describes a dreadful past and present and goes on to predict a glorious future. The original of Dan 7:1–5 probably still stands before us, except for the substitution of "Daniel" for Bêl-balâtsu-uṣur. Those verses set the scene and symbolize the relevant past. As we have it, Dan 7:6 ascribes to the third beast no atrocities from the dreadful present, but only says that it received dominion. Some or all of the third monster's atrocities may have been transferred by the later supplementer to the fourth. If so, the Three-Beast Version had

> **6** . . . and dominion was given to it, **7** and it had great iron teeth; it devoured and broke in pieces and stamped the residue with its feet.

The original writer went on to symbolize the glorious future, beginning with how the Ancient of Days (Marduk) passed judgment[226] on the *third* beast (7:9–10). The first ten words in the Aramaic of 7:11 deal with the fourth beast and are supplement, but the rest of the verse belongs to the original and tells how the *third* beast was slain. The mention of the survival of the other beasts in 7:12 is also a supplement, as we shall show later.[227]

For the original writer, the glorious future involved the establishment of an empire symbolized not by a monstrous beast but by a human being, precisely the true meaning of Aramaic *bar 'ĕnāsh* and Hebrew *ben 'ĕnosh* and *ben 'ādām,* so often translated over-literally as "son of man."[228] The original meaning should be transparent: Whereas the empires of Nabonidus, of the Medes, and of the Persians were beastly and had an earthly or even an infernal origin, symbolized by the sea, the power of chaos, this one will be humane and good and permanent and will have a heavenly origin, established as it will be by Marduk. The Three-Beast Version certainly contained vv 13–14, the coming of the permanent humane kingdom, and perhaps contained the interpretation in vv 15–18, except that the number "four" which appears twice in v 17 certainly comes from a Four-Beast Version; originally, the number would have been "three." In any case, whether the passage originated with Jews or with Babylonians, the word *mlkyn* in v 17, which the Masoretes read as "kings" *(malkhīn)* should be read as "kingdoms" *(molkhīn* or *malk^ewān)*; thus in that verse we should have

> **17** These great beasts, three in number, mean that three kingdoms will arise from the earth.

But there is a feature of v 18 that seems, at least at first glance, to be Jewish rather than Babylonian, the expression *qdysy ʿlywnyn,* "saints [or "holy ones"] of [those] most high."[229] The practice of calling pious Israelite believers in the LORD his "saints" or "holy ones" is well attested in Scripture,[230] and no cognate expression is known in Babylonian texts. "Most high" in the singular *(ʿlywn)* is a frequent epithet of the God of Israel,[231] and the plural here can be explained as an idiom of biblical Hebrew.[232] The symbolism of the Three-Beast Version of Daniel 7 was transparent in its time, so that it is conceivable that no verses of interpretation were needed then. If so, one might suppose that vv 15–18 were added by Jews when they came to adopt the prophecy in Daniel 7.

There is a chance, however, that vv 15–18 belong to the original Babylonian Three-Beast Version. Natives of Babylon, Borsippa, Sippar, Nippur, and Uruk, holy cities of Babylonia, which from early times had been cult-centers, are called *ṣābē kidinni* ("people of *kidinnu*) by the Neo-Assyrian kings from Sargon II on. *Kidinnu* originally meant a portable sacred emblem or standard which could be carried in procession or set up by a gate, and it came to mean divine protection for the citizens of a city that possessed such a standard and carried out the rites associated with it.[233] The related abstract noun *kidinnūtu* ("privileged or protected status") is used in Neo-Babylonian texts in connection with people of Babylon and (by Nabonidus) in connection with certain priests of Ur.[234] With Babylon, Borsippa, Sippar, Nippur, and Uruk, Ur completes the list of great holy cities of Babylonia. In several texts, *ṣābē kidinni* is paraphrased by *šubarē,* a word connoting "protected persons," and *šubarē* in the texts is further qualified by the name of the god or gods conferring the protection, Anu, Enlil, Bel and Beltia and "the Great Gods." These are the most high gods of Babylonia.[235] Nothing tells us what was the Aramaic equivalent of "people of kidinnu," but people of holy cities living under the protection of the most high gods of Babylonia could well have been called *qdyšy ʿlywnyn,* "holy ones of [those] most high."

There is more to be learned from the symbolism of the vision. The Babylonian griffin, symbolizing the empire of Nabonidus, turned human, precisely as beastly Nabonidus did in Mardukist propaganda (Dan 4:33–34[36–37]); the griffin also was lifted from the earth, *heavenward.* The predicted new Babylonian Empire is symbolized by a human being coming on the clouds of *heaven.* Did the writer mean to predict a mere restoration of power to Babylon, in the hands of a righteous dynasty? Or did he mean restoration of power to a resurrected Nabonidus? We do not hear elsewhere of Babylonians believing in the return of kings from the dead, so that the hypothesis is unlikely, but I see no way to prove it impossible.

The Three-Beast Version served another function: It was a divine revelation that ranked Babylon among the great imperial powers, contrary to the Persian philosophy of history, which held that there had been and were to be only three such powers, Assyria, Media, and Persia.[236]

Jews ultimately knew of only four Persian kings, the ones named in the Bible: Cyrus, Darius (I), Xerxes (I), and Artaxerxes (I).[237] Could Jews have created the Three-Beast Version with its third beast having only four heads? The author of the Three-Beast Version is well informed, far beyond the capacities of ignorant later Jews. He knows that the Median and Babylonian Empires were contemporary, and he knows that three kings ruled over the Median Empire. A later Jew would not have seen or fabricated a vision based upon the Babylonian Creation Epic. A Jew would not have presented the Babylonian monster as turning human. Although the figure of the "Son of Man" has been of vital importance in Jewish and Christian tradition, our careful examination of Daniel 7 shows that originally it symbolized a restored righteous Babylonian Empire!

We have displayed the clue that dates the Three-Beast Version: It must have been written after Xerxes's rule came to be felt as monstrous by Babylonians, and before the fifth Persian king, Artaxerxes I, was securely in power in 464. Was it propaganda for the last great Babylonian rebellion, led by Shamash-erîba, which perhaps occurred in 483? There is no evidence that either he or Bêl-shimânni made any effort to connect himself with Nabonidus, whereas the Three-Beast Version speaks of the return of Nabonidus's kingdom if not of Nabonidus himself. On the whole, it seems best to date the Three-Beast Version after the defeat of Shamash-erîba and at a time when Xerxes was so obviously a failure that Marduk's faithful could believe that their god was about to put an end to the Persian Empire. That could have been the case from the time of Xerxes's defeat in Greece in 480 down through the aftermath of his assassination.

The Three-Beast Version probably remained exclusively Babylonian. It is unlikely that Jews adopted it. Xerxes crushed Bêl-shimânni and Shamash-erîba. Whenever the Three-Beast prophecy was published, it was not fulfilled. Artaxerxes I, the fifth Persian king, was secure in power by 464, and that fact sufficed to prove the falsity of the Three-Beast Version. But so much of that present-future prophecy was true! There had, indeed, been three monster-empires; and, down through the time of Xerxes, the Persian Empire had had four kings. Babylonians who were impressed by that fact and who respected the reputation of Bêl-balâtsu-usur preserved the text and hoped that somehow the prediction of a humane Babylonian kingdom would be fulfilled. But there was no reason for Jews to claim that the prophecy was really Daniel's. There is no trace of Jewish restlessness under Xerxes. Xerxes is praised in Esther 10:2 and in the purely Jewish present-future prophecy at Daniel 11:2.

We should bear in mind, however, that in the mid-fifth century B.C.E. many Babylonians and Jews surely had an imperfect knowledge of the history of the sixth century. Such persons did not have to read Dan 7:5 with the same care as we have employed. Incautious readers of Daniel 7 have always tended to take the second beast as coming *after* the griffin, not as being simultaneous with it. Thus, shortly after the publication of the Three-Beast Version, incautious Babylonians, impressed by the accuracy of the present-future prophecy, already must have believed that between Nabonidus and Cyrus an ethnic Median king had ruled. Though Jews did not accept the Three-Beast Version, they could well have learned from those incautious Babylonians that a Median king, however ephemeral, had ruled then. We thus infer that the author of Daniel 1 wrote after the publication of the Three-Beast Version, an inference that fits the dates we derived above by other means.[238]

The sole evidence for the existence of the Babylonian stories and prophecies which we have reconstructed from Daniel 2–7 is those chapters of the Bible. The lack of supporting evidence on clay tablets does not impair the validity of our reconstructions. The pieces probably were composed from the beginning in Aramaic, and Aramaic was written, not on clay tablets, but on the ancient equivalents of paper, which are unlikely to survive down to modern times. Berossus may have refrained from presenting the miracle tales to his Greek audience, whether because he himself was skeptical of them or because he feared that audience would have scoffed at them. He may have ignored the Three-Beast Version of Daniel 7 as a flagrantly false prophecy. We shall find that the existing supplements to it were added long after Berossus's time. As for the present-future prophecy in Daniel 2, by Berossus's time, as we shall see, it had been supplemented to foretell the doom of Macedonian Empires, and he had to be reticent about such predictions as later Josephus had to be reticent about Daniel 2 and 7, which, Jews then believed, foretold the doom of the Roman Empire.

We have now treated all the reflections in the book of Daniel of Jewish and Babylonian history and thought under the kings of the Persian Empire. Let us glance briefly at the meager evidence on how the two *peoples of an almighty god* fared under the later Persian kings.

NOTES

1   See chap 6, n 19.

2   FGH 685, F 6b = Eusebius *Praeparatio evangelica* ix. 41.2. On Abydenos see Stanley M. Burstein, *The Babyloniaca of Berossus* ("Sources and Monographs: Sources from the Ancient Near East," Vol. I, fascicle 5; Malibu: Undena, 1978), 4, and Walther Sontheimer, "Abydenos," *Der kleine Pauly,* I (1964), 22.

3   After making vast conquests; the conquests mentioned immediately before by Abydenos are fictitious.

4   Reading *an aitios estai* with Mras; the manuscripts have the apparently pointless *anaitios estai,* "innocent [of that] will be." In Abydenos's Ionian Greek, the future indicative with *an* expresses that something will happen in the future under certain circumstances. Possible translations are "in that case," "under the prevailing circumstances," "possibly," "perchance," or the construction I have used with "might." See William Watson Goodwin, *Greek Grammar* (rev. by Charles Burton Gulick; Boston: Ginn and Company, 1930), sec. 1303.

5   The manuscripts have *Mêdês;* I do not know what the word could mean. The well-known word for "Mede" is *Mêdos.* It would be easy to emend the text to read thus, but one wonders how the scribes could have gone astray. I do not understand the words "the Assyrian boast," though I can suggest that a key may exist at Sibylline Oracles iv. 54.

6   See Anson Rainey, "Chaldea, Chaldeans," *Encyclopaedia Judaica,* V (1971), 330.

7   See Herodotus i.55, 91, 107–8.

8   W. W. Hallo, "Gutium," RLA, III (1971), 717–19.

9   Media: I. M. Diakonoff, "Media," chap. 3 of CHI, II (1985), 144; Assyria: Roux, 386–87.

10   A. Leo Oppenheim, "The Babylonian Evidence of Achaemenian Rule in Babylonia," chap 10 of CHI, II (1985), 544.

11   See Rainey, "Chaldea, Chaldeans," *Encyclopaedia Judaica,* V (1971), 330–31; Jonas C. Greenfield, "Aramaic in the Achaemenian Empire," chap 15 of CHI, II (1985), 699–700.

12   Stanislaw Segert (*Altaramäische Grammatik* [Leipzig: VEB Verlag Enzyklopädie, 1975], 47) denies that there are any eastern Aramaic features in the language of

Daniel 2–6. Against him, see Eduard Yechezkel Kutscher, "Aramaic," in *Current Trends in Linguistics,* ed. Thomas A. Sebeok, vol. VI: *Linguistics in South West Asia and North Africa* (The Hague and Paris: Mouton, 1970), 362–64. On 362, Kutscher lists eight traits that distinguished eastern (including Babylonian) Aramaic in the period 700–300 B.C.E. from other dialects. Of these, nos. 4, 5, and 6 (matters of word-order) are strikingly present in Daniel, and nos. 1 and 2 (matters of expressing the genitive relationship) and 8 (loans from Akkadian and Persian) are attested there. See also Peter W. Coxon, "The Syntax of the Aramaic of Daniel: A Dialectal Study," *HUCA* 48 (1977), 120–22, and Joseph Naveh and Jonas C. Greenfield, "Hebrew and Aramaic in the Persian Period," chap 6 of *The Cambridge History of Judaism,* ed. W. D. Davies and Louis Finkelstein (Cambridge: Cambridge University Press, 1984–), I, 116–18.

13   There is a reason why Ezra 4:7–6:18, 7:12–26 are in Aramaic: The passages either consist of Aramaic documents and records or are derived from them. In Daniel this could be true only of chap 4.

14   Chap. 1, p. 16.

15   See Jonas C. Greenfield, "Early Aramaic Poetry," *Journal of the Ancient Near Eastern Society of Columbia University* 11 (1979), 46–47. Greenfield cites no examples from Dan 3:1–30, and that story in fact is the most prosaic of the four. Nevertheless, one can find the parallel stichs characteristic of both biblical and Babylonian poetry even there, in vv 12, 14, 18–21, 27. On the other hand, Dan 3:31–6:29 are full of poetic touches. Only in 4:25(28), 5:4, 11–13, 18, 30, 6:1–4, 7–8, 10, 12–13, 16–17, 22, 26, 29 did I fail to find any. See also James A. Montgomery, *A Critical and Exegetical Commentary on the Book of Daniel* (New York: Charles Scribner's Sons, 1927), 220, 224, 228, 229–30.

16   See J. T. Milik, " 'Prière de Nabonide' et autres écrits d'un cycle de Daniel," *Revue biblique* 63 (1956), 407–15; Frank Moore Cross, "Fragments of the Prayer of Nabonidus," *Israel Exploration Journal* 34 (1984) 260–64.

17   See C. B. Welles, R. O. Fink, and J. F. Gilliam, *The Excavations at Dura-Europos: Final Report V, Part I, The Parchments and Papyri* (New Haven: Yale University Press, 1959), 63 ("Barnaeus" shortened from "Bar-Nebus"); cf. 62 ("Iarhabus" shortened from "Iarhaboles"). The phenomenon was widespread among Jews. "Yōnātān" became "Yannāy," "Yōḥānān" became "Yōḥāy," and "Elʿāzār" became "Ilʿāy."

18   Cf. Hab 2:19, Ps 115:4, 135:15.

19   See chap 5, pp. 116–29.

20   Verse Account, col. IV, line 5, in the translation of Oppenheim, *ANET,* 314a; 4Q Prayer of Nabonidus (see n 16).

21 In the Hebrew and Aramaic consonantal text of Daniel the name is spelled *blš'ṣr* (except at 5:30, 7:1, and 8:1, which have the erroneous *bl'šṣr*). The medieval Jewish Masoretes added the vowels, and even the ancient translators who produced the Greek versions of Daniel did not know the correct pronunciation of Babylonian names. Two processes could have resulted in the loss of the first *r*. Later in Babylonian Jewish Aramaic a *resh* which closes a syllable, as in *shar,* is frequently lost; see J. N. Epstein, *A Grammar of Babylonian Aramaic* (Jerusalem and Tel-Aviv: Magnes and Dvir, 1960), 19 (in Hebrew). The process could have already been operating in the vernacular Aramaic of Babylon at the time Daniel 2–6 were composed. Jewish scribes could also have been led into error by the apparent similarity to the name Belteshazzar *(blṭš'ṣr).*

22 As is proved by 4Q Prayer of Nabonidus.

23 See Louis F. Hartman and Alexander A. Di Lella, *The Book of Daniel* ("Anchor Bible," vol. 23; Garden City, N.Y.: Doubleday, 1978), 139; André Lacoque, *The Book of Daniel* (Atlanta: John Knox, 1979), 29–30; Montgomery, 123.

24 See Montgomery, 123, 129–30.

25 On ʿ*abed* as a West Semitic loanword used in Middle Babylonian and Neo-Assyrian personal names, see **"abdu,"** *CAD,* I, 1 (1964), 51a.

26 Not all Jews were so sensitive. The writer of 1–2 Chronicles kept the undeformed names, rightly taking *baʿal* ("lord") to be an epithet of his own God. Other biblical writers freely use the names of pagan deities, whether because they interpreted Exod 23:13 to exclude only spoken mention or for some other reason.

27 ʿ*Abodah zarah* 6(7):4 Zuckermandl.

28 See Johann Jakob Stamm, *Die akkadische Namengebung* (Leipzig, 1939; Reprinted, Darmstadt: Wissenschaftliche Buchgesellschaft, 1968), 211, 232, 236, 370, 372.

29 See Stamm, *Namengebung,* and Knut L. Tallqvist, *Neubabylonisches Namenbuch* ("Acta Societatis Scientarum Fennicae, Tom. XXXII, no. 2; Helsingfors, 1905). From here through n 36 I have received the kind help of Matthew W. Stolper.

30 Albert T. Clay, *Documents of Murashu Sons of Nippur Dated in the Reigns of Darius II* ("University of Pennsylvania, the Museum, Publications of the Babylonian Section," II, 1; Philadelphia: Department of Archaeology and Palaeontology of the University of Pennsylvania, 1912), No. 88, line 6, with transliterated name listed on 36.

31 Stamm, 211; Tallqvist, *Namenbuch,* 187 and 331, cites an example of "Sha-Marduk-shu," at Felix E. Peiser, *Babylonische Verträge des Berliner Museums* (Berlin:

W. Peiser, 1890), No. 49. In a letter to me of July 28, 1989, Matthew W. Stolper writes, "[Peiser's No. 49 is] a duplicate of [his] No. 46. . . . Later [Arthur] Ungnad republished No. 49 as VAS 3 94 and No. 46 as VAS 3 95. . . . [Thereafter the pair of documents were] edited in Ungnad and [Mariano] San Nicolò, *Neubabylonische Rechts- und Verwaltungsurkunden*, I, 438, No. 488. Peiser copied half-broken signs that looked convincingly like - shú-u, but Ungnad—generally the more reliable copyist—saw traces of horizontal wedges at the edge of the break and copied signs that look convincingly like - DU-´, and Ungnad-San Nicolò [at] NRV, I, 438, accordingly read the name as 'Sha-Marduk-banâ,' and for your purposes it is an unreliable datum [for the existence of the name 'Sha-Marduk-shu']."

32 Cf. Montgomery, 129.

33 Montgomery, *Daniel,* 128–29. There are parallels for the weakening of the ʿ to ʾ or nothing. The name *Shimʿāh* of I Chron 2:13 is *Shammāh* at I Sam 16:9, 17:13.

34 See Stamm, 221, n. 1; Tallqvist, *Namenbuch,* 116–18.

35 Cf. Isa 43:11.

36 See Montgomery, 123, 129, and cf. Dan 4:5. One should compare the name of Nabonidus's father, Nabû-balâṭ-su-iqbi ("Nabû decreed his life"). See Stamm, 188. Babylonians frequently shortened such full names by omitting the name of the deity (Stamm, 111), so that Balâṭ-su-uṣur is possible as a Babylonian shortened name. But the formal contexts of the book of Daniel surely require the use of a full name. Matthew W. Stolper in his letter of July 18, 1989, informs me that he has been unable to find an instance of "Bêl-balâssu-uṣur" (= Bêl-balâṭsu-uṣur) in Babylonian documents.

37 Omitting the Masoretic vowels, which are mostly mere guesses, the words are *prt-mym* ("nobles"; 1:3), *ptbg* ("menu"; 1:5), *ʾzdʾ* ("public knowledge"; 2:5, 8), *hdmyn* ("[severed] limbs"; 2:5, 3:29); *rz* ("secret," "mystery"; 2:18, 19, 27, 28, 29, 30, 47, 4:6[9]); the titles, *ʾḥsdrpnyʾ, ʾdrgrzryʾ, gdbryʾ, dtbry, tptyʾ* (3:2–3; *ʾḥsdrpnyʾ* is also in 3:27, 6:2[1]-8[7]); *zny* ("kinds"; 3:5, 7, 10, 15), *ptgm* ("answer," "word"; 3:16, 4:14[17]), *hdbryʾ* ("companions"; 3:24, 27, 4:33[36], 6:8[7]), *hmwnkʾ* ("torque"; 5:7, 16, 29), *dt* ("decree," "law"; 2:15, 6:6[5], 9[8], 13[12], 16[15]. 7:25), *srkyn* ("chief ministers"; 6:2[1]). See Montgomery, 21–22 and his notes to the passages where the words occur, and Maximilian Ellenbogen, *Foreign Words in the Old Testament, Their Origin and Etymology* (London: Luzac, 1962), s.vv.

38 On Esther, see my *I Maccabees,* 13.

39 Contrast especially Exod 5:1–12:36, 2 Kgs 19:22–35, and Ezra 1:2–4.

40   Hab 3:3; Job 3:4, 23, etc.

41   See "**ilu** 2d," *CAD*, VII (1960), 99.

42   Dan 2:47, Deut 10:17; Marduk and Sîn were each called "the god of the gods" (see Knut L. Tallqvist, *Akkadische Götterepitheta* [Helsingfors: Societas orientalis fennica, 1938], 12, 366, 448). The idea occurs, with somewhat different vocabulary, at Nab. 5, col. I, line 29, and col. II, line 5; Nab. 6, col. II, line 50; Nab. 17, col. I, line 1; Nab. 21, col. II, line 7; and cf. Creation Epic, tablet VI, line 149 (*ANET*, 70).

43   Dan 2:23; cf. Deut 26:7, Ezra 7:27, etc.; but see also "**ilu** 1b.4," *CAD*, VII (1960), 95, for Babylonian instances.

44   Dan 3:28–29, 6:27; Gen 26:24, 31:42, 46:3, etc.; Babylonian parallels: "**ilu** 1b.1," *CAD*, VII (1960), 94.

45   Dan 2:47, 3:17, 28, 6:6, 11, 12, 17, 21, 23, 24; biblical examples exist in abundance; Babylonian parallels: "**ilu** 1b.5," *CAD*, VII (1960), 99.

46   Dan 2:18, 19, 37, 44; Neh 1:5, 2:4, 20, etc.; Babylonian parallels: "**ilu** 1a.2," *CAD*, VII (1960), 92, and *ANET*, 332, line 301. See Montgomery, 158.

47   Dan 2:28; e.g., Nabonidus speaks of "the gods in heaven" (Nab. 4*, col. III, line 73); see **šamû** A 1a.1, *CAD*, XVII, Part I (1989), 340–41.

48   Dan 3:26, 32, 4:14(17), 21(24), 22(25), 29(32), 31(34), 5:18, 21, 7:25; Gen 14:18–22, Num 24:16, Deut 32:8, Ps 57:3, 78:35, 92:2, etc.; Babylonian parallels: see "**elû** Ab," *CAD*, IV (1958), 111, and Nab. 17, col. I, line 1; *Cuneiform Texts from the British Museum*, Part XXV (London: Trustees of the British Museum, 1909), Plate 11, line 14 (epithet of the god Ninurta); Woldemar G. Schileico, "Tête d'un démon assyrien à l'"Ermitage impériale de Saint Pétersbourg," *Revue d'assyriologie* 11 (1914), 58–59; take note especially of Isa 14:14. In Daniel the epithet occurs without an accompanying divine name. Therefore, perhaps we should exclude the abundant Babylonian parallels where the epithet accompanies a divine name. Babylonian *elû* and Aramaic ʿ*ilaya* and the synonymous Babylonian *shaqû* meant "exalted" and often were not superlatives. See "**elû**," *CAD* IV (1958); "**šaqû**," *CAD*, XVII, Part II (1990); and "'*ly*," Charles-F. Jean and Jacob Hoftijzer, *Dictionnaire des inscriptions sémitiques de l'Ouest* (Leiden: Brill, 1965), 211, and "'*yl'h*," Marcus Jastrow, *A Dictionary of the Targumim, the Talmud Babli and Yerushalmi, and the Midrashic Literature* (New York and Berlin: Choreb, 1926), 1069. On Hebrew and non-Israelite West Semitic use of ʿ*elyon* and its cognates as noun and adjective, see also Montgomery, 215–16; Hans Wildberger, *Jesaia, 2. Teilband* (Vol. X/2 of *Biblischer Kommentar: Altes Testament*, begrundet von Martin Noth; Neukirchen-Vluyn: Neukirchener Verlag, 1978),

554–555; Cumont, *"Hypsistos," RE,* X (1916), 444–46; Bertram, *"hypsistos* B," *Theological Dictionary of the New Testament,* ed. Gerhard Kittel (Grand Rapids and London: Eerdmans, 1964–74), VIII (1972), 615–16.

49   Deut 7:21, Ps 95.3.

50   It does occur in the Greek of I Esd 4:46, Tob 13:9 (AB), 11 (AB), 16 (S), 3 Macc 2:2. See Montgomery, 245, 247, and my *I Maccabees,* 153.

51   See Tallqvist, *Götterepitheta,* 236. The formula is not found in the inscriptions of Nabonidus, but cf. Nab. 1, col. II, lines 26 and 33, and Nab 24, col. II, line 33 (all speaking of Sîn).

52   Cf. however, Tobit (S) at 6:17, 7:12, 10:13, 11:1, and Tobit (AB) at 1:12. See Tallqvist, *Götterepitheta,* 54 (of Sîn). The formula does not occur in the inscriptions of Nabonidus, but cf. Nab. 4*, col. III, line 73, and Nab. 25, col. I, lines 5–6 (both speaking of Sîn). Marduk at Creation Epic, tablet VI, line 142, is "lord of all the gods of heaven and earth."

53   See n 83.

54   See Deut 32:40, Sir 18:1; cf. Tob 13:1. The writer of Dan 12:7 may have copied the epithet from Dan 4:31.

55   E.g., see Gilgamesh, tablet X, Old Babylonian Version, fragment iii, lines 3–5 (*ANET,* 90).

56   Judg 8:19, 1 Sam 14:39, etc.; **"balātu** 1e," *CAD,* II (1965), 50.

57   **"balātu** 1b.2," ibid., 47.

58   See Creation Epic, tablet IV, lines 4–7; Adapa D, lines 5–6 (*ANET,* 66).

59   There are further difficulties in v 2, "And the Lord gave Jehoiakim, king of Judah into his hand, and some of the vessels of the house of God; and he brought them to the land of Shinar, to the house of his god, and the vessels he brought to the treasure-house of his god."

Does the word "them" include Jehoiakim as well as the vessels? The Greek versions are unambiguous: They include only the vessels. In Hebrew the expression, "the Lord gave King X into the hands of Y," does not always mean that X became a captive of Y; it may mean only that the Lord allowed Y to defeat X (see 2 Chr 28:5, Judg 1:4, 3:10). By so interpreting "gave . . . into his hand" at Dan 1:2, we can prevent the verse from contradicting the account in 2 Kings, where Jehoiakim never suffers exile and receives burial in the company of his ancestors. But the strange syntax of Dan 1:2 argues against so construing it. There is the repetitiousness of the last two clauses, as well as the emphatic placement of "the vessels" before "he brought," as if the vessels were being opposed to something else. In fact, the text appears corrupt, a common phenomenon at the beginning of an ancient book, where scrolls were exposed to much wear. One would expect the passage to read, "and he brought him [Jehoiakim] to the land of Shinar and brought the vessels to the treasure-house of his god." Cf. Montgomery, 116–18. "To the house of his god" can easily be a dittography from the end of the verse, unless it was customary at Babylon to display captive kings to the god.

If the writer meant that Jehoiakim was carried off to Babylon, he could have minimized his disagreement with the account in 2 Kings by imagining that later Jehoiakim was sent back to Judah, just as the Chronicler had King Manasseh of Judah carried off to Babylon and then allowed to return (2 Chr 33:11–13). Though (as we shall see) the original writer of Daniel 1 was well-informed on the regnal years of Nebuchadnezzar and Jehoiakim, he was interested in the boys and the temple vessels and not at all in Jehoiakim.

60 See Tadmor, *"Rēshīt malkhūt," Entsiqlopediah miqra'it,* VII (1976), 312–14.

61 See Tadmor, "The Chronology of the First Temple Period," chap 3 of *Age,* 47–57.

62 See p. 113; Tadmor in *Age,* 49; Malamat, *Israel in Biblical Times,* 244 (in Hebrew).

63 Nisan: Tadmor in *Age,* 49–50; Tishri: Malamat, *Israel in Biblical Times,* 244–47 (in Hebrew).

64 2 Kgs 23:29–34.

65 See chap 4, n 29.

66 D. J. Wiseman, *Chronicles of the Chaldaean Kings (626–556 B.C.) in the British Museum* (London: Trustees of the British Museum, 1956), 20–27, 46, 65–68); Babylonian Chronicles 4 and 5, obverse, lines 1–13 (*ABC,* 97–100).

67 Chronicle 5, obverse, lines 12–13 (*ABC,* 100).

68 Grayson, *ABC,* 100.

69 Wiseman, *Chronicles,* 69.

70 Josephus *Antiquities* x.6.1.84, 2.88, 3.96–97 (see Ralph Marcus, *Josephus with an English Translation,* Vol. VI [Cambridge, Mass.: Harvard University Press, 1937],

205, n. *e*); *Seder ʿolam rabbah* 25; Jerome, *Commentary on Daniel* to Dan 2:1. See also Montgomery, 113–16, 140–41.

71 See p. 118. But take note of Nab. 25, col. III, lines 1–3.

72 Wording: "spirit was troubled": Dan 2:1, 3, and Gen 41:8; "I have dreamed a dream": Dan 2:3, Gen 41:15; Dan 2:27–28 is parallel to Gen 41:16; Dan 2:45(end) is parallel to Gen 41:25, 28. See also Montgomery, 142–43. But there is a close Babylonian parallel to Dan 2:1, 3 at Nab. 25, col. III, lines 1–3 (*ANET*, 563).

73 The terminology, *minḥāh wᵉniḥōḥīn* ("an offering and sweet odors") echoes biblical Hebrew (Exod 29:18 etc., Lev 2:1 etc.; Ezek 20:28) and is not Babylonian.

74 Samuel is not reported to have prayed for information on the she-asses for which Saul was searching (1 Sam 9:3–30). Cf. also 2 Kgs 6:8–12.

75 See Nab. 8, cols. VI-VII (*ANET*, 309–10). On that text, see above, p. 118, as well as Oppenheim, "Interpretation of Dreams," *TAPS*, N.S., 46 (1956), 202–5, and Erica Reiner, "Fortune-Telling in Mesopotamia," *JNES* 19 (1960), 24, n 2. See also the last sentence of n 72, above. Cf. Also "Prayer to the Moon-God," lines 11, 13, 26 (*ANET*, 386); "Prayer of Ashurbanipal to the Sun-God," line 4 (*ANET*, 387); "Hymn to the Sun-God," col. I, line 54 (*ANET*, 388); "Prayer to the Gods of the Night," lines 21–24 (*ANET*, 391); Nab. 4*, col. II, lines 28–74; Nab. 7, col. I, lines 11–12, 41 through col. II, line 40; Nab. 18, lines 1–34; Oppenheim, *Ancient Mesopotamia*, 271–72.

76 Praise to a god for granting a request is a common religious procedure. The Babylonian texts which I was able to find differ from Dan 2:20–23 in being promises to offer such praise if the worshiper's request is granted, rather than the hymn of grateful praise itself. See "Prayer of Lamentation to Ishtar," lines 100–106 (*ANET*, 385); "Hymn to the Sun-God," col. III, lines 50–54 (*ANET*, 389); "Prayer to Every God," line 63 (*ANET*, 392). The change from third to second person or vice versa is common both in biblical and in Babylonian prayer (e.g., 1 Kings 8:12–13; "Prayer to Every God," *ANET*, 391–92).

On 2:20: cf. Ps 41:14, 113:2, Job 1:21, 12:13, Neh 9:5. "Blessing" God's name (using the Semitic root *brk*) is a Jewish trait, but it is also found at pagan Palmyra, where Jewish influence is unlikely (see Jean-Hoftijzer, *Dictionnaire*, 44). Babylonians blessed Marduk, using the anagram and probable cognate verb **karâbu;** see **karābu** 7, *CAD*, VIII (1971), 198b. Though I have found no instance of **karâbu** with *shumu* or *zikru* ("name") as direct object, Matthew Stolper, in letters of July 28 and August 11, 1989, upon searching the files of *CAD*, reported abundant instances of "praising" *(damiqta qabû),* "extolling" *(ullû),* "magnifying" *(shutarbû),* and "glorifying" *(shutammuru)* the name of assorted gods. See also "**dalālu** A," *CAD*, III (1959), 47.

Wisdom and might were attributes of the LORD (Job 12:13) but also of Marduk; see

Creation Epic, Tablet VII, line 104 (*ANET,* 71); "**nēmequ** c.2 c," *CAD,* XI, Part II (1980), 161; Marcus Jastrow, *The Religion of Babylonia and Assyria* (Boston: Ginn & Co., 1898), 240; "**emūqu** 1a.2 c," *CAD,* IV (1958), 158a.

On 2:21: There is no parallel in the Hebrew Bible for "He causes the times to change and the eras to pass; He deposes kings and sets up kings." Though the LORD confers kingship (I Kgs 3:7, 2 Chron 1:8–9) and revokes it (I Sam 15:11, 35, 16:1), so do Sîn and Marduk. See Nab 8, col. IV, line 37 through col. V, line 10; Nab. 25, col. I, lines 8–11; "Hymn to the Moon-God," obverse, line 17 (*ANET,* 385). See also "**malkūtu** a," *CAD* X, Part I (1977), 169, "**malku** Aa," ibid., 166–67, "**malku** Ac," ibid., 168. On wisdom, see above.

On 2:22: In the Hebrew Bible the LORD is said to reveal profundities (Job 12:22) and perhaps secrets (Amos 3:7, though *sōd* there primarily means "counsel"); Babylonian gods certainly are said to reveal secrets; see "**niṣirtu** 1a," *CAD,* XI, Part II (1980), 276, "**niṣirtu** 1e.2," ibid., 277, and Gilgamesh, Tablet XI, lines 187–88 (*ANET,* 95). Light was an attribute of the LORD (Ps 36:10) but also of Marduk (Creation Epic, Tablet VI, lines 128–29, 149, 157 [*ANET,* 69–70]; Temple Ritual for the New Year's Festivals at Babylon, lines 25–26, 288 [*ANET,* 331–32]; "**nūru** A1a," *CAD,* XI, Part II [1980], 348–49).

On 2:23: For "God of my fathers," see n 43. Wisdom and might were treated above, on 2:21.

77   As opposed to *shōq* ("thigh, upper leg"), *regel* means "lower leg, including the foot." On *ḥsp,* see Montgomery, 167.

78   See Elias Bickerman, *Four Strange Books of the Bible* (New York: Schocken, 1967), 68, based on information received from Edith Porada and W. Samolin.

79   Feared: see chap 4, n 47. See also chap 7, n 122.

80   Attested: *mlk* must mean "kingdom" at 7:17, 8:20–21a (but in 8:21b the word means "king"). See H. L. Ginsberg, Review of *A Grammar of the Phoenician Language* by Zellig S. Harris, *JBL* 56 (1937), 142, and " 'King of Kings' and 'Lord of Kingdoms,' " *AJSL* 57 (1940), 71–74.

81   Below, pp. 237–44 and chap 12, pp. 371–78.

82   Sequences of metals in cuneiform texts: See the articles in *CAD:* "**erû** A," IV (1958), 321a–323a; "**ḫurāsu**," VI (1956), 245b–247b; and "**kaspu**," VIII (1971), 245a–247b. Date of Hesiod: See Martin L. West (ed.), *Hesiod: Theogony* (Oxford: Clarendon Press, 1966), 40–46, and *Hesiod: Works and Days* (Oxford: Clarendon Press, 1978), 31; Robert Lamberton, *Hesiod* (New Haven and London: Yale University Press, 1988), 14–15. Hesiod drew on ancient Near Eastern traditions: See Albin Lesky, *A History of Greek Literature* (New York: Crowell, 1966), 94–96.

83   Parallels to Nebuchadnezzar's confession: "God of gods": Deut 10:17; *Creation Epic,* Tablet VI, line 121 (*ANET,* 69); see Jacobsen, *Treasures,* 183.

"Masters of kingdoms" (or "masters of kings") does not occur elsewhere in the Hebrew Bible or in any known Babylonian text. It is found in Phoenician and Aramaic and in the Greek of the Ptolemaic Empire. See H. L. Ginsberg, *AJSL* 57 (1940), 71–74; Franz Rosenthal in *ANET,* 662b, n 4; Herbert Donner and W. Röllig, *Kanaanäische und Aramäische Inschriften* (2d ed.; 3 vols.; Wiesbaden: Harrassowitz, 1966–69), II, 312–13; Montgomery, 171–72.

On "revealer of secrets," see n 76.

Daniel would have had to participate in pagan practices: cf. Montgomery, 182–83.

84   Above, p. 206–7.

85   3:5, 7, 10, 15; see Louis F. Hartman and Alexander A. Di Lella, *The Book of Daniel* ("Anchor Bible" vol. 23; Garden City, N.Y.: Doubleday, 1978), 157. Certainly Greek are the lyre (*'qitaros* in the Aramaic text; Greek *kitharis*), the harp (*pᵉsanterin*) and the "symphony" (*sumphonᵉyah;* Greek *symphônia*), whatever that was. In later Greek it meant "bagpipe." Possibly Greek is the "trigon" (*sabbᵉkha;* = Greek *sambykê?*), a triangular instrument with four strings, a small arched harp.

86   Antiochos IV is known to have come uninvited to parties held by young men, bearing with him his horn *(keration)* and his *sympônia* (Polybius xxvi.1.4). The narrator gives the list of instruments four times. Clearly he wanted his audience to notice it. Two on the list are favorite instruments of Antiochus IV; the names of three and perhaps four are Greek. Can all six named instruments have been favorites of the king? If so, the narrator himself could have inserted the names in the 160s B.C.E. However, we have found good reason to date the tale close to 538 B.C.E. To have inserted the names of the instruments in the 160s might rouse suspicion and skepticism. If so, it is unlikely that the names were then interpolated into the text.

87   Cf. "angel" in v 28 and the Hebrew *bᵉnēy hāʾĕlōhīm* at Gen 6:2, Job 1:6.

88   See "**māru** 1d.1'," *CAD,* X, Part I (1977), 313b. See also Montgomery, 214–15, for the pagan West Semitic use of "son of gods" and "angel."

89   Chap 2, p. 34.

90   Nab. 25, col. I, lines 5–7. On "angels" in Babylonian religion, see J. A. Licht, *"Malʾakh ʾădōnāy, malʾakhīm," Entsiqlopedia miqrāʾit,* IV (1962), 977–78.

91   Nab. 24, col. I, lines 10–16.

92   Nab. 25, col. I, lines 1–2, as translated by Oppenheim, *ANET,* 562.

93   See n 18.

94   See chap 5, p. 114.

95   See Montgomery, 153, 225–26.

96   Ezek. 17:1–10, 23–24, 31:3–18.

97   See Montgomery, 228–29, and my article, "The Central Composition of the West Wall of the Synagogue of Dura-Europos," *Journal of the Ancient Near Eastern Society* 16–17 (1984–85), 134.

98   See Montgomery, 243–44; the best examples come from inscriptions of Nebuchadnezzar. Good examples from Nabonidus may have been lost because of the mutilated condition of Nab. 8, cols. VIII–X. Cf. also Nab. 6, col. II, line 47; Nab. 17, col. I, line 31; Nab. 21, col.I, lines 13–19.

99   On the epithets, see pp. 209–10.

100   See pp. 114–16; chap 5, pp. 132–35.

101   See Deut 26:5, Isa 43:27; "**abu** A 3a," *CAD*, I, Part I (1964), 72. Although most examples are plural, one is cited there from Nebuchadnezzar in the singular. Nabonidus speaks of the kings of Assyria as "my fathers" (Nab. 1, col. II, line 7)! Cf. Jerome, *Commentary on Daniel*, to Dan 5:2.

102   See 2 Kgs 24:13, 25:13–17.

103   Gen 41:40, Esth 10:3.

104   But cf. Montgomery, 71–72, 254, 256–57.

105   See p. 215, and cf. Dan 5:14.

106   Nab. 8, col. V, lines 8–9; Nab. 25, col. I, lines 7–11.

107   See p. 215.

108   See chap 5, pp. 113–16.

109   On Dan 3:16, see Montgomery, 208.

110   Cf. Clermont-Ganneau, "Mané, thécel, pharès et le festin de Balthasar," *Journal asiatique,* 8th series, 8 (1886), 48 (see n 116).

111 *Antiquities* x.11.3.243–44.

112 *Commentary on Daniel* to 5:25–28.

113 Inserted at the head of chap 5.

114 Jerome has "number," "a weighing," "separation."

115 See also Otto Eissfeldt, "Die Menetekel-Inschrift und ihre Deutung," *Zeitschrift für die alttestamentliche Wissenschaft* 63 (1951), 105–14.

116 *Journal asiatique,* 8th series, 8 (1886), 36–67, translated into English as "Mene, Tekel, Peres, and the Feast of Belshazzar," *Hebraica* 3 (1886–87), 87–102.

117 See J. Trinquet, "Métrologie biblique," *Dictionnaire de la Bible: Supplément,* ed. L. Pirot et al. (Paris: Letouzey, 1928–), V (1957), 1243–45.

118 *Journal asiatique,* 8th series, 8 (1886), 54–55, n 2.

119 *Zeitschrift für die alttestamentliche Wissenschaft* 63 (1951), 111–12. Eissfeldt, however, would read the first *mn'* not as the name of a weight, but as a participle, "counted up." Both Clermont-Ganneau and Eissfeldt rightly assume that the inscription contained ordinary phraseology, perhaps terms taken from accounting. Accordingly, H. L. Ginsberg (*"Mᵉne tᵉqel upharsin," Entsiqlopediah miqra'it,* V [1968], 11) pointed out, against Eissfeldt, that in the fairly abundant surviving Aramaic documents of accounting *mn'* never appears with that meaning.

120 See Eliezer Ben Yehuda, *A Complete Dictionary of Ancient and Modern Hebrew,* ed. N. H. Tur-Sinai (New York and London: Thomas Yoseloff, 1960), VI, 5203b, n 1.

121 Robert Biggs.

122 Albert T. Clay, *Letters and Transactions from Cappadocia,* Vol. IV of *Babylonian Inscriptions in the Collection of J. B. Nies* (New Haven: Yale University Press, 1927), no. 92, line 12.

123 "Zur Menetekel-Inschrift," *Vetus Testamentum* 4 (1954), 303–5.

124 See Ginsberg, *Entsiqlopediah miqra'it,* V [1968], 11.

125 Eissfeldt, *Zeitschrift für die alttestamentliche Wissenschaft* 63 (1951), 112.

126 E.g., Eissfeldt, ibid., 109; Clermont-Ganneau, *Journal asiatique,* 8th series, 8 (1886), 60–62.

127 Ibid., 61.

128 *Ta'anit* 21b.

129 See Hartman and Di Lella, *Daniel,* 190; Elias Bickerman, *Four Strange Books of the Bible* (New York: Schocken, 1967), 80; Ginsberg, *Entsiqlopediah miqra'it* V (1968), 12.

130 On the likelihood that *prsyn* is dual, see Clermont-Ganneau, *Journal asiatique,* 8th series, 8 (1886), 51–53. Even if it is plural, the word would represent at least two pieces of small change.

131 Nab. 8, col. II.

132 Nab. 8, col. V, lines 14–16; col. VI, lines 12–29.

133 Nab. 8, col. IV, lines 1–36; col. V, line 15. Although Oppenheim inserted Nergal-shar-usur's name at col. III, line 4 (*ANET,* 309a), he did so only on the insecure basis of col. IV, line 24; more likely the missing antecedent is Nabopolassar or Nebuchadnez-zar. Cf. Hermann Hunger and Stephen A. Kaufman, "A New Akkadian Prophecy Text," *JAOS* 95 (1975), 374, and Wilfred Lambert, *The Background of Jewish Apocalyptic* (London: Athlone Press, 1978), 11.

134 Cf. the verdict of Berossus on both, above, chap 4, end.

135 *ABC,* 109–10; *ANET,* 306.

136 Col. II, line 18.

137 i.190.

138 Herodotus i. 191.

139 Xenophon *Cyropaedia* i.4.16–iv.1.8.

140 Ibid., i.4.16–24, iv.6.2–vii.5.30.

141 Ibid., iv.6.3–5; v.2.28, 4.1.

142 Ibid., iv.6.1–10, v.3.8–19.

143 Ibid, vii.5.24.

144 Ibid., vii.5.1–34.

145 Cf. Montgomery, 70

146 See Hartman and Di Lella, *Daniel,* 35–36; Montgomery, 63–65; Parker-Dubberstein, 13–14; Herodotus i.73.3, 95.2–107.2, 130.1; Darius at Behistun, Persian, pars. 1–4 (col.I, lines 1–11, 26–30).

147 See chap 5, p. 113.

148 Herodotus's narrative (i.123–130) implies that Cyrus was still young when he defeated Astyages in 550 B.C.E., and Nabonidus, too, says that Cyrus was young then (Nab.1, col. I, line 29).

149 See "aḫšadrapannu," *CAD,* I, Part I (1956), 195.

150 As *'ḥšdrpn.*

151 As *exatrapês, xatrapês,* or *satrapês.*

152 Kent, *Old Persian,* 181. On the forms of the word, see I. M. Diakonoff, "Media," chap 3 of CHI, II (1985), 137.

153 For what is known, see Diakonoff, ibid., 124–37.

154 See Cook, *Persian Empire,* 83.

155 Herodotus iii.89–94; see Cook, *Persian Empire,* 77–85.

156 Cf. Montgomery, 268–70. On *bāʿū* as "prayer," see ibid., 270.

157 See my *I Maccabees* ("Anchor Bible," vol. 41A; Garden City, N.Y.: Doubleday, 1976), 137–59.

158 See pp. 183–87.

159 *Babylonian Talmud, Berakhot* 31a; *Palestinian Talmud, Berakhot* 4:1, 7a.

160 Ps 55:17 no more reflects a religious obligation than does Ps 119:64.

161 *Counsels of Wisdom,* lines 135–41, in W. G. Lambert, *Babylonian Wisdom Literature,* 104:

> Every day worship your god.
> Sacrifice and benediction are the proper accompaniment of incense.

> Present your free-will offering to your god,
> For this is proper toward the gods.
> Prayer, supplication and prostration
> Offer him daily, and you will get your reward.
> Then you will have full communion with your god.
> In your wisdom study the tablet.
> Reverence begets favour,
> Sacrifice prolongs life,
> And prayer atones for guilt.

According to Lambert (ibid., 97), the text is probably later than the First Dynasty of Babylon. To him, the tone and piety suggest the Kassite period. The script is typical late Babylonian.

162 See n 88.

163 On "living God," p. 210, end; but cf. Jer 15:20–21, 32:20, Joel 3:3, Ps 135:9, 145:13, Neh 9:10.

164 See above, p. 209.

165 Note, e.g., the mistaken decision of Hartman and Di Lella (*Daniel*, 212) to give them no attention.

166 Note the allusion to the parallel Israelite myth at Isa 51:9–10 and the use there and at Gen 1:2 and at Jonah 2:6 of the Hebrew cognate of *tiâmat, t*ᵉ*hôm* ("the deep").

167 Tablet I, lines 1–104 (*ANET*, 60–62).

168 Ibid., lines 105–8 (*ANET*, 62; cf. tablet IV, lines 42–43, 96–99 (*ANET*, 66, 67).

169 Tablet I, lines 132–45 (*ANET*, 62).

170 Ibid., line 96 (*ANET*, 62).

171 Ibid., line 103 (*ANET*, 62).

172 Tablet IV, lines 39–40 (*ANET*, 66).

173 Tablet VI, lines 53–166 (*ANET*, 68–70).

174 Tablet IV, lines 103–18 (*ANET*, 67).

175 Chap 1, pp. 11–16.

176 See n 101, and cf. Nab. 8, col. V, lines 14–18.

177 Cf. Bickerman, *Four Strange Books,* 62–64, and the views of Eerdmans and Beek, cited in Aage Bentsen, *Daniel* (2d ed.; Tübingen: Mohr [Siebeck], 1952), 31.

178 Views of Nabonidus and Berossus on Awêl-Marduk: see chap 4, last paragraph. Views of Babylonians on Cyrus: See pp. 204–5. The author of 2 Kgs 25:27–30 may have agreed with the Babylonians who valued Awêl-Marduk above Nergal-shar-uṣur.

179 2 Kgs 10:30.

180 Herodotus i.13, iv.163, v.92.

181 See William Kelly Simpson, "Pap. Westcar," *LÄ,* IV (1982), 745. In fact, Khufu was followed by four members of his family (Bickerman, *Four Strange Books,* 63).

182 Ibid., 62.

183 In chap 12, pp. 341–45.

184 Ibid. and chap 12, pp. 347–48.

185 Olmstead, *Persian Empire,* 34; Cook, *Persian Empire,* 25.

186 See chap 7, pp. 168–78.

187 Isa 47:13–14.

188 In a letter of Oct. 20, 1975.

189 Babylonian Chronicle 5, reverse, lines 11–13; 2 Kgs 23:36, 24:8–16 (Jerusalem fell in the last month of Nebuchadnezzar's seventh year, and the exiles were carried off early in his eighth).

190 See pp. 210–12.

191 I do not know why the author set the minimum at three years. Montgomery (122) thought he borrowed it from the three years of the Persian system for educating youth.

192 See pp. 210–11.

193 The text we have could easily have arisen if the original had had *b' nbwkdn'ṣr mbbl* ("Nebuchadnezzar came from Babylon") and a scribe expecting to see a title had added *lk* to make *bʾ nbwkdnʾṣr mlk bbl* ("Nebuchadnezzar, king of Babylon, came"), but I do not think that the original narrator in his first mention of Nebuchadnezzar would have left him without a title.

194   The scribes of Dan 1:1 may well have found at Jer 27:1–6 confirmation for their reading; on the meaning there of *bᵉrēshīt mamlekhet* ("at the beginning of the reign of"), see Hayim Tadmor, "Rēshīt malkhūt," *Entsiqlopediah miqraʾit,* VII (1976), 312–14. On the error in chap 5, see sec 12.

195   The Hebrew idiom occurs also at Jer 1:3.

196   Pp. 224–47.

197   Verse Account, col. V, lines 14–22; cf. chap 5, n 32.

198   See chap 5, pp. 115–16.

199   See chap 5, pp. 114–15.

200   *Cyropaedia* vii.5.29–30.

201   "And silver" is missing from the Aramaic text.

202   See Nab. 24, col. I, lines 10–11 (*ANET,* 560); col. II, lines 10, 14–15 (*ANET,* 561); Nab. 25, col. III, lines 22–23 (*ANET,* 563).

203   See n 101.

204   See pp. 233–35.

205   See chap 7, pp. 168–78.

206   See p. 205.

207   See Dandamaev, *Persien,* 94–95; David Frank Graf, *Medism: Greek Collaboration with Achaemenid Persia* (Ph.D. diss., University of Michigan; Ann Arbor: University Microfilms International, 1982).

208   See p. 158.

209   Nab. 25, col. I, line 42.

210   Demotic Chronicle, cols. III-V, in Wilhelm Spiegelberg, *Die Sogenannte Demotische Chronik des Pap. 215 der Bibliothèque nationale zu Paris nebst den auf der rückseite des Papyrus stehenden Texten* (Leipzig: Hinrichs, 1914), 17–20.

211 See p. 244.

212 Cf. the 127 provinces of the Persian Empire at Esth 1:1; see Muhammad A. Dandamaev and Vladimir G. Lukonin, *The Culture and Social Institutions of Ancient Iran* (Cambridge: Cambridge University Press, 1989), 103.

213 The author of Dan 10:1–12:3 accepted Daniel 1–6 (see below). Therefore, he believed that Darius the Mede reigned immediately after Belshazzar's death. That author makes Daniel date his vision in the third year of King Cyrus of Persia (10:1), and in 11:1 he refers to the first year of Darius the Mede as past. Thus, those Jews who believed there had been a King Darius the Mede dated him after Belshazzar's death and before the third year of Cyrus. They believed that Darius the Mede's reign practically coincided with the early reign of Cyrus.

214 See Jacob M. Myers, *I Chronicles* ("Anchor Bible," vol. 12; Garden City, N.Y.: Doubleday, 1965), lxxxvii–lxxxix; Sara Japhet, "Chronicles, Book of," *Encyclopedia Judaica*, V (1971), 533–34.

215 The author of Dan 8:20–21 named the empires symbolized in that chapter as Media, Persia, and Macedonia *(Yāwān),* and he knew of Daniel 7, to which he alludes in 8:1. Daniel 7 should be interpreted by its internal evidence. On Daniel 8, see chap 14.

216 Sec p. 216.

217 Compare the mistaken procedure of Jewish editors or scribes in Daniel 1 and 5:1–30; see pp. 228-32.

218 See chap 5, sec 2, pp. 115–16.

219 Aramaic: *lśṭr ḥd.* For use of *lśṭr* as "alongside," cf. *Qohelet rabbah* to Qoh 11:2. Aramaic *bśṭr* renders Hebrew *'ṣl* ("alongside") in the Targum to 1 Sam 20:19.

220 See Richard M. Frank, "The Description of the 'Bear' in Dn 7,5," *Catholic Biblical Quarterly* 21 (1959), 505–7, and cf. the commentary of Pseudo-Saʿadya Gaon to Dan 7:5.

221 Pp. 341–45.

222 See Herodotus i. 102–3, 107, 127–30. Astyages fell to Cyrus in 550 B.C.E.

223 Nab. 1, col. I, line 25; on the "Median Wall," see chap 6, n 10.

224 Parker-Dubberstein, 17.

225 Chap 13, pp. 427–34; chap 14, pp. 451–54.

226 Marduk as judge: See Tallqvist, *Götterepitheta,* 363, 366.

227 Chap 13, pp. 427–34.

228 Cf. Helge S. Kvanvig, "Struktur und Geschichte in Dan. 7,1–14," *Studia Theologica* 32 (1978), 102–3.

229 The word "those" does not occur in the Aramaic text, but I insert it to show that the adjective ʿ*lywnyn* is plural. The expression *qdyšy* ʿ*lywnyn* occurs also at Dan 7:22, 25, and 27, verses which will be treated in chap 14, pp. 451–54.

230 See Ps 34:10, Dan 8:24, and cf. Lev 19:2, 20:7, 26; Num 15:40, 16:3.

231 Pss 9:3, 21; 21:8, etc.

232 Either as a "plural of majesty" or as an instance of the pluralization of both nouns in a construct pair where only the first is properly plural; see Montgomery, 308.

233 See "**kidinnu,**" *CAD,* VIII (1971), 342b, 344a; W. F. Léemans, "Kidinnu, un symbole de droit divin babylonien," in *Symbolae ad jus et historiam antiquitatis pertinentes Julio Christiano van Oven dedicatae,* ed. M. David, B. A. von Groningen, and E. M. Meijers (Leiden: Brill, 1946), 36–61 (esp. 36–38, 54–59); Kemal Balkan, *Kassitenstudien: 1. Die Sprache der Kassiten* ("American Oriental Series, vol. 37; New Haven, CT: American Oriental Society, 1954), 159–60.

234 "**Kidinnūtu,**" *CAD,* VIII (1971), 344; Léemans, "Kidinnu," 55.

235 Ibid., 55–56.

236 See pp. 187–88.

237 However, the four Persian kings alluded to at Dan 11:2 are Cyrus, Cambyses, Darius, and Xerxes.

238 P. 237.

~9~

The Jews and the Babylonians from the Death of Xerxes I to the Eve of the Great Expedition of Alexander (465–334 B.C.E.)

1. Introduction

URING THIS PERIOD NEITHER *people of an almighty god* rose in revolt. The Jews continued to believe that God himself had placed his wayward people under the rule of the Persian kings, and they obeyed the divine decree. After four bitter defeats, the Babylonians waited for Marduk himself to act, at first, no doubt, hoping for fulfillment of the Three-Beast Version. Indeed, the subsequent course of history indicates that the defeat of Shamash-erîba was a turning point: Never again would Babylonians rise in mass revolt against a foreign conqueror.[1] Though previously the Assyrians had crushed many Babylonian rebellions, those multiple defeats had not deterred the vanquished from trying again. Nothing tells us why the victories of Darius I and Xerxes I had a greater deterrent effect. In chapter 12, however, we shall find that after the fall of the Persian Empire Marduk's people dared to produce still more present-future prophecies, to predict that the god himself would bring about their miraculous liberation from Macedonian overlords. From the reigns of Xerxes's Persian successors, to my knowledge, no such texts survive and other information on the Babylonians is scarce. We do have some texts and some good information from the Jews. Let us first give a brief treatment of the Babylonians.

2. The Babylonians

WE SHALL FIND in the next chapter that Marduk's people in 331 B.C.E. were viewing Persian rule with favor at the very moment when Alexander the Great was about to overwhelm the last Persian king, Darius III. We would like to know what put an end to their hatred for the heirs of Xerxes I.

Artaxerxes I (465–424) had three Babylonian concubines, each of whom bore him a son. No source tells us whether they influenced him to show favor to Babylon. Herodotus could observe Babylonia under Artaxerxes I. He reports that it was heavily taxed and from the time of Darius I had been joined to Assyria in one province and had to provide 500 boy-eunuchs annually. Babylonian documents confirm the heavy taxation under Artaxerxes I and the later Persian kings and show that most officials bore Persian names and that many foreigners moved in.² Nevertheless, cuneiform tablets give proof that throughout those reigns the temples of Marduk and the other Babylonian deities were in use, received ample income and offerings, and the priests and other cult officials functioned busily there.³

The queen, Damaspia, bore Artaxerxes I his one legitimate son, the future Xerxes II. Children of his three Babylonian concubines had profound effects upon the Persian Empire and may have won some following among Babylonians. Alogune bore him his sons Sekyndianos⁴ and Ochos; Kosmartidene bore him his son Arsites, and Andria bore him a son, Bagapaios, and a daughter, Parysatis. Artaxerxes gave Parysatis to her half-brother, Ochos, in marriage. The king and queen died on the same day in late 424 or early 423, and Xerxes II became king at Susa or Ekbatana.⁵ The new king reigned for only 45 days before being murdered. The reign was so short that Babylonian documents show no recognition of it; indeed, they also take no note of the reign which followed. In a time of insecurity, the scribes of Babylon went on dating by the regnal years of dead Artaxerxes I.⁶ The murderer of Xerxes II was his half-brother, Sekyndianos, who took the throne, whether at Susa or Ekbatana.⁷

Sekyndianos, too, had a brief reign. From the beginning he had to face the hostility of the army for killing both his brother and the influential courtier, Bagorazos, though the king tried to win the soldiers over with bonuses. Artaxerxes I had made his son Ochos satrap of Hyrkania (just south of the Caspian Sea). Babylonia and its resources may well have been important in these dynastic struggles.⁸ No source tells us where Ochos was during the reign of Sekyndianos.⁹ Sekyndianos repeatedly summoned Ochos to come to him, and Ochos each time promised to comply but did not. Meanwhile, Ochos managed to raise a considerable force, and people expected him to try to seize the throne.

Sekyndianos's cavalry commander defected to Ochos, and so did the satrap of Egypt and an influential eunuch. Those three crowned the still reluctant Ochos king. He took the throne name, "Darius," and to us he is known as Darius II (423–405).[10]

Though Ktesias gives 45 days to the reign of Xerxes II and 6 months and 15 days to that of Sekyndianos, a tablet from Babylon attests that Darius II was recognized there as king as early as Feb. 13, 423.[11] Was he already popular with the inhabitants? The assertions that Darius II contributed to repairs at the temple of Ishtar at Uruk and possibly showed other favor to that shrine rest on misinterpretations of documents.[12]

It is possible that Darius and Parysatis learned from their Babylonian mothers to revere Ishtar and Nabû, so that they, in turn, transmitted this devotion, mixed with Persian theology, to their sons, Arsakes (the future Artaxerxes II) and Cyrus;[13] both sons are known to have shown favor to the cult of the Iranian goddess Anahiti (Anahita), who was closely identified with Babylonian Ishtar. Darius, Parysatis, and their sons may also have fostered the worship of Iranian Tiri, who was closely identified with Babylonian Nabû.[14] Artaxerxes II even abandoned the Persian abstention from the use of statues in worship and began, like the Babylonians, to employ them. He set up statues of Anahiti for worship at Babylon, Susa, Ekbatana, Persepolis, Baktra, Damascus, and Sardis.[15] Three inscriptions from Asia Minor, perhaps datable in the fifth or fourth century B.C.E., suggest that Persian Ahuramazda was identified with Babylonian Bêl.[16] It is possible that all these trends pleased Babylonians.

Darius II died in 404 B.C.E., and Artaxerxes II became king (404–359/8). The new Persian monarch lost control of Egypt in 402. Unfortunately, no Egyptian texts of interest for our study of *peoples of an almighty god* survive from the period. Egypt under native rulers remained free for some six decades, until Artaxerxes III reconquered the country. Young Cyrus sought to overthrow his older brother Artaxerxes II and seize the throne. In the war between the two in 401, Babylonia was the king's main base, and the pivotal battle of Kunaxa, in which Cyrus was killed, took place only 60 miles from Babylon. Did public opinion at Babylon favor the ruling monarch? Throughout his long reign, the somewhat inept Artaxerxes II faced severe difficulties, but by the time of his death, except for Egypt, he was holding the entire empire he had inherited. Thereafter, three more Persian monarchs ruled: Artaxerxes III (359/8–338), Arses (338/7–336), and Darius III (336–330). A badly damaged king-list on a clay tablet found at Uruk may mention a Babylonian rebel king just before the accession of Darius III, but, if so, we have no other evidence of this pretender.[17] Only on the eve of the climactic battle with Alexander the Great in 331 do the

Babylonians again give us information valuable for our study, and that belongs in chap 10. Let us turn to examine the history and literature of the other *people of an almighty god* under the later Persian kings.

3. The Jews

EVEN AFTER THE COMPLETION of the building of the temple in 515 B.C.E., Jerusalem still was heavily scarred by the devastation incurred in her fall to Nebuchadnezzar in 586. Her walls were still breached, and raiders could easily penetrate the city and escape with plunder. The ruined condition of Jerusalem was humiliating and evoked contemptuous comments from Gentiles. Cyrus had issued permission only to build the temple. He had said nothing about Jerusalem and her walls. Jews had not displayed the rebellious behavior typical of a *people of an almighty god* since 586. Nevertheless, when they attempted to repair the city and the walls in the first half of the reign of Artaxerxes I, the records of their revolts of long before still impelled the king to issue a rescript putting a stop to the reconstruction.[18]

Soon thereafter, however, the loyal quiescence of the Jews who feared the LORD must have begun to impress the royal government, and we have ample evidence of its benevolent intervention on their behalf in the reigns of Artaxerxes I and Darius II. Artaxerxes himself decreed the rebuilding of Jerusalem and her walls.[19] The instances of Persian benevolence included the careers of Ezra and Nehemiah and, possibly, an order of Darius II to the Jewish military colonists at remote Elephantine in Egypt, that they observe the Feast of Unleavened Bread.[20] There were also the instructions sent by that king's officials to permit the rebuilding of the destroyed temple of the Elephantine community, provided that henceforth only vegetable sacrifices were offered there[21] (according to Deut 12:5–14, if God had chosen the temple at Jerusalem to be His place, only there could Jews offer animal sacrifices).[22]

Mere mention of these topics is enough here. Other scholars have treated them and the complicated problems involved.[23] I wish to stress the importance, in this period, of the incomplete fulfillment of the glorious prophecies of Isaiah, Jeremiah, Ezekiel, Deutero-Isaiah, Haggai, and Zechariah. Jews recognized them all as true prophets: Isaiah had predicted the falls of Assyria and Babylon; Jeremiah and Ezekiel had foreseen the fall, destruction, and rebuilding of Jerusalem; Deutero-Isaiah had foreseen Cyrus's decrees on the reconstruction of the temple and on the return of exiles to Jerusalem; Haggai and Zechariah had proclaimed that the reign of Darius I was the time to rebuild the temple, and, speaking for God, had promised the people good harvests if they rebuilt it;[24] the temple was completed without provoking the wrath of God, and even one bountiful harvest soon after was enough to lead people to believe that the words of the two prophets had been fulfilled.

Glaring, however, was the incompleteness of the fulfillment of the utterances of all these men. We have previously considered examples of how the words of all but Ezekiel were still unfulfilled.[25] It is easy to supply instances for the case of Ezekiel. Contrary to his words, the whole house of Israel had not been restored to the Holy Land to live in safety and prosperity, endowed with new, pious hearts, under their own King David.[26] Jews preserved the utterances of the true prophets, expecting them to be fulfilled eventually, if not now. Meanwhile, the predicted imperial glories did not come to Jerusalem and the Jews. Contrary to God's promises, revealed through Moses and the other true prophets, blight and drought still sometimes came upon the LORD's people, and Israelites still sinned.[27]

Like their predecessors, the prophets of the Persian period held that if the LORD inflicted adversity, he could only be punishing sin, and the people could find the same lesson in Deuteronomy, in the books of Kings, and in any other tendentious histories of their people which were available. Jews at the time faced a challenging question: What sin or sins now impeded the fulfilment of the words of the true prophets? That question evoked two kinds of responses among the LORD's people. One was "piecemeal"; the other, "wholesale."

In a piecemeal response, a Jew would name one or more sins as the cause. Deutero-Isaiah could name many.[28] Haggai and Zechariah had pointed to the failure to rebuild the temple, and Zechariah had taken note of other sins.[29] Ezra feared the disastrous effects of intermarriage with Egyptians, Ammonites, Moabites, and peoples of the Holy Land.[30] Nehemiah agreed and surely was concerned about violations of the Sabbath and of the commandments against usurious moneylending.[31]

We are entitled to be skeptical of some of these diagnoses. For the biblical writers, it was an axiom that only sin could bring on the wrath of God and that the deadliest sin was idolatry. Earlier, Ezekiel, who was not in Jerusalem, had made accusations of rampant idolatry there which find no support in Jeremiah, who was in the city and was equally zealous for the LORD. We deduce that Ezekiel drew his inferences from the axiom and did not report fact. The post-exilic writers had the same tendencies as Ezekiel. On the other hand, some of the "sins" singled out as to blame certainly were prevalent then, as in all periods. Zealous believers tried to put a stop to the sins, but the ever present mass of persons of lesser faith made success impossible.

The piecemeal approach and the explanations in the books of the prophets and in the tendentious histories only floodlighted the failure of the divine promises to be fulfilled. Whatever the amount of Sabbath observance or of free loans to the poor, it did nothing to hasten the end of foreign domination. Hence, some pious Jews tried to provide a "wholesale" cure for their postexilic adversity: If they sought out, collected, authenticated, edited, and taught all revelations of the LORD's will, going back to the times of the creation, the patriarchs, and the career of Moses, they might have a complete list of what would please or offend God, one which would be so impressive that the mass of the people would follow it. Once the will of God was well defined, the Jews' leaders could hope to enforce it.[32]

Clearly, more was required than observance of the commandments in Deuteronomy. King Josiah's covenant to observe those had not averted the catastrophe of 586 B.C.E., and efforts to observe those commandments after the return brought no noticeable abatement of adversity. We have no direct information on the processes of searching, collecting, authenticating, and editing. We are told, however, that at the very beginning of the seventh year of Artaxerxes I, Ezra set out from Babylon for Jerusalem as a learned expert (*spr,* "scribe")[33] on the "Law of the God of Heaven." He was determined to teach it and see to it that it was obeyed. Ezra bore both a copy of that Law and a letter of the king empowering him to teach God's Law and enforce it upon all members of his people in the huge Trans-Euphrates province, which included the land of Judah.[34]

The content of the text that Ezra was carrying, called "the Torah of Moses" at Ezra 7:6, has to be inferred from the accounts of Ezra's actions.[35] It indeed contained more than Deuteronomy. It drew on all three of the main sources of the Pentateuch, now called "JE," "P," and "D." In his memoirs, expressed in the first person, Ezra sharply distinguishes priests from Levites,[36] in accordance with the teaching of the Priestly Code (P),[37] and in contrast to Deuteronomy (D), in which Levites are equated with priests.[38]

Moreover, in confronting intermarriage as Israel's current deadly sin, Ezra in his first-person narrative has his informants saying,[39] "The people of Israel and the priests and the Levites have not separated themselves from the peoples of the lands, doing according to their abominations, even of the Canaanites, the Hittites, the Perizzites, the Jebusites, the Ammonites, the Moabites, the Egyptians, and the Edomites.[40] For they have taken of their daughters for themselves and for their sons, so that the holy seed have mingled themselves with the peoples of the lands." In his own prayer of confession which follows, Ezra says, "We have forsaken your commandments which you have commanded by your servants, the prophets,[41] saying, 'The land, unto which you go to possess it, is an unclean land through the uncleanness of the peoples of the lands, through their abominations, with which they have filled it from one end to another in their filthiness. Now therefore, do not give your daughters to their sons, and do not take their daughters for your sons, and forever do not seek their peace or their prosperity. . . . ' . . . Shall we again break your commandments and make marriages with the peoples that do these abominations?"

Ezra and his interlocutors do not accuse the wives of idolatry or any other heathen practices. They assume, rather, that the wives belong to stocks whom God has forbidden Jews to marry, and Ezra and the community leaders demand that the Jewish husbands divorce their foreign wives and separate from the children born to them.

We should ask what was the real situation and what scriptural justification Ezra and his supporters had for so drastic a step. Did he go beyond legitimate exegesis of the authoritative texts?[42] Let us examine the wording of his first-person account in the book of Ezra to see where it echoes the Pentateuch as we have it. Deuteronomy alone[43] forbids all intermarriage with the Ammonites and Moabites and allows intermarriage with Egyptians and Edomites only with the third generation. The same passage says of the Ammonites and Moabites, "Forever do not seek their peace or their prosperity."

The names of the Canaanites, the Hittites, the Perizzites, and the Jebusites occur together in D and in JE,[44] but not in P. Deuteronomy (7:1–4) expressly forbids intermarriage with those peoples, using the singular, "You shall not give your *daughter* to his *son,* and you shall not take his *daughter* for your *son*," in contrast to the plurals used of the marriage partners at Ezra 9:2, 12, and Neh 10:31.

Although P nowhere forbids intermarriage, Leviticus 18 clearly was an important source for Ezra. There we find plural "abominations" associated with the inhabitants of Canaan (vv 2, 24–28, 30), and those abominations are said to have defiled the land. Both Hebrew words used by Ezra for "uncleanness" *(niddāh, tum'āh)* occur in P, not in JE or D; and *niddāh* is found at Lev 18:19 and the root *ṭm'* occurs repeatedly in Leviticus 18 (vv 24–25, 27–28, 30).

Equally important for Ezra was Exod 34:11–17. I italicize some words of the passage and shall soon explain their importance: "I will drive out before you the Amorites, the Canaanites, the Hittites, the Perizzites, the Hivites, and the Jebusites. Beware of making a covenant with *the inhabitants of the land.* . . . You must not make a covenant with *the inhabitants of the land.* . . . When you take wives from among their daughters for your sons, their daughters will lust after their gods and will cause your sons to lust after their gods." Here we have the peoples of the promised land who were listed in Ezra 9:1 and a prohibition of intermarriage with them, and the prospective spouses are mentioned in the plural, as in Ezra and Nehemiah.

The opponents of Ezra's party would have been quick to point out that few if any of the wives could be shown to be Canaanites, Hittites, Perizzites, or Jebusites, ethnic groups that were extinct or nearly so. But most if not all the wives in question were indeed "inhabitants of the [Holy] land," with no secure claim to be ethnic Israelites. Hence, for Ezra's party, the names of the aboriginal peoples served only to lead the audience to think of the multiple prohibitions, in the authoritative texts, of relations with those peoples; but crucial for the foes of the questionable marriages were the words I have italicized in Exod 34:12 and 15. There a text of the Torah could be read as saying that God himself banned intermarriage with the inhabitants of the land. The expression in the books of Ezra and Nehemiah for such "inhabitants of the land" is "the peoples of the *land* [singular]." [45]

We have thus established that the Torah that Ezra carried with him contained matter from JE, D, and P. We can also be confident that one item from P was surprisingly missing. Although the Day of Atonement is treated in four passages of P,[46] the commandments to observe it cannot have stood in Ezra's Torah. We are told [47] that on the first day of the seventh month Ezra read out the book of the Torah to a mass meeting of the people with Levites acting as interpreters, and "All the people wept when they heard the words of the Torah," surely because they now were aware that they had committed numerous sins. The commandments for the Day of Atonement put it on the tenth day of the seventh month, a convenient time for its rites to serve to remit the sins of a people dismayed by hearing a reading of a version of the Torah on the first day of that month. Yet the narrative in the book of Nehemiah contains no hint of the existence of those rites. Ezra and his associates speak to console the people but say nothing of the Day of Atonement. Clearly, the Torah from which Ezra read cannot have mentioned it.[48]

The "wholesale" approach, which brought about the compilation of Ezra's Torah, was a rational procedure for believers to use. However, skeptics then as now could ask whether the observance of laws of purity and diet, the offering of sacrifices, the keeping of the Sabbath, and being kind to the poor could hasten the end of foreign domination and bring fulfillment of the glorious prophecies. In fact, the compiled Torah brought new difficulties upon those who wished to do God's will.

First, there were abundant contradictions among the laws of the three (originally separate) sources, JE, P, and D.[49] Some passages contained expressions that were of unknown meaning or ambiguous. On many problems of life, the compiled Torah contained nothing whatever, especially when the present brought unprecedented situations. In later Jewish texts, "midrash" came to be the Hebrew word for both the activity and the results of seeking to harmonize the contradictions, remove the ambiguities, discover the unknown meanings, and ascertain the divine will when there was nothing explicit in the Torah.

Already in the time of Ezra, midrash was necessary.[50] The people and their leaders then wished to make sure of obeying the divine will where they perceived problems in the language of the commandments or difficulties in carrying them out. At another mass-meeting, on the twenty-fourth day of the same month, they entered into a "sure covenant" *('ămānāh),* not only to observe the Torah but also to follow a set of provisions intended to solve those problems of interpretation and performance.[51] One of those who signed the *'ămānāh* was Nehemiah, the Jewish governor of Judea.[52]

Even in Ezra's time, one could no longer modify the texts assembled into the Torah. The items of the "sure covenant" could be recorded in the book of Nehemiah, but they could not be added to the Pentateuch. Old passages felt then to be awkward or embarrassing could not be changed.[53] Yet the Day of Atonement was absent from Ezra's Torah but entered the Pentateuch by the third century B.C.E., for the old Greek "Septuagint" translation, made then, has the passages. The Day of Atonement is unlikely to have been an invention to meet the needs of Ezra's generation; rather, its provisions must have stood in a scroll that had a claim to authenticity. Either Ezra and his party for some reason rejected that document (perhaps he found the scapegoat ritual of Leviticus 16 unacceptable) or he did not know of it. If so, the scroll was discovered or accepted later.

Human nature being what it is, neither Ezra nor anyone else could secure perfect obedience to the Torah he brought. Adversity and Persian rule over the Jews continued and had to be blamed on sin. Now the Torah displayed many possible causes for the wrath of God: violation of purity laws, improper or insufficient sacrificial offerings, laxity in tithing, sexual intercourse with menstruant women, failure to impose the death penalty for adultery, etc. After centuries of adversity, it was no wonder that some persons, like members of gnostic sects, learned to hate the Torah. A Jew could draw the conclusion that it was impossible to obey the Torah, that the Torah was a trap set for man by a malevolent deity. We can be surprised at the absence of such opinions from the surviving Jewish literature. There, the Torah is loved.[54]

We should ask why there is no trace of a Babylonian system of divine commandments parallel to the Jews' Torah. It is not hard to suggest an answer. Jews, unlike Babylonians, believed their God would wreak his wrath upon them only if they sinned. Marduk could be angry even if the Babylonians did not sin,[55] so that Babylonians lacked the motivation that impelled the Jews to compile and accept the Torah. I shall not try to explain why Jews insisted that their God was ethical!

The date of the last of the writing prophets, Malachi, is a matter of controversy. Some put him before Nehemiah,[56] some after. The later date seems correct. Malachi takes for granted (2:10) that tithes are obligatory and must be paid into the temple storehouse, an innovation of Nehemiah and the men of his time. Malachi returns to the piecemeal approach, surely using a version of the Torah, for he echoes both D and P.[57] In his short book he singles out, as provocations of God, the offering of unfit sacrifices, lax performance of priestly duties, intermarriage, the grievances of divorced wives, the questioning of God's justice, and failure to bring tithes and heave-offerings. In addition, he mentions (3:5) sorcery, adultery, false oaths, and oppression of the weak. Malachi's interlocutors come close to expressing hatred for the Torah when they complain of the profitlessness of keeping God's charge and of walking mournfully because of the LORD of Hosts (i.e., of obeying the often burdensome commandments).[58]

Difficulties faced the Jews who accepted the Torah, even after the establishment of the rites of the Day of Atonement. Adversity continued and had to be blamed on sins of the present or of the past that were too grievous to be erased by that day. Furthermore, the contradictions, obscurities, and silences of the Torah were real. Ingenuity could and did produce multiple midrashic solutions. There was no infallible way to eliminate all solutions but one. Jews tended to split up into irreconcilable sects, on issues such as the calendar and the festivals, purity laws, tithes and heave-offerings, and sacrifices.

After the careers of Ezra and Nehemiah begins a period for which the sources are extremely scanty, and reasons for the scarcity are not hard to find. Ezra and Nehemiah could tell of remarkable actions of divine providence in response to their prayers. Malachi's audience still believed he was divinely inspired. Thus Jews preserved his prophecies and wrote down and preserved the histories of Ezra and Nehemiah. Thereafter came long decades during which the Persian Empire, though severely challenged, managed to hold together and defeat its enemies. Jews as a nation continued to obey the Persian king and suffered neither the punishments inflicted upon rebels nor any other catastrophe. Nevertheless, their status as subjects of a foreign ruler, so contrary to the glorious prophecies, continually reminded them that their God was punishing them for sin and, for the time being, was otherwise not intervening in their history. Also unfulfilled were the present-future prophecies of the Pentateuch and

Daniel 2.[59] Believers had to hold that the nonfulfillment was temporary and due to sin. Contemporary history was uninteresting. Perhaps no one wrote it down; if anyone did, his work was not preserved.[60] In such a period, would-be prophets could hardly impress their audiences. If any presumed then to utter words of the LORD, not even their names have been preserved.[61] The Jews also experienced no crises then such as might have provoked the writing of present-future prophecy.

The lack of sources from this period is not very restricting for the purposes of this study. The Jews then believed their almighty God, because of their past or present sins, was not intervening on their behalf. As long as they held such a belief, they would not exhibit the phenomena typical of *peoples of an almighty god*. One of the few pieces of information from these times can serve as an illustration. Josephus reports[62] that in the reign of Artaxerxes II (405/4–359/8) fratricidal strife in the *high priestly family* caused a Persian commander to defile the temple and punish the Jews. Despite the apparent injustice, we hear of no protest and no resistance.

Only with the reign of Artaxerxes III (359/8–338/7) do we come upon reports of possible Jewish resistance to the Persian Empire. Christian authors attest that Artaxerxes III captured Jews and deported them to Hyrkania (the region just south of the Caspian Sea) and Babylon. Other texts which have been taken to corroborate that report and add details may rather contain mistakes.[63]

I see no reason why Christian authors or their sources would have invented a deportation of Jews by Artaxerxes III. The report is probably true. Can we date the deportation and determine its circumstances? The deported Jews could have been rebels from Judea, but, if so, they would constitute an exception to my generalization, that Jews after 586 and before 167 B.C.E. would not rebel against the pagan king whom, they believed, God himself had placed over them. No text attests a rebellion in Judea under Artaxerxes III, and the reasoning we used before also should be good here, that the historians and preachers of the LORD's people would not have been silent about such an event but would have used it as an object-lesson on the folly of rebellion, and believers and scribes would have preserved the evidence.[64] Jews were already known to be superb soldiers, and those deported by Artaxerxes III might have been mercenaries serving an enemy of the Persian king. Two such enemies are conspicuous as possibilities: Egypt and the Phoenician city of Sidon.

The sources on the reign of Artaxerxes III are not of the best. Let us first give a brief outline of what is known about his campaigns against Egypt and Sidon.[65] The only continuous account is that of Diodorus. Unfortunately, his narrative is somewhat confused and tells of all the events under the years 351/0 and 350/49 B.C.E., although evidence shows that they extended from the late 350s to 343.[66] Diodorus calls the last native ruler of Egypt "Nektanebos." This monarch is the second by that name in Diodorus's history.[67] He is identical with the king named Nekht-har-hebit on Egyptian monuments.[68]

Artaxerxes III in the late 350s marched against the Egypt of Nektanebos II, penetrated the country, but was ignominiously forced to withdraw. The Athenian orator Demosthenes, in his speech "For the Liberty of the Rhodians" (dated in 352 or in 351/0),[69] alludes to the unsuccessful campaign as a recent event, and a source of Diodorus clearly knew of it.[70] This blow to Persian prestige gave rise to revolts in Phoenicia, led by the Sidonians.[71] At Sidon, the people destroyed supplies accumulated for yet another campaign against Egypt, killed Persian officers, and cut down the trees of the local forest preserve of the Persian king. Artaxerxes intended to make an example of Sidon.[72] The city fell to him and suffered massacre, looting, and burning.[73]

The year perhaps can be fixed as 345 with the help of the fragmentary Babylonian Chronicle 9. It says, "The fourteenth [year] of Umasu, who is called Artaxerxes [III]: in the month Tashrîtu the prisoners which the king took [from] Sidon [were brought] to Babylon and Susa. On the thirteenth day of the same month a few of these troops entered Babylon. On the sixteenth day the . . . women, prisoners from Sidon, whom the king sent to Babylon—on that day they entered the palace of the king."[74] By Babylonian reckoning, the fourteenth year of Artaxerxes III was 345/4 B.C.E., and in that year Tashrîtu began on Oct. 11. One is tempted to infer that the fall of Sidon preceded the dates given in Chronicle 9. If so, it is unlikely that Artaxerxes would have waited many months to send eastward the prisoners he took from Sidon, so that the fall of the city, too, would have occurred in 345. Nevertheless, the Babylonian Chronicle might be referring to prisoners taken in an early stage of Persian operations against Sidon, long before the city fell.[75]

In any case, Diodorus's narrative shows that Artaxerxes took Sidon and afterward invaded Egypt.[76] At first the Persian king's army was unable to cross the Nile at the stronghold of Pelusion, but finally one unit succeeded in doing so. Nektanebos II lost his nerve and withdrew to Memphis from the neighborhood of Pelusion. His withdrawal demoralized his large forces at the frontier, and they soon surrendered to the Persians.[77] Thus ended the ancient history of independent Egypt. There is a report that Artaxerxes cruelly deported many *Egyptians* to Persia.[78]

Can we determine the chronology of these events more closely? The Egyptian priest, Manetho (his name is also given as "Manethon" or "Manethos"), in the mid-third century B.C.E. wrote about the history of his country, giving lists of kings and the lengths of their reigns. According to Manetho, Nektanebos II reigned eighteen years, and, on the basis of the priest's figures, one might date the fall of Egypt to Artaxerxes III in 341 B.C.E.[79] However, Greek texts prove that the Persian king conquered Egypt between November 343 and February 342, and a satisfactory explanation has been found for Manetho's error.[80]

Thus we have multiple possibilities for the Jews deported by Artaxerxes III. If those Jews were not captured after a rebellion in Judea, they could have been mercenaries for Egypt, taken during either of the Persian king's penetrations into that country;[81] or they could have been mercenaries hired by the Sidonians. Let us now examine the texts on the deportations.

Georgius Syncellus (late eighth to early ninth century C.E.) writes, "[Artaxerxes III] Ochos, son of Artaxerxes [II], in the course of an expedition against[82] Egypt, took a partial captivity of Jews. Some of them he settled in Hyrkania by the Caspian Sea, and others, in Babylon, who are still there to the present day, as many of the Greek historians report. This Ochos, two years after he conquered Egypt, was murdered by Bagoas, a Persian, one of the high officials. The same king also destroyed Sidon. This Ochos had launched an expedition against Egypt while his father Artaxerxes was still alive[83] (so say other authorities), but later he did conquer Egypt after Nektanebos [II] had fled."[84] Clearly Syncellus here drew on multiple sources and has done nothing to combine them into a coherent narrative. Therefore, it is most unlikely that he altered what he found in his informants. Thus, one or more sources of Syncellus connected the deportation with an expedition of Artaxerxes III against Egypt. Syncellus offers no support for connecting the deportation with the fall of Sidon. He knew of several expeditions of Artaxerxes III against Egypt, but his words leave it unclear which of the expeditions occasioned the deportation of the Jews.

Orosius (ca. 385–420 C.E.) in his *Histories Against the Pagans* iii.7 treats disastrous events of the mid-fourth century B.C.E. After mentioning the Roman treaty with the Carthaginians (of 348 B.C.E., though Orosius dates it in 352) and the birth of Alexander the Great (356), he goes on to write, "At that time, too, Ochos (alias Artaxerxes), after the end of a long campaign in Egypt on a very large scale, transplanted a great many of the Jews and ordered them to dwell in Hyrkania by the Caspian Sea."[85] Orosius probably had no source beyond those of Syncellus. Orosius locates the campaign in Egypt. Though he mentions its length and scale, he does nothing to tell us whether the Jews were deported at the end of Artaxerxes's unsuccessful campaign of the late 350s or at the end of his successful conquest of Egypt in 343.

Eusebius (ca. 263–339 C.E.) constructed chronological tables. Many of the sources on which he drew are no longer extant. The original Greek of his tables has perished, but an Armenian version of them survives, as does the Latin reedition of them by Jerome. Handwritten, the tables readily suffered corruption, and some of the dates were wrong to begin with. Nevertheless, useful hints can be derived from Jerome's Latin and from the Armenian.

In giving dates, Eusebius used the "era of Abraham," in which the year 1 was equivalent to 2016 B.C.E. His tables do not record the abortive invasion of Egypt by Artaxerxes III. In Jerome's Latin, the deportation is recorded thus: "Ochos captured a portion of the Jews and, after transferring them to Hyrkania, had them settle as dwellers by the Caspian Sea."[86] The item appears in the line for year of Abraham 1658 (359/8 B.C.E.) and for the second year of Olympiad 105 (359/8 B.C.E.) and for the seventh year of Artaxerxes III (353/2 B.C.E.). On the line for year of Abraham 1666 (351/0 B.C.E.), for the second year of Olympiad 107 (351/0), and for the fifteenth year of Artaxerxes III (345/4) appears the note, "Ochos occupied Egypt after Nectanebos fled to Ethiopia, the event in which the kingdom of Egypt was destroyed; thus far Manethos."[87] On the line for year of Abraham 1669 (348/7 B.C.E.) and for the first year of Olympiad 108 (348/7) and for the eighteenth year of Artaxerxes III (342/1) appears this note: "Ochos destroyed Sidon and annexed Egypt to his own empire."[88]

The inconsistencies are not surprising. The spacing of the events is significant. Eleven years separate the deportation from the fall of Sidon, and at least eight years separate the deportation from Artaxerxes's final conquest of Egypt.

The Armenian version of the tables has suffered considerable derangement. The deportation appears on the line for year of Abraham 1652 (365/4 B.C.E.), for the first year of Olympiad 104 (364/3), and for the first year of Artaxerxes III (359/8). Ochos's occupation of Egypt and the end of native dynastic rule in that country appear on the line for year of Abraham 1668 (349/8 B.C.E.), for the first year of Olympiad 108 (348/7), and for the seventeenth year of Artaxerxes III (343/2). Sixteen years separate the two lines. Eusebius's note on the fall of Sidon is not preserved in the Armenian version.

Both versions of Eusebius's tables, therefore, argue against connecting the deportation with Artaxerxes's final conquest of Egypt. Jerome's version is evidence against connecting the deportation with the fall of Sidon. Indeed, no source associates the deportation with the fall of Sidon. Unless further evidence turns up, it seems best to connect the deportation with Artaxerxes's unsuccessful campaign of the late 350s in Egypt. If Nektanebos II paid Jewish soldiers, and those soldiers fell into the hands of Artaxerxes III, the fact is far from showing that Jews in Judea rebelled against the Persian king, even if some of the mercenaries came from Judaea. Most of those Jewish soldiers may have been born in Egypt. Their religion may have driven them to be as loyal to the kings of Egypt as the Jews of the Persian Empire were to Artaxerxes III and his predecessors. We conclude that as long as the Persian Empire existed, the vast majority of the Jewish nation under its rule served it loyally.

NOTES

1 On the revolts to which Babylonian astronomical diaries of 238 and 235 B.C.E. attest, see chap 12, pp. 392–93.

2. Babylonian concubines: Ktesias, FGH 688, F 15.47; Olmstead, *Persian Empire,* 355. Taxation, officials, and foreigners: Herodotus i.192, iii.92; Oppenheim in CHI, II (1985), 568–82; Kuhrt in CAH², IV (1988), 130–31; Olmstead, *Persian Empire,* 298–99, 356, 358; Cook, *Persian Empire,* 202–4, 261 (n 21); Frye, *History,* 129–30, 132–33.

3 See Matthew W. Stolper, "The Governor of Babylon and Across-the-River in 486 B.C.," *JNES* 48 (1989), 295–96. The references given by Olmstead at *Persian Empire,* 291, n 5, do not justify his assertions in the first paragraph of that page, that Artaxerxes I honored Ishtar of Babylon with a stele and that in his reign the priests of Bêl-Marduk had been reinstated and some of their lands restored. I cite the references as given by Olmstead. J. N. Strassmaier, *Actes du huitième congrès international des orientalistes,* II, Sec. IB (1892), 279 ff. (actually, 282), No. 24, contains nothing on the priests of Bêl-Marduk. As Stolper informed me in messages of May 16, 22, and 23, 1990, the fragments mentioned at MDOG XXII (1906), 5, are not from a stele, mention Artaxerxes *II,* and later readings of them say nothing of Ishtar (see Robert Koldewey, *The Excavations at Babylon* [London: Macmillan, 1914], 129 and fig. 78).

4 So he is called by Ktesias (FGH 688, F 15.47). Diodorus (xii. 71.1) gives his name as "Sogdianos."

5 Deaths of Artaxerxes I and his queen: David M. Lewis, *Sparta and Persia* (Leiden: Brill, 1977), 74. On the events between the death of Artaxerxes I and the time that Darius II was securely in power and on their chronology, see Matthew W. Stolper, *Entrepreneurs and Empire* (Leiden: Nederlands Historisch-Archaeologisch Instituut te Istanbul, 1985), 114–20.

6 Parker-Dubberstein, 18; Cook, *Persian Empire,* 129.

7 See Lewis, *Sparta and Persia,* 74.

8   See ibid., 72–76; Cook, *Persian Empire* 129, 136, 250 (n 10).

9   Olmstead's statement, that Ochos had gone from Hyrkania to Babylonia (*Persian Empire,* 355) is a mere guess, though it may be correct. Boyce, HZ, II, 198, depends on Olmstead. See Lewis, *Sparta and Persia,* 74.

10   For the events between the death of Artaxerxes I and the accession of Darius II we depend on Ktesias (FGH 688, F 15.47–50; Diodorus xii.71.1).

11   Parker-Dubberstein, 18.

12   For the assertion, see M. Meuleau, "Mesopotamia under Persian Rule, from the Sixth to the Fourth Centuries," in *The Greeks and the Persians,* ed. Hermann Bengtson (New York: Delacorte, 1968), 378. As Stolper informed me in messages of May 22 and 23, 1990, the documents of the temple archive refer to Darius I, not Darius II.

13   Ktesias, FGH 688, F 15.51; Plutarch, *Artoxerxes* 1.2–3. Plutarch (*Artoxerxes* 1.4) cites the elder son's name from Ktesias as "Arsikas"; Photius's summary of Ktesias gives it as "Arsakas" or "Arsakes" (FGH 688, F 15.51, 55, 56).

14   Anahiti (Anahita): Boyce, HZ II, 196–97, 201–4, 216–21; Tiri: ibid., 204–6; see also ibid., 240–41.

15   Berossus, FGH 680, F 11; Boyce, HZ, II, 217.

16   Ibid., 274–75.

17   Egypt: Edda Bresciani, "The Persian Occupation of Egypt," chap 9 of CHI, II (1985), 512, 522–26. Babylonia in the war between Cyrus and Artaxerxes: Lewis, *Sparta and Persia,* 73; Olmstead, 374. Reigns of Artaxerxes II and his successors: Cook, *Persian Empire,* 211–28; Olmstead, *Persian Empire,* 371–445, 486–524. Babylonian rebel king: See A. Leo Oppenheim in CHI, II (1985), 533.

18   Ezra 4:7–23; on how Ezra 4:6–24 fit into the narrative, see my *II Maccabees,* 174.

19   Neh 2:1–8.

20   Text of the "Passover Letter": Bezalel Porten and Ada Yardeni, *Textbook of Aramaic Documents from Ancient Egypt* (4 vols.; Jerusalem: Hebrew University, 1986–), I, 54. See also Bezalel Porten, *Archives from Elephantine: the Life of an Ancient Jewish Military Colony* (Berkeley and Los Angeles: University of California Press, 1968), 128–30, 132–33, 280–82, 311–14. Cf. Morton Smith, "Jewish Religious Life in the Persian Period," chap 10 of *CHJ,* I (1984), 230–32.

21   Porten, *Archives,* 284–96, and "The Jews in Egypt," chap 13D of CHI, I (1984), 389–90.

22   Some Jews are known to have believed that God had not chosen the second temple; see my *II Maccabees,* 14–17.

23   See the discussions in the works on the Jews cited in chap 6, n 42.

24   Hag 1:5–11, 2:15–19; Zech 1:16, 8:9–12.

25   See pp.159–60, 172–77. Cf. Robert P. Carroll, *When Prophecy Failed: Cognitive Dissonance in the Prophetic Traditions of the Old Testament* (New York: Seabury, 1979), 36, 39–40, 57–58, 112–16, 150–68, 204–5.

26   See Ezek 20:40–42, 29:25–26, 36:8–14, 24–37; 37:15–28.

27   See n 25. Blight and drought: Hag 1:10–11, 2:17, Zech 8:11–12; cf. Mal 3:9–11.

28   See Isa 56:2, 57:1–7, 58:6–13, 59:2–9, 65:3–7, 11.

29   1:2–6, 8:16–17.

30   Ezra 9:1–10:44.

31   Neh 5:1–13; 13:23–27.

32   On the compilation of the Pentateuch as a response to the incomplete fulfillment of the prophecies and to the Jews' postexilic adversity, cf. Kaufmann, *Toledot,* Vol. IV, Part I, 352–53, 396, 408.

33   The king, as usual in ancient narratives, is given no ordinal numeral in Ezra 7:1–8 but is best taken as Artaxerxes I. See Tadmor in Ben-Sasson, 173–75, and in *Historiah shel Eretz-yisrael,* II, 265–67, and Morton Smith, *Palestinian Parties and Politics that Shaped the Old Testament* (New York and London: Columbia University Press, 1971), 120–22, 252–53. On *spr,* see Kaufmann, *Toledot,* Vol. IV, Part I, 275–78.

34   Ezra 7:1–26; the king's letter (surely a response to carefully worded requests) contains most of the important facts. It is a contemporary witness, even if the third-person narrative introduction (7:1–10) was written later.

35   Cf. Widengren in Hayes-Miller, 514–15.

36 Main sources of the Pentateuch: See Samuel R. Driver, *An Introduction to the Literature of the Old Testament* (New York: Meridian, 1957), 10–103, 116–59; Kaufmann, *Religion of Israel,* 153–67.

Ezra distinguishes priests from Levites: 8:15–19, 24, 9:1, 10:18–23.

37 E.g., Num 3:9–10, 16:1–35.

38 17:9, 18; 18:1–8, 24:8, 27:9.

39 Ezra 9:1–2.

40 "Edomites" is the reading at I Esd 8:69, where Ezra 9:1 has "Amorites." The other peoples at the end of the verse, the Ammonites, the Moabites, and the Egyptians, are all drawn from the prohibitions on intermarriage at Deut 23:4–10, where Edomites, not Amorites are also mentioned.

41 The commandments to which Ezra alludes are in the Pentateuch; Moses and Aaron were prophets.

42 Cf. Kaufmann, *Toledot,* Vol. IV, Part I, 284–93.

43 23:4–10.

44 Deut 7:1, 20:17; JE: Exod 3:8, 17, 13:5, 23:23, 28, 33:2, 34:11, Num. 13:29.

45 Ezra 10:2, 11; Neh 9:24, 10:3, 32. Pagan inhabitants of territories outside the Holy Land are called "the peoples of the *lands* [plural]" (Neh 9:30, 10:29). The presence of the plural, "lands," at Ezra 3:3 and 9:11 is probably due to scribal corruption. At 9:1–2, the plural is correct because Ammonites, Moabites, Egyptians, and Edomites are included (see n 40). On all this, see H. Louis Ginsberg, *The Israelian Heritage of Judaism* (New York: Jewish Theological Seminary of America, 1982), 8–9, 15–16.

46 Leviticus 16, 23:26–32, 25:9, Num 29:7–11.

47 Neh 8:1–12.

48 See Smith, *Parties,* 123, 254 (n 118). Menahem Haran's note (*Temple and Temple Service in Ancient Israel* [Oxford: Clarendon, 1980], 291–92 [n 7]) might account for the absence of the Day of Atonement from the Covenant Code *(JE)* and from D, but it does not explain how the Day could fail to appear in the narrative of the book of Nehemiah. Kaufmann (*Religion of Israel,* 210, n 17; *Toledot,* Vol. IV, Part I, 339–40) argues that in Neh 8–10 no priestly temple rituals are mentioned: It was not an occasion for ritual but for learning the Torah, becoming conscious of sin, and resolving to obey the commandments, so that it is not surprising that the narrative is silent about the Day of Atonement, which was primarily a rite for purifying the temple (Lev 16:16, 19–20, 33). Its omission from the narrative of Nehemiah 8–10 "is accidental, or, more likely, owing to the fact that the day had not yet achieved the popular significance it had later." We should bear in mind, on the contrary, that the commandments for the Day of Atonement do not concentrate on the purification of the sanctuary. They give at least equal importance of the act of atoning for the sins of the people (Lev 16:21–22, 30, 33–34, 23:28). In Nehemiah 8–10 we have a people in tears over its sins; there, the silence about the Day of Atonement cannot be accidental or due to the still insufficient popularity of its rites. These considerations also dispose of the argument presented by Jacob Milgrom (*Leviticus 1–16* ["The Anchor Bible," vol. 3; New York: Doubleday, 1991], 1071). A. Demsky (in *Shilton paras,* 265, n 52) argues on the basis of the word *be'āsōr* ("on the tenth day") at Ezek 40:1 that Ezekiel knew Lev 16:29, 23:27, or 25:9, which Demsky there mis-cites as Lev 22:9). But Ezekiel in chap 40 says nothing of the Day of Atonement, and *be'āsōr* occurs elsewhere, both in Ezekiel and in the Torah, with no connection to that Day (Ezek 20:1, 24:1, Exod 12:3). On how the Day of Atonement came into the Torah at some time after Ezra read his version to the mass-meeting, see p. 272.

49   See, e.g., Kaufmann, *Religion of Israel,* 166–200; Moshe Weinfeld, "Pentateuch," EJ, XII (1971), 243–57.

50   See Kaufmann, *Religion of Israel,* 327–28, 346, 350–51.

51   Neh 9:1–10:40; Kaufman, *Toledot,* Vol. IV, Part I, 329–338.

52   Neh 10:2.

53   See Kaufmann, *Religion of Israel,* 209–11; *Toledot,* Vol. IV, Part I, 342–46.

54   See, e.g., Ps 119.

55   See 2:16 and 2:32.

56   See, e.g., Widengren in Hayes-Miller, 527; Bright, *History,* 378; Smith, *Parties,* 117, 250 (n 83). The strongest reason for putting Malachi before Nehemiah is the fact that in Malachi "abuses" supposedly ended by Nehemiah are still present, such as intermarriage and failure to pay tithes into the temple storehouse. However, even a forceful leader could not always enforce the rules. Evidently the governor of Judea in Malachi's time was not Nehemiah, and probably he was not even Jewish (Mal 1:8).

57   Obligatory tithes: Neh 10:38–39, 13:10–13; see Kaufmann, *Religion of Israel,* 189–93; *Toledot,* Vol. IV, Part I, 366–67; B. Oppenheimer in *Shilton paras,* 161–62.

Echoes of expressions from D not found in P are abundant in Malachi. E.g., Mal 2:2, "I will send the curse upon you" (Deut 28:20); Mal 2:8, "you are turned aside from the way" (Deut 11:28, 31:29); Mal 2:9, "you have shown partiality to persons" (Deut 10:17); Mal 2:15–16, "beware for yourselves" (Deut 4:15); Mal 3:22, "Horeb" (P uses "Sinai"), etc. It is important to note that echoes from P and expressions from P not found in D are also abundant (contrast H. L. Ginsberg, *Heritage,* 18). E.g., Mal 1:7, *leḥem* (usually, "bread," but here, "sacrifice"): the word occurs with that meaning only in P (Lev 21:6, Num 28:2, etc.); 1:10, *uminḥāh lo erṣeh miyyedkhem* ("I will not accept an offering from your hand"): in the Torah the use of the root *rṣh* for the acceptance of offerings is peculiar to P (Lev 1:4, 7:18, 19:7, 22:23, 25, 27, but the closest parallel to Mal 1:10 is at Amos 5:22); the expression implied at Mal 1:11–12, *hallēl shēm* ("profane [God's] name") in the Torah is peculiar to P; the root *rṣh* is used at Mal 1:13, as at Lev 22:25, to say that a defective animal is not acceptable as an offering; Mal 1:14, *moshḥat* ("a blemished thing") is paralleled only at Lev. 22:25; Mal 2:11, *hillēl qōdesh YHWH* ("has profaned the holiness of the LORD") has a parallel at Lev 19:8; although Mal 3:5 has a parallel at Deut 24:14 and 17, only at Lev 19:12–14 are false oaths and the fear of God mentioned.

58 Mal 3:14–15.

59 See pp. 9–16, 224–27.

60 See 7.

61 See 1:1–12, 20, 21; I do not believe that the canonical books of the prophets contain the work of seers who were later than Malachi.

62 *Antiquities* xi.7.1.297–301.

63 At Josephus *Against Apion* i.22.194, Hecataeus of Abdera is quoted as saying that the *Persians* deported many myriads of Jews to Babylon, but Hecataeus is probably speaking of the Jews deported by Nebuchadnezzar II and, from ignorance or carelessness, anachronistically names the great eastern power as the Persians. Julius Solinus, who probably lived in the third century c.e. (Diehl, "Julius 492," *RE,* X [1919], 824–25), was a compiler of memorable facts. In his brief description of Palestine, he writes (*Collectanea rerum memorabilium* 35.4), "Judaeae caput fuit Hierosolyma, sed excisa est. Successit Hierichus, et haec desivit Artaxerxis bello subacta" ("The capital of Judaea was Jerusalem, but it was destroyed. Jericho replaced it, and it, too, came to an end on being conquered in war by Artaxerxes"). Solinus in this context otherwise draws his information from Pliny's *Natural History,* but the reference to Jericho is enigmatic. Jericho, as far as we know, never was the capital of Judea, nor is there any other record that an Artaxerxes conquered it. The efforts of D. Barag to find archaeological evidence of a devastating campaign of Artaxerxes III in Judea ("The Effects of the Tennes Rebellion on Palestine," *Bulletin of the American Schools of Oriental Research* 183 [October, 1966], 6–12) have been refuted by Geo Widengren (in Hayes-Miller, 500–502); cf. Ephraim Stern in *CHJ*, I (1984), 77, 114, and Peter Ackroyd, ibid., 154.

64 Nevertheless, scholars have tried to assemble clues to prove that there was such a rebellion in Judea; see, e.g., Morton Smith, *Palestinian Parties*, 60, 156, 185. The clues do not make a good case.

65 Modern discussions: Andrew R. Burn in CHI, II (1985), 385–87; D. Barag's article cited in n 63; Olmstead, *Persian Empire*, 432–40; Cook, *Persian Empire*, 223–24. Detailed studies of the chronology: E. Bickermann, "Notes sur la chronologie de la XXX-ième dynastie," in *Mélanges Maspero* ("Mémoires publiées par les membres de l'Institut français d'archéologie orientale du Caire," LXVI; Le Caire: Impr. de l'Institut français d'archéologie orientale, 1934–36), I, 77–84; Friedrich Karl Kienitz, *Die politische Geschichte Aegyptens vom 7. bis zum 4. Jahrhundert vor der Zeitwende* (Berlin: Akademie-Verlag, 1953), 166–80, 181–84.

66 Diodorus xvi.40.1–45.6, 46.1–51.3. See Charles L. Sherman, *Diodorus of Sicily,* Vol. VII (Cambridge, Mass.: Harvard University Press, 1952), 348, n 2; Burn in CHI, II (1985), 385.

67 See Diodorus xv.42.1 (Nektanebos I) with xvi.93.2 (Nektanebos II).

68 See Herman De Meulenaere, "Nektanebos II," *LÄ*, IV (1982), 451–53.

69 Demosthenes 15.11–12; Dionysius of Halicarnassus (*First Letter to Ammaios* 4) dates the speech in 351/0, but F. Focke gives weighty reasons for assigning it to 352 ("Demosthenesstudien," in *Genethliakon Wilhelm Schmid* ["Tübinger Beiträge zur Altertumswissenschaft," Vol. V; Stuttgart: W. Kohlhammer, 1929], 18). Isocrates, too, alludes to the defeat of Artaxerxes III in Egypt, in his oration to Philip (5.101, of 346 B.C.E.). Demosthenes's phrase, *en Aigyptôi* ("in Egypt"), implies that Artaxerxes invaded the country.

70 Diodorus xvi.40.3, 44.1, 48.1–2.

71 Ibid., 40.5, 41.1–4; cf. Isocrates 5.102.

72 Diodorus xvi.41.5–6.

73 Ibid., 43.1–45.6.

74 *ABC*, 114. John Wilson Betlyon (*The Coinage and Mints of Phoenicia: the Pre-Alexandrine Period* ["Harvard Semitic Monographs," no. 26; Chico, Calif.: Scholars

Press, 1980], 18) dates the fall of Sidon to 348 B.C.E., following the obsolete arguments of Walther Judeich, *Kleinasiatische Studien* (Marburg: Elwert, 1892), 170–75. Judeich did not know of Babylonian Chronicle 9 and ignored the likelihood that Diodorus at xvi.40.4 wrongly ascribed to the reign of Artaxerxes (III) Ochos defeats that occurred in the reign of Artaxerxes II; see C. L. Sherman, *Diodorus,* VII, 348–49, nn 2–3. Judeich took for granted that Isocrates 5.101 refers to a defeat in Egypt suffered by Artaxerxes III in the 340s B.C.E., whereas it probably refers to the king's defeat there in the 350s. Judeich also did not know of Bickerman's determination of the date of the full moon mentioned in the story of the dream of Nektanebos II (see n 80). Betlyon's datings of the reigns of the kings of Sidon and of the fall of the city are insecure. The discovery of a single new dated coin can prolong a reign by a whole year, and Betlyon himself assumes (*Coinage,* 17) that years could go by during which a king of Sidon minted no coins. Thus the numbers of the regnal years of the kings of Sidon presently known from their coins are no obstacle to setting Artaxerxes's capture of the city in 345. Gustave Glotz set the fall of Sidon in the summer of 344 B.C.E., wrongly disbelieving the testimony of the Babylonian Chronicle (Glotz, *Histoire grecque* [4 vols. in 5; Paris: Presses universitaires de France, 1925–38], Vol. IV, Part I, 13 [esp. n 22]).

75 Bickermann, *Mélanges Maspero,* I, 80–81; Kienitz, *Politische Geschichte,* 183–84. Both assigned the fall of Sidon to 343, largely on the basis of the numerals on the coins minted by the Satrap Mazaios at Sidon. They took the numerals to be those of the regnal years of Artaxerxes III, but other interpretations are possible; see Betlyon, *Coinage,* 14–15, 18, 35 (n 70).

76 Diodorus xvi.46.4.

77 Diodorus xvi.46.5–51.3.

78 *Suda* (= Suidas) s.v. *asato.*

79 Kienitz, *Politische Geschichte,* 168–69.

80 Ibid., 170–73, 178–80. An important text for establishing the chronology is the Greek papyrus preserving a story about a dream of a King Nektanebos (Ulrich Wilcken, *Urkunden der Ptolemäerzeit* [2 vols.; Berlin: Walter de Gruyter, 1927–57], no. 81). The story reports that in the king's sixteenth regnal year the moon was full during the night between 21 and 22 Pharmuthi on the Egyptian calendar. The astronomical data fit only 21 Pharmuthi, 343 B.C.E. (July 5), in the reign of Nektanebos II. See Bickermann, *Mélanges Maspero,* 78–79. If the data are correct, 344/3 was the sixteenth regnal year of Nektanebos II, and the king was still ruling Egypt in July 343. But if Manetho is correct in giving that king eighteen regnal years, his last year was 342/1, after the proved date for the fall of Egypt! Bickermann's solution (ibid., 79–81) was to suppose that Nektanebos II continued to be recognized as king in Upper Egypt for two years after the fall of Lower Egypt to Artaxerxes III. Kienitz rejected Bickermann's hypothesis, noting that Diodorus's narrative leaves no room for it and demonstrating that the two-year discrepancy arose from errors of Manetho in reckoning the chronology of the twenty-eighth and twenty-ninth dynasties. Kienitz preferred to suppose that the scribe of the papyrus erred, and, in Greek figures, miswrote "eighteenth" as "sixteenth" (*Politische Geschichte,* 171–73, 178–80). Cf. Alan B. Lloyd, "The Late Period," chap 4 of B. G. Trigger, B. J. Kemp, D. O'Connor, and A. B. Lloyd, *Ancient Egypt: A Social History* (Cambridge: Cambridge University Press, 1983), 179–81.

81 There is no way to demonstrate that the deported Jews, if mercenaries captured from Egypt, were descendants of the community of Elephantine, but the possibility could have interesting consequences; see my *II Maccabees,* 107–9.

82 The Greek preposition *eis* is ambiguous; it can mean either "against" or "into." We have other testimony that Artaxerxes penetrated into Egypt, so that I prefer here the weaker equivalent.

83 See Burn in CHI, II (1985), 380–81.

84 Syncellus *Chronographia* in *Georgius Syncellus et Nicephorus Cp.,* ed. Wilhelm Dindorf (2 vols; Bonn: Ed. Weber, 1829), I, 486–87:

Ὦχος Ἀρταξέρξου παῖς εἰς Αἴγυπτου στρατεύων μερικὴν αἰχμαλωσίαν ἷλεν Ἰουδαίων, ὧν τοὺς μὲν ἐν Ὑρκανία κατώκισε πρὸς τῇ Θαλάσσῃ, τούς δὲ ἐν Βαβυλῶνι οἱ καὶ μέχρι νῦν εἰσιν αὐτόθι ὡς πολλοὶ τῶν Ἑλλήνων ἱστοροῦσιν.
Οὗτος ὁ Ὦχος κρατήσας Αἴγυπτου β΄ ἔτη ἀναιρεῖται ὑπὸ Βαγώου τινὸς Πέρσου τῶν ἐν τέλει. ὁ αὐτὸς καὶ Ξιδῶνα κατέσκαψεν.
Οὗτος ὁ Ὦχος εἰς Αἴγυπτον ἐπιστρατεύσας ἔτι ζῶυτος τοῦ πατρὸς Ἀρταξέρξου, ὡς καὶ ἄλλοι, μετὰ ταῦτα ἐκράτησεν Αἴγυπτου, φυγόυτος Νεκτανεβώ. . . .

Syncellus wrongly dates the king's murder two years after his conquest of Egypt.

85 "Tunc etiam Ochus qui et Artaxerxes, post transactum in Aegypto maximum diuturnumque bellum, plurimos Judaeorum in transmigrationem egit, atque in Hyrcania ad Caspium mare habitare praecipit."

86 *Eusebii Pamphili Chronici Canones, Latine vertit, adauxit, ad sua tempora produxit S. Eusebius Hieronymus,* ed. Iohannes Knight Fotheringham (London: Humphrey Milford, 1923), 203: "Ochus apodasmo Iudaeorum capta in Hyrcaniam accolas translatos iuxta mare Caspium collocavit." Although I am surprised to see *apodasmus* used as feminine, I see no other way of construing the passage.

87   Ibid.: "Ochus Aegyptum tenuit, Nectanebo in Aethiopiam pulso, in quo Aegyptiorum regnum destructum est: huc usque Manethos." Manethos is Manetho, the Egyptian who in the early third century B.C.E. (under Ptolemy I), wrote in Greek the history of his country.

88   Ibid.: "Ochus Sidonem subuertit et Aegyptum suo iunxit imperio."

~10~

The Career of Alexander the Great

1. Introduction

THE PERSIAN PHILOSOPHY OF HISTORY[1] was wrong: The Persian Empire of Asia did not last forever. Indeed, it was not even the third empire in Asia, though the Persians simply did not know of empires that had existed a millennium and more earlier. The Persians were confident that their empire, at least in Asia, would last till the end of time, and they were fairly successful in convincing the subject peoples of that. The Greeks had successfully repelled the Persians by 479 B.C.E., and for the next half-century an alliance led by Athens was a worry to the empire on its western fringe, but from 412 on the Persians were so successful pitting Greek against Greek, that in many ways Persia could be said to have dominated even the Greeks from 412 to 338, even though the Greeks of Europe were not under the direct rule of the Persian king.[2]

We have seen how Egypt revolted at the end of the fifth century and remained independent until 344.[3] Otherwise, the serious upheavals faced by the Persian Empire were, not revolts of subject peoples, but civil wars in which rival groups of Persians fought over who was to rule the empire that was supposed to last forever.[4]

Perhaps the Persians' religious belief that they were destined to rule forever made them complacent and contributed to their fall to Alexander the Great. In Europe there were two vigorous peoples, related to each other, who were still independent of Persian rule. They were the Greeks and the Macedonians. In the fourth century, intelligent observers among the Greeks repeatedly called attention to glaring weaknesses in the structure of the great empire and in the national character of the Persians.[5] Again and again, Isocrates of Athens (436–338) recommended that the Greeks, beset by poverty, solve their problems by invading the great empire and conquering some of its territory.[6]

In fact, the Persians lost almost every battle against Greeks or Macedonians, from Marathon in 490 to Gaugamela in 331. If their weakness was so obvious, the question arises, how were the Persians able to conquer and control so large an empire and rule over so many nations? They were always heavily outnumbered by the conquered peoples.[7] To begin with, they must have had some military excellence: There were the strategic ability of King Cyrus (to be inferred from the magnitude of his achievements), the great skill of the Persian archers and light infantry, and the high quality of the Iranian cavalry.[8] Those archers and infantry were almost invincible until they had to face the heavy-armed infantry ("hoplites") of the Greeks.[9] Greek hoplites and navies (especially the fleet of Athens) accomplished the defeats of the Persians between the battle of Marathon and the victories of Alexander.

Why did the Persian Empire fail to develop its own hoplites?[10] Were too few Persians willing to submit to the arduous training and discipline required? The Persians made heavy military use of the subject peoples.[11] Were they afraid to train such persons to be hoplites, the type of soldier that consistently defeated Persians?[12]

In any case, Cyrus, Cambyses, and Darius I and their nation conquered and consolidated a vast empire. Most of the subject peoples quietly obeyed the Great King, especially from the 380s on. Indeed, they fought in his armies and fleets. The Persians certainly mastered the art of collecting taxes from the conquered, to the extent that Persian treasuries dwarfed any others in the world. Did their skill at taxation include knowing how to limit their demands so that the subject peoples would not feel driven to revolt? Modern writers have condemned the Persian kings for overtaxing the conquered,[13] but the evidence is insufficient either for that conclusion or for its opposite.[14]

We may say that the Persians held their empire through military force, through the willingness of many of their subjects to have them rule,[15] and through the power of their money. If there were any enemies whom they could not defeat, such as the Greek hoplites, usually the Great King could buy them with bribes, often by hiring the enemy troops to fight instead for him.

In the fourth century B.C.E., the Persian combination of archers, light infantry, cavalry, and money was no longer unbeatable. Greek hoplites had long been demonstrating their superiority to the imperial infantry. Iranian cavalry would at last meet its superior in the Macedonian horsemen.[16] Persian money would mean nothing if the enemy power was headed by a leader so charismatic that few if any would switch sides, no matter how much the Great King offered. First-rate hoplites, superb cavalry, brilliant generalship, and a charismatic personality constituted the combination that Alexander the Great used to overrun the Persian Empire.[17]

The Persians had an absolute monarchy. The strength of their state depended upon the strength of the king. The power of the throne, at the time Alexander set out on his invasion of the empire, had been gravely impaired by a series of murders. Bagoas, a powerful eunuch minister, brought about the poisoning of Artaxerxes III late in 338 or early in 337 and put on the throne the dead king's son, Arses. Arses in turn tried to poison the eunuch but instead was poisoned by him after a reign of less than two years. All Arses's children were killed, and Bagoas put on the throne Arses's second cousin, as Darius III. No closer member of the royal line was still alive. Darius III managed to poison Bagoas before Bagoas poisoned him.[18] Under the circumstances, the position of the new Persian king could only have been insecure. Later, he exhibited weakness of character as repeatedly he lost his nerve in times of crisis.

2. Asia Minor, Syria, Palestine, and Egypt

IN THE SPRING OF 334, twenty-two-year-old Alexander crossed the Hellespont and invaded the Persian Empire. He circulated propaganda avowing as his motive a war of revenge for the atrocities suffered by the Greeks at the hands of Xerxes and his army in 480–479, almost a century and a half earlier. At the Granikos River he defeated the forces of the Persian satraps of Asia Minor. Thereafter, he marched easily through the coastal fringe along the Aegean. There was resistance at fortified Miletus, but during the summer he took that city by siege. At Halikarnassos, Persian forces held out in two citadels, though Alexander captured the rest of the city. He left a detachment which, after a protracted siege, succeeded in taking the citadels.

Meanwhile, Alexander with the bulk of his army marched across the interior of Asia Minor. By late autumn 333, Darius had prepared a vast army to face Alexander near the northeast angle of the Mediterranean Sea. The Persian king hoped the battle under his own command would bring decisive victory. He went through elaborate Zoroastrian rituals to assure that his army would have the aid of Ahuramazda and his divine assistants[19]—in vain! Darius lost his nerve and fled, and Alexander and his army at Issos (Map 3) decisively defeated the Persian forces.

By the victory, a huge quantity of Persian gold fell into Alexander's hands, and no important Persian land force was left near the Mediterranean to prevent the Macedonian king from overrunning all the imperial holdings along that sea. Alexander proceeded to do so, though he was slowed by having to besiege Tyre for seven months in the winter and spring of 332 and having to besiege Gaza for two months in the autumn.

Meanwhile, could the Jews have avoided facing a terrifying dilemma? We have seen [20] how they came to believe that their own God would punish them for rebellion against the pagan king he had placed over them. Two pagan kings now had claims to be the ruler God himself had chosen to rule over his wayward people. As long as Darius still held some power, it was not clear whether God would give final victory to Alexander. To obey one king was an act of rebellion against the other! Would Alexander not be quick to call upon the Jews to acknowledge his overlordship, just as he had called upon other peoples in the area?

The pagan writers on Alexander say nothing about the Jews' dilemma at this time. Only the narrative in Josephus's *Antiquities* reflects it, and scholars have been right to doubt the historicity of his account, as well as that of the two other ancient Jewish legends about the encounter of Alexander and the Chosen People.[21] I have analyzed and explained those legends elsewhere, proving that all three are false, but also that a few facts can be gleaned from them to supplement what can be learned from the pagan Alexander-histories and from archaeology.[22] I present those facts in the following three paragraphs.

To the north of Judea, in Samaria, lived another group that claimed to be Israelites, the Samaritans. They did not accept the books of Jeremiah, Ezekiel, and Chronicles, which teach the doctrine requiring that Israelites obey the pagan king whom God has placed over them. It therefore is not surprising that Sanballat, the Samaritan governor at Samaria for Darius, came to Tyre and put himself and his province under the rule of Alexander soon after the battle of Issos. The pleased king, in return, granted Sanballat permission to build a Samaritan temple on Mount Gerizim.

Judea lay farther from Tyre than Sanballat's province, but if the Jews of Judea were to survive unscathed during Alexander's reign (and they did so survive), they had to come to an acceptable agreement with him. Alexander or his agents may well have met a Jewish delegation at the place later called "Antipatris," though in Alexander's time it was called "Kephar Saba." Antipatris lay well to the north of Gaza on the route probably followed by Alexander. Hence, if the meeting occurred there, it probably preceded the siege of Gaza.

The content of the negotiations must have been unremarkable, because no reliable tradition preserves it. Alexander may have appreciated the religious predicament of the Jews. Most of the Jews probably lacked military equipment. No Persian army remained in the area to defend it. As viewed by the Jews and by their God, submission to Alexander's armed soldiers and tax-collectors under those circumstances was not necessarily rebellion against Darius. All doubt would be removed as soon as Alexander completely defeated the Persian king, as he did in 331–330. Alexander may have accommodated the scruples of the local Jewish governing authorities by inviting Jews to volunteer for service under him instead of requiring those authorities to conscript them.

Soon after Gaza fell in the autumn of 332, Alexander and his army marched on Egypt, a major objective for him in his effort to deprive the Persian fleet of its land bases. He met no opposition there. Any forces under Mazakes, the Persian satrap of Egypt, were much too small to fight Alexander. The satrap surrendered. The native Egyptians were bitter over the atrocities Artaxerxes III had committed in reconquering Egypt and over the harsh Persian administration that followed. They welcomed Alexander as their liberator and legitimate king. Then or later, a legend grew up, that Alexander was in reality the son of Egyptian King Nektanebos II. The Macedonian conqueror participated in Egyptian rituals and founded the great city of Alexandria.[23]

Alexander himself temporarily solved the theological problem which otherwise could have perplexed the Egyptians: How could their almighty (or nearly almighty) god, Amon (called "Ammon" in Greek) have permitted Egypt to fall into the hands of yet another conqueror? Alexander made a pilgrimage to the oasis shrine of Amon, where he received oracular messages that he was the son of Amon and surely also, whether explicitly or by implication, that the god approved the Macedonian's conquest of Egypt.[24]

Egypt was a rich and important area, bounded by deserts and sea so as to be easy for a rebel to defend. Alexander took care to divide civil and military authority in that country, assigning functions to Macedonians, Greeks, and native Egyptians, all directly responsible to him. His efforts to prevent a single subordinate from controlling Egypt failed. Kleomenes, a Greek from Naukratis in Egypt, was to be governor of the desert regions east of the Delta and also was the treasurer who was to receive the tribute collected throughout the country. Through his financial power, in the years that followed, Kleomenes was able to dominate the other officials and gain full control of Egypt. He heavily exploited the Egyptians and enormously enriched himself, but took care always to be loyal to Alexander, who gladly maintained him in power.[25] Egyptians under the rule of Kleomenes could hardly continue to view Alexander as their liberator.

In the winter or early spring of 331, news reached Alexander that the Samaritans had burned to death Andromachos, the king's governor of Syria. Samaritans thus again showed that their religion did not require them to be loyal to the pagan king over them. Alexander intended to avenge the murder promptly. He left Egypt in April 331 and marched back across the desert into Palestine. On his arrival at Samaria the perpetrators were surrendered to him. Excavations at Wadi Daliyeh, some fourteen kilometers north of Jericho, and papyri and skeletons found there show how well-to-do refugees from Samaria suffered wholesale massacre there in the time of Alexander, surely as part of his vengeance for Andromachos. Jews certainly did not rebel; there is some slight reason to believe they helped Alexander suppress the Samaritans.[26] After paying respects to the Herakles of Tyre, Alexander marched to the Euphrates, which he reached in midsummer of 331.[27]

3. Mesopotamia

DURING THE INTERVAL between the battle of Issos in 333 and the autumn of 331, Darius made extensive and elaborate preparations for a showdown rematch with Alexander. By the end of those months, he aimed at having the battle occur in the level plains east of the Tigris, ideal for his cavalry and chariotry.[28] By Sept. 30, 331, Alexander and his army indeed had marched into that area, and on Oct. 1, 331, the battle of Gaugamela occurred.

Darius still had faith in the divine powers protecting his empire. During the night before the battle, "accompanied by his commanders and kinsmen, he made the rounds of his army and, while doing so, he called upon the Sun, Mithra, and the Sacred Eternal Fire to inspire the men with courage befitting their ancient glory and their ancestors' monumental achievements. If the human mind could at all comprehend the omens which predicted the aid of the gods," he said, "the deities surely were on his side. The gods had recently brought sudden panic upon the Macedonians," said he, "who were still frightened and throwing down their arms to be carried off as spoils. Thus, the guardian deities of the Persian Empire were inflicting on these madmen a well-deserved punishment. Equally insane was their leader. Like a wild beast, he was setting his mind on the plunder he was seeking and was charging straight ahead toward the annihilation for which the booty was the bait." Darius was unable to carry this religious faith with him into the battle. Again he lost his nerve and fled, and the generalship of Alexander and the valor of his army won the day.[29] The imperial army of Persia was smashed beyond recovery, though local forces in eastern Iran were later to offer vigorous resistance to Alexander.

Before the battle, however, the outcome was in doubt. The fragmentary text of a Babylonian present-future prophecy, one which almost immediately proved false, has survived by some improbable chance. It shows us explicitly that Babylonians came to view Darius III with favor and also lets us infer with probability that Marduk's people continued to believe in their god's almighty power.

The fragments of the Dynastic Prophecy[30] are preserved on a badly broken tablet, but parts of its outline are clear, though the "predicted" kings are not named. As usual, most of the "predicted" events were past in the time of the real author. Easily recognizable in the first preserved portion is the final defeat of Assyria and the glorification of Babylon, surely by King Nabopolassar (column I). After a gap there is mention (column II, lines 1–10) of the 3-year reign of a king some time thereafter (surely of Nergal-shar-uṣur) and of the abortive reign of his son (surely of Labashi-Marduk).

The treatment of Nabonidus which follows (in Column II, lines 11–16) is interesting. Though Nabonidus tried to pose as a legitimate successor of Nabopolassar and Nebuchadnezzar, here he is called a "rebel prince" and his line is called "the dynasty of Harran." The length of his reign is given, correctly, as seventeen years, during which, the prophecy says, he will oppress the land and will cancel the festival of Esagila and will plot evil against Akkad.

A "prediction" of the reign of Cyrus follows (column II, lines 17–24). Instead of "Persia," the writer uses the old name "Elam" for Cyrus's home country. Cyrus will depose Nabonidus and will settle him in another land.[31] The king from Elam will oppress(!) Akkad, and all lands will bring him tribute. One might be surprised to find a Babylonian regarding Cyrus as an oppressor.[32] But as Persian rule over Babylonia became harsher and harsher, Babylonians came to view even Cyrus's victory as a disaster, as can be seen from the "Persian Mule" prophecy.[33]

After a gap, we find the text of the Dynastic Prophecy in column III "predicting" that a eunuch will murder a king (Arses) after a reign of two years, and his successor (Darius III) will reign five years. That king will have to face the army of the "Khanaeans," an archaizing code-name for the Macedonians. The Khanaeans at first will defeat the Persian royal army and will plunder and rob the king. "Afterwards he (the king) will refit his army and raise his weapons. Enlil, Shamash and . . . [a third divine name is broken off; Grayson, the editor, guesses that it was Marduk] will go at the side of his army, and he will bring about the overthrow of the army of the Khanaean. He will carry off his extensive booty and bring it into his palace. The people who had experienced misfortune will enjoy well-being. The mood of the land will be a happy one."

The two battles mentioned from the reign of Darius III are certainly those of

Issos and Gaugamela.³⁴ Alexander did defeat an army of Darius's satraps at the Granikos river in 334 and took spoils on the battlefield. He also captured precious metals accumulated by the satraps as he made his way across Asia Minor in 334/3.³⁵ But Darius himself did not participate in those events; the defeated army was not precisely his; his satraps, not he, were the victims of the robbery and the plundering. The great change in the fortunes of the Persian Empire came at Issos in 333: there, Darius and his own army suffered defeat, and thereafter the king himself was the victim of robbery and plunder.³⁶

Thus, when the author writes of the earlier defeat of the king by the Khanaeans, he must mean the battle of Issos. As we saw, after that battle, for almost two years, Darius prepared for a showdown rematch, action which the author reflects in writing, "Afterward he will refit his army and raise his weapons." The showdown battle clearly is the one at Gaugamela, but the author predicts, falsely, that Darius, with the help of the gods of Babylonia, will win, to the great joy of the Babylonians! The author could have written so obviously false a prophetic work only if the battle of Gaugamela still lay in the future.³⁷

If that battle still lies in the future, so must any subsequent events in the Dynastic Prophecy. Scanty fragments of a fourth column survive. What did the author think would happen after the battle of Gaugamela? In his composition, he gives only figures for the full number of years in a reign. He does not date events within a reign by giving a partial figure in regnal years. Thus the "five years" given to Darius III (column III, line 8) must represent the author's expectation of the full length of that king's reign. The battle of Gaugamela occurred in the middle of Darius's fifth regnal year (331/0). In the author's expectation, the Persian king will reign on for only several months after winning victory over Alexander and bringing joy to the Babylonians!

Grayson may well have been right to guess that at column IV, line 2, the length of a reign was reported. Knowing the patterns of present-future prophecy, we may suppose that the author predicted that Darius somehow (by death or by abdication?) would yield the throne to a member of Marduk's people and that thereafter the god's people would prosper.

Nothing tells us what favors granted to Babylonians by Darius III or his predecessors brought the Babylonian author to believe that the great gods of his country would bring victory at Gaugamela to the Persian king. Not only was the author rash enough to predict such a victory. If our reconstruction is correct, he also committed the treason of predicting the imminent end of the reign of the ruling king! Longman has argued that the speaker in every extant Babylonian present-future prophecy is a god.³⁸ If Marduk is the speaker in the Dynastic Prophecy, the author in his rashness has displayed his faith in his almighty god.

When Alexander won overwhelmingly at Gaugamela, the Dynastic Prophecy was irreparably proved false. The mutilated state of the tablet bearing the disappointing "revelation" is not surprising. It is astounding that the tablet survived at all.

From this point, let us first sketch what is known of Alexander's campaigns and acts down to his death in June 323 B.C.E., and only thereafter let us return in chap 11 to discuss in detail the texts that survive to display the reactions of the subject peoples.

Having vanquished Darius and his empire, Alexander felt justified in having himself proclaimed "king of Asia."[39] The destruction of the Persian imperial army and the flight of Darius from the battleground of Gaugamela also laid open to Alexander the road to Babylon, and he could hope for easy marches to and through the Persian capitals of Susa, Persepolis, Pasargadai, and Ekbatana.[40]

After Darius's imperial army had been destroyed at Gaugamela, only a fanatic ready to put up suicidal resistance could have attempted to use the limited forces at Babylon to oppose the victors' march into Marduk's city. Mazaios, the Persian satrap there, was no fanatic and may well have negotiated with Alexander, offering him a bloodless surrender in return for a promise of office under the new regime. Alexander took due precautions against possible treachery, but he and his army received a splendid welcome to Babylon.

Mazaios himself marched out with his grown children and formally surrendered. "A large number of the Babylonians found places on the walls, eager to catch sight of their new king. Still more of them went out to meet him. So did Bagophanes, the official in command of the citadel and the royal treasury. Not to be outdone by Mazaios in paying respects to Alexander, Bagophanes had strewn the whole route with flowers and garlands and had set up at intervals on both sides silver altars heaped not only with frankincense but with all kinds of aromatic spices. After him came his gifts: herds of cattle and horses and also lions and leopards, carried along in cages. Next came the Magi,[41] chanting a song in their traditional way, and, after them, were the 'Chaldaeans' [i.e., the omen-reading priests of Marduk],[42] and after them marched not only Babylonian priests but also Babylonian musicians with their own kind of stringed instruments."[43]

On entering the city, Alexander ordered the Babylonians to rebuild those temples that were then in ruins, "especially the temple of Bêl [= Marduk]." He reappointed Mazaios satrap of Babylon. The conqueror had a meeting with the

"Chaldaeans" and carried out all their recommendations concerning the temples in Babylon, and, in accordance with their directions, sacrificed to Bêl.[44] Alexander showed he believed in the powers of the priests of Marduk to purify and to forecast the future: When he left Babylon, he took some of them along for those purposes.[45]

4. Iran

ON LEAVING BABYLON, Alexander encountered no resistance at Susa and took over its ample treasury. There, too, he reappointed as satrap a noble Persian, Abulites.[46] Alexander's easy marches on the routes between the chief cities of the Persian Empire ended at Susa. Only luck and his brilliant tactics allowed him and his army to traverse the rugged route from Susa to Persepolis quickly, in winter, despite the determined resistance of a local tribe (the Uxioi), and of a large force of Persians under the satrap Ariobarzanes. The Uxioi fought under the governor of their region, Medates or Madetes, a kinsman of Darius, who intended to be loyal to the utmost.[47] Clearly the inept Persian king still had a following, though it was no match for the Macedonian conqueror and his army.

Alexander met no resistance upon his arrival at Persepolis around the beginning of Feb. 330 B.C.E.[48] We probably should believe the sources which tell us that the conqueror, even so, handed over the riches within the city to his army to be plundered and the inhabitants to be massacred, raped, and enslaved.[49] Among the victims were probably many Zoroastrian priests. At the time, the priests were the "living books" of the faith, because they memorized the sacred texts and transmitted them orally.[50] Alexander exempted only the palace area from this pillage and massacre.

Curtius probably gives an accurate presentation of Alexander's avowed motive for so treating Persepolis: "No city was more hateful to the Greeks than Persepolis, . . . from which Darius and Xerxes had waged an unholy war on Europe."[51] If so, the Macedonian king was still carrying out his proclaimed war of revenge against the Persian Empire, on behalf of the Greeks. An additional motive can be surmised: Alexander had long been restraining his men from plunder, certainly at Babylon and Susa; the hard fighting on the way to Persepolis made them still hungrier for loot.

Alexander stayed four months at Persepolis,[52] and one must ask, why? Darius was in Ekbatana and still had a following, and, left to himself, could have built up a fresh army (in fact, he did nothing). Was Alexander waiting for the snows in mountainous Iran to melt?[53] Alexander is known to have braved snow and ice elsewhere, and only an exceptionally severe winter could have forced him to wait into May.[54] The Alexander historians could not have passed in silence over such an unusual circumstance.

Just before leaving Persepolis, the conqueror burned the palace area, which he had protected when he let his men sack the city. He avowed again that he intended in this enormous act of arson to take vengeance for the destruction which the Persians had wrought in Greece in 480 B.C.E.[55]

As soon as Persepolis fell, the city and its palaces belonged to Alexander. Did he have good reason to sacrifice valuable property of his own to the Greeks' craving for revenge, and to do so twice? He had. As far as Alexander knew, the dangerous anti-Macedonian movement in Greece led by Agis III, king of Sparta, still had not been suppressed by Antipater, the Macedonian commander in Europe.[56] Under the circumstances, it was prudent both to wait at Persepolis for news that Agis had been defeated and to curry favor with Greek public opinion.

What did the burning of the palaces mean to Iranians? Was it for them equivalent to what the burning of the temple at Jerusalem in 586 meant to the Jews? The palaces certainly functioned as residences or audience halls of the kings who ruled by the grace of Ahuramazda. That in itself constituted religious significance. However, some of the sculptures of the palaces at Persepolis have led scholars to believe that the area was the place where the Persian king, like the king of Babylon, reenacted the supreme deity's primeval victory over the powers of chaos.[57] But the evidence from the sculptures is weak and equivocal,[58] and the Greek literary records are absolutely silent on Persepolis as the site for such reenactment and on participation by the Persian king in an analogue to the Babylonian Akîtu. Herodotus, Ktesias, Xenophon, Deinon, and the Alexander historians and other Greek writers were strongly interested in Persian religion. If the annual reenactment at Persepolis had existed, the silence of those authors concerning it would be hard to explain.[59]

Not long after the palace area lay in ashes, Alexander must have received a report that Agis III had been defeated.[60] The conqueror knew he must now proceed against Darius. The Persian king should not be left free to organize resistance in the provinces of the empire which had not yet fallen. If captured alive, Darius might be induced to abdicate in Alexander's favor. If killed, the Persian king would cease to be a focus around whom Iranian resisters could gather.

Alexander received information that Darius had assembled a force of infantry and cavalry at Ekbatana, the capital of Media, and had sent off his women and his property eastward.[61] The conqueror marched quickly toward Ekbatana, only to receive the news that Darius had fled, taking with him a considerable treasure in money and his force of infantry and cavalry.[62]

Arrian states that Alexander nevertheless pressed on to take Ekbatana and make important arrangements there before resuming his pursuit of the Persian king.[63] Curtius, on the other hand, reports that on learning of Darius's flight, Alexander immediately veered away from Ekbatana to pursue him.[64] If so, Alexander left the occupation of Ekbatana to his subordinates.

Meanwhile, high-ranking officials under Darius concluded that if the war was to be prolonged, their king was not a suitable commander, whether because of his ineptitude (as we may suppose) or because of his inherent ill fortune (as Curtius implies).[65] Nabarzanes the "chiliarch" (vizier) and Bessos, the satrap of Baktria, and Barzaentes, the satrap of Arachosia and Drangiana, plotted to have Bessos replace Darius as king. Bessos had a claim to royal legitimacy, inasmuch as he was related to Darius. The conspirators put Darius under arrest, in golden chains, and Bessos took power as king.[66] According to Arrian,[67] even the Persians in Darius's army sided with the plotters. Curtius[68] has those Persians at first bitterly opposed to the conspiracy and later accepting the fait accompli only when there appeared to be no other choice.

Deserters brought the news to Alexander. Still hoping to take Darius alive, the conqueror in a fantastic race across country unknown to him, much of it desert, drove horses to death and finally caught up with the Persian column. The conspirators were too frightened to stand and fight. They tried to persuade Darius to flee with them, but he refused. To prevent him from falling into Alexander's hands, they mortally wounded him with their spears and fled in more than one direction. Darius was still alive when a soldier of Alexander found him, but the deposed king soon died, before Alexander saw him.[69]

The conqueror saw to the royal burial of Darius and from time to time took care to pose as the one who was seeking to avenge the murdered king, for thus he might have hope, however slim, of gaining some legitimacy for his own rule over the Persians.[70]

Remnants of Darius's army, including his formidable Greek mercenaries, had withdrawn into the province of Hyrkania (southeast of the Caspian sea), and so had Nabarzanes the chiliarch. Though Alexander must have known that Bessos had already acted as the Persian king,[71] he chose to eliminate the dangers in Hyrkania, on his flank, before marching to Baktria, against Bessos. The conqueror quickly overran Hyrkania. The opposing forces surrendered. He even pardoned Nabarzanes, as if the chiliarch had not been implicated in the murder of Darius.[72]

On leaving Hyrkania, Alexander marched his army through Parthyaia to Areia, where he was met by the local satrap, Satibarzanes, whom Curtius names as one of the two actual murderers of Darius III. Nevertheless, Alexander renewed the man's appointment as satrap, again failing to show thirst to avenge the murdered king. In Areia, the conqueror received the news that Bessos had put on the royal tiara and vestments of a Persian king and was calling himself Artaxerxes instead of Bessos (for us, that would constitute him Artaxerxes IV).[73] Though he had acted as king before, apparently at first he had not assumed those royal prerogatives. Now he was posing as the legitimate occupant of the Persian throne, against the conqueror's claim to have seized it.

Artaxerxes IV is reported to have made a good beginning of organizing the resources of Baktria to resist Alexander. Darius had appointed Bessos satrap of the province, and the man had become widely known there because of his office. He now called upon the people to defend their freedom, pointing out that the rugged terrain of Baktria and its ample population would aid in their resistance. Artaxerxes IV himself would take command! He proceeded to enroll soldiers and to build up supplies for the coming war.[74]

The Persian pretender's strategy may have been better than that of his murdered predecessor.[75] His implementation of it, however, consisted of withdrawals which resembled those of Darius III. The most effective resistance to Alexander during the reign of Artaxerxes IV was accomplished by his subordinate, Satibarzanes.

Though Alexander forgave Satibarzanes for his involvement in the murder of Darius III and reappointed him satrap of Areia, Satibarzanes quickly gave his allegiance to Artaxerxes IV and massacred the Macedonian detachment the conqueror had assigned to Areia. Not daring to try to hold Areia against Alexander, Satibarzanes fled to Bessos. The pretender gave Satibarzanes 2,000 cavalrymen, with whom he reentered Areia and led the people into revolt.

Alexander sent a force to suppress the rebellion. There was a fierce battle, during which Satibarzanes managed to issue a challenge to the opposing side, inviting any one of them to fight him in single combat. Alexander's commander, Erigyius, accepted the challenge and slew Satibarzanes. The demoralized Areians gave up the struggle.[76]

After the death of Satibarzanes, Bessos's only response to Alexander's advances still was withdrawal. His own subordinates, Spitamenes and Dataphernes, viewed Artaxerxes IV as incompetent and delivered him into the hands of Alexander.[77] Alexander accused the captive pretender of treason against Darius and of murdering him and probably also of taking the title of king, "which did not belong to him."[78] The conqueror had Bessos whipped and cruelly mutilated and turned him over to Darius's brother Oxathres and to Medes and Persians for execution.[79]

Spitamenes, the betrayer of Bessos, proved to be the Iranian who offered the most effective resistance to Alexander. The man was a Baktrian,[80] not a Persian. He had no claim himself to kinship with the Persian Achaemenian dynasty. He never assumed the title of king. From the summer or autumn of 329 to late 328 or early 327, Spitamenes, using a mobile force based upon Baktrian, Sogdian, and Scythian cavalry, made clever use of ambush tactics and mostly managed to avoid fighting pitched battles with superior Macedonian forces. The cost for the Baktrians, Sogdians, and Scythians, however, was heavy, as Alexander and his subordinates with their vast resources won victories, capturing and destroying resistant towns and massacring and enslaving their inhabitants and inflicting heavy casualties on Spitamenes's forces. Finally, his allies among the Scythian Massagetai—or, according to Curtius, Spitamenes's own wife—had enough of the hardships of war. They or she beheaded Spitamenes and delivered his head to Alexander.[81]

A towering nearly impregnable rock remained in Sogdia as a focus of resistance. But skilled mountain climbers in Alexander's army scaled the rock, and their feat so intimidated the defenders that they surrendered even though their manpower was surely adequate for resistance (late winter or spring 327).[82] Among those who had taken refuge on the rock were the wife and daughters of the important Baktrian baron, Oxyartes. Alexander fell in love with Roxane, one of the daughters, and, though as a captive she was in his power, he treated her with respect and soon married her. Oxyartes ever after collaborated loyally with Alexander's rule.[83]

Resistance continued outside Sogdia,[84] at another towering rock in the territory of the Pareitakai, under the commnd of Chorienes. However, with the help of his future father-in-law, Oxyartes, Alexander convinced Chorienes to give up the fight.[85] Alexander's subordinates in a fierce battle destroyed the last rebel Iranian forces in the territory of the Pareitakai (spring 327).[86] He could regard his conquest of Iran as complete.

5. Alexander's Last Years (327–323 B.C.E.)

WE ARE INTERESTED in *peoples of an almighty or near almighty god,* in particular, the Iranians, Babylonians, and Jews. Therefore, we shall not follow in any detail Alexander's victorious campaigns in the Indus valley (summer 327 through summer 325) and his near-disastrous journey back across the deserts of Gedrosia to the Iranian province of Karmania (September[?] 325).[87]

We are also free to make only the briefest mention of the subsequent events among the Macedonians, as corruption among Alexander's officials and the conqueror's own paranoia produced a crop of executions. We ought, however, to list here the facts which show that some Iranians still dared to resist Alexander. Just after Alexander completed his perilous crossing of the deserts of Gedrosia, a message came from his subordinate commander, Krateros, that two Persian nobles, Ozines and Zariaspes, had been fomenting rebellion, but had been captured. They were brought to Alexander, who had them executed (autumn-winter 325/4).[88]

A more interesting and extreme example was the Mede, Baryaxes, who put on the Persian royal tiara and assumed the title of king of the Persians and the Medes, only to be arrested with his supporters by Atropates, the Iranian who was Alexander's loyal satrap of Media. Atropates brought his prisoners to Alexander at Pasargadai, where the king put them to death (early 324).[89]

In the course of 324 B.C.E. it became clear that Alexander could turn to and rely on Persian troops even when his own Macedonians turned mutinous.[90] Clearly, large numbers of Iranians were willing to collaborate with the conqueror.

In the autumn of 324, Alexander's best friend, Hephaistion, died suddenly at Ekbatana. In the months that followed, the grieving king consoled himself by conducting a murderous campaign against the Kossaioi, who lived in the mountains southwest of Ekbatana, and then he marched his army southwestward to Babylon.[91]

Babylonians had been largely demilitarized and disarmed from the time of the quelling of their last revolt under Xerxes.[92] Any of them who were hostile to Alexander knew that physical resistance to the king's army was suicidal. Marduk's people, if they felt aggrieved, could put their hopes in their god; priests of the almighty god could exploit their own reputation to interpret omens (and manipulate them).

Alexander died at Babylon on June 10 (28 Daisios on the Macedonian calendar), 323 B.C.E.[93] Oracles and omens at Babylon in the months before his death were recorded as predicting his demise. Several of them (or the interpretations placed upon them) might reflect Babylonian hostility toward the king.[94] The sources vary in the way they present the omens and predictions.

According to Arrian,[95] after Alexander had crossed the Tigris on his way to Babylon, Chaldaean seers came to meet him and claimed they had an oracle from Bêl warning that the king would suffer harm *(mē pros agathou hoi einai)* if he entered Babylon. The Chaldaeans advised him, surely as a safer course than the direct route of marching westward into the city, to take a circuitous detour, so as to enter marching eastward. Arrian cites the good testimony of Alexander's subordinate, Aristobulos, for the fact that Alexander and his army did attempt to take that detour but found the swampy way impassable.[96]

Arrian also reports that Alexander suspected the Chaldaeans were deliberately trying to prevent his entrance into Babylon for the following reason. Years before (in 331), the conqueror had ordered the rebuilding of ruined Esagila,[97] but those charged with the task had thereafter been slack in handling it. Now, Alexander planned to complete the project with the help of his entire army.[98] He suspected the Chaldaeans of fearing that the upkeep and cult-expenses of the huge rebuilt temple would exhaust the income from the ancient endowment of the shrine, money which hitherto the priests had been taking for themselves.[99] Each Babylonian king in his inscriptions had regularly proclaimed that he was fulfilling his duty of being "caretaker" *(zānin)* of Esagila. Even Macedonian Antiochus I was to do so.[100] Alexander's suspicions show that he intended the expense of caring for the rebuilt temple to fall not upon himself as king but upon the endowment controlled by the priests.

On the other hand, Diodorus reports[101] that when the Chaldaean astrologers, led by Belephantes, declared to Alexander that death awaited him in Babylon, they told him that he could escape the danger if he rebuilt the "tomb" of Bêl (i.e., the ziggurat Etemenanki)[102] and passed the city by, without entering it. The ziggurat could indeed have been in disrepair at the time. At first, Alexander did refrain from entering and only sent his subordinates into Babylon (Diodorus does not say whether he offered to do anything about the "tomb" of Bêl). But the king's philosophic Greeks convinced him to despise Chaldaean superstition, and he boldly entered the city.

According to Justin,[103] as Alexander approached Babylon a magus warned him not to enter the city because the results would be fatal to him. Alexander thereupon turned away from Babylon, crossed the Euphrates, and went to Borsippa, but his philosopher, Anaxarchus, convinced him to ignore the magus's warning, so that he turned back and entered Babylon.

Plutarch[104] adds nothing beyond these accounts. He tells that the Chaldaeans warned Alexander to keep away from Babylon and that Alexander ignored them and marched into the city.

Inasmuch as Arrian based his narrative on the works of Alexander's subordinates, we should accept his statement that the warners were Chaldaeans, priests of Marduk, and that the warning was in vague terms (harm would befall Alexander, rather than death). We also should accept Arrian's report of Alexander's suspicions, but we should ask whether the suspicions were justified.

The conqueror had had no detailed conversations with the Chaldaeans in 323. He could have learned of the endowment to support the expenses of Esagila only in his meeting with them in 331. At that time, he probably also was told how each king over Babylon was supposed to function as caretaker of Esagila. Alexander was pleased to have the temple rebuilt but did not intend to pay the subsequent expenses of the amply endowed shrine and probably so informed the Chaldaeans. In 331, Esagila was still in ruins, and the question of its up-keep and subsequent expenses could be passed over largely in silence, so that Arrian's source could record that Alexander "carried out all the recommenda-tions of the Chaldaeans on the Babylonian temples." But Alexander had to know that the question was a potential sore point between him and the Chal-daeans, and the fact gave rise to his suspicions in 323.

Could the potential sore point have become an actual cause of real hostility? Could it have led the Chaldaeans to prognosticate to Alexander as they did? The suggestion is unlikely. The king suspected the Chaldaeans of wanting to delay or prevent the rebuilding of Esagila (a discreditable intention). One way for them to get Alexander to do their bidding would be to please him, but they, on the contrary, brought him an unwelcome message and induced him to make a burdensome and futile detour. Their oracle, if heeded, could serve only to keep Alexander himself out of Babylon. Alexander by then must have been well known for having projects forcefully and successfully executed by his subordinates in his absence. Even if they succeeded in keeping the king out of Babylon, they would have accomplished nothing toward their suspected aim of delaying or preventing the rebuilding of Esagila. And then they gave him the advice about the detour. Even if, as is likely, they knew the route was impracti-cable, how would proposing it either prevent Alexander from eventually enter-ing the city or please the king?

We can be sure that the Chaldaeans suggested the detour. Aristobulos bears witness that the king attempted to go by that route. The priests' advice to Alexander could thus accomplish nothing for their suspected aim, and we must conclude that Alexander was wrong to suspect their motives. Though they probably were conscious of the one sore point in their relations with the con-queror, it was not strong enough to make them hostile to the king. Like the other Babylonians,[105] the Chaldaeans viewed him with favor. Believing in the oracles of their god, they thought Alexander was in danger and sought to pro-tect him.

As for the report in Diodorus, by substituting "death" for the vague "harm," it shows that it originated after Alexander's death. The story presents the Chal-daeans' prediction not as an oracle of Bêl but as a "scientific" prognostication based upon astrology and goes on to demonstrate the inferiority of Greek phi-losophy to Babylonian astrology. The narrative shows interest in the Chal-daeans also in giving the name of their leader. The story told by Arrian's source could be used to discredit the Chaldaeans by alleging they were not eager to have Esagila rebuilt. As if to correct that impression, the narrative in Diodorus says that they suggested to Alexander that he avert danger by repairing Eteme-nanki. We can infer that Diodorus's account goes back to a report composed by a priest of Marduk. Here again, the Chaldaeans' aim is to protect Alexander.

Justin's version may go back to a magus at Babylon who tried to claim credit for predicting that Alexander would die if he entered Babylon. The report that the king detoured to Borsippa confirms Arrian's account and helps correct its text.[106]

Chaldaean opposition to Alexander has been detected in connection with two other omens preceding Alexander's death,[107] wrongly, in both cases. In one instance, the king was temporarily deprived of his diadem; in the other, an obscure commoner was found sitting on the king's throne. Let us examine the sources on each, taking the omen of the diadem first.

According to Arrian,[108] Alexander on shipboard, accompanied by other ves-sels, explored the marshes near Babylon. Some of the ships lost their way, but Alexander sent them a pilot who brought them through safely (if that is what happened, up to that point nothing ominous had yet occurred). Arrian reports the strange events that followed[109] as "a story that is told"; thus, he voices some skepticism. Nevertheless, he goes on to tell that a strong breeze struck Alexan-der's hat and the diadem attached to it. The heavy Macedonian hat fell into the water. The diadem sailed in the wind until it was caught on one of the reeds which grew on "a tomb of one of the old kings."

Eddy rightly noted[110] that only a Babylonian could have identified a mound in a Babylonian marsh as a tomb of one of the old kings. With that identifica-tion, the diadem caught on the reed readily symbolized the return of imperial power to Marduk's people, surely their dearest desire, even if they liked Alexander. Their similar favor for Darius III had not prevented the Chaldaeans from writing the last section of the Dynastic Prophecy.[111]

Babylonians provided the identification of the mound as a royal tomb, but they could not have caused or predicted the gust of wind that caught the dia-dem, and they would have preferred to have the story end with the diadem caught on the reed. Instead, a sailor then jumped into the water, swam, and re-trieved the diadem, tied it around his own head to keep it dry, and brought it back to Alexander, thus nullifying what would have been a pro-Babylonian omen. Alexander gave him the huge reward of a talent. According to Aristobu-los, the sailor was a Phoenician. Arrian adds (approvingly!) that some say Se-leucus brought the diadem back to the king, and that this portended death for Alexander and vast empire for Seleucus. We can recognize that version as Se-leucid royal propaganda.

Arrian also says the seers who served the king warned that the head which had worn the diadem should not be left alive. Most writers read by Arrian reported that Alexander accordingly ordered the man beheaded, but Aristobulos, who may well have been an eyewitness, said that Alexander gave him the talent and merely had him flogged.

Julius Caesar was a master at the ancient art of improvising actions and interpretations to turn ominous chance events into favorable presages,[112] but he surely did not originate it. Hephaistion's unexpected death surely had oversensitized Alexander to possible intimations of his mortality. Otherwise, he might have been as clever as Caesar and might have perceived the favorable truth: The sailor of his own free will had restored the diadem to the king; Alexander by the huge reward had extinguished any claims the sailor had to it. Those facts should have sufficed to nullify any baneful content of the omen. By flogging the sailor, Alexander had been unjust, but he also demonstrated who was king and who was subject. There was no need to behead the man or to offer special sacrifices to the gods. Only the fact that Alexander soon died restored the incident to the status of a valid omen.

In contrast to Arrian, Diodorus[113] has Alexander himself losing his way in the marshes, a possibly baneful omen; and, as the king sailed through a narrow channel, his diadem got caught on an overhanging reed and fell into the water. An oarsman swam after it and, to keep it safe, placed it on his own head, and brought it back to Alexander, at the same time as the king found his way through the marsh. Alexander put on the diadem and consulted the soothsayers, who advised him to sacrifice to the gods on a grand scale and with all speed, but the king instead was distracted into the carouse that led to his sickness and death.

Diodorus says nothing about a tomb of an ancient king or about the swimmer's identity or about reward or punishment for him. Diodorus or his source simply was not interested in failed pro-Babylonian propaganda, in the ethnic origin of a common sailor, or in Seleucid propaganda. His wish was to present the omen which proved to be fatal. He or his source reversed the order of the stories of the lost diadem and the man on the throne, so that the event of the lost diadem became the one which immediately preceded the king's sickness and death and thus had a claim to be regarded as fatal. We shall see that in Diodorus's version, the omen of the man on the throne was thoroughly nullified. Alexander had the man put to death and offered the prescribed sacrifices. The king had accomplished neither of those actions in Diodorus's version of the story of the diadem. As viewed by Diodorus, Alexander's omissions proved to be fatal.

We have thus accounted for Diodorus's omissions and his transposition of events. Arrian's accounts are generally the most reliable among those of the historians of Alexander. In this case, except for the one piece of Seleucid propaganda, Arrian transmits nothing to arouse suspicion, and we should accept what he wrote.

Eddy saw [114] in the story of the sailor a clue indicating that Chaldaeans were suspected of being hostile to Alexander. Eddy asked, who were the soothsayers *(manteis)* who recommended capital punishment for the swimmer. He reasoned that they must have been Greeks, for, had they been Babylonians, they would have been called "Chaldaeans" (and, we may add, by Eddy's logic, had they been Iranians, they would have been called "magi"). Eddy's reasoning is hardly cogent,[115] but let us grant it for the moment. Then, Eddy could point out that the sailor had done Alexander a good service, with only good intentions. Greeks could recommend he suffer capital punishment only if they wished to give "a warning to someone who wanted to interpret the episode in a particularly exciting way." Eddy can find only the Chaldaeans to be such persons.

However, we have found the Chaldaean element in the story of the diadem. It consists solely of the identification of the mound as a royal Babylonian tomb. The diadem did not remain there! Babylonians would no more welcome transfer of Alexander's empire to a Phoenician than would Macedonians. And even the omen presaging Phoenician rule had been nullified. Thus, the story contains no reflection whatever of Chaldaean hostility to Alexander.

Let us now examine what the sources tell about the incident of the commoner on Alexander's throne, beginning with Arrian.[116] Aristobulos is his authority for the fact that the portent occurred near the time of Alexander's death. Arrian's entire main account of the event may come from Aristobulos. Alexander was assigning newly arrived troops to units when he got thirsty and left the throne to get a drink. A quite obscure person—some say a prisoner under open arrest—marched past the eunuch attendants and went up and sat on the throne. Because of some "Persian custom," the eunuchs did not drag him off the throne but showed their distress as if a terrible disaster had occurred. When Alexander learned what had happened, he ordered the man tortured on the rack, to find out whether his action had been part of a plot. The man would say only that the idea had come to him to do so. His answer made the seers all the readier to view the event as an evil omen for Alexander. Arrian does not say what happened to the man but reports that the king a few days later offered the customary sacrifices for good fortune plus some prescribed by the soothsayers.

According to Diodorus,[117] Alexander was being massaged with oil; he left his royal robe and diadem on a chair. A local person who was being kept in bonds was spontanously freed from his fetters, escaped the notice of the guards and, unhindered, got through the doors of the palace. He went to the chair, put on the royal robe, tied the diadem around his head, and sat upon the chair, without doing anything else. When the king learned of the event, he was panic-stricken over the strange omen but went to the chair and without showing his panic quietly asked the man who he was and what he meant by doing this. The man said absolutely nothing, so Alexander referred the omen to his seers for interpretation and put the man to death in accordance with their judgment, hoping that the evil signified by the omen might thus be turned away from Alexander and turned onto the man. Alexander picked up the clothing, sacrificed to the gods who avert evil, and thought ill of the philosophers who had persuaded him to ignore the Chaldaeans' warning not to enter Babylon.

According to Plutarch,[118] Alexander took off his regalia for a ball game. After the game, the young men who had played with him found a man sitting on the throne in silence, wearing the royal diadem and robe. Asked who he was, the man was speechless for a long time; with difficulty, he came to his senses and said that his name was Dionysios and that he was a Messenian. Because of a charge against him, he had been transported from the seacoast and had been in chains for a long time. Just now, the god Sarapis had come to him and loosed his fetters and brought him here and had commanded him to put on the robe and the diadem and to sit silent on the throne. On hearing this, Alexander had the man executed, as the seers directed.

Sarapis was certainly an Egyptian deity, and later writers, especially Tacitus and Plutarch, say that the cult of Sarapis was an innovation of King Ptolemy I, although, as a local Egyptian deity around the site of Alexandria, the god had been worshiped before.[119] Nevertheless, there is now some reason, besides Plutarch's story here, to believe that the god and his worship existed in Alexander's time and at Babylon.[120] If the name "Sarapis" was not in the story from the beginning, how did a Greek or Macedonian writer come to put it in?

Arrian tells only of the royal throne and says nothing of the other regalia. His readiness to tell the story of the wind-blown diadem shows that he and his source would not have hesitated to tell of the diadem and robe had they been involved in this event. We conclude that this event originally involved only the throne.

On the other hand, we have good reason to believe that the sources of Diodorus and Plutarch added the regalia to the story. Alexander was famous for his readiness to allow a commoner to sit on his throne.[121] The sources of Diodorus and Plutarch supposed that the king could have been dismayed only if the man on the throne possessed the regalia, so as to be viewed as king. But there is a significant difference between an incident in which Alexander *allowed* a commoner to sit on his throne (and had no fear in doing so) and our case, where the man sat on the throne *without permission* (and Alexander was alarmed). Thus, we again conclude that originally the event involved only the throne. Indeed, in Diodorus and perhaps in Plutarch, the throne is not the one regularly reserved for the king, so that the main ominous force lies in the other regalia.

The spontaneous loosing of the prisoner's bonds reported by Diodorus can hardly be viewed as anything but a miracle, and Plutarch says it was an act of the god Sarapis. Normally, one would prefer the unmiraculous account of Arrian. In this case, however, there may be reason to think that Arrian's source tried to rationalize the event, though he, too, told of an improbability: a prisoner kept "under open arrest." We should look carefully at all the evidence.

The omen involves an allegedly Persian custom and a prisoner sitting on the king's throne and perhaps wearing the king's regalia. Greek literature contains a reference to a Persian rite involving a prisoner who sits on the king's throne and wears the king's regalia.

According to Dio Chrysostom,[122] Diogenes, the cynic philosopher, gave Alexander the following account of the "Festival of the Sakai," which the Persians celebrated. "They take one of their prisoners who has been sentenced to death, seat him upon the king's throne, give him the royal apparel, allow him to give orders and to drink and to carouse and to enjoy the royal concubines during those days, and no one prevents him from doing as he wishes. Afterwards, however, they stripped, whipped, and hanged him." The story about Diogenes is fictitious, for otherwise Alexander would have recognized that the event was, at worst, a harmless Persian ritual.

On the other hand, we learn from Berossos[123] that the Sakaia (the usual name for the festival) was a *Babylonian* festival, held on the sixteenth day of the Macedonian midsummer month, Loös. During the festival, in each household a slave ruled and wore a robe similar to the king's.

Nothing prevented Persians and Babylonians from adopting one another's festivals, so that the rite described by Berossos and Dio Chrysostom could well have been both Babylonian and Persian. However, the date in Loös, the second month *after* Alexander's death, renders it impossible that our event was a celebration of the Sakaia.

Cuneiform sources allow us to understand the strange incident as an Assyrian and Babylonian procedure. "If dangerous omens accumulated, and there were no signs that the person of the [Mesopotamian] king was in any way protected, a substitute king was appointed. He reigned for one hundred days, and he was then destroyed, in the hope that he would carry away with him the disasters which had threatened the real king."[124]

In the view of believers, the more complete the substitution was, the more likely it was to be effective,[125] because they thought that the baneful forces would then be more likely to mistake the substitute for the real king. In some cases, a loyal subject might volunteer to face danger and even execution to protect his royal lord. In others, an expendable person, such as a prisoner condemned to death, was used as the substitute.

Dangerous omens against Alexander had accumulated, with little or no sign that the king was being supernaturally protected. We have found reason to believe that the Chaldaeans had already been seeking to protect Alexander. Did they now try to use the rite of the substitute king? Difficult obstacles stood in their way. The procedure of substitution was foreign and perhaps entirely unknown to the Greeks and Macedonians of Alexander's time,[126] so much so that the king and his entourage jumped to the conclusion that the commoner on the throne was at least a baneful omen and perhaps a subversive plot. If the rite would be so hard to explain to Alexander, a good procedure for Chaldaeans who sought to protect the king would be to use the rite without his knowledge. Let us assume they did so and try to reconstruct what happened.

We then find that Chaldaeans sought to contrive a substitute king in order to protect Alexander, who was menaced by adverse omens. They had to keep their procedure secret from Alexander and from Greeks and Macedonians, who would misunderstand it and inform the king. However, we can accept from Plutarch that the substitute was a Greek, Dionysios the Messenian, who had long been imprisoned, clearly on a serious charge. Diodorus's assertion, that the man was a "local person," probably implies that he was a Babylonian and may well be a result of a refusal of Diodorus or his source to believe that a Greek would have done the deed. Arrian and his source were not interested in the man's identity or ethnic status, and, as rationalists, did not record that Sarapis had spoken; rather, the man who sat on the throne had said only that the idea had "come" to him.

A Greek prisoner was not only expendable. His ethnic status was close to Alexander's, making him a good substitute. Greeks had long been worshiping Egyptian deities. Dionysios may have been known for his devotion to Sarapis. We may imagine Chaldaeans contriving for gullible Dionysios to hear a voice, "I am the god Sarapis! I shall loose your bonds! You must then go and sit on Alexander's throne!" A hidden Chaldaean then released Dionysios from his chains.

The eunuchs may well have been Babylonians. If so, they surely knew of the rite of substitution, and the Chaldaeans would have had no trouble explaining their intentions to the eunuchs, who therefore did nothing to obstruct Dionysios on his errand. If the Chaldaeans had known that the diadem and royal robe would be available, they would have had "Sarapis" tell Dionysios to put them on, but how could they have foreseen that availability?

The eunuchs cannot have been dismayed at the sight of the substitute on the throne if they were accomplices of the Chaldaeans. But if, contrary to plan, Greeks and Alexander himself learned of the strange event, the eunuchs could well have been in danger and therefore distressed: How could they explain the protective rite to ignorant persons who could only misunderstand it? They gave an excuse for their failure to drag the man off the throne: A "Persian custom" forbade them. So lame is the excuse that it begs for explanation. Under our hypothesis, the eunuchs in their perplexity were telling something near the truth! Their evident distress and their lame excuse seem to have been enough to preserve them from danger. Alexander saw no reason to question their loyalty.

Normally, the substitute king would have been killed after 100 days. The Chaldaeans, unable to explain the rite to Alexander and unable to conceal the substitute king from him any longer, recommended that Alexander have him executed forthwith. The death of the substitute *might* be a complete fulfilment of the earlier dire omens. However, believers knew that after being killed the substitute could no longer divert from the king any ill fortune that still impended. Thus, under our hypothesis, all three source-narratives make sense, and we have found an explanation for the eunuchs' distress and lame excuse. Our hypothesis as a result looks highly probable, and again we find the Chaldaeans acting to *protect* Alexander.

Eddy[127] took the incident of the commoner on the throne as part of a Chaldaean plot against Alexander. Eddy recognized the rite of the substitute or mock king, but wrongly connected that rite with the *Akîtu,* perhaps because the *Akîtu* at Babylon fell in Nisanu, the month before the one of Alexander's death. The clay tablets which let us know of the rituals of the *Akîtu*[128] say nothing of a rite of a substitute.[129] Though the tablets are fragmentary, we have good reason to believe that even when complete they could not have had anything about a substitute king. The whole point of the *Akîtu* was to have the king himself, not a substitute, suffer and learn to be humble.

Eddy went on to view the man on the throne as part of a clandestine effort of the Babylonians to celebrate the *Akîtu,* at a time when Alexander had made no effort to do so, though, as king over Babylon, he should have. Thus, the conspirators could prove that Alexander's rule over Babylon was illegitimate. In all probability, however, such a procedure would prove nothing of the kind.[130] Eddy found in the drastic responses of Alexander and the Macedonians (involving torture and execution) confirmation for his theory. Our hypothesis is much better founded.

Eddy was probably wrong again when he took a last incident as a sign that Chaldaeans were hostile to Alexander. The king fell into his final illness during a carouse. The disease went on for eleven days. During the last four, Alexander was unable to speak.[131] Two days before the king died, his officers, Peithon, Attalos, Menidas, and Seleucus, and his seers, Kleomenes and Demophon, are said to have slept in the temple of Sarapis. Using the ancient procedure called "incubation," they were seeking an answer from the god, whether it would be better for Alexander to be brought into the god's temple, and, after supplication, to receive care from him. However, an oracle came from the god that the king should not be brought into the temple; rather, it was better for him to stay where he was. Soon thereafter, Alexander died.[132]

Here again it is strange to find Sarapis mentioned in Alexander's time and at Babylon. Even granting that the god was known and worshiped then at Babylon, could he have been important enough there to be involved with the king and his doom? Had the god been Bêl, whose oracle Alexander had defied, one could understand how the king's loyal subjects, in their desperation, sought his help. But how and why would a Greek or Macedonian writer (even Ptolemy I) have turned Bêl into Sarapis?

On the other hand, Amon, the mightiest of the Egyptian gods, had declared through his priest that Alexander was his son.[133] One could expect the king's divine father to care for him. But Amon had no temple at Babylon (at least we know of none). In their desperation, Alexander's loyal subordinates could have turned to another Egyptian god, if that god had a temple there.

Alexander is reported to have founded a temple for Sarapis at Alexandria.[134] It is unlikely that Plutarch's story involves a temple of Sarapis founded at Babylon by Alexander or subordinates of his. Such a temple would have been immediately open to the dying king.

One might conjecture that the worship of Sarapis had been brought to Babylon much earlier, by Queen Nitokris, whose name shows her to have been partly or wholly Egyptian. She may well have been Nabonidus's wife.[135]

Alexander's men knew that their king had fostered the cult of Sarapis in Egypt, and probably also that Sarapis was a god who gave revelations to those who slept in his shrine, that he could cure the sick,[136] and that he was Egyptian and would act for the benefit of Amon's son. Hence, it was natural for them to invoke the aid of Sarapis if indeed he had a temple at Babylon.

Thus, the priests of Sarapis's temple at Babylon were probably not Chaldaeans. But any priests, whether Chaldaeans or not, could only have endangered themselves by allowing the dying Alexander to be brought to their temple in search of a cure. If the god then did not cure him, Alexander's men might blame the priests and exact terrible vengeance. Not hostility, but mere prudence probably determined the priests' course of action.

Alexander's victories posed difficult religious problems for the conquered peoples. Persians, Babylonians, and Jews responded by producing or adopting pieces of literature. Let us proceed to examine what survives.

N O T E S

1 See p. 187.

2 See, e.g., Hermann Bengtson, *History of Greece from the Beginnings to the Byzantine Era* (Ottawa: University of Ottawa Press, 1988), 89–177.

3 See p. 266.

4 Stolper, *Entrepreneurs,* 152; Cook, *Persian Empire,* 229.

5 Isocrates 4.135–56, 160–66; Xenophon *Hellenica* vi.1.12, vii.1.38, *Cyropaedia* vii.8.8–16 (on Xenophon *Cyropaedia* viii.8, see Heleen Sancisi-Weerdenburg, "The Fifth Oriental Monarchy and Hellenocentrism," in *Achaemenid History II,* 117–38).

6 Orations 4, 5 (and cf. 13.77); Epistles 1 (probably), 2.11, 3, 9 (probably).

7 Dandamaev and Lukonin, *Culture,* 223.

8 Archers and light infantry: Dandamaev and Lukonin, *Culture,* 224. Cavalry: ibid. and Cook, *Persian Empire,* 103. According to Xenophon (*Cyropaedia* i.3.3, iv.3.1–23), King Cyrus created the *Persian* cavalry; see Cook, 40–41. In any case, other Iranians, notably the Medes, had a long tradition of horsemanship (Dandamaev and Lukonin, *Culture,* 224).

9 Cook, *Persian Empire,* 102–3, 219.

10 See Dandamaev and Lukonin, *Culture,* 225.

11 Ibid., 230–34.

12 Dandamaev and Lukonin (*Culture,* 225, 229) give a Marxist explanation for the military weakness of the later Empire: The early Persian kings could make successful use of soldiers from the conquered peoples because there was then little class cleavage, whereas the later kings, under whom classes were sharply differentiated, could not.

13 Olmstead, *Persian Empire,* 289–99; Cook, *Persian Empire,* 82–83, 203–4; Dandamaev and Lukonin, *Culture,* 177–95, but cf. 367.

14 See Stolper, *Entrepreneurship,* 143–51.

15 See Cook, *Persian Empire,* 103, 226; Dandamaev and Lukonin, *Culture,* 367.

16 Cook, *Persian Empire,* 103, 226.

17 In this specialized study of mine, I have no intention of giving a detailed treatment of Alexander's career. Such treatments can be found, e.g., in N. G. L. Hammond, *Alexander the Great* (2d ed.; Bristol: Bristol Press, 1989); A. B. Bosworth, *Conquest and Empire: The Reign of Alexander the Great* (Cambridge: Cambridge University Press, 1988); and Peter Green, *Alexander of Macedon, 356–323 B.C.: A Historical Biography* (2d ed., revised and enlarged; Berkeley: University of California Press, 1991).

18 Olmstead, *Persian Empire,* 489–90.

19 Curtius iii.3.8–25; Boyce, HZ, II, 286–88, and III, 3.

20 157–59, 289–98, 455–61.

21 Josephus: *Antiquities* xi.8.3.317–19, 4–5.326–339; the other two legends:
First legend: *Megillat Ta'anit* 21 Kislev and scholium, in Hans Lichtenstein, "Die Fastenrolle," *Hebrew Union College Annual* 8–9 (1931–32), 339–40, and the parallel version at Babylonian Talmud, *Yoma* 69a. In my article, "Alexander and the Jews," *Proceedings of the American Academy for Jewish Research* 59 (1993), 64–66, I reconstruct the probable original reflected by the two versions and present a translation.
Second legend: Pseudo-Callisthenes *Vita Alexandri regis Macedonum* (Recension ε) 20.2–5 in *Anonymi Byzantini Vita Alexandri regis Macedonum,* ed. Juergen Trumpf (Stuttgart: Teubner, 1974), 76–78. For proof that the legend in Pseudo-Callisthenes is Jewish in origin, see Friedrich Pfister, *Eine jüdische Grundungsgeschichte Alexandrias mit einem Anhang über Alexanders Besuch in Jerusalem* ("Sitzungsberichte der Heidelberger Akademie der Wissenschaften, philosophisch-historische Klasse," 1914, 11 Abteilung; Heidelberg: Carl Winter, 1914); Gerhard Delling, "Alexander der Grosse als Bekenner des jüdischen Gottesglaubens," *Journal for the Study of Judaism in the Persian, Hellenistic, and Roman Periods* 12 (1981), 1–51; Daniela Pacella, "Alessandro e gli Ebrei nella testimonianza dello Ps. Callistene," *Annali della Scuola normale superiore di Pisa, classe di lettere e filosofia,* Serie III, Vol. XII, 4 (1982), 1255–69.

22 In my article, "Alexander," cited above, n. 21.

23 Arrian iii.1.2–4; Curtius iv.7.1–5; Diodorus xvii.49.1–2; legend: Pseudo-Kallisthenes i.34, published in *Historia Alexandri Magni (Pseudo-Kallisthenes), Vol. I,*

Recensio Vetusta, ed. Guilelmus Kroll (2d ed., photographed from 1st ed. of 1926; Berlin: Weidmann, 1958), and translated in *The Life of Alexander of Macedon by Pseudo-Callisthenes,* trans. and ed. Elizabeth H. Haight (New York: Longmans, Green, 1955). See also Samuel K. Eddy, *The King Is Dead* (Lincoln: University of Nebraska Press, 1961), 279–80, and Ludwig Koenen, *Eine agonistische Inschrift aus Ägypten und frühptolemäische Königsfeste* ("Beiträge zur klassischen Philologie," 56; Meisenheim am Glan: Anton Hain, 1977), 30–31. Antipatris is located on Map 1.

24 Hammond, *Alexander,* 126–28; Bosworth, *Conquest,* 71–74.

25 Bosworth, *Conquest,* 234–35; Eddy, *King,* 269–70.

26 At *Against Apion* ii.4.43, Josephus quotes a report that he ascribes to Hekataios (surely, Hekataeus of Abdera), "Because of the consideration and loyalty shown to him by the Jews, he [Alexander] added to their territory the region of Samaria, free of tribute." The report and its ascription to Hekataios may or may not be true (see, e.g., Ralph Marcus, *Josephus I* [LCL. Cambridge: Harvard University Press, 1956], 209, n. *d*). If the report is true, it may imply that Jews helped Alexander punish the Samaritans, whether at Samaria or at Wadi Daliyeh. Why else would the king have rewarded the "loyalty" with all or part of that region? There is an obstacle to believing this inference: We can infer it from the report ascribed to Hekataios, but no authority says so directly, not even Josephus, the eager narrator of humiliations that befell the Samaritans.

27 Arrian iii.6.1–7.1.

28 Hammond, *Alexander,* 140–43; Bosworth, *Conquest,* 76–79; Green, *Alexander,* 282–88.

29 Darius during the night before the battle: Curtius iv.13.12–14. Alexander's victory: Hammond, *Alexander,* 138–50; Bosworth, *Conquest,* 74–85; Green, *Alexander,* 282–96.

30 Transliteration and translation: BHLT, 30–37. Introductory commentary: ibid., 24–27.

31 Cf. Berossus *apud* Josephus *Against Apion* i.20.153, where Cyrus is said to have had Nabonidus reside in Karmania.

32 See chap 5, p. 116.

33 See chap 8, pp. 203–5.

34 Grayson (BHLT, 26) does not exclude the battle at the Granikos; for him, it is only "less likely."

35   Arrian i.16.7; Bosworth, *Conquest,* 44; Hammond, *Alexander,* 157.

36   See Hammond, *Alexander,* 157; Green, *Alexander,* 233, 237–38, 244–45.

37   Though Grayson (BHLT, 26–27) did not perceive this fact, M. Tsevat did (in his review of BHLT, *Journal of Biblical Literature* 96 [1977], 277). Grayson (BHLT, 26–27) believes that the author indicated the conclusion of a reign by drawing a horizontal line and that the three horizontal lines in col. IV represent three more historical reigns, so as to bring the date of writing down well past the time of Alexander the Great. But Grayson himself recognized that the Dynastic Prophecy has no horizontal line at the end of the reign of Arses and probably none at the end of the reign of Cyrus. He also recognized that such horizontal lines served the purpose of our paragraph indentations. Thus nothing proves that the events mentioned in col. IV were past in the author's time.

38   See chap 2, n 51.

39   Plutarch *Alexander* 34.1; J. R. Hamilton, *Plutarch, Alexander: A Commentary* (Oxford: Clarendon Press, 1969); 90; Bosworth, *Conquest,* 85.

40   Arrian iii.16.2, Curtius v.1.4–7.

41   Magi (presumably, Zoroastrian priests) had become prominent at Babylon under the Persian kings. See Boyce, HZ, III, 386.

42   See chap 8, p. 204.

43   Curtius v.1.17–22; cf. Arrian iii.16.3.

44   Arrian iii.16.4–5; the text there blames on Xerxes the ruin of the temples, but see chap 7, pp. 178–90.

45   Plutarch *Alexander* 57.3; Green, *Alexander,* 304 and 544, n 5.

46   Arrian iii.16.6–11; Curtius v.2.8–17; Diodorus xvii. 65.5–66.2.

47   Arrian iii.17.1–18.10; Curtius v.3.1–5.4; Diodorus xvii.67.1–69.2; Green, *Alexander,* 310–13.

48   The approximate date is deducible from the information in the sources; see Karl Julius Beloch, *Griechische Geschichte* (2d ed.; Berlin and Leipzig: Walter De Gruyter et al., 1912–27), Vol. III, part 2 (1923), 318. Green (*Alexander,* 314) is too precise in giving the date as January 31.

49   Curtius v.6.1–9; Diodorus xvii.60; Plutarch *Alexander* 37.2; Green, *Alexander,* 315–16; Bosworth, *Conquest,* 92; Hamilton, *Commentary,* 97. Arrian says nothing of Alexander's atrocities on entering Persepolis, but Arrian himself tells us (i.preface) that he follows closely the works of Alexander's admiring subordinates, Ptolemy and Aristobulos, so that in this instance Arrian's report should be discounted; see Bosworth, *A Historical Commentary on Arrian's History of Alexander* (Oxford: Clarendon Press, 1980–), I, 329, and Badian in CHI, II (1985), 443.

50   Boyce, HZ, II, 290–92; III, 14–17.

51   Curtius v.6.1; cf. Diodorus xvii.70.1.

52   Plutarch *Alexander* 37.6 (LCL 37.3).

53   So Bosworth, *Conquest,* 92.

54   See Badian, CHI, II (1985), 444.

55   Arrian (iii.18.11–12) presents the burning as an act of cool judgment; the other sources have it instigated by Ptolemy's mistress, the Athenian courtesan, Thais, when Alexander was drunk (Curtius v.7; Diodorus xvii.72; Plutarch *Alexander* 38). See Badian in CHI, II (1985), 444–45.

56   Until recently, chronological studies gave Alexander's reception of the news, that Antipater had defeated Agis's army at Megalopolis, a date well before the burning of Persepolis, but use of Aeschines 3.133 now shows that the defeat of Agis came some time in the spring of 330, and Alexander had not heard of it by May. See Badian in CHI, II (1985), 445–47.

57   See Dandamaev and Lukonin, *Culture,* 255–56; Eddy, *King,* 51 and Plate IV; Green, *Alexander,* 318–19.

58   Boyce, HZ, II, 107–10, and III, 14.

59   Peter Green has suggested that Alexander stayed so long at Persepolis in hopes that Persian nobles and priests might consent to have him play the role of the king at the Persian New Year's festival, the analogue of the Babylonian *Akîtu* (*Alexander,* 318–21; cf. Boyce, HZ, III, 14–15). We have noted that there is no good evidence that such an analogue existed. If Alexander had truly resented stubborn Persian rejection of his kingship to the point that for that reason he burned the palaces, there was no reason for any of our sources to have been silent about the fact. Alexander thoroughly punished the resistant Persians and the pretenders to Persian kingship. Large numbers of Persians became collaborators under his rule. His unbroken string of victories outdid even great Darius I. The Alexander-historians had no more need to conceal stubborn Persian rejection of his kingship (and Alexander's resentment) than they had to conceal the stubborn refusal of the Tyrians to let Alexander sacrifice to their Herakles. Alexander crushed both Persian and Tyrian resistance. After capturing Tyre, he sacrificed to Herakles, though at least some of the vanquished must have held he had no right to do so or to rule Tyre. Had the conqueror wished, after capturing Persepolis, in the same manner he could have forcibly posed as king and carried out a ritual to Ahuramazda, though many of the vanquished held he had no right to do so or to rule Iran.

60 See n 56.

61 Arrian iii.19.2

62 Arrian iii.19.3–5.

63 iii.19.5–8.

64 Curtius v.13.1; Bosworth (*Commentary,* 335–36) accepts Curtius's version and tries to explain how Arrian could have erred. Badian (CHI, II [1985], 447, n 2) argues for accepting Arrian's account.

65 v.9.4.

66 Arrian iii.21.1–5; Curtius v.9.2–12.20.

67 iii.21.4.

68 v.9.16, 10.7, 12.7, 13, 19.

69 Arrian iii.21; Curtius v.13. According to Curtius, "Bessos and his fellow-conspirators" mortally wounded Darius; according to Arrian, Satibarzanes and Barsaentes did so. Both authorities agree that Alexander punished Bessos as the regicide (Arrian iii.29.4–5; Curtius vii.5.38–43, 10.10).

70 Arrian iii.22.1.

71 See n 67.

72 Arrian iii.23.1–25.1; Curtius vi.4.1–22.

73 Arrian iii.25.1–3; Curtius vi.6.13; cf. Diodorus xvii.83.3, 7.

74 Diodorus xvii.74.1–2.

75   See Green, *Alexander,* 351–53.

76   Arrian iii.25.5–7, 28.2–3; Curtius vii.4.32–38.

77   Arrian iii.29.6–30.5; cf. Curtius vii.5.19–26.

78   Curtius (vii.5.38) adds this third charge to the two recorded by Arrian (iii.30.4; iv.7.3) and Justin (xii.5.10–11). The act of Bessos which most injured Alexander's interests was his assumption of the kingship. As a kinsman of Darius, Bessos had more legitimacy as Persian king than had the conqueror. Either Alexander or his admiring subordinates (the sources for Arrian) may have preferred to have the conqueror presented as disinterestedly seeking to avenge the murdered king. Bosworth (*Conquest,* 108) remarks that Alexander had been prepared to coexist with the regicides in the immediate aftermath of Darius's death; the change of attitude came when Bessos assumed the upright tiara, and the punishment eventually meted out to him was the punishment suffered by usurpers in the Achaemenid period; like Bessos, Fravartish (who was proclaimed king of Media during the struggles which accompanied the rise to power of Darius I) suffered mutilation, public exposure, and death by impalement at Ekbatana.

79   Arrian iii.30.5; Curtius vii.5.40.

80   Arrian (vii.4.6) is explicit on Spitamenes's ethnic status.

81   Arrian iv.1.4–5, 3.5, 5.2–6.4, 16.3–17.7; Curtius vii.6.14–15, 24; 7.31–39, 9.20, viii.3.1–15.

82   Arrian iv.18.4–19.6, 20.4–21.1; cf. Curtius vii.11.

83   Arrian iv.19.4–6, 20.4.

84   As is implied by Arrian iv.21.1.

85   Arrian iv.21; cf. Curtius viii.2.19–33.

86   Arrian iv.22.1–2; cf. Curtius viii.1.3–7.

87   Arrian iv.2.3–vi.27.1; Curtius viii.5.1–ix.10.17.

88   Curtius ix.10.19; x.1.9.

89   Arrian vi.29.3.

90 Arrian vii.11.1–3; Curtius x.3.7–14; Justin xii.12.1–4; Badian in CHI, II (1985), 482–83. Cf. Arrian vii.6.1–5; 23.1, 3–4; 29.4; Badian in CHI, II (1985), 488–89.

91 Arrian vii.110.6–8, 111.4–112.1; Plutarch 72.1–73.1.

92 See Oppenheim in CHI, II (1985), 586, but see also Dandamaev and Lukonin, *Culture,* 230–31, and Cook, *Persian Empire,* 102–3, 111, 245.

93 See my *Letters of Demosthenes* (New York and London: Columbia University Press, 1968), 44, n 44.

94 See Eddy, *King,* 106–12.

95 vii.16.4–17.6.

96 I find the descriptions of the detour at Arrian vii.16.6 and 17.5–6 difficult to understand and suspect that something is missing from the text. Alexander was coming from the east and north and had crossed the Tigris. The normal way for him to enter Babylon would have been from the east, marching westward through the Marduk gate. The detour, as described, has Alexander reaching the Euphrates, surely from the east and north, halting for a night, and then marching as he kept the river on his right (!) past the west side of the city, with the goal of turning around and entering the city marching eastward, perhaps through the Adad gate (see Harry Frank, *Discovering the Biblical World* [Maplewood, NJ: Hammond, 1975], map on 132). Arrian does not say that Alexander crossed the Euphrates. If the king did not cross the river and kept the Euphrates on his right, he would be marching to the south and east, away from Babylon! According to Justin, Alexander did cross the river and, avoiding Babylon, marched to Borsippa. Borsippa lies almost due south of Babylon and little if at all west (historical atlases are annoyingly inaccurate and inconsistent with one another on whether Babylon or Borsippa lies more to the east). But the direction of the Euphrates at Babylon is almost from north to south, and Borsippa by that criterion lies on the west side of the river.

I am also puzzled as to why the Chaldaeans advised the king to take the detour. How could they have failed to know that the route was impassable? Their suggestion and its outcome could serve only to discredit them in Alexander's eyes.

97 The king's order in 331: Arrian iii.16.4.

98 Alexander began to carry out those plans. Jews in his army refused to obey his orders to participate in the rebuilding of the idolatrous shrine and suffered severe punishment until the king finally pardoned them and exempted them from the task (Hecataeus of Abdera *apud* Josephus *Against Apion* i.22.192). Here was an instance where obedience to the Torah clashed with the principle that the Jews in the Age of Punishment must obey the pagan king God had placed over them.

99 Priests in other instances have been known to have been lax in repairing their temples, especially at their own expense; see I Kgs 12:5–16 and above, p. 190, and chap 7, n 133.

It is unlikely that Alexander in 331 ordered the Babylonians to rebuild Esagila at their own expense. Such an order would have been no improvement over Persian rule, and Arrian adds (iii.16.5) that in 331 Alexander had a meeting with the Chaldaeans "and carried out all their recommendations on the Babylonian temples." If the king had not at once volunteered to pay the expenses of rebuilding, the Chaldaeans would have recommended he should. Furthermore, even under Persian rule, nothing prevented the Chaldaeans from offering the obligatory sacrifices on the ruined site of Marduk's temple (on the duty in Babylon of caring for and feeding the gods, see Oppenheim, *Ancient Mesopotamia,* 187–93). The priests and the endowment must already have been covering those costs, though the Chaldaeans may have hoped that Alexander would assume part or all of them. Hence, the issue in 323, as viewed by Alexander (and as described by Arrian), was whether he should pay thereafter for the upkeep and expenses of the well-endowed temple.

100 Kings as caretakers: See, e.g., Nab. 1, line 3, and Nab. 4*, col. I, line 59; Antiochus I: *ANET,* 317.

101 xvii.112.2–5; see also Eddy, *King,* 107.

102 See p. 189.

103 xii.13.3–6.

104 *Alexander* 73.1.

105 Justin xiii.1.1, Diodorus xvii.112.6.

106 Magi at Babylon: Curtius v.1.22.

107 Eddy, *King,* 108–11.

108 vii.22.

109 Appian (*Syriakê* [ix.] 56 [287–91]) has nothing about a ship or ships losing their way in the marshes, but does present the story of the wind carrying off the diadem and of Seleucus retrieving it.

110 108.

111 See sec 3, pp. 293–95.

112   See Suetonius *Julius* 59.

113   xvii.116.4–117.1.

114   108–9.

115   Arrian does call the pronouncements of Chaldaeans *manteiai* (vii.22.1; cf.vii.17.1). The seers *(manteis)* and the Chaldaeans in Diodorus xvii.116.4 may be identical. If so, the passage refutes Eddy's argument. Also, the soothsayers in Arrian's account could well have been magi. The Persians were the ones who held that it was a terrible thing for a non-royal person to wear any of the garments that were royal prerogatives (Plutarch *Artoxerxes* 5.2).

116   vii.24.1–3.

117   xvii.116.2–3.

118   *Alexander* 73.3–4.

119   Tacitus *Histories* iv.83–84; Plutarch *On Isis and Osiris* 362a; John E. Stambaugh, *Sarapis under the Early Ptolemies* (Leiden: Brill, 1972), 12–13.

120   See Hamilton, *Commentary,* 212–13; Stambaugh, *Sarapis,* 1–13.

121   See Otto Seel, *Pompei Trogi Fragmenta* (Leipzig: B. G. Teubner, 1956), 109–10.

122   iv.67.

123   *Babyloniaka,* book i, *apud* Athenaeus xiv.639c.

124   Henri Frankfort, *Kingship and the Gods* (Chicago: University of Chicago Press, 1948), 263–64. Cf. James George Frazer, *The New Golden Bough,* edited and with notes and foreword by Theodor H. Gaster (Garden City, NY: Doubleday, 1961), 135–36, 159. Thorkild Jacobsen (*ZA* 52 [1957], 139) recognized that our incident was an instance of the substitute king *(shar pūḫi)* ritual. Simo Parpola has written the most complete treatment of the substitute king ritual (*Letters from Assyrian Scholars* [Neukirchen-Vluyn: Butzon und Bercker, 1970–83], Vol. II, xxii–xxxii). Parpola (xxix–xxxi) presents and discusses the ancient texts on the Sakaia and on the incident of the commoner on Alexander's throne. For conclusions similar to mine, see Robin Lane Fox, *Alexander the Great* (London and New York: Penguin, 1986), 459–60, 548.

125   The Sakaia clearly was a particular case of the rite of the substitute king; even the royal concubines were turned over to the substitute! Frankfort writes (*Kingship,* 263), "The substitution had to be complete in order to be effective."

126 In the *New Golden Bough,* Frazer and Gaster, who were both well informed on Graeco-Roman antiquity, cite no Greek or Roman parallels for the rite of the substitute king, a good sign that there were none.

127 *King,* 109–11; cf. Green, *Alexander,* 472 (based on Eddy).

128 *ANET,* 331–34.

129 But see Frankfort, *Kingship,* 410, n 41.

130 See Kuhrt in *Achaemenid History II,* 73–76. Add to the evidence adduced by her the fact that Nabonidus for years failed to participate in the *Akîtu,* but in all that time even his enemies did not deny that he was king.

131 Arrian vii.24.4–26.3; Curtius x.5.1–6 (incomplete); Diodorus xvii.117; Plutarch 75.3–76.4.

132 Arrian vii.26.2–3; Plutarch 76.4. Eddy's interpretation: *King,* 111–12.

133 Curtius iv.7.25; Diodorus xvii.51.1; cf. Arrian iii.3.2.

134 *Suda* s.v. *Sarapis;* John Malalas *Chronographia* in *Patrologiae Cursus Completus,* Series Graeca Prior, ed. J. P. Migne (Paris: J. P. Migne, 1865), XCVII, 304.

135 See Raymond Philip Dougherty, *Nabonidus and Belshazzar* ("Yale Oriental Series: Researches," Vol. XV; New Haven: Yale University Press, 1929), 39–62, and cf. I Kgs 11:1–8.

136 Stambaugh, *Sarapis,* 2, 10–13.

⤙ 11 ⤚

How the Persians, Babylonians,
and Jews Reacted to Alexander

1. The Religious Problems that Faced the Conquered Peoples

NO ANCIENT RELIGION really predicted Alexander's conquests, though present-future prophecies were written after the events had occurred. For almost every contemporary observer, there had to be a religious explanation for such superhuman feats: A man of 22 set out from tiny Macedonia and conquered the whole Persian Empire and more. Not surprisingly, some Greeks, some Egyptians, and some others viewed Alexander himself as a god. Even the conqueror's death did not put an end to that point of view.

Jewish prophecy hitherto had said nothing about a heathen monarchy to come after the Persian Empire. Jewish prophecy hitherto seems to have agreed with Persian theory[1] and with the Five-King Version[2] of Daniel 2: the Persian Empire would last at least until God himself brought the era of universal peace. Babylonian prophecy, to judge by the Three-Beast Version of Daniel 7,[3] certainly predicted no foreign rule to come after the hated dynasty of Xerxes.

Egyptians and Babylonians had welcomed Alexander as their liberator from cruel Persian rule. But even those peoples who had welcomed the conqueror soon suffered harsh exploitation under Alexander or under his successors. All the conquered peoples had to find some explanation of why their great gods would let this happen. Indeed, the Macedonian conquerors now had the vast hoards of Persian gold. The Macedonians (and the Greeks who came in large numbers to assist them) had their own great superiority in military skill and weapons. Consequently, the Macedonians and Greeks were long able to keep the conquered peoples in such a state of helplessness that armed rebellion was usually suicidal and long remained hopeless.

There did remain feasible forms of "resistance" for the conquered peoples: They could seek the aid of their gods, and they could write propaganda about those gods. The propaganda would at least strive to show that our great god did really predict another monstrous empire. The propaganda might then try to explain why our great god permitted this dreadful thing to happen, but often the religious teachers decided that only the god could know his own inscrutable purpose. Always, however, the religious teachers would search the national collections of omens and oracles for some sign that Greco-Macedonian domination was temporary, and then the religious teachers would publish their findings, often in the form of present-future prophecy.

2. The Responses of the Persians

THE MOST INTERESTING of the published findings are those of the Persians. Let us examine first their reactions to Alexander's conquests. On the eve of the battle of Gaugamela, Darius III still believed that the gods supported him and his empire and were communicating with him.[4] However, after the disastrous (and unpredicted) defeat there, Darius and the Persians had to conclude that their gods had turned away from them. Despite heavy losses, Iranians went on bravely resisting in eastern provinces from 330 to 327, but Alexander ultimately crushed them. Not just Persians but all Iranians had to conclude, at least for the moment, that their mighty gods had neither predicted nor resisted Alexander.

The Persian reactions to Alexander both in his lifetime and after his death ran through the whole spectrum from violent resistance to enthusiastic acceptance and collaboration. This is not surprising, because Alexander's policies toward the Persians ran through a similar spectrum. His entire enterprise began, at least in propaganda, as an aggressive crusade of brutal revenge against the Persians for the atrocities Xerxes had committed in Greece in 480 and 479 B.C.E. Alexander wantonly burned the imperial Persian palaces and shrines at Persepolis. Whatever the religious significance of Persepolis, Iranians could not fail to resent the massacres and the destruction perpetrated there by Alexander. Some of Alexander's corrupt officials went on to rob Persian temples and extort wealth and commit other atrocities. Though the sources report that Alexander inflicted capital punishment on the culprits,[5] Persians still could have resented the crimes. The bitter bloody struggles in eastern Iran from 330 to 327 must have created abundant resentment.

But if Alexander accepted some of the Graeco-Macedonian prejudices against the "unmanly" conquered peoples, he was almost totally unprejudiced against the Persians. Indeed, he was prejudiced in their favor. (He showed no such favor to the other conquered peoples.) From the aftermath of the battle of Gaugamela on, he made no secret of his desire to be king of a new empire, which would be the heir of the Persian Empire, with a mixed Macedonian-Greek-Persian ruling class. When capable Persian governors, such as Mazaios, governor of Babylon, found themselves left in the lurch by inept Darius III, Alexander welcomed them and confirmed them in office. The conqueror chose as his queen Roxane, daughter of noble Iranian Oxyartes; he married also two Persian princesses and encouraged his officers and men to marry Persian or Iranian women.[6]

Consequently, we shall not be surprised to find some Persians reacting with extreme hostility to Alexander, and others gladly accepting him. The secular Persian literature of the time of Alexander, if there ever was any, is long since lost. As for the religious literature, much if not all of it was transmitted orally, and a large proportion of it was lost.[7] Nevertheless, recognizable pieces of Persian present-future prophecy survive from the time, and Persian works written between the third and eleventh centuries C.E. may well contain authentic traditions on Iranian reactions to Alexander. Let us examine two present-future prophecies first.

Strangely, one of these revelations survives only in Greek dactylic hexameter verses, and the other, only in a present-future composition which was still being supplemented in mediaeval times. Both, however, can be shown to have originated as works composed by Persians during the lifetime of Alexander.

3. Sibylline Prophecy

THE GREEK HEXAMETERS are preserved in the *Sibylline Oracles,* a collection of utterances all of which at first sight have the appearance of having been written by pagans. All, however, are useful for teaching Jewish or Christian doctrines. In fact, the vast majority of the *Sibylline Oracles* were written by Jews or Christians, but a few pieces really are pagan products. Though the etymology of the word "sibyl" (*sibylla* in Greek) has never been explained satisfactorily in any language, women called "sibyls" are a phenomenon peculiar to Greek tradition and literature. All known sibylline texts are in Greek dactylic hexameter.

In Greek tradition, going back beyond 500 B.C.E., a sibyl is an old woman who in an ecstatic trance utters predictions of a predominantly gloomy nature, usually affecting states or kingdoms.[8] Although sibyls are peculiar to Greek tradition, the ancient evidence on them contains conspicuous mention of sibyls who were Persian, Babylonian, or Hebrew! The great Roman scholar, Marcus Terentius Varro (116–27 B.C.E.), drew up a list of ten sibyls, probably in his encyclopedic *Antiquitates rerum humanarum et divinarum* ("Ancient Institutions of Secular and Religious Life"), published in 47 B.C.E. His book has perished. His list, however, was quoted by the Christian Father, Firmianus Lactantius (ca. 260–340), and has survived. It begins as follows: "The first [sibyl] was from the Persians; of her Nikanor, who wrote a book on the deeds of Alexander the Macedonian, made mention."[9] The quoted list does not contain Varro's reason (if he gave any) for regarding the Persian sibyl as the earliest.

Furthermore, there was no reason for a biographer of Alexander to mention a very early Persian prophetess unless she was believed to have predicted some of the feats of the great conqueror. Indeed, Christian writers took what Varro left to be inferred and turned it into an explicit assertion that the Persian sibyl predicted Alexander's deeds. Those writers also gave a reason for regarding the Persian sibyl as the earliest.

There is a clearly Christian prologue to the *Sibylline Oracles,* written no earlier than the end of the fifth century. That prologue says, "First [of the ten sibyls] is the Chaldaean, that is to say, the Persian. Her proper name was 'Sambethe.' She belonged to the family of the most blessed Noah. She is the one who is said to have predicted the deeds of Alexander the Macedonian."[10]

"Scholiasts" in ancient times wrote scholia, i.e., commentaries in the margins of the texts on which they commented. A Christian scholiast on Plato's *Phaedrus* 244B wrote, "There have been ten sibyls, of whom the first was named Sambethe. The older accounts say she was Chaldaean, but others say instead that she was a Hebrew and that she was married to one of Noah's sons and accompanied him and the others into the ark. They say that because she lived before the differentiation of languages she gave her prophecies in Hebrew; furthermore, that she predicted the exploits of Alexander the Macedonian. Nikanor, the biographer of Alexander, mentions her."

Pausanias, a pagan writer of the second half of the second century C.E. knows of a Hebrew sibyl named "Sabbe." He adds that some call her a Babylonian sibyl and others, an Egyptian. He says nothing about a Persian sibyl or about predictions of Alexander's feats.[11]

The author of *Sibylline Oracles* iii.809–29 claims to be a prophetess from Babylon and a daughter-in-law of Noah. Those verses are part of the main corpus of Book iii of the *Oracles,* which is datable in the second century B.C.E.

Pausanias's "Sabbe" can hardly be anything but a shortened form of "Sambethe," and "Sambethe" is certainly a Jewish name derived from "Sabbath." [12] A reference to a sibyl's presence aboard the ark would suffice to date her in very early times not only for Jews but also for Babylonians and Persians, because all three peoples had the story of the deluge or something like it. [13]

Thus, by the times of the prologue-writer and the scholiast, people believed that a prophetess rode aboard the ark and predicted Alexander's feats. Some said she was Persian; others, that she was Babylonian (= Chaldaean), and still others, that she was a Hebrew. The prologue-writer identifies the Persian with the Chaldaean sibyl, and by saying her name was Sambethe gives reason to identify her with the Hebrew. The scholiast, too, gives reason to identify the Chaldaean with the Hebrew. Pausanias speaks of authorities who said that Sabbe, the Hebrew sibyl, was Babylonian. We shall find that there was, indeed, good reason to say that the Persian, Babylonian, and Hebrew sibyls who predicted Alexander's feats were one and the same.

Would Greek scribes allow Sibylline verses to perish if they purportedly were composed in very early times and predicted the feats of Alexander? It is inherently probable that such verses would be preserved somewhere, and scholars have found an instance of them at *Sibylline Oracles* iii.388–95. [14]

In interpreting such texts, we must bear in mind that most present-future prophecies eventually prove false. We should not necessarily reject an interpretation which renders the prediction false. The *Sibylline Oracles* contain a chaotic sequence of passages, so that it can be difficult to determine where one utterance ends and another begins. But iii.388–95 can be shown to be a well-defined unit.

One key to determining the boundaries of oracles can be derived from our study of present-future prophecies. A writer undertakes the hazardous and deceitful task of writing a present-future prophecy if he foresees an imminent glorious future or at least a coming end of the present adversity and also believes that the members of his religious community should hear of it, even though at this time they do not think the gods are communicating with them. An announcement of further adversity or a prediction of events that mattered little to the religious community, even if fulfilled, is unlikely to have followed, in one and the same prophecy, an announcement of an end to adversity or of a coming glorious future.

Let us examine the context of *Sibylline Oracles* iii.388–97. Verses 350–80 are a real (if false) prophecy against Rome, announcing an end to adversity for Asia. Verses 381–87 speak of Macedonia bringing adversity upon Asia, so that those verses do not belong to the oracle in iii.350–80. We shall translate and treat iii.381–87 later,[15] and shall show then that the passage probably reflects a time after Alexander's death. The bringer of adversity is an entire "breed," rather than a single spectacular leader. The passage thus seems to be directed at Alexander's successors rather than at the great conqueror himself. Verses 386–87 predict the end of that breed, whereas verses 388–92 prophesy adversity. Clearly one oracle ends at verse 387 and another begins at verse 388.

Here is a translation of verses 388–95. Let us call the passage *Sibylline A.* English word order makes it impossible to have the lines of translation exactly correspond to the Greek verses.

388	One day an incredible[16] man shall come to Asia's wealthy land
389	Clad with a purple cloak upon his shoulders,
390–91	Savage, unjust, fiery, for he, a thunderbolt, assembled
391–92	Lights ahead of himself.[17] And all Asia will bear An evil yoke,
392	And the earth, drenched, will drink much blood.
393	But even so, Hades will attend to him in all respects when he has altogether vanished.[18]
394	By the stock of those whose stock he wishes to wipe out,
395	By that same stock shall his own stock be wiped out.

The prophecy in verses 393–95 announces an end to adversity and predicts glorious revenge upon the invader. Therefore, when the author wrote *Sibylline A,* he is unlikely to have followed those verses with the (difficult) verses 396–400, which hint at continued adversity and add nothing to the glory. On the other hand, the audacious prediction in verses 394–95, that the stock of the invader's victims will wipe out his line, was never fulfilled, and believers would be likely to supplement the disappointing prophecy.[19]

The fierce and fiery invader, who wears a purple cloak (an attribute of royalty) and conquers all Asia and perpetrates bloody massacres was recognized as Alexander the Great by a later ancient writer of a Sibylline Oracle and by modern scholars.[20] The prophecy must have been transparent to the author's contemporaries.

To what nation did the writer of *Sibylline A* belong? We have noticed that Alexander treated both the Jews and the Babylonians with kindness. Therefore, the sibyl who calls him savage and unjust is unlikely to have been a Jew or a Babylonian. Her interest in all Asia as victims should imply that she was not Greek. Only the Persians claimed to be the legitimate rulers of all Asia. They were the victims of the largest-scale massacres perpetrated by Alexander.

If, moreover, verses 390–91 condemn Alexander for exploiting fire as a mere means for his own self-glorification, the writer must have been a fire-worshiping Persian.[21]

Alexander indeed died, but his body was preserved for centuries after his death; he did not "altogether vanish." Moreover, he did not seek to wipe out Darius III and his family. Alexander was outstandingly kind to the defeated king's brother, wife, mother, and daughters, and even to his little son and heir. The conqueror's relentless pursuit of Darius might lead Persians to think that he sought to destroy their monarch and his dynasty, but Alexander's behavior at the end of that pursuit, when he found Darius slain by *Persians,* left no further room for that belief.[22] Alexander even left it to Iranians to execute Bessos-Artaxerxes IV (though one can easily say that Alexander was responsible for Bessos's death). Furthermore, neither Alexander nor any heir of his owed his death to a Persian. The falsity of verses 393–95 is a strong indication that they belong to the future part of the present-future prophecy. *Sibylline A* was written while Alexander still lived, before June 10, 323 B.C.E., and, indeed, even before Darius III was murdered in 330!

We have accepted the reading of verses 390–91, according to which Alexander is said to have had flaming fire-pans or burning torches carried in front of him.[23] Two problems confront us as a result. First, although later Hellenistic monarchs and Roman emperors had lights carried in front of them, no extant text says that Alexander did so. However, similar practices were known earlier in Greece.[24] The Alexander historians could pass over in silence a practice of Alexander's which did not offend Greeks or Macedonians. Walter Otto has argued from the evidence on Alexander and on the Ptolemies of Egypt that Alexander did have lights carried in front of him.[25]

There is a second problem: Persian kings, too, had fire carried in front of them.[26] If the sibyl is Persian, why does she give prominence to this trait as characteristic of the savage invader? There is a difference between the description of the Persian practice and that of the savage invader: Only one fire was carried in front of the Persian king. Plural lights were carried before Alexander, and pious Persians may have found the plurality disrespectful to the sacred fire, as if it were being exploited by the conqueror as a mere means for his own self-glorification.

Why would Persians spread their own religious propaganda in Greek and use the figure of a sibyl? The old Persian Empire of Darius III and his predecessors was conspicuous for circulating announcements and propaganda in the languages of the intended audiences, including Greek.[27]

Alexander's own propagandist, Kallisthenes, spread the report that the sibyl of Greek Erythrai had uttered prophecies of Alexander's illustrious (or even divine)[28] descent. What would Persians do to counter a prophecy in support of Alexander, placed in the mouth of a Greek sibyl? One might have expected them to reply with a prophecy attacking the Macedonian conqueror, placed in the mouth of great Iranian Zarathushtra. But at first they may have refrained from doing so because the prophet's utterances were so well known that it was difficult to persuade believers that another one had just been discovered. It was better to have a Persian sibyl's oracle be the reply to that of the Greek sibyl.

Pious Persians had settled in the Greek-speaking world, notably at Ephesus. Such Persians at Ephesus may have composed *Sibylline A* in Greek in reply to the verses of the Greek sibyl.[29] Those Persian authors probably said that the Persian sibyl had entered the *var* (the Iranian equivalent of the ark) with Yima (the Iranian equivalent of Noah)[30] and was therefore far more ancient than the Greek prophetess of Erythrai.

No Persian was responsible for the death in 311 of Alexander's posthumous son, Alexander IV, or for the death in 309 or 308 of the conqueror's alleged illegitimate son, Herakles.[31] There were no more members of Alexander's line. Fulfilment of verses 394–95 had become impossible.

But decades had elapsed, during which the oracle in *Sybilline Oracles* iii.388–95 showed Persian believers that the prophetess of mighty Ahuramazda had indeed foretold the feats of Alexander. Jews and Babylonians, too, each needed corresponding reassurance about their almighty god. A prophetess who rode aboard the equivalent of the ark could be one of their own, so Jews and Babylonians quickly laid claim to the sibyl. Pagan and Christian Greeks tell us about a Persian, Babylonian, and Jewish sibyl who predicted the deeds of Alexander. *Sibylline A* can only have been Persian. Greek informants would not have ascribed that oracle to Babylonians and Jews, if Babylonians and Jews themselves had not laid claim to it. Here we have direct evidence for the phenomenon we discovered in Daniel 2 and 7: A religious community took over a present-future prophecy which originally could have belonged only to another community.

4. Texts in Persian

THE EXISTENCE OF A PERSIAN sybil may well have been news even to Persians, though the author of Sibylline Oracles iii.388–95 seems to have thought it prudent to ascribe his present-future prophecy to her. However, another Persian writer was more daring and boldly ascribed his own present-future prophetic composition to great Iranian Zarathushtra. We can trace the Zoroastrian traditions that made it possible for that writer to do so without fear of being disbelieved.

The Persians probably were impressed already between 538 and 522 B.C.E. with the Five-King Version of Daniel 2, for it bore an astonishing resemblance to a text in their own scriptures. We have noted [32] that the series of gold, silver, bronze, and iron has been a fact of metallurgy and chemistry and economics ever since the beginning of the Iron Age. Each metal in the series is nobler, less corrodable, and more expensive than the metals that follow it. Any price-list of metals in ancient times could have had the series. Wherever these metals were known, they could be used to describe a sequence descending from the nobler to the baser.

The *Avesta* contained an instance of the gold-silver-bronze-iron series, or a very similar one, in a section now lost. The section still existed in the ninth century C.E. and may well have been composed by Zarathushtra and be earlier than the instance in Hesiod, [33] though it is very difficult to date Avestan texts and Zarathushtra himself.

Originally the *Avesta* was preserved by being memorized and was transmitted orally. At most a few written copies were kept at important shrines, and even that practice may have begun only under the Sassanian kings of the third through the sixth century C.E. In the ninth century, after the fall of the Sassanian Empire to the Muslim Arabs, Zoroastrian scholars produced a summary of the scriptures for mass circulation, and this summary is preserved in the *Dinkard*. Under the Sassanian kings at the latest, the *Avesta* was divided into sections called *nasks*. [34] The passage interesting for us stood in the *Sudgar Nask* as the seventh *fargard* (chapter). The *Sudgar Nask* has perished, but the *Dinkard* preserves a summary of it, and the interesting passage has been translated [35] as follows:

> The seventh *fargard, Ta-ve-urvata,* is about the exhibition to Zaratusht [= Zarathushtra] of the nature of the four periods in the millennium of Zaratusht. First, the golden, that in which Auharmazd [= Ahuramazda] displayed the religion to Zaratusht. Second, the silver, that in which Vishtasp [= Vishtaspa, Zarathushtra's patron] received the religion from Zaratusht. Third, the steel, the period within which the organizer of righteousness, Aturpad son of Maraspend, was born. Fourth, the period mingled with iron is this, in which is much propagation of the authority of the apostate and other villains, as regards the destruction of the reign of religion, the weakening of every kind of goodness and virtue, and the disappearance of honor and wisdom from the countries of Iran. . . .

We do not possess the full text of the seventh *fargard* of the *Sudgar Nask* and cannot be sure that any aspect missing from the summary also was absent from the original. The summary says nothing of a dream or of a statue or a tree consisting of the metals. But Ahuramazda is said to have *exhibited* the nature of the four periods. The *exhibition* is unlikely to have been of shapeless lumps of metal. It probably took the form of some kind of vision of symbolic objects made of the metals. The metals are said to represent not kings or kingdoms or reigns, but periods. Corspicuous by its absence from the summary of the seventh *fargard* is anything to correspond to the stone of Daniel 2, as something to end the deterioration and restore prosperity.[36] The *Dinkard* was compiled after the Muslim conquest of Iran, in a time of adversity for Zoroastrians. If an Avestan text spoke of an end to adversity, surely the summarizer would not have passed the fact over in silence.

Zarathushtra certainly knew of his own experiences of revelation and of his conversion of his patron, Vishtaspa. But how could he have known of Aturpad son of Maraspend, prime minister and chief Zoroastrian priest under the Sassanian king Shapur II, who reigned 300–79 C.E.?[37]

The answer for nonbelievers is easy: Zarathushtra could not have known of Aturpad. The *Dinkard* and the other Zoroastrian Pahlavi works (i.e., works written in Middle Persian, in the Pahlavi alphabet) are full of *zand* (i.e., translations, paraphrases, and interpretations of Avestan texts), by late hands, often wrong.[38] The identification of the steel period as that of Aturpad is an example of erring *zand,* contributed by a believer in Zarathushtra's prophetic power.

If the predicted periods are symbolized by the series of metals, they should descend from the nobler to the baser. If they are parts of Zarathushtra's millennium, they should be of considerable length. Zoroastrians certainly regarded the period during which Zarathushtra received revelation from Ahuramazda as golden, but it was less than one lifetime in length. Why should the period during which Vishtaspa received the religion from Zarathushtra be only a silver age? Zarathushtra had to face persecution at the hands of opponents during it, but it, too, was less than one lifetime in length. The age of Aturpad, too, lasted only one lifetime, and one can ask, why should it be a steel age, inferior to the silver? All these difficulties suggest that the identifications of the gold and silver periods, too, come from late *zand* and are not part of the original *Nask.* Zarathushtra and the summarizer of the *Nask* were able to use words such as "king," "reign," "dynasty," or "kingdom." There is no reason why the summarizer would have used the vague word "period" if it did not stand in the original *Nask.*

It is surprising to find steel as the third metal, instead of the bronze of Dan

2:32. We shall soon render it probable that originally the third metal in the *Nask* was indeed bronze, but it is also possible that "steel" is the correct reading. A series of metals beginning with silver and gold and continuing with steel and iron can make sense: Steel is more corrodable than silver but is superior to mere iron. That series, indeed, is found in the Pahlavi *Greater Bundahishn,* in a passage "introduced by a formula which suggests that it is a direct Middle Persian translation of a lost Avestan text: 'Of [the legendary fortress of] Kangdiz he says . . . it has seven walls of gold, silver, steel, bronze, iron, crystal and lapis lazuli.' "[39]

Also strange is the expression "mingled with iron" or "mixed up with iron" or "mixed iron." In Dan 2:41 and 43 another material is specified, clay, with which the iron is mixed. A period is not a material, such as would form part of a mixture with iron. Scholars have proposed that the word "clay" has fallen out of the text.[40] In the Five-King Version of Daniel 2, however, iron and clay symbolized Nabonidus, the monstrously cruel weakling. Nothing suggests that the "apostate" and the "other villains" of the *Nask* are weaklings. We shall find in chap 12 that the solution lies elsewhere and that "mixed" or "mingled" is a later supplement.

If we remove from the summary of the seventh *fargard* of the *Sudgar Nask* the materials we have identified as later glosses and supplements, we obtain a Four-Metal Vision that we can call the "original." The original Four-Metal Vision emerges as a *real* prophecy by Zarathushtra. It is not a present-future prophecy by a person pretending to be Zarathushtra. In it Zarathushtra saw symbolic objects (not necessarily a tree [or root] and branches) made of gold, silver, steel (or bronze), and iron, representing four *periods* (*not* kings).

Whenever Zarathushtra was born, his *Sudgar Nask* could have been known to Zoroastrians at the time of the publication of the Five-King Version.[41] Whether the third metal in the *Nask* then was bronze or steel, Zoroastrians would have been surprised at the close resemblance of the strikingly "fulfilled" Babylonian Five-King prophecy to the text in their own scriptures and would have suspected the Babylonians of plagiarism, and all the more, because the *Nask* seems to predict apostasy, the sin which Marduk's worshipers found in Nabonidus. Peculiarities of a Pahlavi text suggest that the Zoroastrians soon told of a revelation to Zarathushtra involving four metals, a revelation which far antedated the prophetic dream-interpretation of Bel-baltsu-usur.

The *Dinkard* is not the only Iranian text to preserve something of the *Sudgar Nask.* The revelation to Zarathushtra is also described and interpreted in an oft-misnamed Pahlavi text. It has been called the *Bahman Yasht.* Bahman (or Vohu Manah) is one of the seven "Bountiful Immortals" who assist Ahuramazda.

Yasht is a religious hymn glorifying an Avestan deity. This text, however, is clearly not a hymn of praise, and otherwise there is no ancient Yasht in honor of any of the Bountiful Immortals.[42] The work received the title, *Bahman Yasht,* from A. H. Anquetil-Duperron, the pioneer of Zoroastrian studies in Europe.[43] B. T. Anklesaria called it *Zand i Vohuman Yasn,* but that title occurs at the beginnings of chaps 2 and 3 of the text, as the name of one of its sources, and therefore should not serve as the title of the text itself. The work contains present-future prophecy and is full of paraphrases and interpretations, so let us call it the *Prophetic Zand.*[44]

The *Prophetic Zand* at its beginning (1:1[1.1]) cites the *Stutgar* (= *Sudgar Nask*)[45] as the source for the following[46] report:

1. Zarathushtra asked for immortality from Ahuramazda.
2. Then, Ahuramazda showed the wisdom of all-knowledge unto Zarathushtra.
3. Through it, he saw the trunk[47] of a tree, on which there were four branches, one of gold, one of silver, one of steel and one of mixed iron.
4. Thereupon he considered that he saw this in a dream. . . .
6. Ahuramazda spoke to Spitaman Zarathushtra: the trunk of a tree, which thou sawest [is the material existence, which I, Ahuramazda, created].[48]
7. The four branches are the four periods which will come.
8. That of gold is that when I and thou will hold a conference of religion and King Vishtaspa shall accept the religion, the figures of the *dîvs* shall totter. . . . [49]
9. That of silver is the reign of King Artakhshir the Kae.[50] and that of steel is the reign of Khˇasruy son of Kavat, of immortal soul.
10. And that of mixed iron is the evil sovereignty of the *dîvs*, having disheveled hair, of the seed of Aêsham,[51] when thy tenth century will be at an end, Spitaman Zarathushtra.

In the *Prophetic Zand,* the exhibition is indeed specified to have been a dream of a tree. Vishtaspa's acceptance of the religion has been moved into the golden period, perhaps because otherwise the golden period would be very short.

The identifications of the kings of the silver and steel periods look to be erroneous *zand.* Khˇasruy son of Kavat (= Chosroes son of Kavad) is a Sassanian king whose reign extended from 531 to 579 C.E. The legendary Kayan kings mentioned in the *Avesta* are said to have ruled before Vishtaspa, and the last of them bore what amounted to the same name as Khˇasruy in an earlier dialect

(Haosravah). But one would expect the steel (or bronze) period to be later than the gold and the silver. In any case, a period of disasters for Iran did not immediately follow either the reign of the legendary Haosravah or that of Chosroes son of Kavad. Artakhshir the Kae is said to have been the successor of Vishtaspa, so that it is hard to see how the named periods could have come close to filling a millennium or why Artakhshir and Chosroes (or, indeed, any two Iranian kings) would have been singled out from among the many who ruled.[52]We shall find that disheveled hair is characteristic of Alexander and his successors and probably was added as a supplement in the time of that conqueror.

Mary Boyce has noted that long-term progressive deterioration is a prospect "essentially alien to [optimistic] orthodox Zoroastrianism." However, in the context of the *Prophetic Zand* (and probably in that of the original *Sudgar Nask*) the prophet before receiving the Four-Branch Vision requests the gift of immortality. Therefore, the grim prospect serves a Zoroastrian purpose, of solving a real problem: Why did Zarathushtra die before Ahuramazda's final victory? After hearing of the dreadful fourth period, the prophet himself asked for death in preference to having to live through it.[53]

Thus far, we have been able to explain away anomalies of the *Prophetic Zand*. But three difficulties do not yield so easily: The reigns of three kings are much too short to fill a considerable part of a millennium; there seems to be no reason to single out for mention the kings of the second and third periods; and a tree with simultaneous branches is a poor symbol for successive periods when the seer fails to report having seen them sprout one after another. The original of the seventh *fargard* of the *Sudgar Nask* did not contain the chronology in terms of kings and may well have lacked the tree-and-branch symbolism. If so, how did the problematic elements get into the *Prophetic Zand?*

The Five-King Version of Daniel 2 had chronology in terms of kings and had, in the statue, an equivalent for the tree-and-branch symbolism, and in the Babylonian present-future prophecy both features were appropriate![54] Can Zoroastrians have taken these elements from the Five-King Version and imported them into the *Prophetic Zand?* They can!

At some time between 538 and 522 B.C.E., Babylonians publicly boasted that their seer, Bêl-balâtsu-uṣur, long before the event, predicted the fall of Nabonidus. Zoroastrians could counter the boast by "proving" that the Babylonian seer had merely plagiarized from a revelation to Zarathushtra. To prove their point, they seem to have produced a version of the vision in the *Nask* which told of the prophet's dream of a tree with four branches. Zoroastrians had good reason to avoid using as a symbol the statue from Daniel 2; it was an idol, prohibited by their religion. They also had good reason to substitute for it a tree, a favorite symbol of imperial monarchy in Assyrian, Babylonian, and Persian art.[55] The Zoroastrians would have found no difficulty with the obvious difference between the *five* kings of the Babylonian present-future prophecy and the four periods of the *Nask* and the *Prophetic Zand,* because the last two kings both were symbolized by iron, and, if necessary, two kings could be symbolized by one branch. If so, we can reconstruct an earliest version of the visionary part of the *Prophetic Zand.* In it Zarathushtra saw a tree trunk (or root) with four branches, gold, silver, steel (or bronze), and iron, symbolizing kings' reigns which grow worse and worse. Using only the evidence in the book of Daniel, we discovered that the original version of Daniel 2 spoke of kings rather than kingdoms.[56] Now we have confirmation from an external source for that discovery.

Cyrus's victory over Nabonidus brought an age of triumph for Iranians. We have inferred that the *Sudgar Nask* contained no prediction of how prosperity would be restored after the fourth period. Zoroastrians in that age of triumph would not have needed then to add an equivalent of the stone of Daniel 2. In implying that Babylonians, in order to predict the downfall of Nabonidus, plagiarized from the *Sudgar Nask,* the Persians did not have to believe that the Babylonian "interpretation" was the correct one. Surely Zarathushtra and Ahuramazda were not interested in kings of Babylon! Furthermore, the Zoroastrian contemporaries of the fall of Nabonidus did not have to produce an acceptable Iranian identification of the periods and kings; all they wanted was to discredit Bêl-balâtsu-uṣur as a plagiarist. Very likely, they believed that the fulfillment of this earliest version of the *Prophetic Zand* lay far in the future.

Believing Zoroastrians found, in the disasters inflicted upon Iran by Alexander, the dreadful evils of the fourth period. According to *Prophetic Zand* 1.11(1.5), the inflicters of the evils belong to the "seed of Aêsham," to the "race of Wrath"; clearly, they are foreigners, not Iranians. Two features of the description there of that fourth period point unequivocally to Alexander and his companions and successors and exclude for us later powers who brought disaster upon Zoroastrians and Iran. First, the foreign rulers are called *dîvs* ("demons"). A *dîv* is an evil superhuman being.[57] The Iranians and the Muslims did not raise human beings above the human, but Alexander and the Seleucid kings (his Macedonian successors who ruled over Iran) claimed and received divine honors.[58] Zoroastrians could not admit the foreign kings were gods but could easily view them as evil demons.

Roman emperors were deified, but the second factor in the description serves to exclude them: The demons are said to have disheveled hair. The statues both of Alexander and of the Seleucids and their portraits on their coins show them with wildly tousled hair, in contrast to the orderly hair styles of the Persian kings and the Roman emperors. The disheveled hair also serves to exclude both pre-Islamic and Muslim Arabs, for they wore headgear that covered their hair.[59]

We infer that Zoroastrians took the version of the *Prophetic Zand* which originally they had used to discredit the boasts of Babylonians concerning the prophetic power of Bêl-balâṭsu-uṣur and added to it the references to the seed of Aêsham, the *dîvs* and the disheveled hair. At this point, we have proved that the *Prophetic Zand* contains a stratum going back to the time of Alexander and his successors and even an earlier stratum going back to the time of the fall of Nabonidus.[60] The interpretation, that the fourth period is the one of the conquest of Iran by Macedonian foreigners, hardly fits the symbolism of the Four-Branch Dream: Trees do not grow foreign branches.

After the description and interpretation of the four-metal vision, the *Prophetic Zand* is heavily encrusted with supplements, as a result of the many invaders and conquerors whom Zoroastrians had to suffer after Alexander and his successors. For example, there would be Romans and Muslim Arabs and Turks. Reasonable procedures can be devised to separate the various strata and strip off the later ones, and Samuel K. Eddy has carried out fairly well the task of reconstructing the version that existed in the time of Alexander's successors. I have included a modified version of Eddy's reconstruction as the Appendix,[61] and henceforth, unless otherwise noted, all references to the *Prophetic Zand* will be to that version.

Zarathushtra (or a later writer), in predicting that before the final victory of Ahuramazda there would be a final period of disasters at the end of the tenth century of the prophet's millennium, would want to protect believers from wrongfully identifying a period of temporary adversity as that final period. Hence, the text (4.2[2.24]) presents Zarathushtra as asking for the "tokens of the tenth century."

Ahuramazda responds with a list of tokens (4.3–64[2.24–53]), several of which fit Alexander's conquest of Iran: The invasion will be on a large scale (4.3[2.24]) and will involve burning and other damage to Iran (4.7[2.26]), as well as great depopulation, presumably by massacres (4.8[2.27]). There will be misrule and religious incompatibility (4.9–10 [2.28]). On the other hand, most of the tokens in the list are commonplaces of ancient Near Eastern descriptions of an evil time, as can be seen from the vivid biblical parallels,[62] and some of the tokens involve departures from the order of nature such as never happened, for example the shortening of the day, month, and year (4.16[2.31]).

If the time of Macedonian rule was indeed the fourth period predicted to

Zarathushtra, Zoroastrians then would search their traditions for a prophecy of consolation: How and when would the demonic rule end? Avestan texts had spoken of the role of the immortal hero, Pishi-shyaothna (called "Peshyotanu" or "Pishyotan" or "Peshyotan" in Middle Persian), and his followers in defeating the powers of evil.[63] Zoroastrian teaching, by the time of Alexander, also told that Hushedar ("Aûsîtar," in Anklesaria's transliteration), the first in the series of Zoroastrian saviors, would win victories over the powers of evil at the end of Zarathushtra's millennium.[64] Nothing had been said in the seventh *fargard* of the *Sudgar Nask* of the victories of those two heroes to end the age of adversity. The Zoroastrians conquered by Alexander, in their distress, combined the revelation of the four periods with the traditions about the two heroes, to produce what we may call the "Core Version" of the *Prophetic Zand* (as opposed to the later "encrusted" versions). The composers ignored the fact that this core hardly fits the Four-Branch Dream, in which nothing symbolizes either Peshyotan or Hushedar.

The "demon with disheveled hair" of *Prophetic Zand* 7.2(3.13) is singular in number[65] and can be only Alexander. On the other hand, the "demons with disheveled hair" are plural[66] in 1.11(1.5), where they are probably Alexander and his successors, and in 4.3–7(2.24–26), 4.10(2.28), and 7.13(3.22), where they include the rank and file of Alexander's army. The change from singular to plural conceivably could be the error of a scribe or of an oral transmitter, but probably it is an instance of the supplementing of a present-future prophecy. The original Core Version had the singular and predicted the doom of Alexander. Thereafter, Zoroastrians found that Macedonian rule lasted beyond the lifetime of Alexander and learned to dread the rank and file of the Macedonian army. Those believers produced a version with plurals. Just as supplementers of the Five-King Version left the word "kings" unchanged to "kingdoms" in Dan 2:44, so Zoroastrians left the singular unchanged at *Prophetic Zand* 7.2(3.13).

Nowhere in the *Prophetic Zand* does a prediction of the death of the singular demon survive, probably because Alexander died at 32, long before the composer of the core version expected him to. In 7.2(3.15), however, Ahuramazda begins to answer Zarathushtra's question, how will the *plural* demons be destroyed?, and says that at the time the *singular* demon with disheveled hair appears, Hushedar will be born. When Hushedar will be thirty years old, according to *Prophetic Zand* 7.7–17(3.17–14), he and his armies will win victories over the demons of the race of Wrath. Clearly, the supplementer wrote before 304 B.C.E. (before thirty years had elapsed from the time Alexander invaded the Persian Empire). *Prophetic Zand* 7.19–9.9(3.25–43) narrates successes of Peshyotanu and his followers over the wicked demonic opposition. Neither Peshyotanu nor Hushedar put in an appearance before 304 B.C.E. or ever. Because of the passages predicting the coming destruction of the plural demons, we can infer that the supplement was composed when Macedonian Seleucids still ruled Iran. Indeed, the death of Alexander and the fall of the Seleucids bore no resemblance to the predictions in the *Prophetic Zand*.

Chapter 3 (2.1–22) of the *Prophetic Zand* is a late supplement to the visionary part of the work. Centuries elapsed, and neither Hushedar nor Peshyotanu appeared. Muslims conquered Iran (642 C.E.) and brought far worse disasters upon Zoroastrians and their religion than had Alexander. A believer, in response, supplemented the Four-Branch Version of the vision in the *Prophetic Zand* and produced the Seven-Branch Version, which we have in chapter 3(2.1–22). Four periods were no longer enough to fill credibly the time that had elapsed between the prophetic career of Zarathushtra and the time of the author(s) of chapter 3, much less four reigns of kings, so three more were added, between the original second and the original third. Here is another clue to show that the Four-Branch Version contains material composed long before the reigns of the Sassanian kings.[67]

The Seven-Branch Vision also supplies us with evidence to make it probable that the third metal in the *Prophetic Zand* was brass or copper, rather than steel. In the Seven-Branch Vision, the metals for the first two periods and the last two remain the same as in the present text of the Four-Branch Vision, and the metals for the third, fourth, and fifth periods are, respectively, brass, copper, and lead (or tin).[68] The kings associated in the Seven-Branch Vision with the first, second, and sixth periods are the same as the three in the Four-Branch Vision. We found, because of chronological difficulties, that it was best to ascribe the association, of those periods with those kings, to late *zand*-writers.[69] The same is true of the kings associated in the Seven-Branch Vision with the brass, copper, and lead period: with the brass, Sassanian kings Artakhshir (= Ardashir) I (224–240) and Shapur I (240–ca. 272); with the copper, the Arsacid Parthian king, Valakhsh (Vologeses I; ca. 51–80)—the name is mutilated in one manuscript and missing in the other; with the lead, the Sassanian king, Vaharam-I Gur (Bahram Gor; 421–439). Though nothing requires the periods to proceed consecutively, the chronological backtracking to the Parthian king is jarring, and no more than in the Four-Branch Vision do the baser metals seem to symbolize deterioration. The text of the Seven-Branch Vision is defective, having lost the reference to "the evil sovereignty of the seed of Aêsham." The missing words are easy to restore, as soon as the reader perceives that the four branches of the Four-Branch Vision and the first, second, sixth, and seventh branches of the Seven-Branch Vision are otherwise identical.

The sequence of metals in the Seven-Branch Vision begins with gold, silver, brass (or bronze; in antiquity, the two were the same, because the copper-zinc alloy now called "brass" was unknown) and ends with mixed iron. Here is the sequence we would have expected in the Four-Branch Vision! Does the Seven-Branch Vision preserve the original sequence of the first four metals? We can argue to render that possibility likely.

Let us suppose that the original seventh *fargard* of the *Sudgar Nask* (from the time of Zarathushtra) and the original Four-Branch *Prophetic Zand* (from the time of Alexander) began with gold, silver, and bronze and ended with iron or mixed iron, as we find in the Seven-Branch *Zand* (from the time of Muslim rule over Iran). If we can show how the present versions of the *Nask* and the *Four-Branch Zand* and the *Seven-Branch Zand* developed from those originals, our supposition will become probable.

Having made our assumptions, let us consider how pious Zoroastrians would have reacted on coming to know the *Seven-Branch Zand*. They would try to figure out how Ahuramazda could have made two revelations to Zarathushtra on the same subject, one with four periods and one with seven. They probably would suppose that the Four-Metal texts were incomplete, perhaps because Zarathushtra let his mind wander. The most important periods for a Zoroastrian are the time of the foundation of the religion and that of Ahuramazda's great victory. If the first revelation as received by Zarathushtra was incomplete, what was omitted was surely neither the beginning nor the end but the middle. (We have taken note of the fact that the content of the present text of the Four-Branch Vision and that of the first two and last two periods of the Seven-Branch Vision are identical.) Both versions of the *Prophetic Zand* have, as the last period, that of iron (or mixed iron). Hence, Zoroastrians probably reasoned, both versions (as well as the seventh *fargard* of the *Sudgar Nask*) should have steel as the next to last metal, and they proceeded to "correct" the text of the *Nask* and the *Four-Branch Zand*. On the other hand, perhaps Ahuramazda had a hidden purpose in revealing the Four-Metal Vision. The possibility was sufficient for Zoroastrians to preserve the emended Four-Metal Revelation, instead of abandoning it. If so, originally the third metal both in the *Sudgar Nask* and in *Prophetic Zand* was bronze, as one would expect.

5. Another Sibylline Prophecy

CONSPICUOUS BOTH IN THE *Sudgar Nask* and in the *Prophetic Zand* is the concept of the four periods. In the summary of the *Sudgar Nask,* the periods are said to be included within the millennium of Zarathushtra, but their length is not specified, and we have found reason to regard, as erroneous late *zand,* the identification of them with the reigns of named kings. In the *Prophetic Zand,* the fourth period comes at the end of Zarathushtra's millennium (1.11[1.5]) and thus could either begin within Zarathushtra's millennium or follow immediately after it. The mention of the "last century" does not necessarily tell us that the periods are centuries. Indeed, the document predicts that Hushedar will put an end to the fourth period *thirty* years after it began (7.2–3[3.13–14], 7.7–17[3.17–24]). Otherwise, the only clues in the *Prophetic Zand* to the lengths of the periods are, again, the identifications of them with the reigns of named kings, which we have dismissed as erroneous late *zand.*

Sibylline Oracles iv survives as evidence for us that in the reign of Darius I, centuries before the time of the Sassanian dynasty, Iranians attempted to identify the four periods of the *Sudgar Nask* and to specify their lengths.[70] Before the time of Alexander, the Iranians had developed the theory that there were destined to be only three world empires, the Assyrian, the Median, and the Persian.[71] Alexander proved it false: His was clearly a fourth. Zoroastrians combined the elements of their previous theories with the hard fact of Alexander's conquests to produce a revised doctrine: There were to be only four world empires, and the fourth, Alexander's, would be evil but would be overthrown by Ahuramazda's final victory. A Persian Sibylline text soon taught the revised doctrine. Jews later supplemented this originally Persian Sibylline oracle in order to predict the doom of Rome, so that the poem survives, somewhat curtailed and disguised, but still recognizable, in *Sibylline Oracles* iv. Let us call *Sibylline Oracles* iv.49–101 *"Sibylline B."* Here is an English translation of the portions of *Sibylline B* that are important[72] for us:

49 First, the Assyrians will rule over all mortals,
50 Holding the world in their dominion for six generations
51 From the time when the heavenly God was in wrath
52 With the cities themselves and all men,
53 And the sea covered the earth when the Flood burst forth.
54 These will the Medes destroy and boast on their thrones.
55 They will have only two generations. In their time the
   following things will take place:
56 There will be dark night in the mid-hour of day.

        . . .

61 But when the great Euphrates is flooded with blood,
62 Then indeed a terrible din of battle will arise for the Medes
62–63 And Persians in war. The Medes will fall under the spears
63–64 Of the Persians and flee over the great water of the Tigris.

65   The power of the Persians will be the greatest of the whole world.

66   They are destined to have one generation of very prosperous rule.

67   But thereafter[73] evils which men pray to be spared will come to pass.

68   Battles and murders, dissensions and exiles,

. . .

70–71   When boastful Greece sails to the wide Hellespont

71   Bringing grievous doom to the Phrygians and Asia.[74]

. . .

76   A king will come from Asia, brandishing a great spear,

77   With countless ships. He will walk the watery paths

77–78   Of the deep, and will cut through a lofty mountain as he sails.

79   Him will wretched Asia receive as a fugitive from war.[75]

. . .

83   There will be strife in Greece. Raging against each other

84   They will cast many cities down headlong and will destroy many men

85   By fighting. But the strife will have equal effect on all parties.[76]

86   But when the race of men comes to the tenth generation,

87   Then there will also be yokes of slavery and terror for the Persians.

88   But when the Macedonians boast of scepters,

89   Thereafter there will also be dire capture for Thebes.[77]

. . .

93   Babylon, great in appearance but insignificant in battle,

94   Will stand, fortified[78] on useless hopes.

95   Macedonians will colonize Baktra,[79] but the colonists from[80] Baktra

96   And Susa will all flee to the land of Greece.

Sibylline B measures its periods in terms of generations (not centuries) and counts altogether 10 of those. It presents a curious mixture of accurate knowledge and ignorant error. If we assume that a generation lasts between thirty and forty years, we find the six generations of Assyrian rule occupy two hundred forty years, a good estimate of the time that elapsed between the reign of Shalmaneser III (858–824 B.C.E.) and the fall of Assyria in 612. On the other hand, the sibyl displays no knowledge of individual facts during the period of Assyrian rule, which certainly did not follow closely upon the deluge. Similarly, two generations, consisting of sixty-two years, are a good estimate of the period of Median imperial rule, from the fall of Assyria in 612 until the fall of Median King Astyages to Persian King Cyrus in 550, and the sibyl knows of the famous solar eclipse predicted by Thales and recorded by Herodotus (i.71). On the other hand, it is unlikely that battles between Astyages's and Cyrus's armies were fought near the Tigris or the Euphrates.[81] The sibyl knows of the spectacular successes of the Persian kings, Cyrus, Cambyses, and Darius ("one generation of very prosperous rule," from 550 to ca. 500). Why, however, does she not credit the Persians with imperial rule thereafter?[82] The Persian Empire lasted at least until the Battle of Gaugamela in 331!

There is only one plausible solution. Early in the reign of Darius I, the Persian king probably believed that Ahuramazda had come closer than ever before to routing the powers of evil.[83] Was his final victory imminent? Writing in the reign of Darius I (521–485), after the peak of his success, the author knew the chronology of the Assyrian and Median Empires but could err on details of events 40 years before. He had seen *only one generation* of Persian imperial rule, and the signs of the times (Darius's defeats in Scythia [ca. 512 B.C.E.]and at Marathon [490] and the rebellion of Egypt [486/5])[84] no longer lent themselves to optimistic predictions concerning the near future. Indeed, overcome by pessimism and perhaps influenced by the portrayal of the fourth period in the *Sudgar Nask,* the author had the sibyl predict slavery and terror for the Persians in the imminent next, tenth, generation, writing a real, though incorrect prophecy. If so, the date of the earliest stratum of *Sibylline B* is the middle or late reign of Darius I, after his first defeats, and we thus have evidence of Persians using the form of Sibylline prophecy long before Alexander's time.[85]

Persian believers would have been impressed by the sibyl's correct "prediction" of the durations of Assyrian and Median imperial rule. If the age of less-than-successful Persian imperial rule dragged on beyond any conceivable tenth generation, the believers gave "generation" an interpretation far beyond its literal meaning. Thus, when Alexander brought slavery and terror upon the Persians, the believers could view the fact as a fulfillment of *Sibylline Oracles* iv.86–87 and could supplement the prophecy with verses 89–101.

Sibylline B gives no specific information about Alexander. Unlike *Sibylline A,* it cannot have been celebrated as a text in which an ancient sibyl predicted the conqueror and his feats. Nevertheless, it alludes clearly to events datable within Alexander's lifetime.

Verses 95 and 96 say that Macedonians will colonize Baktra, but the colonists from Baktra . . .[86] will all flee to the land of Greece. At or near Baktra, Alexander is known to have founded a colony that he named after himself, Alexandria.[87] Remote Baktra was so far from Macedonia that to have Alexander establish a colony there was shocking. Furthermore, Zoroastrians believed that Baktra had sacred associations, that it was Vishtaspa's city, where Zarathushtra converted him to the religion.[88]

While Alexander was in India in 325 B.C.E., discontented Greek colonists, settled in Baktra by Alexander, set out from there, intending to return to Greece.[89] Iranians after suffering grievously at the hands of Alexander and his army must have been glad to take note of the voluntary withdrawal of some of the unwelcome invaders, as a good sign, and thus we find it mentioned by the sibyl. *Sibylline B* contains no later datable event, so we may assign its composition to 325 B.C.E. at the earliest. It was certainly not much later, for the departure of the colonists from Baktra soon proved to be an insignificant event.

6. Later Persian Texts that Preserve Memories of Alexander

WE HAVE SHOWN THAT the *Prophetic Zand* contains matter that was composed in the reigns of Alexander and the Seleucids. Other Zoroastrian Pahlavi works have no claim to contain anything composed at so early a time. They were written, at the earliest, in the age of the Sassanian kings, but some of them preserve memories of the catastrophic effects of Alexander's invasion upon Ahuramazda's people and their religion.

Pahlavi texts, from the ninth century C.E. on, narrate, with some variation in details, how Alexander brought disaster upon Iran and came close to eradicating all memorized or all written texts of the *Avesta* and its *zand*.[90] It is at least doubtful that a written *Avesta* and *zand* existed in the time of Alexander.[91] Thus, the story that the Macedonian king nearly exterminated the Zoroastrian sacred texts may be a fabrication. Generally, however, one *invents* monstrous deeds to blacken further a character who is already thoroughly hated. We are not surprised to find that pious Zoroastrians hated Alexander.

On the other hand, good evidence shows that Iranians in large numbers collaborated with Alexander and his successors. They must have found it possible to have a favorable view of Alexander and to present him somehow as a legitimate ruler of Iran. Beyond the Zoroastrian texts and the verses of the sibyls, no Iranian literature from the time survives. Did the views of Iranian collaborators leave traces in later Iranian literature?

There could be reflections of the collaborators' views in the largely favorable accounts about Alexander, as told in Persian historical and literary works from between the ninth and the fifteenth centuries. These accounts clearly draw upon the *Alexander Romance,* an anonymous work originally composed in Greek, between 200 B.C.E. and 300 C.E., by an author now referred to as "Pseudo-Kallisthenes." With a large component of fabulous fiction, the *Alexander Romance* was very popular, and the transmission of its text has been very complicated. The Persian historical and literary works all drew on the so-called *δ recension of the *Romance.*[92]

The non-Persian versions of the *Alexander Romance* tell how the last ancient king of independent Egypt, Nektanebos (II) fled his country, which was then under threat of irresistible invasion from the east. The fugitive went to Macedonia, where he used his magic arts, first to become widely known as a prophet, and then to have intercourse with Olympias, the wife of King Philip. Alexander was the offspring of this union, and thus was a legitimate king of Egypt. This birth legend may well have been created by Egyptians who viewed Alexander as their own king and as their liberator from Persian rule. Let us call it the "Egyptian birth story."

The lost Pahlavi translation of the *Alexander Romance* belonged to the *δ recension but still had the Egyptian Birth-Story, as can be learned from the fact that the Syriac version, made in the sixth century C.E. from the Pahlavi, has it. Later Persian texts, however, substitute a birth-legend that could well reflect the propaganda of Persians who collaborated with Macedonian rule. Let us call it the "Persian Birth-Story."

According to it, Dara was the last Persian king. His father was King Darab. Darab defeated King Philip of Macedonia, and, as part of the peace terms, demanded that he receive Philip's daughter as his wife. Philip complied. The daughter was very beautiful, but Darab could not bear the odor of her breath and sent her back to her father, Philip. But she was pregnant and eventually gave birth to Alexander. Philip concealed the disgrace of his daughter's having been rejected by her husband and claimed the boy was his own son by a concubine. Later, by another wife, Darab begat Dara. Thus, Alexander, as Dara's older brother, could claim a superior right to the Persian throne.

Persian and Arab historians who wrote during the Muslim era used the *Romance* as a historical source, unaware of its heavily fictitious nature. The historian Abu-Hanifah al-Dinawari (died in 894/5 C.E.) is the earliest author known to have made use of the Persian birth-legend. The Muslim Persian poet Abu al-Qasim Firdausi in 1010 produced a classic literary embodiment of the Persian adaptation of the *Alexander Romance* in his *Shahnamah (Book of Kings).*

Only Persian and Arab accounts contain the Persian birth story. Muslims could present a favorable view of Alexander. Clearly, Muslim Persians substituted the Persian birth-story for the Egyptian.[93] But did they invent it then, in the age of Islam, to give Persians rather than Egyptians a share in the glory of

Alexander? Or was the Persian birth-story an existing tale, going back to Iranian collaborators under Macedonian rule? We lack evidence to decide these questions.

The absence of pre-Islamic attestations of the Persian birth-story proves nothing. The overwhelmingly hostile view of Alexander in Zoroastrian tradition[94] prevented any favorable references to the Macedonian king from entering Zoroastrian literature, whether oral or written. But secular storytellers or minstrels could have preserved the propaganda of the collaborators. Indeed, the lost Pahlavi version of the *Romance,* with its favorable portrayal of Alexander, was written under the Zoroastrian Sassanian kings. Its writer still did not venture to replace the Egyptian birth-story by the Persian (Sassanian kings could have found it offensive), but Muslim Iranians, when Zoroastrians no longer ruled, could have drawn upon an already-existing legend.

We should also take note of the profound differences betweer the two birth-stories. True, each makes Alexander a rightful heir of the native dynasty, but in the Egyptian legend Alexander has no blood relationship to Philip; in the Persian, he is Philip's grandson. In the Egyptian legend, Nektanebos is a refugee who seduces Queen Olympias; in the Persian, the (wholly fictitious) Darab is a mighty ruling king who has intercourse with his own wife. In the Egyptian legend, Alexander's father flees from his native Egypt; in the Persian, Alexander's mother is sent to Darab from her native Macedonia.

Persians had enough access to Greek literature to write the Pahlavi version of the *Alexander Romance.* If Muslim Persians had wished to fabricate a counterpart to the Egyptian birth-story, they could have drawn on the truthful Greek reports of the dynastic murders perpetrated by Artaxerxes III and by Bagoas[95] and could have told of a fugitive Persian prince who managed to escape to Macedonia and to beget Alexander as a more direct heir to the Persian royal line than was Darius III.

To me, it seems unlikely that Muslim Persians felt a need to assert that Alexander had a Persian, not an Egyptian, origin and that they invented the Persian birth-story. But I cannot prove that Muslim Persians did not do so. Therefore, the question remains open.[96]

7. Summary: The Reactions of the Persians, the Babylonians, and the Jews to Alexander

WE HAVE NOTED[97] THAT the Persians' reactions ran through the entire spectrum from bitter resistance to enthusiastic collaboration. Remarkable, however, is the persistence of some Iranians in resisting. The best explanation for the phenomenon is provided by the Persians' dualistic Zaroastrianism.[98] The long resistance at first reflected a belief that the age still belonged to good Ahuramazda. The fall of Spitamenes[99] was a good demonstration that even guerrilla warfare was hopeless, yet even after the death of Spitamenes there were Iranians who dared to rebel,[100] in the belief that Ahuramazda was in control again. They were put down. The fact demonstrated that the age belonged to evil Ahriman.

By the time of Alexander's late reign, most Iranians were quiescent or collaborated with the conqueror's regime. Well they might. The *Prophetic Zand* predicted a period during which Ahriman and evil would prevail; that period would last thirty years and would be ended by the victories of Hushedar and Peshyotanu.[101] The lesson for Iranians was: "Make the best you can of the evil present, and wait for Hushedar and Peshyotanu." The two never came, so that even after the lapse of thirty years, Persians did not rebel. As for *Sibylline A,* with its prediction that Persians would wipe out Alexander's stock, the deaths of Alexander the Great, Alexander IV, and Herakles, for which no Persian was responsible, proved it false. We do not know what doom the original version of *Sibylline B* predicted for the Macedonians; but whatever it was, events probably soon proved the prophecy false.

The Babylonian author of the *Dynastic Prophecy* showed hostility to Alexander in 331 B.C.E., and Babylonians probably were quick to appropriate *Sibylline A.*[102] But Alexander was mostly popular in Babylon. There was no further resistance there, whether physical or literary.

Jews found Alexander no worse than they had found the Persians. Jews, too, probably were quick to appropriate *Sibylline A.* We do not know when they took over *Sibylline B.* They may have done so only when they adopted and adapted it to predict the fall of the Roman Empire. In any case, there is no trace that Jews resisted Alexander. Both Jews and Babylonians adhered to previously established policies. Babylonians, even if discontented with Alexander, waited for Marduk to act.[103] Jews, even if discontented, waited for God to signify that the period of their servitude, the punishment for past sins, was over.[104] There was no such clear sign from God.

NOTES

1   See pp. 187–88.

2   See chap 8, pp. 224–27.

3   See chap 8, pp. 237–44.

4   Curtius iv.13.12–14.

5   Arrian vi.27.4–5; Curtius x.1.9.

6   Arrian vii.4.4–8; see Eddy, *King,* chap 1, n 8.

7   See Boyce, HZ, III, 15–17, esp. n 70.

8   See, e.g., John Collins, *The Sibylline Oracles of Egyptian Judaism* (Missoula, Mont.: Society of Biblical Literature and Scholars' Press, 1972), 1–4; Herbert W. Parke, *Sibyls and Sibylline Prophecy in Classical Antiquity* (New York: Routledge, 1988), 1–10.

9   Fragment *apud* Lactantius *Divinae Institutiones* i.6. Nothing further is known of Nikanor, who may have been a contemporary of Alexander's.

10   Johannes Geffcken (ed.), *Die Oracula Sibyllina* (Leipzig: Hinrichs, 1902), 2, lines 32–36. All my quotations from the *Sibylline Oracles* are based on Geffcken's edition unless I state otherwise. The prologue writer claims to have assembled Books i–viii of the oracles; proof of his date: Rzach, "Sibyllinische Orakel," *RE,* IIA (1921), 2120, and Geffcken, *Komposition und Entstehungszeit der Oracula sibyllina* ("Texte und Untersuchungen zur Geschichte der altchristlichen Literatur," neue Folge, VIII. Band, 1. Heft; Leipzig: Hinrichs, 1902), 76. The tenth-century Byzantine encyclopaedia, the *Suda* (often referred to as "Suidas") in its article on *Sibylla Chaldaia* repeats almost verbatim the information on the ten sibyls given in the prologue to the *Sibylline Oracles.*

11   Pausanias x.12.1–9.

12   Date of the main corpus of *Sibylline Oracles* iii: John Collins, "Introduction to Sibylline Oracles," Book iii, in *The Old Testament Pseudepigrapha,* ed. James H. Charlesworth (2 vols.; Garden City, NY: Doubleday, 1983–85), I, 354–55. "Sabbe": See Parke, *Sibyls,* 42; Victor A. Tcherikover and Alexander Fuks (eds.), *Corpus Papyrorum Judaicarum* (3 vols.; Cambridge, Mass.: Harvard University Press, 1957–64), III, 43–56.

13   On the Babylonian and Sumerian Deluge stories, see Alexander Heidel, *The Gilgamesh Epic and Old Testament Parallels* (Chicago and London: University of Chicago Press, 1949), 224–69. The Iranians told stories of the primeval heroic king, Yima. "It is said that when he [Yima] had reigned for 1,000 years the gods came to an assembly with him and the best of the men whom he had ruled; and they told him that winters were about to come upon the 'bad corporeal world' bringing cruel frosts and snow on mountain and plain. When the snow melted it would carry away stores of fodder, so

that cattle would starve and it would be a wonder thereafter to see the footprint of a sheep. Yima was accordingly to build a *var* beneath the earth, and to bring into it pairs of the best and finest men and women, and the best and finest animals, and the seeds of all the biggest and most fragrant plants, and also of the most edible and delicious ones. . . . The *var* was to be divided into three parts" (*Vendidad,* Fargard 2, secs. 20–end, as summarized in Boyce, HZ, I, 94; on the three parts of the *var,* cf. Gen 6:16). In arid mountainous Iran a cold spell and blizzards are more probable than a deluge. Without flood waters, the *var,* the sheltering vessel, could not float and it would have been buried under the snows. The story in the *Vendidad* says that the *var* was underground. On the position underground and the possible connections of the legend of the *var* with the Babylonian flood story, see Boyce, HZ, I, 95.

14 E.g., W. Bousset, "Die Beziehungen der ältesten jüdischen Sibylle zur chaldäischen Sibylle . . . ," *Zeitschrift für die neutestamentliche Wissenschaft* 3 (1902), 34–41; Geffcken, *Entstehungszeit* 3; Eddy, *King,* 10–14.

15 See pp. 382–83.

16 *Apistos* in v 388 could mean "faithless." Although Alexander in the Greek sources is not conspicuous for breaking his word, the conquered victims conceivably could have viewed him as faithless. However, in v 389 the invader is said to be unjust; "unjust" after "faithless" would be repetitious.

17 I translate here the text as emended by Geffcken, who reads *autou* where all witnesses have *auton.* Otherwise, it is hard to make sense of the passage. The clause beginning with "for" (Greek *gar*) must explain what precedes. In my translation it tells in what way the invader was fiery. With the reading *auton* one can barely make sense of the passage, by deriving the verb *êgeire* from *egeirein* ("rouse") instead of from *ageirein* ("assemble") and construing the noun, *phôta,* as the accusative singular of *phôs* ("human being," "mortal") rather than the accusative plural of *phôs* ("light"), so that the translation would become, "for beforehand a thunderbolt roused him, though a mortal." Can a mortal be roused (rather than stunned or killed) by a thunderbolt and thereby become fiery? On the other hand, Alexander could be said, metaphorically, to be a thunderbolt, and lightning does flash before the sound of a thunderclap. Ancient kings (and Roman emperors) did have fire-pans or burning torches carried in front of them.

18 The passage plays upon the word or prefix "all" or "altogether" *(pan).* Under the circumstances, it is unlikely that *panaïston* (which I have rendered "when he has altogether vanished") can mean "though he knows it not," as Collins renders.

19 Perhaps *Sibylline Oracles* iii.396–400 is such a supplement, but I have not been able to find a fitting interpretation of the verses.

20 *Sibylline Oracles* xi.195–223, where vv 216–18 echo iii.390–92; modern writers: e.g., W. Bousset, "Die Beziehungen der ältesten jüdischen Sibylle zur chaldäischen Sibylle, *Zeitschrift für die neutestamentliche Wissenschaft* 3 (1902), 34–38; Eddy, *King,* 10–12; Collins in *Pseudepigrapha,* ed. Charlesworth, I, 359.

21 Cf. Eddy, *King,* 12.

22 Alexander's kindness: Curtius iii.12.21–26, v.2.20–22, vi.2.11, x.5.19–25, Diodorus xvii.37.6–38.7, 67.1, Plutarch *Alexander* 21, 30, 43. His behavior after Darius's death: Arrian iii.22.1, 6; Diodorus xvii.73.2–3; Curtius vii.5.40–43; Plutarch *Alexander* 43.

23 See n 17.

24 See Xenophon *Constitution of the Lacedaemonians* 13.2.

25 Walter Otto, "Zum Hofzeremoniell des Hellenismus," in Epitymbion: *Heinrich Swoboda dargebracht* (Reichenberg: Stiepel, 1927), 194–200; *Idem* and Hermann Bengtson, *Zur Geschichte des Niederganges des Ptolemäerreiches, Abhandlungen der Bayerischen Akademie der Wissenschaften, Philosophische philologische und historische Klasse,* Neue Folge, Heft XVII (1938), 154, n 1.

26 Xenophon *Cyropaedia* viii.3.12–13 (as a practice of Cyrus the Great).

27 Chap 3, sec 3; Esther 1:22, 3:12, 8:9; Dandamaev and Lukonin, *Culture,* 114–16. A Greek inscription preserves a letter from Darius I to his official, Gadatas (*Sylloge Inscriptionum Graecarum,* ed. W. Dittenberger [3d ed.; Leipzig: Hirzel, 1905–24], No. 22). Darius may have had it published in Greek to be propaganda to demonstrate to the Greeks his piety toward the god Apollo.

28 Strabo xvii.1.43 (C. 814) and xiv.1.34 (C. 645); FGH 124 F 14a; the manuscripts at Strabo xvii.1.43 have *eugeneias* ("illustrious descent"), but Meineke was probably correct in emending the word to *diogeneias* ("descent from Zeus") or *theogeneias* ("descent from the gods").

29 Cf. Eddy, *King,* 11–13. Eddy there notes that a painting of Alexander by Apelles stood in the temple of Artemis-Anahita at Ephesus. Apelles there portrayed Alexander as about to hurl a thunderbolt.

On the possibility that Persians had seen to the production of Sibylline prophecies even before Alexander invaded their empire, see pp. 341–45 and Mary Boyce, "The Poems of the Persian Sibyl and the Zand ī Vahman Yast," in *Études irano-aryennes offertes à Gilbert Lazard,* compiled by C.-H. de Fouchécour and Ph. Gignoux (Paris: Association pour l'avancement des études iraniennes, 1989), 62.

30 See n 13.

31 Alexander IV: Gerhard Wirth, "Alexander 7," *Der kleine Pauly,* I (1964), 250; Herakles: Schoch, "Herakles 2," *RE,* Supplement IV (1924), 309; Paul Cloché, *La Dislocation d'un empire* (Paris: Payot, 1959), 183–84.

32 Chap 8, p. 214.

33 See ibid.

34 Oral transmission of the *Avesta* with few if any written copies: Boyce, HZ, III, 15–17, esp. n 70; Philippe Gignoux, "Sur l'inexistence d'un Bahman Yasht avestique," *Journal of Asian and African Studies* 32 (1986), 53. Summary and division into *nasks:* see E. W. West, *Pahlavi Texts,* Part IV ("The Sacred Books of the East . . . ," ed. F. Max Müller, Vol. XXXVII; Oxford: Clarendon Press, 1892), xxix–xlvi; J. Kellens, "Avesta," *Encylopaedia Iranica* III (1989), 35–37.

35 *Dinkard,* Book ix, chap 8, quoted from E. W. West, *Pahlavi Texts,* Part IV, 180–81.

36 In *other* utterances, Zarathushtra certainly predicted the ultimate victory of Ahuramazda and the forces of good over Ahriman and the forces of evil. We shall soon find that a later Zoroastrian text, the *Prophetic Zand,* partly based on the seventh *fargard* of the *Sudgar Nask,* presents the hero Peshyotanu and his followers as the ones who put an end to the fourth period, and Peshyotanu and his followers are mentioned and described in the summary of the fifteenth *fargard* of the *Sudgar Nask* itself (West, *Pahlavi Texts,* Part IV, 203). But one has only to read the material between the seventh and the fifteenth *fargard* to recognize that the passages are not parts of one and the same revelation.

37 A. Tafażżoli, "Adurbad i Mahrspandan," *Encyclopaedia Iranica* I (1983), 477.

38 "[*Zand* is] nearly always literal and for that very reason often inaccurate and ambiguous. For this reason, too, many translators explain various passages by means of glosses, which, however, very often do not elucidate the sense at all . . ." (Otakar Klíma, "Avesta, Ancient Persian Inscriptions, Middle Persian Literature," in Jan Rypka, *History of Iranian Literature* [Dordrecht, Holland: D. Reidel, 1968], 35).

39 Quoted from Boyce, "On the Antiquity of Zoroastrian Apocalyptic," *Bulletin of the School of Oriental and African Studies* 47 (1984), 63.

40 "Mingled with iron" and "mixed up with iron" are E. W. West's translations of the expression (see nn 35 and 45). Anklesaria renders it by "mixed iron" (see n 45). Belief that the word "clay" has fallen out: See Eddy, *King,* 20.

41   Zarathushtra's birth date: See chap 3, p. 67; date of the publication of the Five-King Version: See chap 8, pp. 224–27.

42   Gignoux, "Inexistence," 56.

43   W. Sundermann, "Bahman Yašt," *Encyclopaedia Iranica,* III (1989), 492a.

44   Pahlavi text with transliteration and English translation: Behramgore Tahmuras Anklesaria, *Zand-î Vohûman Yasn* (Bombay: Bhargava, 1957); another English translation: West, *Pahlavi Texts,* Part I ("The Sacred Books of the East," Vol. V; Oxford: Clarendon Press, 1880), 191–235. I have included a translation of the part of the *Prophetic Zand* which is important for this book as an appendix. I use Anklesaria's translation and chapter and verse numbers, unless I specify otherwise. In parentheses, I add West's chapter and verse numbers.

My caution in naming the text may be unnecessary. See Boyce's arguments ("Antiquity," *Bulletin of the School of Oriental and African Studies* 47 [1984], 68, and "Poems," in *Études irano-aryennes offertes à Gilbert Lazard,* 71–77), that a late Avestan text called the *Vahman Yasht (= Vohûman Yasht)* existed and that what I call the *Prophetic Zand* can properly be called the *Zand-î Vahman Yasht.*

45   See West, *Pahlavi Texts,* Part I, 191–92, n 3.

46   For brevity I have omitted inessential material, and for simplicity and consistency I have normalized some proper names. I have also omitted marks of vowel quantity.

47   The object is called *van-ê bûn* at 1.3(1:1) and *darakht-ê bûn* at 1.6(1.3). Anklesaria renders "trunk of a tree" in both places, and West, "root of a tree." Both translations are justifiable, but normally branches grow from a trunk, not from a root.

48   Anklesaria correctly perceived a gap in the text: The branches, not the trunk, represent the four periods which will come. He filled the gap with appropriate Zoroastrian doctrine.

49   A *dîv* for Zoroastrians is an evil demon who must not be worshiped (Boyce, HZ, III, 85). The text probably means that Vishtaspa destroyed the images of the *dîv*s.

50   The Kayan kings mentioned in the *Avesta* clearly are supposed to have reigned before the time of Vishtaspa. See Arthur Christensen, *Les Kayanides* ("Historisk-filologiske Meddelelser, udgivne af Det Kgl. Danske videnskabernes selskab," Bind XIX, fascicle 2; København: Levin & Munksgaard, 1931), 18. But Vishtaspa's grandson (or son) and successor was said to be Kay Ardashir (= Kay Artakhshir), also called "Vahman" (ibid., 97–98, 124).

51   Aêsham, personified Wrath, is an agent of evil Ahriman; see J. P. Asmussen, "Aēšma," *Encyclopaedia Iranica,* I (1983), 479a–480b.

52   Artakhshir: See n 50; Haosravah: Christensen, *Kayanides,* 3, 18, 29.

53   Boyce: "Poems," in *Études irano-aryennes offertes à Gilbert Lazard,* 74–76. Zarathushtra prefers to die: *Prophetic Zand* 6.2(3.1).

54   Chap 8, pp. 224–27.

55   See Eddy, *King,* 26–29, and add to Eddy's evidence J. Reade, "Neo-Assyrian Monuments in their Historical Context," in *Assyrian Royal Inscriptions,* ed. F. M. Fales ("Orientis antiqui collectio," XVII; Roma: Istituto per l'Oriente, Centro per le antichità e la storia dell'arte del Vicino Oriente, 1981), 147, and my *Semites, Iranians, Greeks, and Romans: Studies in their Interactions* (BJS, No. 217; Atlanta, GA: Scholars Press, 1990), 79.

56   Pp. 224–27.

57   See n 49.

58   Alexander: Bengtson, *History of Greece,* 219; Green, *Alexander,* 451–53; Bosworth, *Conquest,* 278–90. Seleucids: Élie Bikerman, *Institutions des Séleucides* (Paris: Geuthner, 1938), 236–57.

59   Alexander: Eddy, *King,* 19 and Plates I and II. Seleucids: M. Rostovtzeff, *The Social and Economic History of the Hellenistic World* (2d impression; 3 vols.; Oxford: Clarendon Press, 1953), Plates III and IV; Percy Gardner, *Catalogue of Greek Coins: The Seleucid Kings of Syria* ("A Catalogue of the Greek Coins in the British Museum"; Bologna: Forni, 1963), esp. Plates III, V–XI, XIII, XV, XIX, XXI–XXVI. Arab headgear: See Y. K. Stillman, "Libās," *Encyclopaedia of Islam,* New Edition, Vol. V, Fascicules 89–90 (Leiden: Brill, 1983), cols. 732b, 734b–735a, 737b.

60   Alexander is mentioned by name in later supplements to the *Prophetic Zand* (3.26[2.19], as emended [see West, *Pahlavi Texts,* Part I, 200, n.1]; 7.32[3.34]).
     Philippe Gignoux ("Nouveaux regards sur l'apocalyptique iranienne," *Comptes rendus de l'Académie des inscriptions et belles lettres,* 1986, 334–44, and "Inexistence," *Journal of Asian and African Studies* 32 [1986], 53–64) has sought to prove that nothing in the *Prophetic Zand* goes back to such early times: It may contain material from the times of the Sassanian Persian kings (224–651 C.E.) but is mostly post-Sassanian. He has ignored the evidence we have just presented. Gignoux accepts the view that the vision of the four metals in the *Prophetic Zand* is borrowed from biblical Daniel 2 ("Nouveaux regards," 342). We have shown, on the contrary, that it shows the influence

of the Babylonian Five-King Version. Gignoux's arguments to show that there was no Avestan *Bahman Yasht* do not affect our position on the *Prophetic Zand,* which was merely misnamed *Bahman Yasht* by modern scholars. Against Gignoux, see also Boyce, "Antiquity," *Bulletin of the School of Oriental and African Studies* 47 (1984), 57–75, and HZ, III, 383–87; Anders Hultgård, *"Bahman Yasht:* A Persian Apocalypse," in *Mysteries and Revelations: Apocalyptic Studies since the Uppsala Colloquium (Journal for the Study of the Pseudepigrapha,* Supplement Series 9; Sheffield: Sheffield Academic Press, 1991), 114–34. Gignoux has demonstrated that identifiable historical events in the *Prophetic Zand* are Sassanian and post-Sassanian. But Alexander and his successors are also identifiable, and the later events simply belong to later supplements. Gignoux ("Nouveaux regards," 343) knows that Zoroastrian texts were transmitted orally for many centuries but still finds it hard to believe that the early predictions of the *Prophetic Zand* could have been preserved and supplemented for so many centuries without being written down. In fact, what has been preserved is not the original prophetic text, but the many-times-supplemented version. We shall find that the surviving versions of Daniel 2 and 7 in the Bible have each been supplemented at least twice, over a period of centuries. A surprising fact, and a testimony to the stubborn conservatism of Zoroastrian transmitters of tradition, is the survival in the *Prophetic Zand* of the Four-Branch Version (chap 1[1.1–5]) alongside the supplemented Seven-Branch Version (chap 3[2.1–22]). Gignoux rightly criticized Eddy for finding Persian resistance to *Hellenism* ("Nouveaux regards," 341–42). We hold that the *Prophetic Zand* and the other evidence show Persian indignation, not against the spread of Hellenistic culture, but over being conquered by Macedonians. Hence, Gignoux's criticism does not touch our position.

61 *King,* 343–49; Eddy used West's translation. I have taken much from Anklesaria's version and have rejected Eddy's transfer of 4.66(2.54) to stand after 7.2(3.13), his removal of the mention of the birth of Hushedar from 7.2(3.13), and his insertion of "Hystaspes" at 7.5(3:14). Contrary to Eddy's assumptions, Hushedar was indeed the first in the Zoroastrian sequence of three saviors and was regarded as a contemporary of Peshyotanu. See Boyce, "Antiquity," *Bulletin of the School of Oriental and African Studies* 47 (1984), 67–70.

62 See, e.g., Deut 28:54, 56; Isa 13:2–22, 50:2–3; Jer 4:19–31, Joel 2:2–3, 6; Mic 7:1–7.

63 See Boyce, "Antiquity," *Bulletin of the School of Oriental and African Studies,* 47 (1984), 59–62, 65–66.

64 See ibid., 67–68.

65 *Prophetic Zand* 7.11(3.21) has the singular but is probably a late supplement and has been omitted from the Appendix. The "wicked evil spirit" *(ganâk mînôê)* of

4.66(2.54) is Ahriman (see J. Duchesne-Guillemin, "Ahriman," *Encyclopaedia Iranica*, I (1986), 672a. Eddy (*King,* 348) seems to have committed the error of taking it to be Alexander.

66   On 3.29(2.22) and the Seven-Branch Prophecy, see below.

67   The supplementing of present-future prophecies is so common a phenomenon that Gignoux's alternative explanation ("Nouveaux regards," 343; "Inexistence," 59) of the increase to seven branches is inherently much less probable.

68   Tin, according to West; lead, according to Anklesaria.

69   See Boyce, HZ, III, 384, n 97.

70   David Flusser carried out the fundamental analysis of *Sibylline Oracles* iv.49–101 to date the passage after Alexander's conquests and before Rome's great victories over the kingdoms of the Macedonian Antigonids and Seleucids in 197 and 190/89 B.C.E. ("The four empires in the Fourth Sibyl and in the Book of Daniel," *Israel Oriental Studies* 2 [1972], 148–74). But we demonstrate that vv 88–101 are supplement to the still earlier stratum in vv 49–87. Flusser ascribed vv 49–101 to Jews, because of the allusion to the deluge in *Sibylline Oracles* iv.51–53. He was wrong to do so. He himself was aware that numerous clues in the text point to its Persian origin; even the allusion to the deluge can be made to do so (see above, n 13, and Collins in *Pseudepigrapha,* ed. Charlesworth, I, 381).

71   See pp. 187–88.

72   Taken from Collins in *Pseudepigrapha* (ed. Charlesworth, I, 385–86), with a few corrections of my own.

73   If the preceding context mentions only one generation of very prosperous rule and the following context narrates a long series of disasters, the force of the Greek particle *de* at the head of v 67 is "but thereafter."

74   The Greek expedition (500 or 499 B.C.E.) to aid the revolt of the Greeks of Asia against Darius I.

75   Xerxes's disastrous effort to conquer Greece, 480–479 B.C.E.

76   The Greek Wars of the fifth and fourth centuries B.C.E., especially the Peloponnesian War (431–404 B.C.E.). The Persian Empire was involved in much of the fighting.

77   When rebellious Thebes fell to Alexander in 335, the city was totally destroyed.

78   Babylon surrendered to Alexander in 331, without resisting. Collins's "built" is insufficiently literal for *teichistheisa.*

79   The text has *Baktra,* which usually means the city, not *Baktria* or *Baktrianê,* the territory.

80   Reading *apo* instead of *hypo.* It is hard to make any sense of the other reading, and, as we shall see, history records an event which fits the reading with *apo.*

81   See Cook, *Persian Empire,* 26–27.

82   The rabbinic chronology at *Seder ʿolam rabbah* 29–30 and *Babylonian Talmud, ʿAbodah zarah* 9a, allots a similar duration to the Persian Empire, surely under the influence of Daniel 9:24–27; see Joseph Jacobs, "Chronology," *Jewish Encyclopedia,* IV (1903), 70b–71a. We shall demonstrate that the present-future prophecy in Daniel 9 was composed in the mid-second century B.C.E. and cannot have influenced *Sibylline B,* a creation of the time of Alexander.

83   See my treatment of the reign of Darius, pp. 68–70.

84   See Cook, *Persian Empire,* 62–63, 98–99.

85   See n 29.

86   Nothing is known of colonists from Susa fleeing to Greece.

87   Stephanus of Byzantium, *Ethnika,* s.v. *Alexandreia;* cf. Pliny, *Natural History* vi.25.92; Avigdor Tcherikover, *Die Hellenistischen Städtegründungen von Alexander dem Grossen bis auf die Römerzeit* (Leipzig: Dieterich, 1927), 104–5; W. W. Tarn, "Alexander: The Conquest of Persia," chapter xii of *Macedon 401–301 B.C.* (3d impression; Cambridge: Cambridge University Press, 1964), Vol. VI of the *Cambridge Ancient History,* eds. J. B. Bury, S. A. Cook, and F. E. Adcock, 398.

88   See A. V. Williams Jackson, *Zoroaster, the Prophet of Ancient Iran* (London: Macmillan, 1899), 199–201.

89   Curtius ix.7.1–11; Diodorus xvii.99.5–6. See Ludwig Schober, *Untersuchungen zur Geschichte Babyloniens und der Oberen Satrapien von 323–303 v. Chr.* (Frankfurt am Main and Bern: Peter D. Lang, 1981), 28–31. From Curtius, one would deduce that a considerable number of the discontented colonists succeeded in returning to Greece; according to Diodorus, they were massacred by the Macedonians after the death of Alexander.

90   See Boyce, HZ, III, 16–17, esp. n 70; Minoo S. Southgate (trans. and ed.), *Iskandarnamah: A Persian Medieval Alexander-Romance* (New York: Columbia University Press, 1978), 186–89.

91   Boyce, HZ, III, 16–17.

92   See Richard Stoneman, *The Greek Alexander Romance* (London: Penguin, 1991), 11–12, 24; Eddy, *King,* 280. See also chap 10, pp. 290–93, and ibid., n 23.

93   On the Persian and Arab works which drew upon the *Alexander Romance,* see Southgate, *Iskandarnamah,* 167–85, 190–201.

94   See n 90.

95   See chap 10, p. 290; Olmstead, *Persian Empire,* 424, 489–90, and Cook, *Persian Empire,* 222, 225.

96   For the two contrasting views, see Eddy, *King,* 73–75; Boyce, HZ, III, 60, n 40.

97   See pp. 325–26.

98   Eddy (*King,* 1–36) tries to prove that the prolonged resistance of the Iranians and the nature of the literary propaganda reflect Alexander's abolition of Achaemenian kingship as against the tenacious belief in it by Iranians. His theory is improbable. Of those persons with Achaemenian claims to royal legitimacy, Darius III was murdered by Iranians, and Bessos-Artaxerxes IV was betrayed by them. Before Alexander's time, there was a long history of Iranian rebellion against legitimate Achaemenian kings.

99   See pp. 300–301.

100   See chap 10, pp. 301–2.

101   See p. 339.

102   See p. 331.

103   See chap 9, p. 264.

104   See chap 4, pp. 94–95; chap 7, pp. 168–78.

～12～

Babylonians, Jews, and Iranians under the Successor Dynasties

1. Introduction

THE UNRESISTING JEWS AND BABYLONIANS as well as the Iranian collaborators could have a favorable view of Alexander. Not so the victims of his atrocities. In fact, the conqueror and his army, even at their best,[1] were predators, preying on and exploiting the conquered. The army lived off the land and was able to take whatever it needed or wanted from the local inhabitants. The huge hoards of precious metals amassed by the Persian kings through taxation did fall into Alexander's hands, and he was lavish in spending them, but even when he used that money to compensate the conquered peoples for goods and services provided by them, they suffered loss because the outpouring of hoarded cash brought about inflation.[2] Some collaborators among the subject peoples might grow rich and even somewhat powerful, but neither the rulers nor the ruled ever regarded the empire as anything but a system in which the conquerors were ruling and exploiting the conquered through military superiority.

In the absence of modern artillery, aircraft, and bombs, war in antiquity was far from total. In the absence of trucks to transport supplies and the booty accumulated by the soldiers, porters and beasts of burden in large numbers had to be fed, and that fact put limits on the size of armies. Alexander's victories for the most part intimidated the conquered peoples, and his powerful personality overawed his own soldiers. Consequently, there was little disorder while the king lived, and, if he wished, he could set limits to his soldiers' looting. The worst potentialities for making the subject peoples suffer occurred when and where one or more armies were present. If the conqueror succeeded in imposing order, the burdens upon the conquered would be limited to taxes and occasional requisitions. Those, too, could be resented, but we know how few were the rebellions to Alexander's rule.

The king, however, died without establishing who would be his successor, and the lot of the conquered became much worse. Let us examine why. Succession within the male line of the royal family was the norm in Macedonia.[3] When more than one candidate was available, the assembled army would choose which would be king. Few survived of the male line. With the army at Babylon was Arrhidaios, Alexander's feeble-minded half-brother; and the conqueror's wife, Roxane, was pregnant and might give birth to a son. If so, the boy would be a mixed-breed, unacceptable as king to some prejudiced Macedonians. The army factions agreed on a compromise: Arrhidaios should be king and should be renamed Philip (III). If a son should be born to Roxane (as in fact happened), the boy, as Alexander (IV), should reign jointly with Arrhidaios.[4] Thus, the empire was turned over to a moron and a baby!

Among the men who had been Alexander's subordinate commanders were able and ambitious persons. Alexander was no longer there to restrain them, and they were determined to wield whatever power each held. We call them the "Diadochoi" (successors). Though some of them may at first have believed in the compromise, there was no way to keep them loyal to a moron and a baby. A period of almost uninterrupted wars among the great commanders extended from 321 to 301, and even afterwards there were wars among the surviving Diadochoi, down to the battle of Korupedion in 283. The last surviving Diadochos, Seleucus I, was murdered in 280. Of all the great competitors, only Ptolemy I died in his own bed (in 283).

Nationalism did not propel this violence. The great majority of the Diadochoi were Macedonians, but there were too few Macedonians to man all their armies. Greeks of all kinds were a favorite source for recruitment. Besides Macedonians and Greeks, the Diadochoi drew upon a vast mixture of ethnic stocks for their soldiers. The best explanation for this era of violence lies in the nature of "predation," as practiced by Alexander and the Diadochoi. Such predation included war, taxation, and requisitions. This predation can be viewed very much as a business enterprise. The risks were high, but the profits could be fantastic, at the expense of civilians and of enemies (including the armies of rival Macedonians). A successful commander would become a multi-millionaire, able from his own resources to pay a big army. As a result, soldiers would be willing to make the "investment" of fighting for his "corporation," in the expectation of huge profits. Nationalistic and ideological slogans were used as propaganda, but in essence, the savage struggles of the Diadochoi were the cut-throat competition of rival military business organizations.

To participate in the "predation business" one had to have an army. Soldiers tended to enlist under the highest bidder for their services and to desert to his forces. Alexander the Great, with all his talent as a commander, still found it necessary to be spectacularly generous in sharing the vast booty with his men, and he let them know that he would not tolerate insubordination. Over the subject peoples he ruled only as their conqueror, but he possessed an important advantage among Macedonians. He was their legitimate king. The moron and the baby had Macedonian legitimacy but were powerless and eventually perished. The commanders who fought the wars of the Diadochoi lacked that legitimacy and had to work harder to keep the loyalty of the soldiers who held down the subject peoples. They had to provide the men with pay (usually from taxes and requisitions) and with booty.

With Alexander dead, there was no legitimate ruler able to suppress rivalry. Any commander of a sizable army could enter the competition, and from the first there were several such commanders. Not one of them was able to conquer all the others. More than one generation elapsed before a fairly stable state structure developed under the dynasties founded by successful Diadochoi. Until that happened, there was continual war among multiple competitors. In Alexander's time there was usually only one army confronting another; under the Diadochoi there often were multiple fronts with multiple pairs of armies, with all the suffering that implied for the conquered peoples.[5]

Some of the Diadochoi only wanted to be left alone to govern the provinces assigned to each of them. Such was Peukestas, who until the spring of 315 B.C.E. was the satrap of Persis, the nuclear territory of the Persians.[6] Most of the Diadochoi were probably opportunists. If they believed that they possessed adequate means, they would attempt to conquer any territory they coveted. Certainly that description fits Antigonus the One-Eyed (satrap over much of Asia Minor).[7] But it also fits Ptolemy I, who conquered territories far beyond his allotted province of Egypt. Two years, however, went by after Alexander's death before the "business competition" could begin, for in 323 dangerous rebellions of Greeks broke out at both ends of the empire. There was a revolt of the homesick mercenaries Alexander had settled in Baktria. Macedonian forces drowned it in blood. More serious was the last truly great effort of the Greeks to throw off Macedonian domination, the Lamian or Hellenic war of 323–322, but that, too, was crushed. Now the great entrepreneurs of war could begin to fight each other.

Never was it possible for a moron and a small child to be more than token rulers of Alexander's empire. From the beginning the assembled army at Babylon had been required to provide them with a regent or guardian. The first such person was Perdikkas. His clear intention to keep the empire united while seeking his own interests evoked opposition to him. The opponents included Antipater, the Macedonian commander in Europe; Antigonus the One-Eyed, satrap of much of Asia Minor; and Ptolemy, satrap of Egypt. Perdikkas had won the loyalty of the Greek Eumenes of Kardia, who was satrap of Cappadocia, by conquering that region for him (it had been by-passed by Alexander).

A two-front war ensued in 320 B.C.E. Leaving Eumenes to hold Asia Minor, Perdikkas marched from there against Ptolemy. However, his attempts to cross the Nile failed, and his own officers murdered him by the river. At a meeting of Diadochoi in the presence of a large army at Triparadeisos in Syria that same year, Antipater, who had been Macedonian commander in Europe, was appointed guardian of the kings. While he held office, war was limited to the effort to suppress Perdikkas's able ally, Eumenes, in Asia Minor. Antipater died a natural death in 319, and the army, following his wishes, appointed Polyperchon (also called "Polysperchon") as his successor. But the powerful satraps refused to recognize him; indeed, Antipater's own son, Kassandros, destroyed his father's plans and, by 316, had wrested control of Macedonia and Greece from Polyperchon. As soon as Antipater was dead, the era of widespread and continual war was in full swing. Important among the competitors were Antigonus the One-Eyed, Kassandros, Ptolemy, Lysimachos (satrap of Thrace), and Seleucus (satrap of Babylon).

In the course of the struggles, first Philip III Arrhidaios was murdered (in 317); then (in 316), Olympias, the mother of Alexander the Great; and then (in 310), Alexander IV and his mother, Roxane. The legitimate male line of Alexander's dynasty was extinct, but all the rival strong men still claimed to be governing as the satraps of the dead conqueror!

Particularly dangerous for the subject peoples were the episodes in which they and their territories passed from one Diadochos to another, for during those occasions the armies of both might requisition supplies, seize booty, sell captives into slavery, and inflict battle damage and slaughter upon the conquered. Babylon on the Euphrates was on a main route connecting strategic territories and was the center of Babylonia, a rich agricultural area. Jerusalem and mountainous Judea were away from the coast and main roads and escaped the worst predation. Nevertheless, both Babylonians and Jews changed hands too often for comfort in the years between 320 and 301. A turning point came in 301, with the battle of Ipsos. After the battle, conflicts between the surviving competitors became less frequent, and the armies usually were far from Babylon and Jerusalem.

2. The Babylonians and Iranians to 301

THE FRAGMENTARY STATE of Babylonian Chronicle 10 conceals from us the exact number of times Babylon and Babylonia passed from one ruler to another in this period. Archon, of whom little is known, was satrap of Babylonia after Alexander the Great died.[8] By 320 Perdikkas, the regent, no longer trusted Archon and sent Dokimos, whom he knew to be loyal, to take his place. An armed group at Babylon supported Archon and opposed Dokimos. Because the source, in this case a Greek manuscript, is fragmentary, we cannot be sure whether Archon's supporters consisted entirely of his soldiers or included Babylonians. There was a battle in which Archon was mortally wounded, and the Babylonians accepted Dokimos as satrap over themselves.[9]

Antipater, the new regent, appointed Seleucus satrap of Babylon, and he was in power there in November 320.[10] Perdikkas was dead, but his able subordinate, Eumenes, went on fighting, professedly to keep the empire united under Philip III and Alexander IV. While Eumenes was marching eastward toward the Iranian satrapies in summer or autumn 317, and was "near the Tigris river," the "local inhabitants" attacked him by night and killed some of his soldiers.[11] We are not told whether the attackers were members of Marduk's people and what they had in mind when they attacked Eumenes's force. Did they intend to punish the predators?

Eumenes is reported to have spent the winter of 318/7 with his army at villages in Babylonia. He may have captured and held part of Babylon (the "palace") in the autumn and winter of 317/6. Again the fragments of Chronicle 10 leave it uncertain. Nor are we told when such forces of Eumenes no longer held any part of Babylon. Any forces of Eumenes at Babylon were gone long before Seleucus came into difficulties with Antigonus, the powerful satrap over much of Asia Minor, in the summer of 315. Antigonus had captured and executed Eumenes.[12]

Seleucus, knowing that his army was no match for that of Antigonus, fled from Babylon in the summer of 315 and took refuge with his friend, Ptolemy, satrap of Egypt.[13] From 315 to 312, Babylonia belonged to Antigonus. Over it he appointed Peithon the son of Agenor as satrap, a title Peithon held until his death at the battle of Gaza (312).[14]

In that battle, Ptolemy inflicted a severe defeat upon Demetrius, Antigonus's son,[15] and, thus, upon Antigonus's entire system. Furthermore, Peithon, the satrap of Babylon for Antigonus, was dead. The moment was opportune for Seleucus to attempt to reconquer Babylon for himself.

For that attempt, victorious Ptolemy granted Seleucus a force of no more than 1,000 infantry and 300 cavalry. Seleucus rightly believed that most Babylonians strongly preferred him to Antigonus as ruler. He boldly marched with his tiny army and retook Babylon in 311.[16] Though the conquered Babylonians, as usual, did not rebel against Macedonian overlordship, this time they threw their weight to decide a conflict between a Diadochos that they disliked and one that they favored.

Seleucus's position in 312 B.C.E., as a subordinate of Ptolemy I, and his subsequent success in conquering a great empire of his own are reflected in Dan 11:5, "one of his officers will become stronger than he, and he will gain dominion over a domain larger than his." See the translation of Hartman and Di Lella in *AB* vol. 23, p. 257.

One might have thought that Seleucus won and retained the lasting favor of the conquered peoples, especially of the Babylonians and Iranians. He did make an effort to do so. He may have treated his Babylonian subjects with at least relative kindness already in the years from 320 to 315.[17]

Chronicle 10, though mutilated, eloquently testifies that Seleucus was viewed as a good ruler of Babylonia from 311/0 to 309/8. In those years he is said to have "had the dust of [ruined] Esagil . . . removed," surely in preparation for rebuilding it. The Chronicle for 320/9 and 318/7 calls Seleucus "Satrap of Akkad" and for 318/7 calls him "Commander of the Army" and "Custodian of Emeslam [the temple of Nergal]." Sometime after declaring himself king in 304, Seleucus probably had his name given in Babylonian documents with the long unused, good Babylonian title, "King of Babylon, King of the Lands." Even Alexander had not used it.[18] Seleucus's coins, down to 306, followed the patterns of Persian, not of Greek or Macedonian issues![19]

Both Cyrus and Cambyses had had honeymoon periods with the Babylonians, as their legitimate kings. The favorable attitude of the Babylonians to Seleucus was gravely impaired if not destroyed by the difficult period of intensified warfare and the favoritism Seleucus had to show to the Macedonians and Greeks who were the backbone of his army. No matter how much army commanders may have wished to spare civilians, often they had no choice. From 311 to 301 the subject peoples saw repeatedly how they were being made to suffer ruinous warfare only to decide which Macedonian would be their ruler.

Nikanor, whom Antigonus had appointed as satrap of Media and as commander in the Iranian regions, marched against Seleucus and Babylonia in 311 and encamped near where the road from Susa to Babylon crossed the Tigris. Seleucus's army was far inferior in numbers. Nevertheless, he routed the rival force in a surprise attack by night (spring 311). Most of the vanquished soldiers joined the victor, who soon thereafter added to his own domains "Susiane and Media and some neighboring regions."[20] Unwilling to let Seleucus keep all these gains without a fight, Antigonus sent Demetrius eastward with a large force of 15,000 infantry and 4,000 cavalry, giving him the limited objective of reconquering Babylonia, with orders to return quickly thereafter to the Mediterranean coast. By this time (summer 311), Seleucus was in Media with the bulk of his army. In command at Babylon he had left Patrokles.

As Demetrius with his army drew near the city, Patrokles knew he had an insufficient force for holding it. He ordered the civilians to evacuate Babylon, while he himself took to guerrilla warfare in the countryside, exploiting the river courses and the canals. There were still two garrisoned citadels in the city. Demetrius took one by siege and gave it over to his soldiers to plunder. The other citadel held out. According to Diodorus, Demetrius, under orders to return promptly to the Mediterranean coast, left a force of 5,000 infantry and 1,000 cavalry under his friend, Archelaos, to press the siege, while he himself departed with most of his soldiers. From Plutarch's parallel account we can infer that Demetrius gave up on the possibility of holding any part of Babylon and withdrew with all his soldiers after first letting them plunder the entire territory.[21] Clearly, Demetrius's army inflicted suffering on the Babylonians, and Seleucus's men did, too. The evacuated civilians cannot have enjoyed the experience.

There was to be more suffering for the Babylonians as a result of further conflict between Antigonus and Seleucus. In 311, Antigonus made two peace treaties, one with Kassandros and Lysimachos, and one with Ptolemy. The Greek sources mention no treaty with Seleucus, and Chronicle 10 is again too mutilated for inferences. It is hard to see why Greek authors would have passed in silence over a treaty between Seleucus and Antigonus.

If Antigonus remained in a state of war with Seleucus, had Kassandros, Lysimachos, and (especially) Ptolemy, by making peace without Seleucus, deliberately abandoned him to the ambitions of Antigonus? Not necessarily. Seleucus's territory and ambitions lay far to the east of the interests of Kassandros and Lysimachos. There was no reason for them to mention Seleucus in the negotiations for, and in the text of, their treaty with Antigonus. At the time of his treaty, Ptolemy's army had been defeated, and Ptolemy had lost Syria. He was in no position to demand any protection for Seleucus. The sources do not state that Antigonus exploited his two peace-treaties to attack

Seleucus. In fact, Antigonus's peaces with Kassandros and Ptolemy were so soon broken off that they could have been no help to Antigonus in his designs against Seleucus.[22] Even if Antigonus had made a peace with Seleucus in 311, as is most unlikely, he was not above violating it at any moment he considered opportune.[23]

The Greek writer Polyainos describes a conflict between Antigonus and Seleucus, without giving the date or naming the place, and the circumstances make the incidents datable between the end of 311 and the beginning of 307.[24] Babylonia was the most likely area for clashes between the two. If so, their clash again exposed the Babylonians to the presence of two Macedonian armies. Greek sources give no other information on conflict between Antigonus and Seleucus after 311 and before 302 B.C.E., the year which preceded the battle of Ipsos.

Even in its mutilated state, however, Chronicle 10 bears eloquent witness to how Babylonia suffered from years of warfare between Antigonus and Seleucus in that period: "... there was weeping and mourning in the land. The south wind [...] went out from Babylon. He plundered city and countryside. The property [...] On the second day he went up to Cuthah and the plunder of [...] the people retreated. [He set] fire to the store-house of Nergal [...]" (Chronicle 10, lines 26–29; the implied date is 309/8). Chronicle 10 goes on to say, "... there was weeping and mourning in the land ... he plundered city and countryside ..." (lines 39–40; the implied date is 308/7). One can infer from the entire mutilated context that Antigonus conquered Babylonia and Babylon in 309/8. In 309/8 and in 308/7 he plundered the city and the province. Clearly he was not seeking to win the favor of the Babylonians! We have no information on how badly or how well Seleucus's soldiers then treated his subjects.[25]

Seleucus himself introduced a policy which roused Babylonian hostility. He liked the patterns of Greek city-life and wanted to attract Greeks to settle in his kingdom and support it. He founded in Babylonia a city, Seleukeia, named for himself, as capital and as a center for Greeks. Situated on the Tigris river, it was only a few miles from Babylon on the Euphrates. Unfortunately, no source gives us the date within his reign for the founding. It is unlikely he founded it during his first term as satrap (320–315) or at the beginning of his second (312/11), for otherwise surely it would have figured in the war against Eumenes or in the one against Demetrius. It is possible that Seleucus founded his city after feeling secure in Babylon in 311 (upon the withdrawal of Demetrius) or after assuming the royal title in 304. It is, however, more likely that he founded Seleukeia shortly after the battle of Ipsos. Later, the Roman author, Pliny the Elder, was convinced that Seleucus founded the city in order to turn Babylon into a ghost town by siphoning off its population.[26] Perhaps that was not his intention, but that was the ultimate result, and Babylonians of the time may have foreseen it. The priests of Babylon opposed the foundation of Seleukeia, and since they had no army, they used their religion. Seleucus asked them as astrologers to tell him what hour and what day would be luckiest for beginning the work, and they told him precisely the unluckiest time.

We have, not the Babylonian, but the Macedonian version of what then happened. According to it, when the truly lucky moment came, Seleucus's laborers heard a mysterious voice saying that the work should begin, and they dashed to begin construction, despite efforts to stop them. Seleucus is said to have asked the astrologers to explain this astonishing event, and they confessed that they had given him the wrong time because they did not wish the new town to overshadow Babylon. The Greek tradition goes on to say that Seleucus then pardoned the astrologers.[27] The Greek tradition clearly was meant to counteract Babylonian propaganda.

A favorite topic for Babylonian astrologers during the next century was to write clay tablets forecasting the downfall of Seleukeia on the Tigris. To build a new city in the Hellenistic world required the moving of large numbers of natives from the surrounding territory to supply the menial laborers. Though we have no direct evidence, it is likely that Seleucus himself began the depopulation of Babylon by drafting residents of the old city and forcibly moving them to his new one. Three hundred years later, Babylon was a ghost town.[28]

In the spring of 302, Kassandros, Lysimachos, Ptolemy, and Seleucus were to form an alliance against Antigonus and Demetrius. A Babylonian tablet recording astronomical observations of Jupiter is the sole source letting us know that Antigonus again ruled Babylon, at least from August 6, 302, to March 7, 301. Evidently, Antigonus sent an expedition to Babylon in a vain effort to distract Seleucus from bringing his army to join forces with his allies.[29] Thus, the years from the fall of Archon in 320 down to the eve of the battle of Ipsos in 301 were a time of horror for the Babylonians. The years around 301 were an urgent time for Marduk to speak and promise an end to the dreadful Macedonian Empires, and all the more so if the new city of Seleukeia was threatening Babylon herself with depopulation. If Marduk himself did not utter oracles, his priests would have to compose and circulate a present-future prophecy.

In ruling Iranians, Seleucus had an advantage unique among Diadochoi because Apame, the wife Alexander had ordered him to take, remained his queen as long as she lived. She was Iranian, the daughter of Baktrian Spitamenes,

Alexander's dangerous enemy.[30] There is reason to believe that on her mother's side she was descended from the Persian dynasty. Seleucus named cities after her. Many Iranians because of her may have viewed Seleucus' rule as legitimate.[31]

The war between Antigonus and Eumenes (317–315) brought armies and surely some suffering to Iran, but perhaps not very much. It ended in Eumenes's death.[32] By 305 B.C.E., Seleucus had control of all the Iranian provinces. Only in Baktria is he reported to have had to fight, and even there he may have faced little resistance.[33] Seleucus marched on past the Iranian provinces to campaign in India. There, the king, Chandragupta, in large measure held his own and made a peace treaty with Seleucus, who gained from Chandragupta 500 elephants.[34] The Iranians may have suffered little from the wars of the Diadochoi during the last two decades of the fourth century B.C.E., but they still could resent being ruled and taxed by foreigners. They probably continued to believe that the age was an evil one, with Ahriman in power.

3. The Jews and the Greeks to 301

THE LOT OF THE JEWS in that period may have been as bad as that of the Babylonians. After Alexander's death, the regent Perdikkas appointed the Greek, Laomedon of Mitylene, as satrap of Syria, the huge province which included Judea.[35] After the murder of Perdikkas, Antipater (in 321) confirmed Laomedon in office,[36] but in 320 or 319, Ptolemy successfully sent his commander, Nikanor, to seize Syria.[37]

Jerusalem and Judea were inland, but even if unmentioned in the sources, they may have changed hands from one Diadochos to another when the coastal cities did. Thus, we note that in 318 Eumenes marched into Phoenicia.[38] By 315 Ptolemy again dominated Syria as far north as Tyre.[39] But in that same year Antigonus seized Jaffa and Gaza, and in 314 Tyre fell to him.[40] After the battle of Gaza in 312, Ptolemy retook the coastal cities.[41] But when Antigonus moved with his main forces in the same year toward Syria, Ptolemy prudently withdrew to Egypt after razing the fortifications of Jaffa, Samaria, and Gaza and carrying off as much portable property as possible.[42] For a decade Antigonus ruled Syria and Judea.

In 306, Antigonus put an end to the increasingly ridiculous pose of the great Diadochoi, by which they claimed to be mere satraps of the (dead!) King Alexander IV. Antigonus took the royal title and named Demetrius full co-king. Early in 304, Ptolemy took the title "king," followed quickly by Seleucus, Lysimachos, and Kassandros.[43]

In 302, upon the formation of the alliance of the four kings against Antigonus and Demetrius, Ptolemy reoccupied "all the cities of Koilê Syria," except Sidon, which he besieged. "Koilê Syria" included inland as well as coastal regions.[44] While besieging Sidon, he received a false report that Antigonus, having defeated Lysimachos and Seleucus, was marching against Syria. Ptolemy believed the report, made a four-month truce with the Sidonians, put garrisons into the captured cities, and withdrew to Egypt with the bulk of his army.[45] It is likely that forces loyal to Antigonus took over after this withdrawal by Ptolemy. Demetrius did hold Tyre and Sidon after the battle of Ipsos,[46] and the sources leave undated an episode in which Ptolemy I took Jerusalem on the Sabbath, when the Jews would not bear arms, and the city thereupon got a "harsh master." According to another report, Ptolemy I (at an unspecified date) deported thousands of Jews to Egypt, many as slaves.[47]

Let us proceed to demonstrate that those events probably occurred shortly after the battle of Ipsos, when Jews tried tenaciously to be loyal to King Demetrius. If Ptolemy I had to wait for the Sabbath in order to take Jerusalem and treated the inhabitants harshly, clearly the city had been resisting him. The Jews' own beliefs required them to remain loyal to the king ruling over them. After the death of Alexander IV, there were no kings until Antigonus and Demetrius took the royal title. Jews could not have shown such stubborn resistance to Ptolemy before 302. Ptolemy is reported to have met significant resistance in 302 only at Sidon.[48] On the other hand, in the summer of 301, Ptolemy hastened to enter southern Syria after Antigonus fell in the battle of Ipsos.[49] A king, Demetrius, still claimed rule over the area and held Tyre and Sidon.[50] Jews probably felt obliged to be loyal to him and held out against Ptolemy until the Sabbath.[51]

In 20 years, Jerusalem and Judaea may have changed hands nine times: once in 320 or 319, twice in 318, once in 315 or 314, twice in 312, once or twice in 302, and once in 301. Enough sufferings had come upon the Jews to evoke the writing of present-future prophecy!

The wars of the Diadochoi also inflicted severe damage in Macedonia and Greece, and Babylonians were aware of their sufferings,[52] but we do not have to study them in detail here.[53] Down to the battle of Ipsos, the conquered peoples desperately needed theological interpretations of the history of the times. They were being battered by the cruel armies fighting one another. The swords of the soldiers were of strong steel. Throughout the period, the forces of the Diadochoi so outmatched the disarmed subject peoples that revolt was hopeless. But those forces were obviously and madly killing each other, just as the Persians had appeared to be killing each other off at the beginning of the reign of

Darius I. The mania of the armies for fighting among themselves clearly was a weakness. The colossus built by Alexander had plenty of iron in it, but his successors' lack of cohesiveness suggested the cohesiveness of broken pottery!

4. The "Divided Empire" through the Aftermath of the Battle of Ipsos

ALEXANDER'S EMPIRE WAS NOT even nominally a unit after Antigonus and his rivals took the royal title. By that time, Kassandros, Lysimachos, Ptolemy, and Seleucus had long believed that Antigonus's ambitions were dangerous to themselves. In 314 B.C.E. the other four surely believed they were protecting themselves when they provoked war with Antigonus by confronting him with demands they knew were unacceptable to him. The war lasted until 311.[54] Thus, Alexander's kingdom became a "divided empire."

We have given special study to Seleucus's defensive wars against Antigonus. Against Ptolemy, Antigonus and Demetrius in 306 staged a formidable amphibious invasion of Egypt. Ptolemy was lucky: The weather enabled him to beat off the enemy forces.[55]

In early summer of 304, Antigonus sent Demetrius to Greece, where Kassandros had been trying to capture Athens. Demetrius enjoyed spectacular military and diplomatic successes there, into 302.[56] Kassandros sued for peace with Antigonus, who, however, demanded unconditional surrender; to that, Kassandros would not consent.[57] Instead, he urged Lysimachos, who long had been his friend and his help in distress, to join him in resisting Antigonus.[58]

Lysimachos perceived that his own power would be gravely threatened if his neighbor Kassandros should fall to Antigonus. Kassandros and Lysimachos thereupon sent envoys to Ptolemy and Seleucus. The envoys easily persuaded Ptolemy and Seleucus to join in a new alliance against the menace to them all (302).[59]

Though Demetrius had pressed Kassandros hard enough to drive him to sue for peace, Kassandros, nevertheless, took the bold gamble of sending a considerable part of his army across the straits to join Lysimachos in an invasion of Antigonus's Asia Minor.[60] As it turned out, Kassandros was able, with his remaining soldiers, to cope with Demetrius in Europe. Meanwhile, the expeditionary forces in Asia won important victories. Two of Antigonus's commanders, Dokimos and Phoinix, deserted with their men to the enemy.[61] Antigonus had to move against the invaders.[62]

Even with the absence of Demetrius's force as it uselessly confronted Kassandros, Antigonus's army outnumbered that of Lysimachos. Seleucus's large force would be an equalizer, but it was still far to the east. With great skill, Lysimachos avoided battle. He would encamp in a strong position, and when pressed hard, he would escape with his outnumbered army to yet another such position.[63] Antigonus gave up the effort to prevent Lysimachos from linking up with Seleucus, and he recalled Demetrius and his army from Europe.

In 301 occurred the pivotal battle of Ipsos. Lysimachos and Seleucus had some 400 elephants against the 75 of Antigonus and Demetrius. That difference proved to be decisive. The impetuous Demetrius led a cavalry charge and routed the opposing horsemen, but pursued too far and was unable to come to the aid of his hard-pressed aged father, because the horses would not charge against Seleucus's formidable screen of elephants. Antigonus was slain, and his army was routed.[64] Demetrius escaped and managed to retain important military resources but was never again a superpower.[65]

The victorious allies divided the spoils, namely, the bulk of Antigonus's empire. Lysimachos took Asia Minor, from the straits to the Taurus mountains. Seleucus took northern Syria and claimed that his contribution to the victory had earned him southern Syria (including Judea) as well. Ptolemy had seized southern Syria around the time of the battle. In the Ptolemaic Empire, the large region seized became a province with the offical name, "Syria and Phoenicia." In Seleucus's view, Ptolemy, absent from the battle, had done nothing to earn a share of the spoils, but Seleucus would not war against the man who had been his friend. Kassandros was satisfied to have preserved his rule in Macedonia and his domination in Greece.[66] Demetrius was not content with what remained in his hands, but he was no longer a major power. The four strong kings, Lysimachos, Kassandros, Seleucus, and Ptolemy, refrained from fighting one another between 301 and 283.

5. The Four-Plus-Kingdom Version of Daniel 2

CONTRARY TO THE HOPES of the conquered peoples, the armies of the Macedonians stopped killing each other and settled down to an era of relative stability. The period when the conquered peoples suffered bitterly had been a hopeful one, just because the Macedonians and their Greek "junior partners" seemed to be destroying themselves, surely driven mad by the deities of their subjects. Both the suffering and the hopefulness had been good reasons for religious leaders of the conquered peoples to write and publish present-future prophecies. Once the structure of stable kingdoms was achieved, after 301 B.C.E., the disappointed conquered peoples would tend to turn a deaf ear to any such prophecies.

Present-future prophecies of this period should reflect the history of the years just before 301 and should be datable at the latest early in the third century B.C.E. Older prophecies were available for the priests of Marduk to interpret and use for predictions of the fall of the Macedonian empires. There was the Three-Beast-Four-Head version of Daniel 7, foretelling the rise of a new humane Babylonian empire sometime after the death of Xerxes, the fourth Persian king, who was supposed to be the last king of the third monster-empire. One might attempt to supplement that prophecy by adding a fourth monster-empire. But the priests may have avoided doing so at first, for fear of rousing suspicion: Too many people may have known the original text.

The Five-King version of Daniel 2, however, looked promising. It spoke of a series of reigns to be followed by an everlasting rule appointed by Marduk. The original meaning of the Five-King version had been fulfilled by the fall of Nabonidus to Cyrus, but it had not been completely fulfilled, because Cyrus's dynasty did not last forever (contrary to Daniel 2:24) and in reigns of its later members had been inimical to Marduk and his city. The old prophecy, if true, had to mean something else! Already the Persian authors of the *Prophetic Zand* (based on the Five-King version!) had made the wicked fourth reign into the empire of an ethnic group foreign to the first three kings. The foreign branch was inappropriate to the tree-image, but resulted in an interpretation comforting to the conquered Persians: The conquering Macedonian empire would fall.

By a similar procedure, Marduk's Babylonian believers took the Five-King version and with a few supplements transformed it into what we may call the "Four-Plus-Kingdom version." Only Jews or Babylonians could have done so: The scene of the Five-King version is the court of Babylonian King Nebuchadnezzar, and the heroic dream interpreter is Babylonian Bêl-balâtsu-uṣur or Jewish Daniel. We shall soon find proof that though the Jews adopted the Four-Plus-Kingdom version, they did not originate it.

In vowelless Aramaic, it was easy for Babylonian believers to transform each king *(malk-)* into a kingdom *(molk-)* because both words were written *mlk*. The scribe of the new version felt justified in removing all ambiguity by writing *mlkw* ("kingdom," "reign") instead of *mlk* in Daniel 2:39, 40, and 44.

In the resulting prophecy, the first kingdom is indeed golden: It is the Babylonian Empire of Nebuchadnezzar (and the author of the supplement felt no necessity to change the third word of Daniel 2:44, *mlk'* ["kings"], to *mlkwt'* ["kingdoms"]). Jews, on the other hand, had no reason to view Nebuchadnezzar's reign as a golden age. For Babylonians, the second kingdom, the Median Empire could only be inferior, but the Medes had never insulted Marduk or hurt the city of Babylon. Hence, a Median Empire could be silver for Babylonians. Jews had no reason to view the Median Empire as inferior to the Babylonian.

Some Babylonians might still know that the Babylonian and Median empires had been contemporaries, but 200 years had gone by, and the Babylonians knew the Persian theology of history, which had the Medes as rulers of the second great empire. Probably the Babylonians also had the tendency to read the Three-Beast version of Daniel 7 carelessly, so as to view the second beast as coming *after* the first.

To turn the third king into the third empire, the supplementer in 2:39 wrote *mlkw* ("kingdom") for *mlk* ("king") and added "which shall rule over all the earth" to designate clearly the Persian Empire. Bronze is baser than silver, and baser than the Medes the Persians with their dreadful Xerxes certainly had been. Jews had no reason to view the Persian Empire as base.

The original iron reign had been that of Labâshi-Marduk, a mere child, in whom iron symbolized not strength but baseness. The empire that superseded the Persians' was Alexander's, which certainly impressed the conquered peoples with its strength. We may suppose that the Five-King version had consistently used the metals in their sequence as metaphors. The supplementer in v 40 abandoned metaphor for simile: The fourth king*dom* will be *as strong as* iron. The metaphorical metals in the traditional sequence had required no explanation: The progression was from noble to base. Iron in a simile stands for strength, not baseness. There was no need to exclude "baseness" as a meaning. Yet v 40 overelaborately specifies that the meaning is strength.[67] Hence, the change from metaphor to simile and the superfluous explanation are yet more hints that an original prophecy has been supplemented.

In Daniel 2:41–42, after Alexander's empire comes the divided king*dom*, with at least ten divisions, symbolized by toes. That kingdom is hard as iron yet as incapable of unity as a heap of potsherds. The strange circumstance that the toes are mentioned only in the interpretation of the dream (Daniel 2:37–45), not in the description of it (Daniel 2:31–35) is but one more sign that an older prophecy is being supplemented. The supplementer tried to conceal that fact by placing the words *dy ḥzyth* ("whereas you saw) at the beginning of v 41 in which he introduced the toes.

Diodorus gives detailed lists of the satrapies of the empire in the early years of the age of the Diadochoi. From them we learn that the empire, as reorganized by Perdikkas in 323 B.C.E., contained twenty-two satrapies,[68] and, as reorganized after Perdikkas's death in 321 B.C.E., it contained nineteen.[69] By 301 B.C.E. the greatest of the competitors had annexed some ten satrapies: Ptolemy had annexed Syria and had lost it thrice to Antigonus and had reoccupied it twice;[70] Antigonus had annexed Hellespontine Phrygia, Lydia, Cappadocia, and Cilicia;[71] Seleucus had annexed Persis, Susiane, Media, Parthyaia, Areia, Baktria, and Sogdia.[72] Thus, the surviving satrapies were at most twelve in number and could easily be symbolized by the toes of a statue. Clearly, the writer of Daniel 2:41 and 42 had reached the period containing the battle of Ipsos.

The strange circumstance that the divided kingdom is not designated in Daniel 2:41 by its ordinal number ("fifth") also serves to demonstrate that Babylonians, not Jews, were the authors of this version. Let us carry out the demonstration.

The author of the new version of Daniel 2 faced real difficulties in assigning an ordinal number to the divided kingdom. The last of the inferior reigns in the Five-King version was the fifth. However, there are ancient sources that claim or imply, for each of Seleucus, Ptolemy, and Antigonus, that he was a member of Alexander's dynasty, the Argeads (no such claim was made for Lysimachos).[73] If the Diadochoi were legitimate dynastic heirs of Alexander, then the "divided kingdom" over which they ruled could be regarded as the same as his.

We can be sure that the claims of Ptolemy and his descendants (the Ptolemies), of Seleucus and his (the Seleucids), and of Antigonus and his (the Antigonids), to be members of the Argead line are false. The Macedonians had a deep-seated belief in the principle of legitimate dynastic succession. If any of the strong men during the wars of the Diadochoi had been able to make such claims, he would have made them loudly and would have won massive support for himself. Jews knew that there had been a change of dynasty.[74] Surely some Babylonians must have known, too. Nevertheless, nonrebellious Babylonians quickly gave at least lip service to the claims of Seleucus and his descendants, that they were direct heirs of the Argead dynasty.[75]

The author of a present-future prophecy presents himself either as an inspired person or as a god and should not be deceived by false dynastic propaganda. But there could be good reason for a Babylonian prophet or god to regard Seleucus's kingdom as a continuation of Alexander's, even if the claims that Seleucus was the legitimate dynastic successor were false. If one counted the kingdoms by the ethnic groups of their ruling elements, the Diadochoi were just as Macedonian as was Alexander the Great. Should the divided kingdom of the Diadochoi, then, be regarded as the fifth or as a continuation of the fourth? Unable to be sure how Marduk or an inspired person would count the divided kingdom, the composer of the new prophecy took the safe course of giving it no ordinal number, and we, accordingly, give his composition the awkward name of the "Four-Plus-Kingdom version."

Daniel 11:4 testifies that Jews rejected the false claims of Diadochoi to be members of the Argead dynasty. Furthermore, after the death of Alexander IV, Judea had been ruled by two *kings,* Antigonus and Ptolemy. Though Antigonus had ruled Babylon after the death of Alexander IV, he had done so with the title satrap, not king. Jews thus might tend to count, not five kingdoms, but six! The kind of hedging which we find in the new version thus indicates that Babylonians, not Jews, created it.

We called attention before to the false note in Daniel 2:41 and 43: The description of the fifth level of the statue in the *dream* (as opposed to the *interpretation* of it) contains no mention of mixture: In the dream, the legs are *partly* iron, *partly* clay, and the text of Daniel 2:43 itself admits that iron does not *mix* with clay. The references to mixture in Daniel 2:41 and 43 must be supplement. Do they belong to the Four-Plus-Kingdom version?

They do not. Daniel 2:43, by saying, "They shall mix themselves by means of the seed of man," reveals that mixture symbolizes marriage, and the verse goes on to predict that the marriage will not succeed. As we have noted, only Jews or Babylonians could produce versions of Daniel 2. There were no failed dynastic marriages that had significant effects on Jews or Babylonians until well into the third century B.C.E.[76] We shall treat the Mixture Version of Daniel 2 when we reach that later period.[77]

In the Five-King version, the iron part of the fifth level had represented the monstrous cruelty of Nabonidus, as the clay part had represented his weakness. Now, however, as we have the text in vv 40 and 42, the author, a writer of present-future prophecy who had experienced Alexander and the Diadochoi, has made the iron of the fourth and fifth levels symbolize cruel strength and the clay of the fifth level symbolize the fragility of an empire that so obviously was falling apart. Though the supplementer had abandoned metaphor for simile in v 40, in vv 41–42 he returned to metaphor! If people knew the symbolism of the Five-King version, there was strong reason for the supplementer to make clear, in vv 40 and 42, the change in what iron and clay stood for.

The trouble is that the explanation of the symbolism in v 40 contains a historical falsehood. Let us again bear in mind that only Babylonians and Jews could have supplemented the Five-King version. Verse 40 asserts that the fourth kingdom, Alexander's, will crush and shatter all these (preceding kingdoms). In fact, in the time of the fourth kingdom neither the Babylonians nor the Medes had kings. Alexander conquered the *Persian* Empire, inflicting great damage on the Persians but probably little on the Medes. He did not injure the Babylonians and the Jews.[78] We shall find a plausible explanation for the strange content of v 40 when we study the final Mixture version. There we shall take the words of vv 40–43 and reconstruct how they looked in the Four-Plus-Kingdom version and how they were altered in the final version.[79]

In the Five-King version of Daniel 2, the stone in v 34 and in the original of v 45 had symbolized Cyrus and probably also his dynasty. In the new version, the ethnic group of the final kingdom is not specified, but the *people of the almighty god* understood who it would be. In the Five-King version it made sense to say that Cyrus would topple the dynastic succession of Babylon (symbolized by the statue). With the fall of Nabonidus and the death of his sole heir, the dynasty reached its end. But in the Four-Plus-Kingdom version, it was senseless to say that the future kingdom to be established by the almighty god would destroy all the preceding kingdoms—the kingdoms of Nebuchadnezzar, of the Medes, of the Persians, and even Alexander's were dead and gone. Only the divided kingdom of the Diadochoi remained. But the pattern had been established by the Five-King version. To depart from it would invite suspicion that the new version was a forgery. In fact, no one noticed the senselessness and historical falsehood in Daniel 2:44.

For the time being, we shall define the Four-Plus-Kingdom version of Daniel 2 as containing the dream exactly as described in vv 31–35 and the interpretation as in vv. 36–41a (including the references to toes in vv 41 and 42). It did not contain v 43 or the end of v 41 with their references to mixture.

Jews, on seeing that Babylonian revision of the Five-King version *may* still have known that they first learned of their Daniel from Babylonian documents. Jews may still have known that in those documents the great seer was presented as a Babylonian, Bêl-balâtsu-uṣur. After the many captures of Jerusalem, the Jews had seen even more evidence of cruelty and division in the "kingdom" ruled by the Diadochoi than had the Babylonians. Naturally they took the Four-Plus-Kingdom version as a correction of the earlier Babylonian document and again made it their own, by assuming that Bêl-Balâtsu-uṣur was none other than the Jew, Daniel. For them, the predicted final kingdom would be Jewish.

Around the time of the battle of Ipsos, Babylonians and Jews probably had more compelling reasons driving them to produce present-future prophecy than had the Persians.[80] But the Persians did not have to like being ruled by Macedonian foreigners, even if Seleucus's queen was Iranian, though they appear to have accepted his claim to be Alexander's heir. We have already taken note of a text they produced in the time of the Diadochoi: the *Prophetic Zand*, with its references both to a singular demon (Alexander) and to plural demons (the Diadochoi), but without the description of the iron as "mixed."[81] There is no sign that the Four-Plus-Kingdom version so impressed the Persians that they sought to fabricate a counterpart.

We have mentioned the sufferings of the Jews down through the harsh treatment that came upon them when Ptolemy captured Jerusalem after the battle of Ipsos. In reaction to those troubles, Jews produced another piece of literature, perhaps even before the battle of Ipsos; it survives in chaps 6–11 of the book of *1 Enoch*.[82] It is a story of divine intervention, an elaboration on hints in the book of Genesis. In its original form, it told how all the evil before the deluge arose from the giants who were the offspring of human women and wicked angels, led by Shemiḥazah[83] (*1 Enoch* 6:2–7:6; the passages telling of wicked angels led by ʿAsaʾel in *1 Enoch* 8:1–10:8 are clearly intrusive and therefore are interpolations into the original text).[84] The wicked wars and violence of the giants inflicted great damage upon the righteous. When the powers of good cried out to the LORD to take action, God sent the angel Sariel to warn Noah of the coming deluge, the angel Raphael to heal the earth,[85] the angel Gabriel to make the wicked giants kill themselves off,[86] and the angel Michael to imprison the wicked angels who were the fathers of the giants (9:1). Those wicked angels will be punished at the last judgment (9:1–10:15).

In my opinion, the moral of the story is clear: The Diadochoi pretend to be superhuman, descended from gods,[87] but their gods are mere idols, and their claims to be descended from them are false. The LORD in Noah's time brought real giants, descended from superhuman angels, to kill each other off. How much more easily, therefore, will God now bring destruction upon the Diadochoi who even now are killing each other off! The motif of "killing each other off" shows that the story in *1 Enoch* originated in the hopeful period, before it was clear that the Diadochoi had desisted from the internecine warfare.

The message of the story of the giants requires the believer to reason from the greater case (the giants) to the lesser (the Diadochoi). One might instead take that story as merely a tale of the distant past, with no direct bearing on the troubles of the conquered peoples in ca. 301 B.C.E. The giants were extinct; God had destroyed them long before the age of the Diadochoi. The Diadochoi were not giants. Nevertheless, cruel war still beset the conquered peoples, and they still regarded as a scandal the sexual immorality of the conquerors. Perhaps for all those reasons, an interpolator (who may have been the original author) worked into *1 Enoch* 8–10 the passages that speak of ʿAsaʾel (one of Shemiḥazah's associates according to 6:7), as the one who taught mankind mining and metallurgy and the way to make metal weapons and the use of minerals as cosmetics and jewelry.[88]

ʿAsaʾel, says the resultant text, is already being punished and will be destroyed at the time of the Last Judgment (*1 Enoch* 10:4–6), and all the evil that he caused will also then be annihilated (10:16–22). The combined story of

Shemiḥazah and 'Asa'el recognizes that war and sin still exist in the interpolator's present but promises that they will be abolished at some time in the future.

Like Daniel 2–7, *1 Enoch* contains narrative on the wonderful powers of God (6–10) and present-future prophecies (the "Animal Vision" [85:1–90:41], and the "Apocalypse of Weeks" [93:3–10, 91:11–17, in that order]) and was originally written in Aramaic. Also, like Daniel 2–7, *1 Enoch* was heavily influenced by Mesopotamian patterns.[89] Daniel 2–7, however, was adopted from Babylonian originals with slight revision, if any. No part of *1 Enoch* so closely reflects a Babylonian original.

6. From the Aftermath of the Battle of Ipsos (301) to the Death of Antiochus I (261)

BABYLONIA GOT OFF WITHOUT any harsh treatment except perhaps taxes in 301, and thereafter, for a long time, Babylonia and Judea enjoyed the blessings of local peace. But Babylonians were destined to supplement the Four-Plus-Kingdom version, creating the "Mixture" version of Daniel 2, and the Jews would adopt it as their own. Let us give a brief account of the complicated developments.

Seleucus's victory at Ipsos was a disappointment, but no disaster for Marduk's worshipers, though the hated city of Seleukeia would continue to drain population away from Babylon. Seleucid kings would continue to honor Marduk if Marduk's priests did not treat them too sullenly, and perhaps those priests always treated the kings with tact. Whatever the case may be, the reigning Seleucid could win popularity in Babylonia also by favoring other gods honored in the land. Seleucus's successor, Antiochus I (reigned 281–261), repaired and rededicated Nabû's temple in Borsippa and set up a cuneiform tablet there, the last known royal inscription in Babylonian.[90] In it, Antiochus naturally concentrates not on Marduk, but on Nabû. This kindness to Nabû cannot be taken as a sign of bad relations between the king and Marduk, because in this very inscription, Antiochus takes pains to call himself also the builder of Marduk's temple at Babylon.

From 301 to the death of Seleucus in 281, as far as the Persians, Babylonians, Egyptians, and Jews were concerned, there was peace and stability in the Hellenistic kingdoms. The only great event occurred far away from those four peoples: In 281 Lysimachos fell in battle against Seleucus at Kurupedion near Sardis, and Seleucus thereby became ruler of most of Asia Minor.[91]

Seleucus had a grievance against Ptolemy for seizing southern Syria and Palestine in 301, but the two kings were friends and would not war against each other.[92] Ptolemy, however, died in 283 B.C.E., and Seleucus I was murdered in 281. Their heirs, Ptolemy II (283–246) and Antiochus I had no such friendship between them and soon went to war. The conquered peoples had surely viewed as madness the savage conflicts among the members of the first generation of Alexander's successors. Renewed conflict among kings of the second generation of successors must have impressed those peoples as folly, and the more so, if their own king's wars proved profitless to him and costly to his subjects. Let us examine the evidence which shows how Babylonians could believe that the Seleucid Empire, from 281 to 241 B.C.E., was weak compared to the Ptolemaic kingdom.[93]

We shall soon be studying documents dated by the Seleucid era and must pause to give a brief explanation of it. Under Seleucus I, dates had been given by numbering the years from his capture of Babylon in 312 B.C.E., with the beginning of the calendar year being set in late summer or early autumn. Some of the subject peoples (notably the Babylonians and the Jews) had been accustomed to begin the numbered regnal year in the spring and they continued to do so with Seleucus's numbered years. After the death of Seleucus I, it appears that the scribes under Antiochus I found it convenient to go on numbering the years consecutively from 312 B.C.E., and thus arose the Seleucid era, in at least two forms. The royal government used the "Macedonian" form, with year 1 beginning in late summer or early autumn, 312 B.C.E. The Babylonians used the "Babylonian' form, with year 1 beginning in the spring of 311 B.C.E. Jews in their local documents used a form likewise having year 1 begin in the spring of 311 B.C.E., but at least the Jewish author of 2 Maccabees, writing in Greek, dated by the Macedonian form.[94]

There were clashes between the forces of Ptolemy II and Antiochus I already in 280–279, with Antiochus losing territory in Asia Minor to Ptolemy. Between 279 and 274, Antiochus married off his daughter, Apame, to Magas, the half-brother of Ptolemy II. Magas was the Ptolemaic governor of Cyrenaica. After Ptolemy II put to death two of his own brothers, one of whom was a half-brother of Magas, Magas induced his Cyrenaean subjects to rebel against Ptolemy and marched upon Egypt.[95] At an unknown date, very likely at the time of this revolt against Ptolemy II, Magas took the title "king." Antiochus I and his son-in-law Magas were unable to coordinate offensives against Ptolemy. Magas was forced to withdraw from Egypt to fight off Libyan nomads, and Ptolemy's countermeasures sufficed to nullify Antiochus's efforts.[96] Magas was able to rule Cyrenaica securely until the middle of the third century B.C.E.,[97] but the fact probably gave little comfort to Antiochus.

Our information on the next conflict between Ptolemy and Antiochus, the so-called First Syrian War, is very poor. The war broke out in 274 and may have lasted until 271.[98] Antiochus I probably gained nothing from it, and, if so, he lost at least the costs of the conflict, and perhaps considerably more.[99] At about the same time Antiochus, perhaps in 275/4, in a battle in which he used elephants, won glory by defeating the Celtic Galatians, formidable warriors who had invaded Asia Minor.[100] The campaign surely must have been expensive. The king's subjects must have felt the costs of all this warfare. Indeed, there is evidence that they did.

Our best source on the "First" Syrian War is a somewhat damaged clay tablet that contains a Babylonian astronomical diary of the second half of the Babylonian year 38 Sel. (274/3 B.C.E.).[101] Lines 29'–39' and the four lines written an the upper edge of the tablet narrate historical events. One would expect them all to be events of 274/3 B.C.E., but strangely, the writer draws a ruled line and below it, in lines 34'–39', he tells of events of the previous year, 37 Sel. (275/4 B.C.E.).

In lines 29'–33' we learn that in 38 Sel. the king left Sardis in Asia Minor and went against Egyptian forces which had invaded his province called "Beyond-the-[Euphrates]-River" (approximately, northern Syria). Confronted by him, the Egyptian forces withdrew. Nevertheless, the war must have continued. In the last month of that Babylonian year, so the tablet reports, the satrap of Babylonia sent to the king in Syria much silver and cloth, as well as twenty elephants from Baktria, and, in the same month, the *stratêgos* (military commander) mustered troops in Babylonia and brought them to the king as reinforcements. Next the writer tells of two events of 274/3 B.C.E. as if to show how bad a time it was: "That year, purchases in Babylon and the other cities were made with copper coins of Greece" (surely those copper coins were used for lack of silver). "That year, there was much *ekketu*-disease [scabies?][102] in the land."

On the upper edge of the tablet, there are four lines of writing, of which the first two tell of additional distressing facts of the year: "There was famine in Babylonia; people sold their children [as slaves]. People died of . . . [the sign is unreadable; "hunger" would fit the context]."

The writer may have added the events of late 37 Sel. (in lines 34'–39') to supply yet other distressing facts of the time. Doubt arises because of a gap in the text and ambiguity on the language.[103] Let us consider first lines 34'–36':

34'   Year 37 (kings) Antiochus and Seleucus, month XII, the
ninth: the satrap of Babylonia and the appointees of the king,
who had gone before the king to Sardis in year 36,

35' returned to Seleukeia, the royal city which is on the Tigris.
Their message (written on a) leather (scroll) came to the
citizens of Babylon. The twelfth day,

36' the citizens of Babylon went out to Seleukeia. . . .

Should we take this passage to mean that the royal officials brought back to
the citizens of Babylon the order that they must move to Seleukeia and that,
three days later, the citizens complied? We know that the Seleucid kings drew
on the population of Babylon to swell the population of Seleukeia. R. J. van der
Spek[104] considers it improbable that within three days arrangements for such a
transfer of people could have been made. But if the officials had gone to Sardis
to the king bearing a petition from the Babylonians to him that he revoke a previous deportation order, the petitioners had to be prepared for a possible rejection of their appeal.[105] Van der Spek suggests that a delegation of Babylonian
citizens went to Seleukeia in order to welcome the satrap of Babylonia and to
respond to the message from the king. Such a matter of perfunctory courtesy
was probably not worthy of being recorded in the diary, and so it becomes
likely that the diary does refer to a forced transfer of Babylonians to Seleukeia.

Lines 36'–38' are also interesting:

36' That month, the satrap of Babylonia [. . .] the fields which
had been given in year 32 at the command of the king for the
sustenance of the people of Babylon,

37' Borsippa,[106] and Cutha. Bulls, sheep, and everything of the
[cities] and the religious centers at the command of the king
before the citizens

38' [. . .] . . . of the house of the king he made. That year, a large
number of bricks for the reconstruction of Esa[gila] were
molded above Babylon and below Babylon [. . .].

Line 36' probably alludes to the partial or total revocation of gifts made by
the king for the benefit of the people of Babylonian cities.[107] Perhaps line 37'
does so, too. Even if such revocation were justifiable as a wartime measure,
Babylonians could disapprove of it. Line 38', on the other hand, presents the
royal government as performing the pious duty of seeing to the rebuilding of
Esagila. Thus, as viewed by Babylonians, both Ptolemy II and Antiochus I
were guilty of the folly of warring against each other. Antiochus, in addition,
treated Babylonia with an inconsistency that easily could give the impression
of folly.

Only a few years later, Babylonians received another illustration of what they could take to be the folly of their Seleucid king. From 280 B.C.E. through March 268, evidence shows that Seleucus, son of Antiochus I, was co-regent king with his father. But by 266 B.C.E., Antiochus I had had this Seleucus executed on a charge of plotting and had made his younger son Antiochus (the future Antiochus II) co-regent instead.[108]

A Babylonian, on observing the combination of folly and piety in Antiochus I, is the probable author of another Sibylline poem, one that has been preserved in the *Sibylline Books* at iii.381–387, immediately before the verses on Alexander (iii.388–395) that we have called *Sibylline A*. Let us call iii.381–387 *"Sibylline C."*

Here is a translation of those verses:

381   Macedonia shall give birth to grievous woe for Asia,
382   And for Europe there shall sprout very great distress
383   From the race descended fram Kronos, a breed of bastards
       and slaves.
384   It shall rebuild[109] even Babylon the fortified city,
385–386   And, though called mistress of every land on which the sun
       shines, the breed shall perish through ruinous follies.
387   Leaving [its mere] name among far-wandering posterity.

The poet is interested first in woe upon Asia, arising from Macedonia. He considers it remarkable that the baneful conquerors carry out a rebuilding project at Babylon. Surely, then, the poet was a Babylonian, writing after the great victories of Alexander. He is unlikely to have written while Alexander was alive, although the great conqueror did plan to rebuild Esagila (Marduk's temple at Babylon).[110] Alexander was kind to Babylon and mostly had the favor of Marduk's worshipers.[111] Early anti-Macedonian writers in Asia could hardly tell Greeks from Macedonians. Rather, they know Greeks as kinsmen or partners of the conquering stock. Our poet wrote late enough to have known that Europeans (Greeks) were victims of the Macedonians. Greece, except for Sparta, was largely at peace while Alexander marched through Asia. "Europe" began to suffer great distress in the age of the Diadochoi. "Ruinous follies" could be ascribed to the reigns of the Diadochoi, especially to their wars, not to the reign of Alexander.

Seleucus I, too, had a project of rebuilding Esagila,[112] but it is unlikely that the poet in writing *Sibylline C* had him in mind. Seleucus I enjoyed too much favor among Babylonians and was too conspicuously successful to have folly ascribed to him.

We know, however, that Antiochus I suffered losses in war and imposed costly policies on Babylonians. Our poet could easily have ascribed folly to him. Antiochus I is also the last Seleucid known to have had a building project at Babylon. Consequently, *Sibylline C* probably was written in his reign, about the same time as the astronomical diary of 274 B.C.E.[113]

Line 383 of *Sibylline C* deserves comment. Descent from the god Kronos or association with him could connote gruesome cruelty.[114] In many ancient societies, the children of an intermarriage were illegitimate. Antiochus I was the son of Macedonian Seleucus I and Iranian Apame. Writers of present-future prophecy, without justification, could use derogatory epithets such as "bastards and slaves" to refer to the stock they hated.[115]

Toward the end of his reign, Antiochus I suffered a grievous defeat, so that the conquered peoples could perceive one more instance of Seleucid weakness or even folly. In western Asia Minor, Philetairos had long governed the city of Pergamon and its vicinity, rich in timber and minerals. Philetairos was an apparently loyal subject of the Seleucid king, and, in return, the king accorded him a considerable measure of independence. But Philetairos died in 263 B.C.E., and his nephew and heir, Eumenes I, won complete independence by warring against Antiochos and defeating him near Sardis, thus becoming the first ruler of Pergamon's Attalid dynasty. Soon afterward, in June 261 B.C.E., Antiochus I died, and his son, Antiochus II, became king.[116]

7. The Mixture Marriage (252), the War of Laodice (246–241), and the Mixture Version

ANTIOCHUS II AND PTOLEMY II quickly went to war, and the subject peoples probably viewed their renewal of warfare as folly and could resent the renewal of war taxation. Again we have very little information on this, the "Second" Syrian War, but the Seleucid king appears to have made some gains,[117] though perhaps not enough to offset previous beliefs, held by the subject peoples, that his empire was weak.

In the mid 250s, at the earliest in 255 B.C.E., the two kings saw further fighting as futile. Antiochus's wife, Laodice, had borne him two sons, Seleucus and Antiochus. Nevertheless, King Antiochus demoted Laodice from the position of queen, probably without divorcing her, and in 252 married Berenice, daughter of Ptolemy II. Macedonian kings before him had had plural wives.[118] We infer that Antiochus gave up for the time being his claims to Syria and Palestine.[119] A papyrus letter lets us know that Berenice had been escorted to the border between the two kingdoms just before early March 252, on the way to her marriage.[120] Would there be a lasting peace? Would the Seleucid dynasty be torn by strife? There is evidence that Antiochus tried to buy off Laodice's resentment and that of her sons. A Babylonian clay tablet lets us know that the king gave valuable real estate in Babylonia to Laodice (called "his wife" in the document) and to "their sons," Seleucus and Antiochus.[121] Unfortunately, the tablet does not date the act of giving, and some interpreters[122] have believed that because Laodice is called "wife" the gift preceded her demotion. But living Seleucid kings were not known for making such gifts. Antiochus II must have had a strong motivation for doing so. Even if the real estate transfer came well before the king planned to marry Berenice, it still would suggest that he already had good reason to try to mollify a hostile wife and sons. Whatever the case may have been, Babylonians must have been aware of the dissension in the royal family.

We cannot tell whether Babylonians know of other efforts by the king to win Laodice over. A letter in Greek survives from Antiochus II himself. A copy of it is preserved, somewhat mutilated, on stone at Didyma in western Asia Minor.[123] The letter can be used to strengthen the inference that the king had reason to fear his estranged wife. It was written in 59 Sel., before the spring harvest, as can be determined from its content. As a royal letter, its date must be by the Macedonian Seleucid era, as 254/3 B.C.E. Mutilated contexts make it difficult to find how early in the year the king wrote the letter.[124]

By it, the king sells to Laodice, at a low price, valuable real estate in northwest Asia Minor. Unlike the Babylonian document, here Laodice is not called "wife," and the sons are not mentioned. The fact may be a mere result of marital estrangement; it need not reflect a full divorce. If the king sold the land early in 59 Sel., he acted long before his marriage to Berenice (though that project may have been planned well in advance). The marital troubles could already have existed. The later the letter was written, the more likely it represents an effort to buy off Laodice's resentment of her husband's impending marriage to Berenice. In any case, persons who know of the marital estrangement would perceive one more instance of weakness in the Seleucid dynasty.

Eumenes of Pergamum had inflicted that grievous defeat on Antiochus I, a loss which the empire had not yet made good. There were also great losses in the east. Already Seleucus I had given up parts of his holdings in the Iranian provinces, and under the first two Antiochuses the Seleucid hold on those provinces loosened further, and Babylonians could perceive that the empire was crumbling in that region, though we have scanty evidence for the fact.[125]

Thus, to a Babylonian, the Seleucid Empire in the late reign of Antiochus II looked fragile, whereas the empire & relatively successful Ptolemy II,[126] by comparison, could look strong. Ptolemy II died in January 246 B.C.E., and his son, Ptolemy III, became king.[127]

Antiochus II died at Ephesus in the summer of 246 B.C.E.[128] The bizarre circumstances of his passing seemed to herald for Babylonians the hoped-for collapse of the Seleucid Empire. Although Berenice had borne Antiochus a son, the king had returned queenly rank to Laodice and had restored her sons to favor.[129] Before his death, he probably proclaimed her son Seleucus to be his heir, although one source attributes Seleucus's succession to Laodice's machinations after her husband was dead.[130]

Rumor held, perhaps correctly, that Laodice had the king murdered for fear he would again change his mind and favor Berenice and her son.[131] With two strong-minded queens, each one mother to a possible successor to the throne, each having some support within the kingdom,[132] the already weakened Seleucid Empire was ripe to be torn by civil war. Babylonians could hope that at last it was collapsing.

The war that followed was called "The War of Laodice" (246–241 B.C.E.). Berenice's side had a grievous disadvantage: Their candidate for king was a helpless child. The sources contradict one another, so that we cannot be sure of the course of events. Clearly, both Berenice and her son were murdered. Did she survive long enough to send to her brother, Ptolemy III, for help?[133] Or did the message to him come from her supporters, after she and her son were dead?[134] Whether Ptolemy III aimed at rescuing his nephew and sister or at avenging their deaths, he overran much of the Seleucid Empire but had to withdraw to put down a revolt in Egypt, though he took rich spoils.[135] During the War of Laodice, Andragoras, satrap of Parthyene, seceded from the empire (ca. 245?) and asserted his independence by coining in gold and silver, in his own name, though without giving himself the title "king."[136]

Upon Ptolemy's withdrawal, Seleucus II was able to reconquer or win back the loyalty of most of the Seleucid Empire (but not Parthyene). In 241, Ptolemy III made peace with Seleucus II, despite the murders of his sister and nephew. Of the land he had overrun, he retained some territories in Asia Minor and the important city of Seleukeia in Pieria, port of Antioch.[137] Ptolemy III was indeed the great power of the time, but the Seleucid Empire survived and kept firm hold on Babylon.

During the period in which one could hope the Seleucid Empire was collapsing, between 246 and 241, one of Marduk's faithful added to Daniel 2:41 the words I have italicized, and he also put v 43 into the existing text: "[41] And whereas you saw the feet and the toes, part of *potter's* clay, and part of iron, it will be a divided kingdom; but there will be in it of the firmness of iron, *inasmuch as you saw the iron mixed with miry clay*. . . . [43] And whereas you saw the iron mixed with miry clay, they will mix themselves by the seed of man; but they will not cleave to one another, even as iron does not mix with clay.

We proved earlier that these passages must be supplement.[138] Now let us examine them and their context more closely. The added passages in the interpretation use words not found in the description of the vision, the words *phr* ("potter's") and *tyn'* ("miry"). Inasmuch as the word for "clay" *(hsp)* properly means "baked clay, earthenware," "potters" and "miry" fit badly into the context. But they are required for turning the Four-Plus-Kingdom version into the Mixture version, a prophecy of Berenice's marriage to Antiochus II and of the ensuing war of Laodice. Let us call Berenice's marriage the "Mixture Marriage." Miry potter's clay is gooey and is a good symbol for semen, so as to allude to that marriage. The male partner of the couple did come from the clay Seleucid dynasty! But one who knew the earlier meanings of the text would have recognized the inconsistency of having clay first symbolize brittleness or fragility and then a viscous liquid.

In no way could the Mixture version be a more complete text of the earlier versions. The supplementer did his best to conceal the fact. He reused the device employed by the writer of the Four-Plus-Kingdom versions: Within the last clause of v 41 and at the head of v 43 he placed the words *"dy hzyth* ("just as you saw") to give the (false) impression that *mixture* of iron and clay had been in the vision seen by Nebuchadnezzar.[139]

There were, indeed, later "Mixture Marriages," notably that of Ptolemy V to the Seleucid princess Cleopatra I in 194/3 B.C.E., that of Seleucid pretender Alexander Balas to the Ptolemaic princess Cleopatra Thea in 150, that of Seleucid Demetrius II to the same woman in 145, and that of Seleucid Antiochus VII to the same woman in 138. There is good evidence that Jews of the second century B.C.E. interpreted the Mixture version as applying to one of those marriages.[140]

However, to interpret an already existing prophecy as referring to an event of one's own time is not the same as to compose a new version of a present-future prophecy. We can be sure that the supplements in Daniel 2:41 and 43 were added between 246 and 241 B.C.E. The supplements have to be later than the creation of the Four-Plus-Kingdom version and have to involve one dynasty that looked to be strong and one that looked to be soft or fragile; the Mixture Marriage has to prove to be a failure; the ensuing events have to look promising to those Jews or those Babylonians who were hoping for the fall of the Ptolemaic or Seleucid Empire, so much so that they undertook the risky procedure of supplementing a present-future prophecy. The marriage of Antiochus II and Berenice and the ensuing War of Laodice fulfill all these conditions.[141]

A royal "mixture by the seed of man" can be said to have succeeded if an offspring of that marriage inherits the rule of his father's kingdom. By that criterion, the marriage of Ptolemy V and Cleopatra I was not a failure. It ended only with the natural death of Ptolemy (in 180), and Cleopatra lived on until 176 as the regent for their young son, Ptolemy VI. The Seleucid princess, Cleopatra I, thus could be said to have cleaved to the Ptolemaic dynasty.[142]

From the time Cleopatra Thea married Alexander Balas, she stayed within the Seleucid Empire. With each of her three husbands she had the status of Seleucid queen. She thus cleaved to the Seleucid Empire, and sons by each of her husbands reigned over the kingdom: Antiochus VI, son by Alexander Balas (145–142/1); Antiochus VIII, by Demetrius II (125–96); and Antiochus IX, by Antiochus VII (115–95).[143] By that criterion, the marriages were not failures. We need not consider later marriages between the Seleucids and the Ptolemies, because, after the death of Cleopatra Thea, neither dynasty was a great power so as to be ranked with the empires in Daniel 2.

Difficulties still confront us in the extant text of Daniel 2:40–43. We have called attention to the falsehood[144] in 2:40: The fourth kingdom (Alexander's) crushed and shattered only the Persian kingdom, not a Babylonian or a Median one. Indeed, Alexander did little or no damage to the Babylonians and the Medes. The kingdom that inflicted grave damage upon the conquered peoples through internecine warfare was the divided kingdom of the Diadochoi. The Diadochoi were also responsible for breaking up the empire of Alexander. There is another strange aspect in Daniel 2:40–43: The middle of 2:40 is oddly repetitious in content ("just as iron crushes and smashes everything, and like iron that shatters"), and the first clause of 2:43 repeats the last clause of 2:41 almost verbatim. There is good reason to blame the creator of the Mixture version for most if not all of these peculiarities.

From the extant text of Daniel 2:40–43, one can reconstruct how the author of the Four-Plus-Kingdom version, before the author of the Mixture version went to work, probably described Alexander's empire and the divided kingdom of the Diadochoi in a text with none of the aforementioned difficulties. Let us proceed with the reconstruction and consider whether the creator of the Mixture version would have felt a need to bring those difficulties into the text.

In the Four-Plus-Kingdom version, vv 40–42 could have read as follows:

40a And there will be a fourth kingdom, as strong as iron.

41a Inasmuch as you saw lower legs and toes partly of clay[145] and partly of iron, there will be a divided kingdom.

42   The fact that the toes were partly iron and partly clay means that part of the kingdom will be strong and part of it will be fragile.

41b   some of the firmness of iron will be in it.

40b–c   Just as iron crushes and smashes everything, (and like iron
that shatters), it will crush and shatter all these others.

This text would predict both how the Diadochoi broke up Alexander's empire and the grave damage they inflicted upon the conquered peoples, and
would not tell a falsehood about Alexander. I have enclosed "and like iron that
shatters" in parentheses because it is awkward in the context and was probably
added by someone who saw the verb "shatter" near the end of the sentence and
wanted to have it present also in the description of iron. The creator of the Mixture version may have been that person.

One might have thought that to turn this reconstructed text into the Mixture
version one would have only to append Daniel 2:43: "Inasmuch as you saw the
iron mixed with miry clay, they will mix themselves by means of the seed of
man, but they will not cleave to one another, even as iron does not mix with
clay." But there would then be some awkward circumstances. First, the description of the vision contains no reference to mixture and none to plastic clay.
The supplementer coped with that problem by adding the Aramaic for
"potter's" in v 41a, which already had "inasmuch as you saw" *(wdy hzyth)* at its
head in the Four-Plus-Kingdom version, and by adding "inasmuch as you saw
the iron mixed with miry clay" at the end of v 41. It was better to be prompt in
connecting mixture with the dream. The repetition at the beginning of v 43
could be taken as directing the mind of the reader to the interpretation of mixture. As for the words which I have enclosed in parentheses in v 40b–c, they
probably do not go back to the supplementer but to a later reader, who saw the
verb "shatter" *(r⁽⁽)* at the end of v 40 and thought it should appear also in the
description of iron earlier in the verse.

Another awkward circumstance lay in the disproportion in the the words allotted to the predicted kingdoms. In the Aramaic of Daniel 2:37–39 plus our
reconstructed text of vv 40–42 plus verse 43, thirty-one words are devoted to
Nebuchadnezzar (properly: the prophecy is addressed to him); six words, to
the second kingdom; nine words, to the third; five words, to the fourth; and
sixty-eight words,[146] to the divided kingdom. The disproportion is striking.
Furthermore, the divided kingdom is characterized by disunity, by destructiveness and by the Mixture Marriage, whereas the supplementer's attention is focused on disunity and mixture. By moving 40b–c to its present position, where
it refers to Alexander, the creator of the Mixture version could add fourteen
words[147] to the five words of the prediction on the fourth kingdom and leave
the divided kingdom with only fifty-four; also, destructiveness thus is made to

characterize Alexander's empire, leaving disunity and mixture to characterize the divided kingdom. By the middle of the third century B.C.E., a Babylonian or Jewish author could have been sufficiently ignorant of Alexander's gentle treatment of Babylon and Judea to commit such a falsehood. Even in the Four-Plus-Kingdom version, Alexander's empire had been included among the evil kingdoms. We thus have an explanation of how the creator of the Mixture version could have been impelled to modify the text which we have reconstructed and thus could have produced the present version of Daniel 2:40–42. The present version of Daniel 2:37–45 is indeed the Mixture version. There is no reason to think that later hands supplemented the text further.

The author of the Mixture supplement is unlikely to have been a Jew of Judea. Whereas the Babylonians between 246 and 241 B.C.E. lived under the tottering Seleucid Empire, the Jews of Judea lived under the increasingly solid Ptolemaic Empire, with peace in their local area; we have no sign of Jewish protest from this period. Jews probably resented being under the rule of exploiting foreigners, but Jews still believed that under the Ptolemies they were serving out God's sentence upon them.

However, soon after the Mixture version was published by Babylonians, Jews of Babylonia and even Jews of Judea could and did assume it was a more complete text of the revelation by their Daniel. We shall soon find evidence that a Jew of the third century B.C.E. believed the Mixture version and acted upon his belief. Zoroastrians could draw upon it, too. Zoroastrians used it to bring the mixture idea into the *Sudgar Nask* and the *Prophetic Zand* and probably did so promptly, still believing that the Babylonians had plagiarized the prophecy from a Zoroastrian text.

Were the Zoroastrians sloppy in revising their own texts? First, let us take note of the fact that, whereas the Babylonian Mixture version had a fourth kingdom of iron and a fifth (but unnumbered) kingdom of iron mixed with clay, the Zoroastrian versions have only an iron-mixed period and none of only iron. Alexander was indeed cruelly destructive to Iranians, so Daniel 2:40 for them fit Alexander, and they may have felt no need to distinguish the fourth period from the unnumbered divided kingdom by giving them separate symbols: The kings of the two periods were equally Macedonian and non-Iranian.

Second, let us also take note of the fact that in the Zoroastrian texts nothing identifies the substance with which the iron was mixed. It is possible that a word like "clay" fell out of the passages, but could the word have fallen out of all three texts (the *Sudgar Nask* and the Four-Branch and Seven-Branch Versions of the *Prophetic Zand*)? Furthermore, the supplementer in Daniel 2:43 carefully explains what mixture symbolizes. In all the prolix verses of the

Prophetic Zand there is no such explanation. What purposes did the mixture-idea serve for Iranians in the mid-third century B.C.E.? It gave them a recent event after which they could look forward to the collapse of the Seleucid Empire. It also enabled them to claim again that Bêl-Balâṭsu-uṣur plagiarized from a prophecy of Zarathushtra.

The Mixture version of the *Prophetic Zand* is evidence that at least some Zoroastrians in or after the mid-third century believed their age still belonged to evil Ahriman and were so eager for the Seleucid Empire to collapse that they took the risky step of supplementing a present-future prophecy. Present-future prophecies tend to be produced or supplemented in times of dire adversity or in times when adversity seems to be passing away. The forecasts in such prophecies usually would offend the power responsible for the adversity, so that the author or supplementer would have to believe that the good results of his prediction outweighed the risks.

The *Prophetic Zand* spoke of dire tokens of the evil mixed-iron period, including burning, great depopulation, misrule, and religious incompatibility with the rulers from the race of wrath.[148] Iranians probably could remember such facts from the reign of Alexander and the wars of his first successors. But in the years between 246 and 241 B.C.E. and following, it is at least doubtful that Iranians felt they were suffering grave adversity in the present. Rather, it is likely that the supplementer who put mixture into the *Prophetic Zand* believed that the adversity brought upon them by the Macedonians had begun to pass away, even though the liberating heroes, Peshyotanu and Hushedar, had not yet made their appearance.

Indeed, we can tell that Seleucid rule was not terribly burdensome and had some advantages for the Iranian subjects of the empire, though the sources on Iran in the third century B.C.E. are scarce, fragmentary, and often unreliable. One factor lightening the burden was the fact that already Seleucus I moved the chief royal residence from Seleukeia-on-the-Tigris to Antioch-on-the-Orontes, a point too far away for exercising close supervision of Iran,[149] even when the monarchs in Antioch delegated sweeping authority to the crown prince or to other officials overseeing the East. The Seleucid kings usually focused their attention and military resources upon their conflicts with the Ptolemies and upon their interests in Asia Minor. Antiochus I was half Iranian himself. Except for the persecution of the Jews by Antiochus IV, no member of the dynasty interfered with religion.[150] Furthermore, the Seleucids had some successes in protecting their Iranian subjects from the predatory raiders coming out of central Asia.[151]

In the mid-third century B.C.E., the symbolism of the Mixture version must have been transparent. Believers surely expected that the Seleucid and Ptolemaic dynasties would be smashed shortly after the end of the War of Laodice. Nothing of the kind happened. But the events of the next decades nevertheless encouraged belief in the Mixture version and belief that adversity was passing away. The Seleucid Empire was torn by civil war (241?–239? and 227) between Seleucus II and his brother, Antiochus Hierax; and Attalos I, king of Pergamon, conquered Seleucid Asia Minor (238?–227).[152] Diodotos, satrap of Baktria, took advantage of this internecine strife, seceded from the Seleucid Empire, coined in silver in his own name, and made himself king (239 or 238).[153] A reason for his secession may well have been the fact that the Seleucid kings were too far away and too interested in western affairs to give sufficient attention to the menaces from central Asia. Diodotos and his Macedonian or Greek successors, like the Seleucids, belonged to the period of iron but were equally unburdensome to their Iranian subjects.

A group of marauders from central Asia entered Parthyene (a region claimed as their own by the Seleucids), asserted independence, and eventually gave rise to the Arsakid dynasty and its Parthian Empire. The sources on these people are unsatisfactory and often contradict one another. The official era of the dynasty numbered the years from 247 B.C.E., a date too early to be credible. At any rate, the group entered Parthyene around the times of the War of Laodice and the War of the Seleucid Brothers, after 247 and at the latest in 238. They defeated and killed Andragoras, who had been ruling there. The Arsakid dynasty probably was Zoroastrian from the beginning of its rule but also for decades preyed upon its neighbors and probably was at first disliked by civilized Iranians. Seleucus II fought the Parthian kingdom but desisted in order to deal with problems in Asia Minor.[154]

Another set of factors could suggest to the conquered peoples, especially the Iranians, that the Divided Empire was crumbling. Independent states, some ruled by Iranian dynasties, arose within the territories that had been claimed by Alexander. We have mentioned the kingdom of Pergamon, ruled by the non-Iranian Attalid dynasty. Bithynia, in northwestern Asia Minor, was an independent kingdom from 297/6 B.C.E.[155] under an originally Thracian dynasty. In northeastern Asia Minor a dynasty of Persian descent ruled Pontic Cappadocia (often called simply "Pontus") from ca. 302. In east-central Asia Minor Ariarathes III, a member of a dynasty of Iranian descent which had long governed Cappadocia, asserted his independence and took the title "king" in 255 and married the daughter of Antiochus II.[156]

Atropates had governed Media during the reign of Darius III. Alexander appointed Oxydates in Atropates's place but came to distrust Oxydates and reinstated Atropates (328/7), who served the conqueror well. After Alexander's death, Atropates was left in control of only northwestern Media, which came to be called, after him, "Media Atropatene" (now Azerbaijan). Atropates soon became the independent ruler of his province and took the title "king." He founded a dynasty, the Atropatids, which ruled practically independent Atropatene for several centuries.[157] Neither Atropates nor his successors issued coins.[158] The founder and his dynasty were probably active Zoroastrians.[159]

Can the rulers of Persis, the core area for the Zoroastrian Persians, also have asserted independence in the middle of the third century B.C.E.? If they had, how could Iranians have brought the mixture idea into the *Prophetic Zand?* Misrule of Persis by non-Iranians would have been a thing of the past!

There is evidence of such assertive rulers of Persis, but it consists almost solely of silver coins.[160] They bear Zoroastrian and Achaemenid motifs.[161] On some of the coins, the name of the ruler is Achaemenid, as well (Artaxerxes,[162] Darius); all the names of the dynasts are Persian. The first four of these dynasts appear on their coins with the title *prtrk' zy 'lhy'* (*"frataraka* of the gods"[?]). *Frataraka* probably means "deputy" or "governor."[163] From the sixth ruler on, the title becomes *mlk* ("king"). If a legend appears on these coins, it is not in Greek (the official language of the Seleucid Empire) but in Aramaic (the official language of the old Persian Empire) or in Aramaic intended to be read off in Persian, as was Iranian practice.

Coinage in silver was already an assertion of at least a measure of independence, and all the more so was the title *mlk,* though there is evidence that the Persian rulers recognized the overlordship of the Seleucids and later, of the Parthians.[164] It has been extremely difficult to date the coins. Wiesehöfer would put them well inside the second century B.C.E., beginning about the time of Antiochus IV (175–164).[165]

No one hitherto has used the evidence of the Mixture version of the *Prophetic Zand.* The coins must be later than that version. This inference leaves the date imprecise; we shall find a later present-future prophecy helpful.

8. Events Affecting the Jews and the Babylonians, 238–223 B.C.E.

NEITHER THE JEWS nor the Babylonians rose in revolt during those years. Babylonian astronomical diaries of 238 and 235 B.C.E.[166] have been interpreted to mean that "Between 238 and 235 some kind of serious military revolt was taking place, one of the centres being Babylon."[167] But the diaries testify only to brief uprisings of *soldiers,* which do not even extend into the following month, and Babylonians are rarely found in the Hellenistic armies.[168]

After reigning some twenty years, Seleucus II died as a result of a fall from his horse (in 226), and his young son, Seleucus III, ruled only three years before being murdered by one of his officers (in 223).[169] Indeed, Babylonians, Jews, and Zoroastrians were surely disappointed by the delay in the fulfillment of the Mixture version, but they probably had little difficulty believing in it until well into the reign of Antiochus III (223–187), the vigorous younger son of Seleucus II. It is likely that no one who wished to predict the fall of the Seleucid Empire thought of again supplementing the prophecy of Daniel 2. It would have been difficult to symbolize the events of 241–227 (and after). Furthermore, yet another revision of the already twice-supplemented prophecy would have severely strained the credulity of the "predictor's" audience.

The Jews of Judea still were living under the Ptolemaic Empire. The Mixture version promised the fall of both the Seleucids and the Ptolemies (Dan 2:24). The high priest of the Jews, Onias II, seems to have believed, around 227 B.C.E., that fulfillment of the prophecy was imminent, that both Seleucus II and Ptolemy III were doomed. Therefore, he refused to pay to Ptolemy III the required twenty talents of his own income on behalf of the people, much to the people's consternation.[170]

NOTES

1 Alexander's consideration for the conquered was often remarkable among conquerors; see N. G. L. Hammond, *The Macedonian State* (Oxford: Oxford University Press, 1989), 205–8, 217–26. Nevertheless, he and his army were predators. See M. I. Rostovtzeff, *The Social and Economic History of the Hellenistic World* (2d ed.; 3 vols.; Oxford: Clarendon Press, 1952), I, 129–30.

2 Ibid., 165 and 168.

3 The history of the *Diadochi* and the wars among them is a complicated topic, to which I can contribute little or nothing. I intend to provide from that history only that minimum which is necessary for understanding my own project, the histories of the *peoples of an almighty god* and their literatures in the time of those rulers. For general treatments, see Peter Green, *Alexander to Actium: the Historical Evolution of the Hellenistic Age* (2d printing; Berkeley and Los Angeles: University of California Press, 1993); Édouard Will, *Histoire politique du Monde hellénistique (323–30 av. J.-C.)* (2 vols.; 2d ed.; Nancy: Presses universitaires de Nancy, 1982); CAH², Vol. VII, Part I (1984): *The Hellenistic World*, ed. F. W. Walbank, A. E. Astin, M. W. Frederiksen, and R. M. Ogilvie, esp. chaps 1–6, 11.

Succession within the male line: Hammond, *State*, 16–17, 71–76.

4   Will, *Histoire*, I, 20–21; Green, *Alexander to Actium*, 3–8.

5   On the factors driving the *Diadochoi* to fight each other and to inflict suffering on the subject peoples, see also Rostovtzeff, SEHHW, I, 135–42.

6   See Josef Wiesehöfer, *Die 'dunklen Jahrhunderte' der Persis* ("Zetemata," Heft 90; München: C. H. Beck, 1994), 50–55.

7   Antigonus is accused by writers ancient (e.g., Diodorus xviii.50.2; xxi.1.1–2) and modern of intemperately aiming to conquer all of Alexander's empire for himself. Against this view, see Richard A. Billows, *Antigonos the One-Eyed and the Creation of the Hellenistic State* (Berkeley, Los Angeles, and London: University of California Press, 1990).

8   Diodorus xviii.3.3.

9   Arrian *The Successors of Alexander (Hoi met' Alexandron)* 24.3–7, published in *Arrianos: Quae extant omnia*, ed. A. G. Roos (2 vols.; 2d ed.; Leipzig: Teubner, 1967–68), Vol. II; see Andreas Mehl, *Seleukos Nikator und sein Reich* ("Studia Hellenistica," ed. W. Peremans, 28; Leuven, 1986), 39–40.

10   Babylonian Chronicle 10, obverse, lines 5–6 (*ABC*, 115–16); Mehl, *Seleukos*, 40.

11   Diodorus xviii.73.3; Mehl, *Seleukos*, 44 (corrects the date implied by Diodorus).

12   Eumenes's winter quarters in 318/7: Diodorus xix.12.1. Capture of the palace: Chronicle 10, obverse, lines 14–15; Mehl, *Seleukos*, 43–49. Fall of Eumenes: Diodorus xix.39–44. Seleucus's difficulties with Antigonus: Mehl, *Seleukos*, 50–52, Diodorus xix.55.5. Doubts that Chronicle 10 attests Eumenes's possession at this time of any part of Babylon: John D. Grainger, *Seleukos Nikator* (London and New York: Routledge, 1990), 38–39.

13   Diodorus xix.55.5; Mehl, *Seleukos*, 52–62.

14   Diodorus xix.56.4, 69.1, 85.2; Mehl, *Seleukos*, 85, 89.

15   Diodorus xix.81–85.

16   Diodorus xix.90–91, Appian *Syriakê* (ix.)54.273–74, Mehl, *Seleukos*, 89–103. Those priests of Marduk who had uttered prophecy in 315, warning Antigonus not to let Seleucus escape (Diodorus xix.55.7–9), probably opposed Seleucus's return (Mehl, *Seleukos*, 64–68, 90).

17   Diodorus xix.90.1, 91.1; Mehl, *Seleukos*, 41–42.

18 Surely Seleucus's son, Antiochus I, bore those titles. See Elias J. Bickerman, "Notes on Seleucid and Parthian Chronology," *Berytos* 8, Fasc. 2 (1944), 75, nn 16–17.

19 Eddy, *King,* 114.

20 Diodorus xix.92; Mehl, *Seleukos,* 107–10, 118.

21 Diodorus xix.100.4–7; Plutarch *Demetrius* 7; Mehl, *Seleukos,* 112–15, 118 (chronology). Chronicle 10 on those years is too mutilated to add anything to this picture of Babylonian suffering.

22 Ptolemy violated his peace with Antigonus in early spring, 310 (Diodorus xx.19.3–4; Green, *Alexander to Actium,* 139). Kassandros early in 310 made an alliance with Polemaios (= Ptolemaios), Antigonus's rebellious nephew (Diodorus xx.19.2; Green, *Alexander to Actium,* 140).

23 See Mehl, *Seleukos,* 120–28.

24 Polyainos iv.9.1; Mehl, *Seleukos,* 129–30.

25 See Mehl, *Seleukos,* 130–34.

26 Shortly after the battle of Ipsos: See Robert A. Hadley, "The Foundation Date of Seleucia on the Tigris," *Historia* 27 (1978), 228–30. Pliny: *Natural History* vi.122; cf. Pausanias i.16.3.

27 Appian *Syriakê* ix.58.300–7.

28 Forecasts of downfall of Seleukeia: See Theophilus G. Pinches, *The Old Testament in the Light of the Historical Records of Assyria and Babylonia* (2d ed.; London: Society for Promoting Christian Knowledge, 1903), 477; cf. Eddy, *King,* 115–16.

29 Mehl, *Seleukos,* 196–99.

30 Arrian vii.4.6.

31 W. W. Tarn, "Queen Ptolemais and Apama," *Classical Quarterly* 23 (1929), 139–41.

32 Diodorus xix.12.3.–44.3; Billows, *Antigonos,* 89–104.

33 Justin xv.4.11; Mehl, *Seleukos,* 134–37, 166–68; Ludwig Schober, *Untersuchungen zur Geschichte Babyloniens und der Oberen Satrapien von 323–303 v. Chr.* (Frankfurt am Main and Bern: Peter D. Lang, 1981), 147–51.

34 Mehl, *Seleukos,* 166–86.

35 Appointment: Diodorus xviii.3.1; on Syria, see Diodorus xviii.6.3.

36 Diodorus xviii.39.6.

37 Diodorus xviii.43.1; *Marmor Parium,* FGH 239 B, F 12.

38 Diodorus xviii.63.6.

39 Implied by Diodorus xviii.58.1, 61.5.

40 Diodorus xix.59.2, xviii.61.5.

41 Diodorus xix.85.4.

42 Diodorus xix.93.7.

43 Billows, *Antigonos,* 158–59; cf. Green, *Alexander to Actium,* 30–31 and 748, n. 56.

44 On Koilê Syria, see my article, "The Message of Aristeas to Philokrates," in *Eretz Israel, Israel, and the Jewish Diaspora: Mutual Relations,* ed. Menachem Mor (Lanham, New York, and London: University Press of America, 1991), 19, n 12.

45 Diodorus xx.113.1–2.

46 Plutarch *Demetrius* 32.

47 Capture on the Sabbath: Agatharchides *apud* Josephus *Against Apion* i.22.209–11; *Antiquities* xii.1.1.6. Deportation: *Aristeas to Philokrates* 12–14.

48 Diodorus xx.113.1.

49 Diodorus xxi.1.5.

50 Plutarch *Demetrius* 32.

51 Probably, the undated episode narrated at Appian *Syriakê* 50.252 also belongs to Ptolemy's capture of Jerusalem in 301.

52 See below, on *Sibylline Oracles* iii.382.

53 See the works cited in n 3.

54 See Billows, *Antigonus,* 108–34.

55 See ibid., 162–64.

56 Billows, *Antigonus,* 169–73.

57 Ibid., 173–74.

58 Diodorus, xx.106.2–3. Diodorus there attests to Lysimachos's friendship and help. There is no record of a battle between forces of Lysimachos and Antigonus before 302, but Lysimachos had shown where his sympathies lay in 314–311 and later (see Diodorus xx.96.3, 100.2).

59 Diodorus xx.106.3–5.

60 Diodorus xx.107.1.

61 Diodorus xx.107.2–5.

62 Diodorus xx.108.1–3.

63 Diodorus xx.108.4—109.3.

64 Plutarch *Demetrius* 29.3–5.

65 Ibid., 30–52.

66 Diodorus xxi.1.5; Will, *Histoire,* I, 80, 82–83.

67 See Hartman and Di Lella, *Daniel,* 141.

68 xviii.3.

69 xviii.39.5–6.

70 See above, pp. 368–70.

71 Billows, *Antigonos,* 82–83, 198, 206, 238–39.

72 See above, pp. 363–68.

73 Seleucus: See Élie Bikerman (= Elias Bickerman), *Institutions des Séleucides* (Paris: Geuthner, 1938), 5, 7. For Berossus, the Babylonian historian who wrote in Greek, Antiochus I (son of Seleucus I) was the third king after Alexander and thus

was the direct and legitimate heir of Alexander IV (see Tatian, *Against the Greeks* 36.2).

Ptolemy: Pierre Briant, *Antigone le Borgne* (Paris: Les Belles lettres, 1973), 21, and ibid., n 8; W. W. Tarn, "The Lineage of Ptolemy I," *Journal of Hellenic Studies* 53 (1933), 57–61. Contrast A. Bouché-Leclercq, *Histoire des Lagides* (4 vols.; Paris: E. Leroux, 1903–7), III (1906), 26.

Antigonus: Polybius v.10.10.

Lysimachos: see Geyer, "Lysimachos 1," *RE,* XIV (1930), 1.

74 Daniel 11:4: ". . . His kingdom will be broken up and divided toward the four winds of the heavens, but not among his descendants or in keeping with the domain over which he ruled; for his kingdom will be torn asunder for others, rather than for these."

75 On Berossus, see n 73; the Babylonian king list of the Hellenistic period in the British Museum has Seleucus I as the direct successor of Alexander IV (A. J. Sachs and D. J. Wiseman, "A Babylonian King List of the Hellenistic Period," *Iraq* 16 [1954], 202–5).

76 For what dynastic marriages there were, down to the aftermath of the battle of Ipsos, see Green, *Alexander to Actium,* 12, 15, 26, 120–22, 763–64, n 10; and Hermann Bengtson, *Die Diadochen* (München: C. H. Beck, 1987), 77.

77 See pp. 383–92.

78 Jews: pp. 290–93; Babylonians: pp. 293–97; Persians and Medes: pp. 297–301.

79 See pp. 383–92.

80 See p. 368.

81 See chap 11, pp. 331–41.

82 See George W. E. Nickelsburg, "Apocalyptic and Myth in *1 Enoch* 6–11," *JBL* 96 (1977), 383–405.

83 Cf. Gen 6:1–6.

84 Nickelsburg, "Apocalyptic and Myth" *JBL* 96 (1977), 383–86.

85 Raphael's task (curing the earth) should reflect his name ("God has cured"): Shemiḥazah and his followers have brought sin and disease upon the world.

86 Similarly, Gabriel's task of bringing destruction upon the giants befits his name ("God's manly hero").

87 See Nickelsburg, ibid., 396, n 61. Nickelsburg was not so sure of the moral of the story (ibid., 397, n 62).

88 In *1 Enoch* 8:3, other angels, all likewise taken from the list in 6:7, including Shemiḥazah himself, teach mankind various types of magic and divination. Such information, it is assumed, should not have been revealed to mortals. The text of *1 Enoch* does allude to their sinful teachings in 9:8 and 10:7, but those other angels, unlike ʿAsaʾel, are not singled out for punishment. The author of 8:3 probably wrote the verse (and the allusions in 9:8 and 10:7) to smooth the linkage of the story of Shemiḥazah with the tale of ʿAsaʾel. Again, that author may have been the interpolator.

89 Two scholars have amply demonstrated this point: Helge Kvanvig, *The Mesopotamian Background of the Enoch Figure* ("Roots of Apocalyptic," vol. I; Oslo: Skrivestua, Det teologiske Menighetsfakultet, 1983); and James VanderKam, *Enoch and the Growth of an Apocalyptic Tradition* (The Catholic Biblical Quarterly Monograph Series," 16; Washington, DC: The Catholic Biblical Association of America, 1984) esp. 8, 15, 38–75, 141, 188–90.

90 *ANET,* 317.

91 Will, *Histoire,* I, 101–3.

92 See p. 341.

93 Susan Sherwin-White and Amélie Kuhrt (*From Samarkhand to Sardis* [London: Duckworth, 1993]) have labored to demonstrate the real strengths of the Seleucid Empire. Here we are not concerned with real strengths, but with what Babylonians believed.

94 See my *I Maccabees,* 22–25, 544, and William W. Hallo, "The Concept of Eras from Nabonassar to Seleucus," *Journal of the Ancient Near Eastern Society* 16–17 (1984–85), 143–47.

95 Antiochus I loses territory to Ptolemy II: Will, *Histoire,* I, 140–41; H. Heinen, "The Syrian-Egyptian Wars and the New Kingdoms of Asia Minor," chap xi of CAH[2], Vol. VII, Part I, 415–16. Magas's marriage and war on Ptolemy: Pausanias i.7.1, 3; François Chamoux, "Le Roi Magas," *Revue historique* 216 (1956), 21, 29. Magas takes the royal title: Chamoux, ibid., 26–27; Athenaeus xii.550b; Justin xxvi.2.

96 Pausanias i.7.1–3; Heinen in CAH[2], Vol. VII, Part I, 416.

97   Heinen, ibid.

98   Will, *Histoire,* I, 146–48; Green, *Alexander to Actium,* 146; Heinen in CAH², Vol. II, Part I, 416. Some scholars have taken a passage in the Pithom Stele to mean that Ptolemy II in the course of the war sent an expedition to the Persian Gulf, and Will wrongly conceded the possibility of their theory. See David Lorton, "The Supposed Expedition of Ptolemy II to Persia," *JEA* 57 (1971), 160–64.

99   Heinen, ibid.; Will, *Histoire,* I, 147, 150; Green, *Alexander to Actium,* 146.

100   Will, *Histoire,* I, 143–44; Green, *Alexander to Actium,* 140.

101   On astronomical diaries, see chap 2, pp. 45–46. The diary treating the observations and events of 274/3 B.C.E. is no. –273 in Abraham J. Sachs, *Astronomical Diaries and Related Texts from Babylonia* (completed and ed. Hermann Hunger; Wien: Verlag der Österriechischen Akademie der Wissenschaften, 1988–). On that diary see the comments of R. J. van der Spek, "The Astronomical Diaries as a source for Achaemenid and Seleucid History," *Bibliotheca Orientalis* 50 (1993), 97–99.

102   See the translation of Sidney Smith, *Babylonian Historical Texts,* 156 (to line 14) and his note to *murṣu ikkitum* on 158.

103   Cf. van der Spek, "Diaries," *Bibliotheca Orientalis* 50 (1993), 98–99.

104   "Diaries," *Bibliotheca Orientalis,* 50 (1993), 98.

105   Cf. the situation reflected at 2 Macc 11:30–33, and see my *II Maccabees* ("Anchor Bible," vol. 41A; Garden City, NY: Doubleday, 1983), 418–19. In the passage of 2 Maccabees, Menelaus is parallel to the satrap and the appointees in the diary, and a decree of Antiochus V, to subjects expectantly awaiting an answer to a petition, is enforceable within three days. The appointees, if they bear a petition from the Babylonians, are probably Babylonians themselves. See the description of the office of *epistatês,* in Bikerman, *Institutions,* 163. Bikerman there ignored the existence of an *epistatês* at Babylon (see Wilhelm Dittenberger, *Orientis Graeci Inscriptiones Selectae* [Leipzig: Hirzel, 1903–5], no. 254).

106   Van der Spek ("Diaries," *Bibliotheca Orientalis* 50 [1993], 99) gives good reasons for reading "Borsippa" instead of "Nippur."

107   Cf. van der Spek, "Diaries," *Bibliotheca Orientalis* 50 (1993), 99.

108   Will, *Histoire,* I, 150–51.

109   The translations which give here "capture" or "conquer" instead of "rebuild" are the result of Badt's conjectural emendation of the reading of the manuscripts. In a context of woe brought from Europe to Asia, scribes would tend to think of Alexander, and would be much more likely to turn "will rebuild" *(dedomêset')* into "will capture" *(dedamêset')* than vice versa.

110   See pp. 302–3. "No texts or remains testifying to the activity of Alexander [in rebuilding Esagila] . . . have been found, and the reconstruction by Alexander is not mentioned by the excavators in their report" (Rostovtzeff, SEHHW, III, 1427, n 34).

111   See chap 10, pp. 301–13, and chap 11, p. 348.

112   Babylonian Chronicle 10.

113   Cf. Eddy, *King,* 127.

114   See Herbert J. Rose and Herbert W. Parke, "Kronos," *Oxford Classical Dictionary,* ed. N. G. L. Hammond and H. H. Scullard (2d ed.; Oxford: Clarendon Press, 1970), 574; Wolfgang Fauth, "Kronos," *Der Kleine Pauly,* III (1969), 359, 363.

115   Compare the use of "slaves" at *Testament of Moses* 5:5, to refer to the high priest Onias-Menelaus, a member of the legitimate priestly clan Bilgah.

116   Will, *Histoire,* I, 151–52.

117   See ibid., I, 234–43.

118   Notably, Philip II and Alexander the Great.

119   Ibid., 239–40. No ancient source says that there was a divorce (contrast Green, *Alexander to Actium,* 148; Will, *Histoire,* I, 239, 242). Rather, texts assert that henceforth Antiochus had two wives and that Laodice had inferior status (Jerome, *In Danielem* III, to Daniel 11:6; Polyainos viii.50; Appian *Syriakê* 65.345. However, a letter of Antiochus II, of 254/3 B.C.E., mentions Laodice *without* calling her "queen" or even "wife" (C. Bradford Welles, *Royal Correspondence in the Hellenistic Period* [New Haven: Yale University Press, 1934], no. 18).

120   Friedrich Bilabel, *Sammelbuch griechischer Urkunden aus Ägypten,* Vol. III (Berlin and Leipzig: Walter de Gruyter, 1926), no. 6748; for the calendar equivalent, see Elias Bickerman, *Chronology of the Ancient World* (Ithaca: Cornell University Press, 1968), 50.

121 C. F. Lehmann, "Sprechsaal," *Zeitschrift für Assyriologie und verwandte Gebiete* 7 (1892), 330–32; B. Haussoulier, "Les Séleucides et le temple d'Apollon didymien," *Revue de philologie, de littérature et d'histoire anciennes* 25 (1901), 18–19.

122 E.g., Hans Volkmann, "Laodike 3," *Der kleine Pauly,* III (1969), 480.

123 C. Bradford Welles, *Correspondence,* no. 18; Albert Rehm, *Die Inschriften,* Part II of Theodor Wiegand, *Didyma* (2 parts in 4 volumes; Berlin: Verlag Gebr. Mann, 1941–58), no. 492.

124 See Welles, *Correspondence,* 95–96, and (especially) Rehm, *Inschriften,* 294–95.

125 See Domenico Musti, "Syria and the East," chap vi of CAH², Vol. VII, Part I, 210–20; Will *Histoire,* I, 263–90.

126 See ibid., I, 244.

127 Will, *Histoire,* I, 243–44.

128 Date: A. J. Sachs and D. J. Wiseman, "A Babylonian King List of the Hellenistic Period," *Iraq* 16 (1954), 206. Ephesus: Porphyry, *FGH* 260, F 32.6.

129 Jerome *In Danielem* iii, to Daniel 11:6.

130 Probably proclaimed: Polyainos viii.50. According to Jerome (*In Danielem* iii, to Dan 11:6), Laodice, after having Antiochus II murdered, established Seleucus as king.

131 Jerome, ibid.; cf. Phylarchus *apud* Athenaeus xiii.593c–d; Appian *Syriakê* 65.345. See Will *Histoire,* I, 249.

132 Will, *Histoire,* I, 250; Polyainos viii. 50.

133 Probably implied by Justin xxvii.1, which says that Ptolemy III acted *"periculo sororis exterritus."* ("frightened by the danger to which his sister was exposed").

134 Polyainos viii.50.

135 On the murders of Berenice and her son and on the invasion, see Will, *Histoire,* I, 250–54.

136 Will, *Histoire,* I, 281–82, 286–87. Normally, in the Seleucid Empire, coinage in one's own name and in silver or gold was a prerogative of the kings. If a subject person or area coined in silver, it was a mark of independence or near-independence; see Bikerman, *Institutions,* 235.

137 Will, *Histoire,* I, 254–61.

138 See p. 375.

139 See sec 5, p. 373.

140 See my *I Maccabees* ("Anchor Bible," vol. 41; Garden City, NY: Doubleday, 1976), 415.

141 The present-future prophecy in Daniel 11 in vv 6–9 "predicts" the failure of the Mixture Marriage and "foretells" the War of Laodice. The passage should be read as in Hartman and Di Lella, *Daniel,* 257. In Dan 11:6, *lqṣ šnym* may mean that the Mixture Marriage (252 B.C.E.) occurred forty-nine years after the Battle of Ipsos (301), forty-nine years being the period prescribed by Lev 25:8.

142 See Hans Volkmann, "Kleopatra 4," *Der kleine Pauly,* III (1969), 247–48.

143 On Cleopatra Thea, see Edwyn R. Bevan, *The House of Seleucus* (London: Edward Arnold, 1902), II, 212, 220, 233, 237, 248–52; Hans Volkmann, "Kleopatra 14," *Der kleine Pauly,* III (1969), 250.

144 Above, sec 5, p. 376.

145 The Aramaic word translated as "potter's" belongs to the Mixture version, as we stated eight paragraphs ago.

146 Sixty-five, if the parenthesized words in the reconstruction are to be regarded as a later interpolation.

147 Eleven, if the parenthesized words in the reconstruction are to be regarded as a later interpolation.

148 See p. 338.

149 See Bickerman in CHI, III, 4–5; Will, *Histoire,* I, 264.

150 Bickerman in CHI, III, 12–18.

151 Bickerman, ibid., 5–7; cf. Will, *Histoire,* I, 267–70.

152 Will, *Histoire,* I, 294–301.

153   Will, *Histoire,* I, 283, 288, 301–4. See n 136.

154   Strabo xi.9.2–3 ("Euthydemos" there is an error for "Diodotos"); Justin xli. 1, 4, 5.1; Frye, *History,* 206–8; Sherwin-White and Kuhrt, *From Samarkhand,* 84–90. The Arsakids as Zoroastrians: Boyce, HZ, III, 28.

155   Will, *Histoire,* I, 137, 291.

156   Pontic Cappadocia and Cappadocia: ibid., I, 138, 292.

157   Strabo xi. 13. 1 (C. 523); M.L. Chaumont, "Atropates," *Encyclopaedia Iranica,* III (1989), 17–18.

158   Boyce, HZ, III, 110.

159   Boyce, HZ, III, 69–86.

160   See n 136.

161   Wiesehöfer, *Jahrhunderte,* 103–5, 109–13; Boyce, HZ, 110–15.

162   Against Frye, *History,* and Boyce, HZ, III, 114, see Wiesehöfer, *Jahrhunderte,* 109.

163   Wieshöfer, *Jahrhunderte,* 107–8.

164   Strabo xv.3.24.

165   On the efforts to date the coins, see Wiesehöfer, *Jahrhunderte,* 115–24.

166   Sachs-Hunger, *Diaries,* Vol. II, 89 (No. –237) and 95 (No. –234).

167   Sherwin-White and Kuhrt, *From Samarkhand,* 138–39.

168   Marcel Launey, *Recherches sur les armées hellénistiques* (2 vols.; Paris: É. de Boccard, 1950), I, 582–83.

169   Green, *Alexander to Actium,,* 265. Polybius (iv.48.8) names two conspirators, Nikanor and Apaturios.

170   Josephus *Antiquities* xii.4.1.158–59; see my article, "The Tales of the Tobiads," in *Christianity, Judaism and Other Greco-Roman Cults: Studies for Morton Smith at Sixty,* ed. Jacob Neusner (Leiden: Brill, 1975), III, 86–87, 94–98, 101.

~ 13 ~

The Reigns of Antiochus III
and Seleucus IV

1. Introduction

I N 223 B.C.E. ANTIOCHUS III, an able and energetic eighteen-year-old king, came to the Seleucid throne, and in 221 a very intelligent but dissolute and lazy king came to the Ptolemaic throne, Ptolemy IV. The struggles of these two kings were to result in the explosion of the accumulated pressure of generations of frustration as the Egyptians rose in national revolt and some Jews dared to believe that God did not require them to be loyal any longer to the Graeco-Macedonian rulers.

2. Antiochus III Consolidates His Rule

THE CONDITIONS WHICH FACED Antiochus III upon his accession were not promising. He was not yet twenty years old. His brother, the previous king, Seleucus III, had been murdered through a plot of some of his officers.[1] Achaios was a close relative (first cousin or maternal uncle)[2] of Antiochus III and thus had a good claim to be a member of the Seleucid dynasty. Achaios had already proved his competence in important posts. He had participated in the final expedition of Seleucus III and had seen to the execution of the conspirators and had so skillfully presided over the reorganization of affairs after the murder of the king that the soldiers urged him to take over the kingdom himself. However, Achaios insisted on reserving the throne for the more legitimate heir, his younger kinsman.[3] Though Achaios began by displaying exemplary loyalty to

Antiochus III, the fact that Achaios had been the soldiers' first choice for the succession was a peril for the young king. Nevertheless, Antiochus entrusted the government of Asia Minor to Achaios. Achaios proceeded promptly to recover what had been Seleucid Asia Minor, driving Attalos I all the way back to take refuge within the walls of Pergamon (222 B.C.E.).[4] This exhibition of competence rendered Achaios still more formidable to young Antiochus.

Also dangerous to Antiochus was the power and unpopularity of Hermeias, the "prime minister" (*ho proestôs tôn holôn pragmatôn,* "the one who presided over the entire government"). Hermeias had received that powerful post from Seleucus III and jealously protected his own preeminence against any other prominent official, especially by falsely accusing potential rivals. At first young Antiochus did not venture to oppose Hermeias, even when the chief minister's advice appeared to be bad. Antiochus entrusted the government of the "Upper Provinces" (those far away from the Mediterranean, especially the Iranian districts) to Molon, the satrap of Media, who was to be assisted by his brother, Alexandros, satrap of Persis. The two brothers, "despising the king on account of his youth and hoping that Achaios would join them in their plot, dreading at the same time the cruelty and malice of Hermeias, entered upon a revolt."[5]

The news of Molon's uprising reached the king and his court in the summer of 222. The loyal commander, Epigenes, advised the king to move promptly against the rebels: The soldiers would not venture to fight against their rightful king. Hermeias bitterly opposed that counsel, claiming that the king's duty was to conquer Ptolemaic Syria and Palestine, now being ruled by old, inactive Ptolemy III. Furious, Hermeias accused Epigenes of serving the interests of Molon (!), and Hermeias's advice prevailed. A force under two commanders, Xenon and Theodotos, was sent against Molon, and Antiochus prepared to invade Ptolemaic Syria. Molon routed the force sent against him and occupied the territory east of the Tigris. Antiochus was ready to postpone the expedition against the Ptolemaic Empire and to march himself against Molon, but even then Hermeias managed to prevail: The project of invading Ptolemaic Syria was not postponed, and a force under the mercenary commander Xenoitas marched against Molon, but it was crushingly defeated at the Tigris. Xenoitas himself was killed. Molon crossed the river, captured the eastern Seleucid capital, Seleukeia-on-the-Tigris, and controlled the land of the two rivers as far upstream as Dura-Europos. We learn from Molon's coins that, at an unknown date, he also took the title "king."[6]

Meanwhile, in 221, the Ptolemaic army under the command of Theodotos the Aetolian so staunchly held a narrow pass at the entrance to Ptolemaic Syria that Antiochus gave up his expedition. Epigenes again advised the king to go against Molon. At first Hermeias bitterly opposed the advice, but seeing that the king and the majority of the court backed Epigenes, he, too, recommended marching against Molon. Shortly afterward, however, Hermeias was able to have Epigenes framed and executed. Antiochus' campaign against Molon was so successful that Molon and his brother committed suicide, and the young king was able to bring about the murder of dangerous Hermeias, a step that actually increased his popularity.[7]

Molon and his brother Alexander were, respectively, satraps over the Persians and the Medes. One might have thought that those two peoples would have backed the revolt of their satraps. But in fact the evidence shows that the movement was only an insurrection of Macedonian and Greek troops and officers against Antiochus III, probably because he was dominated by Hermeias.[8] Only one piece of evidence indicates that native Iranians supported Molon and Alexander. Polybius says that after the victory over Molon Antiochus wished "to overawe and intimidate the barbarian rulers whose domains bordered on and lay beyond his own provinces, so as to prevent their daring to provide any rebels against him with supplies or armed aid"; accordingly, he "decided to march against them, first against Artabazanes, who was thought to be the most important and energetic of these rulers." Artabazanes ruled Atropatene Media, as a remote successor of Atropates. Aged Artabazanes offered no resistance and accepted whatever terms Antiochus imposed upon him. Polybius clearly implies that Artabazanes did aid Molon, but the aid cannot have amounted to much.[9] For most Iranians, rule by the Seleucids was probably still not very burdensome.[10]

Achaios had been both competent and loyal, but while Antiochus was campaigning against Artabazanes in the summer of 220 B.C.E., Achaios came to think of the likelihood that some misfortune of war could come upon the king, and even if no such thing happened, that Antiochus was now so far away that he himself could invade Syria and seize control over the government with the help of the Kyrrhestai, who were already in revolt. Achaios marched out of Lydia with his whole army. On reaching Laodikeia in Phrygia, he put on a diadem and dared to take the title "king." His soldiers at first did not oppose him, but later, near the border of Lykaonia, they mutinied, unwilling to march against their legitimate king. Achaios immediately abandoned the project of seizing control and marched instead against the rebellious area of Pisidia. By so doing, he won back the loyalty of his soldiers, even though he retained the royal title. The fact made Achaios yet again more formidable to Antiochus. Wishing to conquer Ptolemaic Syria, rather than to war against his kinsman,

Antiochus contented himself with reproaching Achaios for his act of usurpation.[11] The two Seleucid kings, for the time being, were ready to abstain from interfering with one another.

3. Antiochus III versus Ptolemy IV (the "Fourth" Syrian War)

PTOLEMY IV REIGNED UNDER the domination of his ministers, Sosibios and Agathokles, especially the former.[12] Antiochus III was aware of the weakness of that king's personality. The moment looked opportune for a Seleucid attack on the Ptolemaic Empire. Antiochus and his advisors quickly agreed that the first objective was to recover Seleukeia in Pieria, the port of Antioch, which had been in Ptolemaic hands since 246 B.C.E. Antiochus mounted a vigorous siege of the city by land and by sea and judiciously bribed some of the defenders, so that it fell to him in the spring of 219.[13]

Theodotos the Aetolian was the commander who in 221 B.C.E. had held the passes of northern Syria and had blocked the effort of Antiochus III to invade the Ptolemaic province.[14] By 219 Theodotos had received ungrateful, indeed very rough, treatment from Ptolemy and his courtiers and defected to the Seleucid side. As a result, the important towns of Tyre and Ptolemais fell into Antiochus's hands, but other fortified cities held out. Ptolemy was incapable of organizing resistance to the invasion with the resources at hand, beyond having his forces open the sluices, flooding the land and filling the wells of fresh water at Pelusium, the gateway to the Nile valley.

Sosibios and Agathokles resolved to play for time by involving Antiochus in protracted negotiations and meanwhile secretly to prepare for war, especially by hiring mercenaries from Greece, Thrace, Galatia, and Libya and by securing expert Greek commanders to train them. This stratagem of the Ptolemaic ministers was at first successful. Antiochus in pushing southward through Palestine had been balked in his siege of Dor, and he was worried that Achaios might go to war against him; winter was approaching. Antiochus agreed to a truce. Negotiations came to nothing. Meanwhile, the Ptolemaic side acquired a fresh, well-trained army. Ptolemy's ministers also took a fateful step: For the first time in the history of their empire, they not only enrolled native Egyptians in the army, they had them equipped and trained to fight in the massed infantry phalanx, the arm that was usually supposed to be decisive in the battles of the time. There were 20,000 Egyptians in the phalanx, alongside the 25,000 Macedonians.[15]

War broke out again in the spring of 218, and Antiochus at first won more successes against the Ptolemaic forces. He captured strategic points in Phoenicia, Samaria, and Transjordan, though Sidon held out against him, and he set his winter quarters at Ptolemais. By the beginning of spring 217, when both sides were ready for a decisive battle, Antiochus and his army had penetrated past Gaza and were even to the southwest of Raphia (Hebrew *Raphiaḥ*, Arabic *Rafah*), not far from the historical border of Egypt.[16]

The author of the present-future prophecy in Daniel 11, writing around 166 B.C.E.,[17] knew how powerful and devastating Antiochus's invasion of 219–217 appeared to be before the battle of Raphia. In v 10, he applied to that invasion language taken from prophecies of Isaiah and of Jeremiah: "He shall surely come and overflow and pass beyond." "Overflow and pass beyond" has long been recognized as an allusion to Isa 8:8, where it predicts and describes an invasion of Judah by the king of Assyria (a king of the North!), the figurative waters of which will "reach even to the neck."[18] "He shall surely come" *(ubʾ bwʾ)*, a perfect with *waw*-consecutive followed by the infinitive absolute of the same root, is somewhat unusual Hebrew, but it is grammatical,[19] and probably reflects Jer 36:29, "The king of Babylon [again, a king of the North] shall surely come, and he shall destroy this land [Judah] and wipe out from it man and beast." The context of Jer 36:29 speaks of ruin upon Jerusalem (in v 31), and one might assume that Jerusalem suffered during Antiochus's invasion of 219–217. But the seer says nothing explicit of Jerusalem in v 10, whereas we shall see that in vv 14–16 he details how the city suffered in the war between Antiochus III and Ptolemy V. Hence, in the absence of any other information, we may assume, rather, that Antiochus devastated other parts of Judea but by-passed Jerusalem in 217.

To the battle-site near Raphia, Ptolemy IV brought the full strength of his revamped army, including the Egyptian soldiers in the phalanx. Ptolemy himself took command. Present with him was his younger sister, Arsinoë, perhaps because her character was stronger than his. She was soon to become his queen. Ptolemy had 70,000 infantry, 5,000 cavalry, and 73 African elephants. Antiochus had 62,000 infantry, 6,000 cavalry, and 102 elephants. These were the biggest armies to take the field after the battle of Ipsos.[20]

Antiochus posted himself on the right side of the battle line, and the opening stages of the fighting favored him, but he too eagerly pursued the fleeing enemy left. Meanwhile, Ptolemy uncharacteristically took the bold step of displaying himself to the men of his phalanx and inspired them to charge against the enemy. His phalanx, especially the Egyptians, routed the Seleucid forces opposite them and won the battle. The Ptolemaic hold on Syria and Palestine was safe for the time being. Antiochus lost nearly 10,000 infantry and 300 cavalry killed and more than 4,000 men captured. He requested and received from

Ptolemy the customary truce to bury his dead, and then he made haste to return to Antioch with the survivors of his army. On arrival, he sent ambassadors to sue for peace, for he no longer had confidence in his own soldiers and was afraid that Achaios would attack him. Ptolemy granted him surprisingly generous terms. He kept Palestine and southern Syria, but he let Antiochus retain Seleukeia in Pieria. Polybius and, probably, public opinion ascribed this leniency to Ptolemy's weak and indolent character.[21] Whatever the case may be with Ptolemy's handling of the peace terms, a more ruinous factor impaired his victory at Raphia. Polybius writes that Ptolemy's war against the rebellious Egyptians occurred in the near aftermath of the battle: "This king, by providing arms to the Egyptians for his war against Antiochus planned suitably for the needs of the present but failed to perceive the needs of the future. The soldiers, highly proud of their victory at Raphia, were no longer minded to obey orders but were looking for someone with a commanding personality, thinking themselves well able to fight off their enemies. In fact, they did just that not long thereafter."[22] The Egyptians in the phalanx had indeed routed the supposedly invincible conquering stock, the Macedonians, whom Antiochus had posted opposite them, and the Ptolemaic Empire was to be torn by Egyptian revolts (mostly guerrilla warfare) until 186 B.C.E.[23] It was probably the long chain of Egyptian revolts that brought the writer of the present-future prophecy in Daniel 11 (in about 166 B.C.E.) to make his "prediction" concerning the battle of Raphia and its aftermath, using the exasperatingly ambiguous words of vv 11–12. In the translation that follows I have added the words in brackets to remove the ambiguities: "The King of the South [Ptolemy IV] shall be enraged and he shall go forth and war against the King of the North [Antiochus III]; he [Ptolemy] shall have mustered a great multitude, and the multitude [belonging to Antiochus] shall be given into his [Ptolemy's] hand.[24] And though the multitude [belonging to Ptolemy] shall be uplifted[25] and its spirit shall be high and though it shall fell tens of thousands [of Antiochus's men], he [Ptolemy] shall not prove strong."[26]

4. Antiochus Crushes Achaios and Marches to Northwest India and Back

THE PEACE WITH PTOLEMY IV, though ignominious, left Antiochus III free to attack Achaios. He could compensate for the ignominy of his defeat by deposing his usurping kinsman. Though Achaios had not moved against Antiochus during the war against the Ptolemaic Empire, Antiochus had feared that he would do so.[27] Antiochus resolved to reunite the Seleucid Empire and to remove that threat. In 216 B.C.E. he made an alliance with his enemy's enemy, King Attalos I of Pergamon, and invaded Achaios's territory. By 215, even the city of Sardis, Achaios's capital, had fallen, but Achaios held out there in the nearly impregnable citadel. In an attempt to escape, Achaios was betrayed into the hands of Antiochus. As a deterrent example, the prisoner suffered amputation of his extremities and then decapitation. His severed head was sewn into an ass's skin and his mutilated corpse was crucified.[28] From 212 to 205 Antiochus performed near-mighty deeds which brought Greek public opinion to call him "Antiochus the Great." With his army he paralleled the campaigns of his ancestor, Seleucus I, marching from Armenia to what was then the northwestern edge of India (now eastern Afghanistan) and back to Seleukeia on the Tigris. On part of his route he was unopposed. Persis surely remained loyal and was not molested. He gave up the effort to crush his most formidable opponents and made treaties with them. Thus, Antiochus III fell short of the achievements of Alexander the Great and even of Seleucus I, but his prestige now stood high.[29]

Zoroastrians probably felt keenly Antiochus's spoliation of the temple of Anahita at Ekbatana in 210 B.C.E.; they may also have resented his attack on the Parthian kingdom.[30] Perhaps at this point Zoroastrians supplemented the *Sudgar Nask* and the *Prophetic Zand* according to the Babylonian Mixture version, but more likely the supplementing occurred earlier, when the Mixture version was relatively fresh.

5. Antiochus III versus Ptolemy V (the "Fifth" Syrian War)

THE KINGDOM OF THE SOUTH became still weaker when Ptolemy IV, at most 35 years old, died in the summer of 204 and left his realm to his little son, Ptolemy V (born in 210).[31] A kingdom ruled by a child tempts rival states to be aggressive. Already in 203 Antiochus took over cities in southwestern Asia Minor that had been subject to the Ptolemies.[32] In the winter of 203/2, Antiochus and King Philip V of Macedonia made a secret agreement to grab what each could of the holdings of the kingdom ruled by a helpless child.[33] Having made the agreement, Antiochus was probably quick to invade Ptolemaic Syria in the spring of 202. No Greek source tells us of the opening months of his campaign,[34] but the seer who some 36 years later wrote Dan 11:13 was impressed with the size and equipment of the Seleucid army and with the devastation it caused in Judea: "The King of the North shall again muster a multitude, one greater than the first, and at the predicted end *[qṣ]* of the times (years)[35] he shall surely come with a big army and a vast supply train." We have seen before[36] that "He shall surely come" is an allusion to Jer 36:39 and its prediction that Judah will be devastated.

Antiochus did have to conduct a long siege of Gaza, but that city, too, fell to him in the summer or autumn of 201.[37] Did the Seleucid army occupy Jerusalem during the campaign of 202/1? Although Jerome says so,[38] we shall soon see that again (as in Dan 11:10) the seer in Dan 11:13–14 says nothing about the army of the King of the North in Jerusalem. It is best to assume again that Jerusalem, inland and unimportant, was bypassed.

Even after the fall of Gaza, the Ptolemaic Empire was not yet ready to give up. Knowing even in 204 that Antiochus was likely to take advantage of the weakness of the child-king, Agathocles, minister of Ptolemy V, in 203 had sent the seasoned mercenary commander, Skopas of Aetolia, to recruit more Greek mercenaries.[39] Aetolia was a region of northwestern Greece, poor in resources except for its warlike population. War and piracy were mainstays of its economy. Through their victories, the Aetolians built up a league of city-states which was a significant power in Greece at this time.

Skopas returned from his recruiting mission with a force composed especially of his Aetolian countrymen, and took command of the Ptolemaic army after the fall of Gaza. His counteroffensive in the winter of 201/200 overran Judea and Jerusalem and drove Antiochus all the way back to the sources of the Jordan. But the Seleucid army in the spring or summer of 200 won the decisive battle of Panion.[40] Skopas withdrew to Sidon with the 10,000 survivors of his army. Antiochus besieged him there. Starved out, Skopas surrendered in 199 and was allowed with his men to depart.[41] Only local Ptolemaic garrisons were left in Palestine, and they were unable to prevent Antiochus from taking over the whole region. The Jews of Jerusalem went over to him voluntarily and joined his forces in reducing the garrison that Skopas had left in the citadel there. By the summer of 198, Antiochus had control of all of what had been Ptolemaic Syria and Palestine.[42]

The wars of Antiochus III with Ptolemy IV and Ptolemy V had subjected the Jews and the other peoples of Syria and Palestine to the presence of two predatory armies, inflicting intense suffering. The soldiers plundered, took captives, sold persons as slaves, and terrorized many so that they fled from their homes.[43]

6. Events in Jerusalem, 201–198 B.C.E.

WE HAVE SEEN THAT Antiochus probably bypassed Jerusalem in 201. What happened in that city between then and the time it went over to Antiochus?

Texts provide clues to events there, but they have not been properly inter-preted.

One might have expected the Jews to remain, as usual, tenaciously loyal to their pagan royal "warden," for fear God would punish any rebellion. The Ptolemies, like the Persians before them (and like Antiochus III thereafter) knew how to appreciate permanent loyalty, such as the Jews exhibited. Jews very early became members of the privileged ruling group in the Ptolemaic Empire,[44] especially as soldiers, but also (as the history of Joseph the Tobiad and his family shows) as civilian functionaries.[45] Such evidence as we have suggests that the Jews' pagan neighbors in Palestine and Syria mostly stuck to the Ptolemaic side.[46] Yet the proverbially loyal Jews did switch to fight for Antiochus III! We must seek to find how this came about.

In the struggles between the "King of the North" and the "King of the South," between Antiochus III and Ptolemy IV and Ptolemy V, the Jews had to solve again that frightening problem: Which of the contending kings was the one chosen by God to rule over his people? Though they may have feared what God might do to them for the wrong choice, what the human victor might do to them for choosing wrongly was also a dreadful prospect. In 218–217 the Jews of Judea surely suffered for a year at the hands of the Seleucid army, but Antiochus may well have bypassed Jerusalem, or perhaps the city stood firm behind its walls, and the victory of Ptolemy IV at Raphia put an end to the dilemma: God's chosen warden was Ptolemy.

More difficult for the Jews was the crisis of 202–198 B.C.E. Though Antiochus may at first have bypassed Jerusalem, he occupied much of Judea. Skopas certainly overran Judea and Jerusalem. The Jews suffered at the hands of both armies. There is no evidence that anyone claimed to be a prophet speaking on the issue of which king was God's chosen warden. Most if not all Jews believed that the LORD was not at present communicating with them: That was part of their punishment. They believed that the return of real prophecy still lay in the future. Material considerations would not necessarily reflect God's will until the very last moment of the struggle.

For believing Jews, there was only one intelligent method to find the safe way out of these dangers: Search the words of the true prophets. Perhaps they had foreseen just these difficult times. The Jewish adaptation of the Mixture version of Daniel 2 was available. It speaks of the downfall of the Macedonian kingdom after a marriage between the clay and the iron dynasty. But Berenice's marriage to Antiochus II was long past, and now the Seleucid Empire, under vigorous Antiochus III, looked to be the iron dynasty, and the formerly steely Ptolemaic Empire appeared to be as brittle as a heap of potsherds.

If Daniel provided no clear guidance, other prophets from the past might. Though other prophets said nothing of Macedonian empires, Ptolemy V was king of Egypt, and Antiochus III was king over Babylon. In ordinary talk, though not in official terminology, Antiochus was called "King of Syria," and in the ancient world "Syria" and "Assyria" were synonyms. Isaiah, Jeremiah, and Ezekiel were full of prophecies on Assyria, Babylon, and Egypt. The trouble was that Isaiah advised neutrality, which was not feasible, and most of the prophecies of Jeremiah and Ezekiel had been fulfilled and therefore could hardly refer to the dreadful present facing the Jews in 202–198. The details of Jeremiah's prophecies, too, did not fit the situation. Hence, we can guess that the perplexed Jews eagerly seized upon several prophecies of Ezekiel that had not been fulfilled. This guess becomes a near certainty when we find that Jewish texts which reflect the events of 202–198 contain echoes of those prophecies of Ezekiel.

Ezekiel prophesied (30:20–26) that a king of Babylon would conquer Egypt. God, he said, would somehow first break one arm of the Egyptian king, and then, when the king of Babylon was ready to attack, God would break the other arm, leaving Egypt powerless in front of the Babylonian conqueror. Though Nebuchadnezzar was king when Ezekiel wrote, the prophecy does not mention Nebuchadnezzar by name. The prophecy had never been fulfilled in the time of Nebuchadnezzar. Though Cambyses and Artaxerxes III of Persia both conquered Egypt when they were ruling Babylon, neither conquered a "crippled" Egypt. But Ptolemaic Egypt in 202–198 was doubly crippled by the bitter revolt of the native Egyptian soldiers and by having a child as king. Surely it looked as if the unfulfilled prophecy was being fulfilled! One might think that Ezekiel predicted victory for Antiochus.

There was another prophecy of Ezekiel that surely was being read at the time. Ezekiel received his first messages from God in the fifth year of the exile of King Jehoiachin,[47] that is, in 593/2 B.C.E. In one of these earliest visions,[48] God told Ezekiel that the punishment of the house of "Israel" would last 390 years, whereas the punishment of Judah would last 40 years.[49] One who knows of the two kingdoms of Israel and Judah would tend to recognize that Ezekiel refers to the two kingdoms. But in 202/1 B.C.E. it was clear that even after the passing of 390 years there had been no return of the "Ten Lost Tribes" from exile, no end to their punishment. Ezekiel's prediction is false! Believers in 202–200 B.C.E. did not want to accept that possibility, especially when they were seeking prophetic instruction on what to do in their present predicament. There was another way to take Ezekiel 4:5–9. "Israel" in biblical texts composed after the fall of the northern kingdom frequently means "Judah." Although Ezekiel knows that "Israel" can mean "the northern kingdom,"[50] far more often he uses it to mean "Judah."[51] The 40 years for Judah could stand as an approximation of the duration of the Babylonian exile, especially if it was measured from 586 to 538. The exile obviously had not been the total punishment. Even after the return, the chosen people clearly continued to undergo punishment. Ezekiel's prophecy could be taken as predicting that their illustrious status as Israel would be restored to them only after 390 years. 390 years after 593/2 B.C.E. was 203/2 B.C.E., exactly the time of the crisis facing the Jews in the "Fifth" Syrian War. If the age of punishment was over, Jews could assert their freedom. They could be free to rebel against their foreign "warden."

There is good evidence in Daniel 11 on how these two prophecies affected the Jews in 202–201. That chapter is written in outrageously bad Hebrew and is extremely hard to understand.[52] Nevertheless, enough is clear to give an interesting picture of events. Daniel 11:10–12 describes the war that ended in the Battle of Raphia.[53] Verse 13 has strange phraseology which I have italicized: "The King of the North again mustered a multitude, one greater than the first, and *at the predicted end of the times (years) [wlqṣ hʿtym šnym]* he shall come with a big army and and a vast supply train." The word *qṣ* ("end") in Daniel refers to an appointed time, one predicted by prophecy, and not necessarily to the end of the age of punishment.[54] At 11:13, it certainly does not refer to the end of the age of punishment, for the chosen people must go on suffering. "Time" *(ʿt)* in Ezekiel can refer to a period of punishment.[55] The word "years" makes for awkward Hebrew and seems to be redundant. I have enclosed it in parentheses, believing that the author did not care about the awkward syntax and intended the word to be in the sentence, as an allusion to Ezekiel's "[390] years." Thus, Daniel 11:13 can mean that Antiochus III will invade Ptolemaic Syria and Palestine at the time predicted by Ezekiel, 390 years after the prophecy in Ezekiel 4:4–9. On the other hand, in Daniel 11:13–14, the King of the North has not yet overrun Judea and does not yet hold Jerusalem; those events are reflected in Daniel 11:15–16.

Interpreters at least since the times of the Greek versions and Jerome have erred in treating Daniel 11:14. It should say, "And in those times [still periods of punishment!] many shall take a stand with[56] the King of the South, and the men of violence[57] among your own people shall rise up in order to fulfill a vision, but they shall fail." "Many" in Qumran texts is a "code word" meaning "the majority of pious Jews." Our passage thus means, "The majority of pious Jews will take a stand in support of the King of the South," in vivid contrast with the "men of violence" in the next clause. Which vision did the men of violence seek to fulfill? Ezekiel's prophecy concerning the 390 years![58] Believing their years of servitude to foreign rulers were over, they struck for independence in 202/1, only to be crushed, whether by the loyalist majority or, as we shall find, by Skopas's force.

The author of the last chapters of Daniel has no sympathy for these Israelite "martyrs" who wrongly believed that the Jews had served their full sentence. Rather, the author believed that until great miracles showed that the sentence had been lifted, Jews must obey their pagan rulers. He called the rebels "men of violence."

A text written by a member of the Qumran sect reflects the perplexity of the times; this text, the "Covenant of Damascus," also called the "Cambridge Document," is referred to by the abbreviation "CD."[59] One section of it traces important developments in the history of the sect,[60] as follows:

> And now, listen, all you that know righteousness and consider the deeds of God. For he has a quarrel with all flesh, and he will execute justice upon all who despise him. For when they committed treason in deserting him, he hid his face from Israel and from his Temple and gave them over to the sword. But when he remembered the covenant with the forefathers he caused a remnant to remain for Israel and did not give them over to complete destruction. And in the Age of Wrath, 390 years after he had delivered them into the hand of Nebuchadnezzar king of Babylon, he remembered them, and he caused to sprout from Israel and Aaron a root of cultivation to inherit his land and to grow fat in the goodness of his soil. And they contemplated their sin and understood that they were guilty men. But they were like the blind and like those who grope their way, for twenty years. And God contemplated their deeds, that they sought him wholeheartedly, and he raised up for them a Teacher of Righteousness to lead them in accordance with his desire.

Are the "men of violence" identical with those who were "like the blind"? If so, they were "like the blind" in that their interpretation of Ezek 4:4–9 proved to be disastrously wrong. From the quoted passage of the Cambridge Document, we can infer that the career of the Teacher of Righteousness began a bit before 180 B.C.E. The ancestors of the Qumran sect produced a present-future prophecy, the Animal Vision (*1 Enoch* 85:1–90:40), from which we can infer that the "men of violence" were indeed identical with those who were "like the blind." The crucial passage is *1 Enoch* 90:6–19; this passage of the prophecy was later supplemented, so interpreting it is somewhat difficult.

The first sections of the Animal Vision are easy to understand. The seer wrote a summary of the history of humanity and of the chosen people, beginning with Adam and Eve. In the elaborate symbolic scheme, human beings represent angels. Ritually clean animals (bulls) represent the antediluvian patriarchs and Abraham and Isaac—though Noah and Moses do become human. After Isaac, each animal species represents a distinct state or ethnic group. Sheep represent Jacob and his descendants, and blind or wild sheep represent them when they are sinful. God is portrayed as their "Owner" or "Lord." Unclean predatory animals and birds represent the Gentile nations which oppress the children of Israel. At 89:21, the seer spoke of the Exodus. At 89:50, he treated the building of the first temple. At 89:54–58, he dealt with the sins of King Manasseh of Judah and his generation and with God's abandonment of his people to be the prey of the Gentile nations.[61]

The Owner turns the wayward "blind" sheep over to seventy angelic shepherds, who each in turn are to supervise their punishment for one period. The shepherds, however, transgress the bounds of their mission: They allow too many of the sheep to be slain and even join in killing them (*1 Enoch* 89:59–60, 65, 68–69),[62] though the Owner also sees to it that an angel records all the misdeeds of the shepherds (89:61–64, 70–71). In 89:65–67, lions (Assyria) and tigers (Babylon) devour the sheep and destroy the temple ("that tower") and Jerusalem ("that house") and the sheep pass out of sight (into exile). By 89:72, twelve shepherds have pastured the sheep. In 89:72–77, the seer is treating the period of Persian rule. The sheep return from exile and rebuild a temple, but they offer unclean sacrifices and suffer more punishment at the hands of the shepherds.

No species of beast represents the Persians! Indeed, they were mostly gentle, or even benevolent, to the Jews, yet the seer reports (89:72, 74–75) great losses of the sheep to the beasts under that empire. In fact, the Persian kings were surprisingly tolerant of local strife among the subject peoples, and under those kings the Jews suffered at the hands of Edomites, Ammonites, Moabites, Arabs, Philistines, and Samaritans and were dispersed and did mingle (i.e., intermarry) with the Gentiles.[63] By 90:1, thirty-five[64] shepherds have pastured the sheep. Thereafter, birds of prey, including eagles, vultures, kites, and ravens (Alexander and the Hellenistic kingdoms and their mercenary soldiers), attack the sheep, with the eagles leading all the birds. By 90:5 fifty-eight shepherds have pastured the sheep.

Paraphrase and summary are not sufficient for treating *1 Enoch* 90:6–19. A complete translation[65] follows:

> 6 And small lambs were born from those white sheep, and they
>   began to open their eyes and to see and to cry to the sheep.

7   But they afflicted them, and did not listen to what they said to them but were extremely deaf, and their eyes were extremely blinded, and they prevailed.[66]

8   And I saw in the vision how the ravens flew upon those lambs and took one of those lambs and dashed the sheep in pieces and devoured them.

9   And I looked until horns came up on those lambs, but the ravens cast their horns down; and I looked until a big horn grew on one of those sheep, and their eyes were opened.

10   And it looked at them, and their eyes were opened, and it cried to the sheep, and the rams saw it, and they all ran to it.

11   And besides all this those eagles and vultures and kites were still continually tearing the sheep in pieces and flying upon them and devouring them; and the sheep were silent, but the rams lamented and cried out.

12   And those ravens battled and fought with it and wished to make away with its horn, but they did not prevail against it.

13   And I looked at them until the shepherds and the eagles[67] and those vultures and kites came and cried to the ravens that they should dash the horn of that ram in pieces; and they fought and battled with it, and it fought with them and cried out that its help might come to it.

14   And I looked until that man who wrote down the names of the shepherds and brought them up before the Owner of the sheep came, and he helped that ram and showed it everything; he had come down for the help of that ram.

15   And I looked until the Owner of the sheep came to them in anger, and all who saw him fled and they all fell into the shadow before him.[68]

16   All the eagles[69] and vultures and ravens and kites gathered together and brought with them all the wild sheep, and they all came together and helped one another in order to dash that horn of the ram in pieces.

17   And I looked at that man who wrote the book at the command of the Owner until he opened that book of the destruction which those twelve last shepherds had wrought, and he showed before the Owner of the sheep that they had destroyed even more than (those) before them.

18   And I looked until the Owner of the sheep came to them and took in his hand the staff of his anger and struck the earth; and

the earth was split, and all the animals and the birds of heaven fell from those sheep and sank in the earth, and it closed over them.

19 And I looked until a big sword was given to the sheep, and the sheep went out against all the wild animals to kill them, and all the animals and the birds of heaven fled before them.

In 90:20–39 a Last Judgment and a perfecting of the world occur.

We can identify most of the events that are symbolized in 90:1–19. We know that Alexander did not harm the Jews. The seer says as little of him as of the Persians. Ptolemy I was conspicuous for harshly treating the Jews during the wars of the Diadochoi.[70] If "the eagles led all the birds," they should represent Ptolemy I and his dynasty. Indeed, the eagle is the almost universal emblem on the reverse side of Ptolemaic coins. Jews down to the late third century B.C.E. believed Jeremiah and Ezekiel and were afraid to rebel against their pagan overlords. The lambs who "began to open their eyes" and grew horns only to have the ravens cast those horns down can hardly be other than the "men of violence," the "root of cultivation," who were *like* the blind" in their disastrously wrong interpretation of Ezekiel 4:4–9. Unfortunately, there is nothing to help us identify the "one of those lambs" in v 8 who was taken by the ravens.

Ravens are birds of prey and must represent Gentiles, whereas "the majority of pious Jews" reflected in Daniel 11:14 would have been represented by sheep. On the basis of our knowledge of the history of 201/200 B.C.E., we infer that the horned lambs were crushed by Greek Skopas and his Greek mercenaries and that ravens represent Greeks. In 90:9 (first half), the seer is treating events of the middle of the war between Antiochus III and Ptolemy V. This fact enables us to infer who is represented by the vultures and the kites. The seer chose his symbols carefully. Large and strong animals represent great powers. Lions and tigers represent Assyria and Babylon. Smaller animals symbolize weaker ethnic groups. It is easy to show that dogs represent Philistines and boars, Edomites.[71] Vultures and eagles are large birds, about equal in strength. If eagles represent Ptolemies, vultures in events of 201/200 B.C.E. represent Seleucids. Greek mercenaries came from small city-states and therefore are represented by a smaller bird species, the ravens. Kites, too, are a smaller bird species and should represent a mercenary stock, employed by the Ptolemies or the Seleucids or both. Both dynasties made considerable use of Thracians, so the kites probably represent Thracians.[72] No other source tells us of the event symbolized by *1 Enoch* 90:8. The verse speaks of the plural lambs and cannot date from the time of Judas Maccabaeus, a fact which renders it impossible that the seer is speaking of the murder of the deposed high priest, Onias III, narrated at 2 Maccabees 4:32–34. Furthermore, Onias was not seized by Greeks before being murdered.

The passage 90:9(second half)–19 contains puzzling problems. In 90:9 an invincible horned ram appears, representing a great fighter and leader of the chosen people against their enemies. There was no such person until the rise of Judas Maccabaeus in 166–165 B.C.E. Could he have called to the horned rams of 201/200? Even if he could have, what is the point of twice saying that the eyes of the horned rams were opened (90:9–10) after his great horn grew? Their eyes had been opened already in 90:6! In the time of Judas Maccabaeus the Ptolemies no longer held Judea; only the Seleucids and their mercenaries could molest the Jews. Yet in 90:11 eagles are still attacking the sheep! In 90:10 the horned rams all join the great horned ram, yet in 90:11–12 the plural horned rams do nothing but bleat, while the great horned ram alone fights the ravens. The bleating surely represents prayer. Are we to regard the prayers as inefficacious? In 90:13 and 16, eagles join in fighting the great horned ram, at a time when Ptolemies could not have been fighting Judas Maccabaeus! Very strange is the way in which the foreign oppressors are "completely" destroyed several times over in 90:15(perhaps), 18, and 19.

In fact, the verses involving the plural horned rams treat events of 201/200, and the verses involving the single great horned ram treat events of 166–161.[73] The two sets of verses are incompatible with one another. We infer that the original writer said nothing of the single horned ram. He wrote 90:6–9(first half) and 11 to tell of the inspired enlightenment of the plural horned rams and of their misfortunes; then, he went on to predict their ultimate victory in 90:15, 17–18, an event which did not happen. But he or a member of his sect found it possible to supplement the false prophecy with successive "predictions" of the great deeds of Judas Maccabaeus in 90:9(second half), 10, 12–14, 16, 19. The supplementer even found it possible to make 90:17–18 refer to Judas's surprising survival in 163–162 B.C.E. (1 Macc 6:28–63) and to the destruction of the regime of Lysias and Antiochus V in 162 (1 Macc 7:1–3).

As for the eagles who attack the great horned ram in 90:13 and 16, manuscripts exist which omit the eagles from those verses,[74] surely correctly, in a context in which the inclusion or omission of a bird species fits historical fact. Thus, the omission of vultures in 90:4 is correct: Seleucids at first did not molest Judea, which was subject to the Ptolemies. In 90:11, both eagles and vultures attack the sheep, truly reflecting the war between Antiochus III and Ptolemy V. Later scribes are unlikely to have known Seleucid and Ptolemaic history; but, after reading 90:2, they expected to have eagles also in 90:13 and 16 and, perhaps without thinking, inserted them there.

Having identified the events symbolized in the Animal Vision and having shown when and in what passages it was supplemented, we must also try to understand its peculiar chronological scheme of seventy periods, subdivided into sections of twelve, twenty-three, twenty-three, and twelve units. Scholars were tempted to think that at the end of every subdivision must stand a significant event. But, on that basis, no one could find an acceptable explanation.[75] George Nickelsburg found the key to a solution:[76] One must pay more attention to the events within each subdivision than to the endpoints. It is likely that the unit-periods are all equal. We must try to deduce from the Animal Vision itself the length of the unit.[77] From *1 Enoch* 89:54–58, one can infer that the terms of the seventy shepherds began in the reign of King Manasseh of Judah (698–642 B.C.E.).[78] Within the first twelve periods fell the destruction of Jerusalem and exiling of her people (89:66–67), so those periods extend from some time within 698–642 and include 586 and may extend down to just before the first return from the Babylonian exile (538 B.C.E.; 89:72). At the longest, one period would be 698 minus 538 (= 160) divided by 12, or 13 1/3 years, and, at the shortest, 642 minus 586 (= 56) divided by 12, or 4 2/3 years.

The next twenty-three periods extend from some time after 586 B.C.E. and include the dedication of the second temple (515). After the end of thirty-five periods (= 12 + 23) the harsh rule of Judea by Ptolemy I began (*1 Enoch* 90:2; 320 B.C.E. at the earliest, 301 at the latest). Alexander was gentle to the Jews. He may be included in "all the birds of heaven" (90:2), but none of the mentioned birds of prey symbolizes him. The twenty-three units contain at most 285 years (586 minus 301), so that a unit would contain at most 12.39 years. The minimum figure of 4 2/3 years which we calculated from the first twelve periods is far too short to cover in twenty-three units even the time from 515 to 368–362 B.C.E. (the date of the satraps' revolt, the most chaotic years of the reign of Artaxerxes II).

The next twenty-three periods begin before 301 and possibly well before 334, the year of Alexander's first conquests in Asia; they end before the crushing of the "horned rams" in 201/200 (90:2–9). If they begin in the chaotic years of the satraps' revolt, the unit would be 7.3 years. If they begin in 334, the unit would be 5.826. It is extremely unlikely that the author reckoned with a unit that was not a whole number of years. If the unit was 7 years, the destruction and exile of 586 do fall within 84 (12·7) years after the reign of Manasseh (698–642), and the first twelve periods end between 586 and 558 (558 = 642 minus 84).

If so, the next twenty-three periods begin between 586 B.C.E. and 558 and end between 425 and 397, and within that span does fall the dedication of the second temple. The next twenty-three periods would then begin between 425 and 397 and end between 264 and 236, and within that span do fall the years of the harsh reign over Judea of Ptolemy I (between 320 and 283, the year of his death). The last twelve periods would then begin between 264 and 236 and would end between 180 and 152. Since the "root of cultivation," the "men of violence," were "like the blind" for twenty years after 200 B.C.E., an endpoint near 180 suits the original version, addressed to the "root of cultivation," and one in the 160s would suit the supplemented version, addressed to Judas Maccabaeus and his contemporaries.

Though the symbolized events do fit chronologically the divisions into twelve, twenty-three, twenty-three, and twelve units, I do not know why the author chose to have such divisions. On the other hand, a seven-year unit fits the thought-world of believing Jews; the Torah provides for a seven-year cycle (Leviticus 25, 26:34–35). The failure to mention Jeremiah's seventy-year prediction is only natural: Enoch lived long before Jeremiah. The fact that in Daniel 9 there is no mention of Enoch's seventy hebdomads is easily explained: To the author of Daniel 9, the book of Enoch was a forgery by heretics, containing predictions that had proved false.

Another present-future prophecy in *1 Enoch* runs largely parallel to the Animal Vision,[79] the "Apocalypse of Weeks" (93:1–10, 91:11–17, in that order), but its exact date is hard to determine. It contains no allusion to the Hellenistic empires or to the crushing of the men of violence. There is reason to believe that it was written earlier and that the seer of the Animal Vision in part used it as a model.[80]

Not all Jews took Ezekiel 4 as their guide in the troubled years 202–200 B.C.E. Some preferred to look to Ezekiel 30, as we learn from the difficult words of Daniel 11:15–17. The seer in Daniel 11:15 goes on telling of the events of the war between Ptolemy V and Antiochus III; I have italicized crucial words:

> **15.** Then the king of the North shall come and throw up siegeworks and take the fortified city, and the *arms* of the south shall not stand . . . , [81] for there shall be no strength to stand. **16.** He who comes against him shall work his will, and no one shall stand before him. He shall stand in the *glorious land,* and all of it shall be in his power.[82] **17.** And he shall set his face to come with the might of his entire kingdom and the Upright shall be with him, and he shall succeed.

The "fortified city" in v 15 is probably Sidon, Skopas's last foothold in Asia, because the "glorious land" has not yet fallen to the king of the North. The word for "arms" in v 15 is the Hebrew word for upper limbs, not that for weapons. In the course of nature, arms do not "stand." The unnatural expression in Daniel 11:15 plays upon the prophecy of Ezekiel 30:21–26. Antiochus III, king of Babylon, will defeat doubly crippled Ptolemaic Egypt. According to v 16, temporarily invincible Antiochus III shall stand in Judea, the "glorious land" (an expression derived from Ezekiel 20:6, 15), and all of it shall be in his power. According to v 17, Antiochus shall come with overwhelming power and take Jerusalem with the help of the Upright (the majority of righteous Jews).

The seer of Daniel here records the switch of even the loyalist pious Jews, now powerless, to the Seleucid side. A Jewish leader, perhaps the high priest, Simeon II, surnamed the Just, convinced his fellow Israelites in the nick of time that Ezekiel's prophecy at 30:20–26 proved that God's chosen "warden" was now Antiochus III. A Jewish writer in the 180s B.C.E., Jesus Ben Sira, praised Simeon II in the highest terms for his leadership during this difficult period.[83]

Antiochus III was grateful for the switch of loyalty, and the Jews, badly battered by both sides in the war, now received generous concessions and tax cuts from the victor.[84] One should note how great were the privileges that Antiochus now conferred upon the Jews. From then on, until Antiochus IV revoked the privileges, the Jews enjoyed the status of a recognized *ethnos* ("nation"). Peoples with that status possessed local government under their own officials, and taxes levied upon them even by the royal government were collected only by their own authorities, not by royal tax gatherers.[85]

7. The Later Years of Antiochus III (198–187 B.C.E.)

THE PTOLEMIES HAD REFERRED to their holdings in Syria and Palestine as the province of "Syria and Phoenicia." Antiochus renamed the area as the province of "Koilê [= Coele-] Syria and Phoenicia."[86] His ambitions were not limited to gaining this territory, which Seleucids from the time of Seleucus I and the battle of Ipsos had claimed as theirs by right of conquest. Seleucus I had ruled most of Asia Minor, and Antiochus III now also aimed at reconquering that heritage, parts of which were being held by the Ptolemaic Empire, by Philip V of Macedonia, by Attalos I of Pergamon, and by small free Greek states.

The strongest of the holders of the territories in Asia Minor was Antiochus's supposed partner and ally, Philip. Philip, however, became involved in a desperate war (200–197) with the Roman republic (historians call it the "Second Macedonian War"), and he could not spare any forces to fight Antiochus. Attalos I, an active ally of Rome, appealed to the Romans, and their senate sent a message to Antiochus which induced him to withdraw from territories of Pergamon.[87] But the Seleucid's army had reached the Hellespont by 196, and his fleet had overwhelmed the Ptolemaic holdings on the south coast of Asia Minor. Many of the free Greek cities accepted his overlordship or went over to his side.[88]

In the spring of 196, Antiochus crossed the Hellespont and occupied Lysimacheia, demonstrating his claim to Thrace, which, he insisted, was part of the heritage of Seleucus I. Rome had just defeated Philip V and had imposed a rather harsh peace upon him. Two Roman delegations now presented demands to Antiochus, that he refrain from bringing an army into Europe and from waging war against any free city of Asia and that he withdraw from the cities captured by him which previously had been subject to Ptolemy V and Philip. Antiochus, however, stood his ground and complied with none of the demands. The Romans had, indeed, made no threat of force.[89] Polybius reports[90] that to the second Roman delegation Antiochus declared his intention to settle his relations with young Ptolemy "in a manner agreeable to that king. He himself had decided not only to establish friendship with him but to unite him to himself by marriage" (that is, Antiochus would give his daughter as wife to Ptolemy).

Antiochus's military and diplomatic successes and the internal difficulties of Egypt (especially the native revolts) demonstrated to young Ptolemy V and his ministers that it was time to make peace, and the two kingdoms made a treaty (195 B.C.E.). The Ptolemaic Empire gave up all its possessions in Syria, Palestine, Asia Minor, and Thrace.[91] Antiochus did betroth his daughter, Cleopatra (the first of that name to be in the Ptolemaic dynasty), to Ptolemy V, and the marriage took place in the winter of 193.[92]

All those Jews, Babylonians, and Zoroastrians who believed in a Mixture version[93] surely took note of the marriage, even though much time had elapsed since the original Mixture Marriage and the publication of the prophecy. It may have been at this point that Zoroastrians brought mixture into the *Prophetic Zand*. The end of v 17 of the present-future prophecy in Daniel 11, when properly understood, attests that Jews hoped this second Mixture Marriage would bring destruction upon at least one Hellenistic empire, but it also attests that those hopes were disappointed. The passage should be read to mean "And he [Antiochus III] shall give him [Ptolemy V] his daughter in marriage in order to destroy him, but it shall not succeed, and it shall not be." The renewed prospect of a fulfillment of the Mixture version may have emboldened Zoroastrians to produce yet another present-future prophecy, the original of the *Oracle of Hys-*

taspes, if Samuel K. Eddy's dating of that text is correct.[94] Antiochus was now clearly a great power, but he still had not satisfied his urge to recover the heritage of Seleucus I in Europe as well as in Asia. The new superpower of the Mediterranean world, Rome, had used diplomacy in an effort to set limits to the Seleucid's ambitions. The voters of the Roman republic were weary after the extremely costly Second Punic War against Carthage (218–201) and after the Second Macedonian War (200–197). Diplomacy between the two great powers might have produced a peaceful solution if Antiochus's ambitions had been the only destabilizing factor, but there was another, the Aetolian League! Let us briefly trace how that league came to be a destabilizer.

After the terrible Roman defeat at Cannae in 216 during the Second Punic War, Philip V concluded that the Carthaginians under their commander, Hannibal, would be the ultimate winners. In 215, Philip made a treaty of alliance with Carthage.[95] Philip could do no harm to the Romans in Italy if he could be tied down by a war in Greece. In 212 or 211, the Romans made an alliance with the Aetolian League, which had recently (220–217) fought a bitter war against Philip.[96] Philip was indeed tied down in Greece by what historians call "the First Macedonian War." The major burden of that war fell upon the Aetolians, who, contrary to their treaty of alliance with Rome, made a separate peace with Philip in 206.[97] In 205, Rome, too, despite her treaty with the Aetolian League, made a separate peace with Philip.[98] Thus, one could argue that the treaty had lapsed for both parties. The Romans became a superpower by defeating Carthage in 201.

Philip V was intelligent, impulsive, and ambitious. He embarked upon an aggressive military policy in the Greek world. Those who suffered from his attacks, especially Attalos I, king of Pergamon (241–197), and the republic of Rhodes, sent ambassadors to Rome, appealing for aid. We need not go into the vexed problem of why the Romans went to war against Philip in 200 (in the "Second Macedonian War").[99] At first, Philip was able to fight them off. The Aetolians waited to see which side would prevail. By August 199, the Romans were winning victories, and the Aetolians voted to join them.[100] An Aetolian spokesman was later to argue that the terms of the alliance of 212 or 211 were still in force.

In 198, the tide in the war turned with the arrival in Greece of the young Roman consul, Titus Quinctius Flamininus. Philip's Greek allies went over to the Romans. Philip staked all on the final battle of Kynoskephalai (June 197). The Romans won,[101] and their Aetolian supporters distinguished themselves in the battle and made no secret of their readiness to lay claim to rewards.[102] Flamininus, however, had no wish to see the unsavory Aetolians grow to be the dominant power in Greece.[103] Accordingly, during the peace talks that followed, he rebuffed the suggestion of an Aetolian spokeman that Philip be deposed or killed[104] and blocked Aetolian efforts to secure the return of cities in Philip's hands which formerly had been members of the Aetolian League. An Aetolian spokesman held that the terms of the treaty of 212 or 211 provided for the Aetolians to gain those territories, but Flamininus rejected the claim: That treaty was void.[105] These frustrations were what embittered the Aetolians against Flamininus and Rome.[106]

Flamininus liked Greeks and admired Greek culture. He bid for Greek support by proclaiming, at the Isthmian Games of 196, that henceforth all Greek cities were to be free, under their own governments and laws, and ungarrisoned by any foreign power. In 194 he personally led the invincible Roman army out of Greece. Surely the Greeks would support such benefactors and fight for their own liberty![107]

The embittered Aetolians sought to upset this Roman settlement of Greek affairs. They captured the important port of Demetrias and invited Antiochus to use it as his base for a campaign in Europe, telling him (falsely) that Greeks would flock to support him against the "hated" Romans. The opportunity looked too good to Antiochus. He would not waste it. Trusting the Aetolians, he sailed to Demetrias with a force much too small to compete with the Romans and their allies. No Greeks flocked to join him. Even the Aetolians brought him little support.[108]

Philip V had not withdrawn from Greece in order to make room for the ambitions of Antiochus III. He sided firmly with the Romans. Antiochus with his small force could not face the armies of both Macedonia and Rome in open battle. He moved his army and occupied the strategic pass of Thermopylae, the route from Macedonia into central Greece. The events of the Persian invasion of Greece in 480 were repeated: The bulk of the Roman army attacked the Seleucid lines in the pass, while a second column took by surprise the Aetolians who were supposed to hold the alternative routes through the mountain ridge. This second column attacked the rear of Antiochus's forces, routing them. Antiochus fled with only 500 men to the sea and back to Asia (end of April 191).[109]

The seer of the present-future prophecy in Daniel 11 referred to these events in v 18, "Afterwards, he shall direct his attention to the lands by the sea and capture many of them. But a magistrate [the Roman consul, Manius Acilius Glabrio] shall put a stop to his insolence. He [the Roman consul] shall turn upon him [Antiochus] the contrary of his insolence."[110]

Antiochus's flight to Asia did not protect him. The fleets of Pergamon and

Rhodes smashed the Seleucid fleet, so that the Roman army could easily cross from Europe. Near Magnesia on the Hermos, the Roman army administered the final defeat to Antiochus. At Apameia in Phrygia he had to accept the terms proposed by the Romans. The terms of the Peace of Apameia required surrender of all his territory north and west of the Taurus mountains; payment of the costs of the war (15,000 talents, a very heavy burden); delivery of his son (the future Antiochus IV) to be a hostage at Rome; restrictions upon the number of his war elephants and of his warships and upon the seas into which his navy could sail.[111]

Having surrendered his most lucrative territories, Antiochus found it difficult to pay the Romans the required talents. He took to sacrilegious means, attempting to rob the rich temple of Bêl in Elymaïs, where the indignant natives slew the Seleucid king and massacred his army.[112] The event is reflected in Daniel 11:19.

8. The Four-Beast-Ten-Horn Version of Daniel 7 and the Reign of Seleucus IV (187–175 B.C.E.)

ELYMAÏS WAS THE ANCIENT LAND of Elam (mentioned in the Bible[113]). It lay near Babylonia and had long been influenced by it. The cult of Marduk (= Bêl) existed in Elymaïs, too. We can imagine the impact when the news reached Babylon that the once-great Antiochus III, king of the Macedonian monster Seleucid Empire, had fallen while trying to rob Marduk's own temple in Elam! Many must have been ready to view it as a miraculous deed of Marduk himself; Marduk had returned to act upon human history! True, the Seleucid army and government apparatus remained loyal to the dynasty, so that the eldest surviving son of Antiochus III could ascend the throne as Seleucus IV. But the new king's position was weak. He was weighed down by the terms of the Peace of Apameia. He just managed to make ends meet and could undertake no ambitious foreign or domestic projects.

In the British Museum there is a copy of the list that Babylonians kept of their foreign rulers. It lets us know how the Babylonians could have been ready to compare Seleucus IV with Darius III, the last Persian king. The Persian line was counted as one dynasty even though Darius I was not closely related to Cyrus and Cambyses. Just so, the Babylonians had accepted the Seleucids' claims to be the legitimate direct heirs of Alexander the Great,[114] even though Seleucus I was not related to Alexander. Darius III was the tenth Persian king to rule over Babylon in the line that began with Cyrus. The Babylonian list of Macedonian kings[115] ran as follows:

1. Alexander the Great
2. Philip III Arrhidaios
3. Alexander IV
4. Seleucus I
5. Antiochus I
6. Antiochus II
7. Seleucus II
8. Seleucus III
9. Antiochus III
10. Seleucus IV

Antigonus's name does not appear in the list. Even though he ruled over Babylon from 315 to 312, he did not then bear the title "king," but was only satrap (of the dead Alexander IV!). Although there is evidence that Antigonus held Babylon from about August 6, 302, to March 7, 301,[116] he did not succeed then in deposing Seleucus, who continued to rule an empire which probably included much of Babylonia outside the city of Babylon, and the period of Antigonus's hold on the city was short enough to be ignored or forgotten.

If the Persian Empire fell with its tenth king, perhaps Marduk, who had just revealed his power by bringing about the death of Antiochus III, would now make the Macedonian Empire fall with its tenth king! The expectations were so high that the priests of Marduk took the risk of supplementing the old Three-Monster version of Daniel 7. In the early 180s B.C.E., that prophecy still had only three monsters, with the third monster still having only four heads. No one was interested in adding six more heads to the third monster to make up the historical ten Persian kings. If one had wished, one probably could have found two other Persian kings besides Darius I and Xerxes who could be singled out as having injured or insulted Marduk.[117] Marduk's rhythm was obvious: he would tolerate rule over his city by no more than ten kings of a foreign dynasty. Marduk's purpose was clear. He had already eliminated Antiochus III. Surely one could not go wrong in supplementing the old prophecy by adding one more monster, this time one with ten horns to symbolize the Macedonian kings.

Those who put the Aramaic vowels into the text of Daniel 7:17 erred. We know that the monsters symbolize not kings but kingdoms. Hence the word in that verse should not be *malkhīn* ("kings") but *molkhīn* ("kingdoms"). Our text of Daniel has, not ten horns, but eleven on the fourth monster. But the eleventh horn in Daniel 7:8 and thereafter can be proved to be a later supplement. The normal thing in such a prophecy would be simply to say, "I saw a fourth beast with eleven horns." Furthermore, in no ancient dynasty did an eleventh king cause the removal of three of his predecessors! We shall find out later what the "uprooting of the three horns" means. Moreover, the normal thing in such prophecies is to describe what the beast did and how it finally was defeated. It is not normal to describe what the beast's body parts did. Finally, the vision itself just barely describes the eleventh horn, whereas the interpretation tells all sorts of things that the eleventh horn did (7:20–21, 24–25). When we found the Mixture version of Daniel 2 only in the interpretation of the vision and not in the description of it, we knew that the Mixture version of Daniel 2 must be a later supplement.

Hence, there was a stage of Daniel 7 when it had four monsters, with the fourth monster having ten horns. The supplementer who produced the ten-horn stage added a few more symbols to the dream. With the death of Antiochus III, the Iranian peoples became mostly free. Thereafter, they no longer had need to supplement the *Prophetic Zand*. The supplementer knew that in his own day the bestial Median and Persian kingdoms were free, but not yet the Babylonian kingdom (though it had long since ceased to be beastly). After the killing of the last beast in Daniel 7:11 and the humanization of the first beast in Daniel 7:4, only two beasts remained. Accordingly, the supplementer wrote in 7:12, "The other beasts lost their empires, but their lives were prolonged for a period and a time"; probably "for a period and a time" means "until Marduk's appointed time." This supplement to the dream, in the opinion of the supplementer, was self-evident. He did not bother to explain it in the interpretation of the dream.

Babylonians, not Jews, lived near the free Medians and Persians and needed to hear how their god allowed Medians and Persians but not his own favored people to be free. The Jews in far-off Judea could hardly have cared about Marduk's victory over Antiochus III or about the good fortune of the Medes and the Persians. Indeed, in the Jewish present-future prophecy at Dan 11:19 there is no claim that a miracle brought about the king's death.

Let us summarize what material in Daniel 7 belongs to what we should now call the "Four-Beast-Ten-Horn version." The vision consists of vv 1–7, 9–10. The beginning of v 11 talks about the eleventh horn, but the end of v 11, speaking of the death of the fourth beast, should belong to the Four-Beast-Ten-Horn version. Verses 12–14 complete the vision and certainly belong to the Four-Beast-Ten-Horn version, and vv 15–18, the general interpretation, also certainly belong to it. The Four-Beast-Ten-Horn version is complete in v 18. Its symbolism was clear to its audience. Only the author of the Four-Beast-Eleven-Horn version had to give a special interpretation of the fourth beast and its mixed-up symbolism in which he called attention to the superlatively dreadful present.

The Jews probably had not yet accepted the Three-Monster-Four-Head version of Daniel 7, so, if only for that reason, they were unlikely to have been the authors of the Four-Beast version. Thus, there is a good case that the Four-Beast-Ten-Horn version of Daniel 7 was originally Babylonian. We shall see that the eleventh horn certainly represents Antiochus IV Epiphanes, successor of Seleucus IV, so that the tenth horn indeed represents Seleucus IV. But if so, the prophecy soon proved false: The death of Seleucus IV in 175 did not bring the fall of the Seleucid Empire. It brought the reign of the strong king, Antiochus IV. The Four-Monster-Ten-Horn version, therefore, must have been composed after the "miraculous" death of Antiochus III in 187 and before the death of Seleucus IV in 175.

There could be an alternative to this hypothesis. After all, Daniel 7 is known to us only from the Bible. Could not Jews, despite all we have said, have been the ones who first produced the Four-Monster-Ten-Horn version? Consider the Hellenistic kings who ruled over the Jews, down through Seleucus IV:

1. Alexander the Great
2. Philip III and Alexander IV (they reigned jointly!)
3. Antigonus (as king, 306–302!)[118]
4.–8. Ptolemies I–V
9. Antiochus III
10. Seleucus IV

The Jews, too, were ruled by ten kings. But the Jews, unlike the Babylonians, knew that the kings were not all from the same dynasty.[119] Jewish supplementers would have added not just one but three monsters!

The victory of Marduk over Antiochus III in 187 B.C.E. would have meant nothing to the Jews, but in the 180s or early 170s, some Jews thought they had, at last, a miracle of their own God to cheer about. There had not even been any prophets since the fifth century B.C.E., and the latest miracle the Jews could speak of was Daniel in the lions' den! The supposed miracle in the time of Seleucus IV was the thwarting of Heliodorus, narrated in 2 Maccabees 3.

The background of that event is interesting. Joseph, the Tobiad, was the nephew of the high priest, Onias II. Onias II refused to pay out to Ptolemy III the tribute required of him, probably because he believed that fulfillment of the Mixture version of Daniel 2 was imminent. Ptolemy threatened to punish the whole Jewish nation. Joseph, the Tobiad, delivered the tribute and won the favor of Ptolemy and thus became the tax farmer for the region, a post in which he gained great wealth. In 210, upon the birth of a son (who became Ptolemy

V) to Ptolemy IV, Hyrcanus, youngest son of Joseph, won the favor of Ptolemy IV when he cleverly carried out his duties as family delegate to the celebrations at the Ptolemaic court. So over-clever was the young man in winning the king's favor that he provoked the violent jealousy of his brothers and the anger of his father. On his way back to Judea, Hyrcanus narrowly escaped being killed by his brothers and had to flee from Jerusalem. We next hear of Hyrcanus in Transjordan. Josephus does not tell us so, but from Egyptian papyri and other sources we now know that the Tobiad family had long held this area of Transjordan in a manner resembling a feudal fief and had a castle or stronghold there;[120] an earlier member of the family is mentioned in the book of Nehemiah as living in "Ammonite" territory, that is, in Transjordan.[121] Hyrcanus seized the family stronghold, and the Ptolemaic government recognized him as the tax collector for that area.

Josephus failed to identify correctly the Ptolemies of the stories of Joseph and Hyrcanus. His errors are explainable.[122] Because of those errors, Josephus did not realize that Hyrcanus's flight from Jerusalem in 210 B.C.E. was only a few years before the dangerous chaos in the Ptolemaic Empire which followed the death of Ptolemy IV. In 205, Jews were reading the Mixture version of Daniel 2, which could predict the fall of the successor kingdoms of the whole Macedonian Empire of Alexander. They were also reading Ezekiel 4, which could mean the end of Jewish subjection to foreign empires. Jews were also reading the prophecy of Ezekiel 30, which could predict the fall of the Ptolemaic Empire to the Seleucid Antiochus III. Tax farming was essentially an investment scheme. In cold reality, the Ptolemaic Empire was torn by native revolts, and the government of the child-king Ptolemy V at first could accomplish little. With such real prospects and such prophecies, who would invest in Ptolemaic Egypt? Hence, it is not surprising that the Tobiad family's career as tax farmers for the Ptolemies ended abruptly in 205/4 B.C.E., after 22 years. Most of the family deserted the Ptolemaic ship immediately. Only Hyrcanus, who had enjoyed Ptolemaic support in Transjordan, held staunchly to the Ptolemies.

Before Antiochus III won his final victory over the forces of Ptolemy V, Hyrcanus may have been viewed by the weak Ptolemaic government as their most reliable man in an area they could not hold with their own military resources. Antiochus, upon conquering Palestine in 201/200, may have ignored as insignificant the small area controlled by Hyrcanus, or perhaps Hyrcanus followed temporarily the interpretation of the prophecies that brought the Jews of Judea to switch to the Seleucid side. If so, Antiochus may have been satisfied with a pledge of loyalty from Hyrcanus.

But what happened? First, Antiochus gave his daughter in marriage to Ptolemy V, thus bringing another possibility of the fulfillment of the Mixture version of Daniel 2. Clearly, Ezekiel 30:20–26 had not been completely fulfilled, for it predicted that the Egyptians would be scattered in exile. Perhaps the prophecies of Ezekiel did not really apply! As time went by, the Mixture version more and more seemed to be in the process of fulfillment: Ptolemaic Egypt continued to totter from native revolts, and Rome stunned the Seleucid kingdom with that disastrous defeat in 189, and then Antiochus III himself fell in 187. Jews, including Hyrcanus, could well believe that the days of such empires were numbered, that Jewish loyalty either to the Ptolemies or to the Seleucids would be necessary, if at all, only for a short time.

Under these circumstances, Hyrcanus acted with full independence. As a sort of robber baron in the later reign of Seleucus IV, he collected taxes from the indigenous population for his own profit. As for the Jews of Judea, they were now led by their high priest, Onias III, the hero of 2 Maccabees 3. We find him presented there as a discreetly loyal subject of Seleucus IV, so loyal that in return the king, despite his own shortage of money, gladly paid the heavy expenses of the obligatory daily sacrifices at the Jewish temple. Onias III also impressed the historian in 2 Maccabees as a scrupulous enforcer of Jewish law. From the narrative, it is very clear that in this period the high priest was responsible for collecting the taxes of the Jews and for delivering the money to the king. We may assume that Onias III scrupulously collected the taxes and paid them to the royal treasury. Yet he, too, had read the prophecies and probably viewed the days of the Hellenistic empires as numbered. Though in no way a rebel, Onias III dared to accept, for safe deposit in the temple, money belonging to the now independent chieftain Hyrcanus.

Temples were favorite places for safe-deposit; the gods and public opinion would severely punish anyone, even a king, who dared to rob a temple. Hyrcanus probably had surrounded himself with mercenaries of doubtful loyalty and needed a safe place to keep his money. Onias III allowed his second cousin, Hyrcanus, to use the temple for safe-deposit. The weak government of Seleucus IV securely held Jerusalem but was in no mood to invade Transjordan in an effort to suppress Hyrcanus. The Seleucid garrison did not interfere with local affairs like the deposit or withdrawal of private money at the temple. Hyrcanus probably thought his funds would be safe there.

All would have gone smoothly, but for a quarrel over a political appointment at Jerusalem, between the high priest, Onias III, and the second ranking priest, Simon of the priestly clan Bilgah.[123] Simon lost the political struggle, but in revenge, he went to the royal government and let the authorities know of Hyrcanus's huge sums on deposit. The author of the story in 2 Maccabees wished to portray Onias III and the temple of Jerusalem as entirely innocent victims of Simon's slander and Seleucus's greed for money. But when we see the narrative presenting Onias himself as admitting that the temple holds large funds belonging to Hyrcanus, we know that he is admitting that the temple holds large funds belonging to a man who is in fact a rebel against the empire, though the Seleucid government is now too weak to suppress him. Under all systems of royal law, the money of a rebel could be confiscated by the king. The only question was whether the sanctity of the temple overrode royal law. Onias held that it did. The royal government held that in this case royal law applied—surely the just God of Jerusalem would not shelter the funds of a rebel against the legitimate king.

Seleucus entrusted the task of collecting the money to his minister, Heliodorus. The dramatic narrative of 2 Maccabees 3 reports how distressed were Onias III and the Jews of Jerusalem over the prospect that money deposited for safekeeping in the LORD's temple might be confiscated. Jews still believed that their own God would punish them grievously for any act of disobedience against the pagan king he had placed over them. So they opposed Heliodorus only by the resistance of prayer. Surprisingly, Heliodorus failed to seize the deposits. According to 2 Macc 3:24–25, 27, a supernatural being mounted on a horse felled the king's minister as he was about to enter the temple treasury. Two supernatural beings, visible only to Heliodorus, whipped him where he lay (2 Macc 3:26). The twofold nature of this report invites suspicion. Indeed, it is clear that some Jews, including the author of 1 Maccabees and Josephus, believed that no miracle had occurred.[124] One cannot prove that the miracle-tale is false, but one can suggest that Heliodorus feared that he would suffer the fate of Antiochus III and colluded with Onias III to produce the miracle-tale, which could serve as his excuse to Seleucus IV for failing to seize the money.

Nevertheless, it is clear that many Jews believed a miracle had occurred. Certainly Jason of Cyrene and his audience so believed, as did the author of Dan 11:20 and his.[125] An important question arose: Was the term of punishment, of serving foreign kings, over? When would it no longer be necessary to obey the pagan king? An error on this issue had proved disastrous to Jewish rebels between 203 and 201 B.C.E. Few if any wanted to repeat that error. In particular, the high priest Onias III remained unswervingly loyal to Seleucus IV. Those Jews who believed that the foiling of Heliodorus was indeed a miracle were quick to notice that Babylonians had published the Four-Monster-Ten-Horn version of the prophecy of Bêl-balâtsu-uṣur. Unhesitatingly those Jews claimed the prophecy as Jewish and insisted that its author was none other than the Jew, Daniel. For such Jews, the time for resisting pagan outrages by prayer only, not by fighting, seemed nearly over. Events at first seemed to confirm their expectations.

Miracle or not, the thwarting of Heliodorus did not deter Simon of the clan of Bilgah from pursuing his feud with Onias III. A henchman of Simon's even perpetrated murders, and Simon could count on support from the governor of the province that included Judea. Under such pressure, Onias went to Antioch to appeal to the king to intervene. But Seleucus did not live long enough to act on Onias's appeal.[126] Nothing indicates that Onias ever returned to Jerusalem.

Heliodorus himself appears to have murdered Seleucus IV in 175 B.C.E. and to have put Seleucus's available heir, an infant, on the throne as King Antiochus (historians give him no numeral), though an older son, Demetrius, was then a hostage in Rome. Heliodorus clearly intended to be the real power behind the infant. However, the expectations of Jews and of Heliodorus were disappointed. Antiochus IV, the capable and forceful brother of Seleucus IV, had just been released from being a hostage in Rome and marched in. Heliodorus disappears—Antiochus IV probably had him killed. Antiochus IV adopted the infant and eventually had him killed, too (170 B.C.E.).[127] So forcefully did Antiochus IV set about ruling the kingdom that bold Hyrcanus, after years of being independent in Transjordan, gave up the contest with the Seleucid king and committed suicide, probably in 169 B.C.E.[128] But the hitherto inflexibly loyal Jews were soon to rise in revolt.

NOTES

1   See chap 12, n 169.

2   Hatto H. Schmitt, *Untersuchungen zur Geschichte Antiochos' der Grossen und seiner Zeit* (Wiesbaden: Steiner, 1964), 30–31.

3   Polybius iv.48.

4   Polybius iv.48.10; Will, *Histoire,* II, 16–17.

5   Polybius v.40.7–41.3; Will, *Histoire,* II, 17–18.

6   Polybius v.41.6—45.6, 46.5—48.16; Will, *Histoire,* II, 18–20.

7   Antiochus's abortive expedition: Polybius v.45.7—46.5, 48.17; Will, *Histoire,* II, 19–20. The present-future prophecy in Daniel 11 takes no note of the expedition, per-

haps because it so soon failed or perhaps because it had no effect on Jewish territory. Deaths of Epigenes and Hermeias and victory over Molon: Polybius v.49.1–56.15.

8   See Elias J. Bickerman, "The Seleucids and the Achaemenids," in his *Religions and Politics in the Hellenistic and Roman Periods,* ed. Emilio Gabba and Morton Smith (Como: Edizioni New Press, 1985), 497; Will, *Histoire,* II, 21.

9   Polybius v.55.1–2; see Schmitt, *Antiochos,* 124.

10   See chap 12, p. 390.

11   Polybius v.57; Will, *Histoire,* II, 23–26.

12   Polybius v.34–39; Will, *Histoire,* II, 26–27.

13   Polybius v.58.1–61.2; Will, *Histoire,* II, 29–30.

14   Above, pp. 406–7.

15   Polybius v.61.3—66.9; Will, *Histoire,* II, 29–37.

16   Polybius v.68–71, 79–80; Will, *Histoire,* II, 37. See map 1 inset.

17   For the date, see my *I Maccabees,* 43.

18   Montgomery, *Daniel,* 456.

19   Montgomery, ibid.

20   Polybius v.79, 82–83; Green, *Alexander to Actium,* 289(last paragraph)–90.

21   Polybius v.82–87; Will, *Histoire,* II, 37–40. On the supposed weakness of Ptolemy and on the information provided by the "Raphia Decree" on the Pithom Stele, see Heinen in CAH[2], Vol. VII, Part I, 437–38.

22   Polybius v.107.1–3.

23   Will, *Histoire,* II, 40–44, 302. The rebellious Egyptians may well have been behaving in a manner similar to a *people of an almighty god.* However, the important present-future prophecy (the *Oracle of the Potter*) belongs to a later period (see the articles of Ludwig Koenen, cited above in chap 3, n 12). Though in beginning my research I had planned to treat the Egyptian revolts against the Ptolemies, I no longer intend to do so. Life is too short!

24 One might also render the words after "against the King of the North" as follows: "Though he [Antiochus] shall have mustered a great multitude, that multitude shall be given into his [Ptolemy's] hand."

25 When accompanied, as here, by the Hebrew root *rwm* ("be high"), the verb *nissa'* means "be lifted up," "be lofty"; cf. Isa 2:13, 6:1, 57:15, and especially 52:13 (of a person).

26 The change of grammatical subject here, from the Egyptians in the phalanx to Ptolemy, is harsh, though in keeping with the poor syntax of Daniel 11–12. Alternatively, one might retain the multitude of Egyptians in the phalanx as the subject, "It shall not prove strong"; despite crushingly defeating Antiochus's forces at Raphia, the Egyptians were unable to conquer portions of the Seleucid Empire or even to retake Seleukeia in Pieria, and their revolts in Egypt were mostly limited to guerrilla warfare and were ultimately fought down.

27 Polybius v.87.2 (cf. v.66.3, 67.12); Will, *Histoire,* II, 47.

28 Polybius v.107.4, vii.15–18; viii.15–21; Will, *Histoire,* II, 49–50.

29 Persis: Will, *Histoire,* II, 63–65; shortfall: Polybius viii.23; x.27–31, 49; xi.34; xiii.9; Will, *Histoire,* II, 51–65.

30 Spoliation: Polybius x.27 and Boyce, HZ, III, 90–91; attack on Parthian kingdom: Polybius x.28–31; Justin xli.5.7.

31 Will, *Histoire,* II, 108–11.

32 Will, *Histoire,* II, 113–14.

33 Polybius iii.2.8, xv.20; Will, *Histoire,* II, 114–17.

34 Maurice Holleaux, *Études d'épigraphie et d'histoire grecques,* Tome III: Lagides et Séleucides (Paris: E. de Boccard, 1942), 320.

35 The word *shānīm* (years) looks superfluous, but can be shown to serve a purpose of the author. On this and on *qṣ,* see pp. 412–27.

36 Pp. 408–9; cf. Josephus *Antiquities* xii.3.3.129–30.

37 Holleaux, *Études,* III, 320–21; B. Bar-Kochva (*The Seleucid Army* [Cambridge: Cambridge University Press, 1976], 146 and 256, n 2) has misread both of his authorities.

38 *In Danielem* iii, to Dan 11:14.

39 Polybius xv.25; Will, *Histoire,* II, 109.

40 Josephus *Antiquities* xii.3.3.131–36; Dan 11:15–16; Polybius xvi.18; Holleaux, *Études,* III, 321–26; Frank W. Walbank, *A Historical Commentary on Polybius* (Oxford: Clarendon Press, 1957–), II (1967), 523. On the battle of Panion, see Bar-Kochva, *Seleucid Army,* 140–57. See map 1 inset.

41 Jerome *In Danielem* iii to Daniel 11:15–16; Holleaux, *Études,* III, 326–27.

42 Jews join in reducing the citadel: Josephus *Antiquities* xii.3.3.129–33, 138, 143–44. Antiochus in control by summer, 198: Livy xxxiii.19.8; Holleaux, *Études,* 327.

43 Josephus *Antiquities* xii.3.3.129–30, 138, 143–44.

44 See my *II Maccabees,* 151.

45 Josephus *Antiquities* xii.4.1–11.157–236, to be corrected by my article, "The Tales of the Tobiads," in *Christianity, Judaism, and Other Greco-Roman Cults: Studies for Morton Smith at Sixty,* ed. Jacob Neusner (4 vols.; Leiden: Brill, 1975), Part III, 85–123.

46 After telling of the Ptolemaic victory at Raphia in 217, Polybius (v.86.10) says that the populations of Koilê Syria continually tend to favor the Ptolemies.

47 Ezek 1:2.

48 Ezek 4:4–5; cf. ibid., v 9.

49 On *ʿwn* as "punishment," see Moshe Greenberg, *Ezekiel, 1–20* ("Anchor Bible," vol. 22; Garden City, NY: Doubleday, 1983), 105. The Hebrew text of Ezek 4:5–9 has "390," whereas the Greek version has "190"; cf. Greenberg, *Ezekiel,* 105–6. There can be no doubt that the Greek version there represents the original reading: The punishment of Israel is to be 150 years longer than the punishment of Judah. The first exile from the northern kingdom occurred in the reign of Pekah (2 Kings 15:29). Pekah reigned ca. 736–732 B.C.E., about 150 years before 593/2 B.C.E. Ezekiel envisioned the 190-year exile of Israel and the forty-year exile of Judah as ending simultaneously. Judah's exile actually lasted fifty-nine years, from 597 to 538, counting from the exile of Jehoiachin as befits Ezekiel. The duration clearly was more than forty years, but the discrepancy could be tolerated, especially in view of the longstanding belief that punishments lasted forty years (see chap 1, p. 10). But with the passing of 403/2 B.C.E. the prediction of 190 years in Ezekiel 4:5–9 was clearly false; we may assume that a believer changed the text to read "390."

50 See Ezek 37:19.

51 E.g., Ezekiel 2:3, 3:4, 4:13, 6:5, 9:8, 12:27, 14:9.

52 On the defective Hebrew, see H. L. Ginsberg, *Studies in Daniel* (New York: Jewish Theological Seminary of America, 1948), 41–61.

53 Above, pp. 411–12.

54 See Dan 8:17, 19; 9:26; 11:35, 40; 12:6, 13. At 11:6, *qṣ šnym* ("an appointed span of years") probably means a jubilee of forty-nine or fifty years, the time between the Battle of Ipsos and the Mixture Marriage.

55 Ezek 7:7, 12; cf. Ezek 21:30, 34; 35:5.

56 Here is the error of the translators. They have taken *rbym yʿmdw ʿl mlk hngb* to mean that the majority in Jerusalem rebelled against Ptolemy. But Josephus says (xii.3.3.132) that the Jews, on being attacked by Skopas, *joined* him. Interpreters have not noticed that the expression in the passage is *yʿmdw ʿl*, not *yqwmw ʿl. qwm ʿl* regularly means "rise up against, "attack," but *ʿmd ʿl* more often means "stand over," "serve," "act in behalf of," "protect the interests of"; cf. Num 7:2, Deut 27:13, Zech 4:14, Dan 12:1, 1 Chr 6:17, and perhaps even 1 Sam 1:9–10. See also Saul Lieberman, *Greek in Jewish Palestine* (New York: Jewish Theological Seminary of America, 5702 = 1942), 64.

57 The expression "men of violence" (*bny pryṣy;* literally, "sons of the violent") is derived from Ezek 18:10.

58 "Vision" (Hebrew *ḥāzōn*) in Ezekiel means a prophecy, not necessarily something seen; see Ezek 12:23, 27.

59 The text has been edited by Chaim Rabin, *The Zadokite Documents* (Oxford: Clarendon Press, 1958), and by Philip R. Davies, *The Damascus Covenant: an Interpretation of the "Damascus Document"* (JSOTSup 25; Sheffield: JSOT Press, 1983); for the fragments found at Qumran, see Joseph M. Baumgarten, *Qumran Cave 4, XIII: The Damascus Document (4Q266-273)* ("Discoveries in the Judean Desert," XVIII; Oxford: Clarendon Press, 1996).

60 CD 1:1–11. The Qumran versions are in Baumgarten, *Damascus Document,* 14, 119.

61 2 Kgs 21:1–16.

62 Psalm 82 reflects the same sort of thinking.

63 Suffering at the hands of neighbors: Mal 1:1–4, Joel 4:19. Zech 9:5–6; Neh 1:3, 2:10, 19; 3:33–35, 4:1–2, 6:1–9, 16–19. Intermarriage: Ezra 9–10; Neh 9:23–29.

64 On the twelve shepherds of 89:72, see George W. E. Nickelsburg, *Hermeneia: A Commentary on 1 Enoch* (forthcoming), note on 89:59–90:19. In 90:1, all manuscripts have "thirty-seven" as the number of the shepherds, but it is an error, as is implied by 90:5.

65 Based largely upon M. A. Knibb, *The Ethiopic Book of Enoch* (2 vols.; Oxford: Clarendon Press, 1978), II, 212–14.

66 See Patrick A. Tiller, *A Commentary on the Animal Apocalypse of I Enoch* ("Society of Biblical Literature: Early Judaism and Its Literature," Number 4; Atlanta, GA: Scholars Press, 1993), 351–52.

67 Two manuscripts omit "eagles"; they were probably correct to do so, as we shall soon find.

68 The expression "fell into the shadow" is strange. "Into the shadow" in Aramaic is *bṭl'*; I suspect that the original Aramaic had the verb *bṭlw* ("they ceased"); cf. H. L. Ginsberg, *Studies in Koheleth* (New York: Jewish Theological Seminary of America, 5711 = 1950), 22, and see chap 14, pp. 459–60, on Judas Maccabaeus's "victory" over Lysias.

69 One manuscript omits "eagles"; it was probably correct to do so, as we shall soon find.

70 See chap 12, pp. 368–70.

71 See Robert H. Charles, *The Book of Enoch* (2d ed.; Oxford: Clarendon Press, 1912), 195.

72 On Greeks in the Ptolemaic armies of the third and second centuries B.C.E., see Marcel Launey, *Recherches sur les armées hellénistiques* (2 vols.; Paris: E. de Boccard, 1949–50), I, 92–93, 100; Greeks in the armies of Antiochus III: ibid., 98. Thracians in the Ptolemaic and Seleucid armies: ibid., 49, 92, 98, 374–80; Jeanne and Louis Robert, "Bulletin épigraphique, 1979," *Revue des études grecques*, 92 (1979), 532 (No. 635); V. Velkov and A. Fol, *Les Thraces en Égypte gréco-romain* ("Studia Thracica," 4; Sophia, 1977).

73   The allusions to the deeds of Judas Maccabaeus will be treated in chap 14.

74   In 90:13, Tana Ethiopic ms. 9 and EMML 6281 omit "eagles."; in 90:16, Abbadianus 55 omits the word. See Tiller, *Commentary,* 31, 142–43.

75   See Robert H. Charles, *The Book of Enoch or 1 Enoch* (2d ed.; Oxford: Clarendon Press, 1912), 201.

76   See Charles's note on *1 Enoch* 89:59–90:19.

77   One should not jump to the conclusion that the unit is seven years on the basis of Daniel 9:24. We shall find in chap 14 that the author of Daniel 9 wrote in 164/3 B.C.E., long after the original writer of the Animal Vision, and he knew that Enoch lived long before Daniel. Yet he treats the seventy weeks of years as a new revelation!

78   See Mordechai Cogan and Hayim Tadmor, *II Kings* ("Anchor Bible," vol. 11; n.p.: Doubleday, 1988), 341. Can a Jewish composer of a present-future prophecy have known even the approximate dates of the reign of King Manasseh? Certainly the rabbis erred greatly on the chronology of the times between the reign of Manasseh and the late third century B.C.E. See especially their fantastic misconception of the length of the period of Persian rule, *Seder ʿolam rabba,* ed. Ber Ratner (New York: Talmudical Research Institute, 1966), chap 30, 136–37, 141, or *Babylonian Talmud, ʿAbodah zarah* 9a. But the rabbis probably followed the Pharisees; other Jewish sects may have had better reckoning of historical dates. Whether by luck or by skill, the Men of Violence knew that 390 years had elapsed since the time of Ezekiel's prophecy, and we are about to find that the author of the Animal Vision knew that the crushing of the Horned Rams occurred during the last twelve-period division of the seventy periods of seven years beginning in the reign of Manasseh. Similarly, we shall find that the author of Daniel 9 measured forty-nine years (v 25) from Jeremiah's prophecy about the resettlement and rebuilding of Jerusalem (587 B.C.E.; Jeremiah 32–33) down to the decree of Cyrus to rebuild the temple (538 B.C.E.; Ezra 1:1–4), and knew (v 24) that almost 490 years had elapsed between the reign of King Manasseh and his own present (164/3 B.C.E.).

79   See Nickelsburg, *Commentary,* excursus in the note on *1 Enoch* 89:59–90:19, Table 3.

80   I hope to treat the problems elsewhere.

81   I have omitted *wʿm mbḥryw* from my translation because I do not know what the words mean.

82   Or "A final destruction shall be in his power."

83 Wisdom of Ben Sira 50:1, 4; see my "Alexander and the Jews," *PAAJR* 59 (1993), 92–94. On the other hand, Will (*Histoire,* II, 119) takes note of the fact that Antiochus III in the documents at Josephus *Antiquities* xii.3.3.138 does not even mention the high priest, so that one may doubt that Simeon's influence was the decisive factor in inducing most Jews to support Antiochus.

84 Josephus xii.3.3–4.138–146.

85 See my *I Maccabees,* 194–96.

86 Will, *Histoire,* II, 119. See also my article, "The Message of Aristeas to Philokrates," in *Eretz Israel, Israel, and the Jewish Diaspora: Mutual Relations,* ed. Menachem Mor (Lanham, New York, and London: University Press of America, 1991), 19–20, n 12.

87 Livy xxxii.8.9–16, 27.1; Will, *Histoire,* II, 179–81.

88 Will, *Histoire,* II, 181–85.

89 Polybius xviii. 47.1–4, 49–52; Livy xxxiii.34.1–4, 39.3–40.6; Will, *Histoire,* II, 186–89.

90 xviii.51.10.

91 Will, *Histoire,* II, 190–93.

92 Livy xxxv.13.4.

93 See chap 12, pp. 385–92.

94 On Dan 11:17, see Ginsberg, *Studies,* 57, 61; Hartman and Di Lella, *Daniel,* 258. On the *Oracle of Hystaspes,* see Eddy, *King,* 32–36; Boyce, HZ, III, 376–81.

95 Will, *Histoire,* II, 82–85.

96 Previous bitter war: Will, *Histoire,* II, 71–76; Rome makes alliance with Aetolians, ibid., 87–89.

97 Will, *Histoire,* II, 91.

98 Will, *Histoire,* II, 94–97.

99 See Will, *Histoire,* II, 131–49.

100   Livy xxxi.40.9–10.

101   On the course of the war, see Will, *Histoire,* II, 149–60.

102   Polybius xviii.21.5–22.7; Livy, xxxiii.6.6, 7.13.

103   Polybius xviii.34.1–2; Livy xxxiii.11.8–10.

104   Polybius xviii.36.5–37.12; Livy xxxiii.12.3–13.

105   Polybius xviii.38.3–9; Livy xxxiii.13.6–12.

106   Polybius xviii.39.1–2; Livy xxxiii.13.13.

107   Will, *Histoire,* II, 169–78.

108   Will, *Histoire,* II, 200–206.

109   Will, *Histoire,* II, 206–7.

110   See Hartman and DiLella, Daniel, 258, 268.

111   Polybius xxi.42, 45; Will, *Histoire,* II, 221–31.

112   Diodorus xxviii.3, xxix.15; Justin xxxii.2.1–2; Will, *Histoire,* II, 238–40.

113   Gen 10:22, 14:1 and 9; Isa 21:2, Jer 49:34–39, etc.

114   Bikerman, *Institutions,* 5.

115   Darius III as the tenth Persian king to rule over Babylon: Babylonian dated documents show that Xerxes II was not recognized as king over Babylon, leaving only ten Persian kings in the list of those who ruled Babylon See Parker and Dubberstein, *Babylonian Chronology* ("Brown University Studies," XIX; Providence, RI: Brown University Press, 1956), 18.

Babylonian list in the British Museum: Abraham J. Sachs and D. J. Wiseman, "A Babylonian King List of the Hellenistic Period," *Iraq* 16 (1954), 202–12.

116   Above, chap 12, p. 367.

117   Cf. the procedure in the four-branched *Prophetic Zand,* where three kings had to be symbolized by the three Persian branches, though ten to twelve kings had reigned.

118   See p. 369.

119 See pp. 374–75.

120 B. Mazar, "The Tobiads," *Israel Exploration Journal*, 7 (1957), 137–45, 229–38, and see especially my treatment of the Tobiads in my *Semites, Iranians, Greeks, and Romans*, 115–51.

121 Neh 2:10, 19, 3:35, etc.

122 See my article in my *Semites*, 119–42.

123 See my *II Maccabees*, 201–3.

124 See my *II Maccabees*, 197–99.

125 See my *II Maccabees*, 196–97.

126 2 Macc 4:1–7 with my *II Maccabees*, 220 (next to last paragraph)–223 (line 2).

127 See Will, *Histoire*, II, 304–6. Dan 11:20 bears witness to the accession of Seleucus IV and to the brevity of his reign. Dan 11:21 reports the accession of Antiochus IV, who hitherto had not been the heir to the throne. H. L. Ginsberg suggested to me reading *bšlwh* in Dan 11:21 and 24 as derived from *šlw* ("deceit"), parallel to *bḥlqlqwt*, the last word of 11:21. Then, Dan 11:21(end) becomes "And he [Antiochus IV] shall come deceitfully and seize royal power by trickery." For *haššetef* in Dan 11:22, read *hiššātēf* (cf. Hartman and Di Lella, Daniel, 258, n ii–ii). Attach the last three words of Dan 11:22 to v 23. Then, Dan 11:22(end)–23 becomes, "The forces shall melt completely away before him, and also the prelate of the Covenant [Menelaus] through association with him [Antiochus IV] shall work treachery and thus rise to rule over the small people [Israel; cf. Deut 7:7]"; cf. my *II Macccabees*, 262.

128 See my *II Maccabees*, 208.

14

The Reigns of Antiochus IV and V

1. The Civic Policy of Antiochus IV

WHILE HE WAS A HOSTAGE at Rome, the future Antiochus IV was forbidden to leave Italy, but he was left free to observe the institutions there that had made Rome invincible.[1] Especially important had been the military manpower of the great republic. How far could a conquering power expand its holdings? Surely it had to keep under its control the populations already conquered. Would not a point be reached at which there would be insufficient manpower to perform the two tasks, of keeping the conquered under control while going on to further conquests? Roman policy in Italy went far toward the successful accomplishment of both tasks. Some conquered communities there were Latin—they spoke the same language as did the Romans. Others did not, and are called Italic. But all conquered communities in Italy became allies of Rome, obligated to provide manpower for Rome's wars, but free from paying taxes to her. The allies could feel discontent over having to fight in Rome's wars, but they were compensated by the protection Rome faithfully gave her allies. Any discontent felt by the allies was much less than that which would have arisen from having to pay taxes to a government they necessarily regarded as foreign. Thus, Rome gained the manpower of her subject allies and usually did not have to waste her own to keep them under control. There was another result of this Roman policy. If a conquered people was subjected to taxation, it became a tempting field for exploitation by Rome and her officials. If it instead contributed to Rome's military manpower, it became an ally to be valued and to be kept favorable to Rome. In contrast, Hellenistic empires that pursued aggressive policies could pursue them and simultaneously keep control of the conquered only by hiring mercenaries of dubious loyalty, and their financial resources for hiring them were quickly exhausted. Some Latin and Italic communities in Italy received full Roman citizenship.

Antiochus also observed how Rome's practice of conferring power on *elected* magistrates contributed to civic loyalty and reduced the danger of civil strife. On becoming king of the Seleucid Empire, Antiochus proclaimed an Antiochene republic. He invited many groups of his subjects to accept Antiochene citizenship with attendant privileges. Even though he was an absolute monarch, he campaigned to be elected to magistracies of his republic!

Both under Jewish law[2] and under the law of the Seleucid Empire, the death of the ruling king terminated all his appointments. Whoever was to be high priest under Antiochus IV had to receive his office from the new king.

2. Jason Usurps the High Priesthood

THE JEWS' HIGH PRIEST, Onias III, had a clever and ambitious brother, Joshua or Jesus, called in Greek Jason.[3] By heredity, Jason was as eligible to be high priest as was Onias. And Onias had too long been in Antioch and absent from Jerusalem. On learning of Antiochus's Antiochene republic, Jason saw opportunities for himself. He knew the ambitious king needed much money and offered him increased tribute plus an ample payment for the privilege of being the founder of a community of Antiochene citizens at Jerusalem. Pleased, Antiochus accepted the offers and made Jason high priest in place of Onias. Jason's project might have been impeded by "humane concessions" *(philanthrôpa)* granted by Antiochus III. Those concessions had ratified rigorist interpretations of Jewish laws against close association with Gentiles, but Antiochus IV issued decrees nullifying the concessions. Furthermore, Jason and his followers must have argued that the Torah itself did not forbid their "reforms."[4] Indeed, even pious Jews did not resist Jason's program, surely believing that to do so would be to resist the king placed over them by God.[5]

At first, all went smoothly. Jason paid the tribute. A delegation from the Antiochenes of Jerusalem attended the quinquennial games at Tyre. Jason sent with them the 300 drachma admission fee, ignoring the fact that normally the money would go for a sacrifice to Tyrian Herakles. The members of the delegation were more scrupulous and insisted that the money be spent on a non-idolatrous purpose.[6] Antiochus IV paid a cordial visit to Jerusalem,[7] showing that relations between him and the Jews were amicable.

3. Menealus Usurps the High Priesthood

JASON'S POLICIES WERE CLEARLY different from those of his deposed brother Onias. In 172 B.C.E., three years after becoming high priest, Jason used, as his agent for dealing with the king, Menelaus, the brother of Onias's enemy, Simon of the clan of Bilgah. That was a mistake. Menelaus belonged to a priestly clan and had some backing in Jerusalem. He proceeded to outbid Jason for the high priesthood and became high priest and head of the Antiochene community at Jerusalem. Jason withdrew to the Ammanitis, to Transjordan, probably to the stronghold of his second cousin, Hyrcanus, the Tobiad, who may still have been alive. However, Menelaus found it impossible to deliver the promised increased revenue and stole temple vessels. Summoned to the king, he left as substitute high priest his brother, Lysimachos. However, Antiochus left Antioch to put down uprisings in Cilicia. Andronikos was left in charge at Antioch, as the king's deputy. Menelaus sold some of the stolen vessels in Tyre and neighboring cities and delivered others to Andronikos.[8] Both Jews and Greeks viewed temple robbery as a heinous sin. Pious Jews and probably even Antiochene Jews must have been indignant. Onias, fully informed of Menelaus's acts, withdrew to the place of asylum at Daphne by Antioch, where he thought he would be secure, and denounced him. Menelaus begged Andronikos to do away with Onias, and treacherously Andronikos did so.[9]

Onias was famous among the Jews and Gentiles of Antioch for his probity, and public opinion was enraged at his murder. When Antiochus returned from Cilicia, the Jews of Antioch, supported by the Greeks, presented a petition to him, charging that Onias had been killed unjustly. Antiochus responded immediately by having Andronikos executed at the site of the murder, thus still displaying amity toward righteous Jews.[10] Back at Jerusalem, many temple vessels had been stolen by Lysimachos (Menelaus's brother and deputy) with the connivance of Menelaus. When reports of the matter spread to the countryside, the unarmed people massed against Lysimachos. Though Lysimachos was Menelaus's deputy, he had not been appointed by Antiochus. The people felt that God would tolerate a rebellion against the deputy and his 3,000 armed men.

The rebels improvised weapons from stones and rubbish, defeated Lysimachos's force, and slew the temple robber himself at the treasury, the site of his thefts. These events became the basis for a suit against Menelaus. Three delegates from the Council of Elders argued the case before Antiochus at Tyre. Menelaus in his peril promised a large bribe to the important official, Ptolemy son of Dorymenes, and Ptolemy privately induced the king to acquit Menelaus and to condemn to death the innocent delegates of the Council of Elders. Antiochus and his officials by now had committed acts against the interests of righteous Jews.[11] Menelaus retained the high priesthood, having proved himself to be a temple robber, suborner of murder, and briber. Both the *ethnos* of the Jews and the Antiochenes at Jerusalem must have had misgivings about such a leader, but as long as Menelaus could pose as the king's appointee, many of the *ethnos* and of the Antiochene community would hold that both God's law and man's law forbade rebellion against the high priest. But the king might change his mind about Menelaus, or the king might die; then Menelaus would be vulnerable.

4. Antiochus IV in Egypt

IN 170 B.C.E., THE REGENTS in Ptolemaic Egypt planned to undo the results of the Battle of Panion. Three children then shared the Egyptian throne: Ptolemy VI, his younger brother Ptolemy (the future Ptolemy VIII) and their sister, Cleopatra II. Even so, the regents felt ready to go to war. Antiochus, however, struck first and overran all of Egypt except Alexandria. Ptolemy VI fell into Antiochus's hands. Diehards in Alexandria rallied around the younger Ptolemy and Cleopatra. Antiochus responded to the challenge by deposing Ptolemy VI and having himself crowned king of Egypt at Memphis. He then reinstated Ptolemy VI as king of Egypt. No longer did Ptolemy VI rule as heir of the Ptolemaic dynasty. Rather, he now owed his royal title to Antiochus. If we may borrow the language of medieval European feudalism, Ptolemy VI now reigned as Antiochus's vassal, and Antiochus could pose as the defender of the interests of Ptolemy VI against the claims of his brother and sister.[12]

5. Jason's Coup at Jerusalem

ANTIOCHUS PROCEEDED TO TRY to reduce the diehards in Alexandria. Unfortunately, Polybius's account of what happened then is lost. Our next information comes from 2 Maccabees: A false rumor of Antiochus's death reached Jerusalem. All who loathed Menelaus now could feel free to strike against him, at least until a new king should reappoint Menelaus as high priest. The deposed Jason saw his opportunity. Accompanied by some 1,000 armed followers, he moved back across the Jordan and took Jerusalem, with great brutality.[13] Thus, civil war broke out between the partisans of Jason and those of Menelaus. The non-Antiochene Jews were caught in the middle. Fed up with the sins of the Antiochenes and their leaders, the pious Jews appear to have struck against both parties of Antiochenes. They drove Jason out of Jerusalem and drove Menelaus to take refuge in the old citadel.[14]

From Antiochus's point of view, Jason's coup was an act of rebellion against his kingdom, and the attack of the people on Menelaus was an attack on the king's appointed official. Both uprisings appeared to be revolts against the king.[15] The violence at Jerusalem was sufficient to make Antiochus withdraw with his army from Egypt. Why? I have considered this problem before and have concluded that, as a usurper distrusted by invincible Rome, he had much to fear if he failed to suppress and punish revolts in his kingdom.[16] Though the Romans were temporarily tied down by the Third[17] Macedonian War, they might be quick to send their hostage, Demetrius, to be a rival pretender to the Seleucid throne. Putting down the unruly Jews at Jerusalem was therefore no task to entrust to a subordinate. Antiochus postponed his project of completing his conquest of Egypt. He left his "vassal," Ptolemy VI, in charge of that country and hastened with his army to Jerusalem.

6. Antiochus Sacks Jerusalem

THE PIOUS MILITANTS in Jerusalem may have felt themselves still loyal to Antiochus when he proved to be alive. They may even have been the ones who obeyed their king and opened the gates of the city to him.[18] Antiochus, however, stood by his appointee Menelaus and by Menelaus's Antiochene supporters and hence cruelly suppressed the pious militants, sacked the city, and despoiled the temple.[19] Indeed, as even pious Jews could have viewed it, there had been a sinful rebellion, by Jason, against Antiochus IV, the sovereign chosen by God to rule over them. The sin could well require as expiation the surrender of the temple treasures, as before, when Rehoboam had surrendered them to Shishak.[20] Not all Jews, however, believed that the sin responsible for the cruel sack was Jason's rebellion against the king or the siege by the pious of Menelaus in the citadel. A piece of present-future prophecy survives from the period. *Jubilees* 23:11–31 (and perhaps the entire book of *Jubilees*) was written betweem 169 and 167 B.C.E., and thus, in the aftermath of Antiochus's punishment of Jerusalem.[21] I have demonstrated that the writer of *Jubilees* 23:13–25 "predicts" that pious young Israelites will strive in vain to use the sword to turn sinning Jews back into the path of righteousness and that some wicked Jews will escape from these bloody clashes and will go on to exalt themselves to deceit and wealth and to defile the holy of holies. Thereafter he predicts that "the sinners the Gentiles" will punish Israel cruelly. I have demonstrated that these "predictions" reflect the events narrated in 2 Macc

4:39–5:16.[22] To judge by *Jubilees* 23:13–25, the sins that brought on the disasters were general violation of the Torah[23] and the failure of most Jews to follow the teachings of the sect of *Jubilees* regarding the Jewish calendar.[24]

Many Jews must have deduced that another factor was the disastrous sin. Even with all the changes of ruler that Jerusalem experienced in the years after 323 B.C.E., the city had not had so to suffer large-scale massacres, captivity, and enslavement. Indeed, no such disaster had occurred since the fall of Jerusalem to Nebuchadnezzar in 586 B.C.E. Only a new deadly sin could be responsible for this kind of disaster. The program of Jason and his Antiochenes was unprecedented and new; its compatibility with the Torah was very doubtful. How could it not be the reason why God in his wrath allowed such a catastrophe to befall his people?[25]

For Jews who reasoned in this manner, the course to take was clear: The practices of the Antiochenes were perilously close to idolatry and had brought upon Jerusalem the wrath of God. Jews must therefore strive to eliminate the Antiochenes, in accordance with Deut 17:7 ("You shall sweep out the evil from your midst"). Pious Jews still refrained from rebelling against the king, but no religious principle forbade them to attack Jewish Antiochenes. Antiochus, on the other hand, felt bound to protect his "citizens." We are not surprised that on leaving conquered Jerusalem, Antiochus left "in charge of maltreating our race"[26] (i.e., of preventing or punishing attacks on Antiochenes) Philip the Phrygian and Menelaus.

Pious Jews, however, could only infer, from the actions of Philip and Menelaus and the continued presence of the Antiochenes, that God was still angry. All the more, then, were the pious impelled to try to eliminate them, and all the more did the pious infuriate the king.

7. Rome Forces Antiochus, Embittered, to Withdraw from Egypt

MEANWHILE, PTOLEMY VI MADE common cause with his brother and sister in Alexandria and broke his agreement with Antiochus. The Seleucid would have to return to Egypt with his army if he was to retain his conquests there.[27] Antiochus's army again overran Egypt except for Alexandria. However, confronted by a Roman demand to withdraw, he bitterly complied.[28] For what followed, we must combine the evidence of Daniel 11 with that of 1 and 2 Maccabees. The procedure is difficult. At Daniel 11:30, one must read "and he shall pass by" *(wʿbr)* for "and he shall take action *(wʿśh,* from Aramaic *wʿbd).*[29] Once we do that, we find that Antiochus, as he passed through Judea after withdrawing from Egypt in 168, "spoke in anger" *(wzʿm)* against the turbulent Jews (who had deprived him of his opportunity to complete the conquest of Egypt in 169) but passed them by *(w'br)* and on his return to Antioch "gave a sympathetic hearing" to the insecure Antiochenes of Jerusalem who had "deserted the Holy Covenant."[30]

8. The Expedition of Apollonius the Mysarch

THE KING'S RESPONSE was the expedition of Apollonius the Mysarch in February or March 167 B.C.E.[31] Apollonius taught the pious Jews of Jerusalem a harsh lesson, turning his army loose on them as if they were a population conquered in war. He is said to have attacked on the Sabbath.[32] Sabbath observers may have been his special target. Probably following Roman precedents,[33] Apollonius established now for the first time an Antiochene city at Jerusalem, called "the Akra" in 1 Maccabees. It was based on the old fortress just north of the temple. Apollonius dispossessed the "non-Antiochene" Jews who still survived at Jerusalem and turned their property over to new military colonists, loyal to the king.[34]

The new military colonists were a group of heterodox Jews; their religion was polytheistic and was not based upon the Torah.[35] At Dan 11:39 there is an allusion to the establishment of the garrison in the Akra: "And he shall transfer the fortifiers of strongholds, the people of a foreign god, whom he recognizes and honors greatly, and he shall place them in rule over the pious Jews and shall parcel out land as wages."[36] The verses of Dan 11:30–39 are out of order. The seer intended them to be read in the order 30, 39, 36 (through *npl'wt,* "past belief"), 31, 36(end)–38, 32–35.[37]

9. The Imposed Cult

PIOUS JEWS MIGHT INFER that the punitive acts of Apollonius's force only proved that God was still angry at them for allowing the Antiochenes to exist! Some Jews still went on attacking Antiochenes. We are therefore not surprised that Antiochus viewed them as stubborn rebels (even though they still would not dream of rising against the king). Antiochus surely must have been aware that the pious Jews were acting from a religious motivation (they would have told him so). It would be only natural for Antiochus to act to curb such a religion. The simplest procedure would have been a direct ban on attacking Antiochenes, but Antiochus chose a much more extensive and drastic course. The next actions of the king upon the Jews have been most puzzling, and so is their timing.

We have said that the expedition of the Mysarch occurred in February or March 167 B.C.E. By some time in April 167, as we shall see, the king had issued decrees telling the Jews, "Since you have used your religion as a pretext for acts of rebellion against me, I impose the following changes upon your religion by way of punishment and to prevent you from bringing evil upon my kingdom. On pain of death by torture, you are forbidden to circumcise your sons, to bring the daily burnt offerings and meal offerings, to keep the Sabbath and the festivals prescribed in the Torah, and to obey the dietary laws; you must worship, in addition to your own great God, deities, who I say are his female consort and son." This imposed cult was not at all Greek or Macedonian and was intended to be a corrected version of Judaism; probably it was based upon the religion of the heterodox Jews in the Akra.[38] In contrast, Nabonidus imposed his own religion on his subjects. So did the Christian princes of Europe in ancient, medieval, and early modern times. But where else in human history can one find another example of a ruler imposing on subjects of his a religion that was not his own?

10. The Four-Beast-Eleven-Horn Version of Daniel 7

FROM THE MOMENT the decrees were issued, pious Jews found them frightening. If they disobeyed the decrees, both the king and their own God would punish them severely. If they obeyed the decrees, their own God would punish them severely. We may be able to date the king's decrees because they were so horrifying to pious Jews that a Jew created another present-future prophecy: He supplemented the Four-Beast-Ten-Horn version of Daniel 7 (a text that was originally Babylonian) to create the Four-Beast-Eleven-Horn version, which now stands in our Bibles (Babylonians contributed to the earlier versions, but had no role in composing the final one).

On this basis, we can understand Daniel 7:8 and 24. Seleucus IV was the tenth king in the line that began with Alexander the Great and Philip III and Alexander IV and thereafter went down the Seleucid dynasty.[39] Accordingly, Antiochus IV would be the eleventh such king. But he was also the eleventh king in the line counted from Alexander the Great through the kings who reigned over Judea; and after Antiochus IV deposed the three child-monarchs (of Egypt) and at Memphis had himself crowned king of Egypt in 169 B.C.E., he was also the eleventh monarch in the line counted from Alexander the Great through the monarchs of the Ptolemaic dynasty,[40] and three of his predecessors (the child-monarchs) had been "uprooted." These events occurred in 169 B.C.E. One who had believed in the Four-Beast-Ten-Horn version would feel impelled to supplement it as soon as it was clear that the version could not be true because the Seleucid Empire did not fall before the reign of the eleventh monarch. Changes of imperial dynasty were believed to be events of cosmic importance.[41]

Accordingly, the seer first brought into the vision of Daniel 7 the events of 169 B.C.E. in Egypt (Daniel 7:8, "As I was gazing at the horns, another horn, a small one, sprouted up among them, and three of the previous horns were uprooted from before it"). The dynastic manipulations of Antiochus IV were convenient for the seer. They made it possible for him to go on believing that the Four-Beast-Ten-Horn version had not proved to be false: Because Antiochus had reappointed Ptolemy VI to be king of Egypt, the tenth monarch was still alive and still ruling. Immediately after these mentions of Antiochus's actions in Egypt, the seer alluded to events still earlier in the reign of the eleventh monarch, "In this horn there were eyes like the eyes of a man, and a mouth that spoke grandiloquently." We can guess that reflected here are the facts that Antiochus's announcement of his program of Antiochene citizenship made his subjects think that he intended to treat them humanely, and that the king in speeches asserted his expectations of how the program would contribute to the power of his kingdom.

Dan 7:8 probably was published before Antiochus drastically punished Jerusalem in 169 and 167 B.C.E. Thereafter, it became awkward to add those later events to the vision in chap 7. The seer used the same expedient that had been used earlier: He brought those events into the questions about the meaning of the vision and into the interpretive answers (Dan 7:19–21, "But I wished to make certain about the fourth beast . . . and about the ten horns on its head, and the other that sprouted up, before which three of the previous horns had fallen—the horn with eyes in it and a mouth speaking grandiloquently. . . . As I watched, that horn waged war against the Saints and was prevailing over them"). The procedure was clumsy, but there is no trace that it aroused skepticism. Antiochus's sack of Jerusalem and the Mysarch's expedition were certainly acts of war against pious Jews (called "holy ones" or "saints" in accordance with Lev 19:2).

The decrees on the imposed cult could be subsumed under the utterances of the "mouth that spoke grandiloquently." Thus the seer wrote in 7:25, "He shall speak words concerning the Most High and shall devastate the Saints of the Most High, and he shall think to change the feast days and the Law." Mere "thinking to change the feast days and the Law" was not the same as the forceful implementation of the decrees which occurred Dec 6–16, 167 B.C.E. (1 Macc 1:54–59). Thus, the seer must have produced his new version before then.

The composer of a present-future prophecy could not allow the war on the saints and even the unenforced atrocious decrees to be viewed as permanent. At most they could endure for three and a half years. Accordingly, the seer went on to predict the glorious future to come within three and a half years, with God intervening to rescue his faithful worshipers and to destroy the monstrous heathen empire and to confer imperial power instead upon them (Dan 7:25–27), "They will be handed over to him for a year, two years, and half a year. But when the court sits in judgment, his dominion will be taken away, by a final and utter destruction. Then the kingship and the dominion and the glory of all the kingdoms under heaven will be given to the people of the Saints of the Most High."

Why did the seer believe that Antiochus's atrocities could endure for three and a half years? Jews in the dreadful time of the persecution were driven to think of God's most recent large-scale intervention on behalf of his menaced people, the repulse of the Assyrian king Sennacherib from Jerusalem around the end of the eighth century B.C.E.[42] The word *sāphīah* ("aftergrowth," "what grows of itself [without plowing or sowing]" occurs at 2 Kings 19:29 and at Isaiah 37:30 as well as in the law of the Sabbatical Year (Lev 25:5, 15; aftergrowth was the chief source of food in Sabbatical Years). The seer took that fact as a clue that the repulse of Sennacherib occurred in a Sabbatical Year. He assumed that God would intervene now also in a Sabbatical Year.

There are some ambiguities of which we must take account. We have found reason to believe that the endpoint of the three and a half years was the beginning of the Sabbatical Year. Certainly the Sabbatical Year began in the month of Tishri, the seventh month of the biblical Jewish year, though perhaps Jewish sects, on the basis of Lev 25:8–9, disputed whether it began on the first day of that month (now called Rosh ha-shanah) or on the tenth (the Day of Atonement). What was the initial point? Let us examine Dan 7:25: "He shall devastate the Saints of the Most High and he shall think to change the feast days and the Law, and they shall be handed over to him for a year, two years, and half a year." The words define the three and a half years as the length of the period of the victimization of the Saints of the Most High. The years, therefore, might begin with the "war against the Saints" or with the decrees on the imposed cult. The war against the Saints might begin with the sack of Jerusalem in 169 B.C.E. (1 Macc 1:20) or with the expedition of the Mysarch some two years later, in 167 (1 Macc 1:29). Furthermore, how long was the year envisaged by the seer? It was probably a lunar year of 354 days, because evidence suggests that during the period of the imposed cult Jews were unable to insert intercalary months, whereas we know that the Babylonian years 145 and 148 Sel. Bab.

(167/6 and 164/3 B.C.E.) each contained an intercalary month. If no intercalary month had been inserted, the Sabbatical Year after 169 B.C.E. began Aug. 23 or Sept. 2, 164. If there had been an intercalary month, the Sabbatical Year began Sept. 22 or Oct. 2.[43]

Reckoning backwards from Aug. 23, 164 B.C.E., we find that the three and a half lunar years of Daniel 7:25 began on April 1, 167. They cannot have been measured from the sack of 169 B.C.E. They may have been measured from the expedition of the Mysarch or from the issuance of the decrees.

What was the message of the seer of the Four-Beast-Eleven-Horn version for pious Jews? Patiently suffer and die for three and a half years! In April 167, the decrees were merely published. They were not enforced until December (1 Macc 1:54–57). Even in the chapters of Daniel written later, the seer nowhere issues a call for national revolt, though he takes it for granted that the king's orders to violate the Torah must not be obeyed. The seer did observe *wicked* Jews using the old Jewish principle, "obey the king," to justify acceptance of the imposed cult (Dan 11:32, "Those who act wickedly against the covenant will perform polluting acts[44] by using slippery principles"). But the seer still holds that armed resistance to the king is forbidden by God! In chaps 9–11, the writer makes clear his belief that Antiochus's policy is part of God's punishment of Israel for ancient sins, committed in the seventh century B.C.E., in or before the time of Jeremiah. Nowhere in Daniel is present sin said to be the cause of the persecution. Even the sins of the Antiochenes should not have brought Antiochus's prohibition of the Jewish religion! Psalm 79 may reflect the bewilderment of a pious Jew in that crisis.[45]

We shall find in the book of Daniel predictions (8:14, 9:27, 12:11–12) that God's great intervention to end the persecution would come still later than the beginning of the Sabbatical Year in August 164 B.C.E. The message that came with the prediction in Dan 7:25 was grim enough. What motive could there be for predicting that the great intervention would come still later? It is hard to suggest any except for the pressure of the course of history. If the great miracles had not come within three and a half years, they must, if truly to come, occur at a later date. Thus, "predictions" of a later date for God's great intervention can have been written only after the lapse of the three and a half years, at the earliest in August 164 B.C.E.

11. The Forcible Implementation of the Decrees

WE SHOULD PAUSE HERE and attempt to explain the delay in the forcible implementation of the decrees. Antiochus did the normal thing in sending them to the Jews. He sent them through the high priest, Menelaus. Menelaus owed his position and his safety to the king, and the king had a right to expect obedience from him. Menelaus certainly was no saint, but he knew how Jews would react to the imposition of idolatry upon them. He went through such perfunctory motions as appointing officials to administer the imposed cult but otherwise dragged his feet as long as he could, just as later he was to petition for an end to its imposition. By late 167 B.C.E., however, the failure to implement the decrees came to the attention of the king. Still reluctant to depose the high priest who had cost him so much effort to keep in office, Antiochus now sent from Antioch his own agents to enforce compliance with the decrees.[46]

On 15 Kislev (December 6) 167 B.C.E., the king's agents saw to it that an "Abomination from Desolation" (a structure containing three meteorites, "Abominations from the Sky," representing the God of the Jews, his female consort, the "Queen of Heaven," and their son, "Dionysus") was built upon the sacrificial altar of the temple, and Jews by cruel force were compelled to obey the decrees. The meteorites were also called the "Host [of Heaven]" (in Daniel 8).[47]

12. The Testament of Moses

THERE WAS ANOTHER GROUP of pious Jews who agreed that armed resistance was forbidden but who could not agree to suffer and die for three-and-one-half years. This group produced the so-called "Assumption of Moses." A more correct title for the work is the *Testament of Moses,*" because it does not tell how Moses was taken up into heaven but claims to present Moses' last instructions to Joshua. A later writer has supplemented the work. Chapter 7 is almost completely illegible and may or may not be supplement. Parts of chap 6 certainly are supplement. If we omit the supplementary material, we recover the original work, written in 166 or early 165 B.C.E.[48]

Chapter 1 sets the scene of Moses' last words. In chaps 2–4 Moses surveys the history of the Israelites down to 167 B.C.E. Unlike the seer of Daniel 7-11, who believed passionately in the sacredness of the second temple, the author of the *Testament of Moses* believed that the second temple was not completely holy, for, according to him (4:8), valid sacrifices could not be offered there. The author of the *Testament of Moses* also believed (5:2–6) that the persecutions were a punishment for the recent sins of the Jewish Antiochenes, especially the sins of the high priests, Jason and Menelaus. He was unwilling to believe that the unbearable persecutions had to last until the Sabbatical Year.

There was a special dreadfulness to Antiochus's decrees: Jews were being compelled to sin and were forbidden to repent. Repentance usually consisted of renewed determination to obey the commandments and of acts to fulfill them, procedures forbidden by the king on pain of death. Jews could still fast and pray and bring sin-offerings, but those procedures might not be sufficient to win God's forgiveness. How could they bring God to rescue his people and punish the enemy if they could not repent? The sect that produced the *Testament of Moses* found the solution waiting for them at Deuteronomy 32:36, 42–43. No act of repentance is mentioned there. As read by the sect, those verses predict that, if the wicked persecutor shed enough of the blood of the Jews ("the LORD's servants"), the LORD himself will arise and avenge them and raise the Israelites to heaven (*Testament of Moses* 9:6–10:10). The project of arousing God to act, on the basis of Deuteronomy 32:36, 42–43, was probably attempted more than once, as members of the sect and other Jews deliberately let themselves be slaughtered by the Seleucid authorities in that hope.[49] Indeed, several groups of pious Jews whose dogmas were incompatible with one another did so. The sect of the *Testament of Moses* did not regard the second temple as fully holy. The other groups probably did. Hence, even if they rebelled against the king, they might have found it difficult to put up a united front. All these groups who let themselves be slaughtered believed that armed resistance was sinful and forbidden. At most they resisted by refusing to obey the king's decrees and by letting themselves be killed in the hope of rousing God to avenge them.

13. The Revolutionary Policies of Mattathias

TO ENGAGE IN OPEN ARMED resistance to the king's troops required breaking with the long tradition of nonrebellion by Jews. The priest Mattathias took this audacious step. How could he do it? No prophecy predicted that God's requirement to obey the pagan kings would be repealed before the miraculous end of the Age of Wrath. Even in Zech 9:9–13, before Jews fight Greeks, the Jews have their own king in Jerusalem. As far as we know, pious Jews other than Mattathias believed that the dreadful programs of Antiochus IV were part of the atrocities of the last days predicted by the prophets. Such Jews believed that with the end of the persecution would come such things as the Last Judgment and the resurrection. Hence, all they could do was search the literature of real prophecy and present-future prophecy for consolation. Mattathias's descendants constituted the Hasmonean dynasty. An ardent partisan of that dynasty wrote 1 Maccabees some seventy years after the events.[50] Only from 1 Maccabees can we know anything of Mattathias's ideology. Nevertheless, it is probable, despite the lapse of seventy years, that the author of 1 Maccabees reports Mattathias's views accurately.

According to 1 Maccabees, the persecutions were an ordinary punishment, brought on by the recent sins of the Antiochene Jews (especially the gymnasium), but wicked Antiochus went on to punish the people more severely than God willed (as Assyria had according to Isa 10:5–34). We may imagine Mattathias as theorizing that a Jew might dare to resist a pagan ruler who had overstepped the mandate given him by God. Mattathias's religious approach was quite different from that of his pious contemporaries. If the persecution was merely an ordinary punishment of recent sin but God's punishing tool had exceeded his mandate, it would do no good to study prophecies about the last days. If the present persecution posed unprecedented problems, it would do no good to look in the laws of the Bible for solutions. But the heroes of the biblical narratives themselves had to face problems which for those heroes were unprecedentd. Mattathias's religious approach was to follow the glorious examples of improvisation exhibited by the heroes of the past. No law, no prophecy justified rebelling against Antiochus. The author of 1 Maccabees carefully describes what Mattathias did. If Mattathias had based his actions on a scriptural law or prophecy, our author surely would have quoted it. He does not do so. Instead, our author does everything possible to portray Mattathias's act of zeal as equivalent to Phineas's act of zeal in Numbers 25.[51]

Many pious Jews refused to agree with Mattathias. The seer of Dan 11:34 views Mattathias's movement as only a "small help." Indeed, Mattathias's act of zeal was inspiring for some pious Jews but also led many of them helpless to their deaths. There had already been militant pious Jews, such as those who fought Menelaus and the Antiochenes. Now some of them may have turned to follow Mattathias's example and fight the king's soldiers and officials. But their efforts always ended in defeat. The Seleucid forces merely waited for the Sabbath and then attacked, at the time at which pious Jews believed they were forbidden to defend themselves. At least one sect of pious Jews also believed that if they were attacked on the Sabbath and did not resist, God would quickly avenge them.[52]

Mattathias's response to the massacre of the unresisting Sabbath-observers was to declare that self-defense against attack on the Sabbath was permitted.[53] Some pious Jews accepted his declaration,[54] but the seer of Dan 11:34 regards Mattathias's principles as "contemptible slippery things" *(ḥlqlqwt)*,[55] and goes on to "predict" the sufferings of the unresisting pious (11:35, 41). We learn only from 1 Macc 2:27–48 how Mattathias and his followers enforced observance of the Torah in Judea, down to the day of the zealous priest's death in

166/5 B.C.E. According to 1 Macc 2:65–66, Mattathias on his deathbed appointed his son, Simon, as "father" and "man of counsel," at the same time as he entrusted the conduct of the "war against the Gentiles" to his son, Judas Maccabaeus. Nothing indicates that either man was the eldest son.

14. Judas Maccabaeus's Career

JUDAS MACCABAEUS PROVED TO BE a remarkably talented leader. Mattathias could conduct no more than guerrilla warfare. Judas was long able to win victories over the forces of the Seleucid Empire and over hostile neighboring peoples, and increasingly he was able to unite the bitterly divided sects of pious Jews to support these enterprises.[56] Even the author of Dan 12:7 did not regard Judas and his force as a "small help." He calls them "the Hand of the Holy People." The seer of the *Testament of Moses* probably wrote no more after the probable deaths of Taxo and his sons failed to be followed by God's great intervention and thus proved his prophecy false. The seer of Daniel 11 wrote nothing to reflect the victories of Judas Maccabaeus; unforeseen in Daniel 7, they could not be part of God's plan. The seer contented himself with elaborating on the atrocious deeds of Antiochus against God (indeed, against all gods!) and on the sufferings of the pious (11:35–39) and then passed to the events he expected would happen in the last days (11:40–12:3), all totally fictitious. He knows that the persecution lasted at least a year (11:33)[57] but not that Antiochus marched eastward intending to make lucrative conquests in Iran (probably between May 20 and June 18, 165 B.C.E.), leaving his little son, Antiochus, as co-regent king of the western half of the empire, with Lysias as guardian of the co-regent and as chief minister in the west.[58] Though one might suggest that the seer omitted reference to the expedition because it was contrary to his expectations and predictions, his interest in the aggressive expansion of Hellenistic empires is such (cf. Dan 11:5–9, 10–11, 13–18, 25–29, 40, 42–43) that his omission here is a probably a sign of lack of knowledge. We thus learn that the seer wrote before that expedition. Fortunately, other authorities preserved through long decades details of Judas's victories so that they could be written down in 1 and 2 Maccabees. But another seer writing present-future prophecy alluded to those great events shortly after they happened.

15. The Supplementing of 1 Enoch 90

THE SEER OF *1 Enoch* 90:9–31 admired Judas Maccabaeus and believed that Judas was a key agent in God's plans. The version of the Animal Vision from

201/200 B.C.E. had proved false. The seer sought to supplement it: The vanquished righteous sheep could be vindicated by the victories of Judas. The seer's product did violence to the symbolism of the Animal Vision. In the symbolism of the original vision, each species of animal represented a different state or ethnic group. In the wars of Antiochus III and his Ptolemaic contemporaries, two empires were involved, and several mercenary stocks. The original seer predicted ultimate victory for the hard-pressed sheep in 90:9a, 11, 17–18. In the battles of Judas Maccabaeus, only one empire was involved, the Seleucid. Nevertheless, *within* the career of Judas Maccabaeus, the seer followed a consistent symbolism: The great horned ram is Judas, and ravens represent officials of low rank in the Seleucid empire; often such low officials were members of conquered peoples; the highest royal Macedonian officials the seer represents as eagles or vultures, and those of intermediate rank as kites.

In this manner, the seer was able to "predict" Judas' victories, in 90:9b-10, 12–16. Ultimately he was able to work even 90:17–18 into Maccabaeus's career. In 90:12 we find ravens, probably the local officials Apollonius and Seron, fruitlessly trying to defeat Judas (as in 1 Macc 3:10–24). The text of 90:13–14 has probably suffered alteration. We may guess that the seer intended to present one or more local officials (Philip, as at 2 Macc 8:8) seeking help from superiors and receiving it through the campaign of Gorgias and Nicanor, in the course of which Judas mysteriously learned of Gorgias's stratagem to take him by surprise and instead routed the Seleucid forces (1 Macc 3:38–4:25). The seer ascribed Judas's information to the action of a supernatural being. In 90:15, the seer probably alludes to the sudden withdrawal of Lysias after the battle of Beth-Zur which ended his expedition of 164 B.C.E. (1 Macc 4:34–35), a battle at which pious believers reported a supernatural apparition (2 Macc 11:8–13).[59] In 90:16 the seer alludes to the wars with neighboring peoples (1 Maccabees 5) and to the campaign of Lysias and Antiochus V, in which collaborationist Jews ("sheep of the field") participated and Judas was hard pressed (1 Macc 6:21–54). Finally he found it possible to make 90:17–18 allude to Judas's surprising survival after defeat and to the destruction of Lysias and Antiochus V (1 Macc 6:55–7:4). The finality of the destruction mentioned in 90:18 suggests that the seer thought no more struggles would follow. However, when Nicanor's expedition came (1 Macc 7:26–48), the seer added 90:19, with its references to the miraculous sword (2 Macc 15:15–16) and to the rising of the village Jews who cut down the fugitives from Nicanor's force (1 Macc 7:46).

16. How the Persecution was Brought to an End

NONE OF THE SEERS wrote anything to reflect the actual circumstances of the end of the persecution or those of the persecuting king's death. How could they? The seers had predicted it would be followed by miraculous interventions by God, which had not occurred, such as a resurrection of the dead.[60]

In fact, Judas Maccabaeus and his men in 164 B.C.E. had fought a bloody battle at Beth-Zur against a Seleucid force under Lysias, the chief minister of the west of the empire and guardian of the little co-regent king (the future Antiochus V). The heavy casualties probably made both Lysias and many fighters on the Jewish side think the time had come for negotiations. Before the battle Lysias had probably been confident he could suppress the rebellious Jews. His heavy losses showed him that the campaign would be long and costly, at a time when he could ill afford to be away from Antioch, for political rivals might try to seize control. Many of Judas's pious supporters may have had misgivings about further resistance to the royal government. Would it not be better for the Jewish rebels to try to negotiate with Lysias, offering to stop fighting if Lysias would end the persecution? There were Jews who saw no sign of the fulfillment of the words of the prophets and hence believed that God's sentence of subjection to foreign rulers still stood. Such Jews continued to view rebellion against the king as impious. Hard hit by the persecution, they now also faced the wrath of Judas and his men. There were also Jews, including Menelaus, who had collaborated with the regime, willingly or unwillingly, and now faced the threat of pitiless punishment at the hands of Judas's band.

In 1 Maccabees there is no report of negotiations or of a peace agreement. Lysias there is reported to have withdrawn, intending to come back to invade Judea with a stronger force (4:35). In the documents of negotiation which are presented in 2 Maccabees 11, Judas is not mentioned. We conclude that the Hasmonaeans did not seek the negotiated peace. Enough pious Jews welcomed a negotiated peace and were willing to stop supporting Judas so that Judas for a time was unable to continue to fight the empire and so that Lysias could see there was reason to negotiate. In fact, Lysias, the ministers at Antioch, and those Jews who wanted peace by negotiations succeeded in coming to an agreement. A document of the little co-regent king (2 Macc 11:27–33) brought the persecution to an end without divine intervention, by March 27, 164 B.C.E., long before Aug. 23. Of all the attendant circumstances, only Judas's victories had a claim to be miraculous, and only the seer of *1 Enoch* had "predicted" them.

17. The Death of Antiochus IV

As FOR THE DEATH of Antiochus IV, it occurred after he failed ignomin-iously[61] to plunder the temple of Nanaia in Elymais. In chagrin, he probably died of a psychosomatic disease.[62] Anything miraculous in that event would have tended to be attributed to Nanaia, an unacceptable possibility for monotheistic Jews.[63] Certainly the event contradicted the predictions of the seers.[64] Though the government of Lysias for the little co-regent heir may have tried to conceal the fact that Antiochus IV had died, the truth could not be con-cealed for long. A Babylonian record lets us know that the news reached Bab-ylon in Kislev (Nov. 20–Dec. 18), 164 B.C.E.[65]

18. Embarrassing Factors

THE END OF THE PERSECUTION must have been welcomed by all pious Jews, but it was embarrassing because none of the prophecies circulating among the faithful had predicted that the troubles would cease in so unspectacular a man-ner. Divine judgment should have first been visited upon Antiochus, and pun-ishment upon the Gentiles and wicked Jews. The Seleucid Empire should have been replaced by an eternal empire of the saints. There should have been a res-urrection of the dead Jews, to reward the righteous and punish the wicked. A new Jerusalem and a new temple should have descended from heaven to re-place the desecrated temple built by men (*1 Enoch* 90:28–29). What now should be done about Jerusalem, the temple, and the temple service? Would it not be dangerous to restore the temple before the predicted earthquake and nat-ural upheavals? Would it not be presumptuous to resume services in a temple that God himself was going to remove and replace? God himself, the predic-tions said, would destroy all idols. Would it not be rash for mere flesh and blood even to destroy the Abomination from Desolation?

19. How the Festival of Ḥanukkah Came to Be

THE AUTHORS OF MOST of those predictions had been so confident of their own inspiration that they had set time limits for their fulfillment. Prudence de-manded that the Jews wait until those time limits had passed. Daniel predicted great miracles for the beginning of the Sabbatical Year, in Tishri 164/3. Zechariah 14 contains a prediction of a great manifestation of God's power just before and during the Festival of Tabernacles. Hence, Jews had to wait through the full Festival of Tabernacles, including the Eighth Day of Solemn Assembly, through 15–22 Tishri. Other uncertainties imposed still further delay. Antiochus IV had made it impossible to intercalate the Jewish calendar, and now that calendar was probably two months off. What month would God regard as the month for performance of miracles? The month called "Tishri" on the unintercalated Jewish calendar? Or the astronomically correct Tishri, called "Kislev" on the unintercalated calendar? The only safe procedure was to wait through the astronomically correct Tishri, through the "Festival of Tabernacles in the Month of Kislev."

When the hopes of pious believers that miracles were coming had been dashed, by 23 Kislev 164, Judas Maccabaeus seems to have felt the appropriateness of dedicating a new temple altar on the day of the monthly sacrifices which had profaned the old, the twenty-fifth. He seems also to have wished to follow earlier precedents set by Moses, Solomon, Hezekiah, and Zerubbabel. These complicated developments gave rise to the eight-day Jewish observance of ḥanukkah, beginning on 25 Kislev.[66]

20. Daniel 8 and 9

THE SEER (OR SEERS) of Daniel 8 and 9 felt it necessary to cover up the falsity of the predictions in Dan 7:25 and 11:40–12:3. The procedure used shows that at first the seer (or seers) believed that fulfillment of 7:25 and 11:40–12:3 had merely been somewhat delayed. The beginning of the Sabbatical Year, three and a half years after Antiochus IV victimized the Saints of the Most High, was long past. The observance of ḥanukkah had focused the attention of believing Jews upon the desecration that arose from the sacrifices offered to the Abominations from the Sky on the twenty-fifth of the month.[67] Evidence suggests that only after an idol had been worshiped could it become an object which was forbidden to Jews and which could desecrate the temple.[68] Consequently, the seer of Daniel 8 took, as the beginning point of his measured period, the sacrifices offered on 25 Kislev (Dec. 16, 167 B.C.E.). Such is implied, for example, by Dan 8:13–14, " 'For how long is the vision, the [removal of] the continual offering as a result of sin [read *bappesaʿ*], the imposition of the Host from the Sky and the sanctuary being a trampling ground."[69] And he said to me, 'Until two thousand three hundred days and nights—then the sanctuary shall be vindicated.' " The interval is equal to 1,150 days, and 1,150 days after 25 Kislev 167 B.C.E., brings the date down to Feb. 8, 163. We must guess what event served to vindicate the sanctuary around that date. My guess is that it was the arrival at Jerusalem of the letter of Antiochus V (2 Macc 11:23–26) announcing that Antiochus IV was dead and that Jews were free to obey the Torah and that the temple was to be returned to their control. "Daniel foretold" that event!

The seer of Daniel 9 also sought to preserve belief in other predictions of prophets. It had long been clear, to those who had access to accurate chronology, that Jeremiah's predictions of a seventy-year Babylonian exile had been inaccurate. Cyrus's decree for a return of Jews to Jerusalem had come in 538 B.C.E., only some forty-eight years after the destruction in 586, and only some sixty-six years after the date of Jeremiah 25 (604/3) and some fifty-six years after the date of Jeremiah 29 (594/3). The seer (Dan 9:1–2) presents Daniel in the reign of "Darius the Mede," after the fall of Babylon, as being puzzled over the figure of seventy years in Jeremiah.[70] The seer has Daniel utter a fervent prayer of confession and contrition, imploring God to act to show mercy to Jerusalem and to his people, Israel (9:4–20). Thereupon, the angel Gabriel comes to Daniel and tells him, "Seventy weeks of years are decreed for your people and your holy city, to end the effects of transgression, to complete the expiation for sin, and to absolve iniquity, and to bring about everlasting justification and to put a seal upon vision and prophet and to anoint the holy of holies." The substitution of "Seventy weeks of years" for "Seventy years" was plausible. Hebrew and Aramaic could be written without vowels. In vowelless Hebrew and Aramaic, "seventy" and "weeks" had exactly the same spelling (*sbᶜym* or *sbᶜyn*) so that the extant texts of Jeremiah could have arisen from one of the most common scribal errors, haplography. Alternatively, a Jewish principle of exegesis is known to have prescribed reading a text, the vowels of which were ambiguous, in both ways.[71] For the seer, each week of years was a Sabbatical week, ending in a Sabbatical Year. Since 164/3 probably was a Sabbatical Year,[72] the seer of Daniel 9 thereby had transferred the deadline for fulfillment of Dan 7:25 from the beginning of the Sabbatical Year to its end.

In his complicated sentence, Dan 9:24, the seer has also provided for a protracted age of punishment, far longer than the seventy years. Indeed, the long adversity suffered by Jews after the return from the exile belied the prophecies of prosperity uttered by Jeremiah, Deutero-Isaiah, Haggai, and Zechariah. Now the seer could explain the long adversity. It served as expiation for heinous sin. We can date Daniel 9 by the event which made the seer feel he should write it: the negotiated peace of 164 B.C.E. One might be tempted to date the beginning of his Age of Punishment 490 years before 164 B.C.E., in 654, a date which falls within the reign of King Manasseh of Judah. The sins of that reign could well require such protracted expiation (see Jer 15:1–4). The seer may have been pleased with the way in which that calculation would agree with that of the seer of *1 Enoch*,[73] but if he carefully read the texts in Jeremiah 25 and 29, he cannot have believed the 490 years began in the reign of Manasseh. He derived them from the seventy years in Jer 25:11–12 (dated as if they began in 604/3 B.C.E.) and in 29:10 (datable as if they began in 594/3 B.C.E.).[74] But 490 years from those points would put the end of the Age of Punishment, at the earliest, around 114/3 B.C.E., a date much too late to bring confidence to believers at the time of the negotiated peace of 164. We could only conclude either that the seer did not have access to accurate chronological information, or else, that he did not read carefully the texts in Jeremiah.[75]

In fact, the seer goes on, in vv 25–27, to make clear what he viewed as the beginning and endpoints of the 490 years.

> 25 Know and understand this: from the utterance of the word regarding the return to Jerusalem and its rebuilding, to the coming of an anointed prince there will be seven weeks. Then, during sixty-two weeks, there will be a return to Jerusalem and she will be rebuilt with street and moat, but in times of distress.
>
> 26 After the sixty-two weeks an anointed one will be cut down, though he will not possess,[76] and the soldiers of the successor prelate will ruin the city and the temple. And his end will be by the flood, and until the End there will be war determined with desolations.
>
> 27 It will take one week to make strong[77] the covenant for the Many, and half of that week will see the cessation of animal sacrifice and meal-offering, and upon their base[78] will be Abominations from the Sky[79] until a decreed destruction is poured down upon [the Abominations from the] Sky.

In Jeremiah, the two verbs "return" and "[re]building" occur together only in 33:7, datable in 587/6 (see 32:1). Cyrus (called "the anointed" by Deutero-Isaiah)[80] did decree that Jews could return to Jerusalem and rebuild the temple forty-nine years later (538 B.C.E.). Thus, the seer appears to have taken 587/6 as the beginning point of his seventy weeks of years. The disappointing years that followed were indeed a time of distress because of the failure of the glorious prophecies to be fulfilled. However, 490 years after 587/6 brings one to 97/6 B.C.E., long after the negotiated peace of 164 B.C.E. We must conclude that the seer did not have access to accurate chronology here!

Still, we know that the writers of present-future prophecy normally expect the climactic glorious events to occur in the near future. Thus, the making the covenant strong for the Many and the pouring of decreed ruin upon the Abominations from the Sky, predicted in Daniel 9:27, should have occurred by 164/3

B.C.E. The murder of Onias III, the anointed high priest, probably occurred some seven years earlier, in 170.[81] The destructive coup of Jason the Oniad, the man who usurped the high priesthood from Onias III, came in 169 B.C.E., the year after the murder.[82] Within the final week of years, the seer placed the interruption of the perpetual daily sacrifices and the imposition of the Abominations from the Sky, in 167 B.C.E. Half a week of lunar years after the imposition of Dec. 6, 167 B.C.E. brings the date down to March 31, 163 B.C.E. If the beginning point was the worship of the Abominations on Dec. 16, 167 B.C.E., the three and a half years would end on April 9, 163. Neither date revealed miracles. There is reason to assume that the end of the seventy weeks of years as reckoned by the seer was the end of the Sabbatical Year on the defective calendar, 1,335 days after the desecration of 25 Kislev, 167 (Aug. 12, 163 B.C.E.; Dan 12:12).[83] Could the miracles come by then?

21. The Akra Besieged

IN THE MONTHS that followed the negotiated peace, forces under Judas and his brother, Simon, won an unbroken series of victories over hostile neighboring peoples, who sometimes received the support of officials of the Seleucid kingdom (1 Maccabees 5). Irritating to pious Jews was the presence of the garrison of heterodox Jews and Gentile pagans in the citadel of Jerusalem near the temple. According to the author of 1 Maccabees, the garrison had been perpetrating provocative acts. Judas resolved to put them under siege (1 Macc 6:18–19), an act of open rebellion against the kingdom.[84]

22. The Royal Government Reacts

ANTIOCHUS V AND LYSIAS, his chief minister, responded vigorously, marching with a large force, intending to break the siege and put down the rebels. The column marched through loyal Idumaea, to approach Jerusalem from the south and thus avoid the difficult roads to Jerusalem from the coastal plain, which had brought about so many defeats of Seleucid forces. Judas had previously fortified Beth-Zur against any danger from Idumaea (1 Macc 4:61). The column laid siege to Beth-Zur. The invading force was too big to be opposed by a mere detachment. Judas withdrew his army from the siege of the Akra, and encamped at Beth-Zechariah, north of Beth-Zur, blocking the road to Jerusalem ahead of the king.

The Seleucid force made an early morning dash to Beth-Zechariah. There, a bloody battle ensued. Perceiving the power of the empire and the warlike spirit of the imperial army, Judas and his men withdrew (1 Macc 6:33–47). The royal army marched after them to Jerusalem and besieged them on the Temple Mount. The king and his minister tried to avoid the position of persecutors. They had the hated high priest, Menelaus, executed (2 Macc 13:3–8) in order to gain the support of pious Jews. It was a difficult time for Jews to be besieged, because in this, the Sabbatical Year, there was a shortage of food (1 Macc 6:49, 53–54).

23. Daniel 12:11–12

BY JUNE 28, 163 B.C.E., 1,290 DAYS AFTER the sacrifices to the Abominations from the Sky which had been offered on Dec. 16, 167, the seer of Dan 12:11 believed that the troubles predicted in Dan 12:1 had come. He also believed that within a relatively short time (45 days) the "hand of the Holy People" would be smashed but also that God would intervene with the predicted miracles. He specified that the interventions would have come by Aug. 12, 163 B.C.E., 1,335 days after the sacrifices to the Abominations because, on the unintercalated calendar, that day would be 1 Tishri, the first day of the next week of years after the week of years which the seer of Daniel 9 had predicted would be the last of the Age of Wrath.

24. How the Siege of the Temple Mount Ended

UNFORTUNATELY, THAT DAY, TOO, PASSED without any miracle. Surprisingly, however, the small force still withstanding siege on the Temple Mount was spared the need to surrender. Philippos, the official who had been left in charge at Antioch, rebelled. In order to put down that revolt, Lysias advised the king to make peace with the Jews. The king agreed and offered peace to the besieged Jews, who accepted (2 Macc 13:23).[85] The day the Seleucid force withdrew from Jerusalem (28 Sheʿbat, 162 B.C.E.) was remembered and became a day on which fasting was forbidden.[86] There was no way to cover up the failure of the predictions in Daniel 7–12 to be fulfilled. Those who maintained faith in them had to assume that the plain meanings of the dates were erroneous and that the predictions would be fulfilled at some future time. The seer or seers of Daniel may have lived on, but they published no more predictions.

The seer of *1 Enoch* 90:31 had predicted that Judas, the great horned ram, would live to see God's miraculous vindication of the Jews. The surprising end of the siege of the Temple Mount made it look as if Judas's survival was indeed part of God's plan. The Seleucid policy of conciliation led to the execution of

Menelaus and the appointment of Alcimus to the high priesthood. The evidence suggests that Alcimus was a pious priest who had refrained from rebellion even as he risked his life by refusing to participate in the imposed cult.[87] Though the Hasmonean party benefited from the peace, they recognized neither it nor the right of Alcimus to be high priest. If the age of Israel's subjection was over, Antiochus V had no right to appoint the high priest. And even if God still willed that Israel be subject to foreign rulers, the reign of the son of the monstrous persecutor might be illegitimate and brief (Isa 14:21), and Alcimus's loyalty to the impious Seleucid regime could have disqualified him for the high priesthood. Lysias did prevail over the rebel Philippos at Antioch, but the regime of Antiochus V and Lysias was doomed.

25. Demetrius I Becomes King

A MORE FORCEFUL SELEUCID came in the autumn of 162 B.C.E.,[88] and for him the soldiers of the kingdom put an end to Lysias and the boy king. The seer of *1 Enoch* 90:18 probably alluded to the event.[89] Demetrius I, son of Seleucus IV, had been kept as a hostage in Rome precisely because the Romans believed he would be a stronger ruler of the Seleucid Empire than Antiochus V and Lysias. He escaped from Italy and made his way to the Seleucid realm.[90]

NOTES

1 On what Antiochus IV learned at Rome, see my *I Maccabees,* 104–121, 125–40.

2 See, e.g., 2 Sam 20:25 with 1 Kgs 2:26–27 and my *I Maccabees,* 75–76.

3 See my *II Maccabees,* 223.

4 See my *II Maccabees,* 227, 233.

5 See my *Semites, Iranians, Greeks, and Romans,* 22–25.

6 2 Macc 4:18–20.

7 2 Macc 4:21–22.

8 2 Macc 4:23–32, with my commentary.

9 2 Macc 4:33–34.

10 2 Macc 4:35–38.

11 2 Macc 4:39–49. On the allusion, at *Jub.* 23:16–19, to the riot against Lysimachos, see my *Semites*, 167–68.

12 See my *I Maccabees*, 203, 425–28, and my *II Maccabees*, 252–53. Add to the sources Abraham J. Sachs, *Astronomical Diaries and Related Texts from Babylonia* (completed and ed. Herman Hunger; 2 vols. and 2 vols. of plates; Wien: Verlag der Österreichischen Akademie der Wissenschaften, 1988–89), II, No. –168, 471. Daniel 11:25–26 reflects the war between Ptolemy VI and Antiochus IV and the ineffective resistance of the Ptolemaic side; Daniel 11:27 plays upon the hypocrisy of both kings: Ptolemy never intended to be a loyal vassal, and Antiochus never intended to act for the interests of Ptolemy. With the end of Daniel 11:27 (*"'wd qṣ lmw'd"*, "there is still time till the appointed date") the seer expresses his belief that Antiochus's thorough conquest of Egypt still lay in the future (as he says in 11:40–43).

13 2 Macc 5:5–6.

14 2 Macc 5:5, 7. See also my *II Maccabees*, 250. In a future article I shall demonstrate that the old citadel stood to the north of the temple, on the same site as the stronghold that Josephus called *baris* (*Antiquities* xviii.4.3.92). *Baris* is another word for "citadel"; it is a loanword in Greek, borrowed from Egyptian.

15 2 Macc 5:11.

16 In my *II Maccabees*, 252–53.

17 At my *II Maccabees*, 252, the war is erroneously called the "Second Macedonian War."

18 Josephus *Antiquities* xii.5.3.218.

19 1 Macc 1:20–24; 2 Macc 5:11–21; Dan 11:28 as treated at my *I Maccabees*, 209. Dan 11:28–30 seems to imply that Antiochus IV in person punished Jerusalem both in 169 B.C.E. (after his first invasion of Egypt) and in 168 B.C.E. (after his second). First Macc 1:20–24 has the king attacking the Holy City in 169 and says nothing about 168. Second Macc 5:1, 11–21 seems to have him attacking in 168 and says nothing about 169. Other things being equal, Daniel, if comprehensible, would be the best source. The seer was there, in Jerusalem, observing the events he put into his present-future prophecy, whereas the authors of the histories in 1 and 2 Maccabees wrote many decades later, on the basis of the sources available to them. But other things are not equal. On how these passages should be interpreted, see my *I Maccabees*, 45–46, 209.

20 2 Chr 2:2–9. For the view that Jason's coup was the fateful sin, see 2 Macc 1:7 and my *II Maccabees,* 144–45.

21 See my *Semites,* 161–79. The article there contains bad misprints. In the last line of the text of 162, delete "170." The first line of 163 should not be indented. In the fourth line from the end of the text of 168, "the" should be "of." On 178, par. 2, fourth line from end, "n." should be "pages"; and in par. 3, line 3, "was" should be "has."

22 At my *Semites,* 167–68.

23 *Jub.* 23:14, "Their works are uncleanness and fornication and pollution and abominations."

24 *Jub.* 23:19, "For they have forgotten commandment and covenant and feasts and months and Sabbaths and jubilees."

25 Such is the view in 2 Maccabees (4:13–17); cf. 1 Macc 1:11–15, 64.

26 2 Macc 5:22.

27 Will, *Histoire,* II, 320–23; Dan 11:29 and the first five Hebrew words of 11:30, "At the appointed time, he will again invade the South, but the second invasion will not be like the first. When ships of Kittim come against him, he will lose heart and retreat."

28 Dan 11:29–30; Will, *Histoire,* II, 322–23.

29 See my *I Maccabees,* 213. In the Hebrew and Aramaic alphabets, *d* is often indistinguishable from *r.* On the Hebrew of Daniel 11 as a translation from Aramaic, see Ginsberg, *Studies,* 41–49.

30 See my *I Maccabees,* 212–13.

31 1 Macc 1:29–40; 2 Macc 5:24–26. For the date see my *Semites,* 194–97.

32 2 Macc 5:25.

33 See my *I Maccabees,* 123.

34 1 Macc 1:33–38.

35 See my *II Maccabees,* 105–9.

36 See my *II Maccabees,* 106–7.

37 See my *II Maccabees*, 90 (with notes) and my *I Maccabees*, 45–46.

38 See my *II Maccabees*, 98–112; daily offerings: See my *I Maccabees*, 221.

39 See chap 13, sec 8, p. 429.

40 Kings who reigned over Judea: Alexander the Great, Philip III and Alexander IV (reigned jointly), Antigonus, Ptolemies I–V, Antiochus III, Seleucus IV, Antiochus IV. Monarchs counting through the Ptolemaic dynasty: Alexander the Great, Philip III and Alexander IV (reigned jointly), Ptolemies I–V, Ptolemies VI and VIII and Cleopatra II, Antiochus IV.

41 See Dan 10:13, 20–21.

42 Repulse of Sennacherib: 2 Kgs 18:13–19:35, Isa 36:1–37:37. In the minds of Jews in and around the time of the persecution: See my *I Maccabees*, 239, 261–62, 263, 264, 341, and my *II Maccabees*, 330, 496, 500.

43 Jews could not intercalate during the persecution: See my *I Maccabees*, 274–80. Table of the first days of lunar months in those years: Parker and Dubberstein, *Babylonian Chronology*, 41. See also my *I Maccabees*, 315–18; there is a small error in the day count in my *I Maccabees*.

44 Read a plural verb, *yaḥănīphū*, for the singular verb, *yaḥănīph*. Then, the first four words of Dan 11:32 mean "And those who render the covenant wicked will perform polluting acts by use of slippery principles."

45 See my *I Maccabees*, 332–36.

46 See my *II Maccabees*, 103–4.

47 1 Macc 1:54–64, Dan 8:12–13, 9:27, 12:11; On the "Abomination from Desolation" and the "Host," see my *I Maccabees*, 143–57.

48 See my *Semites*, 181–85.

49 *Testament of Moses* 9:6–7; 1 Macc 2:29–38; 2 Macc 6:11, 7:2–42, and my *II Maccabees*, 294–96.

50 See my *I Maccabees*, 4–12, 62–77, and my *II Maccabees*, 4, 71–83.

51 See my *I Maccabees*, 5–7.

52 See my *I Maccabees*, 235–36.

53 1 Macc 2:39–41.

54 Dan 11:34; 1 Macc 2:42–43.

55 In Dan 11:32 ḥlqlqwt is a contemptuous diminutive of ḥlqwt ("slippery things"), which itself is a pejorative term. The same contemptuous diminutive is used to refer to the legal deceits of Antiochus IV in usurping the Seleucid throne (Dan 11:21). It is possible that Mattathias, like the rabbis, used *halakhah* ("the way one should go"; cf. Lev 26:3) for the religiously proper course and that *hălaqlāqōt* is a pejorative pun. The Qumran sect called the Pharisees *dōwrᵉšēy hălāqōt* ("seekers of-" or "interpreters of slippery things"; 4QpNahum, Hodayot 2:15 and 32; cf. CD 1:18). The author of 2 Maccabees probably shares this contempt for Mattathias; he never deigns to mention him.

56 Victories: 1 Macc 3:1–26, 38–60; 4:1–35, 5:1–54, 63–68; 7:26–50. Increasing ability to unite pious Jews: Note the increasing size of Judas's army in 1 Macc 3:16, 4:6, 29, 5:20, and the mass support his victorious 3,000 men (7:40) received in 7:46.

57 See my *II Maccabees*, 323.

58 See my *I Maccabees*, 251.

59 See my *II Maccabees*, 403.

60 According to Dan 11:24–25, Antiochus IV would perish during a campaign to wipe out the Jews of Judea. Soon afterward would occur a resurrection of the dead (Dan 12:2–3). In *1 Enoch* 90, there is no prediction about the king's death unless 90:18 is to be taken literally and the king and his subordinates were all to be swallowed up by the earth; though the seer may have predicted a resurrection in 90:33, it is not clear whether he predicted a resurrection or merely an ingathering of the living exiles (see my *Semites*, 226). The seer of the *Testament of Moses* predicts (10:9) that Israel (the people) will be raised to heaven and will look down upon their enemies in the earth (Charles read for "earth [Greek *gê*]," "*Ge[henna]*").

61 Ignominious failure: See my *II Maccabees*, 348.

62 Psychosomatic disease: See ibid., 352.

63 The authors of 1 and 2 Maccabees exercised their imaginations to avoid that problem. See my *I Maccabees*, 307, and my *II Maccabees*, 352–53.

64 See n 60.

65 The event contradicted the predictions of the seers: See my *I Maccabees*, 274–76. Babylonian record: Sachs and Wiseman, "King List," *Iraq* 16 (1954), 202–4, 208–9.

66 See my *I Maccabees*, 278–82.

67 1 Macc 1:59.

68 See *Mishnah, ʿabodah zarah* 4:4.

69 Read *ʿd mty hḥzwn hrym htmyd bpšʿ tt ṣbʾ šmm wqdš mrms*.

70 Jeremiah's predictions: Jer 29:10 and 25:12, and see above, p. 176–77. Cyrus's decree: Ezra 1:1–4.

71 See *Babylonian Talmud, Sanhedrin* 4b, near end.

72 See my *I Maccabees*, 315–18.

73 See above, p. 417.

74 On Jeremiah 25, see John Bright, *Jeremiah* ("Anchor Bible," vol. 23; Garden City, NY: Doubleday, 1978), 160. On Jeremiah 29, see ibid., 210.

75 Cf. Hartman and Di Lella, *Daniel*, 250–54.

76 The text of "though he will not possess" is probably defective. We may guess that what the anointed one did not possess was either guilt or his rightful office as high priest. Either description would fit Onias III (see my *II Maccabees*, 239–40).

77 For *wᵉhigbīyr* read *wᵉhagbēyr*.

78 For *kᵉnap* read *kannām*; cf. Hartman and Di Lella, *Daniel*, 240 and my *I Maccabees*, 147.

79 See my *I Maccabees*, 147–48.

80 Isa 45:1.

81 See my *II Maccabees*, 239.

82 See ibid., 239–240.

83 Half a week of lunar years: It is easy to count off the forty-two lunar months using p. 41 of Richard A. Parker and Waldo H. Dubberstein, *Babylonian Chronology, 626 B.C.–A.D. 75* (Providence, RI: Brown University Press, 1956). Reason to assume: See below, p. 466.

84 Some Jews bitterly opposed the act of rebellion, for fear of offending God. A piece of their propaganda survives in the apocryphal book of *Baruch*. See my *Semites*, 191–207.

85 The version given at 2 Macc 13:23 is probably correct against 1 Macc 6:55–61. See my *II Maccabees*, 467.

86 *Megillat Ta'anit* 28 Sh°baṭ. See my *II Maccabees*, 470.

87 See my *I Maccabees*, 332–36.

88 See my *II Maccabees*, 477–78.

89 See p. 459.

90 1 Macc 7:1–4. See my *I Maccabees*, 329–30.

15

The Last Struggles of
Judas Maccabaeus and Conclusion

1. Judas's Last Struggles

A S USUAL, UPON THE DEATH of the king ruling the Jews, the successor king had the right to appoint a new high priest or to reappoint the
incumbent.[1] Alcimus promptly applied to Demetrius I and received
the reappointment. Pious Jews had good reason to reject Alcimus when he
owed his appointment to Antiochus V, the son of the monstrous persecutor.[2]
But Demetrius I was no persecutor and was a legitimate Seleucid. It is likely,
however, that the Hasmoneans believed that their victories proved that the Age
of Israel's subjection was now over, and no Seleucid now had the right to appoint the high priest.

Not surprisingly, the Hasmoneans and their followers regarded Alcimus's
appointment as invalid and conducted guerrilla warfare against him and
against those who collaborated with the regime of Antiochus V and Demetrius
I. Alcimus led a delegation who appealed to Demetrius to intervene. Demetrius
consented and dispatched Bacchides with a large force, to reinstall Alcimus as
high priest and to establish order (1 Macc 7:5–9; 2 Macc 14:3–10).[3] Bacchides
was the governor of the huge province of Koilê Syria and Phoenicia, of which
Judea was a part.

Bacchides tried to pose as having peaceful intentions. The power of the Jews
to resist was now well known. But the size of his force belied his pose, so that
the Hasmoneans did not trust him. The sect of pious Jews who were called
"Asidaioi" were ready to trust Alcimus, whose priestly lineage was indis-

putable and who had a reputation for piety and swore that he and the force with him intended no harm to them or to their friends; the members of the pious sect were also ready to trust Bacchides. But Alcimus immediately arrested sixty of them and had them executed, despite his oath. Bacchides moved with his force to Beth-zaith. There he had many of the "turncoats" who had gone over to him arrested, as well as some supporters of the Hasmoneans. Aiming at the elimination of troublemakers of every kind, he had all of them killed. Leaving Alcimus in power as high priest, Bacchides returned to the king (1 Macc 7:3–20).[4]

Anti-Hasmonean Jews rallied to Alcimus, but the Hasmoneans and their supporters remained opposed to him. Judas and his force drove the supporters of Alcimus from the countryside. Unable to cope, Alcimus went again to King Demetrius and accused of atrocities those opposed to him. The king sent Nicanor with a large force to support Alcimus (I Macc 7:21–26).

There was a brief skirmish at Dessau, in which Simon, Judas's brother, suffered a slight setback (2 Macc 14:16–17). Thereafter, however, Nicanor posed as having only peaceful intentions toward Judas and his band. There was a meeting of the two sides. But Judas grew suspicious and refused to have any further meetings. Judas and his men won a battle near Chapharsalama. Surely the sympathies of the pious had made it possible for Judas and his men to survive and prosper! Hence, Nicanor attempted to intimidate the pious; he threatened to destroy the temple if Judas was not delivered into his hands. Nicanor marched out from Jerusalem to Beth-Horon, where he met reinforcements and conducted them back toward Jerusalem.

At Adasa, Judas blocked the road in front of the superior force, so confident was he of God's aid. In 1 Maccabees (7:43) we are told that Nicanor was killed at the very beginning of the battle. He may have been an over-bold man, and his fall would go far to explain how Judas's outnumbered men were able to rout the enemy. Upon the rout of the Seleucid force, the sympathetic pious Jews of the countryside joined forces with the Hasmonean band in annihilating the survivors. The man who had threatened to destroy the temple suffered condign punishment along with his army. Pious Jews saw a miracle in the victory, so like the triumphs of Gideon and Saul's son, Jonathan. The seer of *1 Enoch* 90:19 presented Enoch as having predicted it and went on to have him predict that God's great triumph over the wicked would occur soon, indeed within the lifetime of Judas.

The great victory over Nicanor's force led the seer of *1 Enoch* and Judas to believe that the Age of Israel's servitude to foreign rulers was past. The official organs of the Jews dared to send ambassadors to Rome to seek an alliance against Demetrius I. According to 1 Macc 8:1–17, Judas took the initiative in seeking alliance with Rome, but the text of the treaty that resulted shows that the ambassadors represented a wider consensus, perhaps that of the Jewish council of elders.[5]

Demetrius I was bold enough even to risk Rome's displeasure. If the Hasmonean party should attempt to deny legitimacy to the rule of Demetrius and to his appointed high priest, Alcimus, Rome probably would not help the Hasmoneans, for the Romans might well view Alcimus as the legitimate head of the Jewish nation. Judas' band continued to resist Alcimus. Like his predecessors, Demetrius could not tolerate rebellion near the sensitive border with Ptolemaic Egypt. Again he sent Bacchides to pacify Judea, this time with half the elite infantry of the imperial army.

At first Judas was confident that God had ended Israel's servitude to foreign rulers. A prediction at *1 Enoch* 90:31 implied that Judas would live to see God's miraculous triumph over the forces of evil. However, even the 3,000-man nuclear Hasmonean force was intimidated by the size of Bacchides's army. All but 800 melted away from Judas's camp at Elasa. The author of 1 Macc 9:9 holds that Judas's loyal comrades and brothers urged him to withdraw and wait for a better day, but Judas saw that course as beneath him. His tiny force fought bravely, but Judas was slain, and the survivors fled. Clearly he had been mistaken as to God's will.

Some Jews probably understood Dan 12:7, "When the shattering of the power of the holy people comes to an end," to mean that after Judas's death the glorious triumph of God and Israel would come. The Hasmonean propagandist (1 Macc 9:23) reflected bitterly that Judas's death led only to the flourishing of evildoers as Bacchides placed Alcimus and his supporters firmly in power and a crop failure made even guerrilla resistance difficult. The surviving members of the Hasmonean party agreed to follow the leadership of Judas's brother, Jonathan.

2. Conclusion

EVEN BEFORE JUDAS'S DEATH, the plain meaning of the predictions in Daniel 2, 7–12 had proved to be false. Now the plain meaning of the predictions in *1 Enoch* 89–90 also proved to be false. Most Jews had viewed Maccabaeus's victories as miraculous. Some viewed them as fulfillments of prophecies. Long years would elapse before such large numbers of Jews saw the hand of God operating in the history of their own time. For both reasons, the failure of the present-future prophecies and also the apparently unmiraculous times that followed the death of Judas, I end here my study of *peoples of an almighty god.*

Another reason to stop here is that the Babylonians apparently gave up hope. We have no further evidence of their behavior as a *people of an almighty god.* They did not rebel against their foreign masters. Even their last present-future prophecies have been preserved only by Jews. Impressed by Marduk's long failure to act, they may have turned to Judaism, Christianity, and Islam. In contrast, Jews later went on to rebel repeatedly against their conquerors and composed more present-future prophecies. A sect of Jews believed that Jesus of Nazareth was the Messiah. Why was there this contrast between Jews and Babylonians? The victories of the Hasmoneans, especially those of Maccabaeus, go far to explain it. Marduk did nothing for centuries, but Judas's victories over supposedly invincible Macedonians demonstrated the activity of the God of the Jews and suggested that the Age of Punishment was past.

A stronger indication that the Age of Punishment had come to its end occurred in 142 B.C.E., when Judas's brother, Simon, was chief of the Jews and the Seleucid Demetrius II released the LORD's people from all taxation. According to 1 Macc 13:41, at that point "the yoke of the Gentiles was lifted from Israel." The phraseology suggests that the author saw in the event the fulfillment of Isa 10:27. In the immediate context (chap 11) Isaiah predicted that soon after the yoke was removed, Israel's native king would be an ideal righteous figure (11:1–5) and the nation would overrun all of its neighbors (11:14). The nation and its ruler would be immune from sinning (11:9).[6]

Under those circumstances, many Jews would believe that the Age of Punishment had ended, never to return. Unless God acted to protect them, the Jews and anyone who ruled as their king were exposed to all the terrible risks inherent in the status of a *people of an almighty god.*[7] Their misadventures and the literature to which those gave rise can be the subject of another book. This one is long enough!

NOTES

1   Chap 14, n 2.

2   See Chap 14, pp. 466–67.

3   On the absence of Bacchides's expedition from the account in 2 Maccabees, see my *II Maccabees,* 479–81.

4   On the omission of this episode from 2 Maccabees, see my *II Maccabees*, 479–81.

5   See my *I Maccabees*, 359–60, and *CHJ*, II, 310–11.

6   Deut 30:1–8; Isa 11:9 (immunity of the king from sinning: Isa 11:2–5); Jer 31:30–34, 32:39–40, 50:4–5; Ezek 16:60–63, 37:26–27.

7   See p. 5.

APPENDIX: THE PROPHETIC ZAND [1]

CHAPTER I

1:1 (1:1). As is manifest from the Stûtgar [= *Sudgar Nask*]: Zaratûhst [= Zarathushtra] asked for immortality from Aûhrmazd [= Ahuramazda]. 1:2. Then, Aûhrmazd showed the wisdom of all-knowledge unto Zaratûhst. 1:3. Through it, he saw the trunk of a tree, on which there were four branches: one of gold, one of silver, one of steel, and one of mixed iron. 1:4 (1:2). Thereupon, he considered that he saw this in a dream.

1:5. When he arose from sleep, he, Zaratûhst, spoke: "Lord of the spiritual and material existences! it seems that I saw the trunk of a tree, on which there were four branches."

1:6 (1:3). He, Aûhrmazd, spoke to Spîtâmân Zaratûhst: "The trunk of a tree, which thou sawest, is the material existence, which I Aûhrmazd, created [2]. 1:7. The four branches are the four periods which will come. 1:8 (1:4). That of gold is that when I and thou will hold a conference of religion, King Vistâsp shall accept the religion, the figures of the demons shall totter, and the demons . . . [3] into distant and concealed movements. 1:9 (1:5). That of silver is the reign of King Artakhšîr the Kae. 1:10. And that of steel is the reign of Kh ͮasrûy son of Kavât, of immortal soul. 1:11. And that of mixed iron is the evil sovereignty of the demons, having disheveled hair, of the seed of Aesham, when thy tenth century will be at an end, O Spîtâmân Zaratûhst! . . .

CHAPTER 4⁴

4:1 (2:23). He, Zaratûhst, asked: "O spiritual and beneficent Creator of the material existence! What will be the tokens of the tenth century? 4:2 (2:24). He, Aûrmazd, replied: "O Spîtâmân Zaratûhst! I will explain the tokens that will be at the end of thy millennium.

4:3. "During that basest of periods, a hundred kinds, a thousand kinds, and ten thousand kinds of demons⁵ having disheveled hair, of the seed of Aêsham, will arrive. 4:4. Those men of the basest origin will rush from the direction of Khᵛârâsan to Airân-sahr⁶ . . .

4:5 (2:26). "O Spîtâmân Zaratûhst! the offspring of Aêsam will be ill-born, their lineage will not be manifest. 4:6. They will rush, with sorcery, on these Iranian villages which I, Aûhrmazd, created. 4:7. Since they will burn and damage many things, the houses of the house-owners and the villages of the village chiefs, prosperity, nobility, husbandry, fidelity to religion, faith, security, joy, and all the productions which I, Aûhrmazd created . . . 4:8 (2:27). The great country will become a town, the great town a village, the great village a family, and the [great] family a single threshold.⁷ 4:9 (2:28). "O Spîtâmân Zaratûhst! they will raze these Iranian villages which I, Aûhrmazd, created, with harmful desires and despotism [misgovernment]." 4:10. "These demons having disheveled hair are deceivers so that what they say they do not do and they are of a vile religion, so that what they do not say, they do." . . . ⁸

4:13 (2:30). "During that period, O Spîtâmân Zaratûhst! all men will become deceivers and great friendship will be of a different hue. 4:14. And reverence, love, and regard for the soul will depart from the world. 4:15. The affection of the father will depart from the son, and that of the brother from his brother; the son-in-law will be severed from the father-in-law; and the mother will be separated from the daughter and of a different will."

4:16 (2:31). "When it is the end of thy tenth hundredth winter, O Zarathushtra Spîtâmâ, the sun is more unseen and more spotted; the year, month, and day are shorter; 4:17. and the earth of Spendarmad⁹ is more barren and fuller of highwaymen; 4:18. and the crop will not yield the seed, so that of the crop of the corn fields in ten cases, seven will diminish and three will increase, and that which increases does not become ripe; 4:19. and vegetation, trees, and shrubs will diminish; when one shall take a hundred, ninety will diminish and ten will increase, and that which increases gives no pleasure and flavor. 4:20 (2:32). And men are born smaller and their skill and strength are less; they become more deceitful and more given to vile practices; they have no gratitude and respect for bread and salt, and they have no affection for their country."¹⁰ . . .

4:43 (2:42). "And a dark cloud makes the whole sky night, 4:44. and the hot wind and the cold wind arrive and carry away the crops and the seeds of corn. 4:45. The rain, too, will not rain at the proper season; it will rain the noxious creatures more than water. 4:46. And the water of rivers and springs will diminish, and it will have no increase. 4:47 (2:43). And the beast of burden and ox and sheep bring forth more painfully and awkwardly, and acquire less fruitfulness, and their hair is coarser and skin thinner; their milk does not increase and they will have little fat. 4:48. And the plowing ox will have little strength; the swift horse will have less speed, and it will win less in a race."

4:49 (2:44). "And, in that perverse period, O Spîtâmân Zaratûhst! men, who will have the sacred thread-girdle on their waist, will desire death as a boon, on account of the hurtful demands of the evil rule and many a false regulation which they have come up to, whereby their life will not be worth living, 4:50. and youths and children will be apprehensive, and gossiping chitchat and gladness of heart do not arise among them."

4:51 (2:45). "And they will perform the feasts and the institutes of the ancients, the votive offerings to God, the worship, the ritual, the season festivals and the ceremonies of remembering the guardian spirits in various places, and they will not believe unhesitatingly in that which they do perform. 4:52. They do not give rewards as required by law; they bestow no gifts and alms, and even those they bestow they repent of again. 4:53 (2:46). And even those men of the good faith, who will have professed this good Religion of Mazda-worship, proceed in conformity with those ways and customs and do not believe their own religion. 4:54 (2:47). And the noble, great, and charitable who are the virtuous of their own country and locality will depart from their own original place and family as idolatrous; through want they beg something from the ignoble and vile and come to poverty and helplessness. 4:55. Nine out of ten of these men will perish, in the direction of the north." . . . [11]

CHAPTER 6

6:1 (3:1). Zaratûhst asked Aûhrmazd, "O spiritual and beneficent Aûhrmazd! holy Creator of the material existence! from whence will they restore this good Religion of Mazda-worship? and by what means will they smite these demons having disheveled hair of the seed of Aêsham? 6:2 (3:2). O Creator! give me death, and give my grandsons death, that they may not live in that perverse period. Give them holy life, that they may not prepare wickedness and the way to hell!"

6:3 (2:3). He Aûhrmazd replied, "O Spîtâmân Zaratûhst . . . [12]

CHAPTER 7

7:1 (3:12). Zaratûhst asked Aûhrmazd, "O spiritual and beneficent Auhrmazd! holy Creator of the material existence! O Creator! as they will be so immense in number, by what means may they be destroyed?"

7:2 (3:13). He, Aûhrmazd, replied: "O Spîtâmân Zaratûhst! when the demons having disheveled hair of the seed of Aêsham will appear, first a black token will become manifest in the direction of the East, Aûsîtar (= Hushedar) the Zaratuhstian will be born on the Lake Frazdân . . . "[13]

7:3 (3:14). "At thirty years of age, he will come to a conference with me, Aûhrmazd, O Spîtâmân Zaratûhst.[14] 7:4. In the East a prince will be born. 7:5. His father, Vishtâsp, will be a prince of the Kayan race, who approaches the women, and a religious prince is born to him. He calls his name Peshyotanu.[15] 7:6. In the night when the prince will be born, a token will come to the earth: a star falls from the sky. The life of the father of that prince will come to an end; they will bring him up with the damsels of the king, and a woman will be the ruler."[16]

7:7 (3:17). "When that prince will be thirty years old, he comes with innumerable banners and divers armies of the East[17] having upraised banners, having erect weapons; they hasten up with speed as far as the [Oxus?][18] river.[19]"

7:8 (3:18). "When the star Jupiter comes up to its culminating point and casts Venus down, the sovereignty comes to the prince. (3:19). Quite innumerable are the champions, furnished with arms and with banners displayed, from Persis."[20]

7:11 (3:21). "So that with mutual help and under the same banner they will come to these Iranian villages and will slay an immense number of those §êtâspans of the seed of Aêsham, the terrible army with the wide front of the two-legged wolves and the leathern-belted demons."[21]

NOTES

1   For an introduction to this text, see chap 11, pp. 334–41.

2–2   These words ("is the material existence, which I Aûhrmazd, created") have been supplied by Anklesaria from Zoroastrian doctrine.

3   Something is missing from the manuscripts. West conjectured that the original text implied that the demons remained, in a spiritual state, to produce evil.

4 Eddy argued persuasively (*King*, 345, n 21) that chapters 2–3.29 are additions of Sassanian date or later.

5 On "demon" *(dîv)* see p. 337.

6 From Khorosan (Afghanistan and northeastern Iran) to the main body of Iran. Eddy argued persuasively (*King*, 345, n 22) for omitting material here as later interpolations.

7 I have chosen to follow West's translation of *ast-ê bê-bahot* here. Anklesaria rendered, "a skeleton."

8 In v 10 I have followed West, and I have omitted from the end of v 10 through v 12, a passage that merely expands on vv 8–10.

9 Spendarmad was the Zoroastrian deity who was the especial guardian of earth.

10 Eddy (*King*, 346, n 32) argued for omitting 4:21–41 (2:33–41) on the ground that the passage is a denunciation of Islam.

11 Eddy (*King*, 346–47, n 36) argued persuasively for regarding 4:56–63 (2:48–52) as a late doublet of 4:7–13 (2:26–30) in which the tyranny and misrule are ascribed to the Byzantines and the Turks (4:58 [2:49]). On the omission of 4:64–68, 5:1–11 (2:53–64), see Eddy, *King*, 347, n 36.

12 On 6:3–13 (3:3–11), see Eddy, *King*, 347–48, nn 38–39.

13 Two sentences have been omitted as mere glosses.

14 Two sentences have been omitted as mere glosses.

15 The text actually has "Bahram the Vargavand; some have said Shapur." These two Sassanian kings cannot have been named in the original. Eddy argues that the original name was Peshyotanu (*King*, 348, n 45.).

16 For the omissions, see Eddy, *King*, 348, nn 45–47.

17 Eddy (*King* 348, n 43) here and in 7:3 (3:14) substitutes "the East" for "Kinistan" and "Hindus," which were not likely regions for the birth of a Zoroastrian savior in the Hellenistic period.

18 On the conjecture of "Oxus" for "Veh," see Eddy, *King*, 348, n 53.

19 The rest of 7:7 (3:17) consists of glosses.

20   Eddy, *King,* 349, n 55, for the list of suggested Iranian regions, substituted "Persis" as the most logical. 7:9 (3:19 end) consists entirely of glosses.

21   Eddy presented a little more of the text of the "Bahman Yasht" (3:22–23), but that additional matter only magnifies the victory. For his reasons for omitting 3:20(first part) and 3:24–63, see *King,* 349, nn 57–65. We have another good reason to stop: From this point on there are no interesting parallels to the Babylonian and Jewish present-future prophecies.

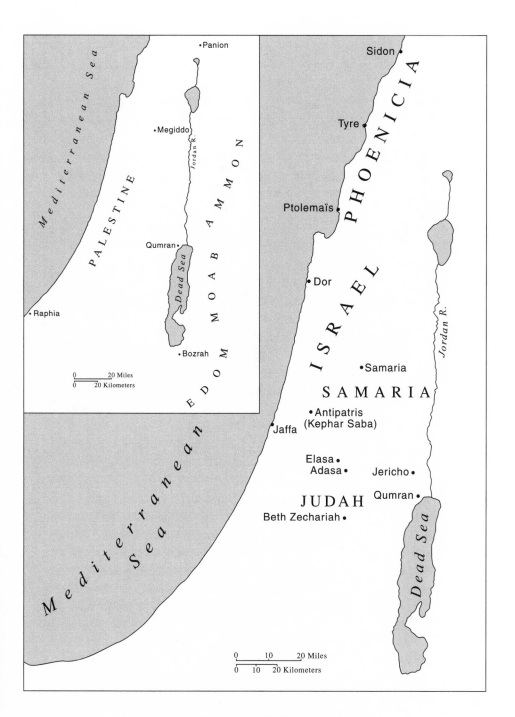

MAP 1: Palestine in the Hellenistic Period

485

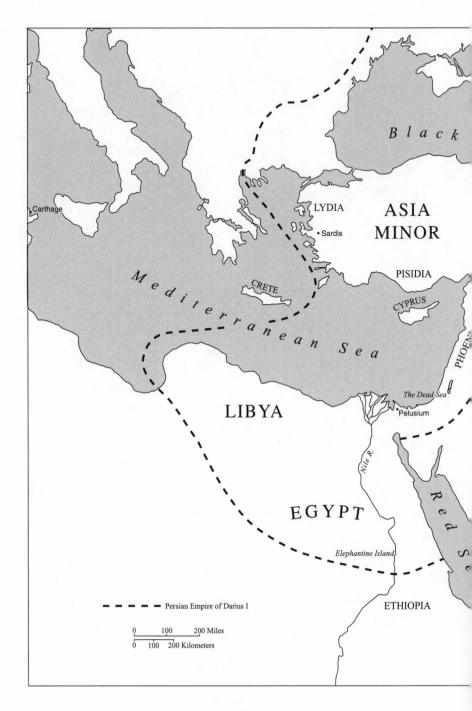

MAP 2: Empire of Darius I

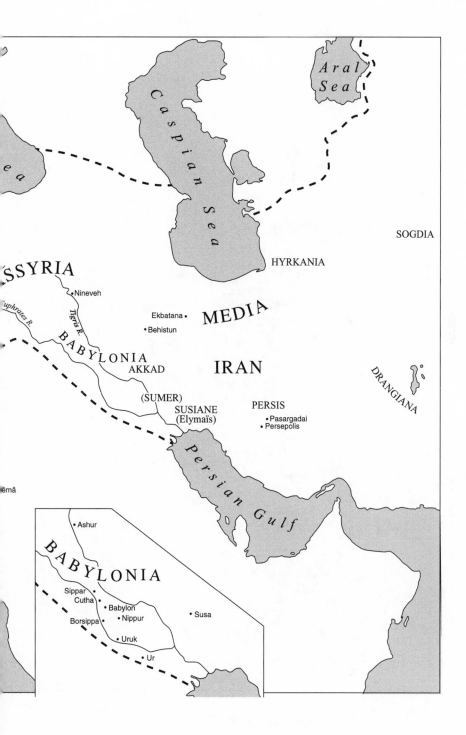

MAP 3: Alexander's Empire

488

NIA

MIA

KOSSAIOI

UXIOI

Caspian Sea

Aral Sea

Oxus R.

BAKTRÍA
• Baktra

HYRKANIA

MARGIANE   AREIA

ARACHOSIA

• Opis

KARMANIA

GEDROSIA

Indus Valley

Indus R.

Persian Gulf

Indian Ocean

```
0      100      200 Miles
0    100    200 Kilometers
```

MAP 4: Hellenistic States

Aral Sea

Caspian Sea

Sea

Sea

MEDIA
ATROPATENE

PARTHIA

DEMETRIAS

S E L E U C I D   E M P I R E

Euphrates R.

RIA
ura-Europos

Tigris R.

PAREITAKAI

DRANGIANA

Seleukeia

ELAM

Persian Gulf

a

BIBLIOGRAPHY

Al-Rawi, Farouk N. H. "Nabopolassar's Restoration Work on the Wall Imgur-Enlil at Babylon." *Iraq* 48 (1985).

———. "Tablets from the Sippar Library: II." *Iraq* 52 (1990).

Alt, Albrecht. "Zur Menetekel-Inschrift." *Vetus Testamentum* 4 (1954).

Andersen, Francis I., and Freedman, David Noel. *Hosea.* Anchor Bible, vol. 24. (Garden City, NY: Doubleday, 1980).

Anklesaria, Behramgore Tahmuras, ed. *Zand-î Vohûman Yasn.* (Bombay: Bhargava, 1957).

Asmussen, J. P. *"Aešma," Encyclopaedia Iranica,* I (1983).

Assyrian Dictionary. edited by Ignace J. Gelb et al. (Chicago: Oriental Institute. Glückstadt: J. J. Augustin, 1956–).

Astour, Michael C. "Symbolism in Genesis 14." in *Biblical Motifs.* Edited by Alexander Altmann. (Cambridge, MA: Harvard University Press, 1966).

Balkan, Kemal. *Kassitenstudien: I. Die Sprache der Kassiten.* American Oriental Series, vol. 37. (New Haven: American Oriental Society, 1954).

Barag, D. "The Effects of the Tennes Rebellion on Palestine." *Bulletin of the American Schools of Oriental Research* 183 (October, 1966).

Bar Kochva, B. *The Seleucid Army.* (Cambridge: Cambridge University Press, 1976).

Bartlett, John R. "Edom and the Edomites." Journal for the Study of the Old Testament: Supplement Series, 77. (Sheffield, England: JSOT Press, 1989).

Batto, Bernard. "When God Sleeps." *Bible Review* 3–4 (1987).

Baumgarten, Joseph M. *Qumran Cave 4, XIII:: The Damascus Document (4Q266–273).* Discoveries in the Judaean Desert, XVIII. (Oxford: Clarendon Press, 1996).

Baumgartner, W. "Herodots babylonische und assyrische Nachrichten." *Archiv Orientální* 18 (1950).

Beaulieu, Paul Alain. *The Reign of Nabonidus, King of Babylon, 556–539 B.C.* (Ph.D. diss., Yale, 1985, Ann Arbor: University Microfilms, order no. DA 8612940).

———. *The Reign of Nabonidus, King of Babylon, 556–539 B.C.* (New Haven: Yale University Press, 1940).

Beloch, Karl Julius. *Griechische Geschichte.* 2d ed. (Berlin and Leipzig: Walter de Gruyter, 1924–27).

Bengtson, Hermann. *Die Diadochen* (München: Beck, 1987).

———. *The Greeks and The Persians.* (New York: Delacorte, 1968).

———. *History of Greece from the Beginnings to the Byzantine Era.* (Ottawa: University of Ottawa Press, 1988).

Ben-Sasson, H. H., ed. *A History of the Jewish People.* (Cambridge, MA: Harvard University Press, 1976).

Bentzen, Aage. *Daniel.* 2d ed. (Tübingen: Mohr [Siebeck], 1952).

Ben Yehuda, Eliezer. *A Complete Dictionary of Ancient and Modern Hebrew.* Edited by N. H. Tur-Sinai. (New York and London: Thomas Yoseloff, 1960).

Berger, Paul-Richard. *Die neubabylonischen Königsinschriften.* Alter Orient und Altes Testament, Band 4/1. (Kevalaer: Butzon & Bercker; Neukirchen-Vluyn: Neukirchener Verlag, 1973).

Bertram. *"hypsistos* B." *Theological Dictionary of the New Testament.* Edited by Gerhard Kittel. (Grand Rapids and London: Eerdmans, 1964–74).

Betlyon, John Wilson, *The Coinage and Mints of Phoenicia: The Pre-Alexandrine Period.* Harvard Semitic Monographs, No. 26. (Chico, CA: Scholars Press, 1980).

Bevan, Edwyn R. *The House of Seleucus.* (London: Edward Arnold, 1902).

Bianchi, Ugo. "L'Inscription 'des daivas' et le Zoroastrisme des Achéménides." *Revue de l'histoire des religions* 192 (1977).

Bickerman, Elias J. *Chronology of the Ancient World.* (Ithaca, NY: Cornell University Press, 1968. Reprint 1980).

———. *Four Strange Books of the Bible.* (New York: Schocken, 1967).

———. *Studies in Jewish and Christian History,* Part One. (Leiden: Brill, 1976).

———. "Notes sur la chronologie de la XXX-ième dynastie." In *Mélanges Maspero.* Mémoires publiées par les membres de l'Institut français d'archéologie orientale du Caire, 66. (Le Caire: Impr. de l'Institut, 1934–36).

———. "Notes on Seleucid and Parthian Chronology." *Berytos* 8, Fasc. 2 (1944).

———. *Religions and Politics in the Hellenistic and Roman Periods.* Edited by Emilio Gabba and Morton Smith. (Como: Edizioni New Press, 1985).

———. *Studies in Jewish and Christian History,* Part 3. (Leiden: Brill, 1986).

——— and Tadmor, H. "Darius I, Pseudo-Smerdis, and the Magi." *Athenaeum,* n 56 (1978).

Billows, Richard A. *Antigonos the One-Eyed and the Creation of the Hellenistic State.* (Berkeley, Los Angeles, and London: University of California Press, 1990).

Bilabel, Friedrich, ed. *Sammelbuch griechischer Urkunden aus Ägypten.* (Berlin and Leipzig: Walter de Gruyter, 1926).

Böhl, F. M. Th. de Liagre. "Die babylonische Prätendenten zur Zeit des Xerxes." *Bibliotheca Orientalis* 19 (1962).

Bongenaar, A. C. V. M. "The Regency of Belsazzar." *Nouvelles assyriologiques brèves et utilitaires,* June, 1993, item no. 41.

Borger, Rykle. *Handbuch der Keilschriftliteratur.* (Berlin: Walter de Gruyter, 1967–).

Bosworth, A. B. *Conquest and Empire: The Reign of Alexander the Great.* (Cambridge: Cambridge University Press, 1988).

———. *A Historical Commentary on Arrian's History of Alexander.* (Oxford: Clarendon Press, 1980–).

Bouché-Leclercq, A. *Histoire de la divination dans l'antiquité.* 4 vols. (Paris: E. Leroux, 1877–82).

———. *Histoire des Lagides.* 4 vols. (Paris: E. Leroux, 1903–7).

Bousset, W. "Die Beziehungen der ältesten jüdischen Sibylle zur chaldäischen Sibylle. . . ." *Zeitschrift für die neutestamentlichen Wissenschaft* 3 (1902).

Boyce, Mary. *A History of Zoroastrianism.* Handbuch der Orientalistik. Edited by B. Spuler. Erste Abteilung: Der nahe und mittlere Osten, Band 8: Religion, Abschnitt 1: Religionsgeschichte des alten Orients, Lieferung 2. (Leiden/Köln: Brill, 1975, 1982, –).

———. "On the Antiquity of Zoroastrian Apocalyptic." *Bulletin of the School of Oriental and African Studies* 47 (1984).

———. "The Poems of the Persian Sibyl and the *Zand i Vahman Yašt.*" *Études irano-aryennes offertes à Gilbert Lazard.* Compiled by C. H. de Fouchécour and Ph. Gignoux. (Paris: Association pour l'avancement des études iraniennes, 1989).

Briant, Pierre. *Antigone le Borgne.* (Paris: Les Belles Lettres, 1973).

Bright, John. *A History of Israel* 3d ed. (Philadelphia: Westminster Press, 1981).

———. *Jeremiah.* Anchor Bible, vol. 21. (Garden City, NY: Doubleday, 1965).

Brinkman, John A. *Materials and Studies for Kassite History.* (Chicago: Oriental Institute, 1976–).

———. "Merodach Baladan II." *Studies Presented to A. Leo Oppenheim.* (Chicago: Oriental Institute, 1964).

———. *A Political History of Post-Kassite Babylonia* Analecta Orientalia, 43. (Roma: Pontificium Institutum Biblicum, 1968).

Budde, K. "Über die Capitel l und li des Buches Jeremia." *Jahrbücher für deutsche Theologie* 23 (1878).

Burn, Andrew Robert. *Persia and the Greeks.* 2d ed. (London: Duckworth, 1984).

Burstein, Stanley M. *The Babyloniaca of Berossus.* Sources and Monographs: Sources from the Ancient Near East, vol. 1, fascicle 5. (Malibu: Undena, 1978).

Cambridge Ancient History. 1st ed. Edited by J. B. Bury, S. A. Cook, F. E. Adcock, et al. (Cambridge: Cambridge University Press, 1923–39). 2d ed. Edited by John Boardman, I. E. S. Edwards, N. G. L. Hammond, E. Sollberger, et al. (Cambridge: Cambridge University Press, 1970–96). 3d ed. Edited by I. E. S. Edwards, C. J. Gadd, N. G. L. Hammond, et al. (Cambridge: Cambridge University Press, 1970–).

The Cambridge History of Iran. Edited by W. B. Fisher and Ilya Gershevitch, et al. 8 vols. (Cambridge: Cambridge University Press, 1968–).

The Cambridge History of Judaism. Edited by W. D. Davies and Louis Finkelstein. (Cambridge: Cambridge University Press, 1984–).

Charlesworth, James H., ed. *The Old Testament Pseudepigrapha.* 2 vols. (Garden City, NY: Doubleday, 1983–85).

Childs, Brevard S. *Isaiah and the Assyrian Crisis.* Studies in Biblical Theology, Second Series, 3. (Naperville, IL: Allenson, 1967).

Christensen, Arthur. *Les Kayanides* Historisk-filologiske Meddelelser, udgivne af Det Kgl. Danske videnskabernes selskab. Bind 19, fascicle 2. København: Levin & Munksgaard, 1931).

Clay, Albert T. *Documents of Murashu Sons of Nippur Dated in the Reigns of Darius II* . . . University of Pennsylvania, the Museum, Publications of the Babylonian Section, II/1. (Philadelphia: Department of Archaeology and Palaeontology of the University of Pennsylvania, 1912).

———. *Miscellaneous Inscriptions in the Yale Babylonian Collection.* Yale Oriental Series, Babylonian Texts, vol. 1. (New Haven: Yale University Press, 1915).

———. *Letters and Transactions from Cappadocia.* Babylonian Inscriptions in the Collection of J. B. Nies, Vol. 4. (New Haven: Yale University Press, 1927).

Clements, R. E. *Isaiah and the Deliverance of Jerusalem* Journal for the Study of the Old Testament, Supplement Series, 13. (Sheffield, England: JSOT Press. 1980).

Clermont-Ganneau, Charles. "Mané, thécel, pharès et le festin de Balthasar." *Journal asiatique,* 8th series, no. 8 (1886).

Cloché, Paul. *La Dislocation d'un empire.* (Paris: Payot, 1959).

Cogan, Morton (Mordechai). *Imperialism and Religion: Assyria, Judah, and Israel in the Eighth and Seventh Centures B.C.E.* Society of Biblical Literature Monograph Series 19; (Missoula, MT: Society of Biblical Literature and Scholars Press, 1974).

——— and Tadmor, Hayim. *II Kings.* Anchor Bible, vol. 11. (Garden City, NY: Doubleday, 1988).

Collins, John. *The Sibylline Oracles of Egyptian Judaism.* (Missoula, MT: Society of Biblical Literature and Scholars Press, 1972).

Cook, J. M. *The Persian Empire.* (London, Melbourne, and Toronto: Dent, 1983).

Cross, Frank Moore. "Fragment of the Prayer of Nabonidus." *Israel Exploration Journal* 34 (1984).

Cumont, F. "Hypsistos." *RE,* 10 (1910).

Dandamaev, Muhammad. "The latest evidence for Nebuchadnezzar III's Reign." *NABU* 7 (1993). Pp. 8–9, item no. 11.

———. *Persien unter den ersten Achämeniden: 6 Jahrhundert v. Chr.* Beiträge zur Iranistik. Edited by Georges Redard. Band VIII. (Wiesbaden: D. Ludwig Reichert Verlag, 1976).

————. Review of *Achaemenid History, I–III. Bibliotheca Orientalis* 46 (1984–1989).

————. *Slavery in Babylonia from Nabopolassar to Alexander the Great.* (DeKalb, IL: Northern Illinois University Press, 1984).

————. and Lukonin, Vladimir G. *The Culture and Social Institutions of Ancient Iran.* (Cambridge: Cambridge University Press, 1989).

Davies, Philip R. "The Damascus Covenant: An Interpretation of the 'Damascus Document.' " Journal for the Study of the Old Testament: Supplement Series, 25. (Sheffield: JSOT Press, 1983).

————. "Qumran and Apocalyptic or Obscurum per Obscurius," *JNES* 49 (1990).

Delling, Gerhard. "Alexander der Grosse als Bekenner der jüdischen Gottesglaubens." *Journal for the Study of Judaism in the Persian, Hellenistic, and Roman Periods* 1 (1981).

De Meulenaere, Herman. "Nektanebos II," *LA,* 4 (1982).

Dentan, Robert C. *The Idea of History in the Ancient Near East.* (New Haven and London: Yale University Press, 1955).

Dhorme, É., "La mère de Nabonide." *Revue d'assyriologie et d'archéologie orientale* 41 (1947).

Dhorme, P. "La fille de Nabonide." *Revue d'assyriologie et d'archéologie orientale* 11 (1914).

Dittenberger, W., ed. *Sylloge Inscriptionum Graecarum.* 3d ed. (Leipzig: Hirzel, 1905–24).

Donner, Herbert. "The Separate States of Israel and Judah." *Israelite and Judaean History.* Edited by John H. Hayes and J. Maxwell Miller. (Philadelphia: Westminster Press, 1977).

Dougherty, Raymond P. *Nabonidus and Belshazzar.* Yale Oriental Series: Researches, vol. 15. (New Haven: Yale University Press, 1929).

————. *The Sealand of Ancient Arabia.* Yale Oriental Series: Researches," vol. 19. (New Haven: Yale University Press, 1932).

Driver, Samuel R. *An Introduction to the Literature of the Old Testament.* (New York: Meridian, 1957).

Duchesne-Guillemin, "Die Religion der Achämeniden." *Acta Antiqua* 19 (1971).

Eddy, Samuel K. *The King Is Dead.* (Lincoln, NE: University of Nebraska Press, 1961).

Eissfeldt, Otto. "Die Menetekel-Inschrift und ihre Deutung." *Zeitschrift für die alttestamentliche Wissenschaft* 63 (1951).

————. *The Old Testament: An Introduction.* (New York and Evanston, IL: Harper & Row, 1965).

Ellenbogen, Maximilian. *Foreign Words in the Old Testament, Their Origin and Etymology.* (London: Luzac, 1960).

Ellis, Richard S. *Foundation Deposits in Ancient Mesopotamia.* Yale Near Eastern Researches, 2. (New Haven and London: Yale University Press, 1968).

Encyclopaedia Iranica. Edited by Ehsan Yarshater. (London, Boston, and Henley: Routledge & Kegan Paul, 1985–).

Entsiqlopediah miqra'it. Edited by E. L. Sukenik and M. D. Cassuto et al. 8 vols. (Jerusalem: Bialik Institute, 1955–82).

Ermann, Adolf. *The Literature of the Ancient Egyptians.* Reprint. (New York: Benjamin Blom, 1971).

———. *Die Märchen des Papyrus Westcar.* (Berlin: W. Spemann, 1890).

Fewell, Danna Nolan. "Sennacherib's Defeat: Words of War in 2 Kings 18:13–19:37." *Journal for the Study of the Old Testament* 34 (1986).

Finkel, Irving L. "Bilingual Chronicle Fragments." *JCS* 32 (1980).

Flusser, David. "The four empires in the Fourth Sibyl and in the Book of Daniel." *Israel Oriental Studies* 2 (1972).

Focke, F. "Demosthenesstudien." In *Genethliakon Wilhelm Schmid.* Tübinger Beiträge zur Altertumswissenschaft, Vol. 5. (Stuttgart: W. Kohlhammer, 1929).

Fontenrose, Joseph. *The Delphic Oracle.* (Berkeley, Los Angeles, and London: University of California Press, 1978).

Fox, Robin Lane. *Alexander the Great.* (London and New York: Penguin, 1986).

Frank, Harry. *Discovering the Biblical World.* (Maplewood, NJ: Hammond, 1975).

Frank, Richard M. "The Description of the 'Bear' in Dn 7,5." *Catholic Biblical Quarterly* 21 (1959).

Frankfort, Henri. *Ancient Egyptian Religion.* (New York: Columbia University Press, 1948).

———. *Kingship and the Gods.* (Chicago: University of Chicago Press, 1948).

Frazer, James George. *The New Golden Bough.* Edited with notes and foreword by Theodor M. Gaster. (Garden City: Doubleday, 1961).

Frye, Richard N. *The Heritage of Persia.* (Cleveland and New York: World Publishing Company, 1963).

———. *The History of Ancient Iran.* Handbuch der Altertumswissenschaft. Begründet von Iwan von Müller, Abteilung 3, Teil 7. (München: Beck, 1984).

Gadd, C. J. "Hammurabi and the End of His Dynasty." Chap. 5 in *CAH*³, Vol. 2, part 1 (1973).

———. "The Harran Inscriptions of Nabonidus." *Anatolian Studies* 8 (1958).

——— and Legrain, Leon. *Ur Excavations: Texts, I: Royal Inscriptions.* Publications of the Joint Expedition of the British Museum and of the University of Pennsylvania to Mesopotamia. (London: Harrison and Sons, 1928).

Gardiner, Alan. *Egypt of the Pharaohs.* (Oxford: Clarendon Press, 1961).

Gardner, Percy. *Catalogue of Greek Coins: The Seleucid Kings of Syria.* A Catalogue of the Greek Coins in the British Museum. (Bologna: Forni, 1963).

Geffcken, Johannes, ed. *Die Oracula Sibyllina.* (Leipzig: Hinrichs, 1902).

———. *Komposition und Entstehungszeit der Oracula sibyllina.* Texte und Untersuchungen zur Geschichte der altchristlichen Literatur." Neue Folge, 8, Band 1. (Leipzig: Hinrichs, 1902).

George, A. R. *Review of Literarische Texte aus Babylon* by Jan van Dijk. *Bibliotheca Orientalis* 46 (1989).

Gershevitch, Ilya. "The False Smerdis." *Acta Antiqua* 27 (1979).

————, *Literatur,* in "Handbuch der Orientalistik," ed. B. Spuler, Erste Abteilung: Der nahe und mittlere Osten, Band IV: Iranistik, Abschnitt II, 2 lieferung (Leiden/Köln: Brill, 1968–81).

Geyer. "Lysimachos 1." *RE,* 14 (1930).

Gignoux, Philippe. "Nouveaux regards sur l'apocalyptique iranienne." *Comptes rendus de l'Académie des inscriptions et belles lettres* (1986).

————. "Sur l'inexistence d'un Bahman Yasht avestique." *Journal of the School of Asian and African Studies* 33 (1986).

Ginsberg, H. L. *The Book of Isaiah: A New Translation.* (Philadelphia: Jewish Publication Society, 1973).

————. "Gleanings in First Isaiah." *Mordecai M. Kaplan Jubilee Volume,* English Section. (New York: Jewish Theological Seminary of America, 1953).

————. "Isaiah: First Isaiah." *Encyclopaedia Judaica,* 9 (1971).

————. *The Israelian Heritage of Judaism.* (New York: Jewish Theological Seminary of America, 1982).

————. " 'King of Kings' and 'Lord of Kingdoms.' " *AJSL* 57 (1940).

————. "M^{e}ne, t^{e}qel upharsin." *Entsiqlopediah Miqra'it,* 5 (1968).

————. "Reflexes of Sargon in Isaiah after 715 B.C.E.," *JAOS* 88 (1968).

————. Review of *A Grammar of the Phoenician Language* by Zellig S. Harris. *JBL* 56 (1937).

————. *Studies in Daniel.* (New York: Jewish Theological Seminary of America, 1948).

————. *Studies in Koheleth.* (New York: Jewish Theological Seminary of America, 1950).

Glasson, T. Francis. "What Is Apocalyptic?" *New Testament Studies* 27 (1980).

Glotz, Gustave. *Histoire grecque.* 4 vols. (Paris: Presses universitaires de France, 1925–38).

Goedicke, Hans. *The Protocol of Neferyt.* (Baltimore, MD: Johns Hopkins University Press, 1977).

Goldstein, Jonathan A. "Alexander and the Jews." *Proceedings of the American Academy for Jewish Research* 59 (1993).

————. "The Central Composition of the West Wall of the Synagogue of Dura-Europos." *Journal of the Ancient Near Eastern Society* 16–17 (1984–85).

————. "Even the Righteous Can Perish by His Faith." *Conservative Judaism* 41, no. 3 (Spring, 1989).

————. "The Historical Setting of the Uruk Prophecy." *JNES* 47 (1988).

————. *The Letters of Demosthenes.* (New York and London: Columbia University Press, 1968).

————. *I Maccabees.* Anchor Bible, vol. 41. (Garden City, NY: Doubleday, 1976).

————. "The Message of *Aristeas to Philokrates." Eretz Israel, Israel, and the Jewish Diaspora: Mutual Relations.* Edited by Menachem Mor. (Lanham, NY, and London: University Press of America, 1991).

————. *II Maccabees.* Anchor Bible, vol. 41A. (Garden City, NY: Doubleday, 1983).

————. *Semites, Iranians, Greeks, and Romans: Studies in their Interactions* Brown Judaic Studies, no. 217. (Atlanta, GA: Scholars Press, 1990).

————. "The Tales of the Tobiads." in *Christianity, Judaism, and Other Greco-Roman Cults: Studies for Morton Smith at Sixty.* Edited by Jacob Neusner. (Leiden: Brill, 1975).

Gonçalves, Francolino. *L'Expédition de Sennachérib en Palestine dans la littérature hébraïque* Publications de l'Institut orientaliste de Louvain, 34. (Paris: Librairie Lecoffre; J. Gabalda, 1986).

Goodwin, William Watson. *Greek Grammar.* Revised by Charles Burton Gulick. (Boston: Ginn and Company, 1930).

Graf, David Frank. *Medism: Greek Collaboration with Achaemenid Persia.* (Ph.D. diss. Univ. of Michigan. Ann Arbor: University Microfilms International, 1982).

Grainger, John D. *Seleukos Nikator.* (London and New York: Routledge, 1990).

Gray, John. *I & II Kings: A Commentary.* 2d ed. (London: SCM Press, 1970).

Grayson, Albert Kirk. *Assyrian and Babylonian Chronicles.* Texts from Cuneiform Sources, vol. 5. (Locust Valley, NY: J. J. Augustin, 1975).

————. *Babylonian Historical-Literary Texts.* (Toronto and Buffalo: University of Toronto Press, 1975).

————. "History and Historians of the Ancient Near East: Assyria and Babylonia." *Orientalia,* n. s., 49 (1980).

———— and Lambert, Wilfred G. "Akkadian Prophecies." *JCS* 18 (1964).

Graziani, Simonetta. *I testi mesopotamici datati al regno di Serse, 485–465 a.c.* Istituto universitaria orientale—Napoli, supplemento 47 agli Annali—vol. 46, fasc. 2. (Roma: Herder, 1986).

Green, Peter. *Alexander of Macedon, 356–323 B.C.: A Historical Biography.* 2d ed., revised and enlarged. (Berkeley: University of California Press, 1991).

————. *Alexander to Actium: the Historical Evolution of the Hellenistic Age.* 2d printing. (Berkeley and Los Angeles: University of California Press, 1993).

Greenberg, Moshe. *Ezekiel 1–20* Anchor Bible, vol. 22. (Garden City, NY: Doubleday, 1983).

Greenfield, Jonas C. "Early Aramaic Poetry." *Journal of the Ancient Near Eastern Society of Columbia University* 11 (1979).

———— and Porten, Bezalel. *The Bisutun Inscription of Darius the Great: Aramaic Version.* Corpus Inscriptionum Iranicarum, Part I: Inscriptions of Ancient Iran. Vol. 5: The Aramaic Versions of the Achaemenian Inscriptions etc., Texts I. (London: Lund Humphries, 1982).

Gruen, Erich. *Heritage and Hellenism.* (Berkeley, Los Angeles, and London: University of California Press, 1998).

Hadley, Robert A. "The Foundation Date of Seleucia on the Tigris." *Historia* 27 (1978).

Hallo, William W. "Akkadian Apocalypses." *Israel Exploration Journal* 16 (1966).

————. *The Bible in the Light of Cuneiform Literature.* (Lewiston/Queenston/Lampeter: Edwin Mellen Press, 1990).

————. "The Concept of Eras from Nabonassar to Seleucus." *JNES* 16–17 (1984–85).

————. *Early Mesopotamian Royal Titles.* American Oriental Series, vol. 43; (New Haven: American Oriental Society, 1957).

————. "From Qarqar to Carchemish." *Biblical Archaeologist* 23 (1960).

————. "Gutium." RLA 3 (1971).

————. "The Limits of Skepticism." *JAOS* 110 (1990).

————. "The Nabonassar Era and Other Epochs in Mesopotamian Chronology and Chronography." *A Scientific Humanist: Studies in Memory of Abraham Sachs.* Edited by Erle Leichty et al. Occasional Publications of the Samuel Noah Kramer Fund, 9. (Philadelphia, 1988).

————. "Sumerian Historiography." *History, Historiography, and Interpretation: Studies in biblical and cuneiform Literatures.* Edited by H. Tadmor and M. Weinfeld. (Jerusalem: Magnes Press, 1982).

———— and van Dijk, Jan. *The Exaltation of Inanna.* Yale Near Eastern Researches, 3. (New Haven: Yale University Press, 1968).

Halpern, Baruch. *The First Historians.* (San Francisco: Harper and Row, 1988).

Hamilton, J. A. *Plutarch, Alexander: A Commentary.* (Oxford: Clarendon Press, 1969).

Hammond, N. G. L. *Alexander the Great.* 2d ed. (Bristol: Bristol Press, 1989).

————. *The Macedonian State.* (Oxford: Oxford University Press, 1989).

Haran, Menahem. *Temple and Temple Service in Ancient Israel.* (Oxford: Clarendon Press, 1980).

————. "The literary structure and chronological framework of the Prophecies in Is xl–xlviii." *Vetus Testamentum,* Suppl. 9 (1963).

Harmatta, J. "The Literary Patterns of the Babylonian Edict of Cyrus." *Acta Antiqua* 19 (1971).

Hartman, Hans. "Zur neuen Inschrift des Xerxes von Persepolis." *Orientalistische Literaturzeitung* 40 (1939).

Hartman, Louis, and Di Lella, Alexander A. *The Book of Daniel* Anchor Bible, vol. 23. (Garden City, NY: Doubleday, 1978).

Haussoulier, B. "Les Séleucides et le temple d'Apollon didymien." *Revue de philologie, de littérature et d'histoire anciennes* 25 (1901).

Hayes, John H., and Miller, J. Maxwell, eds. *Israelite and Judaean History.* (Philadelphia: Westminster Press, 1977).

Heidel, Alexander. *The Gilgamesh Epic and Old Testament Parallels.* (Chicago and London: University of Chicago Press, 1944).

Herzfeld, Ernst. *Altpersische Inschriften.* (Berlin: Reimer, 1938).

Holleaux, Maurice. *Études d'épigraphie et d'histoire grecques.* Lagides et Séleucides, Tome III. (Paris: É. de Boccard, 1942).

How, W. W., and Wells, J. *A Commentary on Herodotus.* 2 vols. (Oxford: Clarendon Press, 1912).

Hultgård, Anders. *"Bahman Yasht:* A Persian Apocalypse." *Mysteries and Revelations: Apocalyptic Studies since the Uppsala Colloquium. Journal for the Study of the Peudepigrapha.* Supplement Series 9. (Sheffield: Sheffield Academic Press, 1991).

Hunger, Hermann. *Spätbabylonische Texte aus Uruk,* Teil I. Ausgrabungen der

Deutschen Forschungsgemeinschaft in Uruk-Warka, Band 4. (Berlin: Gebr. Mann, 1976).

———— and Kaufman, Stephen A. "A New Akkadian Prophecy Text." *JAOS* 95 (1975).

Jackson, A. V. Williams. *Zoroaster, the Prophet of ancient Iran.* (London: Macmillan, 1899).

Jacobsen, Thorkild. "The Eridu Genesis." *JBL* 100 (1981).

————. *The Sumerian King List.* Assyriological Studies, No. 11. (Chicago: University of Chicago Press, 1939).

————. *The Treasures of Darkness: A History of Mesopotamian Religion.* (New Haven and London: Yale University Press, 1976).

Japhet, Sara. "Chronicles, Book of." *Encyclopaedia Judaica,* 5 (1971).

Jastrow, Marcus. *A Dictionary of the Targumim, the Talmud Babli and Yerushalmi, and the Midrashic Literature.* (New York and Berlin: Choreb, 1920).

Jastrow, Morris. *The Religion of Babylonia and Assyria* (Boston: Ginn and Co., 1898).

Jean, Charles-F., and Hoftijzer, Jacob. *Dictionnaire des inscriptions sémitiques de l'ouest.* (Leiden: Brill, 1965).

Jeremias, Alfred. *Das Alte Testament im Licht des alten Orients.* 3d ed. (Leipzig: Hinrichs, 1916).

————. "Die sogenannten Kedorlaomer-Texte." MVAG 21 (1916).

Jordan, Julius. *See* Schott, A.

Judeich, Walter. *Kleinasiatische Studien.* (Marburg: Elwert, 1892).

Kaiser, Otto, "Die Verkündigung des Propheten Jesaja im Jahre 701." *Zeitschrift für die alttestamentlichen Wissenschaft* 81 (1916).

Kaufmann, Yehezkel. *The Religion of Israel.* (Chicago: University of Chicago Press, 1960).

————. *Toledot ha-emunah ha-yiśre'elit.* Vol. 3, part 1, and Vol. 4, part 1. (Tel-Aviv: Bialik Foundation and Dvir, 1938–1947).

Kautsch, E., reviser. *Gesenius' Hebrew Grammar.* Translated by A. E. Cowley. 2d English ed. (Oxford: Clarendon Press, 1949).

Kellens, J. "Avesta," *Encyclopaedia Iranica,* 3 (1989).

Kent, Roland G. *Old Persian.* American Oriental Series, vol. 33. (New Haven: American Oriental Society, 1950).

Kienitz, Friedrich Karl. *Die politische Geschichte Aegyptens, vom 7. bis zum 4. Jahrhundert vor der Zeitwende.* (Berlin: Akademie-Verlag, 1953).

King,, L. W. *Babylonian Boundary Stones and Memorial Tablets in the British Museum.* (London: British Museum, 1912).

Kittel, Rudolf, ed. *Biblia Hebraica.* 4th ed. (Stuttgart: Privilegierte Würtembergische Bibelanstalt, 1949).

Knibb, M. A. *The Ethiopic Book of Enoch.* 2 vols. (Oxford: Clarendon Press, 1978).

Koenen, Ludwig. *Eine agonistische Inschrift aus Ägypten und frühptolemäische Königfeste.* Beiträge zur Klassischen Philologie, 56. (Meisenheim am Glan: Anton Hain, 1977).

―――. "Die Prophezeiungen des 'Töpfers.' " *Zeitschrift für Papyrologie und Epigraphik* 2 (1968).

―――. "A Supplemental Note on the Date of the Oracle of the Potter." *Zeitschrift für Papyrologie und Epigraphik* 54 (1984).

Kramer, Samuel Noah. "Sumerian Historiography." *Israel Exploration Journal* 3 (1953).

―――. *The Sumerians*. (Chicago and London: University of Chicago Press, 1963).

Krecher, Joachim, and Müller, Hans Peter. "Vergangenheitsinteresse in Mesopotamien and Israel." *Saeculum* 26 (1975).

Kutscher, Eduard Yechezkʿel. "Aramaic." in *Current Trends in Linguistics*. Edited by Thomas A. Sebeok. Linguistics in South West Asia and North Africa, vol. 6. (The Hague and Paris: Mouton, 1970).

―――. *The Language and Linguistic Background of the Isaiah Scroll 1Q Isaᵃ*. Studies of the Texts of the Desert of Judah, vol. 5. Edited by J. van der Ploeg. (Leiden: Brill, 1974).

Kvanvig, Helge, *The Mesopotamian Background of the Enoch Figure* Roots of Apocalyptic, vol. 1. (Oslo: Skrivestua, Det teologiske Menighetsfakultet, 1983).

―――. "Struktur und Geschichte in Dan. 7, 1–14." *Studia Theologica* 32 (1978).

Lacoque, André. *The Book of Daniel*. (Atlanta, GA: John Knox, 1979).

Lambert, Wilfred G. *Babylonian Wisdom Literature*. (Oxford: Clarendon Press, 1967).

―――. *The Background of Jewish Apocalyptic*. (London: Athlone Press, 1978).

―――. "A Catalogue of Texts and Authors. *JCS* 16 (1962).

―――. "Nabonidus in Arabia." *Proceedings of the Fifth Seminar for Arabian Studies*. (London: Seminar for Arabian Studies, 1972).

―――. "Nebuchadnezzar, King of Justice." *Iraq* 27 (1965).

―――. "A New Source for the Reign of Nabonidus." *Archiv für Orientforschung* 27 (1968–69).

―――. "The reign of Nebuchadnezzar I: A Turning Point in the History of Ancient Mesopotamian Religion." *Seed*.

―――. "Studies in Marduk." *Bulletin of the School of Oriental and African Studies* 47 (1984).

Lamberton, Robert. *Hesiod*. (New Haven and London: Yale University Press, 1988).

Landsberger, Benno. "Assyrische Königsliste und 'Dunkles Zeitalter.' " *JCS* 8 (1954).

―――. "Zu neuveröffentlichten Geschichtsquellen der Zeit von Asarhaddon bis Nabonid." *Zeitschrift für Assyriologie* 37 (1926–27).

―――― and Kinnier-Wilson, J. V., "The Fifth Tablet of *Enuma Eliš*." *JNES* 20 (1961).

Langdon, Stephen. *Babylonian Liturgies*. (Paris: Geuthner, 1913).

―――. *Die neubabylonischen Königsinschriften*. (Leipzig: Hinrichs, 1912).

―――. "New Inscriptions of Nabuna'id," *AJSL* 32 (1915–16).

―――. *Oxford Editions of Cuneiform Inscriptions*. Vol. 1: *The H. Weld-Blundell collection in the Ashmolean Museum*. Vol. 1: *Sumerian and Semitic Religious and Historical Texts*. (London and New York: Oxford University Press and H. Milford, 1923).

Lanternari, Vittorio. *The Religions of the Oppressed: A Study of Modern Messianic Cults*. (New York: Knopf, 1963).

Larsen, Mogens Trolle. *Power and Propaganda* Mesopotamia: Copenhagen Studies in Assyriology, vol. 7. (Copenhagen: Akademisk Forlag, 1979).

Lasswell, Harold D., Lerner, Daniel, and Speier, Hans, eds. *Propaganda and Communication in World History*. (Honolulu, HI: University Press of Hawaii, 1979).

Latte, Kurt. *Römische Religionsgeschichte*. (München: Beck, 1960).

Launey, Marcel. *Recherches sur les armées hellénistiques*. 2 vols. (Paris: É. de Boccard, 1950).

Léemans, W. F. "Kidinnu, un symbole de droit divin babylonien." *Symbolae ad jus et historiam antiquitatis pertinentes Julio Christiano von Oven dedicatae*, Edited by M. David, B. A. van Gröningen, and E. M Meijers. (Leiden: Brill, 1946).

Legrain, Léon. *Royal Inscriptions and Fragments from Nippur and Babylon*. The Museum of the University of Pennsylvania, Publications of the Babylonian Section, vol. 15. (Philadelphia: Museum of the University of Pennsylvania, 1926).

Leichty, Erle. "Two New Fragments of 'Ludlul Bel Nemeqi.' " *Orientalia*, n. s., 28 (1959).

Lesky, Albin. *A History of Greek Literature*. (New York: Crowell, 1966).

Lewis, David M. *Sparta and Persia*. (Leiden: Brill, 1977).

Lewy, Hildegard. "The Babylonian Background of the Kay Kâûs Legend." *Archiv Orientální* 17, part 2 (1949).

Lewy, Julius. "The Late Assyro-Babylonian Cult of the Moon and Its Culmination at the Time of Nabonidus." *HUCA* 19 (1945–46).

Lexikon der Ägyptologie. Edited by Wolfgang Helck and Eberhard Otto. (Wiesbaden: Harrassowitz, 1975–).

Licht, J. A. *"Mal'akh 'adonay, Mal'akhim. Entsiqlopediah Miqra'it*, 4 (1962).

Lichtenstein, Hans. "Die Fastenrolle." *HUCA* 8–9 (1931–32).

Lieberman, Saul. *Greek in Jewish Palestine* (New York: Jewish Theological Seminary of America, 1940).

Lipiński. *"b'hryt hymym* dans les texted préexiliques. *Vetus Testamentum* 20 (1970).

Livingstone, Alasdair. *Mystical and Mythological Explanatory Works of Assyrian and Babylonian Scholars*. (Oxford: Clarendon Press, 1986).

Longman, Tremper, III. *Fictional Akkadian Autobiography*. (Winona Lake, IN: Eisenbrauns, 1991).

Lorton, David. "The Supposed Expedition of Ptolemy II to Persia." *Journal of Egyptian Archaeology* 57 (1971).

Luckenbill, Daniel D. *Ancient Records of Assyria and Babylon*. 2 vols. (Chicago: University of Chicago Press, 1926–27).

———. *The Annals of Sennacherib*. (Chicago: University of Chicago Press, 1924).

———. "The Black Stone of Esarhaddon." *AJSL* 41 (1925).

Malamat, Abraham, ed. *The Age of Monarchies: Political History The World History of the Jewish People*, vol. 4, part 1. (Jerusalem: Massada Press, 1979). First Series: Ancient Times. Edited by Benjamin Mazar and Alexander Peli.

————. "The Historical Background of the Assassination of Amon King of Judah." *Israel Exploration Journal* 3 (1953).

————. *Israel in Biblical Times: Historical Essays.* (Jerusalem: Bialik Institute and Israel Exploration Society, 1983). In Hebrew.

————. "The Last Kings of Judah and the Fall of Jerusalem." *Israel Exploration Journal* 18 (1968).

————. "The Twilight of Judah: in the Egyptian-Babylonian Maelstrom," *Vetus Testamentum,* Suppl. 28 (1975).

Mattingly, Gerald L., "The Pious Sufferer: Mesopotamian Traditional Theodicy and Job's Counselors." *The Bible in the Light of Cuneiform Literature.* Scripture in Context, III: Ancient Near Eastern Texts and Studies, vol. 8. Edited by William W. Hallo. (Lewiston/Queenston/Lampeter: Edward Mellen, 1990).

Mau. "Einbalsamierung," *RE,* 5 (1905).

Maul, Stefan M. *Herzberhigungsklagen: Die sumerisch-akkadischen Eršahunga-Gebete.* (Wiesbaden: Harrassowitz, 1988).

Mazar, B. "The Tobiads." *Israel Exploration Journal* 7 (1957).

McCullough, W. S., ed. *The Seed of Wisdom: Essays in Honor of T. J. Meek.* (Toronto: University of Toronto Press, 1964).

McKay, John W. *Religion in Judah under the Assyrians 732–609 B.C.* Studies in Biblical Theology, series 2, 26; (Naperville, IL: Allenson, 1973).

McKenzie, John L. *Second Isaiah.* Anchor Bible, vol. 20. (Garden City, NY: Doubleday, 1968).

Mehl, Andreas. *Seleukos Nikator und sein Reich.* Studia Hellenistica. Edidit W. Peremans, 28; Leuven, 1986).

Meyers, Eric and Carol. *Haggai, Zechariah 1–8.* Anchor Bible, vol. 25B. (Garden City, NY: Doubleday, 1987).

Milgrom, Jacob. *Leviticus 1–16.* Anchor Bible, vol. 3. (Garden City, NY: Doubleday, 1991).

————. *Leviticus 17–22.* Anchor Bible, vol. 3A; (New York, London, Toronto, Sydney, and Auckland: Doubleday, 2000.

————. *Leviticus 23–27.* Anchor Bible, vol. 3B. (New York, London, Toronto, Syndney, and Auckland: Doubleday, 2001).

Milik, J. T., " 'Prière de Nabonide' et autres écrits d'un cycle de Daniel," *Revue biblique* 63 (1956).

Montgomery, James A. *A Critical and Exegetical Commentary on the Book of Daniel.* (New York: Charles Scribner's Sons, 1927).

Moore, Carey A. *Esther.* Anchor Bible," vol. 7B. (Garden City, NY: Doubleday, 1971).

Morenz, Siegfried. *Egyptian Religion.* (Ithaca, NY: Cornell University Press, 1973).

Myers, Jacob M. *I Chronicles* Anchor Bible, vol. 12. (Garden City, NY: Doubleday, 1965).

Nickelsburg, George W. E. "Apocalyptic and Myth in 1 Enoch 6-11." *Journal of Biblical Literature* 96 (1977).

————. *Hermeneia: A Commentary on 1 Enoch* (Philadelphia: Fortress, 2001).

————. *Jewish Literature between the Bible and the Mishnah*. (Philadelphia: Fortress Press, 1981).

Nilsson, Martin P. *Geschichte der griechischen Religion,* I. 3d ed. (München: Beck, 1960).

Nyberg, Henrik S. *Die Religionen des alten Irans*. (Leipzig: Hinrichs, 1938).

Oded, Bustenai. "The Babylonian Embassy Narrative (Isaiah 39 = 2Kgs 20:12–18." *Shnaton* 9 (1985).

————. "Judah and the Exile." in Hayes-Miller.

Olmstead, Albert Ten Eyck. "Darius and His Behistun Inscription." *AJSL* 55 (1938).

————. *History of the Persian Empire*. (Chicago: University of Chicago Press, 1948).

————. *History of Syria and Palestine to the Babylonian Conquest*. (New York and London: Charles Scribner's Sons, 1931).

Oppenheim, A. Leo. *The Interpretation of Dreams in the Ancient Near East*. Transactions of the American Philosophical Society, vol. 46, part 3. Philadelphia: American Philosophical Society, 1956).

————. *Ancient Mesopotamia: Portrait of a Dead Civilization*. Revised edition. (Chicago and London: University of Chicago Press, 1977).

Otto, Walter. "Zum Hofzeremoniell des Hellenismus." Epitymbion: *Heinrich Swoboda dargebracht*. Edited by M. San Nicolò. (Reichenberg: Stiepel, 1927).

———— and Bengtson, Hermann. *Zur Geschichte des Niederganges des Ptolemäerreiches*. Abhandlungen der Bayerischen Akademie der Wissenschaften, philosophische und historische Klasse," neue folge, heft 17 (1938).

Oxford Classical Dictionary. 2d ed. Edited by N. G. L. Hammond and H. H. Scullard (Oxford: Clarendon Press, 1970). 3d ed. Edited by Simon Hornblower and Antony Spawforth. (Oxford: Clarendon Press, 1996).

Pacella, Daniela. "Alessandro e gli Ebrei nella testimonianza dello Ps. Callistene." *Annali della Scuola normale superiore di Pisa, classe di lettere e filosofia*, Serie 3, vol. 12, 4 (1982).

Parke, Herbert W., *Sibyls and Sibylline Prophecy in Classical Antiquity*. (New York: Routledge, 1988).

Parker, Richard A., and Dubberstein, Waldo H. *Babylonian Chronology, 626 B.C.–A.D. 75*. (Providence, RI: Brown University Press, 1956).

Parpola, Simo, ed. *Letters from Assyrian Scholars*. (Neukirchen-Vluyn: Butzon und Bercker, 1970–83).

————. "The Murder of Sennacherib." *Death in Mesopotamia*. Edited by Bendt Alster. (Copenhagen: Akademisk Forlag, 1980).

Peat, Jerome. "Cyrus 'King of Lands,' Cambyses 'King of Babylon', The Disputed Co-regency." *JCS* 41 (1989).

Peiser, Felix E. *Babylonische Verträge des Berliner Museums*. (Berlin: W. Peiser, 1890).

Peterson, David C. *Haggai and Zechariah 1–8: A Commentary*. (Philadelphia: Westminster Press, 1984).

Pfister, Friedrich. *Eine jüdische Grundungsgeschichte Alexandrias mit einem Anhang über Alexanders Besuch in Jerusalem*. Sitzungsberichte der Heidelberger Akademie der Wissenschaften, philosophisch-historische Klasse, 11 Abteilung. (Heidelberg: Carl Winter, 1914).

Pinches, Theophilus G. *The Old Testament in the Light of the Historical Records of Assyria and Babylonia*. 2d ed. (London: Society for Promoting Christian Knowledge, 1903).

Porten, Bezalel. *Archives from Elephantine*. (Berkeley and Los Angeles: University of California Press, 1968).

———— and Yardeni, Ada. *Textbook of Aramaic Documents from Ancient Egypt*. 4 vols. (Jerusalem: Hebrew University, 1986–).

Pritchard, James B. *Ancient Near Eastern Texts Relating to the Old Testament*. 3d ed. with supplement. (Princeton, NJ: Princeton University Press, 1969).

Rabin, Chaim. *The Zadokite Documents*. (Oxford: Clarendon Press, 1958).

Reade, Julian. "Ideology and Propaganda in Assyrian Art." *Power and Propaganda*. Edited by Mogens Trolle Larsen. Mesopotamia: Copenhagen Studies in Assyriology, vol. 7. (Copenhagen: Akademisk Forlag, 1979).

————. "Neo-Assyrian Monuments in Their Historical Context." *Assyrian Royal Inscriptions*. Edited by F. M. Fales. Orientis antiqui collectio," 17. (Roma: Istituto per l'Oriente, Centro per le antichità e la storia dell'arte del Vicino Oriente, 1981).

Rainey, Anson. "Chaldea, Chaldeans." *Encyclopaedia Judaica*, 5 (1971).

Reiner, Erica. *Die akkadische Literatur*. Wolfgang Röllig, *Altorientalische Literaturen*. Neues Handbuch der Literaturwissenschaft. Edited by Klaus von See. Band I. (Wiesbaden: Akademische Verlagsgesellschaft Athenaion, 1978).

————. "Fortune-Telling in Mesopotamia." *JNES* 19 (1960).

————. "More Fragments of the Epic of Era." *JNES* 17 (1958).

————. "Plague Amulets and House Blessings." *JNES* 19 (1960).

Robert, Jeanne and Louis. "Bulletin épigraphique, 1979." *Revue des études grecques* 92 (1979).

Röllig, Wolfgang, "Erwägungen zu neuen Stelen König Nabonids," ZA 56 (1964).

Ross, A. G., ed. *Arrianos: Quae extant omnia*. 2d ed. 2 vols. (Leipzig: Teubner, 1967–68).

Rostovtzeff, M. I. *The Social and Economic History of the Hellenistic World*. 2d ed. 3 vols. (Oxford: Clarendon Press, 1952).

Roux, Georges. *Ancient Iraq*. 3d ed. (New York: Penguin, 1992).

Rypka, Jan. *History of Iranian Literature*. (Dordrecht, Holland: D. Reidel, 1968).

Rzach, "Sibyllinische Orakel." *RE*, 2A (1921).

Sachs, Abraham J. *Astronomical Diaries and Related Texts from Babylonia*. Completed and edited by Hermann Hunger. 2 vols. and 2 vols. of plates. (Wien: Verlag der Österreichischen Akademie der Wissenschaften, 1988–89).

———— and Wiseman, D. J. "A Babylonian King List of the Hellenistic Period." *Iraq* 16 (1954).

Saggs, Henry W. F. "A Cylinder from Tell al Laḥm." *Sumer* 13 (1957).

Sancisi-Weerdenburg, Heleen, and Kuhrt, Amélie, eds. *Achaemenid History II: The Greek Sources.* (Leiden: Nederlands Instituut voor het Nabije Oosten, 1987).

San Nicolò, Mariano, and Ungnad, Arthur. *Neubabylonische Rechts- und Verwaltungsurkunden,* Vol. I. (Leipzig: Hinrichs, 1935).

Schileico, Woldemar G. "Tête d'un démon assyrien à l'Ermitage impériale de Saint Pétersbourg." *Revue d'assyriologie* 11 (1914).

Schmitt, Hatto H. *Untersuchungen zur Geschichte Antiochos' des Grossen und seiner Zeit.* (Wiesbaden: Steiner, 1964).

Schober, Ludwig. *Untersuchungen zur Geschichte Babyloniens und der Oberen Strapien von 323–303 v. Chr.* (Frankfurt am Main and Bern: Peter D. Lang, 1981).

Schott, A. "Abhandlungen der Preussischen Akademie der Wissenschaften, philologisch-historische Klasse," *Erster Vorläufiger Bericht über die von der Notgemeinschaft in Uruk-Warka unternommenen Ausgrabungen.* Edited by Julius Jordan. (Berlin: Verlag der Akademie der Wissenschaften. 1929, no. 7; 1930, no. 30).

Seder ʿolam rabba = Midrash seder ʿolam. Edited by Dov Ber Ratner (New York: Machon Tel Orot, 5726 = 1966).

Segert, Stanislaw. *Altaramäische Grammatik.* (Leipzig: VEB Verlag Enzyklopädie, 1975).

Seux, M.-J. "Cyrus serviteur de Marduk?" *Revue biblique* 76 (1969).

Sethe, Kurt. *Amun und die acht Urgötter von Hermopolis.* Abhandlungen der Preussischen Akademie der Wissenschaften, 1929, no. 4.

Shea, William H. "Rewriting Jerusalem History: Jerusalem under Siege; Did Sennacherib Attack Twice?" *Biblical Archaeology Review* 25, 6 (Nov.–Dec., 1999).

———. "Sennacherib's Second Palestinian Campaign," *JBL* 104 (1985).

Sherman, Charles L., ed. *Diodorus of Sicily,* vol. 7. (Cambridge, MA: Harvard University Press, 1952).

Sherwin-White, Susan, and Kuhrt, Amélie. *From Samarkhand to Sardis.* (London: Duckworth, 1993).

Simpson, William Kelly, "Pap. Westcar," *LA,* 4 (1982).

Smith, Morton. *Palestinian Parties and Politics that Shaped the Old Testament* (New York and London: Columbia University Press, 1971).

———. "The Veracity of Ezekiel, the Sins of Manasseh, and Jeremiah 44:18." *Zeitschrift für die alttestamentliche Wissenschaft* 87 (1975).

Smith, Sidney. *Babylonian Historical Texts Relating to the Capture and Downfall of Babylon.* (Hildesheim and New York: Georg Olms, 1975).

———. In CAH, Vol. III. 1st ed., reprinted with corrections. Edited by J. B. Bury, S. A. Cook, and F. E. Adcock, (Cambridge: University Press, 1929).

———. "Miscellanea." *Revue d'assyriologie et d'archéologie orientale* 22 (1925).

Soden, Wolfram von. "Etemenanki vor Asarhaddon." *Ugarit Forschungen* 3 (1971).

————. "Gibt es ein Zeugnis dafür, dass die Babylonier an die Wiederauferstehung Marduks geglaubt haben?" *ZA* 51 (1955).

Sommerfeld, Walter. *Der Aufstieg Marduks.* Alter Orient und Altes Testament. Band 213. (Neukirchen-Vluyn: Kevalaer: Verlag Butzon und Bercker, 1982).

Sontheimer, Walther. "Abydenos." *Der kleine Pauly,* 1 (1964).

Southgate, Minoo S., trans. and ed. *Iskandarnamah: A Persian Medieval Alexander-Romance.* (New York: Columbia University Press, 1978).

Speiser, Ephraim A. *Genesis.* Anchor Bible, vol. 1. (Garden City, NY: Doubleday, 1969).

Spieckermann, Hermann. *Juda unter Assur in der Sargonidenzeit.* Forschungen zur Religion und Literatur des Alten und Neuen Testaments." (Göttingen: Vandenhoeck und Ruprecht, 1982).

Spek, R. J. van der. "The Astronomical Diaries as a source for Achaemenid and Seleucid History." *Bibliotheca Orientalis* 50 (1993).

Spiegelberg, Wilhelm, ed. *Die sogenannte Demotische Chronik des P. 215 der Biblothèque national zu Paris.* Demotische Studien, Heft 7. (Leipzig: J. C. Hinrichs, 1914).

Stambaugh, John E. *Sarapis under the Early Ptolemies.* (Leiden: Brill, 1972).

Stamm, Johann Jakob. *Die akkadische Namengebung.* (Leipzig, 1939. Reprinted, Darmstadt: Wissenschftliche Buchgesellschaft, 1968).

Stillman, Y. K. *"Libās,"* *Encyclopaedia of Islam,* vol. 5. New Edition. Fascicules 89–90. (Leiden: Brill, 1983).

Stokholm, Niels. "Zur Überlieferung von Heliodor, Kuturnakhkhunte und anderen missglückten Tempelräubern." *Studia Theologica* 22 (1968).

Stolper, Matthew W. *Entrepreneurs and Empire.* (Leiden: Nederlands historisch-archeologisch Instituut te Istanbul, 1985).

Stoneman, Richard, trans. *The Greek Alexander Romance.* (London: Penguin, 1991).

Sundermann. "Bahman Yašt," *Encyclopaedia Iranica,* 3 (1989).

Tadmor, Hayim. "The Babylonian Exile and the Restoration." *A History of the Jewish People.* Edited by H. H. Ben Sasson. (Cambridge, MA: Harvard University Press, 1976).

————. "The Campaigns of Sargon II of Assur: A Chronological Study." *JCS* 12 (1958).

————. "The Historical Background to Cyrus' Proclamation." *Oz.*

————. "Historical implications of the correct rendering of Akkadian *dâku." JNES* 17 (1958).

————. "History and Ideology in Assyrian Royal Inscriptions." *Assyrian Royal Inscriptions: New Horizons in Literary, Ideological, and Historical Analysis.* Edited by Frederick Mario Fales. Orientis antiqui collectio, 17. (Roma: Istituto per l'Oriente, Centro per le antichità e la storia dell'arte del Vicino Oriente, 1981).

————. "The Inscriptions of Nabunaid: Historical Arrangement." *AS* 16.

————. "Kronologiah." *Entsiqlopediah miqra'it,* 4 (1962).

———. *"Reshit Malkhut." Entsiqlopediah miqra'it,* 7 (1976).

———. "Sennacherib's Campaign to Judah: Historical and Historiographical Considerations." *Zion* 50 (5745 = 1985).

———. "The 'Sin of Sargon.' " *Eretz-Israel* 5 (1958).

———, Eph'al, I, and Greenfield, J. C., eds. *Historiah shel 'am, yiśra'el.* Kerekh 5: Shivat tsiyyon—y°mey shilton paras. (Jerusalem: Alexander Pel'i, 5743 = 1983).

——— and Weinfeld, M., eds. *History, Historiography, and Interpretation.* (Jerusalem: Magnes Press, 1983).

Tafazzoli, A. "Adurbad i Mahrspandan." *Encyclopaedia Iranica,* 1 (1983).

Tallquist, Knut L. *Neubabylonische Namenbuch.* Acta Societatis Scientiarum Fennicae, tom 32, no. 2. (Helsingfors, 1905).

Tarn, W. W. "The Lineage of Ptolemy I." *Journal of Hellenic Studies* 53 (1933).

———. "Queen Ptolemaïs and Apama." *Classical Quarterly* 23 (1929).

Tawil, Hayim. "The Historicity of 2 Kings 19:24 (=Isaiah 37:25)." *JNES* 41 (1982).

Tcherikover, Victor A., and Fuks, Alexander, eds. *Corpus Papyrorum Judaicarum.* 3 vols. (Cambridge, MA: Harvard University Press, 1957–64).

———. (Avigdor). *Die hellenistischen Städtegrundungen von Alexander dem Grossen bis auf die Römerzeit.* (Leipzig: Dieterich, 1927).

Tiller, Patrick A. *A Commentary on the Animal Apocalypse of I Enoch.* Society of Biblical Literature: Early Judaism and Its Literature, no. 4. (Atlanta, GA: Scholars Press, 1993).

Trigger, B. G., Kemp, B. J., O'Connor, D., and Lloyd, A. B. *Ancient Egypt: A Social History.* (Cambridge: Cambridge University Press, 1983).

Trinquet, J., "Métrologie biblique." *Dictionnaire de la Bible: Supplément.* Edited by L. Pirot et al. (Paris: Letouzey, 1928–); 5, 1957.

Trumpf, Juergen, ed. *Anonymi Byzantini Vita Alexandri regis Macedonum.* (Stuttgart: Teubner, 1974).

Tsevat, M. Review of BHLT, by A. K. Grayson. *JBL* 96 (1977).

Ungnad, Arthur. "Bêl-¢imânni, ein neuer König Babylons und der Länder." *Orientalistische Litteratur-Zeitung* 10 (1907).

———. "Neubabylonische Privaturkunden aus der Sammlung Amherst." *Archiv für Orientforschung* 19 (1959–60).

———, ed. *Vorderasiatische Schriftendenkmäler der Königlichen Museen zu Berlin,* vol. 6. (Leipzig: Hinrichs, 1908).

VanderKam, James. *Enoch and the Growth of an Apocalyptic Tradition.* The Catholic Biblical Quarterly Monograph Series, 16; (Washington, D.C.: Catholic Biblical Association of America, 1984).

Van Seters, John. *In Search of History.* (New Haven and London: Yale University Press, 1953).

Vaux, Roland de. *Ancient Israel: Its Life and Institutions.* (New York, Toronto, and London: McGraw Hill, 1961).

Velde, Herman te. *Seth, God of Confusion.* Probleme der Ägyptologie, Band VI. Edited by Wolfgang Helck. (Leiden: Brill, 1967).

Voigtlander, Elizabeth N. von. *The Bisitun Inscription of Darius the Great: Babylonian Version* Corpus Inscriptionum Iranicarum. Part I: Inscriptions of Ancient Iran, Vol. II: The Babylonian Versions of the Texts of the Achaemenian Inscriptions, Texts I. (London: Lund Humphries, 1978).

Walbank, Frank W. *A Historical Commentary on Polybius.* (Oxford: Clarendon Press, 1957–).

Walker, C. B. F. "A Chronicle of the Kassite and Isin II Dynasties." *Zikir ¢umim: Assyriological Studies Presented to F. N. Kraus on the Occasion of His Seventieth Birthday.* (Leiden: Brill, 1982).

Waterman, Leroy. "The Camouflaged Purge of Three Messianic Conspirators," *JNES* 13 (1954).

Webb, Robert L. "Apocalyptic: Observations on a Slippery Term." *JNES* 49 (1990).

Weinfeld, Moshe. *Deuteronomy and the Deuteronomic School.* (Oxford: Clarendon Press, 1972).

———. "Pentateuch." *Encyclopaedia Judaica,* 12 (1971).

Welles, C. Bradford. *Royal Correspondence in the Hellenistic Period.* (New Haven: Yale University Press, 1934).

———, Fink, R. O., and Gilliam, J. F. *The Excavations at Dura-Europos: Final Report V, Part I, The Parchments and Papyri.* (New Haven: Yale University Press, 1959).

West, E. W., trans. *Pahlavi Texts,* Part I. The Sacred Books of the East, vol. V. Edited by F. Max Müller. (Oxford: Clarendon Press, 1880).

———. *Pahlavi Texts,* Part IV. The Sacred Books of the East, Vol. 37. Edited by F. Max Müller. (Oxford: Clarendon Press, 1892).

West, Martin L., ed. *Hesiod: Theogony.* (Oxford: Clarendon Press, 1966).

———, ed. *Hesiod: Works and Days.* (Oxford: Clarendon Press, 1978).

Westermann, Claus. *Isaiah 40–66: A Commentary.* (Philadelphia: Westminster Press, 1969).

Wetzel, Friedrich, and Weissbach, F. H. *Das Hauptheiligtum des Marduks in Babylon, Esagila und Etemenanki.* (Leipzig: Hinrichs, 1938).

Widengren, Geo. *Die Religionen Irans.* (Stuttgart: Kohlhammer, 1965).

Wiegand, Theodor. *Didyma.* 2 parts in 4 volumes. (Berlin: Verlag Gebr. Mann, 1941–58).

Wiesehöfer, Josef. *Die 'dunklen Jahrhunderte' der Persis* Zetemata, Heft 90. (München: Beck, 1994).

Wilcken, Ulrich. *Urkunden der Ptolemäerzeit.* 2 vols. (Berlin: Walter de Gruyter, 1927–57).

Wildberger, Hans. *Jesaia,* 2. Teilband. Vol. 10/2 of *Biblischer Kommentar: Altes Testament.* Begrundet von Martin Noth. (Neukirchen-Vluyn: Neukirchener Verlag, 1978).

Will, Édouard. *Histoire politique du Monde hellénistique (323–30 av. J.-C.).* 2d ed. 2 vols. (Nancy: Presses universitaires de Nancy, 1982).

Wilson, Alfred M. "The Particle *'et* in Hebrew." *Hebraica* 6 (1889–90).

Wilson, John A. *The Culture of Ancient Egypt.* (Chicago: University of Chicago Press, 1951).

Wirth, Gerhard. "Alexander 7." *Der kleine Pauly,* 1 (1964).

Wiseman, D. J. *Chronicles of the Chaldaean Kings (625–556 B.C.) in the British Museum.* (London: Trustees of the British Museum, 1956).

INDEX OF AUTHORS

Ackroyd, Peter, 284
Adcock, F. E., 103, 357
Al-Rawi, Farouk N. H., 51, 52, 59, 102
Alster, Bendt, 59
Alt, Albrecht, 219
Altmann, Alexander, 59
Andersen, Francis I., 24
Anklesaria, Behramgore Tahmuras, 335, 339, 352, 353, 355, 356, 482, 483
Anquetil-Duperron, A. H., 335
Asmussen, J. P., 354
Astin, A. E., 393
Astour, Michael, 54, 59

Badian, 317, 318, 320
Badt, 401
Balkan, Kemal, 263
Barag, D., 283, 284
Bar Kochva, B., 436, 437
Bartlett, John R., 140, 162
Batto, Bernard, 60
Baumgarten, Joseph M., 438
Baumgartner, Walter, 198
Beaulieu, Paul-Alain, 57, 111, 113, 116, 117, 121, 122, 123, 128, 129, 132, 134, 137–153, 162
Beckerath, Jürgen von, 72
Beek, 260
Beloch, Karl Julius, 316

Bengtson, Hermann, 279, 313, 351, 354, 398
Ben-Sasson, H. H., 98, 99, 100, 101, 110, 111, 165, 280
Bentsen, Aage, 260
Ben Yehuda, Eliezer, 256
Berger, Paul-Richard, 136, 147, 149
Bertram, 250
Betlyon, John Wilson, 284, 285
Bevan, Edwyn R., 403
Bianchi, Ugo, 186, 199, 200
Bickerman, Elias J. (Bikerman, Élie), 73, 74, 137, 142, 163, 172, 192, 193, 194, 253, 260, 284, 285, 286, 395, 397, 400, 401, 403, 435
Biggs, Robert D., 61, 256
Bikerman, Élie. see Bickerman, Elias J. (Bikerman, Élie)
Bilabel, Friedrich, 401
Billows, Richard A., 394, 395, 396, 397
Black, J. A., 59
Blumenthal, Elke, 71
Böhl, F. M. Th. de Liagre, 195, 196, 197, 200
Bongenaar, A. C. V. M., 140–141
Borger, Rykle, 51, 54, 55, 56
Bosworth, A. B., 202, 314, 315, 316, 317, 318, 319, 354
Bouché-Leclerq, A., 398

Bouché-Leclerq, Louis, 20
Bousset, W., 350, 351
Boyce, Mary, 73, 74, 163, 187, 199, 200, 201, 202, 279, 314, 316, 317, 336, 349, 350, 351, 352, 353, 354, 355, 356, 358, 404, 436, 441
Bresciani, Edda, 279
Briant, Pierre, 398
Bright, John, 98, 101, 102, 103, 108, 165, 282, 472
Brinkman, John A., 49, 50, 55, 56, 57, 58, 60, 103, 192
Budde, K., 108
Bull, Ludlow, 70
Burn, Andrew Robert, 198, 284
Burstein, Stanley M., 245
Bury, J. B., 103, 357

Cagni, Luigi, 59, 60
Cameron, George G., 192, 193, 196, 197, 198
Chamoux, François, 399
Charles, Robert H., 439, 440
Charlesworth, James H., 349, 351
Chaumont, M. L., 404
Childs, Brevard S., 98
Christensen, Arthur, 353, 354
Clay, Albert T., 136, 197, 247, 256
Clements, R. E., 98
Clermont-Ganneau, Charles, 219, 255, 256, 257
Cloché, Paul, 352
Cogan, Mordechai (Morton), 99, 101, 440
Cohen, Mark E., 57
Collins, John, 349, 351, 356
Cook, J. M., 73, 74, 164, 191, 193, 198, 202, 258, 260, 278, 279, 284, 313, 314, 320, 357, 358
Cook, S. A., 103, 357
Coxon, Peter W., 246
Cross, Frank Moore, 246
Cumont, F., 250

Dandamaev, Muhammad A., 73, 74, 164, 191, 192, 201, 261, 262, 313, 314, 317, 320, 351
David, M., 263
Davies, Philip R., 438
Davies, W. D., 165, 246
De Gruyter, Walter, 316

Delling, Gerhard, 314
De Meulenaere, Herman, 284
Demsky, A., 282
Dentan, Robert C., 21, 70
Dhorme, Édouard, 138
Dhorme, P., 136
Diakonoff, I. M., 245, 258
Dijk, Jan J. A. van, 42, 50, 58
Di Lella, Alexander A., 247, 254, 257, 258, 259, 364, 397, 403, 441, 442, 443, 472
Dindorf, Wilhelm, 286
Dittenberger, W., 351
Donner, Herbert, 98, 254
Dougherty, Raymond Philip, 23, 103, 137, 138, 139, 323
Driver, Samuel R., 281
Dubberstein, Waldo H., 192, 258, 263, 278, 279, 442, 470, 473
Duchesne-Guillemin, É., 199
Duchesne-Guillemin, J., 356

Eddy, Samuel K., 305, 307, 311, 312, 315, 320, 321, 322, 323, 338, 351, 354, 355, 356, 358, 395, 401, 425, 441, 483, 484
Eerdmans, 260
Eissfeldt, Otto, 22, 23, 98, 102, 108, 162, 163, 219, 256
Ellenbogen, Maximilian, 248
Ellis, Richard S., 147
Epstein, J. N., 247
Erman, Adolf, 70

Fales, Frederick Mario, 147, 354
Fauth, Wolfgang, 401
Fewell, Danna Nolan, 99
Fink, R. O., 246
Finkel, Irving L., 52, 53, 198
Finkelstein, Jacob J., 51
Finkelstein, Louis, 165, 246
Flusser, David, 356
Focke, F., 284
Fol, A., 439
Fontenrose, Joseph, 22
Fotheringham, Iohannes Knight, 286
Fouchécour, C.-H. de, 351
Fox, Robin Lane, 322
Frank, Harry, 320
Frank, Richard M., 262
Frankfort, Henri, 72, 201, 322, 323
Frazer, James George, 322, 323

Frederiksen, M. W., 393
Freedman, David Noel, 24, 99
Fried, Lisbeth S., 99
Frye, Richard N., 74, 195, 198, 278, 404
Fuks, Alexander, 349

Gabba, Emilio, 435
Gadd, C. J., 55, 136, 140, 150
Gardiner, Alan, 71
Gardner, Percy, 354
Gaster, Theodor H., 322, 323
Geffcken, Johannes, 349, 350
George, A. R., 50, 51
Gershevitch, Ilya, 73, 142, 198
Gerth, Bernhard, 139
Geyer, 398
Gignoux, Philippe, 351, 352, 354–355, 356
Gilliam, J. F., 246
Ginsberg, H. Louis, 102, 104, 106, 107,
    164, 253, 254, 256, 257, 281, 283, 438,
    439, 441, 443, 469
Glasson, T. Francis, 25
Glotz, Gustave, 285
Goedicke, Hans, 71, 72
Goetze, A., 59
Goldstein, Jonathan A., 21, 23, 24, 99, 110,
    165, 195, 200, 248, 250, 258, 279, 280,
    286, 314, 354, 396, 399, 400, 403, 404,
    435, 437, 441, 443, 467–473, 477, 478
Gonçalves, Francolino, 98, 101
Goodwin, William Watson, 245
Graf, David Frank, 261
Grainger, John D., 394
Gray, John, 98
Grayson, Albert Kirk, 36, 50, 51, 52, 53,
    54, 55, 56, 58, 74, 104, 111, 137, 138,
    142, 202, 251, 294, 295, 315, 316
Graziani, Simonetta, 197, 198
Green, Peter, 314, 315, 316, 317, 318, 323,
    354, 393, 394, 395, 396, 400, 401, 404,
    435
Greenberg, Moshe, 22, 104, 437
Greenfield, Jonas C., 74, 137, 245, 246
Groningen, B. A. von, 263
Gulick, Charles Burton, 245

Hadley, Robert A., 395
Haight, Elizabeth H., 315
Hallo, William W., 8, 22, 45, 46, 50, 52, 53,
    55, 57, 58, 59, 60, 101, 245, 399

Halpern, Baruch, 21, 22, 99
Hamilton, J. A., 316, 317, 322
Hammond, N. G. L., 314, 315, 316, 393,
    401
Hansman, J., 164
Haran, Menahem, 163, 164, 281
Harmatta, J., 73, 142, 162, 163
Harris, Zellig S., 253
Hartman, Hans, 199
Hartman, Louis F., 247, 254, 257, 258, 259,
    364, 397, 403, 441, 442, 443, 472
Haussoulier, B., 402
Hayes, John H., 98, 100, 101, 165, 195,
    280, 282, 284
Heidel, Alexander, 349
Heinen, H., 399, 400
Herzfeld, Ernst, 199
Hoftijzer, Jacob, 249, 252
Holleaux, Maurice, 436, 437
How, W. W., 198
Hultgård, Anders, 355
Hunger, Hermann, 56, 60, 111, 257, 400,
    404, 468

Jackson, A. V. Williams, 357
Jacobs, Joseph, 357
Jacobsen, Thorkild, 20, 21, 51, 59, 60, 61,
    100, 254, 322
Japhet, Sara, 262
Jastrow, Marcus, 253
Jean, Charles-F., 249
Jeremias, Alfred, 42, 53, 54, 58, 59
Jones, Bruce William, 53
Judeich, Walter, 285

Kaiser, Otto, 98
Kákosy, László, 71
Kaplony, Peter, 71
Karst, 138
Kaufman, Stephen A., 111, 257
Kaufmann, Yehezkel, 22, 23, 24, 104, 106,
    107, 108, 109, 110, 165, 280, 281, 282
Kautsch, E., 105
Kellens, J., 352
Kemp, B. J., 286
Kent, Roland G., 74, 199, 201, 258
Kienitz, Friedrich Karl, 284, 285, 286
King, L. W., 136
Kittel, Gerhard, 250
Kittel, Rudolph, 103

Klíma, Otakar, 352
Knibb, M. A., 439
Koenen, Ludwig, 71, 72, 315, 435
Koldewey, Robert, 278
Kramer, Samuel Noah, 8, 20, 22, 55
Krecher, Joachim, 52
Kroll, Guilelmus, 315
Kühner, Raphael, 139
Kuhrt, Amélie, 191, 197, 201, 202, 278, 323, 399, 404
Kutscher, Eduard Yechezkel, 105, 246
Kvanvig, Helge S., 263, 399

Lacoque, André, 247
Lambert, Wilfred G., 20, 48, 49, 50, 51, 52, 53, 54, 56, 57, 58, 60, 61, 111, 112, 137, 144, 146, 149, 151, 257, 258, 259
Lamberton, Robert, 253
Landsberger, Benno, 42, 51, 55, 109, 136
Lane Fox, Robin, 322
Langdon, Stephen H., 60, 104, 135, 136, 137, 140, 145, 162
Lanternari, Vittorio, 20
Larsen, Mogens Trolle, 104
Lasswell, Harold D., 51
Latte, Kurt, 101
Launey, Marcel, 404, 439
Léemans, W. F., 263
Legrain, Léon, 136
Lehmann, C. F., 402
Leichty, Erle, 53, 58, 61
Lerner, Daniel, 51
Lesky, Albin, 253
Lewis, David M., 278, 279
Lewy, Hildegard, 139, 143, 144
Lewy, Julius, 138, 143, 148, 151
Licht, J. A., 254
Lichtenstein, Hans, 314
Lieberman, Saul, 438
Lipi ski, E., 25
Livingstone, Alasdair, 51
Lloyd, Alan B., 286
Longman, Tremper, III, 36, 50, 51, 53, 54, 55, 56, 57, 58
Luckenbill, Daniel D., 55, 100
Lukonin, Vladimir G., 262, 313, 314, 317, 320, 351

Malalas, John, 323
Malamat, Abraham, 101, 102, 103, 254

Marcus, Ralph, 251, 315
Mattingly, Gerald L., 53, 61
Mau, 201
Maul, Stefan M., 60
Mazar, B., 443
McCullough, W. S., 20
McKay, John W., 101
McKenzie, John L., 162
Mehl, Andreas, 394, 395, 396
Meijers, E. M., 263
Meineke, 351
Meuleau, M., 279
Meyers, Carol, 193, 194, 195
Meyers, Eric, 193, 194, 195
Migne, J. P., 323
Milgrom, Jacob, 282
Milik, J. T., 246
Miller, J. Maxwell, 98, 100, 101, 165, 195, 280, 282, 284
Montgomery, James A., 246, 247, 248–255, 258, 260, 263, 435
Moore, Carey A., 195
Mor, Menachem, 396, 441
Morenz, Siegfried, 70, 71, 72
Mulder, M. J., 101
Müller, F. Max, 352
Müller, Hans Peter, 52
Musti, Domenico, 402
Myers, Jacob M., 262

Naveh, Joseph, 246
Neusner, Jacob, 404, 437
Nickelsburg, George W. E., 26, 398, 399, 421, 439, 440
Nilsson, Martin P., 101
Noth, Martin, 21
Nyberg, Henrik S., 186, 187, 199, 200

O'Connor, D., 286
Oded, Bustenai, 23, 24, 98, 100, 101
Ogilvie, R. M., 393
Olmstead, Albert Ten Eyck, 193, 194, 198, 200, 202, 260, 278, 279, 284, 314, 358
Oppenheim, A. Leo, 20, 51, 57, 60, 71, 104, 135, 136, 137, 140, 141, 142, 143, 144, 145, 150, 153, 191, 197, 199, 202, 246, 252, 254, 257, 278, 279, 320, 321
Oppenheimer, B., 282
Otto, Walter, 351

Pacella, Daniela, 314
Parke, Herbert W., 349, 401
Parker, Richard A., 192, 258, 263, 278, 279, 442, 470, 473
Parpola, Simo, 59, 322
Peiser, Felix E., 247
Peremans, W., 394
Peterson, David C., 194
Pfister, Friedrich, 314
Pinches, Theophilus G., 395
Pirot, L., 256
Ploeg, J. van der, 105
Porada, Edith, 253
Porten, Bezalel, 74, 105, 279, 280

Rabin, Chaim, 438
Rainey, Anson, 245
Ratner, 99
Reade, Julian, 104, 354
Redard, Georges, 73
Redford, Donald B., 71
Rehm, Albert, 402
Reiner, Erica, 54, 60, 105, 252
Renger, J., 228
Robert, Jeanne, 439
Robert, Louis, 439
Röllig, W., 138, 140, 152, 254
Rose, Herbert J., 401
Rosenthal, Franz, 254
Ross, A. G., 394
Rostovtzeff, M. I., 393, 394, 401
Roux, Georges, 54, 55, 56, 59, 60, 100, 101, 102, 103, 104, 105, 111, 143, 152, 165, 192, 193
Rypka, Jan, 352
Rzach, 349

Sachs, Abraham J., 60, 398, 400, 402, 404, 442, 468
Saggs, Henry W. F., 136
Samolin, W., 253
Sancisi-Weerdenburg, Heleen, 191, 201, 313
San Nicolò, Mariano, 179, 196, 197, 248
Schileico, Woldemar G., 249
Schlichting, Robert, 71
Schmitt, Hatto H., 434
Schober, Ludwig, 357, 395
Schott, A., 135
Schwartz, Martin, 199, 200

Scullard, H. H., 401
Sebeok, Thomas A., 246
See, Klaus von, 54
Seel, Otto, 322
Segert, Stanislaw, 245
Seters, John Van, 52
Sethe, Kurt, 72
Seux, M.-J., 146
Shea, William H., 99
Sherman, Charles L., 284, 285
Sherwin-White, Susan, 191, 197, 202, 399, 404
Simpson, William Kelly, 70, 260
Smith, Morton, 21, 73, 109, 111, 157, 163, 165, 279, 280, 281, 282, 284, 435
Smith, Sidney, 103, 136, 400
Snell, Daniel C., 57
Soden, Wolfram von, 44, 51, 59, 100
Sommerfeld, Walter, 49, 50, 51, 54
Sontheimer, Walther, 245
Southgate, Minoo S., 358
Speier, Hans, 51
Speiser, Ephraim A., 21, 104, 110
Spek, R. J. van der, 381, 400
Spieckermann, Hermann, 101
Spiegelberg, William, 71, 261
Spuler, B., 73
Stambaugh, John E., 322, 323
Stamm, Johann Jakob, 201, 247, 248
Starr, I., 60
Stern, Ephraim, 284
Stillman, Y. K., 354
Stokholm, Niels, 54
Stolper, Matthew W., 196, 197, 198, 202, 248, 252, 278, 313, 314
Stoneman, Richard, 358
Strassmeier, J. N., 278

Tadmor, Hayim, 55, 58, 59, 73, 74, 98, 99, 100, 101, 103, 106, 110, 111, 123, 125, 135, 137, 138, 142, 143, 145, 146, 147, 149, 152, 162, 163, 164, 165, 166, 191, 192, 193, 196, 251, 261, 280, 440
Tafazzoli, A., 352
Tallqvist, Knut L., 247, 248, 249, 250, 263
Tarn, W. W., 357, 395
Tawil, Hayim, 98
Tcherikover, Victor A., 349, 357
Tiller, Patrick A., 439
Timm, Stefan, 101

Trigger, B. G., 286
Trinquet, J., 256
Trumpf, Juergen, 314
Tsevat, M., 316
Tur-Sinai, N. H., 256

Ungnad, Arthur, 196, 197, 248

VanderKam, James, 399
van der Spek, R. J., 381, 400
van Dijk, Jan J. A., 42, 50, 58
Van Seters, John, 52
Vaux, Roland de, 20
Velde, Herman te, 72
Velkov, V., 439
Voigtlander, Elizabeth N. von, 74
Volkmann, Hans, 402, 403
von Soden, Wolfram, 44, 51, 59, 100

Walbank, Frank W., 393
Walker, C. B. F., 57
Waterman, Leroy, 193, 196
Webb, Robert L., 25
Weidner, E., 56
Weinfeld, Moshe, 58
Weisberg, David B., 57
Weissbach, F. H., 200, 201, 202

Welles, C. Bradford, 246, 401, 402
Wells, J., 198
West, E. W., 352, 353, 354, 355, 356, 483
West, Martin L., 253
Westermann, Claus, 23, 165
Wetzel, Friedrich, 200, 201, 202
Widengren, Geo, 165, 186, 195, 199, 200, 280, 282, 284
Wiegand, Theodor, 402
Wiesehöfer, Josef, 392, 394, 404
Wilcken, Ulrich, 285
Wildberger, Hans, 249
Will, Édouard, 393, 394, 397, 400, 401, 402, 403, 404, 434, 435, 436, 437, 441, 442, 443, 469
Wilson, Alfred M., 105
Wilson, J. V. Kinnier, 100
Wilson, John A., 70, 71, 72
Wirth, Gerhard, 352
Wiseman, D. J., 251, 402, 442

Yardeni, Ada, 279
Young, T. Cuyler, Jr., 199

Zauzich, Karl-Theodor, 71
Zibelius, Karola, 71
Zuckermandl, 247

INDEX OF SCRIPTURAL SOURCES

Pentateuch, 12, 269, 270, 272, 273, 280, 281

Genesis, 110
1:1–2:3, 62, 95, 223
1:1–2:7, 21
1:2, 259
6:1–6, 398
6:2, 254
6:16, 350
10:1–11:9, 21
10:22, 442
Ch 14, 59
14:1, 442
14:9, 442
14:18–22, 249
15:12–16, 20
15:13–16, 14
26:24, 249
31:42, 249
40:5–20, 20
40:5–41:57, 22
41:1–6, 20
41:1–44, 212
41:8, 229, 252
41:15, 252
41:16, 229, 252
41:25, 229, 252
41:28, 252

41:40, 255
41:45, 207
46:3, 249

Exodus, 6, 19
3:8, 281
3:17, 281
5:1–12:36, 248
10:13, 194
12:3, 282
13:5, 281
14:21, 194
15:7, 107
23:13, 207
23:23, 281
23:28, 281
29:18, 252
33:2, 281
34:11, 281
34:11–17, 270
34:12, 271
34:15, 271

Leviticus, 16, 100
1:4, 283
2:1, 252
7:18, 283
Ch 16, 195, 272, 281
16:16, 282
16:19–20, 282

Leviticus (*cont.*)
  16:21–22, 282
  16:29, 282
  16:30, 282
  16:33, 282
  16:33–34, 282
  Ch 18, 270
  18:2, 270
  18:19, 270
  18:24–25, 270
  18:24–28, 270
  18:27–28, 270
  18:30, 270
  19:2, 263, 452
  19:7, 283
  19:8, 283
  19:12–14, 283
  20:7, 263
  20:26, 263
  21:6, 283
  22:9, 282
  22:23, 283
  22:25, 283
  22:27, 283
  Ch 23, 12, 195
  23:26–32, 281
  23:27, 282
  23:28, 282
  Ch 25, 422
  25:1–12, 100
  25:5, 99, 453
  25:8, 403
  25:8–9, 453
  25:9, 282
  25:11, 99
  25:15, 453
  25:29, 281
  Ch 26, 16, 25, 26
  26:3, 471
  26:3–13, 13
  26:18, 21, 24, 28, 13
  26:32–33, 13
  26:34–35, 13, 422
  26:39–40, 13
  26:41–42, 13
  26:44–45, 13

Numbers
  7:3, 438
  13:29, 281

  14:33–34, 22
  15:40, 263
  16:3, 263
  17:19, 195
  19:9, 195
  21:29, 101
  24:26, 249
  Ch 25, 457
  27:21, 20
  28:2, 283
  29:7–11, 281
  32:13, 22

Deuteronomy, 16, 28, 80, 93, 94, 100, 209,
      268, 269, 270
  1:30–33, 101
  2:4–39, 101
  3:21–22, 101
  3:24, 101
  4:7, 101
  4:15, 283
  4:15–19, 109
  4:19–20, 101
  4:25–31, 14, 16
  4:30, 14, 25
  4:32–39, 101
  6:18–19, 101
  7:1, 281
  7:1–4, 270
  7:6–10, 101
  7:7, 443
  7:18–22, 101
  7:21, 250
  9:1–3, 101
  10:14, 101
  10:17, 101, 249, 254, 283
  11:2–7, 101
  11:23–25, 101
  11:28, 283
  12:1–14, 93
  12:5–14, 267
  13:2–4, 22
  16:21, 109
  17:7, 449
  18:9–14, 109
  18:15–22, 22
  19:1, 101
  20:1–4, 101
  20:17, 281
  23:4–10, 281

24:14, 283
24:17, 283
26:4, 195
26:5, 255
26:7, 249
26:8–9, 101
26:10, 195
26:15, 101
26:19, 101
27:9, 101
27:13, 438
28–30, 16
28:1–68, 12
28:12–13, 101
28:15–30:14, 24–25
28:15–68, 12, 13, 94
28:15–69, 101
28:20, 283
28:36, 105
28:49–50, 105
28:54, 355
28:56, 355
28:59–29:20, 13
28:63, 13
28:63–68, 13
28:68, 13
28:69, 12, 24
29:1–20, 24
29:17–20, 12
29:19–20, 13
29:20, 13
29:21, 12, 13
29:21–27, 12, 13, 24, 94
29:21–28, 12
29:21–30:10, 12
29:27, 13
29:28, 12, 13
30:1, 12
30:1–8, 23, 478
30:1–10, 12, 13, 101
30:11, 13
31:6–8, 101
31:29, 283
32:1–43, 25
32:8, 21, 249
32:12–15, 25
32:36, 25, 456
32:40, 250
32:42–43, 456
33:26, 107

Joshua, 21, 32
5:6, 22
7:13, 107

Judges, 21
1:4, 250
3:8, 14, 22
3:10, 250
4:3, 22
6:1, 22
8:19, 250
Ch 9, 8
10:8, 22
13:1, 22
Chs 17–21, 8

1 Samuel, 109, 207
1:9–10, 438
Ch 9, 20
9:3–30, 252
14:3, 20
14:39, 250
15:11, 253
15:35, 253
16:1, 253
16:9, 248
17:13, 248
20:19, 262
23:6, 20
30:7, 20

2 Samuel, 109, 207
6:6–8, 26
11:1, 197

1 Kings, 7, 8, 21, 22, 32, 79, 86, 87, 92, 94, 100, 109, 156, 268
3:7, 253
8:9, 195
11:5, 101
11:7, 101
13:2, 10, 16
14:18, 20
14:41, 20
18:27, 60
19:15–17, 21

2 Kings, 6, 7, 8, 21, 22, 32, 79, 86, 87, 92, 94, 100, 109, 156, 216, 237, 250, 251, 268, 440

2 Kings (*cont.*)
  1:31–37, 22
  6:8–12, 252
  7:2, 141
  7:19, 141
  8:11–13, 21
  10:30, 260
  13:1–5, 22
  14:25–27, 25
  14:26, 25
  15:3, 98
  15:17–17:6, 20
  15:19, 86
  15:29, 98, 437
  16:6–9, 98
  16:9, 98
  17:1–6, 98
  17:7–18, 109
  17:16–17, 109
  18:2, 99
  18:13, 99
  18:13–16, 77, 98
  18:13–19:35, 470
  18:13–19:37, 98, 99
  18:13–20:19, 156
  18:14–16, 98
  18:19–25, 104
  19:10–13, 104
  19:21–24, 104
  19:21–34, 78, 98
  19:22–35, 248
  19:24, 98, 105
  19:29, 78, 453
  19:34, 79
  20:1, 99
  20:6, 99
  20:8–11, 99
  20:12–19, 192
  20:16–18, 211
  21:1–16, 439
  21:1–18, 99
  21:2–16, 109
  21:2–17, 79
  21:3, 100
  21:5, 100
  21:7, 100
  21:10–15, 102
  21:16, 100
  21:19–23, 101
  21:24, 101

  22:16–20, 109
  22:23–24, 21
  23:12–13, 100
  23:15–18, 10
  23:25–27, 102
  23:26–27, 109
  23:29–25, 21
  23:29–34, 251
  23:30–35, 102
  23:34–24:6, 211
  23:36, 260
  23:37, 211
  24:1–2, 107
  24:1–4, 109
  24:1–7, 103
  24:3–4, 102
  24:8–16, 260
  24:13, 255
  24:17–25:21, 103
  24:19–20, 109
  24:31–34, 13
  25:8–21, 162
  25:13–17, 255
  25:27, 109, 213
  25:27–30, 21, 96, 111, 260
  Chs 36–39, 159

Isaiah, 9, 16, 41, 73, 76, 82, 95, 267, 409,
    414, 463
  Chs 1–33, 159
  Chs 1–35, 24
  Chs 1–39, 23, 87, 154, 161
  1:1, 85
  1:20, 98
  1:28, 98
  Ch 2, 85
  2:1–5, 85, 98
  2:2–5, 85
  2:10, 107
  2:10–22, 104
  2:12, 442
  2:13, 436
  2:19, 107
  2:21, 107
  3:24, 98
  4:2, 107
  4:2–6, 98
  5:25–30, 98
  Ch 6, 77
  6:1, 107, 436

6:9–13, 98
6:11–13, 104
Ch 7, 77
Ch 7–8, 98
7:1–9, 22
7:14–16, 76
7:15–25, 98
Ch 8, 77
8:1–4, 100
8:8, 409
9:1–6, 98
9:18–20, 104
10:5, 108
10:5–15, 21
10:5–27, 81, 91, 109
10:5–34, 457
10:7, 104, 108
10:7–16, 104
10:14, 108
10:20, 81
10:22–23, 104
10:26, 91
10:27, 91, 109, 477
Ch 11, 477
11:1–12, 163
11:1–15, 477
11:2–5, 478
11:6, 164
11:9, 164, 477, 478
11:11, 105
11:12, 164
11:14, 477
11:15, 162
11:15–16, 164
11:16, 105, 162
12:3, 162
12:5, 107
Ch 13, 106, 107
Chs 13–14, 164, 193
13:1, 85, 87, 90, 107
13:1–14:27, 107
13:2, 87, 88, 90, 107, 108, 164
13:2–4, 108
13:2–5, 162
13:2–14:7, 158, 159
13:2–14:23, 109
13:2–14:27, 104, 106, 107, 109, 154, 156, 158, 159, 162, 164, 173, 175
13:2–22, 84, 88, 104, 109, 355
13:2–14–27, 83–91

13:3, 106, 107
13:4, 105, 108, 164
13:4–5, 107, 108
13:4–9, 90
13:4–14, 84
13:5, 164
13:5–17, 164
13:5–18, 85, 104
13:6, 107, 108, 165
13:9, 88, 90, 107, 108, 162
13:9–10, 107
13:10, 107
13:11, 105, 107, 165
13:11–12, 162
13:13, 91, 107, 108, 162, 173
13:14, 91, 107, 108
13:14–15, 108
13:15–16, 162
13:15–18, 107, 108
13:17, 84, 88, 105, 107, 108, 165, 201, 235
13:17–18, 107, 108, 164
13:17–19, 108, 158
13:18, 91, 108
13:18–22, 84
13:19, 84, 85, 87, 107, 108, 156, 165, 174
13:19–20, 91, 107, 162
13:19–22, 89, 108, 164, 173
13:19–23, 108
13:20, 89
13:21, 89, 108
13:21–22, 162
14:1, 108, 165, 173
14:1–2, 22–23, 84, 88, 89, 91, 104, 107, 108, 109, 158, 163, 164, 173
14:1–3, 107
14:1–4a, 104
14:2, 107, 160, 165, 173
14:3–6, 16–17, 87
14:3–20, 89
14:3–21, 88
14:4, 105
14:4–6, 108
14:4–20, 89
14:4–21, 89
14:5–6, 86, 104, 108
14:6, 16–17, 89
14:7, 173, 175
14:8, 87, 89

Isaiah (*cont.*)
14:11–12, 108
14:12, 108
14:12–14, 108
14:13, 86, 89
14:13–14, 158
14:17, 108
14:18–20, 105
14:20, 85, 87, 155, 158
14:21, 158, 467
14:22, 87, 89, 90, 107, 108
14:22–23, 84, 91, 104, 173
14:22–27, 109
14:23, 87, 89, 108, 162
14:24, 108, 165
14:24–25, 108, 164
14:24–26, 108
14:24–27, 84, 108, 109
14:25, 86, 91, 155
14:27, 108
14:28, 106
14:29–32, 106
15:14, 163
16:13, 104
17:1–6, 104
18:6, 104
19:2, 104
19:5–7, 104
Ch 21, 193
21:1, 23
21:1–9, 173
21:1–10, 23, 158
21:2, 23, 165
21:3–6, 23
21:6, 165
21:7, 23
21:8, 108, 165
21:9, 101, 107, 108, 159, 164, 165, 173
21:10, 164
23:11–12, 104
27:8b, 194
29:17, 162
29:18, 162
30:17, 105
32:13, 106
33:9, 162
Ch 34, 194
Chs 34–35, 154–162
34:1–2, 162
34:3, 162

34:4, 162
34:5, 162
34:5–6, 155, 156
34:6–7, 162
34:7, 162
34:8, 162
34:9–10, 162
34:11–14, 162
34:15, 162
34:16, 155, 162
34:17, 162
Ch 35, 194
35:1, 162
35:2, 162
35:3–4, 194
35:4, 162
35:5–6, 162
35:6b, 162
35:8, 162, 164
35:10, 162, 165
Chs 36–37, 22
Chs 36–39, 156
36:1–37:37, 470
36:1–37:38, 98
36:1–38:8, 24
36:4–20, 104
37:10–13, 104
37:22–25, 104
37:22–35, 78, 98
37:24, 105
37:25, 99
37:30, 78
37:31–32, 77
38:7–8, 99
38:21–39:8, 24
38:22, 99
39:1–8, 192
39:5–7, 23, 24
39:6–7, 102
Chs 40–48, 156, 157, 159, 163
Chs 40–55, 11, 160
Chs 40–66, 23, 154–162, 173, 175, 193
40:1, 26
40:1–2, 166
40:2, 173
40:3–4, 164
40:7, 194
40:12, 111
40:19–20, 165
40:21–22, 111

40:26, 111
40:28, 111
41:1–4, 163
41:2, 163, 165
41:4, 111
41:8–9, 165
41:21–29, 163
41:25, 165
41:26, 163
42:1–8, 163
42:5, 111
42:16, 164
42:17, 165
43:1, 111
43:5, 164
43:7, 111
43:10–15, 2
43:11, 248
43:15, 111
43:19–20, 164
43:27, 255
44:1–2, 165
44:2, 111
44:3, 111
44:6–8, 163
44:7–8, 163
44:9–20, 165
44:21, 111, 163
44:24, 111
44:24–28, 163
45:1, 472
45:3, 111
45:3–7, 163
45:4, 163
45:7, 163
45:7, 11–12, 21
45:7–9, 111
45:9–13, 160
45:12, 111
45:13, 165
45:14, 111, 163, 165, 212
45:18, 111
45:20, 165
45:20–21, 163
46:1, 101
46:1–2, 159, 165, 167, 173
46:1–7, 110
46:8–11, 163
46:10, 163, 165
46:11, 165

Ch 47, 95, 160, 168
47:1–15, 159, 165, 167, 173
47:2, 160
47:3–5, 160
47:8, 165
47:10, 165
47:12–13, 163
47:13–14, 144, 260
48:3–15, 163
48:10, 165
48:12–13, 111
48:20, 174
48:22–23, 111
48:39, 163
49:10, 165
49:11, 164
49:13, 165
49:22, 165
49:22–23, 165
49:25, 165
50:2, 160, 171, 176
50:2–3, 355
50:6–11, 160
51:9–10, 259
51:11, 165
51:13, 111
52:5, 105
52:8, 165
52:13, 436
52:26–30, 105
54:3, 111
54:7–10, 23
54:8, 165
54:10, 165
54:11–12, 111
54:16, 165
54:60, 165
55:8, 25
Chs 56–66, 11, 162
56:1–2, 160
56:2, 280
56:3, 165
56:6–8, 165
56:7, 174
56:9–12, 160
57:1–7, 280
57:1–59:15, 160
57:14, 164
57:15, 436
57:18, 166

Isaiah (*cont.*)
58:6–13, 280
59:2–9, 280
59:19, 194
60:1–22, 23
60:3–4, 165
60:5–12, 174
60:5–17, 111
60:7, 174
60:10, 165
60:12, 165
60:13, 174
60:14, 165
60:15, 107
60:16, 165
60:17, 214
61:2–3, 166
61:5, 165
61:6, 174
61:8–9, 23
Ch 62, 160
62:3, 165
62:10, 164
63:3–4, 171, 176
63:11–64:12, 160
Ch 65, 160
65:3–7, 280
65:11, 280
65:14, 165
65:25, 164
Ch 66, 161
66:6, 164
66:10, 166
66:12, 111
66:20, 165

Jeremiah, 10, 13, 16, 79, 82, 83, 87, 92, 93,
    94, 95, 97, 109, 157, 158, 164, 171,
    176, 201, 216, 237, 267, 268, 291,
    409, 414, 419, 422, 454, 463, 464
1:14, 108
3:12–14, 105
4:6, 105, 108
4:19–31, 355
4:21, 108
5:15, 105
6:1, 108
6:4, 107
7:1–15, 21
7:4, 103

7:4–8, 100
8:22, 108
10:11, 95
14:13, 103
15:4, 102, 110
15:20–21, 259
22:7, 107
22:24, 194
23:3–8, 103
23:14–21, 22
23:20, 25
23:24, 105
23:28–29, 105
Ch 25, 463, 472
25:1, 210
25:1–11, 102
25:8–9, 110
25:11–12, 22, 103, 155, 171, 463
25:12, 472
25:15–28, 108
26:1–24, 103
26:7–16, 102
27:1–6, 261
27:6–7, 22, 103, 156
27:7, 110
27:8, 110
27:11, 110
28:1–4, 103
28:1–17, 103
Ch 29, 463, 472
29:1–19, 103
29:1–32, 103
29:10, 22, 155, 171, 472
29:28, 22, 103
30:10, 173
30:25, 25
Ch 31, 173
31:7, 162
31:7–8, 162
31:7–14, 163
31:8, 162
31:10–12, 162
31:12–13, 174
31:23, 174
31:27, 174
31:28, 102
31:30–34, 478
31:31–32, 105
31:31–40, 23
31:36–37, 105

Chs 32–33, 440
32:20, 259
32:37, 23
32:39–40, 478
Ch 33, 173
33:7, 173, 464
33:8, 173
33:9, 173, 174
33:11, 174
33:13, 174
33:14–18, 103
33:14–25, 174
36:20–26, 102
36:29, 409
36:31, 409
37:5, 103
37:7, 103
38:17–23, 110
39:1–11, 103
Ch 44, 110
44:18, 109
44:30, 111
46:11, 108
46:27, 173
47:38–39, 105
48:7, 101
48:13, 101
49:7–22, 163
49:17–18, 156
49:34–39, 442
Chs 50–51, 105, 154, 158, 164, 173, 175
50:1, 90, 107
50:1–51:58, 90, 91, 107, 109
50:2, 90, 101, 107, 110, 165, 173
50:2a, 162
50:3, 105
50:4–5, 107, 163, 174, 478
50:5, 162, 164
50:6–9, 107, 108
50:8, 174
50:9, 91, 105, 107, 165
50:10–11, 108
50:10–13, 107
50:11, 162
50:12–13, 162
50:14–16, 107
50:15, 162, 173
50:16, 107
50:17, 103

50:17–18, 107
50:19, 162, 163
50:19–20, 107
50:20, 173
50:21, 107
50:22, 108
50:23, 108
50:24, 108
50:25, 162
50:25–27, 108
50:26, 108
50:27, 162
50:28, 108, 162, 173, 174
50:29, 107
50:29–30, 108
50:31–32, 86
50:33–34, 108, 173
50:34, 173
50:35, 108
50:35–37, 107, 108, 162
50:38–40, 108
50:39, 162
50:40, 156, 162
50:41–42, 108
50:44, 108
50:44–45, 108
50:45, 107, 173
50:46, 108, 173
51:1, 108, 165
51:2–4, 108
51:4, 162
51:5–6, 163
51:6, 108, 162, 174
51:7, 108
51:8, 108
51:8–9, 108
51:9, 108
51:10, 108, 163, 173
51:11, 103, 105, 108, 165
51:11, 27–28, 91
51:12, 105, 108
51:17–19, 108
51:20–23, 21, 108
51:24, 108
51:24–25, 105
51:25, 90, 108
51:27, 105, 108
51:27–28, 107, 108
51:28, 103, 105, 108
51:29, 108, 173

Jeremiah (*cont.*)
  51:30, 173
  51:31, 108
  51:34, 103, 111
  51:34–35, 108
  51:35, 162
  51:36, 162
  51:37, 108
  51:38–39, 108
  51:39, 108
  51:40, 162
  51:41, 108
  51:42, 108, 110
  51:43, 108, 162
  51:44, 101, 108, 110, 165, 173
  51:45, 174
  51:46, 173
  51:47, 173
  51:49, 108
  51:50, 108, 173, 174
  51:52, 108, 173
  51:53, 108
  51:57, 108
  51:58, 108, 173
  51:59–63, 155, 162
  51:59–64, 90, 91
  51:62, 90, 91
  52:1–30, 103
  52:12–30, 162
  52:31–34, 111

Ezekiel, 10, 13, 16, 79, 83, 87, 92, 93, 94,
  95, 96, 171, 216, 237, 267, 268, 291,
  414, 415, 419, 432, 440
  Chs 1–20, 437
  1:2, 22, 437
  Chs 2–24, 94
  2:3, 438
  2:5–8, 110
  3:4, 438
  Ch 4, 422
  4:4–5, 437
  4:4–6, 9, 22
  4:4–6:9, 23
  4:4–9, 419
  4:5–9, 414, 437, 438
  4:9, 437
  4:13, 438
  4:14, 438
  5:13, 194

6:5, 438
7:7, 438
9:8, 438
11:17–20, 23
12:23, 438
12:27, 438
14:9, 438
16:60–63, 478
17:1–10, 255
17:10, 194
17:11, 110
17:11–21, 110
17:15, 103
17:23–24, 255
Ch 18, 23
18:2, 102
18:10, 438
19:12, 194
20:1, 282
20:6, 423
20:15, 423
20:28, 252
20:32–44, 110
20:40–42, 280
21:30, 438
21:34, 438
24:1, 282
24:13, 194
25:12–14, 163
29:17, 95
29:25–26, 280
Ch 30, 422, 431
30:20–26, 414, 423, 432
30:21–26, 423
31:3–18, 255
Ch 33, 94
33:10–20, 23
35:1–15, 163
35:5, 438
36:5, 163
36:8–14, 280
36:24–25, 23
36:24–27, 280
37:1, 195
37:15–28, 280
37:19, 438
37:26–27, 478
Ch 40, 282
40:1, 282
40:2, 195

40:5–43:11, 174
44:19, 195

Hosea, 24
  2:18, 207
  7:3–7, 20
  8:3–4, 20
  10:3,7, 20
  13:10–11, 20
  13:15, 194

Joel
  2:2–3, 355
  2:6, 355
  3:3, 259
  4:9, 107
  4:19, 439
  4:20–21, 100

Amos, 9, 19
  1:1, 22, 107
  3:7, 253
  4:10, 21
  5:8, 21
  6:14, 105
  8:8, 22
  8:11–12, 23
  9:7, 21

Jonah
  2:6, 259
  4:8, 194

Obadiah, 163

Micah, 9
  3:5, 107
  3:6–7, 23
  5:5, 88
  7:1–7, 355

Nahum, 82
  1:12–13, 81
  2:12–13, 104
  2:12–14, 108
  3:1, 104
  3:19, 104

Habakkuk, 86, 87, 158, 164
  Chs 1–2, 90
  1:1–2:17, 19

1:6–10, 107
1:6–17, 89
1:13–14, 25
1:15–17, 107
2:5, 8, 13, 89
2:5–17, 89
2:9, 89
2:13, 108
2:16, 89
2:19, 246
3:3, 249

Zephaniah, 79, 91, 106, 109, 158,
  164
  1:4, 107
  1:7, 107
  1:11, 107
  1:15, 107
  1:18, 107
  2:2–3, 107
  2:12–13, 89
  2:13, 88, 108
  2:13–15, 88, 89, 107
  2:14, 89, 108
  2:15, 89, 104, 165
  3:8, 107
  3:9, 89, 107
  3:11, 106
  3:14, 89
  3:19–20, 89, 107

Haggai, 11, 41, 161, 171, 172, 174,
  175, 176, 193, 194, 195, 267,
  268, 463
  1:2, 161
  1:5–11, 280
  1:6, 171
  1:9–11, 194
  1:10–11, 280
  2:4–5, 194
  2:6–7, 174, 176
  2:7, 175
  2:15–17, 194
  2:15–19, 280
  2:17, 280
  2:21–22, 175
  2:21–23, 175, 176
  2:22–23, 175
  2:23, 194
  9:11, 171

Zechariah, 41, 161, 171, 172, 174,
    175, 193, 194, 195, 267, 268,
    463
  Chs 1–8, 193, 194
  1:2–6, 280
  1:5, 17
  1:7–11, 193
  1:10–11, 174
  1:11, 174
  1:12, 111, 161
  1:16, 280
  2:8, 175
  2:12–13, 175
  2:14, 175
  2:15, 175
  3:1–10, 175
  3:8, 175
  4:1–3, 175
  4:5, 195
  4:6, 11, 195
  4:6–10a, 175, 195
  4:6a, 195
  4:6b–10a, 176, 194, 195
  4:10b, 194
  4:11–14, 175
  4:12–14, 175
  6:1–8, 194
  6:6, 194
  6:8, 195
  6:9–13, 175
  8:9, 194
  8:9–12, 280
  8:10, 171, 194
  8:11–12, 280
  8:13, 194
  8:16–17, 280
  9:5–6, 439
  9:9–13, 456
  13:2–6, 17
  13:9, 175
  Ch 14, 461
  14:4, 107

Malachi, 273, 282
  1:1–4, 439
  1:1–12, 283
  1:7, 283
  1:8, 282
  1:10, 283
  1:11–12, 283

  1:13, 283
  1:14, 283
  1:20, 283
  1:21, 283
  2:2, 283
  2:8, 283
  2:9, 283
  2:10, 273
  2:11, 283
  2:15–16, 283
  3:5, 273, 283
  3:8–24, 17
  3:9–11, 280
  3:14–15, 283
  3:22, 283

Psalms, 46
  9:3, 263
  9:21, 263
  21:8, 263
  34:10, 263
  41:14, 252
  44, 14, 18
  44:24, 60
  47:5, 107
  48:8, 194
  55:17, 258
  57:3, 249
  78:35, 249
  Ps 79, 454
  Ps 82, 18, 26, 439
  92:2, 249
  113:2, 252
  115:4, 246
  Ps 119, 282
  119:64, 258
  121:3–4, 60
  135:9, 259
  135:15, 246
  137:7, 163
  145:13, 259

Job, 19, 25, 26
  1:6, 254
  1:21, 252
  3:4, 249
  3:23, 249
  12:13, 252
  12:22, 253

Lamentations, 87, 92
  2:9, 14, 20, 92
  2:14, 103
  3:60–66, 103
  4:12, 100
  4:13, 92
  4:20, 103
  4:21, 163

Qohelet (Ecclesiastes), 18
  11:2, 262

Esther, 177, 195, 209, 248
  1:1, 262
  1:22, 351
  3:2–5, 177
  3:12, 351
  3:13, 177
  3:21–23, 177
  8:3–13, 177
  8:9, 351
  10:2, 244
  10:3, 255

Daniel, 15, 16, 97, 190, 414, 472
  Ch 1, 205, 210–212, 228–229, 233, 237,
    244, 251, 262
  Chs 1–2, 229
  Chs 1–5, 208, 209
  Chs 1–6, 237, 262
  Chs 1–7, 203–263
  1:1, 212, 261
  1:1–2, 210, 237
  1:1–4, 102, 210, 211
  1:2, 250, 251
  1:3, 248
  1:3–18, 229
  1:5, 212, 248
  1:7, 207, 208, 209
  1:18, 212
  1:19, 207, 229
  1:21, 222, 229
  Ch 2, 16, 20, 205, 212–215, 224–229,
    232, 233, 238, 244, 273, 324, 331, 332,
    333, 334, 336, 337, 354, 355, 371–378,
    393, 413, 429, 430, 431, 432, 476
  Chs 2–5, 235
  Chs 2–6, 205, 246
  2–7, 113, 137, 154, 205, 209, 244, 378
  2:1, 212, 222, 252

2:1–3, 229
2:1–3a, 229
2:3, 252
2:4, 205
2:5, 248
2:8, 248
2:13, 215
2:15, 248
2:17, 207, 227
2:17–18, 215
2:18, 248, 249
2:19, 248, 249
2:20, 252
2:20–23, 212, 252
2:21, 253
2:22, 253
2:23, 249, 253
2:24, 372, 393
2:26, 208
2:27, 248
2:27–28, 229, 252
2:28, 248, 249
2:29, 207, 248
2:30, 248
2:31–35, 212, 225, 373, 376
2:32, 333–334
2:34, 376
2:36–41a, 376
2:37, 249
2:37–38, 213
2:37–39, 387
2:37–40, 213
2:37–45, 212, 373, 388
2:39, 226, 372, 373
2:39–41, 226
2:39–43, 213
2:40, 226, 372, 373, 375
2:40–42, 386, 387, 388
2:40–43, 376, 386
2:40b-c, 387
2:41, 213, 226, 334, 373, 374, 375, 376,
  385, 386, 387
2:41–42, 213, 373, 375
2:41–43, 226
2:41a, 387
2:41b, 387
2:42, 213, 374, 375, 376
2:43, 213, 334, 375, 376, 385, 386, 387,
  388
2:44, 213, 226, 249, 339, 372, 376

Daniel (*cont.*)
  2:45, 229, 252, 376
  2:47, 210, 214, 248, 249
  2:48, 214
  2:49, 215
  Ch 3, 227, 229
  Chs 3–5, 207
  Chs 3–6, 205, 229
  3:1, 215
  3:1–30, 205, 206, 215, 232–233, 234
  3:2–3, 248
  3:5, 215, 248
  3:7, 215, 248
  3:10, 215, 248
  3:12, 215, 246
  3:12–14, 207
  3:14, 215, 246
  3:15, 248
  3:16, 207, 248, 255
  3:17, 249
  3:18, 215
  3:18–21, 246
  3:19, 207
  3:20, 207
  3:22, 207
  3:23, 207
  3:24, 248
  3:25, 215
  3:26, 249
  3:26–30, 233
  3:26a, 207
  3:26b, 207
  3:27, 246, 248
  3:28, 207, 215, 249
  3:28–29, 249
  3:29, 207, 215, 248
  3:31–4:34 [4:1–37], 205, 209, 215–217,
    232, 233–235
  3:31–6:29, 246
  3:32, 249
  Ch 4, 206, 216, 235, 246
  4:5–6, 207
  4:5[8], 208, 216
  4:5[8]-6[9], 216
  4:6[9], 248
  4:7–14, 234
  4:13[16], 216
  4:14[17], 248, 249
  4:16[19], 207, 208
  4:20[23], 216

  4:21[24], 249
  4:22[25], 216, 249
  4:23, 210
  4:25[28], 246
  4:27, 216
  4:29[32], 216, 249
  4:31, 210
  4:31–32[34–35], 216
  4:31[34], 249
  4:33–34[36–37], 242
  4:33[36], 248
  4:34, 210
  4:34[37], 216
  Ch 5, 55, 205, 206, 222, 231
  5:1–30, 217–222, 229–232, 233, 234,
    262
  5:2, 217, 230, 232, 255
  5:2–3, 217, 234
  5:2–4, 217, 230
  5:3, 231
  5:4, 217, 246
  5:5–7, 217
  5:7, 217, 231, 248
  5:8–9, 217
  5:10–12, 217
  5:11, 217, 231, 232
  5:11–13, 246
  5:12, 207, 208
  5:13–29, 217
  5:14, 255
  5:16, 217, 231, 248
  5:18, 218, 246, 249
  5:18–21, 232, 234
  5:18–22, 218, 232
  5:19, 218
  5:20–21, 218
  5:21, 249
  5:22, 232
  5:23, 217, 231
  5:25, 218, 219
  5:26–28, 218
  5:29, 217, 231, 248
  5:30, 220, 246, 247
  Ch 6, 205
  6 [5:31–6:28], 222–223, 235–237
  6:1–4, 246
  6:1[5:31], 222, 236
  6:2–3[1–2], 222, 235, 237
  6:2[1]-8[7], 248
  6:3–10[2–9], 222

6:3[2], 222
6:4[3], 222
6:6, 249
6:6[5], 248
6:7–8, 246
6:8[7], 248
6:9[8], 248
6:10, 246
6:11, 249
6:11[10], 223, 235
6:12, 249
6:12–13, 246
6:13[12], 248
6:16–17, 246
6:16[15], 248
6:17, 249
6:17[16], 223
6:21, 249
6:22, 246
6:23, 223, 249
6:24, 249
6:26, 246
6:27, 249
6:27–28[26–27], 223
6:28, 208
6:29, 246
Ch 7, 16, 201, 205, 209, 223–224,
    237–244, 262, 324, 331, 355, 372,
    373, 428, 429, 430, 451–455, 458
Chs 7–11, 455
Chs 7–12, 466, 476
7:1, 209, 223, 247
7:1–5, 241
7:1–7, 429
7:2, 209, 239
7:2–14, 224
7:3, 223
7:4, 239, 429
7:5, 239, 244, 262
7:6, 239, 241
7:7, 239, 240, 244
7:7–8, 241
7:8, 428, 451, 452
7:9–10, 241, 429
7:11, 224, 241, 429
7:12, 241
7:12–14, 429
7:13, 239
7:13–14, 241
7:15, 209

7:15–18, 241, 242, 429
7:16, 224
7:17, 238, 241, 253, 428
7:17–18, 224
7:18, 242, 429
7:19–21, 452
7:19–22, 224
7:19–26, 241
7:20–21, 429
7:22, 263
7:23–26, 224
7:24, 239, 240, 451
7:24–25, 429
7:25, 209, 248, 249, 263, 452, 453, 454,
    462, 463
7:25–27, 453
7:27, 263
7:28, 223
Ch 8, 262, 455, 462
8–9, 462–465
8–12, 205
8:1, 247, 262
8:12–13, 470
8:13–14, 462
8:14, 454
8:17, 438
8:19, 438
8:20–21, 262
8:20–21a, 253
8:21b, 253
8:24, 263
Ch 9, 17, 357, 422, 440, 466
Chs 9–11, 454
9:1–2, 463
9:2–20, 195
9:4–16, 111
9:4–20, 463
9:24, 440, 463
9:24–27, 357
9:25, 440
9:25–27, 464
9:26, 438
9:27, 454, 464, 470
10:1, 262
10:1–12:3, 262
10:13, 470
10:20–21, 470
Ch 11, 409, 410, 415, 434, 449, 458, 469
Chs 11–12, 436
11:1, 262

Daniel (*cont.*)
  11:2, 263
  11:4, 375, 398
  11:5, 364
  11:5–9, 458
  11:6, 403, 438
  11:6–9, 403
  11:10, 409, 412
  11:10–11, 458
  11:10–12, 415
  11:11–12, 410
  11:12, 244
  11:13, 411, 415
  11:13–14, 412, 415
  11:13–18, 458
  11:14, 415, 437
  11:14–16, 409
  11:15, 422, 423
  11:15–16, 415, 437
  11:15–17, 422
  11:16, 423
  11:17, 423, 424, 441
  11:18, 426
  11:19, 427, 429
  11:20, 433, 443
  11:21, 443, 471
  11:22, 443
  11:22–23, 443
  11:24, 443
  11:24–25, 471
  11:25–26, 468
  11:25–29, 458
  11:27, 468
  11:28, 468
  11:29, 469
  11:29–30, 469
  11:30, 449, 450, 469
  11:30–39, 450
  11:31, 450
  11:32, 454, 470, 471
  11:32–35, 450
  11:33, 458
  11:34, 457
  11:35, 438
  11:35–39, 458
  11:36, 450
  11:36–38, 450
  11:39, 450
  11:40, 438, 458
  11:40–12:3, 458, 462

  11:40–43, 468
  11:42–43, 458
  12:1, 25, 438, 466
  12:2–3, 471
  12:6, 438
  12:7, 250, 458, 476
  12:11, 466, 470
  12:11–12, 454, 466
  12:12, 465
  12:13, 438

Ezra, 7, 172, 178, 267, 268, 269, 270, 271,
    272, 273, 281
  1:1–4, 142, 440, 472
  1:2–4, 73, 164, 165
  1;2–4, 248
  3:3, 281
  Ch 4, 161
  4:1–24, 177
  4:2, 177
  4:4, 177
  4:6, 177, 195
  4:6–24, 279
  4:7–6:18, 229, 246
  4:7–23, 279
  4:10, 177
  4:12, 15, 19, 21
  4:15, 177
  4:19, 177
  5:13–15, 165
  5:16, 165
  6:2–5, 142, 164, 165
  6:15, 176
  6:18, 176
  7:1–8, 280
  7:1–10, 280
  7:1–26, 280
  7:6, 269
  7:12–26, 246
  7:27, 249
  8:15–19, 281
  8:24, 281
  Ch 9, 195
  Chs 9–10, 439
  9:1, 270, 281
  9:1–2, 281
  9:1–10:44, 280
  9:2, 270
  9:7–9, 110, 111
  9:11, 281

9:12, 270
10:2, 281
10:11, 281
10:18–23, 281

Nehemiah, 7, 178, 267, 271, 272, 273, 431
1:3, 439
2:1–8, 279
2:10, 439, 443
2:16, 282
2:19, 439
2:32, 282
3:33–35, 439
4:1–2, 439
5:1–13, 280
6:1–9, 439
6:16–19, 439
Chs 8–10, 281, 282
8:1–12, 281
9:1–10:40, 282
9:5, 252
9:6–37, 195
9:10, 259
9:23–29, 439
9:24, 281
9:26–37, 111
9:30, 281
9:30–37, 110
10:2, 282
10:3, 281
10:29, 281
10:31, 270
10:32, 281
10:38–39, 282
13:10–13, 282
13:23–27, 280

1 Chronicles, 32, 87, 109, 247, 262, 291
2:13, 248
3:17–20, 24
6:17, 438
20:1, 197
29:2, 214

2 Chronicles, 32, 87, 109, 216, 247, 291
1:8–9, 253
1:14, 195
2:2–9, 469
9:25, 195
28:5, 250

32:1–23, 79
32:10–19, 104
33:1–11, 99
33:11, 101
33:11–13, 251
36:6–7, 102, 237
36:10–20, 103
36:11–14, 110
36:21, 25

NEW TESTAMENT

Revelation, 15, 16, 238

APOCRYPHA AND
PSEUDEPIGRAPHA

Baruch, 473

1 Enoch, 378, 422, 440, 460, 463
Chs 6–11, 377–378, 398
6:2–7:6, 377
6:7, 377, 399
Chs 8–10, 377
8:1–10:8, 377
8:3, 399
9:1, 377
9:1–10:15, 377
9:8, 399
10:4–6, 377
10:7, 399
10:16–22, 377
85:1–90:40, 416
85:1–90:41, 378
Chs 89–90, 476
89:21, 417
89:50, 417
89:54–58, 417, 421
89:59–60, 417
89:59–90:19, 439, 440
89:59–90:25, 17, 45
89:61–64, 417
89:65, 417
89:65–67, 417
89:68–69, 417
89:70–71, 417
89:72, 417, 439
89:72–77, 417
89:74–75, 417
Ch 90, 458–459, 471

1 Enoch (*cont.*)
  90:1, 417, 439
  90:2, 420, 421
  90:2–9, 421
  90:4, 420
  90:5, 417, 439
  90:6, 420
  90:6–9, 420
  90:6–19, 416, 417–423
  90:8, 419
  90:9, 419, 420
  90:9–10, 420
  90:9–31, 458
  90:9a, 459
  90:9b-10, 459
  90:10, 420
  90:11, 420, 459
  90:11–12, 420
  90:12, 459
  90:12–14, 420
  90:12–16, 459
  90:13, 420, 440
  90:13–14, 459
  90:15, 420, 459
  90:16, 420, 459
  90:17–18, 420, 459
  90:18, 420, 467, 471
  90:19, 420, 459, 475
  90:20–39, 419
  90:28–29, 461
  90:31, 466, 476
  90:33, 471
  91:11–17, 378, 422
  93:1–10, 422
  93:3–10, 378

1 Esdras 4:46, 250

Jubilees, 448–449
  23:11–31, 448
  23:13–25, 448
  23:14, 469
  23:16–19, 468
  23:19, 469

1 Maccabees, 7, 24, 99, 200, 210, 248,
    250, 258, 399, 403, 441, 449,
    450, 456–458, 458, 460, 465,
    467–473
  1:11–15, 469

1:20, 453
1:20–24, 468
1:29, 453
1:29–40, 469
1:33–38, 469
1:54–57, 454
1:54–59, 452
1:54–64, 470
1:59, 472
1:64, 469
2:27–48, 457
2:29–38, 470
2:39–41, 471
2:42–43, 471
2:65–66, 458
3:1–26, 471
3:10–24, 459
3:16, 471
3:28–60, 471
3:38–4:25, 459
4:1–35, 471
4:6, 471
4:29, 471
4:34–35, 459
4:35, 460
4:61, 465
Ch 5, 459, 465
5:1–54, 471
5:20, 471
5:63–68, 471
6:18–19, 465
6:21–54, 459
6:28–63, 420
6:33–47, 466
6:49, 466
6:53–54, 466
6:55–7:4, 459
6:55–61, 473
7:1–3, 420
7:1–4, 473
7:3–20, 475
7:5–9, 474
7:26–48, 459
7:26–50, 471
7:43, 475
7:46, 459, 471
8:1–17, 476
9:9, 476
9:23, 476
13:41, 477

2 Maccabees, 7, 165, 195, 200, 279, 280,
    286, 379, 432, 433, 437, 443, 447,
    449, 458, 467–473, 477, 478
1:7, 469
Ch 3, 430, 432, 433
3:24–25, 433
3:27, 433
4:1–7, 443
4:13–17, 469
4:18–20, 467
4:21–22, 467
4:23–32, 467
4:32–34, 420
4:33–34, 467
4:35–38, 468
4:39–5:16, 448–449
4:39–49, 468
5:1, 468
5:5, 468
5:5–6, 468
5:7, 468
5:11, 468
5:11–21, 468
5:24–26, 469
5:25, 469
6:11, 470
7:2–42, 470
8:8, 459
Ch 11, 460
11:8–13, 459
11:23–26, 462
11:30–33, 400

11:37–33, 460
13:3–8, 466
13:23, 466, 473
14:3–10, 474
14:16–17, 475
15:15–16, 459

3 Maccabees 2:2, 250

Tobit, 6, 19, 26
1:12, 250
3:3–5, 26
6:17, 250
7:12, 250
10:13, 250
11:1, 250
13:1, 250
13:2–18, 26
13:9, 250
14:4–7, 26

Wisdom of Jesus Ben Sira (Sirach), 64,
    423
1–5, 19
18:1, 250
48:22–25, 166
48:24, 166
50:1, 441
50:4, 441

Versions
    Septuaguint, 272

INDEX OF ANCIENT SOURCES

Abbadianus 55, 440
Abu al-Qasim Firdausi, *Shahnamah,*
    346
Abydenos, 203, 245
  Megsthenes *apud* Abydenos
    FGH 685, F 6.4, 137
    FGH 685, F 6b, 138–139
Achaemenian Inscriptions, 74
Adad, Psalm to, 60
Adad-shuma-uṣur Epic
  col. I, line 10, 53
  col. II
    line 15, 53
    line 16, 53
    line 19, 53
    lines 20–29, 53
    line 22, 53
    line 28, 53
  col. III, lines 16–17, 53
Adapa D, lines 5–6, 250
Aelianus, 202
  Varia historia xii.3, 188–189
Aeschines 3.133, 317
Aeschylus, *Prometheus Bound,* 20
Agatharchides *apud* Josephus *Against*
    Apion i.22.209–11, 396
Alexander Romance, 346–347,
    358
  δ rescension, 346

Pahlavi translation, 346, 347
Pseudo-Kallisthenes, *Vita Alexandri*
    regis Macedonum, 346
  i.34, 314
  (Recension ϵ) 20.2–5, 314
  Syriac version, 346
Antiochus I Royal Inscription, *ANET* 317,
    199, 321, 399
Appian
  Lybikê [viii] 80–93.371–441, 100
  Syriakê [xi.]
    50.252, 396
    54.273–74, 321
    56, 321
    58.300–7, 395
    65.345, 401, 402
Aristeas to Philokrates, 12–14, 396
Arrian, 182, 190, 299, 302, 303–310, 317,
    319, 320, 321
  Anabasis
    i.16.7, 316
    iii.1.2–4, 314
    iii.3.2, 323
    iii.6.1–7.1, 315
    iii.16.2, 316
    iii.16.3, 316
    iii.16.4, 202, 320
    iii.16.4–5, 316
    iii.16.5, 321

iii.17.1–18.10, 316
iii.18.11–12, 317
iii.19.2, 318
iii.19.3–5, 318
iii.19.5–8, 318
iii.21, 318
iii.21.1–5, 318
iii.21.4, 318
iii.22.1, 318, 351
iii.22.6, 351
iii.23.1–25.1, 318
iii.25.1–3, 318
iii.25.5–7, 319
iii.28.2–3, 319
iii.29.4–5, 318
iii.29.6–30.5, 319
iii.30.4, 319
iii.30.5, 319
iv.1.4–5, 319
iv.2.3–vi.27.1, 319
iv.3.5, 319
iv.5.2–6.4, 319
iv.7.3, 319
iv.16.3–17.7, 319
iv.18.4–19.6, 319
iv.19.4–6, 319
iv.20.4, 319
iv.20.4–21.1, 319
iv.21, 319
iv.21.1, 319
iv.22.1–2, 319
vi.27.4–5, 349
vi.29.3, 319
vii.4.4–8, 349
vii.4.6, 319, 395
vii.6.1–5, 320
vii.11.1–3, 320
vii.16.4–17.6, 320
vii.16.6, 320
vii.17.1, 322
vii.17.1–2, 198
vii.17.2, 202
vii.17.5–6, 320
vii.22.1, 322
vii.23.1, 320
vii.23.3–4, 320
vii.24.1–3, 322
vii.24.4–26.3, 323
vii.26.2–3, 323
vii.29.4, 320

vii.110.6–8, 320
vii.111.4–112.1, 320
Hoi met' Alexandron, 24.3–7, 394
Assumption of Moses. see Testament
    of Moses
Assyrian royal correspondence, 196
Athenaeus
    xii.550b, 399
    xiii.593c–d, 402
    xiv.639c, 322
the Avesta, 68, 73, 332, 333, 334, 335, 339,
    345, 352, 353

Babylonian *Akîtu* (New Year's Festival)
    clay tablets
    ANET 331–34, 323
    lines 25–26, 288, 253
Babylonian astronomical diaries, 45–46,
    278, 367, 392, 400
    lines 29'–39,' 380
    lines 34'–36,' 380
    lines 34'–39,' 380
    line 36,' 381
    lines 36'–38,' 381
    line 37,' 381
    line 38,' 381
Babylonian Chronicles, 8, 50, 137, 211, 215
    1, col. IB, line 9, 51
    2–5, *ABC* 87–102, 111
    3, 120
        lines 1, 16, 31, 58, 197
        lines 59–64, 145
        lines 66–69, 102
    4 and 5, Obverse, lines 1–13, 251
    5
        Obverse, lines 12–13, 251
        Obverse, line 21, 197
        Reverse, lines 6–7, 102
        Reverse, lines 11–13, 103, 260
    6, *ABC* 103–4, 111
    7, 112, 115, 123, 124, 127, 134, 137,
        140, 141, 147, 152, 162, 168,
        204, 220, 221
    ABC 104–11, 137
    col. I, line 7, 139
    col. II
        lines 1–4, 140, 146
        line 5, 10, 19, 23, 150
        lines 13–15, 140
        lines 21–22, 152

Babylonian Chronicles (*cont.*)
  col. III
    lines 1–4, 142
    lines 5–8, 142
    lines 5–16, 152
    lines 9–12, 142
    lines 12–15, 142
    lines 16–28, 142
    lines 21–22, 142
  9, 275, 285
  ABC, 114, 284
  10, 363–366, 394, 395, 401
    lines 26–29, 366
    lines 39–40, 366
    Obverse, lines 5–6, 394
    Obverse, line 6, 202
    Reverse, line 13, 202
    Reverse, line 33, 202
  21 (Synchronistic History), 30, 50, 51,
    52
  Adad-shuma-uṣur Epic (*see* Adad-
    shuma-uṣur Epic)
  Chronicle P, 32, 52, 53
    col. III, line 8, 53
  Dynastic Chronicle, 33, 53
  Early Kings, Chronicle of, 52
  "objective" chronicles, 32–33, 52–53
  Synchronistic History (Chronicle 21),
    30, 50, 51, 52
  Weidner Chronicle, 31–32, 52
Babylonian Creation Epic, 50, 51, 62,
    223–224, 238
  Tablet I
    line 96, 259
    line 103, 259
    lines 1–104, 259
    lines 105–108, 259
    lines 132–45, 259
  Tablet II, 51
  Tablet IV
    lines 39–40, 259
    lines 103–18, 259
  Tablet IV, lines 4–7, 250
  Tablet V, 224
  Tablet VI
    line 121, 254
    lines 53–166, 259
    lines 128–29, 149, 157, 253
  Tablet VI, line 142, 250
  Tablet VI, line 149, 249

Tablet VII
  line 104, 253
Tablet VII, line 35, 102
Babylonian King List, Hellenistic period
    (British Museum), 398, 427–428,
    442
  FGH 260, F 32.6, 402
Babylonian record of death of Antiochus
    IV, 472
Babylonian Talmud, 220
  ʿ*Abodah zarah* 9a, 357, 440
  Berakhot 31a, 258
  Sanhedrin 4b, 472
  Yoma 69a, 314
*Bahman Yasht/Vahman Yasht/Vohûman
    Yasht (Prophetic Zand),*
    334–335, 353, 355, 484. *see also
    Prophetic Zand*
Behistun Inscription, 69, 74, 171, 172, 176,
    193
  Babylonian Version, lines 36–40, 192
  Persian Version
    col. I
      lines 1–11, 258
      lines 26–30, 258
      lines 27–28, 193
      lines 33–35, 191
      lines 35–42, 193
      lines 35–43, 191
      line 43, 191
      lines 55–61, 191, 193
      lines 71–75, 194
      lines 77–81, 192
    col. I, line 83–col. II, line 5, 192
    col. II, lines 5–8, 192
    col. III, lines 76–92, 192
    col. IV
      lines 80–86, 191
      lines 88–92, 74
Bêl-shimânni documents, 178, 179
  Tablet 3, 179
Berlin Nr. 615, 197
Berossus, 97, 112, 152, 203, 225, 244, 257,
    260, 309, 315, 397, 398
  Babyloniaka, book i, *apud* Athenaeus
    xiv.639c, 322
  FGH 680, F 9, 111
  FGH 680, F 9a, 138
  FGH 680, F 11, 279
  FGH 685, F 6b, 245

British Museum
  Babylonian King List, Hellenistic
      period, 398, 427–428, 442
    FGH 260, F 32.6, 402
  CT 22:68, 149–150
  Spartoli tablets (*see* Spartoli tablets,
      British Museum)
  Tablet BM 35526 (from Xerxes' reign),
      180, 198
  VAT 17020, 58

Chronicle P (Babylonian Chronicles), 32,
      52, 53
  col. III, line 8, 53
Counsels of Wisdom, lines 135–41, 258
Covenant Code (JE), 269, 270, 271, 281
Covenant of Damascus/Cambridge
      Document (CD)
  1:1–11, 438
  1:18, 471
Cuneiform texts
  British Museum CT 22:68, 149–150
  University of Pennsylvania Cuneiform
      Text no. 1, lines 6–7, 197
Curtius, 297, 299, 301
  iii.3.8–25, 314
  iii.12.21–26, 351
  iv.7.1–5, 314
  iv.7.25, 323
  iv.13.12–14, 315, 349
  v.1.4–7, 316
  v.1.17–22, 316
  v.1.22, 321
  v.2.20–22, 351
  v.3.1–5.4, 316
  v.6.1, 317
  v.6.1–9, 317
  v.7, 317
  v.9.2–12.20, 318
  v.9.16, 318
  v.10.7, 318
  v.12.7, 318
  v.13, 318
  v.13.1, 318
  v.19, 318
  vi.2.11, 351
  vi.4.1–22, 318
  vi.6.13, 318
  vii.4.32–38, 319
  vii.5.19–26, 319
  vii.5.38, 319
  vii.5.38–43, 318
  vii.5.40, 319
  vii.5.40–43, 351
  vii.6.14–15, 319
  vii.6.24, 319
  vii.7.31–39, 319
  vii.9.20, 319
  vii.10.10, 318
  vii.11, 319
  viii.1.3–7, 319
  viii.2.19–33, 319
  viii.3.1–15, 319
  viii.5.1-ix.10.17, 319
  ix.7.1–11, 357
  ix.10.19, 319
  x.1.9, 319, 349
  x.3.7–14, 320
  x.5.1–6, 323
  x.5.19–25, 351
Cuthaean Legend of Narâm-Sin, 36–37
Cyrus Cylinder, 73–74, 112, 115, 127, 133,
      143, 152, 162, 225
  lines 1–8, 127
  lines 1–11, 142, 153
  line 9, 142
  line 11, 153
  lines 12–14, 142
  line 13, 163
  lines 15–16, 142
  lines 17-end, 142
  line 18, 163
  line 20, 191
  lines 22–30, 191
  lines 30–32, 142
  lines 38–43, 191

D. *see* "Deuteronomy" in index of biblical
      sources
"Daiva Inscription" (XPh), 183–186,
      199
  ANET 316–17, 199
  ANET 317, 199, 321
Daniel commentaries
  Jerome, *In Danielem* iii (*see* Jerome)
  Pseudo-Sa'adya Gaon, Commentary to
      Daniel, 7:5, 262
Darius' Inscription at Behistun. *see*
      Behistun Inscription
Deinon, 297

Delphic Oracle, 225
Demosthenes, 320
   15.11–12, 284
   "For the Liberty of the Rhodians," 275
Demotic Chronicle, 64, 71
   cols. III–V, 261
Dinkard, 332–333, 334
   Book ix, chap 8, 352
Dio Chrysostom, 309
   iv.67, 322
Diodorus, 22, 274, 275, 286, 303–310, 365,
      373
   ii.2, 32.5–34.6, 201
   ii.9.4–9, 202
   xii.71.1, 278, 279
   xv.42.1, 284
   xvi.40.1–45.6, 284
   xvi.40.3, 284
   xvi.40.4, 285
   xvi.40.5, 284
   xvi.41.1–4, 284
   xvi.41.5–6, 284
   xvi.43.1–45.6, 284
   xvi.44.1, 284
   xvi.46.1–51.3, 284
   xvi.46.4, 285
   xvi.46.5–51.3, 285
   xvi.48.1–2, 284
   xvi.93.2, 284
   xvii.37.6–38.7, 351
   xvii.49.1–2, 314
   xvii.51.1, 323
   xvii.60, 317
   xvii.67.1, 351
   xvii.67.1–69.2, 316
   xvii.70.1, 317
   xvii.72, 317
   xvii.73.2–3, 351
   xvii.74.1–2, 318
   xvii.83.3, 318
   xvii.83.7, 318
   xvii.99.5–6, 357
   xvii.112.2–5, 321
   xvii.112.3, 201
   xvii.112.6, 321
   xvii.116.2–3, 322
   xvii.116.4, 322
   xvii.116.4–117.1, 322
   xvii.117, 323
   xviii.3.3, 394

xviii.6.3, 396
xviii.39.6, 396
xviii.43.1, 396
xviii.50.2, 394
xviii.58.1, 396
xviii.61.5, 396
xviii.63.6, 396
xviii.73.3, 394
xix.12.1, 394
xix.12.3–44.3, 395
xix.39–44, 394
xix.55.5, 394
xix.55.7–9, 394
xix.56.4, 394
xix.59.2, 396
xix.69.1, 394
xix.81–85, 394
xix.85.2, 394
xix.85.4, 396
xix.90–91, 394
xix.90.1, 394
xix.91.1, 394
xix.92, 395
xix.93.7, 396
xix.100.4–7, 395
xx.19.2, 395
xx.19.3–4, 395
xx.96.3, 397
xx.100.2, 397
xx.106.2–3, 397
xx.106.3–5, 397
xx.107.1, 397
xx.107.2–5, 397
xx.108.1–3, 397
xx.108.4–109.3, 397
xx.113.1, 396
xx.113.1–2, 396
xxi.1.1–2, 394
xxi.1.5, 396, 397
xxviii.3, 397
xxviii.39.5–6, 397
Dionysius of Halicarnassus, *First Letter to
     Ammaios* 4, 284
Dynastic Chronicle (Babylonian
     Chronicles), 33, 53
Dynastic Prophecy, 112, 137, 294–296,
     305, 316, 348
   BHLT
     30–37, 315
     31–37, 137

col. I, 294
col. II
   lines 1–10, 294
   lines 11–16, 294
   line 12, 138
   lines 17–24, 294
col. III, 294
col. IV, 316
   line 2, 295

Early Kings, Chronicle of (Babylonian
   Chronicles), 52
Egyptian text of ca. 1300 B.C.E., *ANET*
   431–32, 71
EMML 6281, 440
Enlil, Psalms to, 60
Enûma elish, 31, 51, 100
   Tablet V, 100
Erra Epic, 43–46, 55
   Tablet III, 44
   Tablet IV, 44
      52–62, 44
      54, 44
      69, 44
      133, 44
   Tablet V, 27, 44
Eusebius
   Chronika
      Armenian version, 277
         FGH 685, F 6a.13, 138–139
      Latin edition of Jerome *(Pamphili
         Chronici Canones),* 277,
         286–287
      Syncellus, *Chronographia,*
         286
   Praeparatio evangelica
      ix.41.2, 245
      ix.41.4, 137, 138

Gilgamesh Epic, 28, 349
   Tablet X, Old Babylonian Version,
      fragment iii, lines 3–5,
      250
   Tablet XI, lines 187–88, 253
Graziani documents. *see* Xerxes' reign,
   Babylonian documents
   from
Greater Bundahishn, 334
Greek papyrus with dream of King
   Nektanebos, 285–286

Hecataeus of Miletus, 8
Herodotus, 8, 22, 81, 112, 123, 152, 168,
   171, 181–182, 184, 187–190,
   201, 204, 220, 265, 297
i.4.3–4, 201
i.4.95, 201
i.4.130, 201
i.13, 260
i.55, 91, 107–8, 245
i.71, 344
i.73.3, 258
i.95.2–107.2, 258
i.102–3, 107, 127–30, 262
i.107–8, 120, 73
i.123–130, 258
i.130.1, 258
i.131.2, 201
i.140, 201
i.177–78.1, 153
i.181.1, 200
i.181.3–5, 200
i.183.2–3, 202
i.183.3, 202
i.185, 103, 162
i.190, 257
i.191, 257
i.192, 278
ii.87, 201
iii.1–26, 191
iii.61–62, 191
iii.64–66, 191
iii.68, 191
iii.68–88, 191
iii.89–94, 258
iii.92, 193, 278
iii.150–60, 191, 192, 198
iii.159, 192, 200, 202
iv.163, 260
v.92, 260
vii.1.3, 199
vii.7, 199
vii.19, 73
vii.20, 199
ix.101–8, 198
xvi.1.5, 201
Hesiod
   Theogony, 40–46, 253
   Works and Days
      31, 253
      109–201, 214

Homer
  Iliad, 28, 60, 65
    i.565–94, 20
    xiv.157–xv.33, 60
  Odyssey, xxiv.71–73, 201
Hymn to Amon-Reʿ, ANET 365–67, 72
"Hymn to the Moon-God," Obverse, line
    17, 253
"Hymn to the Sun-God," col. I., line 5,
    252
Hystaspes, Oracle of, 424–425, 441

Isocrates, 289
  Epistles 1
    2.11, 313
    3, 313
    9, 313
  Orations
    4, 313
    4.135–56, 313
    5, 313
    5.101, 284
    5.102, 284
Israel Stela, ANET 377, 72

Jason of Cyrene, 433
JE (Covenant Code), 269, 270, 271,
    281
Jerome
  In Danielem iii, 218, 412, 415
    2:1, 252
    5:2, 255
    5:25, 256
    5:25–28, 256
    11:6, 401, 402
    11:14, 437
    11:15–16, 437
Josephus, 244, 274, 431, 433
  Against Apion
    i.20.146–47, 111
    i.20.148–49, 111, 138
    i.20.150, 152
    i.20.153, 315
    i.22.192, 320
    i.22.194, 283
    i.22.209–11, 396
    ii.4.43, 315
  Antiquities, 218, 291
    x.6.1.84, 251
    x.6.2.88, 251

    x.6.3.96–97, 251
    x.11.3.243–44, 256
    xi.7.1.297–301, 283
    xi.8.3.17–19, 4–5.326–339, 314
    xi.8.3.317–19, 314
    xii.1.1.6, 396
    xii.3.3–4.138–146, 441
    xii.3.3.129–30, 436, 437
    xii.3.3.129–33, 437
    xii.3.3.131–36, 437
    xii.3.3.132, 438
    xii.3.3.138, 437, 441
    xii.3.3.143–44, 437
    xii.4.1–11.157–236, 437
    xii.4.1.158–9, 404
    xii.5.3.218, 468
    xviii.4.3.92, 468
  War
    ii.16.4.390–94, 21
    vi.5.4.312–13, 21
Justin, 303, 305, 320
    xii.5.10–11, 319
    xii.12.1–4, 320
    xii.13.3–6, 321
    xiii.1.1, 321
    xv.4.11, 395
    xxvi.2, 399
    xxvii.1, 402
    xxxii.2.1–2, 442
    xli.1.4, 404
    xli.5.1, 404
    xli.5.7, 436

Kalû, Rituals of the, 149–150
Ktesias of Knidos, FGH 688, 168, 171,
    181–182, 185–189, 202, 204,
    266, 297
  F. 1.2, F 5–7, 201
  F. 1.9.4–9, 202
  F. 13.33–14.35, 202
  F. 15.47, 278
  F. 15.47–50, 279
  F. 15.51, 279
Kurigalzu Epic, 50, 53

Lactantius, Divinae Institutiones, 327
  i.6, 349
Lambert's Text, 112, 121, 127, 137, 162
  col. IV, lines 57–61, 148
  Obverse, col. III, lines 2–9, 146

Livy
  xxv.12, 22
  xxxi.49.9–10, 442
  xxxii.8.9–16, 441
  xxxii.8.27, 441
  xxxiii.6.6, 442
  xxxiii.7.13, 442
  xxxiii.11.8–10, 442
  xxxiii.12.3–13, 442
  xxxiii.13.6–12, 442
  xxxiii.13.13, 442
  xxxiii.19.8, 437
  xxxiii.34.1–4, 441
  xxxiii.39.3–40.6, 441
  xxxv.13.4, 441
Ludlul bêl nêmeqi, 47–48
  Tablet III, 50–51, 47
  Tablet IV, 47

Manetho, 70, 275–276, 277, 286, 287
Marduk, Psalm to, 46, 60
Marduk, Speech of, 29–30, 37–41, 51,
  66
Marmor Parium, FGH 239 B, F 12,
  396
Megillat Taʿanit
  21, 314
  28 *Shᵉbaṭ*, 473
Megasthenes *apud* Abydenos, *FGH* 685
  F 6.4, 137
  F 6b, 138–139
Memphite Theology of Creation, 62–
  63
midrash, 272
Mishnah, ʿAbodah zarah 4:4, 472

Nab. 1, 122, 123, 124, 125, 126, 128, 129,
  131, 132, 134, 135, 137, 139,
  147, 148–149, 152, 165
  col. I
    line 2, 141
    line 3, 321
    line 7, 138
    lines 8–13, 146
    lines 18–22, 146
    lines 18–27, 148
    lines 21–22, 149
    lines 23–35, 146
    line 24, 150
    line 25, 262

    line 26, 147
    lines 28–30, 140
    line 29, 146, 258
    lines 50–52, 144
  col. I, line 38–col. II, line 25, 146
  col. I, line 50–col. II, line 25, 141
  col. II
    line 7, 138, 255
    lines 8–9, 149
    lines 11–21, 153
    lines 26–27, 146
    line 33, 146
    line 37, 153
    lines 39–42, 153
    line 41, 146
    lines 43–46, 147
    lines 60–61, 144
  col. III
    line 73, 250
    lines 8–10, 147
    line 11, 147
    lines 27–36, 148
    line 38, 147
    lines 43–45, 147
    line 50, 153
Nab. 1–15, 135
Nab. 1–26, 135–136, 137
Nab. 2, 121, 127, 128, 137, 146, 149–
  150
  col. II, line 27, 153
Nab. 3, 128, 135, 137, 140
Nab. 4*, 134, 135, 136, 137
  col. I, line 59, 321
  col. II
    lines 16–21, 141
    lines 28–74, 252
  col. III
    line 73, 249
    line 79, 153
Nab. 5, 134, 137
  col. I, line 29, 249
  col. II
    line 5, 249
    lines 9–11, 141
    lines 13–30, 153
Nab. 6, 121, 127, 128, 134, 135, 137, 149
  col. II
    line 47, 255
    line 50, 249
    lines 32–46, 153

Nab. 7, 121, 128, 137
  col. I
    line 11, 145
    lines 11–12, 252
  col. I, line 41–col. II, line 40, 252
  col. II
    lines 2–32, 144
    lines 46–49, 153
Nab. 8, 117, 120, 121, 122, 123, 124, 125,
        128, 135, 137, 143, 144, 145,
        151, 152, 165, 220
  col. I, 143
    lines 35–41, 152
  col. I–IX, 119
  col. II, 118, 119, 143, 257
  col. III, 143
  col. IV
    lines 14–33, 143
    line 24, 257
    lines 34–41, 143
  col. IV, line 37–col. V, line 10, 253
  col. IV, line 37–col. V, line 13, 138
  col. V
    lines 1–7, 139
    lines 1–34, 143
    lines 8–9, 255
    lines 14–16, 257
    lines 14–18, 260
    line 15, 257
  col. VI, 144
    lines 1–36, 257
    lines 12–29, 257
  col. VI, line 31-col. VII, line 4, 143
  col. VI–VII, 252
  col. VII, 144
    lines 1–38, 144
    line 49, 144
  col. VII, line 39–col. VIII, line 1, 144
  col. VIII–IX, 119, 255
  col. IX, lines 31–37, 139
  col. X, 119
    lines 1–31, 144
    lines 12–24, 141, 144
    lines 32–47, 145
  col. XI, 121
Nab. 9, 137
Nab. 10, 137
Nab. 11, 137
Nab. 12, 137
Nab. 13, 137

Nab. 14, 132, 137, 152
  line 1, 141
Nab. 15, 121, 137
Nab. 16, 136, 137
Nab. 17, 136, 137, 140
  col. I
    line 1, 249
    line 31, 255
    line1, 249
Nab. 18, 121, 128, 136, 137
  col. I
    lines 1–21, 144
    lines 1–34, 252
Nab. 19, 136, 137, 140
Nab. 20, 136, 137
Nab. 21, 136, 137, 153
  col. I, lines 13–19, 255
  col. II
    line 7, 249
    lines 17–19, 153
Nab. 22, 121, 136, 137
Nab. 23, 136, 137
Nab. 24, 136, 137, 141, 145, 152
  col. I
    lines 6–9, 145
    lines 7–8, 145
    lines 10–11, 261
    lines 10–16, 254
    lines 29–44, 145
  col. I, line 39–col. II, line 21, 139
  col. II
    line 5, 141
    lines 10, 14–15, 261
    lines 11–12, 141
    lines 45–48, 144
    lines 45–50, 138
  col. III, lines 5–7, 140
Nab. 25, 121, 122, 123, 124, 125, 127, 128,
        129, 130, 132, 133, 136, 137,
        151, 152, 165, 216
  col. I
    lines 1–2, 254
    lines 1–6, 27–30, 146
    lines 1–22, 143
    lines 5–6, 250
    lines 5–7, 254
    lines 7–9, 137, 139
    lines 7–11, 255
    lines 8–11, 253
    lines 10–12, 146

lines 10–22, 120
lines 11–14, 144
lines 12–14, 139
lines 14–20, 139
lines 14–21, 150
lines 14–22, 151
lines 14–25, 151
lines 22–27, 150
line 23, 150
lines 24–25, 139
line 26, 145
line 27–col. II, line 10, 151
lines 28–45, 140
line 42, 140, 261
line 43–col. II, line 2, 152
col. II
  line 5, 150
  line 12, 150
  lines 14–42, 133
col. II, line 11–col III, line 10, 151
col. II, line 11–col. III, line 6, 152
col. II, line 11–col. III, line 10, 151
col. II, lines 13–col. III, line 6, 140
col. III
  lines 1–3, 252
  lines 2–3, 150
  lines 21–31, 141
  lines 22–23, 261
Nab. 26, 136, 137
Nabonidus
  Chronicle (*see* Babylonian Chronicle 7)
  prayer of (*see* Qumran texts)
  steles 1–26 (*see* Nab. 1, etc.)
  Verse Account (*see* Verse Account of
    Nabonidus)
nasks, 332, 352. *see also Sugdar Nask*
Neferti, Prophecy of, 64–67, 71, 72
Nektanebos, Greek papyrus with dream of,
  285–286
Nikanor, 327, 349

"objective" chronicles (Babylonian
  Chronicles), 32–33, 52–53
Odyssey, xxiv.71–73, 201
Oracle of Hystaspes, 424–425, 441
Orosius, *Histories Against the Pagans,*
  iii.7, 276

P (Priestly Code), 25, 95, 269, 270, 271,
  273

Pahlavi texts, 333, 334, 345, 346, 347, 353.
  see also specific texts
Palestinian Talmud
  Berakhot 4:1, 258
  Berakhot 4:7a, 258
Papyrus Westcar, 70, 225, 260
Pausanias, 327, 328
  i.7.1, 399
  i.7.1–3, 399
  i.7.3, 399
  i.16.3, 395
  x.12.1–9, 349
Phlegon of Tralles, *FGH* 257, F 36, III, 22,
  26
Photius, *FGH* 688, 181–182, 188
  F 13.25, 198
  F 15.51, 55, 56, 279
  F 26–27, 198
Phylarchus *apud* Athenaeus, xiii.593c-d,
  402
Pithom Stele, 400, 435
Plato, *Phaedrus* 244B, 327
Pliny, *Natural History,* 283, 367
  vi.25.92, 357
  vi.122, 395
Plutarch, 190, 303, 308, 309, 310, 312, 365
  Alexander
    21, 351
    30, 351
    34.1, 316
    37.3, 317
    37.6, 317
    38, 317
    43, 351
    57.3, 316
    72.1–73.1, 320
    73.1, 321
    73.3–4, 322
    75.3–76.4, 323
    76.4, 323
  Artoxerxes
    1.2–3, 279
    1.4, 279
    5.2, 322
  Demetrius
    7, 395
    29.3–5, 397
    30–52, 397
    32, 396
  On Isis and Osiris, 362a, 322

Plutarch (*cont.*)
  Regum et imperatorum apophthegmata
      173c, 198, 202
Polyainos, 366
  iv.9.1, 395
  viii.50, 401, 402
Polybius, 407, 424, 447
  iii.2.8, 436
  iv.48, 434
  iv.48.8, 404
  iv.48.10, 434
  v.10.10, 398
  v.34–39, 435
  v.40.7–41.3, 434
  v.41.6–45.6, 434
  v.45.7–46.5, 434
  v.46.5–48.16, 434
  v.48.17, 434
  v.49.1–56.15, 435
  v.55.1–2, 435
  v.57, 435
  v.58.1–61.2, 435
  v.61.3–66.9, 435
  v.68–71, 435
  v.79, 435
  v.79–80, 435
  v.82–83, 435
  v.82–87, 435
  v.86.10, 437
  v.87.2, 436
  v.107.1–3, 435
  v.107.4, 436
  vii.15–18, 436
  viii.15–21, 436
  viii.23, 436
  x.27, 436
  x.27–31, 436
  x.28–31, 436
  x.49, 436
  xi.34, 436
  xiii.9, 436
  xv.20, 436
  xv.25, 437
  xvi.18, 437
  xviii.21.5–22.7, 442
  xviii.34.1–2, 442
  xviii.36.5–37.12, 442
  xviii.38.3–9, 442
  xviii.39.1–2, 442
  xviii.47.1–4, 441

  xviii.49–52, 441
  xviii.51.10, 441
  xxi.42, 442
  xxi.45, 442
  xxvi.1.4, 254
  xxix.15, 442
"Prayer of Ashurbanipal to the Sun-God,"
      line 4, 252
"Prayer of Lamentation to Ishtar," lines
      100–106, 252
"Prayer to Every God"
  ANET, 391–392, 252
  line 63, 252
"Prayer to the Gods of the Night," lines
      21–24, 252
"Prayer to the Moon-God," lines 11, 13, 26,
      252
Priestly Code (P), 25, 95, 269, 270, 271,
      273
Prophecy of Neferti, 64–67, 71, 72
Prophetic Zand, 335–342, 345, 348, 352,
      353, 354–355, 372, 376, 389,
      390, 392, 411, 424, 429, 442,
      479–482
  "Core Version," 339
  full text, 479–482
  1, 479
  1.1, 335
  1[1.1–5], 355
  1.3[1.1], 353
  1.6[1.3], 353
  1.11[1.5], 337, 339, 342
  3[2.1–22], 340
  3:20, 483
  3:22–23, 483
  3:24–63, 483
  3.26[2.19], 354
  3.29[2.22], 356
  4, 480–481
  4.2[2.24], 338
  4.3–7[2.24–26], 339
  4.3–64[2.24–53], 338
  4.3[2.24], 338
  4:7–13 (2:26–30), 483
  4.7[2.26], 338
  4:8–10, 483
  4.9–10[2.28], 338
  4:10, 483
  4:10–12, 483
  4.10[2.28], 339

4.16[2.31], 338
4:21–41 (2:33–41), 483
4:56–63 (2:48–52), 483
4:64–68, 5:1–11 (2:53–64), 483
4.66[2.54], 355, 356
6, 481
6.2[3.1], 354
6:3–13 (3:3–11), 483
7, 482
7.2–3[3.13–14], 342
7.2[3.13], 339, 355
7.2[3.15], 339
7:3 (3:14), 483
7:7 (3:17), 483
7.7–17[3.17–14], 339
7.7–17[3.17–24], 342
7:9 (3:19), 484
7.11[3.21], 355
7.13[3.22], 339
7.19–9.9[3.25–43], 339
Psalm to Adad, 60
Psalms to Enlil, 60
Psalm to Marduk, 46, 60
Pseudo-Kallisthenes, *Vita Alexandri regis Macedonum,* 346
    i.34, 314
    (Recension ε) 20.2–5, 314
Pseudo-Sa'adya Gaon, Commentary to
    Daniel, 7:5, 262

Qohelet rabbah, 11:2, 262
Qumran texts, 415
    4Q Prayer of Nabonidus (4QPrNab),
        112, 137, 147, 205–206, 216,
        222, 233, 234, 235, 246, 247
    lines 2–3, 216
    4QpNahum
        Hodayot 2:15, 471
        Hodayot 2:32, 471
    Covenant of Damascus/Cambridge
        Document (CD), 416, 438
        1:1–11, 438
        1:18, 471
    pᵉshārīm, 17

Rituals of the *Kalû,* 149–150

Seder 'olam rabbah
    23, 99
    29–30, 357

Seleucid royal correspondence, 383, 384
    18, 401, 402
Shahnamah (Abu al-Qasim Firdausi),
    346
Shulgi, Speech of, 38–41, 50
Sibylline Oracles, 326–331, 341–345
    iii, 349
    iii.350–80, 327
    iii.381–87 *(Sibylline C),* 327, 328, 382,
        383
    iii.382, 396
    iii.383, 383
    iii.386–87, 328
    iii.388, 328, 350
    iii.388–92, 328
    iii.388–95 *(Sibylline A),* 327, 328–331,
        344, 348, 382
    iii.388–97, 327
    iii.389, 350
    iii.390–1, 330
    iii.390–91, 330
    iii.390–92, 351
    iii.393–95, 329, 330
    iii.394–95, 330
    iii.396–400, 329, 350
    iii.809–29, 327
    iv, 74, 342
    iv.49–87, 356
    iv.49–101 *(Sibylline B),* 342–345, 348,
        356, 357
    iv.51–53, 356
    iv.54, 245
    iv.86–87, 344
    iv.88–101, 356
    iv.89–101, 344
    iv.95, 344
    iv.96, 344
    xi.195–223, 351
    xi.216–18, 351
Solinus, *Collectanea rerum memorabilium*
    35.4, 283
Spartoli tablets, British Museum, 41–42,
    50, 53–54, 58, 59
    158, 53–54
    II, 962, 53–54
    II, 987, 41, 42, 50, 58
    III, 2, 41, 42, 50, 58, 59
Speech of Marduk, 29–30, 37–41, 51,
    66
Speech of Shulgi, 38–41, 50

Stephanus of Byzantium, *Ethnika,* s.v.
    Alexandreia, 357
Strabo, 189, 190
    FGH 124 F 14a, 351
    xi.9.2–3, 404
    xi.13.1, 404
    xiv.1.34 (C.645), 351
    xv.3.24, 404
    xvii.1.43 (C.814), 351
Sudgar Nask, 332–342, 344, 352, 389, 411,
    479
Suetonius, *Julius* 59, 322
Sumerian King List
    ANET
        265–66, 21
        266, 50
Sumerian lamentations
    ANET
        455–63, 21, 50
        611–19, 21, 50
Syncellus, *Chronographia,* 276, 286
Synchronistic History (Chronicle 21,
    Babylonian Chronicles), 30, 50,
    51, 52

Tacitus, 308
    Histories iv.83–84, 322
Talmud
    Babylonian (*see* Babylonian Talmud)
    Palestinian (*see* Palestinian Talmud)
Jubilees Tana Ethiopic ms 9, 440
Targums, 1 Samuel 20:19, 262
Tatian, *Against the Greeks,* 36.2, 398
Testament of Moses, 455–456, 458
    1, 455
    2–4, 455
    4:8, 455
    5:2–6, 455
    5:5, 401
    6, 455
    7, 455
    9:6–7, 470
    9:6–10:10, 456
    10:9, 471
Text A, 40–41, 56–57
    col. II
        lines 2–8, 56
        lines 2–9, 57
        lines 9–14, 56
        lines 10–20, 57

lines 14–18, 57
line 19, 57
lines 20–23, 57
col. III, lines 9–11, 57
Theodicy, 48–49
Torah, 269, 271, 272, 273, 282, 283, 320,
    422, 449, 450, 451, 457
Tosefta, 207
    'Abodah zarah 6(7):4, 247

University of Pennsylvania Cuneiform Text
    no. 1, lines 6–7, 197
Uruk Prophecy, 41, 56, 57, 97, 111

*Vahman Yasht/Bahman Yasht/Vohûman
    Yasht (Prophetic Zand),*
    334–335, 353, 355, 484. *see also
    Prophetic Zand*
Varro, *antiquitates rerum humanarum et
    divinarum,* 327
VAT 17020, British Museum, 58
Vendidad, Fargard 2, secs. 20-end, 350
Verse Account of Nabonidus, 52, 112, 115,
    125, 126, 127, 130, 131,
    133–134, 136, 142, 147,
    148–149, 162, 220, 225
    col. I
        lines 1–16, 148
        line 2, 148
        line 11, 148
        line 17, 142
        lines 17–18, 151
        lines 17–29, 148
        line 21, 148
        lines 22–26, 139
        line 23, 148
        line 117, 125
        col. I line 1-col. II line 15, 127
        col. I lines 10–11, 140
        col. I line 17-col. II, line 17, 143
        col. I line 19-col. II, line 16, 148
    col. II
        lines 2–3, 148
        lines 4–7, 149
        line 7, 148
        lines 10–11, 142, 148, 151
        lines 13–15, 149
        lines 16–17, 149
        line 18, 257
        lines 22–29, 150

col. III, lines 3–4, 148
col. IV, 147, 148
   line 5, 246
col. V
   lines 4–7, 141, 153
   lines 9–14, 144
   line 11, 148
   lines 14–22, 261
   lines 16–22, 143
col. VI, 142
   lines 12–15, 142
Vohûman Yasht/Vahman Yasht/Bahman
      Yasht. see also Prophetic Zand
      (Prophetic Zand), 334–335, 353, 355,
      484

Weidner Chronicle (Babylonian
      Chronicles), 31–32, 52
Westcar (Papyrus), 70, 225, 260

Xenophon, 112, 152, 221, 230, 297
  Anabasis
    i.7.15, 162
    ii.4.12, 162
  Constitution of the Lacedaemonians
    13.2, 351
  Cyropaedia
    i.3.3, 313
    i.4.16–24, 257
    i.4.16–iv.1.8, 257
    i.6.2–vii.5.30, 257
    iv.3.1–23, 313
    iv.6.1–10, 257
    iv.6.3–5, 257
    v.2.28, 4.1, 257

v.3.8–19, 257
vii.4.6–vii.5.34, 220
vii.4.16, 152
vii.5.1–34, 257
vii.5.24, 257
vii.5.29–30, 261
vii.8, 313
vii.8.8–16, 313
viii.3.12–13, 351
Hellenica
    vi.1.12, 313
    vii.1.38, 313
Xerxes' reign, Babylonian documents
    from, 180, 195–196, 197–198
Berlin Nr. 615, 197
"Daiva Inscription" (XPh), 183–186,
    199
    ANET 316–17, 199
    ANET 317, 199, 321
Graziani no. 40, 197
Graziani no. 41, 197
Graziani no. 67, 197
Graziani no. 69, 197
Graziani no. 72, 197
Lord Amherst of Hackney, tablet once
    owned by, 196
Tablet BM 35526, 180, 198
University of Pennsylvania Cuneiform
    Text no. 1, lines 6–7, 197

zand, 332, 335, 341, 345, 352. *see also*
    Prophetic Zand
Zand i Vohuman Yasn or *Zand-î Vahman*
    Yasht (Prophetic Zand), 335,
    353. *see also Prophetic Zand*

INDEX OF SUBJECTS

Aaron, 281
Abednego/Azariah/Abed-Nabû, 207, 211, 215, 227, 229, 232–233
Abomination from Desolation/Abomination from the Sky, 455, 461, 462, 464, 465, 466, 470
Abraham, 14, 19, 277, 417
Abu al-Qasim Firdausi, 346
Abulites, 297
Achaemenids, 74, 358, 392
Achaios
    feared by Antiochus III following battle of Raphia, 410
    initial loyalty to Antiochus III, 405–406
    king, taking title of, 406–407
    overthrow by Antiochus III, 410–411
    revolt against Antiochus III, 406–407
acrostics, 48
Adad-apla-iddina, 44, 49
Adad-guppî, 113, 114, 120, 131, 137, 138, 141, 215
Adad-nirâri III, 115, 169
Adad, psalm to, 60
Adad-shuma-uṣur Epic, 53
Adad-shuma-uṣur (Kassite king), 34, 39, 40, 53
Adam and Eve, 417
Adasa, 475

adversity, explanations for
    divine intervention, see divine intervention, stories of
    failure of predictions regarding, reaction to, 476–477
    need for, 5
    prophetic texts regarding, see prophetic texts
Aêsham (Wrath), seed of, 337, 338, 339, 340, 354, 479–482
Aetolian League, 425–426
Afghanistan, 411
Agathokles, 408, 412
Age of Punishment, calculation of, 463–464, 477
Agis III, 298, 317
Agum II Kakrime, 50
Ahasuerus identified with Xerxes, 177
Ahaz of Judah, 22, 76–77, 81, 84
Ahriman, 68–70, 348, 352, 355–356, 368, 390
ahura, 186
Ahuramazda, 68–70, 74, 157, 163, 183–187, 201, 266, 298, 318, 331, 332, 334, 335, 337, 338, 339, 341, 344, 345, 348, 352, 479–482
Akîtu (New Year rituals of Marduk), 44, 100, 114–115, 127–128, 131, 142, 148, 149, 197, 298, 311, 317, 323

Akkad as name for Babylonia, 27, 32
Akkadian language, 46, 246
Akkadian oracles, 41, 58
"the Akra" (Antiochene city at Jerusalem), 450, 451, 465
Alcimus the High Priest, 467, 474, 475, 476
Alexander Balas, 386, 387
Alexander III the Great, 112, 182, 190, 202, 214, 264, 265, 266, 276, 288–358, 430, 451, 470
   "Animal vision," 1 Enoch, 417, 419
   Antiochus III, campaigns of, 411
   Asia Minor, conquest of, 290–293
   atrocities committed by, 359–361
   Babylon, warning not to enter city of, 302–305, 308, 320
   Babylonians
      Indus Valley campaign, events following, 301–313
      Iran, conquest of, 297–301
      Marduk, followers of, 295, 296, 297, 298, 302–313, 348
      Mesopotamia, conquest of, 293–297, 357
      omens, dreams, and astrological signs, 302–313
      responses to conquest, 324, 329, 331, 347–348
   birth stories, Persian and Egyptian, 346–347
   burning of Persepolis, 298, 317, 325
   commoner on the throne tradition, 307–312, 322
   conquered peoples' responses to, 325–348
   death of, 302, 313
   demon (dîv) with disheveled hair, as, 337–340, 353
   diadem landing on royal tomb mound, 305–307
   Diadochoi, see Diadochoi
   Egypt
      birth story, Egyptian, 346–347
      conquest of, 290–293
      response to conquest, 324
      Sarapis story, 308–312
   fire or lights carried in front of, 330, 350
   god, viewed as, 324, 337

Hephaistion, death of, 302, 306
Indus Valley campaign, following events, and death of Alexander, 301–313
Iran, conquest of, 297–301
Jews/Israelites and
   attitude of Alexander towards, 417, 421
   legends about Alexander, 291
   Palestine, conquest of, 290–293
   responses to conquest, 324, 325, 329, 331, 347–348, 356, 417, 419, 421
Macedonian officers, mutiny of, 301–302
map of empire, 488–489
Media and Medes, 298, 300, 302
Mesopotamia, conquest of, 293–297
military prowess of, 289–290, 313, 359–360
omens, dreams, and astrological signs, 302–313
Palestine, conquest of, 290–293
Persians
   Alexander's personal attitude towards, 326
   birth story, Persian, 346–347
   both hostile and favorable responses of, 326
   demon (dîv) with disheveled hair, Alexander as, 337–340, 353
   Indus Valley campaign, events following, 301–313
   Iran, conquest of, 297–301
   Mesopotamia, conquest of, 293–297
   responses to conquest, 325–348
   Sibylline prophecies, use of, 327–331, 341–345, 351
   Zoroastrians, 297, 331–347
religious problems faced by peoples conquered by, 313, 324–325
Sarapis and, 308–312
Seleucids' claim to be heirs of, 427–428
Sibylline oracles and, 326–331, 341–345
substitute king tradition, 307–312, 322, 323
successor dynasties, see Diadochoi
Syria, conquest of, 290–293
Zoroastrians, responses of, 297, 331–347
Alexander IV, 331, 348, 352, 360, 363, 368, 369, 375, 397, 428, 430, 451, 470

Alexander Romance, 345–347, see also index of ancient sources
Alexandros, brother of Molon and satrap of Persis, 406–407
Allah-ed-din Muḥammad, 225
Ameny (Amenemhet I), 66–67
Ammanitis, 446
Ammon, Oasis of, 168, 292
Ammonites, 268, 269, 270, 281, 417, 431
Amon (Egyptian god), 63, 65, 66, 67, 292, 312
Amon (successor of Mannasseh), 80
Amon Reʿ, 65, 72
Amorites, 270, 281
Amurru, 155
Amytis, 181
Anahiti (Anahita), 266, 279, 351, 411
Anaxarchus, 303
Andragoras, 385, 391
Andria, 265
Andromachos, 293
Andronikos, 446
Angra Mainyu, 68–70, see also Ahriman
"Animal Vision," in 1 Enoch, 378, 416–423, 458–459, 476
Anshar, 79, see also Ashur
Antigonids, 356, 374
Antigonus the One-Eyed, 361, 362–371, 373–375, 394, 395, 398, 428, 430, 470
Antioch, 385, 390, 408, 445, 446, 460
Antiochene community at Jerusalem, 445–450
Antiochene heterodox Jews settled at Jerusalem, 450, 455, 457
Antiochene republic, Antiochus IV's founding of, 445
Antiochus I, 57, 303, 321, 378–383, 384, 390, 395, 397, 428
Antiochus II, 382, 383–386, 391, 401, 402, 413, 428
Antiochus Hierax (son of Antiochus II), 384, 391
Antiochus III, 393, 405–427, 430, 459, 470
   Achaios and, see Achaios
   consolidation of rule following accession, 405–408
   death of, 427
   defeat of, 426–427
   Egypt, treaty with, 423–424

epithet "The Great," 411
European invasions of, 423–427
Fifth Syrian War against Ptolemy V, 411–412
final years of, 423–427
Fourth Syrian War against Ptolemy IV, 408–410
Indian campaigns of, 411
Jews' alignment with, 405, 409, 412–423
Zoroastrians, 411
Antiochus IV Epiphanes, 200, 254, 390, 392, 423, 428, 443, 444–461, 470
   civic policy of, 444–445
   death
      actual, 461
      false rumor of, 447, 448
      psychosomatic disease, possible death from, 461, 471
   Egypt and, 447, 449–450
   Elymais, attempt to plunder temple of Nanaia at, 461
   Jews and
      civic policy of Antiochus, effect of, 445
      high priesthood, machinations regarding, 445–449
      Jerusalem, sack of and suppression of revolt at, 447–450, 452, 453
      Judas Maccabaeus, career of, 458–467
      Mattathias, rebellion of, 456–458, 471
      religious impositions of, 390, 450–461
   republic, founding of Antiochene, 445
   Roman Empire and, see Romans/Roman Empire
Antiochus son of Seleucus IV, 434
Antiochus V, 400, 420, 458–462, 465–467, 474
Antiochus VI, 387
Antiochus VII, 386
Antiochus VIII, 387
Antiochus IX, 387
Antipater, 317, 362, 363, 368
Antipatris, 291
Anu, 33, 35, 210, 242
Anunîtum, 118, 119, 124, 153
Apame (daughter of Antiochus I), 379
Apame (wife of Seleucus I), 367–368, 376, 383
Apameia, Peace of, 427

Apaturios, 404
Apelles, painting of Alexander the Great by, 351
"apocalypse" as term, rejection of, 15
"Apocalypse of Weeks," 1 Enoch, 378, 422, 476
Apollonius the Mysarch, 450, 451, 452, 453, 454, 459
apparent injustices of deity, meditations on
    Babylonians, 47–49
    Egyptians, 63–64
    Jews/Israelites, 18–19
Appian, *See* index of ancient sources
Apsu, 223
Arabia
    Alexander Romance, Arab works drawing on, 346–347, 358
    headgear of Arabs, 338
    Muslim Arabs, 332, 338
    Nabonidus' campaigns in, 114, 123, 124, 126–132, 139, 145, 151, 152, 156, see also Têmâ, Nabonidus at
    pre-Islamic Arabs, 338, 417
Arachosia, 299
Arakha, 170
Aramaic language, 69, 95, 176, 204, 205, 206, 208–210, 216, 218, 219, 222, 229, 231, 232, 233, 241, 243, 245–246, 247, 378, 388, 392, 403, 428, 438, 449, 463, 469
Aramaic texts, terms for gods used in, 210, 254
Archelaos, 365
Archon, 363, 367
Ardashir (Artakhshir), 335, 336, 340, 353, 354, 479
Areia, 299–300, 374
Argeads, 374, 375
Ariarathes III, 391
Aristobulos, 302, 303, 305, 306, 307, 317
the ark, sibyl taking passage on, 327, 328, 331
Arkesilas, 225
Armenia, 411
Arrhidaios (Philip III), 360, 362, 363, 428, 430, 451, 470
Arrian, *See* index of ancient sources
Arsakes/Arsikas/Arsakas, 266, 279
Arsakids, 340, 391, 404
Arses, 266, 294, 315

Arsinoë, 409
Arsites, 265
Artabazanes, 407
Artakhshir (Ardashir)/Artakhshir the Kae, 335, 336, 340, 353, 354, 479
Artaxerxes I, 177, 188, 190, 200, 240, 243, 265, 267, 269, 278, 279, 280, 392
Artaxerxes II, 181, 266, 274, 278, 279, 285, 421
Artaxerxes III Ochos, 266, 274–278, 283, 284, 285, 286, 290, 292, 347, 414
Artaxerxes IV Bessos, 299–300, 318, 319, 330, 358
Artemis identified with Anahiti (Anahita), 351
'Asa'el, 377–378, 399
Asherra, 79
Ashpenaz, 207
Ashur, 32, 37, 38, 79, 80, 100, 104
Ashurbanipal, 46, 60, 138, 179
Asia Minor, *see also* specific areas
    Alexander the Great's conquest of, 290–293
    Antiochus III and, 406, 411, 423, 424
    Galatians, invasion by, 380
    Lysimachos, taken by, 371
    map of, 490
    Seleucid rule of, 378, 390, 391
Asidaioi, 474
Assumption (Testament) of Moses, 455–456, *see also* index of ancient sources
Assyria and Assyrian empire, 5, 39, 65, 74, 100, 104, 242, 294, 342, 343, 344, *see also* individual kings
    Abydenos on Nebuchadnezzar II, 203–204
    Babylonian attitude towards, 117, 120, 127, 133, 152, 169–179
    creation epics, 79, 100
    Egypt, conquest of, 79
    fall of Judah and, 76–83
    first great empire, viewed as, 187–188
    Isaiah's prophecy of fall of, 76, 83–91
    Jerusalem's preservation from, 77–79
    lions in "Animal vision," of 1 Enoch representing, 417, 419
astrological signs, *see* omens, dreams, and astrological signs
Astyages, 115, 123, 240, 258, 262, 344

Athena, 4
Athens, 4, 101, 289
Atropates, 302, 391–392, 404, 407
Atropatids, 392
Attalid dynasty and kingdom, 383, 391, 491
Attalos I, 391, 411, 423–424, 425
Atum Reʿ, 63
Aturpad son of Maraspend, 332, 333
Aûṣîtar (Hushedar), 339, 340, 342, 348, 355
authoritative utterances as to cosmic might of deity
  Babylonians, 31
  Egyptians, 62–63
  Jews/Israelites, 6
  need for, 5
the Avesta, *see* index of ancient sources
Awêl-Marduk (Evil-Merodach), 21, 57, 92, 96, 97, 118, 138, 156, 213, 220, 224, 225, 226, 239, 260
Azariah/Abednego/Abed-Nabû, 207, 211, 215, 227, 229, 232–233
Azerbaijan, 302

Baal, 79
Babylon (city of), 122, 124, 159–160, 170, 242, 266, 296, 297, 302–305, 308, 320, 362, 365, 367, 372, 378, 379, 381
Babylonians, 6, 27–30, 49, *see also* individual kings
  Alexander the Great and, see Alexander III the Great
  Antiochus III
    fall of, 427–434
    viewed as king of Babylon, 413
  apparent injustices of deity, meditations on, 47–49
  Assyria, attitude towards, 117, 120, 127, 133, 152, 169–179
  authoritative utterances as to cosmic might of deity, 31
  Chronicles, see index of ancient sources
  chronological system of, 113
  connected histories, 31–33
  creation epic and Marduk's supremacy, 31, 50, 51, 62, 72, 79, 95, 102, 110, 223–224, see also index of ancient sources

Cyrus/Cambyses to Artaxerxes I, 167–190
Daniel 1-7 as Jewish retelling of Babylonian story, see Daniel 1-7 as retelling of Babylonian story
Darius, rebellions under, 169–171, 173
Deutero-Isaiah, responses to, 203–205
Diadochoi, under, see Diadochoi
divine intervention, stories of, 33–37
evil, Babylon as Jewish symbol for, 238
exile of Jews in Babylonia, see exile of Jews in Babylonia
failure of predictions, reaction to, 477
fall of
  Deutero-Isaiah's prediction of, 154–162, 175
  First Isaiah's prediction of, 83–91
  Nabonidus and, 115–116, 133, 135
  historical epics, 33–36, 205
  Judah, conquest of, 75–83
  Ludlul bêl nêmeqi, 47–48
  Marduk, followers of, see Marduk
  Mixture Version of Daniel, 375, 378, 383, 385–393, 403, 424
  moralizing first-person narratives, 33, 36–37, 205, 233
  Nabonidus, reign and fall of, see Nabonidus
  omens, dreams, and astrological signs, belief in, 118, 161, 228
  Persian period, during, 264–267
  prayers to deity, 46–47
  prophetic texts, 37–46
  Sakaia and Festival of the Sakai, 309
  sibyls, Babylonian, 327–331
  Sodom, prediction that Babylon would be destroyed like, 164
  theodicy, Babylonian, 48–49
  tigers in "Animal vision," of 1 Enoch representing, 417, 419
  titles used by kings of, 179–180, 183, 196
  Xerxes and, 178–190
Bacchides, 474–477
baga, 186
Bagapaios, 265
Bagoas, 276, 290, 347
Bagophanes, 296
Bagorazos, 265

Bahman (Vohu Manah), 334
Bahram Gor (Vaharam I Gur), 340
Baktra, 266, 344–345, 357
Baktria, 299, 300, 301, 356, 361, 367, 368, 374, 391
Bardiya, 68, 69, 168–169, 171, 240
Barsaentes, 318
Baryaxes, 302
Bashan, 104
bear beast (Daniel 7), 239–240
Behistun Inscription, 69, 74, *see also* index of ancient sources
Bêl
    Ahuramazda identified with, 266
    Antiochus III's robbing of temple of, 427
    Cyrus, images paraded to honor, 160
    kidinnu, 242
    Marduk, as name for, 32, 35, 54, 188, 216, 278, 296, 427
    Sarapis and Alexander the Great, 312
    tomb of Belitanas (Bêl), 181, 188–189, 198, 303
    Xerxes' destruction of temple of, 182, 188–190
Bêl-shar-uṣur (Belshazzar), 114–115, 116, 126, 131, 133, 134, 135, 139, 140, 141, 149, 158
    Daniel 1–7 and, 206, 207, 217–222, 223, 226, 230, 231, 232, 234, 238, 262
Bêl-shimânni, 178, 179, 182, 185, 186, 196, 236, 240, 243
Belephantes, 303
Belitanas (Bêl), tomb of, 181, 188–189, 198, 303
Belteshazzar (Bêl-balâṭsu-uṣur), Daniel known as, 206, 207–209, 216, 222, 227, 228, 229, 230, 232, 234–238, 241, 243, 247, 248, 334, 336, 337, 376, 433
Beltia, 242
Berenice, 383, 384, 386, 402, 413
Bessos (Artaxerxes IV), 299–300, 318, 319, 330, 358
Beth-Horon, 475
Beth-zaith, 475
Beth-Zechariah, 465
Beth-Zur, 459, 460, 465
Bilgah, priestly clan of
    Onias-Menelaus, 401
    Simon, 432, 434, 446

Bithynia, 391
Borsippa, 35, 36, 122, 178, 179, 196, 197, 242, 303, 378
"Bountiful Immortals," 334–335
Bozrah, 156
brass
    bronze, identified with, 341
    metals sequence, in, 340–341
bronze in metals sequence, significance of, *see* metals, sequence of
Bunene, 149–150

Cambyses, 68, 167–169, 172, 173, 204, 222, 226, 263, 289, 344, 414, 427
Canaanites, 88, 101, 268, 269, 270, 271
Cannae, Roman defeat at, 425
Cappadocia and Cappadocians, 152, 362, 391, 404
Carthage and Carthaginians, 100, 276, 425
cavalry, Persian, 289
cedars of Lebanon, 87, 104
Celtic Galatians, 380
Chaldaeans
    Babylon known as "proud splendor" of, 84, 107, 165
    ethnic group/Nabopolassar and dynasty, 86, 169, 170, 205, 327, 328
    priests of Marduk, 203, 204, 229, 245, 296, 297, 302–313, 322
Chandragupta, 368
Chorienes, 301
Chosroes son of Kavad, 336
Christianity, 65, 75, 274, 326, 327, 331, 451, 477
Chronicle P, 32, 52, 53, *see also* index of ancient sources
chronological systems
    "Animal Vision," 1 Enoch, 421–422
    Babylonians, 113
    Daniel 1, chronological problems with, 210–212
    Daniel 7, Four-Beast-Eleven-Horn Version of, 453–454
    Daniel 8 and 9, 462–465
    date-formulas, titles used by kings of Babylonia in, 179–180, 183, 196
    Persians under Darius, 172
    Seleucus I, under, 379
Cilicia, 446

clay/earthenware, significance of, 212–215, 334, 370, 375, 413

Cleopatra daughter of Antiochus III, 424

Cleopatra I, 386, 387

Cleopatra II, 447, 470

Cleopatra Thea, 386, 387, 403

"Coele-Syria ("Koilê Syria"), 369, 423, 437, 474

coinage/money
Diadochoi period, 364, 392, 402–403, 404
handwriting on wall in Daniel as, 219–220

commoner on the throne tradition and Alexander the Great, 307–312, 322

communication between gods and man, belief in, 4

Coniah (Jehoiachin/Jechoniah), 21, 24, 81, 82, 96, 194, 239

connected histories
Babylonians, 31–33
Egyptians, 63
Jews/Israelites, 7–8

copper in metals sequence, significance of, 340–341

Corinth, King Kypselos of, 225

corpses, preservation of, 188, 201

creation epics
Assyrian, 79, 100
the Avesta, 68
Babylonian creation epic and Marduk's supremacy, 31, 50, 51, 62, 72, 79, 95, 102, 110, 223–224, see also index of ancient sources
Egyptian, 62–63, 72
Jewish/Israelite, 62, 95, 110, 223

Curtius, *See* index of ancient sources

Cuthaean Legend of Narâm-Sin, 36–37

Cuthah, 366

Cyaxares, 80, 240

Cyrenaica, 379

Cyrene, King Arkesilas of, 225

Cyrus Cylinder, *see* index of ancient sources

Cyrus of Persia, 3, 10, 22, 25, 67, 68, 73, 74, 103, 173, 177, 194, 267, 294, 315, 351, 427, 440, 463, 464
age at defeat of Astyages, 258

Daniel 1–7 and, 203, 204, 220–222, 225, 226, 229, 234–238, 243, 244, 258, 260, 262, 263
Deutero-Isaiah and, 154–162
Euphrates diverted by, 220–221
"the First Things," Cyrus' victory over the Babylonians referred to as, 157
Marduk, viewed as vindicator of, 140, 154, 157, 159, 161, 187
Medes, overthrow of, 123–125, 131, 140, 188, 344
military abilities of, 289, 313
Nabonidus, overthrow of, 112, 115, 116, 123, 124, 133, 135, 142, 146, 149, 152, 220–221, 337, 372, 376
reign of, 167–169
titles used by, 179, 196

Cyrus son of Darius II, 266, 279

dactylic hexameter, *Sibylline Oracles* written in, 326

Dadanu, 129

daiva-worship, Xerxes' suppression of, 183–190, 223, 235–237, 240

Damascus, 266

Damaspia, 265, 278

Daniel, *see also* index of Biblical passages
8–9 and end of religious persecutions of Antiochus IV, 462–465, 476
11, 415–416, 419, 422–423, 476
12, 466, 476
Belteshazzar (Bêl-balâṭsu-uṣur), Daniel known as, 206, 207–209, 216, 222, 227, 228, 229, 230, 232, 234–238, 241, 243, 247, 248, 334, 336, 337, 376, 433
falsity of predictions in, 476

Daniel 1–7 as Jewish retelling of Babylonian story, 203–244, *see also* index of Biblical passages
acceptance by Jews of stories in Daniel, 237
Babylonian/Jewish versions of names, 207–209, 227, 232–233
beasts, vision of, 223–224, 237–244
daiva-worship, Xerxes' suppression of, 223, 235–237, 240
Deutero-Isaiah, Babylonian responses to, 203–205

dream of Nebuchadnezzar, 212–215,
224–227
fiery furnace, three men in, 215, 232–
233
"Five-King Version" interpretation of
dream of Nebuchadnezzar,
224–229, 230, 232, 237, 238, 324,
332, 334, 336, 355, 372, 375, 376
Four-Beast-Ten-Horn Version of Daniel
7, 427–434, 451, 452
Four-Beast-Eleven-Horn Version of
Daniel 7, 451–454
Four-Plus-Kingdom version of Daniel 2,
371–378, 386, 387, 389
gods, epithets for, 209–210, 216, 242
lion's den, Daniel in, 222–223, 235–
237
madness/disease of Nebuchadnezzar,
206, 215–217, 233–235
Mixture Version of Daniel 2, 375, 378,
383, 385–393, 403, 411, 413, 424,
429, 430, 432
money, handwriting on wall in Daniel as,
219–220
Nabonidus, Nebuchadnezzar substituted
for, 205–207, 210–212, 217, 218,
221–222, 228–232, 233–235,
238–241, 244
poetic nature of, 205, 246
prayer and worship, 217, 222–223,
235–237, 240, 252
strange features of Daniel, 205–210
temple vessels and handwriting on wall,
217–222, 229–232, 236, 250–251
"Three-Beast Version" of vision of
beasts, 237–244, 264, 324, 372,
373, 428
tree symbolism in Nebuchadnezzar's
dream, 216, 234
Daphne by Antioch, 446
Dara/Darab, 346–347
Darius I, 11, 68–70, 74, 168, 169–178, 181,
184, 190, 192, 264, 265, 267, 289,
318, 319, 342, 344, 356, 370, 427,
428, 463
Apollo, piety towards, 351
Daniel 1-7 and, 209, 221, 222, 235, 236,
237, 240, 262, 263
map of empire, 486–487
Darius II Ochos, 266, 267, 278, 279

Darius III, 69, 265, 266, 290, 292,
293–295, 298–300, 305, 318, 319,
325, 330, 347, 351, 391, 392, 427,
442
Dataphernes, 300
daughter-religion state, parent religions
dwelling in, 75
David, 7, 18, 19, 21, 268
Day of Atonement, 271–273, 281–282,
435
deformation of Babylonian names by
Jewish writers, deliberate, 207–209,
247
Demetrias, port of, 426
Demetrius I, 467, 474, 475, 476
Demetrius II, 387, 477
Demetrius son of Antigonus, 363–371
demons (*dîvs*) with disheveled hair, foreign
rulers of Zoroastrians known as,
337–340, 353, 481, 482, 483
Demophon, 312
Demosthenes, 320
Dessau, 475
Deutero-Isaiah, 3, 11, 23, 95, 111,
154–162, 168, 173, 194, 203–205,
214, 225, 226, 231, 235, 267, 268,
464
Diadochoi, 359–393
"Animal vision," 1 Enoch, 417
Babylonians under, 359, 362–363
battle of Ipsos to death of Antiochus I,
378–383
death of Alexander to 301, 363–368
Mixture Marriage and War of Laodice,
383–392
Mixture Version of Daniel, 375, 378,
383, 385–393, 403
238–235 b.c.e., 392–393
Daniel, versions of, 371–378, 385–
393
"the divided empire," 370–371, 374,
388, 391
Egyptians under
battle of Ipsos to death of Antiochus I,
378, 379, 380
Diadochoi, invasion of Ptolemy I's
Egypt by, 370
Ptolemy I and Ptolemies, see Ptolemy
I, Ptolemies
Greeks under, 361

Diadochoi (*cont.*)
    battle of Ipsos, following, 371
    death of Alexander to 301, 368–
        370
    Ipsos, battle of, see Ipsos, battle of
    Iranians under
        battle of Ipsos to death of Seleucus I,
          378
        death of Alexander to 301, 363–368
        Four-Plus-Kingdom version of Daniel
          2, 376
        Seleucid rule, 390–391
        Zoroastrians and Mixture Version of
          Daniel, 389–393
    Jews under, 359, 362–363, 422
        battle of Ipsos to death of Seleucus I,
          378, 379
        death of Alexander to 301, 368–
          370
        Four-Plus-Kingdom version of Daniel
          2, 371–378, 386, 387, 389
        Mixture Version of Daniel, 378, 389,
          393, 403
        238–235 b.c.e., 392–393
    Laodice, War of, 383–392
    map of Hellenistic states, 490–491
    Marduk's followers and, 363, 367, 372,
        374, 378, 382, 385, 394
    Media under, 391–392
    Mixture Marriage, 383–392, 403, 424,
        438
    Mixture Version of Daniel, 375, 378,
        383, 385–393, 403
    money/coinage during period of, 364,
        392, 402–403, 404
    Persians under, see "Iranians under,"
        this heading
    Zoroastrians and Mixture Version of
        Daniel, 389–393
Dilbat, 178
Dinkard, Alexander the Great and,
    331–341, *see also* index of ancient
    sources
Diodorus, *See* index of ancient sources
Diodotos, 391, 404
Diogenes, 309
Dionysios the Messenian, 308, 310, 311
Dionysus (Abomination from
    Desolation/Abomination from the
    Sky), 455

disheveled hair, demons (*dîvs*) with,
    337–340, 353, 481, 482, 483
"the divided empire" under Diadochoi,
    370–371, 374, 388, 391
divine intervention, stories of
    Babylonians, 33–37
    Egyptians, 63
    Jews/Israelites, 6
dîvs, foreign rulers of Zoroastrians known
    as, 337–340, 353, 481, 482, 483
Djoser, 71
Dokimos, 363, 370
doorposts of temple, rituals involving,
    149–150
Dor, siege of, 408
Drangiana, 299
dreams, *see* omens, dreams, and
    astrological signs
dualism, 65, 347
Dûr-MAKH-ilâni, 59
Dura-Europos, 406

Ea, 33, 48, 72, 223
the Eadgege, 34
Early Kings, Chronicle of, 52
earthenware/clay, significance of, 212–215,
    334, 370, 375, 413
Ebabbar, 128, 134, 150
Edom and Edomites, 114, 140, 155, 156,
    269, 270, 281, 417, 419
Egishnugal, 134
Egyptians, 62–67
    Alexander the Great's conquest of, see
        Alexander III the Great
    Antiochus III and, 405–416, 423–424
    Antiochus IV Epiphanes, 447, 449–450
    apparent injustices of deity, meditations
        on, 63–64
    authoritative utterances as to cosmic
        might of deity, 62–63
    Cambyses' campaign against, 168
    connected histories, 63
    Darius I, rebellion against, 344
    Diadochoi, under, see Diadochoi
    divine intervention, stories of, 63
    Ezekiel's prediction of scattering in exile
        of, 432
    intermarriage with, Jewish fears over,
        268, 270, 281
    Macedonian Ptolemies, rule of, 70

national revolt against Ptolemies, 405, 410, 414, 432, 435

Nektanebos II, campaigns of Artaxerxes III against, 274–278, 284–286, 288

people of a nearly almighty god, as, 64–67

people of an almighty god, Middle Kingdom Egyptians as, 67

practices of, Jewish fears over involvement in, 269, 281

prayers to deity, 63

prophetic texts, 64

Ptolemies, see entries at Ptolemaic, Ptolemy

Sarapis and Alexander the Great, 308–312

sibyls, Egyptian, 327

Xerxes as king of, 183, 184

Ekbatana, 181, 265, 266, 295, 297, 298, 299, 302, 319, 411

Ekhulkhul, destruction and rebuilding of, 114, 115, 116, 117, 119, 120–126, 128–131, 133, 134, 141, 142, 144, 147, 148, 149

the Ekur, 34, 46, 56

Ekursagila, 37, 38

Elam and Elamites, 23, 28, 32, 34–35, 36, 37, 42, 158, 167, 294, 427

Elamite language, 158, 182

Elasa, 476

Elephantine (Egypt), 267

Eliakim, 81

Elisha, 6

Elymaïs, 427, 461

Emesal dialect of Sumerian, 46

Emeslam, 364

Enlil, 20, 29, 31, 33–38, 40, 47, 49, 50, 51, 54, 56, 60, 61, 242, 294

Enlil-nâdin-akhi, 57

Enlil-nâdin-apli, 57

Enlil-nâdin-shumi, 39, 56

Enlil-texts, 48, 49

Ennundagalla, 34, 54

1 Enoch, visions in, 377–378, 416–423, 458–459, 476

Enûma elish, 31, 51, 150

Ephesus, 331, 351, 402

Epicureans, 4

Epigenes, 406–407, 435

Era/Erra (Irra), 36, 43–46, 55

Erîba-Marduk, 44, 57

Erigyius, 300

Erra Epic, 43–46, 55

Erythrai, Greek prophetess of, 331

Esagila, 38, 42, 46, 48, 119, 120, 127, 187, 189, 190, 202, 230, 294, 303, 304, 321, 364, 382, 401

Esarhaddon, 79

Esharra, 34, 36

Etemenanki, 90, 187, 189–190, 199, 200, 202, 303, 305

Ethiopia (Sudan), 168

ethnos, Jews recognized by Antiochus III as, 423

Eulmash, 134, 135

Eumenes of Kardia, 362, 363, 368, 394

Eumenes of Pergamon, 383, 384

Euphrates diverted by Cyrus of Persia, 220–221

Eusebius, *See* index of ancient sources

Euthydemos, 404

evil, Babylon as Jewish symbol for, 238

Evil-Merodach (Awêl-Marduk), 21, 57, 92, 96, 97, 118, 138, 156, 213, 220, 224, 225, 226, 239, 260

exile of Jews in Babylonia, 10, 22, 75–76, 83, 92–97, 283, 415, 421

Daniel 1-7 and, 228–229, 260

return from exile, 155, 158, 160–161, 166, 173, 177, 463, 464

Ezida, 35, 46, 119, 127

Festival of Tabernacles, 461–462

Fifth Syrian War, 411–412

fire or lights carried in front of kings, 329–330, 350

First Isaiah, 76, 81 et seq., 106, 154 et seq., 267

First Macedonian War, 425

First Syrian War, 380

"the First Things," Cyrus' victory over the Babylonians referred to by Deutero-Isaiah as, 157

"Five-King Version" interpretation of dream of Nebuchadnezzar in Daniel, 224–229, 230, 232, 237, 238, 324, 332, 334, 336, 355, 372, 375, 376

Flamininus, 425–426

Four-Beast-Ten-Horn Version of Daniel 7, 427–434, 451, 452

Four-Beast-Eleven-Horn Version of Daniel 7, 451–454

"Four-Metal/Four-Branch Vision" prophecy of Zarathushtra, 334, 335, 336, 337, 339, 340, 341, 354–355, 389

Four-Plus-Kingdom version of Daniel 2, 371–378, 386, 387, 389

Fourth Syrian War, 408–410

frataraka of the gods, 392

Fravartish, 319

Gabriel (angel), 377, 399, 463

Gadatas, 221, 351

Galatia and Galatians, 380, 408

ganâk mînôê, 355

Gaugamela, battle of, 112, 289, 293, 295, 296, 325, 344

Gautama, 168, 172

Gaza, 291, 292, 363, 368, 412

Gedrosia, 301, 302

Gideon, 475

Gilgamesh Epic, see index of ancient sources

Glabrio, 426

Gobryas, 204, 221

gods, *see also* individual gods
  ancient beliefs regarding, 3–4
  epithets for, 209–210, 216, 242, 249
  kingship conferred by, 253

gold in metals sequence, significance of, *see* metals, sequence of

Gorgias, 459

Granikos River, 290

Greece/Greeks
  Alexander the Great and, 288–289, 307, 308, 310, 323, 324–325, 329, 330, 343, 344, 345, 355, 356, 357
  beliefs and gods of, 4, 20, 101
  Cyrus to Artaxerxes I, 183, 184, 186, 187, 189, 201
  Diadochoi, under, 361
    battle of Ipsos, following, 371
    death of Alexander to 301, 368–370
  Egyptian use of mercenaries from, 408
  lights/fire carried in front of rulers of, 330

navy of, 289

present-future prophecies of, 65, 72

substitute king ritual, no parallel for, 323

Greek language, 204, 392

Gubaru, 204

Gutium, 204, 245

Gyges, 225

gymnasium at Jerusalem, 457

Haldita, 170

Halikarnassos, 290

Haman, 177

Ḥammurapi, 27, 29, 32, 46, 49, 60

Hananiah/Shadrach/Sha-Marduk, 207–208, 211, 215, 227, 229, 232–233, 247–248

"Hand of the Holy People," Judas Maccabaeus and forces known as, 458

Hannibal, 425

µanukkah, 461–462

Haosravah, 336, 354

haplography, 463

Harran, 114, 116, 117, 119, 120, 121, 122, 124, 126, 130, 131, 138, 144, 145, 146, 147, 151

Hasmonean dynasty, 456, 460, 467, 474–477

Hatshepsut, 64

Hebrew language, 205, 206, 209–210, 216, 218, 229, 241, 247, 249, 250, 409, 415, 423, 436, 438, 463, 469

Hecataeus/Hekataios of Abdera, 283, 315, 320

Hecataeus of Miletus, 8

Heket, 70

Heliodorus, 430, 433

Hellenes, *see* Greece/Greeks

Hellenistic period, *see* Alexander III the Great, Diadochoi, Greece/Greeks

Hellespontine Phrygia, 374

Hephaistion, 302, 306

Herakles son of Alexander the Great, 331, 348

Herakles, Tyrian, 293, 318, 445

Hermeias, 406–407, 435

Herodotus, *See* index of ancient sources

Hezekiah, 21, 77–78, 79, 84, 100, 462

High Priesthood, *see also* priests
  (Jewish/Israelite)
  Antiochus IV, machinations under,
    445–449
  Seleucid right to appoint high priest,
    445, 467, 474
Hindus, 483
historical epics of Babylonians, 33–36, 205
history and historiography, 7
  connected histories, see connected
    histories
  Jews, survival and literary productivity
    of, 3
  Marxist view of, 7, 21–22, 313
  "objective" chronicles, see also index of
    ancient sources
    Babylonians, 32–33, 52–53
    Jews/Israelites, 8
  Persian philosophy of history, 187–188,
    243, 288, 324, 342
  "tendentious histories," 8
Hittites, 29, 37, 55, 59, 269, 270, 271
Hivites, 270
honey, preservation of corpses in, 201
hoplites, 289
Horus, 63, 66
Hoshea, 76
"Host (of Heaven)", 455, 470
Hushedar (Aûsîtar), 339, 340, 342, 348,
  355
Hyksos kings of Egypt, 65, 70
Hyrcanus the Tobiad, 431–434, 446
Hyrkania, 265, 274, 277, 299
Hystaspes, 355

Idumaea, 465
Igigi, 29
Iliad, See index of ancient sources
Ilte'ri, 126, 148
imperial interests of Nabonidus, 132, 143,
  145, 151
Inanna (Ishtar), 118
India
  Alexander the Great's Indus Valley
    campaign, 301–302
  Antiochus III's campaigns in, 411
  Hindus, 483
  Seleucus I's campaign in, 368
inert raw materials, pagan gods described
  by Jews as, 206, 217, 231, 234

injustices of deity, apparent, *see* apparent
  injustices of deity, meditations on
Intaphernes, 170–171
intermarriage
  Jewish concern over, 268–271, 439
  Mixture Marriage amongst Diadochoi,
    383–392, 403, 424, 438
  Persian-Macedonian, Alexander's
    encouragement of, 326
Ipsos, battle of, 362, 366, 369, 371, 374,
  376, 377, 378, 395, 398, 403, 409,
  438
Iran and Iranians, *see also* Persians and
  Persian Empire
  Alexander the Great's conquest of Iran,
    297–301
  Antiochus III
    fall of, 427–434
    revolt against, 407
  Diadochoi, under, see Diadochoi
  Zoroastrians, see Zoroastrians
iron in metals sequence, significance of,
  see metals, sequence of
Irra (Erra, Era), 36, 43–46, 55
Isaac, 417
Isaiah, *see also* index of Biblical passages
  Assyria and Assyrian empire, prophecy
    of fall of, 76, 83–91
  Deutero-Isaiah, 3, 11, 23, 95, 111, 154–
    162, 168, 173, 194, 203–205, 214,
    225, 226, 231, 235, 267, 268, 464
  First Isaiah, 76, 81 et seq., 106, 154 et
    seq., 267
  Media and Medes, treatment of, 84, 85,
    86, 88, 91, 155, 156, 158, 161, 164,
    165
  "Trito-Isaiah," 11, 23, 160, 162
  Zoroastrians, parallels between Deutero-
    Isaiah and writings of, 157
Ishtar, 39, 80, 118, 119, 124, 143, 252, 266,
  278
Ishum, 44
Isin, Second Dynasty of, 28, 57
Islam/Muslims, 75, 332, 333, 338, 340,
  341, 346, 347, 358, 477
Israel and Judah, 414–415
Israelites, *see* Jews/Israelites
Issos, battle of, 293, 295
Isthmian Games, 426
Itti-Marduk-balâṭu, 60

Jacob, 417

Jaffa, 368

Japheth, sons of, 15

Jason of Cyrene, 433

Jason the High Priest, 445, 446, 447–448, 449, 455

Jebusites, 269, 270, 271

Jechoniah (Jehoiachin/Coniah), 21, 24, 81, 82, 96, 194, 239

Jehoahaz, 81, 82

Jehoiachin (Coniah/Jechoniah), 21, 24, 81, 82, 96, 194, 239

Jehoiakim, 81, 82, 89, 91, 92, 102, 211, 217, 228, 229, 237, 250, 251, 414

Jeremiah, *see* index of Biblical passages

Jericho, 283

Jerome, *See* index of ancient sources

Jerusalem

    Abomination from

        Desolation/Abomination from the Sky built on temple altar, 455, 461, 462, 464, 465, 466, 470

    "the Akra" (Antiochene city at Jerusalem), 450, 451, 465

    Antiochene community at, 445–450

    Antiochene heterodox Jews settled at, 450, 455, 457

    Antiochus III, during reign of, 409, 412–423

    Antiochus IV Epiphanes' sack of and supression of revolt at, 447–450, 452, 453

    besieging of Judas Maccabaeus' forces on temple mount, 466–467

    defilement of temple during reign of Artaxerxes II, 274

    destruction of temple, 200, 298, 421

    Diadochoi period, during, 362, 368, 369

    fall of, 83, 92, 260, 267, 449

    gymnasium at, 457

    Jason's coup and overthrow, 447–448

    rebuilding of temple after exile in Babylon, 160–161, 166, 173, 174, 175, 176, 177, 267–268, 421–422, 440, 464

    refortification of, 177, 267

    restoration of temple after Abomination of Antiochus IV, 461, 462

Sabbath invasions of

    Apollonius the Mysarch, 450

    Mattathias, rebellion of, 457

    Ptolemy I, 369, 396

temple vessels, theft/desecration of

    handwriting on wall in Daniel 1–7 regarding, 217–222, 229–232, 236, 250–251

    Menelaus the High Priest, 446

Jesus ben Sira (Sirach), 162, *see also* index of Biblical passages

Jesus of Nazareth, 477

Jews/Israelites, 3–6, *see also* individual kings

    Ahaz to Zedekiah, 75–83

    Alexander the Great and, see Alexander III the Great

    Antiochus III, alignment with, 405, 409, 412–423

    Antiochus IV Epiphanes and, see Antiochus IV Epiphanes

    apparent injustices of deity, meditations on, 18–19

    authoritative utterances as to cosmic might of deity, 6

    connected histories, 7–8

    creation epic, 62, 95, 110

    Cyrus/Cambyses to Artaxerxes I, 167–190

    Cyrus, reaction to overthrow of Babylon by, 136, 154–162

    Daniel 1–7 as retelling of Babylonian story, see Daniel 1-7 as Jewish retelling of Babylonian story

    Darius, reaction to rule of, 171–178

    Deutero-Isaiah's reaction to Nabonidus and Cyrus, 154–162

    Diadochoi, under, see Diadochoi

    divine intervention, stories of, 6

    ethnos, recognized by Antiochus III as, 423

    exiles/deportations

        Artaxerxes III, by, 274, 276, 277, 283

        Babylonian exile, see exile of Jews in Babylonia

        Ptolemy I, by, 369, 396

    failure of predictions, reaction to, 476–477

    High Priesthood, see also priests (Jewish/Israelite)

Antiochus IV, machinations under, 445–449
Seleucid right to appoint high priest, 445, 467, 474
inert raw materials, pagan gods described as, 206, 217, 231, 234
Jerusalem, see Jerusalem
medieval period, during, 65, 75
Mixture Version of Daniel, 378, 389, 393, 403, 424
Nabonidus, reaction to reign of, 135, 154–162
name shortening in Aramaic, 206, 233
origins of grandiose beliefs regarding, 19–20
Palestine, see Palestine
people of an almighty god, as, 19–20
Persian period, during, 264, 267–278
prayers to deity, 18
priests, see priests (Jewish/Israelite); individual priests and high priests
prophetic texts, 8–18
religious persecution by Antiochus IV, 390, 450–461
Sibylline Oracles written by Jews, 326
sibyls, Hebrew, 327–331
Xerxes, reaction to rule of, 177–178
Jonathan brother of Judas Maccabaeus, 476
Jonathan son of Saul, 475
Joseph, 14, 207, 217
Joseph the Tobiad, 413, 430
Joshua, 455
Josiah, 10, 21, 80–83, 91, 92, 101, 102
Jotham, 84
Jubilee Years, 99–100
Judah, fall of, 76–83, 156, 414–415
Judas Maccabaeus, 419–420, 422, 438, 439, 458–467, 474–477
judge, Marduk as, 241, 263
Julius Caesar, 306
Justin, *See* index of ancient sources

Kabti-ilî-Marduk, 43, 44
Kae, Artakhshir the, 335, 336, 340, 353, 354, 479
Kallisthenes, 330
Kangdiz, 334
Karduniash as name for Babylonian region, 27
Karmania, 301, 315

Kassandros, 362, 365–367, 368, 370–371, 395
Kassite Dynasty, 27, 28, 34, 36, 39, 40, 48, 49, 50, 52, 56, 57, 259
Kay Ardashir (Kay Artakhshir or Vahman), 335, 336, 340, 353, 354, 479
Kayan kings, 335–336, 353
Kephar Saba, 291
Khanaeans (Macedonians), 294, 295
Kh˘asruy, 335, 479
Khibrâ, 129
Khnum, 63, 70
Khonsu, 70
Khorusan, 480, 483
Khshathrita (Phraortes), 81, 240
Khufu, 70, 225, 260
Kidin-Hutrutash, 39
kidinnu, 242
kingship conferred by gods, 253
Kinistan, 483
Kleomenes, 292, 312
"Koilê Syria," 369, 423, 437, 474
Korupedion, battle of, 360
Kosmartidene, 265
Kossaioi, 302
Krateros, 302
Kronos, 383, 401
Kunaxa, battle of, 266
Kurigalzu Epic, 50, 53
Kurigalzu II, 34
Kurupedion, 378
Kutur-nakhkhunte, 28, 29, 34–35, 36, 40, 42, 52, 58
Kuyunjik, 88
Kynoskephalai, battle of, 425
Kypselos, 225
Kyrrhestai, 407

Labâshi-Marduk, 97, 114, 117, 118, 120, 138, 139, 156, 220, 224, 225, 226, 294, 373
Laluralimma of Nippur, 47, 48
Lamian war, 361
Laodice and War of Laodice, 383–392, 401, 402, 403
Laodikeia, 407
Laomedon of Mitylene, 368
Larsa, 122, 128
lead in metals sequence, significance of, 225, 340

Lebanon, cedars of, 87, 104
leopard beast (Daniel 7), 240
leprosy/madness of Nebuchadnezzar, 206,
    215–217, 233–235
Levites
    priests distinguished from or identified
        with, 269, 281
    Torah, interpretation of, 271
Libya, 408
Libyan nomads, 379
light as attribute of gods, 253
lights or fire carried in front of kings,
    329–330, 350
"like the blind," 416, 419, 422
lion-griffin beast (Daniel 7), 239
Ludlul bêl nêmeqi, 47–48
Lydia, 225, 374, 407
Lysias, 420, 438, 458–460, 465–467
Lysimacheia, 424
Lysimachos, 362, 365, 367, 368–371, 374,
    378, 398, 446

Macedonia and Macedonians, *see also*
        individual rulers
    Aetolian League, 425–426
    Alexander the Great and, 288–290, 294,
        295, 298, 301, 302, 308, 310,
        324–325, 330, 343, 344, 355, 356,
        357
    Daniel 2 foretelling decline of, 244,
        262
    Diadochoi, see Diadochoi
    First Macedonian War, 425
    Kassandros' preservation of rule in,
        371
    Khanaeans, 294, 295
    Second Macedonian War, 423, 425
Madetes/Medates, 297
Magas, 379, 399
Magi, 68, 296, 303, 305, 315, 321
Magnesia, 427
Mami, 48, 61
Manasseh, 77–80, 81, 82, 92, 93, 100, 101,
    109, 417, 420, 439, 463
manteiai, 322
"many" in Qumran texts, 415
maps, 485–491
    Alexander the Great, empire of, 488–
        489
    Attalid empire, 490

Darius I, empire of, 486–487
Hellenistic states, 490–491
Palestine in Hellenistic period, 485
Ptolemaic empire, 490
Seleucid empire, 491
Marathon, battle of, 184, 289, 344
Mardonius, 181
Marduk, *see also* Babylonians
    Ahuramazda identified with, 187
    Akîtu (New Year rituals of Marduk), 44,
        100, 114–115, 127–128, 131, 142,
        148, 149, 197, 298, 311, 317, 323
    Alexander the Great's conquests and
        followers of, 295, 296, 297, 298,
        302–313, 348
    anger even without sin of people, 273
    Antiochus III, fall of, 427–434
    Bardiya, murder of, 169, 170
    Bêl as name for, 32, 35, 54, 188, 216,
        278, 296, 427
    birth of, 223
    creation epics and supremacy of, see
        creation epics
    Cyrus viewed as vindicator of, 140, 154,
        157, 159, 161, 187
    daiva-worship, Xerxes' suppression of,
        183–190
    Daniel 1-7 as Jewish retelling of
        Babylonian story about supremacy
        of, see Daniel 1-7 as Jewish
        retelling of Babylonian story
    deformation of Babylonian names by
        Jewish writers, deliberate, 207
    Diadochoi and, see Diadochoi
    failure to act, reaction to, 477
    judge, as, 241, 263
    martyrdom of followers by Nabonidus,
        125, 127, 133, 155, 158
    Nabonidus and, 112–135, 216
    Nabopolassar and, 80
    Persian period, during, 264–267, 278
    Persian philosophy of history and,
        187–188
    Psalm to, 46, 60
    Shazu as name for, 102
    Speech of, 29–30, 37–41, 51, 66
    supreme deity, development as, 27–49,
        72, 79
    titles used by kings of Babylonia,
        significance of, 183

Marduk-apla-iddina I, 23, 41
Marduk-apla-iddina II (Merodach-
    Baladan), 23, 41, 84, 97, 169–170,
    192
Marduk-kâbit-akhkhêshu, 57
Marduk-nâdin-akhkhê, 41, 57
Mari, prophecies from, 58
marriage, *see* intermarriage
Marxist view of history, 7, 21–22, 313
Masoretes and Masoretic vowels, 218, 241,
    248
Massagetai, 301
Mattaniah (Zedekiah), 81, *see also*
    Zedekiah
Mattathias, rebellion of, 456–458, 471
Mazaios, 285, 296
Mazakes, 292
Medates/Madetes, 297
Media and Medes, 23, 81, 103
    Abydenos on Nebuchadnezzar II,
        203–204
    Alexander the Great and, 298, 300, 302,
        342, 344
    Antiochus III, revolt against, 407
    Cambyses, discontent with, 168
    Cyaxares, 80
    Cyrus to Artaxerxes I, 168, 170, 183,
        187–188, 201
    Daniel 1–7 and, 213, 214, 218, 222, 235,
        236, 237, 239, 240, 241, 244, 245,
        262, 372, 375, 376, 387, 429
    Darius and, 170
    Diadochoi, under, 391–392
    Ekhulkhul, destruction by, 114
    horsemanship, tradition of, 313
    Isaiah, in, 84, 85, 86, 88, 91, 155, 156,
        158, 161, 164, 165
    Nabonidus and, 114, 115, 117, 122,
        123–125, 126, 129, 131, 140, 147
    pre-Cyrene history, 67
Media Atropatene, 302
medieval Christians and Jews, 65, 75
meditations on apparent injustices of deity,
    see apparent injustices of deity,
    meditations on
Megabyzos (Megabyxos), 181, 182
Megalopolis, battle of, 317
Megiddo, 81
Meli-Shipak, 56
Melishikhu, 56

Memphis, 275, 451
Memphite Theology of Creation, 62–63
"men of violence," 415, 416, 419, 422, 438,
    439
Menelaus the High Priest, 400, 401,
    446–447, 448, 455, 457, 460, 466
Menidas, 312
Merodach-Baladan (Marduk-apla-iddina
    II), 23, 41, 84, 97, 169–170, 192
Mesekhent, 70
Meshach/Mishael/Mushêzib-Marduk,
    207–208, 211, 215, 227, 229,
    232–233
Mesopotamia, Alexander the Great's
    conquest of, 293–297
metals, sequence of
    Daniel, in, 212–215, 225, 373, 375–376,
        385, 388, 413
    Diadochoi period, during, 369–370, 373,
        375–276, 385, 388
    1 Enoch, in, 377
    "Four-Metal/Four-Branch Vision"
        prophecy of Zarathustra, 334, 335,
        336, 337, 339, 340, 341, 354–355,
        389
    "Seven-Branch Vision" prophecy of
        Zarathustra, 340, 341, 355, 356,
        389
    Sudgar Nask and Prophetic Zand, in,
        332–341
meteorites placed at temple altar
    (Abomination from the Sky), 455
Michael (angel), 377
midrash, 272
might as attribute of gods, 252–253
Miletus, 290
military prowess
    Alexander the Great, 289–290, 313,
        359–360
    Ipsos, battle of, 371
    Nabonidus, military interests of, 132,
        143, 145, 151
    Persia versus Macedonians, 289–290,
        313
    Spitamenes, 301
^{m}IR-^{d}É-a-ku, 59
Mishael/Meshach/Mushêzib-Marduk, 207–
    208, 211, 215, 227, 229, 232–233
Mithras, 293
Mixture Marriage, 383–392, 403, 424, 438

Mixture Version of Daniel 2, 375, 378, 383, 385–393, 403, 411, 413, 424, 429, 430, 432

mlk/mlkw/mlkwth (king/kingdom/dynasty), 213–214, 226, 253, 372, 373, 392, 428

Moabites, 268, 269, 270, 281, 417

Molon, satrap of Media, 406–407, 435

money/coinage
  Diadochoi period, 364, 392, 402–403, 404
  handwriting on wall in Daniel as, 219–220

moneylending, 268

monotheism, 4

moralizing first-person narratives of Babylonians, 33, 36–37, 205, 233

Mordecai, 177, 217

Moses, 15, 19, 25, 268, 269, 281, 417, 455, 462

Mount Gerizim, 291

Murshilish I, 59

Mushêzib-Marduk/Meshach/Mishael, 207–208, 211, 215, 227, 229, 232–233

Muslims, 75, 332, 333, 338, 340, 341, 346, 347, 358, 477

Mykale, battle of, 182, 184

Nabarzanes the chiliarch, 299

Nabonidus, 57, 97, 103, 111, 112–132, 173, 201, 294, 315, 323, 334, 336, 375, 451
  Cyrus, overthrow by, 112, 115, 116, 123, 124, 133, 135, 142, 146, 149, 152, 220–221, 337, 372
  Daniel 1–7, Nebuchadnezzar substituted for in, 205–207, 210–212, 217, 218, 221–222, 228–232, 233–235, 238–241, 244
  departure from Babylon, 129–132
  Deutero-Isaiah and, 154–162
  fall of Babylon and, 115–116, 133, 135
  imperial interests of, 132, 143, 145, 151
  Jews/Israelites, reaction to reign by, 135, 154–162
  Marduk and, 112–135, 216
  martyrdom of followers of Marduk by, 125, 127, 133, 155, 158
  military interests of, 132, 143, 145, 151

neo-Babylonian empire's dependence on, 224

omens, dreams, and astrological signs, importance of, 118, 119, 121, 123, 129–130, 131, 141, 145

reign, overview of, 113–116

religious beliefs of, 114–115, 116–129

return to Babylon, 132–135

Sîn, veneration for, 114–135

Têmâ, at, 114, 115, 123, 124, 126–132, 133, 140, 145, 146, 148, 149, 151, 153, 206, 216

Verse Account of, see index of ancient sources

wealth, interest in, 132, 151, 152

Nabopolassar, 57, 80–81, 87, 96, 97, 102, 117, 118, 120, 170, 205, 220, 228, 229, 230, 257, 294

Nabû, 35, 36, 44, 80, 119, 127, 159, 160, 207, 208, 210, 266, 378

Nabû-apla-iddina, 44

Nabû-balâṭsu-iqbi, 113, 248

Nabû-shumu-libur, 57

name shortening in Aramaic, 206, 233, 246, 248

Nanaia, 461

Nanna, 4, 125, 126, *see also* Sîn

Narâm-Sin, Cuthaean Legend of, 36–37

Narru, 48, 61

Naukratis, 292

navy, Greek, 289

Nebi Yunus, 88

Nebuchadnezzar I, 28–31, 33–46, 48–49, 220, 224

Nebuchadnezzar II, 57, 81–83, 85, 86, 87, 91, 92–97, 102, 117, 118, 156, 188, 200, 201, 267, 283, 294, 372, 376, 388, 449
  Daniel 1–7 and, see Daniel 1-7 as Jewish retelling of Babylonian story
  Ezekiel and, 414

Nebuchadnezzar III, 170, 192, 240

Nebuchadnezzar IV, 170, 171, 240

Neco II of Egypt, 81

Neferti, Prophecy of, 64–67, 71, 72

Nekht-ḥar-ḥebit (Nektanebos II), 274–278, 284, 285, 292, 346, 347

Nektanebos I, 284

Nektanebos II (Nekht-ḥar-ḥebit), 274–278, 284, 285, 292, 346, 347

Neo-Assyrian oracles, 58
Nephthys, 70
Nergal, 364, 366
Nergal-shar-uṣur (Neriglissar), 97, 118,
    120, 138, 139, 224, 225, 226, 257,
    260, 294
New Year rituals of Marduk (Akîtu), 44,
    100, 114–115, 127–128, 131, 142,
    148, 149, 197, 298, 311, 317, 323
Nicanor (military leader against Judas
    Maccabaeus), 459, 475
Nidintu-Bêl, 170, 232, 234
Nikanor (author), 327, 349
Nikanor (murderer of Seleucus III), 404
Nikanor (satrap of Media), 364, 368
Nimrod, 88
Nineveh, 38, 46, 81, 86–90, 105
Ningal, 119, 230
Ninhursaga, 48
Ninlil, 38, 80
Ninshatapada, 58
Ninurta-tukulti-Ashur, 52
Nippur, 29, 32, 34, 36, 38, 39, 40, 46, 47,
    54, 122, 242
Nitokris, 103, 312
Noah
    1 Enoch, in, 377, 417
    sibyl from family of, 327, 331
Nusku, 119, 230

"objective" chronicles, *see also* index of
    ancient sources
    Babylonians, 32–33, 52–53
    Jews/Israelites, 8
Ochos (Artaxerxes III), 266, 274–278, 283,
    284, 285, 286, 290, 292, 347, 414
Ochos (Darius II), 266, 267, 278, 279
olive oil, preservation of corpses in, 188,
    201
Olympias, 346, 347, 362
omens, dreams, and astrological signs
    Adad-guppî, 141
    Akkadian oracles, 41, 58
    Alexander the Great and, 302–313
    Babylonian belief in, 118, 161, 228
    Nabonidus, importance to, 118, 119,
        121, 123, 129–130, 131, 141,
        145
    Neo-Assyrian oracles, 58
    Seleukeia, founding of, 367

Sibylline oracles, see also index of
    ancient sources; Sibylline oracles
Onias II, 393, 430
Onias III, 419–420, 432–434, 445, 465,
    472
Onias-Menelaus, 401
Opis, battle at, 115–116, 220–221, 230
oracles, *see* omens, dreams, and
    astrological signs
Oxathres, 300
Oxyartes, 301
Oxydates, 391
Ozines, 302

Padakku, 129
Palestine
    Alexander the Great's conquest of,
        290–293
    Antiochus III's campaigns to regain,
        406, 408–412, 423–424
    map for Hellenistic period, 485
    Ptolemy's seizure of, 378, 406
Panion, battle of, 412, 447
Papyrus Westcar, 70, 225, 260
Pareitakai, 301
parent religions dwelling in daughter-
    religion state, 75
Parthians, 340, 391, 392, 411, 436
Parthyaia, 299, 374
Parthyene, 385, 391
Parysatis, 265, 266
Pasargadai, 295, 302
Patrokles, 365
Peithon son of Agenor, 312, 363
Pekah, 76, 437
Peloponnesian War, 356
Pelusion, 275
Pelusium, 408
people of an almighty god
    adversity, explanations for, see adversity,
        explanations for
    Assyrians not treatable as, 79
    authoritative utterances as to cosmic
        might of deity, see authoritative
        utterances as to cosmic might of
        deity
    Babylonians as, 49
    connected histories written by, see
        connected histories
    consequences of belief in, 4–5

people of an almighty god (cont.)
  defined, 3
  divine intervention, stories of, see divine
    intervention, stories of
  Egyptians
    people of a nearly almighty god, as,
      67–67
    people of an almighty god, Middle
      Kingdom Egyptians as, 67
  failure of predictions, reaction to,
    476–477
  Jews/Israelites as, 19–20
  prayers to deity, see prayers to deity
  prophetic texts written by, see prophetic
    texts
  recognition of god by other peoples, see
    recognition of god by other peoples
  Zoroastrian Iranians as people of a
    nearly almighty god, 67–68
Perdikkas, 362, 363, 368, 373
Pergamon, 383, 391, 423–424, 425
Perizzites, 269, 270, 271
Persepolis, 266, 295, 297, 317, 318, 325
Persians and Persian Empire, 65, 67–70,
    94, 123, 131, 133, 152, 158, 160,
    168, 169, 176, 177, 183, 186,
    187–188, 201, *see also* individual
    kings
  Abydenos on Nebuchadnezzar II, 204
  Alexander the Great and, see Alexander
    III the Great
  Allah-ed-din Muḥammad, 225
  "Animal vision," of 1 Enoch, 417, 419
  Antiochus III, revolt against, 407
  Babylonians during Persian period,
    264–267
  Daniel 1-7 and, 209, 214, 218, 221,
    226, 233, 237, 239, 240, 241,
    262, 429
  Diadochoi, under, see Diadochoi
  fire-worship of, 330
  history, Persian philosophy of, 187–188,
    243, 288, 324, 342
  Jews/Israelites during Persian period,
    264, 267–278
  military skills of, 289–290
  Sakaia and Festival of the Sakai, 309
  sibyls, Persian, 327–331, 341–345,
    351
Persis, 361, 374, 392, 484

Peshyotan (Pishi-shyaothna, Pishtoyan,
    Peshtoyanu), 339, 340, 348, 355,
    482
Peukestas, 361
Philetairos of Pergamon, 383
Philip II of Macedonia, 21, 346–347, 401
Philip III Arrhidaios of Macedonia, 360,
    362, 363, 428, 430, 451, 470
Philip V of Macedonia, 411, 423–426
Philip the Phrygian, 449, 459
Philippos, 466
Philistines, 417, 419
Phineas, 457
Phoenicia and Phoenicians, 210, 254, 274,
    275, 277, 285, 305, 307, 368, 371,
    408–409, 423, 474
Phoinix, 370
Phraortes (Khshathrita), 81, 240
Phrygia and Phrygians, 152, 343, 374, 407
"piecemeal" response of Jews to sins
    impeding fulfillment of prophecies
    during Persian period, 268–271
Pishyotan (Pishi-shyaothna, Peshyotan,
    Peshyotanu), 339, 340, 348, 355,
    482
poetic nature of Daniel narratives, 205, 246
Polemaios, 395
Polyperchon, 362
polytheism, 3–4, 65, 79, 80, 209, 450
Pontic Cappadocia (Pontus), 391, 404
prayers to deity
  Babylonians, 46–47
  Daniel 1-7, prayer and worship in, 217,
    222–223, 235–237, 240, 252
  Egyptians, 63
  Jews/Israelites, 18
"predation" practices of Alexander the
    Great and Diadochoi, 359–361, 363
present-future prophecies
  Alexander the Great and, 294, 324, 326,
    330, 331, 336, 337
  "Animal Vision," of 1 Enoch, 378,
    416–423, 458–459, 467, 476
  Antiochus IV Epiphanes and, 453, 464;
    see also *Testament of Moses*
  "Apocalypse of Weeks," of 1 Enoch,
    378, 422, 476
  Babylonians, 38
  Daniel 2 and 7, 205, 224, 238, 241, 244,
    273, 453

Daniel 8–9, 464
Daniel 11–12, 434, 457–58, 468, 469, 470, 471
Diadochoi and, 369, 372, 376, 378, 390, 403
Dynastic Prophecy, 112
Egyptians, 66, 71
failure of, 476
Greeks, 65, 72
Jews/Israelites, 15–16
Jubilees, book of, 448–449
Oracle of Hystaspes, 424
Pentateuch, 273
Prophetic Zand and, 484
Romans/Roman Empire, 65, 72
Uruk prophecy, 97
preservation of corpses, 188, 201
Priestly Code (P), *see* index of ancient sources
priests (Jewish/Israelite), *see also* individual priests and high priests
Antiochus IV, machinations under, 445–449
Bilgah, clan of
Onias-Menelaus, 401
Simon, 432, 434, 446
fratricidal strife in high priestly family during reign of Artaxerxes II, 274
Levites distinguished from or identified with, 269, 281
Seleucid right to appoint high priest, 445, 467, 474
Prophecy of Neferti, 64–67, 71, 72
prophetic texts
Babylonians, 37–46
Egyptians, 64
Jews/Israelites, 8–18
present-future prophecies, see present-future prophecies
vaticinium ex eventu, 9–14, 16, 23, 24, 25, 39
Prophetic Zand, see also index of ancient sources
Alexander the Great and, 331–341
full text, 479–482
Psalm to Marduk, 46, 60
psychosomatic disease, Antiochus IV's possible death from, 461, 471
Ptah, 63, 72

Ptolemaic dynasty and empire, 70, 330, 386, 389, 390–391, 393, 419–420, 490, *see also* Egypt
Ptolemaic texts, terms for gods used in, 210, 254
Ptolemaios, 395
Ptolemais, 408, 409
Ptolemy I, 287, 308, 317, 361, 362, 363–366, 368–371, 373–375, 377, 378, 379, 398, 419, 422, 430, 470
Ptolemy II, 379, 381, 383–384, 399, 400, 430, 470
Ptolemy III, 384, 385, 393, 402, 406, 430, 470
Ptolemy IV, 405, 408–410, 413, 430, 431, 470
Ptolemy V, 386, 387, 409, 411–412, 414, 419, 420, 422, 424, 430–431, 432, 470
Ptolemy VI, 387, 447, 449, 452, 468, 470
Ptolemy VIII, 447, 470
Ptolemy son of Dorymenes, 446
Pul (Tiglath-pileser III), 12, 35, 76, 86, 115, 169
purity laws, violations of, 272
pyramids, 189

Queen of Heaven, worship of, 109, 455
Qumran texts, *see* index of ancient sources

Raphael (angel), 377, 398
Raphia, 409, 413, 415, 435, 437
Raṣyan (Rezin), 76
Reˁ, 63, 65, 66, 67, 70
recognition of one's god by other peoples, importance attached to, 5
Rehoboam, 448
religious persecution of Jews by Antiochus IV, 390, 450–461
Remaliah, 76
repentance, 456
Rezin (Raṣyan), 76
Rhodes, 427
Rim-Sîn of Larsa, 58
Romans/Roman Empire
Antiochus IV Epiphanes
civic policy derived from Rome by, 444–445
Egypt, forced by Rome to withdraw from, 449–450

Romans/Roman Empire (*cont.*)
    hostage of Rome, as, 427, 434,
        444–445
    beliefs of, 4, 20, 101, 337
    Carthaginian wars, 100, 276
    Daniel believed to foretell doom of, 244
    deification of emperors, 337
    Demetrius I as hostage of, 467
    disheveled hair, no identification of
        emperors with demons with,
        337–338
    Jewish revolts against, 5
    Judas Maccabaeus and, 475, 476
    Julius Caesar, 306
    lights/fire carried in front of rulers of,
        330, 350
    Philip V and Antiochus III, 423–427,
        432
    present-future prophecies of, 65, 72
    Sibylline prophecy possibly predicting
        doom of, 328, 342, 356
    substitute king ritual, no parallel for, 323
"root of cultivation," 419, 422
Rosh ha-shanah, 453
Roxane, 301, 360, 362

Sabbath invasions of Jerusalem, *see*
    Jerusalem
Sabbath violations, 268
Sabbatical Years, 99–100, 453, 454, 455,
    461, 462, 463, 465, 466
Sabbe, 327–328
Sadarnunna, 119, 230
Saggil-kînam-ubbib, 48
Sakaia and Festival of the Sakai, 309, 322
Samaritans and Samaria, 177, 291, 293,
    315, 368, 409, 417
Sambethe, 327–328
Samsu-ditana, 27
Samuel, 252
Sanballat, 291
Sarapis and Alexander the Great, 308–312
Sardis, 266, 378, 380
Sargon II, 59, 100, 106, 117, 169, 170, 242
Sargon of Agade, 36
Sariel (angel), 377
Sarpânîtum, 47, 48
Sassanian kings, 332, 333, 340, 342, 345,
    347, 354, 355
Satan, 65

Satibarzanes, 299, 300, 318
satraps, 222, 237
Saul, 252, 475
scholiasts and scholia, 327
Scythia and Scythians, 301, 344
Second Isaiah, *see* Deutero-Isaiah
Second Macedonian War, 423, 425, 468
Second Punic War, 425
Second Syrian War, 383
Sekyndianos (Sogdianos), 240, 265, 266,
    278
Seleucid Brothers, War of, 391
Seleucids, 33, 210, 305, 306, 337, 340, 345,
    356, 374, 378, 379, 383–393,
    419–420, 427, 491
Seleucus I, 305, 312, 321, 360, 362,
    363–371, 374, 376, 378–379, 382,
    384, 390, 394, 395, 397, 398, 411,
    423, 424, 428
Seleucus II, 383, 384, 385, 391, 393, 402,
    428
Seleucus III, 393, 405, 428
Seleucus IV, 427–434, 428, 451, 467, 470
Seleucus son of Antiochus I, 382
Seleukeia in Pieria, 385, 408
Seleukeia on the Tigris, 366–367, 378, 381,
    385, 390, 395, 411
Sennacherib, 22, 23, 31, 59, 77–79, 88, 99,
    100, 105, 117, 152, 170, 453, 470
Seron, 459
Seth, 65–67
"Seven-Branch Vision" prophecy of
    Zarathustra, 340, 341, 355, 356,
    389
Shadrach/Hananiah/Sha-Marduk, 207–208,
    211, 215, 227, 229, 232–233,
    247–248
Shalmaneser I, 59
Shalmaneser III, 115, 138, 169, 343
Shalmaneser V, 76, 169
Shamash, 39, 124, 127, 133, 150, 153, 294
Shamash-erîba, 178, 179, 180, 182, 184,
    186, 189, 190, 193, 195–196, 197,
    198, 236, 240, 243, 264
Shapur I, 340
Shapur II, 333
Shazu as name for Marduk, 102
shêdu, 34, 35, 125, 215
sheep in "Animal Vision," 1 Enoch, 378,
    416–423, 458–459, 476

Shemiḥazah, 377–378, 398, 399
Shisak, 448
Shubshi-meshrê-Shakkan, 47, 48
Shulgi, Speech of, 38–41, 50, 55
Sibylline oracles, Alexander the Great and,
  326–331, 341–345, *see also* index
  of ancient sources
sibyls
  defined, 326–327
  Greek tradition of, 326–327
  Persian, Babylonian, and Hebrew sibyls,
  327–331
Sidon, 274, 275, 277, 285, 369, 409, 412,
  422
silver in metals sequence, significance of,
  see metals, sequence of
Simeon II the Just, 423
Simon of priestly clan Bilgah, 432, 434,
  446
Simon son of Mattathias (brother of Judas
  Maccabaeus), 458, 465, 475, 477
Sîn
  Daniel 1–7 and, 215, 218, 230, 231, 249,
  250, 253
  Nabonidus' veneration for, 114–135
Sîn-kâshid of Uruk, 58
Sippar, 118, 122, 124, 127, 128, 129, 134,
  140, 149–150, 242
Sirach (Jesus ben Sira), 162, *see also* index
  of Biblical passages
Skopas, 412, 413, 419, 422
Smerdis, 168, *see also* Bardiya
Snefru, 66
Sodom, 164, 174
Sogdia, 374
Sogdianos (Sekyndianos), 240, 265, 266,
  278
Sogdians, 301
Solomon, 19, 462
Sosibios, 408
Sparta, 298
Spartoli tablets, British Museum, 41–42,
  50, 53–54, 58, 59, *see also* index
  of ancient sources
Speech of Marduk, 29–30, 37–41, 51, 66
Speech of Shulgi, 38–41, 50
Spendarmad, 480, 483
Spitamenes, 300–301, 319, 348, 367
steel in metals sequence, significance of,
  333–334

substitute king tradition and Alexander the
  Great, 307–312, 322, 323
successor dynasties to Alexander the Great,
  see Diadochoi
Sudan (Ethiopia), 168
Sudgar Nask, Alexander the Great and,
  331–341, *see also* index of ancient
  sources
Sumerians, 4, 8
Susa, 265, 266, 295, 297, 365
Susiane, 374
Sutû, 44
Synchronistic History (Chronicle 21), 30,
  50, 51, 52
Syria, 362, 368, 369, 371, 378, 380, 383
  Alexander the Great's conquest of,
  290–293
  Assyria, as representation of, 414
  "Coele-Syria ("Koilê Syria"), 369, 423,
  437, 474
  Ptolemaic Syria, Antiochus III's
  campaigns against, 406, 407,
  408–412, 423–424

Tarshish, ships of, 104
Tashmêtum-Gula, 119
Taurus Mountains, 371, 427
Taxo and his sons, death of, 458
Teacher of Righteousness, 416
Têmâ, Nabonidus at, 114, 115, 123, 124,
  126–132, 133, 140, 145, 146, 148,
  149, 151, 153, 206, 216, 234,
  235
temple at Jerusalem, *see* Jerusalem
Ten Lost Tribes of Israel, 414
"tendentious histories," 8
Testament of Moses, 455–456, *see also*
  index of ancient sources
Text A, 40–41, 56–57, *see also* index of
  ancient sources
Thais, 317
Thebes, 343, 356
theodicy, Babylonian, 48–49
Theodotos the Aetolian, 406, 408
Thermopylae, 426
Thoth, 63
Thrace and Thracians, 391, 408, 424
"Three-Beast Version" of vision of beasts
  in Daniel, 237–244, 264, 324, 372,
  373, 428

Tiâmat, 223, 224
Tiglath-pileser III, 12, 35, 76, 86, 115, 169
tin in metals sequence, significance of,
225, 340
Tiri, 266
titles used by kings of Babylonia,
significance of, 179–180, 183, 196
Tobiad Family, 413, 430–434
tomb mound, Alexander's diadem landing
on, 305–307
tomb of Belitanas (Bêl), 181, 188–189,
198, 303
Torah, 269, 271, 272, 273, 282, 283, 320,
422, 449, 450, 451, 457
Transjordan, 409, 431, 432, 434, 446
trees
imperial monarchy, symbolizing, 337
Nebuchadnezzar's dream in Daniel, 216,
234
Sudgar Nask and Prophetic Zand, in,
333, 334, 336, 337, 353
Triparadeisos, 362
"Trito-Isaiah," 11, 23, 160, 162
Tudkhaliyash, 59
Tudkhula, 59
Tukulti-Ashtur, 32, 52
Tukulti-Ninurta I, 29, 32, 39, 52, 59
Turks, 338
Typhon, 65
Tyre, 291, 293, 318, 368, 369, 408, 445, 446
Tyrian Herakles, 293, 318, 445

Ugbaru, 204
Ur, 4, 121, 122, 128, 130, 131, 242
Ur-Nammu, 55
Urnindinlugga of Babylonia, 47, 48
Uruk, 50, 56, 57, 58, 97, 118, 119, 128,
143, 242, 266
Uruk Prophecy, 41, 56, 57, 97, 111
usury, 268
Uxioi, 297
Uzziah, 84

Vaharam I Gur (Bahram Gor), 340
Vahman (Kay Ardashir/Artakhshir), 335,
336, 340, 353, 354, 479
Valakhsh (Vologeses I), 340
vaticinium ex eventu, 9–14, 16, 23, 24, 25,
39
Vespasian, 200

vessels of temple in Jerusalem,
theft/desecration of
handwriting on wall in Daniel 1-7
regarding, 217–222, 229–232, 236,
250–251
Menelaus the High Priest, 446
Vishtaspa, 332, 333, 336, 345, 353, 479,
482
Vohu Manah (Bahman), 334
Vologeses I (Valakhsh), 340

Wadi Daliyeh, 293, 315
wax, preservation of corpses in, 201
wealth, Nabonidus' interest in, 132, 151,
152
Weidner Chronicle, 31–32, 52, see also
index of ancient sources
Westcar (papyrus), 70, 225, 260
"wholesale" response of Jews to sins
impeding fulfillment of prophecies
during Persian period, 268, 269,
271 et seq.
wisdom as attribute of gods, 252–253
Wrath (Aêsham), seed of, 337, 338, 339,
340, 354, 479–482

Xenon, 406
Xerxes I, 70, 177–190, 264, 265, 428
Alexander the Great's revenge for
campaigns of, 290, 297, 302, 316,
325, 356
daiva-worship, suppression of, 183–190,
223, 235–237, 240
Daniel 1–7 and, 223, 233, 235–240, 243,
244, 263, 372, 373
Xerxes II, 240, 265, 442
xshaçapâvan (satrap), 222

Yadikhu, 129
Yasht, 335
Yatribu, 129
Yima, 331

Zababa-shuma-iddina, 57
Zarathustra/Zoroaster, 67–70, 157, 186,
331–345, 352, 353, 479–482
Zariaspes, 302
Zazannu, 170
Zedekiah, 81–82, 92, 93, 94
Zerubbabel, 11, 175, 194, 462

Zeus (Persian) as Ahuramazda, 201
ziggurat of Babylon (Etemenanki), 90,
    187, 189–190, 199, 200, 202,
    303, 305
Zopyros, 171, 181, 182
Zoroastrians, 67–70
  Alexander the Great and, 297, 331–47
  Antiochus III and, 411
  Arsakid dynasty as, 391, 404
  Atropatids as, 392
  Cyrus, claims regarding, 157, 163
  daiva-worship, Xerxes' suppression of,
    184, 186

  dualistic nature of, 347
  Magi, 68, 296, 303, 305, 315, 321
  Mixture Version of Daniel, 389–393,
    424
  parallels between Deutero-Isaiah and
    writings of, 157
  people of a nearly almighty god, as,
    67–68
  Vishtaspa, 332, 333, 336, 345, 353, 479,
    482
  Zarathustra/Zoroaster, 67–70, 157, 186,
    331–345, 352, 353, 479–482
Zulummar, 48, 61